MASTER TRAPPERS

Tom Miranda Honors The Master Trappers

BY TOM MIRANDA

ILLUSTRATIONS BY
JOE GOODMAN

Master Trappers

PLEASE SUPPORT YOUR
STATE AND NATIONAL
TRAPPING ASSOCIATIONS
THANK YOU

J. GOODMAN

A young Tom Miranda honors the legacy of the "Master Trappers"

Master Trappers

A definitive, in-depth look into the romantic history of the fur-men who mapped the Continent. The passion and entrepreneurial spirit which continues even to this day in these

Wild Expanses of North America.

Follow the French fur traders into wild native lands; The formation of Hudson's Bay Company, Mountain men, pioneers cottage industry trappers.Braving wilderness , risking life and limb in pursuit of precious , prime pelts from the Adirondacks to Alaska, Louissiane to Hudson's bay. The Allagash to Athabaska.

Coulter, Bridger, Glass, Smith, Johnson

The Cottage Industry

Newhouse, Harding, Dailey, Wood, Thompson, Lynch, Hawbaker

Longliners & Furmen

Butcher, Nelson, O'Gorman, Carman, Thorpe, Corr, Milligan, Askins Krause, Lenon, Grigg, Powell, Negus, Weiland, Dunnier, Smythe Leggett, June, Sterling, Grawe, Arnold, Pedersen, Grimshaw, Cronk Trepus, Stearns, Spencer, Herbst, Zagger, Boddicker, & more

The amazing journey of a schoolboy trapper who followed in the footsteps of these amazing men to fulfill his own destiny as a trapper, hunter and outdoorsman.

Tom Miranda

Published by
Tom Miranda Outdoors Incorporated
P.O. Box 806 | Englewood, FL 34295
www.tommiranda.com
www.mastertrappers.com
www.adventurebowhunter.com

To order books or DVDs visit www.tommiranda.com

Cover art and illustrations by Joe Goodman
Book design by Jessica Angerstein

ISBN: 1-978-1-64687-038-7

Second edition

Printed in Canada

DEDICATION

The sights and smells found along the trapline trail are akin to the colored lights, tinsel and sweet pine aroma of the Christmas tree. The anticipation of a trapper tending traps is identical to the excitement of a youngster opening the gifts of Christmas morning. No matter a trappers age, the wonder and prospect of what illusive animal may await in the traps gives promise to every step. Trapping is hard work, yet the rewards far outweigh any drudgery. Master Trappers is a tribute to all the trappers, novice and professional, who directly or indirectly influenced me to follow the path less traveled—to become a trapper & bowhunter.

—Tom Miranda

TABLE OF CONTENTS

FOREWORD

Perhaps the schoolboy knows of a small stream on the outskirts of the city. When fall comes 'round he may be seen in the early morning with a packsack on his back and a .22 rifle across one shoulder making his way to the stream. Here on the soft oozy banks of that creek and on the slippery logs that cross it, his watchful eye detects a likely set for muskrat with the possible chance of getting that "rara avis" the mink. I believe this boy is impelled by exactly the same forces as the professional trapper who runs a hundred-mile trap line thru a trackless wilderness numbering his traps in the hundreds. I know—because I have been there—I have trapped in my spare time as a school boy and for six years have held no less than fifty and sometimes over a hundred miles of trap lines in the Canadian wilderness.

The point I wish to emphasize is there are two factors that go into the making of any trapper, pastime or professional. These are the two P's in t-r-a-p-p-i-n-g—Pleasure and Profit.

Very rare is one considered without the other, but in my own way of looking at things, I believe the pleasure has more influence over the prospective trapper than profit.

Well then, what pleasure is there in trapping? "Oh", you say… "all kinds!" You're right, there are all kinds, yet these same pleasures are hard to define. There is that eon-old harkening back to nature—that inherited call of the wild, if you please. There is an old saying, "Once a trapper, always a trapper," and I believe this to be true in the majority of cases. I know that there will come a time for me when it will be impossible to trap, yet I will always have a warm spot in my heart for the trapper. Who has not listened to the "loon that laughs and cries, down to those reflected skies" and not has been moved to the innermost depths of the soul? Who was not been thrilled by the harsh rasping call of the raven— the bark of a fox in mating time or the howl of a wolf pack?

Let me say that one feature dominates in every phase of trapping as far as pleasure is concerned. This is Anticipation. It is the shy goddess of chance that waits around each bend of the trail— to be wooed and won by the daring woodsman. And once won, she scatters her favors with a lavish hand— now in the shape of a beautifully furred fisher pelt, now in a long hoped for marten run…. and the—Oh never-to-be-forgotten day, she has left a full-furred silver fox. It is Anticipation that spurs the trapper on, hour after hour. Though he may be tired and hungry—surely there will be a reward for his perseverance in the next trap. It is always the NEXT trap—for thus Hope keeps her shining face ever before us by instantaneously transferring our thoughts one object to another.

There yet remains another P in t-r-a-p-p-i-n-g, which spells Profit. Right on the word "Go" let me say that there is a vast amount of ignorance connected with the amount of money that professional trappers make. Trapping is like any other profession; it has varying degrees of success. Thus we find one trapper barely making his grubstake while another right alongside, may be making a "real" stake. Some men have the idea that trapping isn't work. To all I say, "try it." In a few months they will be ready to take up grave digging, tunnel making or some other light profession: they will be convinced that there is neither pleasure or profit in trapping—for them.

If I considered giving any advice to a father regarding his son, I would say, "Watch closely the good he does of his own free will during his spare hours and encourage him in that particular line."

~Raymond Thompson, Trapping as a Profession, 1922

INTRODUCTION

The experiences, lessons and memories of running a trapline has molded my entire life. My first passion as a youngster was baseball, yet trapping eventually replaced ball and bat with tracks, trails and dreams of wilderness. A well placed trap turned adventure into enterprise with the catch of a silky-furred rudder-tailed rat.... or the snarl of a ring-tailed bandit, his eyes glowing as my headlamp shined up the dark riverbank. Trapping was exciting and challenging. It was hard work but immensely rewarding.

A week of "full on" trapping taught me more about life than a month of the best lessons of reading, writing and arithmetic. The trapline was on the job training that brought together meteorology, engineering, physics and biology with a heavy dose of common sense. Mistakes were quickly realized and corrected. Successes were celebrated both in self satisfaction as well as reinforced with congratulations from parents. In the early years I had no idea what work ethic was, yet learned that if I pulled unproductive trap sets and added additional sets each day, my catch would increase. Trapping taught me to take negatives and turn them into positives. The equation was simple... hard work coupled with knowledge paid off. Life lessons.

What trapper doesn't look back into their memories and visualize the solace of the woods during a winter snow fall. Or remember the sounds of quacking mallards flushing from the cattails. Or the sweet musky smell of the skunk, his tail held high in defiance. Or even the feeling of cold water rushing into a pair of leaky waders.... as frozen fingers add another 'rat to the basket. Memories often have a way of molding themselves to leave the discomfort and hardships out-to help us remember the best of everything, while making the not so good..... not so bad.

My romance of the trapline first came to me in the form of Harding's Magazine. Fur-Fish-Game took my love of the outdoors, my obsession of trapping, my heart and my soul and wrapped it all into a dream to become a wilderness trapper. I craved to witness the virgin forests, crystal streams and untapped fur pockets. To watch the smoke sift from the chimney of my own "hand built" log cabin. The crackle of burning wood, bacon in the skillet and the aroma of drying pelts. Fur-Fish-Game magazine became my bible, my recipe for the future. Like the cravings of a chocolate sundae or a pepperoni pizza.. I looked forward to each month's issue and the adventures every page revealed.

Of course it's easy to look back now some fifty years later and try to make sense of it all, yet why I acted upon my dreams with such a pioneering spirit I don't know.. That said, maybe a better question is why don't more inspired individuals act upon their dreams? Why wonder what the wild places are like when one can make it a goal to experience it for themself.

My mission with-in the pages of this book is not so much a scholarly look into trapping and it's history, but a tribute to the trappers and trapping which have so influenced my life. Master Trappers is a motivational treatise for the outdoorsman who craves the romance and knowledge of the woodsmen who used their skills to make a living in the wilds of North America. Many famous and influential trappers are chronicled in this volume, yet the knowledgable reader may not hear the mention his or her favorite trapper. The individuals included here are ones who's methods I have followed and who's careers and writings influenced me to become the best trapper and bowhunter I could be. My sincere hope is this book inspires both trappers and non-trappers with an appreciation for those with the calling to follow a trail less traveled.

~Tom Miranda

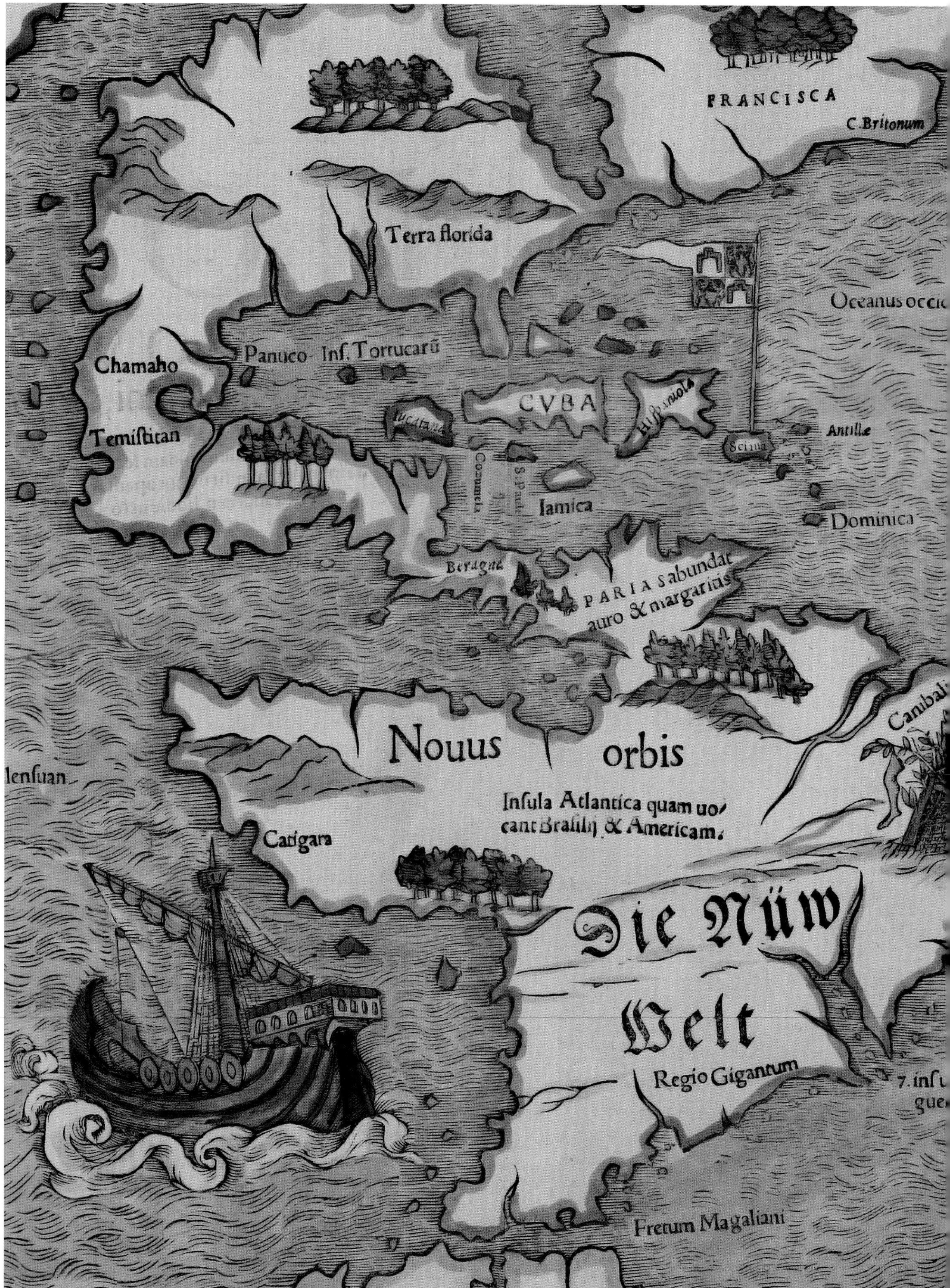
FRANCISCA
C.Britonum
Terra florida
Chamaho
Panuco
Inſ. Tortucarũ
Temiſtitan
Iucatana
CVBA
Hiſpaniola
Antillæ
Cozumela
S.Pauli
Iamica
Dominica
Beragna
PARIA s abundat auro & margaritis
Nouus orbis
Inſula Atlantica quam uocant Braſilij & Americam.
Catigara
Die Nüw Welt
Regio Gigantum
Fretum Magaliani

CHAPTER 1

FUR TRADERS

The best way to understand the roots of trapping is to travel back into history and look at its origins. In the dawn of time early man survived by eating resident plants and animals, clothing themselves with the hides and pelts of the animals they ate. Archeologists have found clues that show most early indigenous peoples were hunter-gatherers. However, as time passed and tribes grew in size, villages where established in areas rich in resources. Tribes enjoyed the added security of strength through numbers, assigning tasks to individuals to accomplish the day-to-day needs of the clan.

Hunters were particularly important to the tribe. The most proficient hunters rose to be the most revered members. Hunters provided animals which became food and hides to make clothing and shelter. As time passed, farming evolved in areas where tribes had permanently settled. Tribes who were adept at growing food could grow more than they needed and trade the excess. Trade often included meat for sustenance and hides for clothing.

Of course, all humans need food and water daily, yet tribes in equatorial areas required less food and more water to survive. But as tribes settled in the northern latitudes, these people experienced colder climates and required more of everything. Early man learned quickly that cooler climates tended to be healthier environments for habitation, yet required warm clothing and insulated shelter.

> Sebastian Münster's Map of America, 1561

EARLY ASIA

Pre-History–900

Although animal skins where traded and used extensively in prehistory, likely the earliest commercial enterprises in fur trading began in the Chinese dynasties. As the Roman Empire expanded, trade routes were established where furs were trafficked with other textiles along the Silk Road from the Orient through Constantinople into Europe. By the middle ages, all of Asia was trading skins and furs. The spruce forests of central Russia were rich in fur-bearing animals and these Russian hunters traded pelts at outposts on the Baltic and Black seas. Martens, beavers, foxes, squirrels and hares where exported into the garment trades as trims and linings.

Wikimedia Commons

This early 14th Century photo depicts a camel train with Chinese trade goods traveling on the Silk Road.

The Chinese invented gun powder in the 9th century and subsequently, the firearm in the 10th century. These weapons eventually evolved to where hunters could use them with proficiency in the collection of meat and furs. Following this, commerce in meat and skins began in earnest.

Siberian hunters eventually crossed the area known today as the Bering Strait and expanded their range into new territories which are now modern-day Alaska. Sea otters and seals thrived along these bountiful coasts rich in fish and crustaceans. In these days of the fur trade, marine mammal skins were exceedingly popular. Seals and sea otter pelts offered the unique characteristics of water-resistance and warmth. These animals were also relatively easy to obtain as they were found in large numbers. In the virgin forests of the mainland, martens as well as other fur bearers were in abundance.

The pine marten was particularly popular for its silky, soft fur and light weight which was worn by wealthy Europeans as trim to their cold-weather garments. Weasels taken in deadfalls were tanned and used to trim the coats of kings, their silky white fur and black-tipped tails accenting these colorful robes of royalty. Peoples of the far north dressed in seal skins, polar bear hides and used decorative wolverine fur ruffs as trim on parka hoods that are still used today by Inuit peoples of the arctic regions.

Wikimedia Commons

Native American encampment on Lake Huron.
Oil on Canvas by Paul Kane, 1945.

Wikimedia Commons

Royal robe made with red velvet, gold thread and ermine trim.

Wikimedia Commons

Neanderthal Flintworkers. Le Moustier Cavern, Dordogne, France.
Oil painting by Charles R.Knight, 1920.

THE NEW WORLD

900–1670

Likely the first potential fur traders to see North America were the Norsemen. Archeological finds and ancient texts confirm that Vikings not only visited Iceland, Greenland, Labrador, Nova Scotia, Newfoundland and even as far south as Cape Cod, Massachusetts—they also built outposts in these areas and most certainly saw natives, and would have traded with them. The warm furs and leathers possessed by America's native tribes would have interested Norsemen, and the iron items these Vikings possessed in swords, knives and nails would have interested the natives as well.

Wikimedia Commons

French Explorer Jacques Cartier landed near the mouth of the St. Lawrence River in modern-day Quebec and claimed the land for France in 1534.

Photo by Author

In 1960, archeological remains of Norse buildings were found on the north coast of Newfoundland. L'Anse aux Meadows is now a National Historic Site of Canada. The original site including the remains of seven Norse buildings are on display and near the remains of the reconstructed buildings.

Fast forward to the early 15th century and Europe was a busy place. The oldest settlements like London, Paris, Seville and Lisbon were now bustling cities. Maritime commerce flowed between European seaports trading African, Indian and Oriental trade goods. During this time period, many people believed the earth was flat. Sailors feared sea monsters and the unknown. Some thought that by sailing west to the horizon, ships would sail off the edge into eternity.

With the four Spanish voyages of Columbus between 1492–1504 and the subsequent discovery of the Caribbean Islands, Cuba, Jamaica and points west, the table was set for Spain to claim the entire Caribbean and Central America. Known as New Spain,

Wikimedia Commons

Norse Vikings visited and settled fringes of the North American continent 500 years before Christopher Columbus saw San Salvador in the present-day Bahamas.

Author's Collection

This plate is the first depiction of Niagara Falls, found in the book *New Discovery,* 1698 by Father Louis Hennepin. Hennepin was sent to Canada in 1675 as a member of the expedition under the command of René-Robert Cavelier and Sieur de La Salle to explore the Great Lakes and rivers of France's Louisiana Territory. Thomas Jefferson had a copy of this book and maps taken from it were used to plan the Louis and Clark expedition.

soon many Spanish explorers and conquerors were sent to the New World in search of virgin lands, treasure and gold, including Ponce De Léon who discovered Florida in 1513, Hernando Cortez who conquered the Aztec empire in 1521, and more. Where Spain dominated in the south, France dominated in the north.

Sailing for England in 1504, Italian explorer Sebastian Cabot set out on one of the first voyage attempts to discover the Northwest Passage, in hopes of finding a shortcut route to the East Indies. Cabot sailed into schools of codfish near modern day Newfoundland which were so dense, he wrote in his journal that shipmates could walk to shore on the backs of the fish. Upon Cabot's return to England and the disclosure of this incredible resource, voyages began in earnest by many countries to capitalize on this New World bounty. The French in particular traveled west and their sights were set on much more than codfish. French fisherman traded knives for beaver pelts. Known as *castor gras* in the French language, these fishermen's beaver blankets and pelts became the catalyst to the North American fur trade. By scraping the fur from the skins, hatters in Europe could make a high-quality, refined felt to craft their fancy hats.

In 1534 French explorer Jacques Cartier planted the French flag on the coastline of present day Quebec and proclaimed the land "New France." French explorers built smaller vessels and navigated the rivers of North America charting the unknown lands. Explorers like Samuel de Champlain founded the first early settlements in North America north of Florida, in areas now known today as St. John, New Brunswick and Quebec City, Quebec.

Champlain made well over 20 voyages to the New World and charted the northeast coast as well as the Great Lakes and more. And more explorers came.—Jesuit missionary Father Jacques "Pere" Marquette, Louis Joliet and René La Salle explored the Great Lakes and Mississippi River. Father Louis Hennepin was the first to see the great falls of Niagara. The French eventually controlled eastern Canada, the Great Lakes region and the entire Mississippi River corridor.

When it comes to the "New World" explorations the British were a little late to the party. The first English attempt to stake claims in America was the Roanoke Colony in 1585. Yet this colony vanished and what happened to it remains a mystery. (Likely the settlers were killed by natives or a devastating hurricane). Captain John Smith established Jamestown in 1607 and William Bradford's puritan congregation known as the Pilgrims, settled at what was called Plymouth Colony after landing at Plymouth Rock in the ship Mayflower, November 1620.

NORTH AMERICAN EXPLORERS

YEAR	EXPLORER	NATIONALITY	AREA EXPLORED
982	Erik Thorvaldsson	Norse Viking	Greenland
986	Bjarni Herjólfsson	Norse Viking	Northeast Coast
1000	Leif Eriksson	Norse Viking	Newfoundland
1473	João Côrte-Real	Portugal	Newfoundland
1492	Christopher Columbus	Italy for Spain	Bahamas
1497	John Cabot	Italy for England	Northeast Coast
1498	João Fernandes Lavrador	Portugal	Labrador
1508	Sebastian Cabot	Italy for England	Northwest Passage
1513	Juan Ponce de León	Spain	Florida
1519	João Álvares Fagundes	Portugal	Nova Scotia
1534	Jacques Cartier	France	Northeast Coast
1539	Hernando de Soto	Spain	Florida
1574	Martin Frobisher	England	Northwest Passage
1585	White/Cavendish	England	Roanoke Island
1603*	Samuel de Champlain	France	Great Lakes
1604*	Pierre Dugua de Mons	France	Northeast Coast
1607*	Henry Hudson	England	Northwest Passage
1607	John Smith	England	Jamestown Virginia
1615*	William Baffin	England	Northwest Passage
1669*	René-Robert de La Salle	France	Mississippi River
1678*	Louis Hennepin	France	Great Lakes
1673*	Louis Jolliet	French-Canadian	Mississippi River
1673*	Jacques Marquette	France	Mississippi River
1683*	Antoine de la Cadillac	France	Great Lakes
1769*	Samuel Hearne	English	Hudson Bay
1789*	Alexander Mackenzie	Scotland	Canada
1804*	Louis & Clark	American	American West
1806*	Zebulon Pike	American	American West
1842*	John C. Frémont	American	American West

* Denotes Fur Trade

FRENCH FUR TRADERS

1590–1769

It didn't take long for the French to see the vast potential of New France. Profiting from the fur trade looked to be a "no-brainer" and easy pickings. Native tribes of America were adept at harvesting animals for food and utilizing their skins for clothing and shelter. French fur traders didn't trap, but traded items for the pelts taken by the natives. And the French were smart—many of the most successful fur traders learned to speak the native language. They dressed in native style deerskin and wore moccasins. Some married natives and were accepted into the family and culture. Often children were born into these mixed unions creating a new race with native and European traits. Called the Métis, these ancestors are one of three recognized aboriginal peoples in Canada today. (The other two aboriginal peoples include Inuit and First Nations which comprise 634 separate indigenous peoples speaking 50 languages.)

Many trappers look at the fur industry as pelts for fur coats or trim. Although some fur was used in this manner, the original North American fur trade was for beaver pelts in which the underfur was scraped off and made into a felt that was molded into hats. In Europe, hats were all the rage and the fine underfur of the beaver was the perfect medium for making the felt.

The French fur traders were known as coureurs des bois or *runners of the woods.* French fur traders used small prams and birch bark canoes to travel by rivers and lakes to native villages in an attempt to create pacts and alliances with them primarily to trade for beaver pelts. Because these men knew their territories well, often they where employed by explorers who where charting the untamed lands of North America. Samuel de Champlain was one such explorer and his French-Canadian guide Étienne Brûlé is thought to be the first European to see the Great Lakes.

The french established a settlement on the St. Lawrence River in 1632 just to build birchbark canoes to be used for freighting furs on the many lakes and rivers too small for ship navigation. They built three sizes—the *North* canoe 26 feet in length. The *Bastard*

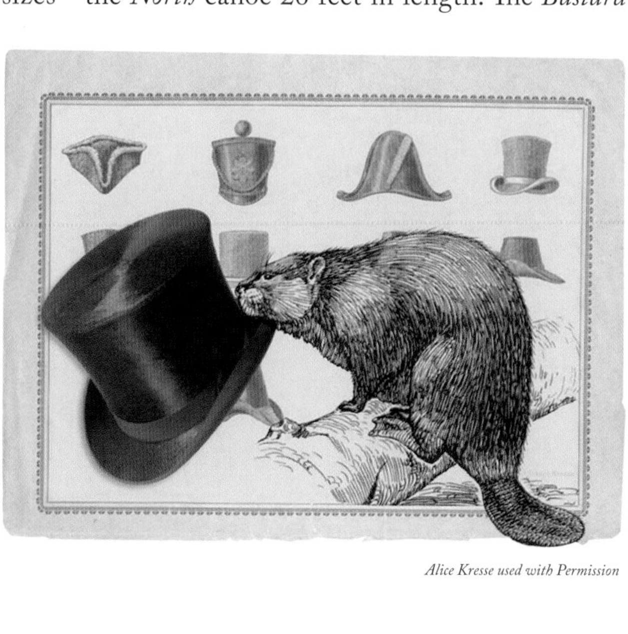

Alice Kresse used with Permission

canoe 28–32 feet in length, and the largest called the *Montreal* canoe—it was 36 feet in length and could carry 8,000 pounds of cargo plus paddlers. These huge Montreal freight canoes were used on long routes from western Lake Superior to Montreal and the Great Lakes trips from Fort Michilimackinac down the Mississippi River system.

The history and pioneering spirit of these fur traders is quite interesting. It must have been amazing to witness the raw, unspoiled beauty of North America.

Wikimedia Commons

1900 depiction of Sieur de La Vérendrye's 1735 re-supply convoy from Michilimackinac was forced to spend the winter at Grand Portage because of a navigational error by the crew. A mistake that ended in tragedy as La Vérendrye died in 1736. Painting by Canadian artist Arthur H. Hider.

HUDSON'S BAY COMPANY

For more than a century (approximately 1540–1650) the French controlled the North American fur trade. Utilizing the St. Lawrence River, French traders gained access to the rich fur areas of what is now Labrador, Quebec and New Brunswick. Utilizing smaller boats and canoes, rivers allowed easy travel to the Great Lakes and points west including the lands now known as the province of Ontario, New York, Michigan, Ohio, Wisconsin and Minnesota.

Hudson's Bay Company arms crest Motto in Latin Pro Pelle Cutem. "Skin For Leather."

In approximately 1658, French fur traders Pierre Radisson and Médard des Groseilliers had gotten word from a trader who had explored the Cree Nation and noted exceptional fur pockets. The Cree Nation includes the territory directly north of Lake Superior

Wikimedia Commons

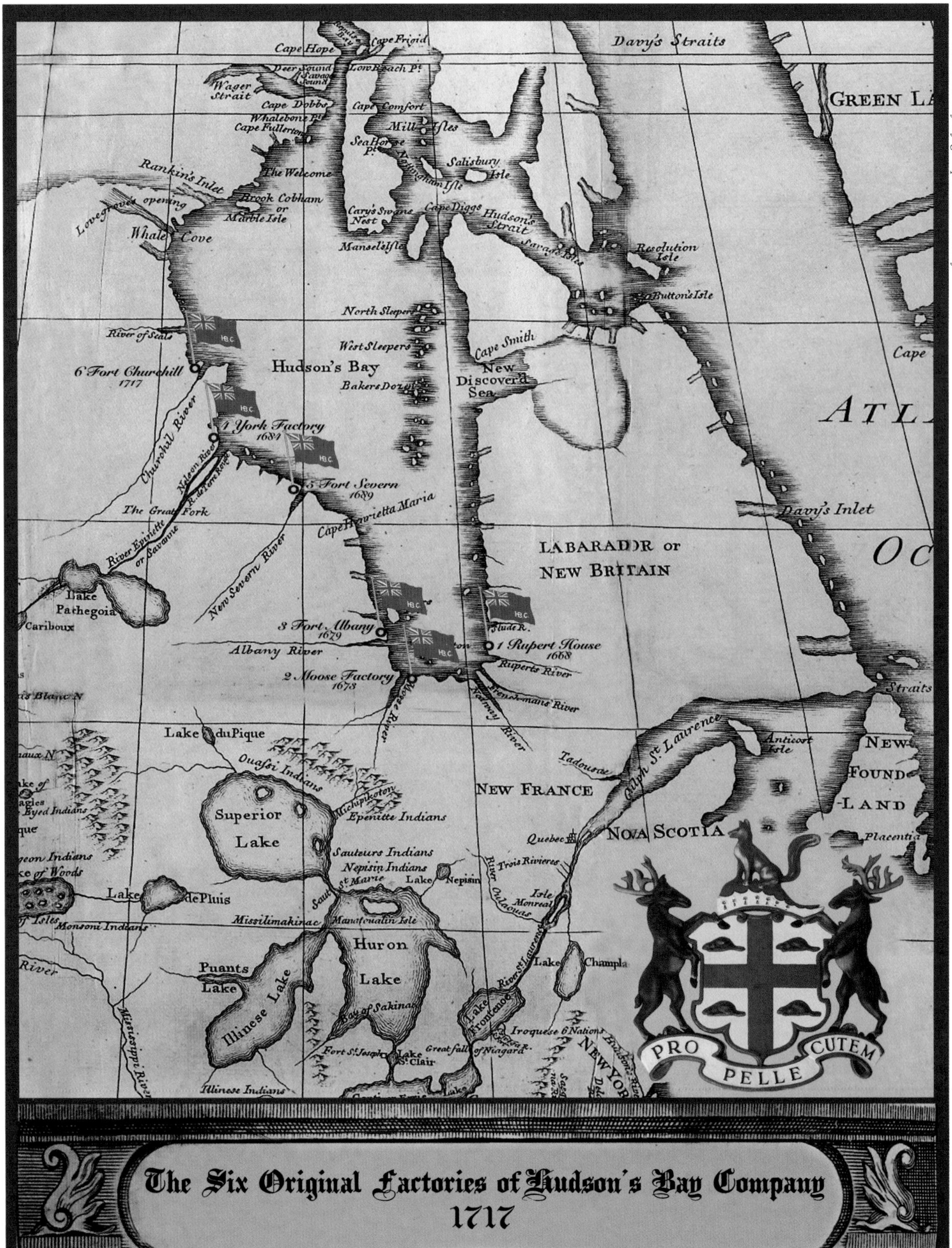

1744 Dobbs Hudson Bay Voyage map with HBC overlay.

This map shows much of the Hudson's Bay Company's Rupert Land Grant area and the six original outposts or Factories. Charles Fort (later named Rupert House)—1668, Moose Factory—1673, Fort Albany—1679, York Factory—1684. Fort Severn—1689 and Fort Churchill—1717. York Factory eventually became the main outpost because of its convenient location of the Saskatchewan and Red River waterways.

Author's Collection

This fur trade gorget was given to the Hudson's Bay Company fur traders and trappers who went deep into the wilderness to trap furs. This gorget was issued at Fort (Port) Albany Factory in 1683 and was highly prized by the trappers and fur traders. Stamped on the reverse is the phrase, "Loyal to the Kings Government," which meant the person issued this gorget would be given full protection and safe passage at any English fort.

to the "frozen sea" and west to the "prairies." Realizing that this area may be more easily accessed by large ships entering into Hudson's Bay, Pierre and Médard applied to the French administration to establish a trading post in the bay. With their request refused, the men traveled to the area on expedition and returned with a good quantity of prime pelts. However, neither Radisson nor des Groseilliers had a license to trade in the area and were heavily fined by the French *powers to be* and their pelts confiscated.

Now with even more determination to succeed in Hudson's Bay, Pierre and Médard sought out English investors in Boston to finance a voyage into the Bay. Securing financing and a ship proved easy, but as luck would have it, the scouting voyage ended early when the ship struck an ice flow in Hudson Strait ending the expedition. Dejected, broke and at ends with the project, Radisson and des Groseilliers received a windfall when Colonel George Cartwright learned of their misfortune and decided to invest in the Frenchmen by taking them to London to meet with Prince Rupert in the hopes of gaining sufficient finance. The 1665 the trip to England was an overwhelming success and by 1668 "Charles Fort" was established on James's Bay (the southernmost extension to Hudson's Bay) at the mouth of the newly named Rupert River (named after Prince Rupert). The fort was renamed Rupert House and became the first trading post of Hudson's Bay Company.

Hudson's Bay Company was established in 1670 by royal charter from King Charles II. The charter granted the company a whopping 1.5 million square miles of land around Hudson's Bay, the area which was considered the drainage basin. This huge tract of land included all rivers and streams that flowed into Hudson's Bay, which is an area nearly one-third the size of all of Canada. This land grant area was named Rupert's Land after Prince Rupert who was appointed as the first governor of the Hudson's Bay Company by the king. By 1717 HBC had built six trading posts or *factories* in key locations of Rupert's Land. This era was the beginnings of the English influence in North America's fur trade.

Hudson's Bay Company utilized the Made Beaver as the standard of trade and its form of currency. A Made Beaver (MB) was considered a prime beaver pelt which had been worn for at least one season. This allowed most of the long guard hairs to wear off revealing the dense underfur. This greasy underfur was easily shaved off the hide by hatters and was turned into a luxurious felt used for making fine European hats.

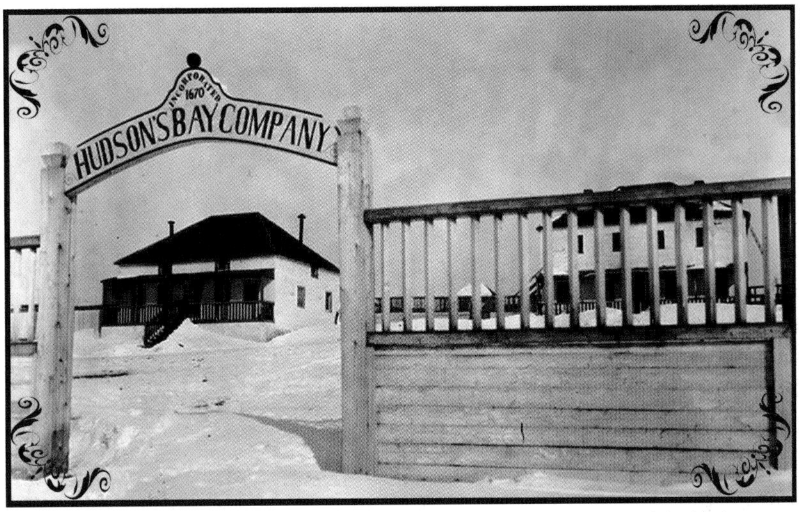

Wikimedia Commons

Fort Chipewyan was the fur hub of the Athabaska region. This Hudson Bay Company post is nestled on the shore of Lake Athabaska, Alberta. However, when Fort Chipewyan was built this area was considered the Northwest Territory.

All trade goods issued by Hudson's Bay Company were assigned a value in Made Beaver, as were other animal skins which the Bay sought to acquire. For example, 3 marten pelts might equal one MB. Hudson's Bay Company traded many useful items to the natives in exchange for their pelts including knifes, kettles, sewing supplies and their famous point blankets. The heavy wool blankets were typically adorned with 4 stripes (red, blue, yellow and green) and were often used to make what's known as a traditional capote. The capote is a 3/4 length, hooded, loose-fitting coat worn by many of the fur traders. Today the older Hudson's Bay point blankets found in excellent condition are quite valuable, especially the blankets woven around 1890, which were the first blankets to carry a stitched-on label. Unfortunately, blankets made before 1890 are all but impossible to date. As with most valuable items, counterfeit blankets have been made and dispersed into the marketplace.

After many owners and numerous transformations over the years, Hudson's Bay Company still exists today primarily as a retail brand associated with Saks Fifth Avenue as well as Lord & Taylor, the oldest department store chain in the United States (founded in 1826).

1733 HUDSON'S BAY COMPANY TRADE ITEMS

Item	Quantity For One Made Beaver
Colored Beads	3/4 Lb.
Brass Kettle	1
Black Lead	1 Lb.
Gun Powder	1 1/2 Lb.
Shot	5 Lb.
Sugar	2 Lb.
Brazilian Tobacco	2 Lb.
Ditto Roll	1 1/2 Lb.
Thread	1 Lb.
Vermilion	1 1/2 Oz.
Brandy	1 Gallon
Broad Cloth	2 Yard
Hbc Blanket*	1
Flannel Cloth	2 Yard
Gartering	2 Yard
Awl Blades	12
Buttons	12 Dozen
Breeches	1 Pair
Combs	2
Egg Boxes	4
Red Feathers	2
Fish Hooks	20
Fire Steel	4
Flint	20
Gun	1 (10-12 Mb)
Pistol	1 (4 Mb)
Gloves / Yarn	1
Goggles	2
Laced Hat	1
Hatchet	2
Hawk Bells	8
Rings	6
Stone Rings	3
Shoes	1
Shirts	2

Wikimedia Commons

Fur Trader at Fort Chipewyan in Canada's Northwest Territory grading fur. The value of this lot is written as $35,000. Value in today's dollars would be $940,000.

NORTH WEST COMPANY

(1779–1821)

The North West Company began in 1779 with an agreement between wealthy Montreal merchants to push back on the monopoly created by Hudson's Bay Company. By 1783 the company saw they were making inroads in the fur business especially in the Lake Superior region and west along the Saskatchewan and Red rivers. Thus the company officially structured with Simon McTavish, along with Joseph and Benjamin Frobisher and a few investors. In 1787 North West merged with another entity, McLeod and Company—eventually famed explorer Alexander Mackenzie joined the ranks seeing the potential of the operation moving west.

Competition was fierce between Hudson's Bay Company and North West, so much so that Hudson's Bay moved into the middle of North West territory's Red River in 1811 (in present-day Manitoba and Saskatchewan), building a settlement known as the colony of Assiniboia. By 1816 tempers were at a boil and North West trappers and traders raided Hudson's

North West Fur Company Coat of Arms — circa 1800.

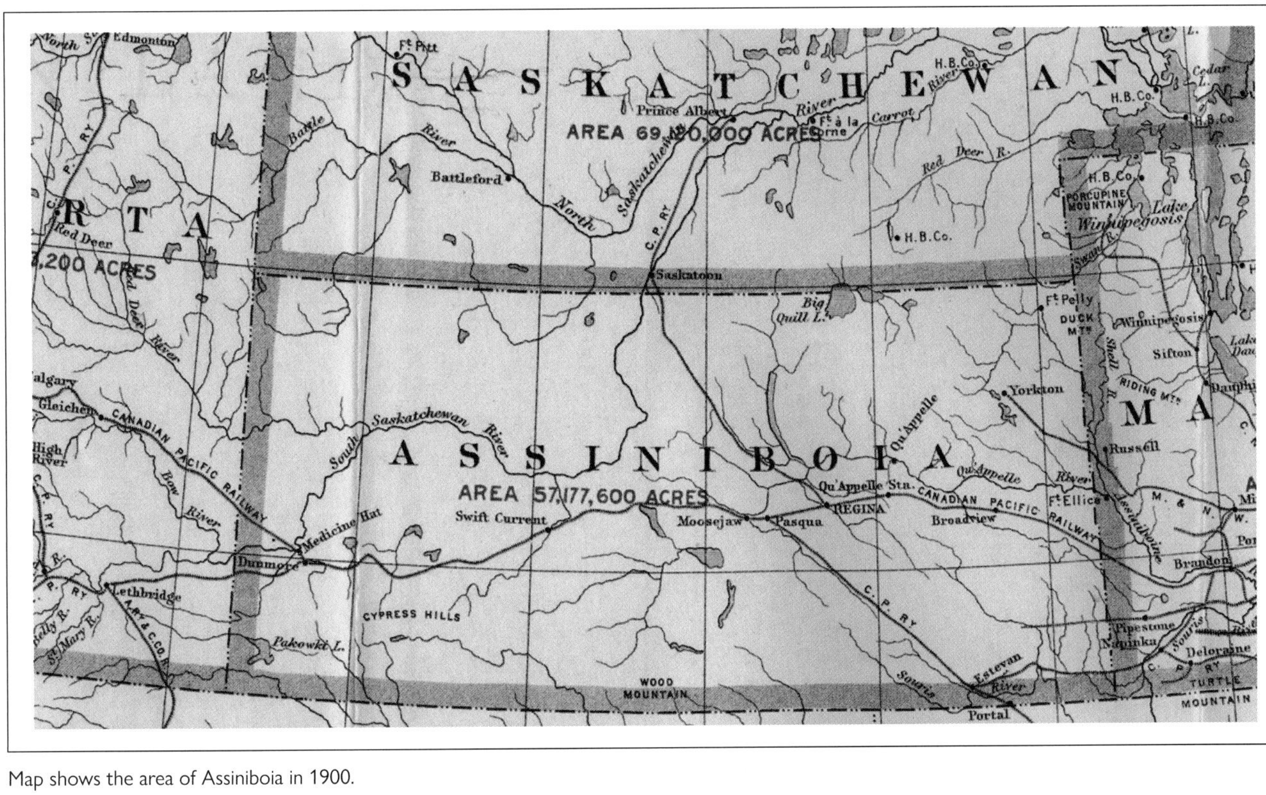

Wikimedia Commons

Map shows the area of Assiniboia in 1900.

Bay settlement and destroyed Assiniboia in what's known as the Seven Oaks Massacre. The Bay retaliated and destroyed The North West Company's post Fort Gibraltar in what is now Winnipeg.

These events led to dissent in the management of the North West Company and many of the wealthy investors pulled away from the enterprise. Hudson's Bay Company bought the North West Company in the summer of 1821.

Sketch of film icon Charlton Heston as Bill Tyler from the 1980 movie *The Mountain Men*.

CENTENNIAL

In 1974, Pulitzer Prize-winning author James Michener published the book *Centennial.* The novel is a chronicle of a group of families living in northeastern Colorado across several generations. Based somewhat on factual events, the story is a riveting tale of adventure and romanticizes the grit of the American west and the resolve of the early settlers.

In October 1978, NBC released a 12-part mini-series of the same name casting a host of famous actors. In the first episode, A French Canadian fur trader named Pasquinel (played by Robert Conrad) travels into wild Indian territory to trade for beaver pelts. Pasquinel's character is modeled after real life French Canadian pioneer and mountain man Jacques LaRamee who trapped and traded on the north Platte River in the area of southern Wyoming and northeastern Colorado in the early 1800s.

I graduated from high school in 1976 and was running extensive traplines in the farmlands on central Ohio during the time *Centennial* originally aired on television. I can remember watching the episodes and being mesmerized about this early history of trapping, about the adventure and dangers that existed in those times. As I pen this book, I can still envision the vivid memories of Pasquinel paddling his canoe up the Platt River, trapping and trading beads and blankets for beaver pelts.

At this time in my life, I was hopelessly hooked on trapping and watching these well-known actors portray trappers, gave me grand ideas that my chosen career should be trapping. Trapping is a huge part of our American history and this romantic portrayal of trappers and the early pioneers brought me feelings of American patriotism and a sense of keeping the trapping tradition.

The Centennial mini-series is available on DVD and if you haven't seen it, consider checking it out. The entire series is over 26 hours in length and is a very interesting watch.

Courtesy Universal Studios

J. GOODMAN

CHAPTER 2

SCOUTS AND MOUNTAIN MEN

In 1972, the film *Jeremiah Johnson* was released, featuring Robert Redford as "Liver-eating" Johnson and Will Geer as "Bear Claw" Chris Lapp. The movie script was a screenplay crafted from the 1959 book *Crow Killer,* a factual treatise of the life of John Jeremiah Johnson, a trapper and mountain man who seeks revenge for the murder of his family. As with most Hollywood movies, the film sensationalized true events (and made up others), but as a 14-year-old trapper, I was mesmerized by the imagery.

The film is a classic today among those of us hunters and trappers who grew up watching it. My oldest son was named Jeremy as sort of a tribute to my kinship with the movie.

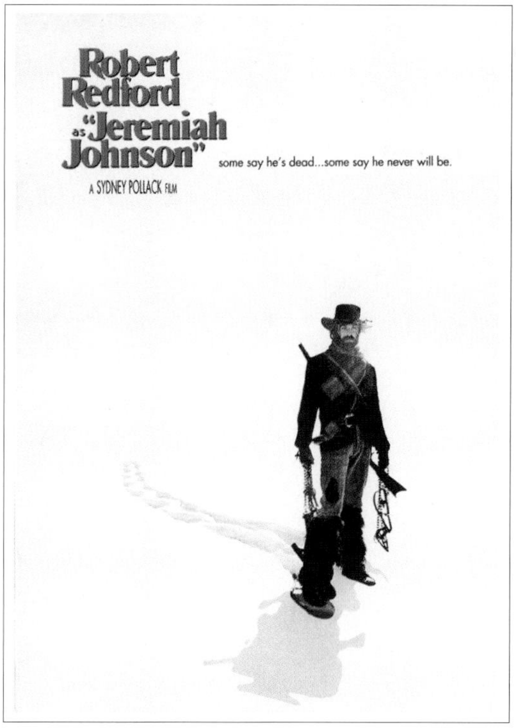

Courtesy Universal Studios

THE EXPANSION WEST

1750–1900

When president Thomas Jefferson tasked James Monroe and Robert Livingston to buy New Orleans from the French, Napoleon countered by offering the opportunity to buy all of Louisiana. In 1803 the United States paid $18 per square mile, or $15 million for the Louisiana Purchase. Later that same year, Jefferson commissioned Army Captain Meriwether Lewis as the leader of "The Corps of Discovery." The second in command would be William Clark. Their famous expedition would follow the Missouri River from Camp Dubois just north of St. Louis—to its headwaters, then over the Rocky Mountains and down the Columbia River to the Pacific Ocean. The goal of the expedition was to begin

< Artist Joe Goodman's sketch depicting Will Geer as "Bear Claw" Chris Lapp from the film, *Jeremiah Johnson.*

to chart the resources of this huge area while declaring sovereignty over the many native tribes found along the route.

Wikimedia Commons

Artist, scout, soldier and writer Edgar Samuel Paxson (1852–1919) was one of the premiere frontier artists of his time and depicted many scenes of the old west including Lewis and Clark's adventures, Custer's Battle of the Little Bighorn which he called "Custer's Last Stand," was a painting that took him six years to complete.

who learned the ways of the natives lived a life of solitude in the back country. The journals of Lewis and Clark tell a story of vast, tall-grass prairies, oceans of buffalo and elk, deer and beavers.

Friday September 15, 1804
At the confluence of the White River with the Missouri is an excellent position for a town. the land rising by three gradual assents, and the neighborhood flourishing more timber than usual in this country.

Monday September 17, 1804
To the westward, a high range of hills about twenty miles distant runs nearly north and south, but not to any great extent, as their rise and termination is embraced by one view, and they seem covered with a verdure similar to that of the plains. All around the country has been recently burnt, and a young green grass about four inches high covers the ground, which was in enlivened by herds of antelopes and buffalo, the last of which were in such multitudes that we cannot exaggerate in saying that at a single glance we saw three thousand of them before us.

—Louis and Clark Journals

Taking a page from the many French explorers from the previous century, Lewis and Clark used native guides and interpreters on their adventure. In fact, many of the most important explorations of the North American continent where led by guides and scouts who where trappers. Lewis and Clark's expedition is by far the most famous expedition of discovery in North America, yet it was just one of many. Trappers established most of the trails west which eventually became the wagon routes and ultimately, the railroad lines. Frontiersman trappers

This area described above was to be the location of Fort Kiowa (also called Fort Lookout) built in 1822 by Joseph Brazeau Jr. of the Berthold, Chouteau, and Pratte French Company. In 1823 it was the official jumping off point of Ashley's hundred trading expedition. Fort Kiowa has a special place in my history as in 1984, I took the government trapper position at Chamberlain, South Dakota, a settlement built only a few miles south of Fort Kiowa. More about this later in the book.

Wikimedia Commons

A portion of the famous painting of Lewis and Clark at Three Forks by Edgar Samuel Paxson.

JOHN COLTER

1775–1812

As a scout for the Lewis and Clark expedition, Virginia-born John Colter is considered among the first generation of mountain men who hunted and trapped in the American West. Known as one of the best hunters in the "The Corps of Discovery," the story goes that Colter decided that he would return to the west once the expedition was complete. As luck would have it, as the expedition was headed back to St. Louis, Colter met trappers Joseph Dickson and Forest Hancock in the Mandan Villages of present-day North Dakota. At their loyal scout's request, Louis and Clark honorably discharged Colter so he could guide trappers Dickson & Hancock back upriver to show them the rich fur pockets—for a cut of profits from the pelts.

Wikimedia Commons

Lewis's first Glimpse of the Rockies — Everett.

The original first edition documentation of Lewis and Clarks, journey is titled, *History of the Expedition Under the Command of Captains Lewis and Clark, to the Sources of the Missouri, Thence Across the Rocky Mountains and Down the River Columbia to the Pacific Ocean. Performed During the Years 1804-5-6.* It's a valuable and scarce 2-volume set that was printed in Philadelphia, released in 1814 and includes the famous map of the west. In top condition these books are very valuable and often sell for over $100 thousand. However, an excellent and affordable biography of the "Corps of Discovery" is the 1996 book, *Undaunted Courage* by Stephen Ambrose and is fascinating reading.

John Colter was likely the first white man to see the areas now known as Yellowstone and Grand Teton National Parks. Trekking in the region, Colter found much geothermal activity and in one area along the Shoshone River, found geysers and thermal vents so hot the area was nicknamed "Colter's Hell."

One story told of Colter's time as a scout is that he was captured by a band of Blackfeet tribesmen near Three Forks, Montana in 1809. The warriors killed Colter's partner John Potts, then stripped Colter naked and set him loose to run while they chased him in a game of hide-and-seek. Colter ran for his life, eventually killing one warrior and outsmarting

Author's Collection

This map shows the approximate location on the Grand River where Hugh Glass was attacked and left for dead. The "track" illustrates the likely movements of Glass as he crawled, then floated with the aide of a log the over 200-mile distance to Fort Kiowa on the Missouri River. Jedediah Smith was also mauled by a grizzly and this location is also marked on the map. 1814 Lewis and Clark map inset.

the others. With his feet raw and bleeding from the sharp rocks and cactus, Colter traveled over 200 miles before finding shelter, clothed with only a blanket he had taken from the warrior he killed.

John Colter trapped and guided in the area until his return to St. Louis in 1810, where he discussed his travels into the Yellowstone and Teton areas to William Clark. Known as Colter's Route, Colter's travels are included as a dotted line in the master version of Clark's map, titled *A Map of Lewis and Clark's Track Across the Western Portion of North America from the Mississippi to the Pacific Ocean*, which was published in 1814.

John Colter was said to have died of a yellowing skin condition caused by tumors or other serious issues within the body (jaundice) in 1812 at Miller's Landing, Missouri, but this has also been disputed.

HUGH GLASS

1783–1833

Many early mountain men and their adventures have been sensationalized in books, movies and television. Pennsylvania-born Hugh Glass would be considered one of the more famous. Featured in numerous books, several movies and at least one television serial, Glass and his wild adventures are the makings of legend. The Hugh Glass resume includes capture and escape from the famous New Orleans pirate John Lafitte, as well as escaping capture from the Pawnee tribe (in the area of present-day Nebraska). Of course neither event was ever documented and may only be embellished stories.

We do know that Glass became a "hired hunter" in 1823 for the Ashley-Henry Fur Company (eventually to be known as the Rocky Mountain Fur Company) and was known as one of Ashley's one hundred fur traders to ascend the Missouri River in search of prime pelts. Glass operated in the area of present day North and South Dakota, Wyoming and Montana. Hugh Glass is the mountain man portrayed by Leonardo DiCaprio in the 2015 film *Revenant*.

With increased conflicts by the native tribes along the upper Missouri, Ashley and Henry decided that the Missouri wasn't a viable travel way to access the Rocky Mountains. Andrew Henry decided to take a party in search of a new route by traveling up the Missouri to the Grand River and west along the Grand, continuing overland to the Yellowstone River. A second party led by Jedediah Smith would follow the Cheyenne River west. Story has it that Glass—who was scouting and hunting game ahead of the Henry party—was mauled by a sow grizzly when he stumbled onto the bear with her two cubs along the Grand River in present-day South Dakota. Severely mauled and eventually left for dead, Glass amazingly overcame his wounds enough to struggle for 6 weeks while he ate berries, crawling and eventually fashioning a crude raft to float his way down the Missouri River to Fort Kiowa, which was located just up river from present-day Chamberlain, South Dakota.

Glass recovered from his wounds and vowed to seek revenge on the fur traders who left him to die, yet eventually returned to the service of the Ashley-Henry Fur Company participating in many expeditions up the Platte, Powder and Yellowstone rivers in search of pelts and trade. Glass had many adventures before he was killed along with several trappers in a raid of Arikara natives on the Yellowstone River in the spring of 1833.

JEDEDIAH SMITH

1799–1831

One of the more educated of the mountain men, Jedediah Smith was born in South Central New York, his parents descended from families of puritans that came to America around 1620, possibly on the *Mayflower*. Like Hugh Glass, Jedediah joined the Ashley-Henry Fur Company and traveled up the Missouri. Where Glass trapped more in the region of western South Dakota and Wyoming, Smith traveled farther upriver to the Yellowstone and further to the Musselshell River in present-day Montana where Smith and a group of Ashley's trappers built a

cabin to trap the winter.

Like Hugh Glass, Jedediah Smith was also mauled by a grizzly and nearly killed. (The location of Smith's mauling is shown on the Glass map, previous page). Smith's scalp and one ear had been chewed off and once his men arrived to help him they located the scalp and sewed it back on his head. Smith also broke several ribs in his wrestle with the bruin. After healing from his wounds, Jedediah wore his hair very long to hide the deep scars of the attack. Jedediah Smith was a tall man with business savvy. Liked and trusted by Ashley and being somewhat of a legend after his surviving of the grizzly attack, Smith went on to lead many parties west in quest of furs and be among the first of the mountain men to see the Back Hills and the Mojave Desert as well as discover the best routes over the Rockies into the Pacific Northwest and California.

Likeness of the well-traveled Jedediah Smith in a birch bark canoe. Pencil sketch by artist Joe Goodman.

Wikimedia Commons

Explorer John C. Fremont employed many trappers and mountain men in his explorations, including Jedediah Smith and Kit Carson. This engraving is from the book, *Life, explorations, and public services of John Charles Fremont"* by Charles Wentworth Upham, 1856.

Rather than building trading posts as the Hudson's Bay Company did throughout the north, the Ashley-Henry Fur Company held Fur Rendezvous to barter and buy pelts. The first rendezvous was held in 1825 north of modern-day McKinnon, Wyoming on the Henry Fork River. It was here at this first rendezvous that Jedediah Smith was offered a partnership with Ashley. Upon accepting, the name was changed to Ashley-Smith Fur Company.

Jedediah Smith kept a diary and also drew maps of his travels which impressed his peers and allowed others to follow his routes. In fact, Smith's 1831 map of the west was used by many including the famous overland explorer John C. Fremont for his expeditions of the early 1840s. Smith made several trips into the California Territory and is thought to be one of the most traveled of all the mountain men having explored regions tied to modern-day Washington, Oregon, California, Nevada, Idaho, Utah, Montana, Wyoming, Colorado, New Mexico, North and South Dakota, Nebraska, Kansas, Missouri and poins east.

Smith was killed by Comanches while scouting for water near a junction of the Santa Fe Trail and a spring fork of the Cimarron River in present-day Kansas. To learn more about Jedediah Smith, check out this book-*The Ashley-Smith Explorations and the Discovery of a Central Route to the Pacific, 1822–1829:* With the Original Journals by Harrison Clifford, 1918.

JIM BRIDGER

1804–1881

Jim Bridger's name is synonymous with trappers of the mountain man age. Often referred to as the Daniel Boone of the Rocky Mountains, Bridger was born in Richmond, Virginia but as a youngster moved with his family to St. Louis about 1812. Like many of America's second generation mountain men, Jim learned the ways of the wilds by answering the call to Ashley's one hundred fur traders. Bridger actually was on the fur expedition with Hugh Glass when Glass was mauled by the grizzly and by contemporary accounts was thought to be one of the men who was left to care for Glass and then abandoned him. In the Glass account, John Fitzgerald and a man only identified as "Bridges" were the two volunteers who stayed with Glass after the attack—yet they later abandoned him to die. The similarity of Bridges and Bridger is likely where the association stems, yet today no one really knows the truth.

Jim Bridger hunted, trapped and explored new areas in the west beginning in 1822. Establishing Bridger's Trading Post (Fort Bridger) with Lewis Vasquez, the men would guide traveling settlers from the fort west to California. The fort was situated at the junction of the Oregon Trail, California Trail and Mormon Trail and was perfect location for buying pelts. Fort Bridger also acted as an essential resupply outpost for wagon trains and was a stop for the Pony Express.

Jim Bridger eventually purchased the Ashley-Smith & Sublette Fur Company and renamed it the Rocky Mountain Fur Company in 1830. A grand historical narrative about Jim Bridger can be found in the book *Jim Bridger* by J. Cecil Alter, 1925.

KIT CARSON

1809–1868

Kit Carson led a full life. As a mountain man, frontiersman, fur trapper and guide, Carson was a standout and much has been written about his amazing life. Born Christopher H. Carson, his mother struggled with her pregnancy and when Carson was born he was a small baby and nicknamed "Kit"—a name that obviously stuck. His parents moved from Madison County, Kentucky to Boone's Lick, Missouri settling on land owned by Daniel Boone's sons.

Young Kit grew up with the stories of Daniel Boone and eventually took an apprenticeship as a saddle-maker at the head of the Santa Fe Trail in the small settlement of Franklin, Missouri. Saddle making wasn't of interest to Kit and he soon left the apprenticeship to tend the livestock for a group of trappers headed west. Carson never looked back. Settling in Taos, New Mexico, Carson was mentored

Wikimedia Commons

by one of the trappers that he traveled west with, Mathew Kinkead.

Wikimedia Commons

Kit Carson

Carson joined Ewing Young's expedition into the Rocky Mountains in 1829 and his career as a mountain man, Indian fighter and guide was in the making. Trapping in the Rockies, Kit would eventually meet Jim Bridger and many other "now famous" trappers on the banks of the Green River, Wyoming at the annual Fur Rendezvous.

Carson was an excellent woodsman and trapper. Quick-witted and well-traveled, a good memory allowed Kit to engage with anyone and quickly gain respect. As fate would have it, Carson met John Charles Frémont on a Missouri river steamboat and was hired by Frémont as a guide of his first expedition of the west, beginning in 1842. Paid $100 a month, Carson earned his keep navigating the expedition through rugged terrains and hostile Indian territories. Kit Carson guided all three of John Frémont's expeditions to cement his name in annals of history.

Kit Carson continued to guide groups of settlers west, run traplines and fight Indians when needed. His adventures and fame grew in newspapers and reports until the stories fell into the hands of publishers who printed dime novels sensationalizing Carson's life as the "fighting trapper." Make no mistake, Kit Carson was the "real deal" and will always be an icon of the early American West.

JOHN JOHNSON

1824–1900

Known as "Liver-eating" Johnson, John Johnson is not remembered for his trapping, prospecting or as a frontiersman. Johnson is best remembered as an Indian fighter. Although there are many tales and legends associated with Johnson, it's thought that he served during the Mexican-American War and deserted after striking an officer. His family name was said to be Garrison and upon the desertion was changed to Johnston and later Johnson. John ran west into the Montana Territory where he dug for gold and cut wood for the paddlewheel steamers (known as woodhawking).

Johnson was said to have married a Flathead native and about 1847 she was found alone by members of a Crow tribe hunting party and murdered.

Montana Tourism

John Johnson's Montana cabin in whichhe lived during the 1880s.

Wikimedia Commons

John Johnson here dressing the part of the legendary frontier Indian fighter he was, complete with Jim Bowie knife, 1880s.

Johnson sought to avenge her death and set out on a killing spree that according to biographers led to the deaths of more than three hundred crow warriors. Johnson would kill each warrior in mortal combat, scalp them and cut out their liver and eat it. A ritual that led to his nickname "Liver-Eating" Johnson. This practice was done as an insult to the natives, as their belief was the liver was a vital organ in the afterlife. Johnson became feared by the Crow as he was seemingly a ghost to them and could not be killed.

One campfire tale that is associated with Johnson is that one winter he was ambushed by a party of Blackfoot warriors. The plan was the warriors would sell Johnson to his enemy the Crow. Tied with leather straps in a teepee, Johnson managed to escape, killing his native guard and then travel over 200 miles to reach the cabin of his trapping partner Del Gue. A journey in the dead of winter with little clothing, food or possibles. Johnson eventually made peace with the Crow after twenty five years of vengeance.

Johnson joined the Calvary in the 1860s and eventually became the Sheriff of Coulson, Montana and the Marshall of Red Lodge, Montana. Johnson died in 1900 at a veteran's home in San Monica, California. However, his remains were moved to Cody, Wyoming in 1974 two years after the release of Pollack & Redford's *Jeremiah Johnson* film.

SEWELL NEWHOUSE

1806–1888

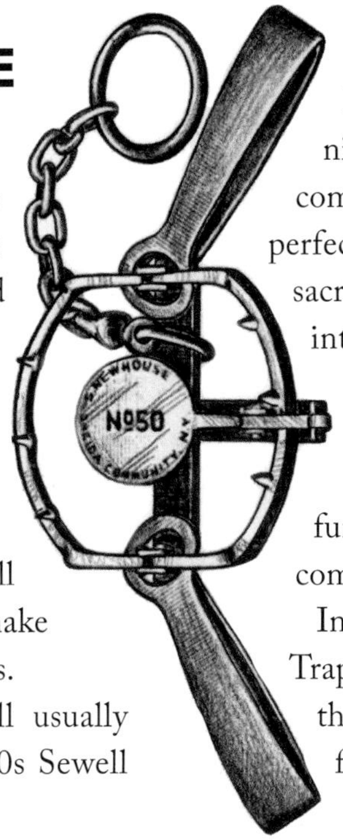

The son of a blacksmith, Sewell Newhouse loved the wild places and as a youngster spent much time outdoors. Sewell's family moved from their home in Vermont to Oneida, New York when he was 14. About 1823 at the age of 17, Newhouse crafted his first steel trap using metal scraps found lying around his father's shop. One trap led to another and over the next twenty or so years. Sewell perfected his craft, learning to temper steel, make chain and he would sell traps to local trappers.

As trap building is hard work, Sewell usually worked with a partner and by the late 1840s Sewell met Oneida Community leader John Humphrey Noyes. The Oneida Community was a religious experiment, an early commune created under the auspice that a perfect life on earth was one where individuals sacrificed personal wants for the needs and interests of the entire community. Oneida Community was known originally for the making of fine silver table service. The added trap business would help fund the approximately 250 families of the community.

In 1852 the initial Oneida Community Traps were hand made, yet by about 1855 the demand was such that Newhouse went full into manufacturing mode (with the

Authors Collection

Sewell Newhouse. Portrait from the book "Trappers Guide" 1867

community's blessing). He built a modern (for the time) manufacturing facility in 1863-64. Records show that in 1865 the Oneida Community recorded sales of over 200,000 traps of various sizes. By 1870, over 400,000 traps.

In 1881 sales were such that the community formed the company Oneida Community Limited. In 1886 Oneida Community LTD launched a new, less-expensive line of traps which they named Victor. By 1900 the company was by far the largest trap manufacturer in the world.

Today, trap collectors are keen to locate original Newhouse traps in fine condition. Sewell Newhouse's handmade traps 1840–1849 and the Community traps 1850–1864 were made with trap pans which were not embossed. Known as slick pan traps, these authentic Newhouse traps are prized by collectors. After 1865, trap pans were stamped with the traps, size as well as Newhouse Community N.Y.

Newhouse traps built between 1880–1925 were stamped S. Newhouse Oneida Community LTD, although some traps in this era were stamped Kenwood N.Y. Sewell Newhouse passed away in 1888 but his traps continued to be manufactured and sold. After 1911, traps carried the patient date of Sept. 26–1911. In 1925 several former community employees bought the trap division of Oneida Ltd. moving the entire business to Lititz, Pennsylvania forming Animal Trap Company. From 1925 onward, all Newhouse trap pans were stamped Animal Trap Company Lititz, PA. There are many nuances in identifying and valuing antique Newhouse traps. Trap historian Tom Parr has several good books on the subject and information on Tom and his museum is found at the end of this chapter.

Authors Collection

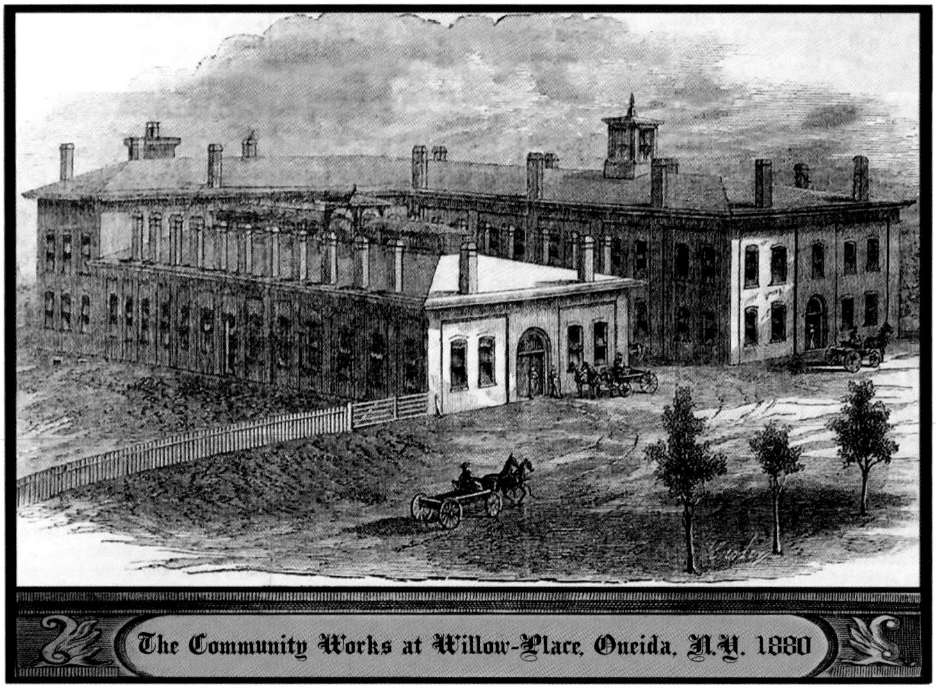

Artists rendition of the factory where Newhouse traps were made, circa 1880.

THE FUR COMPANIES

During the westward push for expansion and discovery, many fur companies were established, first in New York and Chicago then St. Louis and finally, on the northwest coast. Trappers needed outlets to sell their collections of furs. The raw pelts needed care and safe transport to tanneries and manufacturers. Manufacturers needed reliable suppliers. Fur Companies became the "middleman" between the trappers and the furriers. Some of these companies thrived, others were mismanaged and all were susceptible to the ups and downs of the fur markets. Often these companies were sold and merged into existing companies or the company name changed as if to start anew.

AMERICAN FUR COMPANY

1808–1842

The American Fur Company was founded by John Jacob Astor, a German immigrant who is considered the first millionaire businessman in North America. Astor made his fortune in Real Estate, Opium and fur trade.

Astor's family business in Germany was in the meat industry as a butcher. When John arrived in 1783, he set up a butcher shop in New York and would buy furs or trade for meat from trappers as well as indigenous peoples. In 1794 Astor opened a fur shop, selling warm fur garments to wealthy New York patrons.

Soon Astor purchased a dozen ships and began an import/export business which quickly increased his prowess—his fur business grew. Trading opium, tea and sandalwood with the Chinese allowed John Jacob to establish the American Fur Company in 1808 controlling fur trade along the Columbia River in present-day Oregon as well as in the Great Lakes. The American Fur Company was a direct competitor to Hudson's Bay Company and the Northwest Company. Astor's wealth amassed and so did his prowess in the fur trade. Eventually Astor set up Fort Astoria, the first permanent community on the Pacific coast—a strategic move that allowed him to eventually grow into one of the wealthiest men in American history.

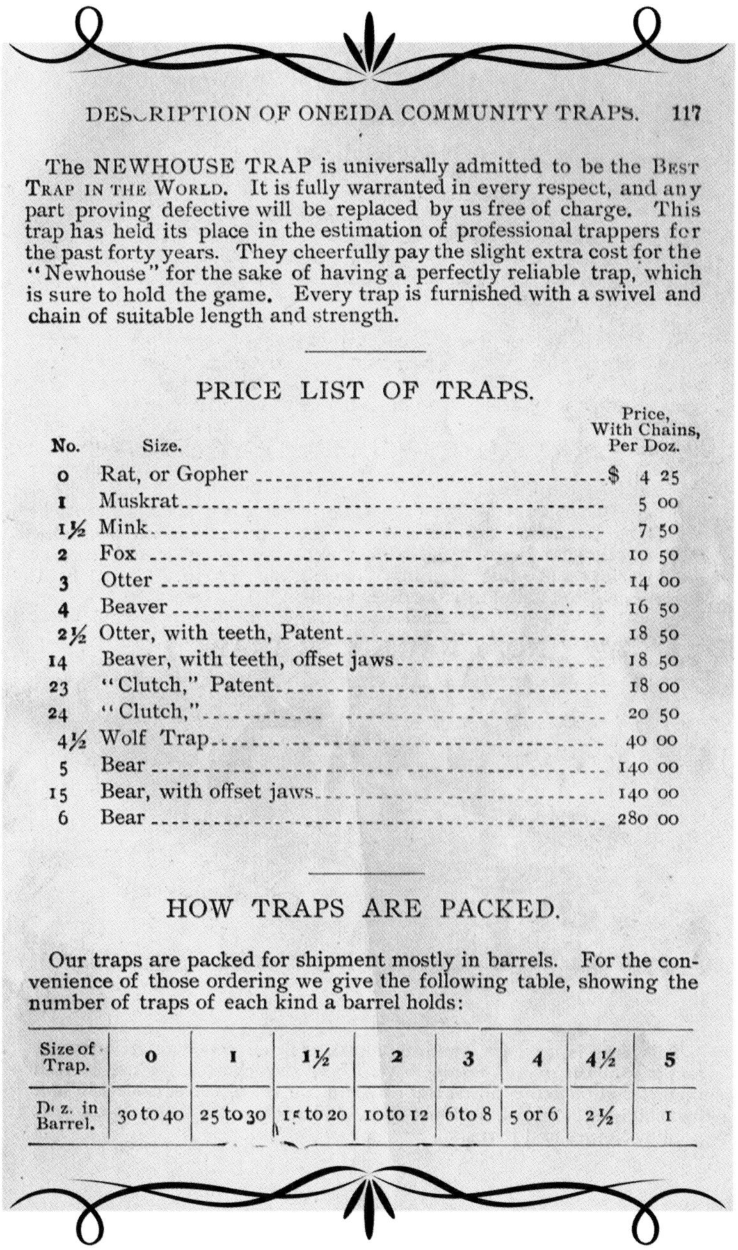

DESCRIPTION OF ONEIDA COMMUNITY TRAPS. 117

The NEWHOUSE TRAP is universally admitted to be the BEST TRAP IN THE WORLD. It is fully warranted in every respect, and any part proving defective will be replaced by us free of charge. This trap has held its place in the estimation of professional trappers for the past forty years. They cheerfully pay the slight extra cost for the "Newhouse" for the sake of having a perfectly reliable trap, which is sure to hold the game. Every trap is furnished with a swivel and chain of suitable length and strength.

PRICE LIST OF TRAPS.

No.	Size.	Price, With Chains, Per Doz.
0	Rat, or Gopher	$ 4 25
1	Muskrat	5 00
1½	Mink	7 50
2	Fox	10 50
3	Otter	14 00
4	Beaver	16 50
2½	Otter, with teeth, Patent	18 50
14	Beaver, with teeth, offset jaws	18 50
23	"Clutch," Patent	18 00
24	"Clutch,"	20 50
4½	Wolf Trap	40 00
5	Bear	140 00
15	Bear, with offset jaws	140 00
6	Bear	280 00

HOW TRAPS ARE PACKED.

Our traps are packed for shipment mostly in barrels. For the convenience of those ordering we give the following table, showing the number of traps of each kind a barrel holds:

Size of Trap.	0	1	1½	2	3	4	4½	5
Doz. in Barrel.	30 to 40	25 to 30	15 to 20	10 to 12	6 to 8	5 or 6	2½	1

Author's Collection

Turn-of-the-century price list showing the cost of Newhouse traps by the dozen.

Wikimedia Commons

Painting by Gilbert Charles Stuart of America's first multi millionaire, John Jacob Astor.

ASHLEY-HENRY FUR COMPANY

1822–1830

William Henry Ashley had participated as a Brigadier General in the War of 1812. Meeting Major Andrew Henry during the war, the two became friends and after the war formed the Ashley-Henry Fur Company. Their premise was simple, outfit one hundred fur trappers and mountain men and send them into the Rocky Mountains to trade and trap, then buy their furs at a rendezvous strategically held near a Hudson's Bay outpost. No trading posts needed to be built. Profit could be made on the outfitting as well as the pelts. Natives who traded with long time fur mogul Hudson's Bay Company, could attend the the event and sell their goods as well. It was a great idea and it worked.

Ashley would hire the better scouts, hunters and trappers to lead trapping parties into virgin areas making alliances with new tribes as well as training tenderfoot's (newcomer's) to the ways of trapping. The most accomplished mountain men where on the Ashley-Henry payroll including Jedediah Smith, Jim Bridger and Kit Carson to name a few.

SAINT LOUIS MISSOURI FUR COMPANY

1808–1830

After Lewis and Clark returned from their expedition, expert river boat pilot and entrepreneur Manuel Lisa learned of the potential for trapping and trade upriver and pulled together a party of fifty-plus men to travel north in 1807 to where the Bighorn River meets the Yellowstone. It was in this location where the crew built Fort Raymond and ran a trapping expedition from the headquarters.

Returning to St. Louis the following year loaded with pelts, the idea to form a fur company to sell their large haul soon became the St. Louis Missouri Fur Company. Using Manuel Lisa's fleet of prams, river boats and an association with both Louisiana Territory Governor Meriwether Lewis and William Clark, the company flourished by commissioning and out-

Author's Collection

Tribute marker for river boat entrepreneur Manuel Lisa and his fort built on the Missouri River at the start of the American West fur trade.

fitting trappers and traders along the upper Missouri and buying their pelts.

The War of 1812 made fur trading difficult in the upper Midwest and soon the St. Louis Missouri Fur Company dissolved. After the war in 1819 the company was re-established as the Missouri Fur Company and operated effectively until May 1823 when one of its partners Joshua Pilcher and his men were ambushed by a Blackfoot war party killing several men, taking their traps, horses and pelts. The event was the proverbial straw that broke the camel's back as the company never recovered from the losses although it was reconstituted under other names until 1830.

TRAP HISTORY MUSEUM

Located just southwest of Columbus, Ohio in the small berg of Galloway, is a collection of traps and trapping memorabilia worth investigating. The collection and holdings of trapper, collector and entrepreneur Tom Parr are nothing short of incredible.

The museum, laid out to resemble an old hardware store, includes over 4,000 traps of various makes, models and sizes. From the oldest of Newhouse bear traps to mouse-catching devices, books, calendars, photos and everything in-between.

Parr began his trap collector binge in 1987 and was soon ravaging every swap meet, yard sale and auction he could find looking for just that one trap he didn't have.

This passion turned into an obsession. By 1995 Tom Parr's collection had grown to where he had so many people interested in his traps, he needed to set up a display which would make it easier to see each relic of his massive hoard. This was the start of the Trap History Museum. Of course it would stand to reason that the "King of Trap Collecting" would also be the president of the North American Trap Collectors Association, N.A.T.C.A.

Tom's museum has also acquired access to the famous Richard Gerstell collection of 189 unique traps built by the Animal Trap Company of Lititz, Pennsylvania. Gerstell was the trap research pro at Animal Trap Company in the late 1940s and authored the definitive trap collectors book, *The Steel Trap in North America.* Hopefully this fantastic addition has found a home in Parr's fine museum.

Tom Parr also authors the antique trap collecting column in *Fur-Fish-Game* magazine with each issue featuring one of his unique traps. Frankly, it's awesome to see how much of a difference one man can make toward documenting and cataloging the history and heritage of trapping. Thank you Tom. For more information on visiting Tom Parr's museum, visit www.traphistorymuseum.com.

Author's Photo

Antique trap expert and trapping history buff Tom Parr and some of his amazing Trap History Museum Collection.

CHAPTER 3

PIONEER TRAPPERS

The turn of the century introduced so many innovations into society—it must have been a grand era to be alive. Electric lights, motor cars, airplanes and an incredible host of technologies that must have made life very exciting. Industrialization had begun moving populations from rural areas into cities where factories were built and jobs available.

It was the idea of the American dream and having your own business. A time when an enterprising person could work their way up from sweeping floors to management. Competition for high-paying trade and supervisory jobs was keen. A "white-collar" workforce expanded as factories and businesses grew.

The workforce needed to man these factories created business opportunities for builders, restaurant owners, supermarkets, and a host of service oriented businesses sprang up. The factory foremen, supervisors and upper management were well paid and had disposable income. The status of their job required supervisors and upper management to dress the part. Men bought suits, for the wives fur coats and fancy hats. At the turn of the century, there were no stigmas about furs—in fact, fur was a status symbol and those who could afford authentic fur, wore it. With so many moving to the city to find work, the countryside was left for farmers, ranchers and enterprising trappers.

> Adirondack Trapper E.J. Dailey admires a dandy winter-caught reynard.
Photo by Dick Wood

Authors Collection

Illustration from the book *Art of Trapping* published by A.B. Shubert Fur House, 1917.

A NEW ERA
1890 —1935

In the early 1900s there was much territory that remained wild. Places like the Allagash wilderness of Maine, the Adirondacks of New York, the White and Green Mountains, Michigan's Upper Peninsula and wild stretches of the Mississippi River. Further west there were the Black Hills, Bighorns, Rockies the Cascade Mountains, Canada's Northwoods and Pacific Northwest all rich in furs.

One of the most intriguing aspects of the fur business in the early years was the demand for certain species. While all furs had value, different eras found a much higher demand for some species. Where the beaver was the most sought in the earliest years, by 1820 their population had plummeted. Buffalo robes became popular from 1820–1860. Raccoons about 1860. Mink became popular after the Civil War, with North America shipping approximately 34,000 mink annually to London. By 1890 mink exports were over 3 million skins. Skunk pelts were also popular in the "mink years" after the war. In fact, fur farming for mink and skunks became popular around 1880. Fur seals were also in demand during the last three decades of the 19th century. Documents show the fur seal harvest in Alaska from 1870–90 at 1.8 million with an estimated profit of nearly $19 million.

Furs were valuable but only where you found them. The days of hiring and outfitting trappers as William Henry Ashley did were long gone. As the fur industry matured, fur companies became keen to recruit new trappers into their system and build loyalty with them.

F.C. TAYLOR FUR COMPANY

St. Louis 1870–

In the pioneering days of trapping, most of the knowledge and equipment came from the larger fur companies who knew that if they could provide books and pamphlets which taught trapping methods, likely they would sell supplies to trappers and eventually buy the pelts. F.C. Taylor began buying furs in 1870. To put that in perspective, famous mountain man "Liver-Eating" Johnson was just 46 years old.

F.C. Taylor was one of the first trapping supply houses to sell trap guns, also known as set guns. I know this sounds crazy by todays standards, but set guns were loaded rifles which used a bait hook in front of the muzzle. When an animal pulled the bait, the rifle fired and killed it. The trappers set gun was refined and patented by Charles D. Lovelace in 1905 and sold first by the Texas Firearm Company.

Taylor's Sure Shot Trap Gun was originally made by Mossberg. Its operation was simple. The weapon was staked into the ground via a large screw. The angle of the weapon was adjusted depending on the animal

Even though the west was still wild, by 1874 St. Louis had grown into a thriving city.

Wikimedia Commons

to be hunted (raccoon, possum, mink, coyote, etc.). Bait is used on the hook. When the animal takes the bait, the trigger discharges and the animal is usually shot in the head. The fact that this firearm uses a small 22 caliber round helps ensure that the animals pelt remains undamaged.

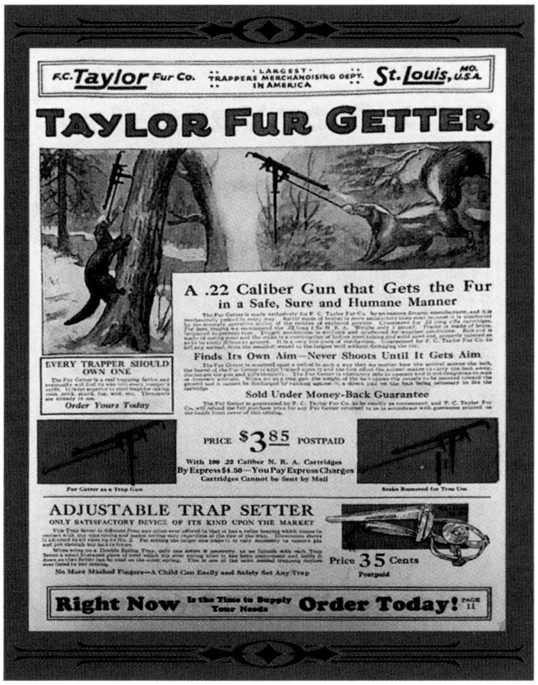

Author's Collection

F.C. Taylor's Fur Getter was a popular item at the turn of the century.

Author's Collection

Early fur company catalogs where nicer than some books at the time

F.C. Taylor helped champion game laws by listing regulations by state in their advertising pamphlets. (Game laws, which eventually did away with the set gun.)

F.C. Taylor outlasted all the St. Louis-based fur businesses until it was purchased in the 1960s by

S. Goodman & Son of Louisville, Kentucky. Today, the F.C. Taylor brand is owned by Keith Winkler's Sterling Fur and Tool Company in Sterling, Ohio.

FUNSTEN BROTHERS

St. Louis, 1881

Author's Collection

The fur business in St. Louis became quite competitive. Here's a full-page Funsten Furs ad from *Boys' Life* magazine, October 1918.

Because nearly all the furs gathered in North America were exported to Europe, New York City had been the fur business epicenter almost since its existence. St. Louis however, became the fur hub in the west. Founded in 1764 by French fur traders, St. Louis was strategically located on the mighty Mississippi River at the mouth of the Missouri River. With Louis & Clark's expedition starting from St. Louis in 1804, the small river town would quickly expand as the "Gateway to the West." Many fur businesses opened in St. Louis. Funsten Brothers along with F.C. Taylor were two of the largest and most aggressive competitors. St. Louis held the World's Fair in 1904 and the fur business was center stage. Funsten Brothers ran huge magazine ads to attract trappers from all across the country to sell them furs and they printed a large supply catalog, chock full of trapping tips. After the fur boom of the 1920s, the fur industry slumped and the Great Depression took its toll on fur businesses as well.

ANDERSCH BROTHERS

Minneapolis, 1884

The Minneapolis based Andersch Brothers was another well-known hide and fur company. Based in Minneapolis, Andersch bought hides, wool, furs and medicinal plants. They also tanned hides, sold trapping supplies and much more. One key element that made Andersch different was Louis Andersch wrote and published a hunters and trappers guide in 1903. At the time, lavish catalogs, pamphlets, softcover mini books and calendars which all included how-to trapping tips were being used by fur companies to lure in new trappers and build brand allegiance. But a hardcover book about trapping published by a large fur company was unheard of. Louis Andersch's book was large—over 430 pages detailed valuable information about all fur bearers, along with illustrations of the most productive sets as well as in-depth descriptions of pelt preparation.

Andersch Bros. Hunters and Trappers Guide also included information about fur farming which was quite popular at the turn of the century. The guide from Newhouse in 1867 and Shubert Fur House *Art of Trapping* were both small books compared to Andersch's treatise which was reprinted in a second edition in 1906. Andersch was a clever businessman in the sense that his book could be added into school libraries, which offered an opportunity to sell books to outlets giving his information instant credibility within the shelves of school text and research books. Many a young trapper sold furs to the Andersch Brothers because of their well-written book. As a note, *Andersch Bros. Hunters and Trappers Guide* becomes available from time to time on eBay in both its 1903 and 1906 editions or can be found at used bookstore websites like abebooks.com.

Authors Collection

ANDERSCH BROS.

Hide-Fur Report

Minneapolis Northwest **Market Prices** Minneapolis Northwest

Quoting Today's Market for Goods We Handle and Consume

Hides-Furs-Wool-Pelts-Tallow, Etc.

Minneapolis, November 20, 1909 Minnesota

The Above Building and Premises are Owned by Us and Exclusively Used for Our Hide and Fur Business in Minneapolis, Minnesota.

We solicit and welcome new patrons. Our 25 years of continued and considerate service is a significant and agreeable endorsement to our policy: "Prompt Cash Returns, Honorable Weights and Selection at Highest Prices." The steady growth of our shipping trade with customers scattered thru all parts of the United States and Canada, with many in Europe, Australia and some in China and Japan must appeal to those who handle Hides, Furs, Etc.

Below is a List of Our Bankers Showing Capital and Surplus:

First National Bank,	Minneapolis, Minn.	$4,000,000
Northwestern National Bank	" "	5,000,000
Security National Bank,	" "	2,300,000
East Side State Bank,	" "	106,000
Continental National Bank, Chicago, Ill.		7,900,000
Second National Bank, Minot, No. Dak.		85,000
Merchants Bank of Commerce, Winnepeg, Man.		9,000,000

Our Checks are Made Payable Without Exchange at Chicago, Denver, St. Louis, Grand Forks, Aberdeen, Winnepeg, Etc.

Ship Your Hides and Furs Where You Get the Most Money

1884 – 1909

25 YEARS IN THE HIDE & FUR BUSINESS 1884 – 1909 MINNEAPOLIS, MINN.

Andersch Bros. 411-413-415-417-419 Main St. Minneapolis, Minn.

The Minneapolis-based Andersch Brothers operated right out of downtown Minneapolis.

Both the 1903 & 1906 (red cover) editions of the *Andersch Bros. Hunters and Trappers Guide* are shown along with the first edition title page.

SEARS, ROEBUCK & COMPANY

Chicago, 1893

Several retail merchandizing businesses got into the fur trade. The biggest was Sears, Roebuck and Company. Sears venture into the fur business began in 1925. Based in Chicago, Sears could supply just about anything in trade for furs from their general merchandise catalog. At the time, Sears also sold kit homes and motor cars.

Sears had an edge on many companies with their widely distributed catalog and network of retail stores expanding into rural areas during the 1930s. The popularity of automobiles at the time allowed rural residents the flexibility to travel to adjoining towns where the newest Sears store was located.

By the mid-1940s Sears Roebuck boasted over $45 million in fur trade business. Just like other fur companies did, Sears used booklets to teach trappers successful trapping methods and build loyalty. Sears creatively invented a character named "Johnny Muskrat" to tell its trapping story and offered cash, pocket knives and other rewards for trappers selling quantities of pelts to Sears.

I actually owned the Sears catalog store in Chamberlain, South Dakota in the late 1980s and early 90s. These stores were a cash cow as Sears paid a commission for all orders purchased from the local ZIP codes that were included with the store franchise. Sears sold many appliances under its Kenmore name such as re-

Authors Collection

Here's a copy of the 1930–31 Sears "Tips to Trappers" featuring Johnny Muskrat.

Author's Collection

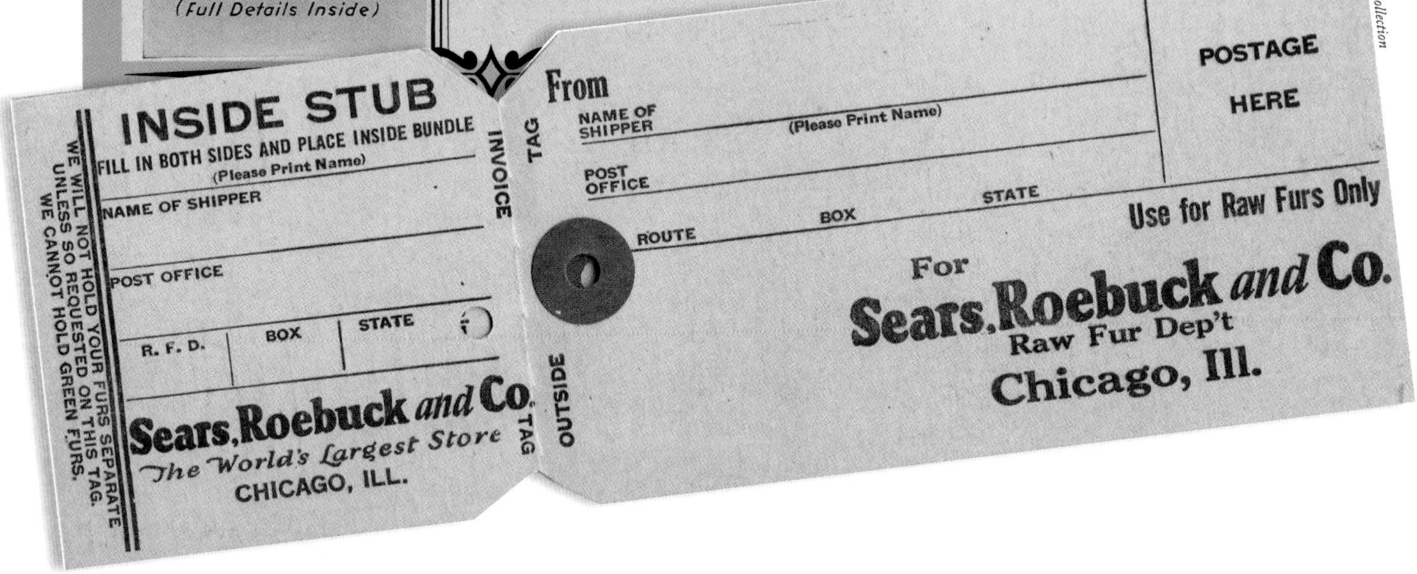

Many raw fur buyers included fur tags with their catalogs for easy shipping. Sears was no different. All you needed were furs, a burlap bag and a stamp.

frigerators, freezers, washers and dryers which were big ticket items and needed by everyone.

With the invention of the motor car, transportation companies went from wagon carts to trucks. The freight business exploded. United Parcel Service traces its history back to 1907. This opportunity for rural trappers allowed them the freedom to sell pelts to the highest-paying buyer instead of the most convenient. Fur companies realized that national marketing campaigns were essential for expansion. With North America's fur industry expanding and so many fur, gun and trap companies looking for national exposure, by the late 1800s the time had come for a monthly outdoor magazine. *Field and Stream* magazine began in 1895, *Outdoor Life* in 1898. This would offer exponential exposure for advertisers looking for new clients. These new magazines also created a need for writers who specialized in hunting and trapping—writers who would give equipment companies credibility and endorsement. Opportunities for a select few industrious trappers were on the horizon.

ARTHUR ROBERT HARDING

1871 –1930

Courtesy Fur-Fish-Game

What Sewell Newhouse was to North America trapping equipment in the 1800s, Arthur Robert Harding was to trapper recruitment in the 1900s. A.R. Harding was born in July 1871 in Gallia County near the Ohio River. Learning to trap at a young age, A.R. began his first entrepreneurial enterprise buying furs from neighboring school pals. By age 20, he was a traveling fur buyer for the L. Frank & Sons Hide and Fur Company of Zanesville, Ohio. A.R. loved everything about the outdoors, especially furs and trapping.

Making acquaintance with a local printer in Gallipolis, Robert Harding started the *Gallia Times* newspaper around 1898. The publishing business soon opened Harding's eyes to the possibilities of combining his passion for the outdoors and the written word. A.R. founded *Hunter-Trader-Trapper* magazine (also known as H-T-T) two years later. The rare October 1900 issue of *H-T-T* had only 24 pages and is a valuable magazine today. An issue of *H-T-T* cost a nickel in those days and the magazine was chock full of articles and advertisements on fur trapping, fur farming, hunting, the fur market report and especially letters from readers. A.R. knew that readers seeing their letters within the pages would endear them to the publication—he was right.

Hunter-Trader-Trapper was an instant sensation. Harding sold his interest in the *Gallia Times* and moved his new magazine offices to Columbus, Ohio. Columbus allowed better access to printing and distribution. By 1906, the magazine had grown to well over 100 pages in some issues. As *H-T-T* expanded

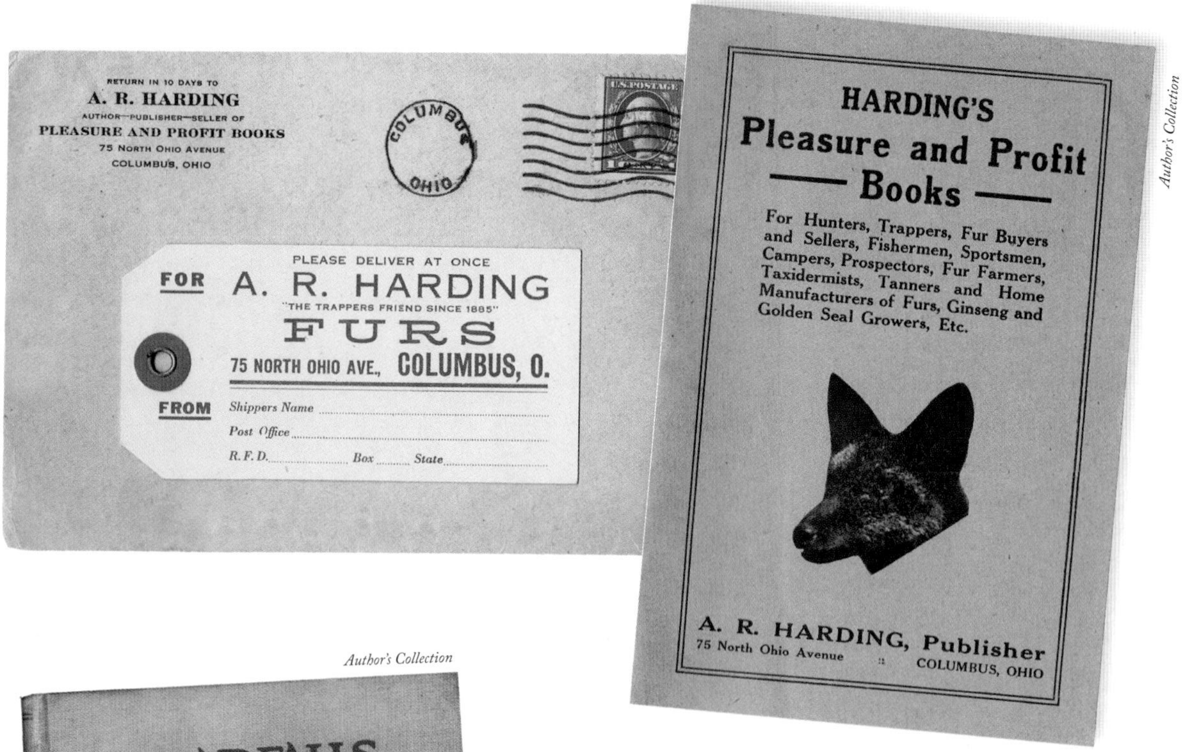

Author's Collection

After Harding sold *H-T-T* in 1914 he marketed his "Pleasure and Profit" books from home. Here's a very rare catalog from the pre-*Fur-Fish-Game* days, complete with the envelope, and Harding Fur Tag.

Author's Collection

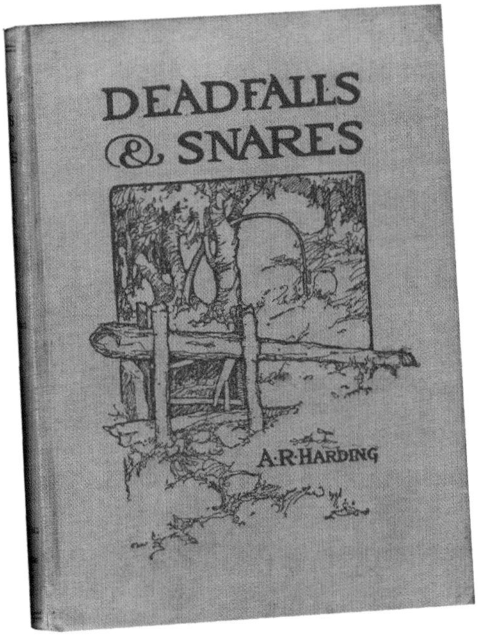

1907 First Edition copy of *Deadfalls and Snares*, one of Harding's many "Pleasure and Profit" books. The early editions were hardcover books but later became softcover to keep the price of printing and postage affordable.

circulation and magazine size, A.R. realized that he could offer his own merchandise to sell within the pages. The perfect items to sell were books about trapping and the outdoor lifestyle, as Harding had authors on the payroll and many photos of trapping and hunting sent to him by readers. Thus, A.R. began writing and publishing small books he called "Harding History and Pleasure" books.

Hunter-Trader-Trapper was a very successful enterprise and so was Harding's book business. So good that in 1909 A.R. added a weekly publication which he called *Camp and Trail,* a series about the outdoor lifestyle. *Camp and Trail* was distributed until 1913 when harding realized that the topic could just be a section in *H-T-T* and expand that magazine's base rather than have the huge load of two magazines to compile. So A.R. stopped publishing the weekly and in turn added similar camping articles into a special section of *Hunter-Trader-Trapper.*

In 1914 Harding fell ill and he decided to sell his *Hunter-Trader-Trapper* magazine. Upon its sale, Harding decided to keep the rights to his book manuscripts and continued to sell the small Pleasure and Profit books. Selling them from home for the next ten years, A.R.recovered from his illness and by 1924 he began to try and buy back *Hunter-Trader-Trapper.* But the owners would not sell, so Harding bought another publication titled *Fur News and Outdoor World,* ultimately changing the name to *Fur-Fish-Game.*

Courtesy Fur-Fish-Game

5 cents a Copy, 50 cents a Year.

HUNTER-TRADER-TRAPPER

LEOPOLD WEIL & BROTHERS,

33-35 WEST HOUSTON STREET,
NEW YORK,

EXPORTERS OF

RAW FURS.

CAN USE YOUR COLLECTIONS AND WILL PAY FULL MARKET VALUE FOR ALL SHIPMENTS. PRICE LIST ON APPLICATION.

Vol. I. Gallipolis, Ohio. No. 1.

October, ... 1900.

The rare First Edition of Hunter-Trader-Trapper, 1900.

Courtesy Fur-Fish-Game

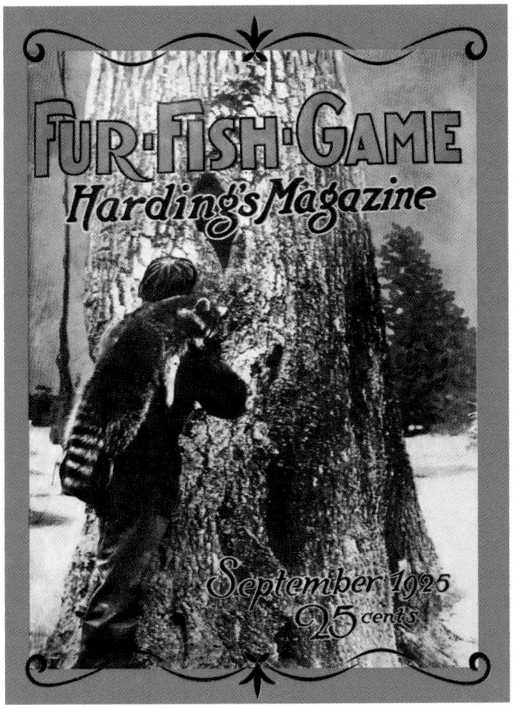

The rare First Edition of Fur-Fish-Game 1925.

September 1925 was the first issue of *Fur-Fish-Game* magazine and just like *H-T-T* it quickly became a hit. Unfortunately A.R. Harding passed less than five years later in 1930. Thankfully *Fur-Fish-Game* has stayed in the family and continues to this day.

The writings and success of A.R. Harding's books and magazines were no doubt the catalyst of many a youngster getting into trapping—his writings are forever woven into the annals of North America's trapping heritage. A.R. Harding made several trappers famous by including them in his books and publications including E.J. Dailey, Raymond Thompson, V.E. Lynch and Dick Wood to name a few. Of course these men were at the top of their game when Harding began publishing their works and all were likely heroes in their perspective locals. Nonetheless, both *Hunter-Trader-Trapper* and *Fur-Fish-Game* catapulted these men into trapping pioneers and icons.

ICONS OF THE WILDERNESS

The trappers who operated at the turn of the century era are the absolute most interesting to me. I refer to this time as the "Pioneer Trappers" as this was the golden era of trapping that spun up a "cottage industry" which was experienced after 1940 and still is today. These men were the first generation of trapping promoters. The first professional businessmen trappers not only trapped fur, but wrote books, magazine articles, made trapping scent, sold trapping supplies and some even bought fur. They built their reputations on their name while documenting adventures in books and articles for the rest of us to read, learn and dream. These rugged men put words to paper describing remote wilderness traplines and bountiful catches of martens and lynx, fishers and foxes—every fur-bearer with a magnificent rich, prime pelt. Their stories so well-written, that the adventures still come to life today.

E.J. DAILEY

1889 –1973

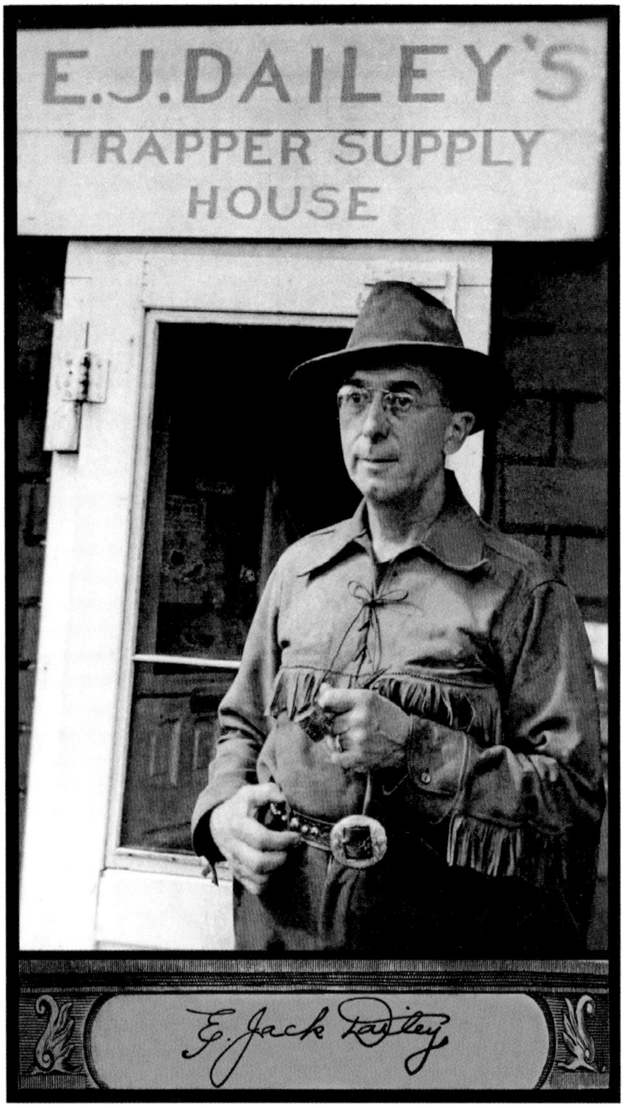

E.J. poses at the entrance to his trappers supply house.

There were no doubt many excellent trappers in this era whose names will never be known. But likely the most well-known of the "Pioneer Trappers" was Elric John Dailey. Born September 27, 1889 near the historic trapping grounds of the St Lawrence River in Lisbon, New York. His parents were cattle farmers from Irish decent, which was a combination that made sure young Elric would grow up with a proper work ethic. Elric's older brother ran a trapline with a school pal and this is how E.J. got interested.

In 1900 at 11 years old, E.J. began to run his own trapline. First catching skunks, then muskrats, mink and foxes. Skunk was a prized pelt at the turn of the century and good money for a farm boy. At 16, E.J. quit school to work the farm and follow his ambitions of being a trapper. Keep in mind, in 1905 fur price records show large, well-furred specimens of muskrat 25 cents, raccoon $1.70, Red Fox $4.00, skunk $1.75, and mink $5.50. The average wage in the United States in 1905 was between $200–$400 per year. Thus a good trapper could make "wages" on the trapline—E.J. knew it was his calling.

E.J. married Maude Weegar in 1910 and that same year, traveled north on an expedition to trap the wilds of Northern Ontario. Dailey built a log cabin, prospected and ran his own trapline. His primary target was mink, but he would catch other species as well. E.J. continued to trap each year and especially enjoyed the challenge of catching red foxes. Dailey was becoming proficient at dry land trapping and was one of only a handful of trappers who could take ole' reynard in numbers. Dailey was always learning and adapting methods as well as the scents he used. By 1915 Dailey was 26 years old and considered himself a professional trapper. E.J. opened his trappers supply shop in 1915.

On April 6, 1917 the United States declared war on Germany (WWI) and soon after, E.J. was called to service. However, E.J. had poor eyesight and was disqualified. That same year, Dailey started his first auto trapline purchasing a fancy, but used National Roadster. In this era, the auto trapline was in its infancy and E.J. knew it would be a game changer. His first auto-line season included 250 traps, often spread over 100 miles. Tent camping allowed E.J. to stay "on the road" and scout new territory—a tactic he called "Spot Trapping." Likely he had learned this strategy on his many wilderness expeditions walking trap lines in the Adirondacks and the utilization of line cabins. Dailey's auto-line was a huge success and he bought a Ford Model T in 1919 and affectionately named his motorcar "Lizzie."

Dailey trapped with many partners over his long career, but no one influenced his life more than Dick Wood. Wood was a master woodsman with a talent of

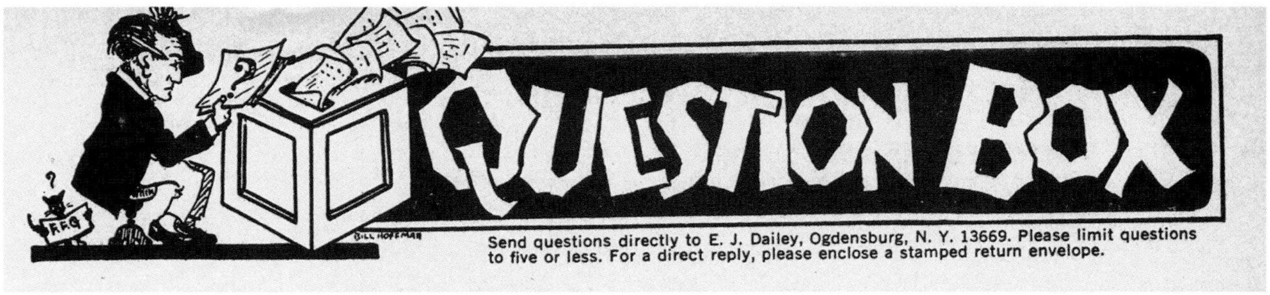

QUESTION BOX
Send questions directly to E. J. Dailey, Ogdensburg, N. Y. 13669. Please limit questions to five or less. For a direct reply, please enclose a stamped return envelope.

Courtesy Fur-Fish-Game

E.J. Dailey's Question Box header taken from one of the authors childhood *Fur-Fish-Game* magazines, circa 1973

Authors Collection

The Trappers Partner by E.J. Dailey, 1938–First Edition, the 1925 First Edition of Dailey's *Traplines and Trails*

putting words to paper. Dailey was a trapper. Together Wood would learn the "art of trapping" from Dailey, while E.J. learned the "craft of writing" from Wood. Don't get me wrong, Dailey was a good writer but Wood made him better. Conversely, Wood was a good trapper but Dailey made him better. Their relationship was beneficial and they enjoyed each others company.

Dailey and Wood trapped the Adirondacks together during the 1919–20 and 1920–21 seasons. These exploits where chronicled in many a *Hunter-Trader-Trapper* article and the experiences spun off into materials for several books including Dailey's *Traplines and Trails*. By 1925 Dailey had assumed the role of Question Box editor for the Harding Publishing Company and *Fur-Fish-Game* magazine. In fact, Dailey was the first *F-F-G* Question Box editor and was on the masthead until his death in 1973.

E.J. Dailey is credited in many circles with the idea of the "dirt-hole" set for foxes. However, three centuries of trapping had occurred in North America before Dailey's time, so it's likely he did not "invent" the dirt-hole set. Adirondack Trapper Johnny Thorpe mentions in his book that Art Crane taught E.J. the dirt-hole set. Crane was a fox trapper extraordinaire and had several fox trapping articles published within the pages of *Hunter-Trader-Trapper* before 1920. However, coining the name to the most popular predator set known in print and describing

Legendary Adirondack fox trapper Art Crane may have shown Dailey the "dirt-hole" set.

it as such to the huge trapper audience of *Fur-Fish-Game* and *H-T-T*, not to mention Dailey's early books on trapping where he discusses the dirt hole —there's no doubt that the dirt-hole set and E.J. Dailey go hand in hand.

Dailey made his own scents and had a lure brochure in 1930. E.J. also offered personal trapping instructions. In 1932 his price was $10 for the three-day course. It's said that Dailey gave trapping lessons to icons Pete Rickard (Rickard also was instructed by Art Crane) and O.L. Butcher. Pennsylvania fox trapper Monty Close took lessons from E.J. to learn Dailey's method of making the dirt-hole set. Close is thought to have later shown the set to Stanley Hawbaker. E.J. released his first catalog in 1935 stating—Dailey's Trapper Supply House listing his "*personally* made trapping lures 'for sale" as well as trapping supplies he considered essential for the trapline."

Dailey was actively involved in the preservation of trapping. He was the first president of the New York State Trappers Association (founded 1938) and did much to support conservation, trapping and state wildlife agencies.

E.J. fox trapped with Vaughn Tingley during the 1940s and eventually turned over his lure and supply business to Vaughn. Dailey mailed his last trapping supply catalog in 1972. Today, Tingley's Northland is operated by Robert Dewey. However, Dailey's lure formulas and business were purchased in 1996 by Rob Erickson of Wildlife Control Technologies and are still made today in Illinois.

Dailey turning "Lizzie's" crank on his Spot Trap Line, circa 1920s from Traplines and Trails -Courtesy Fur-Fish-Game

The Adirondack region is easily accessible, yet there are some of the remotest mountain fastnesses in America to be found there. The scenery is truly wonderful, and is less barren and more forest covered than many other wilderness sections. Trappers however, cannot exist on beautiful scenes, but are more interested in the fur-bearers that make their home there.

The professional Adirondack trapper often has a line of traps out that extends fifty miles. This distance covered in two or three days, depending on the traveling. The necessities a headquarters camp and one or two overnight camps. The temperature gets very low at intervals during the winter, and its not unusual for fifty degrees below zero to remain for a week. Being well sheltered, there is no wind excepting on the mountain tops, and the natives, provided as they are with an abundance of hardwood, rarely suffer from the cold.

The mainstay of the Adirondack trappers are mink and fox. Blind trapping is used by the expert for both of these animals. A few of the best trappers average two foxes each day during the best of the season.

—E.J. Dailey 1925 "Traplines and Trails"

RAYMOND THOMPSON

1896–1979

Arthur Raymond Thompson was born in Lincoln County Washington on May 15, 1896. Industrious at a young age, Raymond Thompson was most at home in the outdoors. At 16, Raymond traveled into the Athabaska region of Alberta, Canada and spent time with trappers his first winter in the far north. It was this experience that set Raymond on his course to become a wilderness trapper. Raymond returned to Almira, Washington the following spring to work and earn money to return to the Athabaska to run his own trapline. Raymond brought along his best friend Cliff Knowles as a partner in the venture.

From A Land of Fur and Gold

Raymond Thompson with his new wife Ruby, May 1918

The Athabaska region was a fur-rich area at the turn of the century. The Athabaska River, Peace River and Slave River all meet at a group of large lakes in northeastern Alberta. This hub is at the junction of the heavy conifer forests of the south and the tree-less tundra of the north. Moose, bears, deer, caribou and an abundance of fur bearers including, foxes, wolves, lynx, martens, beavers, otters and wolverines abound. The Athabaska region was the perfect learning ground for

Author's Collection

Land of Fur and Gold, Raymond Thompson's autobiography,1980, Snares and Snaring by Raymond Thompson 1946, 1924 First Edition of *Wilderness Trapper* by Raymond Thompson

Author's Collection

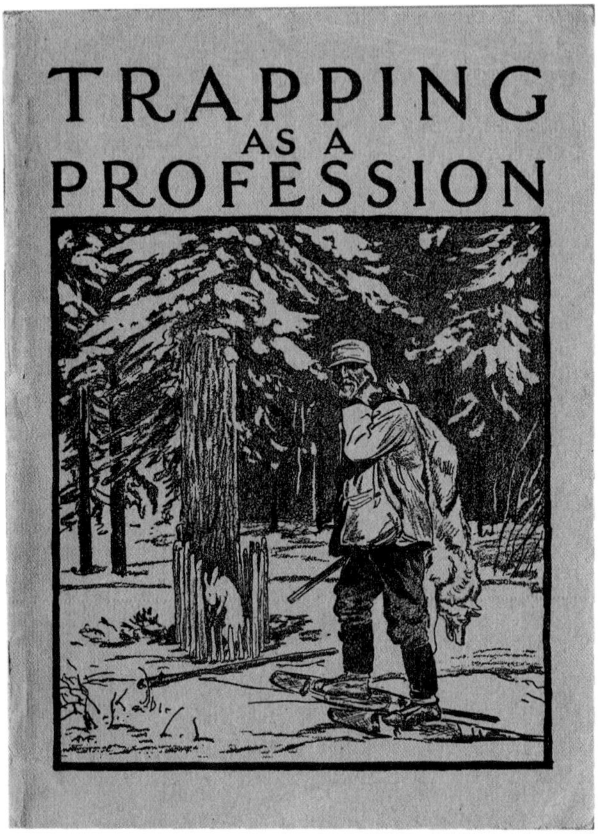

1922 First Edition copy of *Trapping as a Profession.* Raymond Thompson was a contributor in this booklet of professional trapper stories.

a young Raymond Thompson. By the time Raymond was 23, he was in love with 19-year-old Ruby Trench. They married in Canada on May 25, 1918.

Raymond and Ruby lived in cabins along the Peace and Athabaska rivers with Raymond running extensive wilderness traplines there, honing his skills as an expert woodsman and snare-man. Raymond also was prolific in his writing and documented his adventures in the Athabaska putting his thoughts to paper. Thompson was particularly adept at snaring, which was the most effective way of catching predators in the deep snow found in the region. In fact, Thompson created his namesake company in 1927 devoted to trapping supplies, his writings and signature snares which used a self-locking mechanism to choke down the quarry and prevent chew-outs.

Most of Raymond's traplines were run on snowshoes or with a dog team and sled. Native trappers were a big influence on Thompson and his trapping techniques. The Raymond Thompson Company was passed on to Raymond's grandson and at this writing the company is known as Thompson Snares, owned and operated by Brian Davis of Missouri.

Raymond Thompson was a talented writer, describing his adventures in such a way that you felt like you were on the trapline with him. His writings flowed with the authenticity of someone who knew what he was talking about because he had been there and done it. I used Raymond Thompson's articulation about trapping as the foreword of this book as it rings as true today as it did in 1922 when he penned it. Many wilderness trappers will be described in this book, yet Raymond Thompson stands out to me as an iconic figure in the annals of our trapping heritage.

Profits of Trapping in the Canadian Northwest

I caught 21 marten that season, which together with $200 worth of weasels, a fisher, lynx, red fox and caught a few muskrats in the spring brought my catch up to a figure of $1,460. This sum with that of $1,122 (Hackett's and Eckholm's catch) makes $2,582 or an average of $1,291 per man for the season. In summing up we find the averages in the following table.

TRAPPERS	LOCATION	SEASON	AVERAGE
Nelson Brothers	Ponce Coupe and Pine Pass	1915-16	$ 643.00
O. Assen	Athabaska Crossing	1915-16	$ 751.00
T. Walters	Tony River	1918-19	$1,405.00
Hendrickson, Lingrell & Parnell	Athabaska	1918-19	$1,000.00
Hackett and Eckholm	Old Main River	1919-20	$1,122.00
Raymond Thompson	Moose Mountains	1919-20	$1,460.00
Total (six averages)			$6,381.00
Final average per man per season			$1,063.50

In 1915-16 it took an average of 200 marten to make $1,000; in 1917, 150 marten; in 1918 ; 100 marten ; in 1919 ; 40 marten and in 1920 it took 20 marten at $50 each to make $1,000. Like-wise in 1915, I sold lynx for $3.40 and $4.00, and got $45.00 for a lynx in 1920. The trapper makes more money when the fur-bearers are scarce and the market is high. But whether there is more pleasure in collecting 200 marten at $5.00 each or 20 marten at $50 each is a matter open for discussion. Certainly the smaller more valuable catch entails less work in the handling, skinning, drying and shipping.

—Raymond Thompson 1922 "Trapping as a Profession"

V.E. LYNCH

1884–1953

Virgil Everett Lynch was a trapper, woodsman and hunting guide who became a legendary outdoorsman in the wilds of northern Maine. Lynch himself chronicles his early years growing up in the Ozark Mountains by saying, "I began the trapline at age nine, killed my first turkey at age 14 and my first deer when I was fifteen with one of those old time muzzleloading rifles." V.E. Lynch also ran hounds in his early years for coons, bobcats and mountain lions in east and south Texas. However Lynch soon heard the calling of the wild places and ended up in Ashland, Maine.

Known as "Wildcat" Lynch, Virgil trapped, hunted and guided moose, bear and deer hunters out of his camp on the Machias River in the northern Maine wilderness. From 1917–1923 Lynch lived the life of a guide and trapper. "Wildcat" had a gift of crafting stories with pen and paper and as a talented woodsman, Lynch walked the walk.

1927 First Edition of *Lynch's Scientific Methods of Trapping* by V.E. Lynch and 1928 First Edition copy of Lynch's Thrilling Adventures.

Lynch quickly learned that his writing could help his hunting camp business and in 1923 became the editor of *National Sportsman* magazine. As editor, "Wildcat's" reputation grew and with it, so did his guiding business. Lynch wrote many articles for *Hunter-Trader-Trapper* magazine about his hunting exploits and trapline success. These articles often chronicled his adventures as a guide and skills as a trapper. "Wildcat" also wrote several trapping books including *Lynch's Scientific Methods of Trapping* in 1927, *Thrilling Adventures* in 1928 *and Trails to Successful Trapping* in 1935 which was written for A.R. Harding's "Pleasure and Profit" books and sold by Fur-Fish-Game.

The following scent is what I use for bobcat. Take 1/2 pint of trout oil, one half of a beaver castor, one beaver oil sac, which is found alongside the castor and ten drops of oil of catnip... and you will have a scent that a lion, bobcat or line will never pass up without investigating. Wherever you catch one of these cats is a good place to catch another one as they will often nose around where they get the scent of the trapped cat.

— Virgil E. Lynch, 1927 Lynch's Scientific Methods of Trapping

"Wildcat's" Maine hunting camp with hunters guides and game. Circa 1920s. From *Thrilling Adventures* 1928.

I have trapped and guided big game hunters over sections where you could travel the dense forest on a straight line for three days or more with out seeing a road or any signs of civilization. Several inexperienced woodsmen of late years wandered too far into the vast wilderness, got lost and were never heard from again. Most all non-resident big game hunters who come to this region employ experienced guides who are skilled in woodscraft and familiar with the habits and nature of the big game and their haunts.

—Virgil E. Lynch 1928
Thrilling Adventures-Guiding, Trapping, Big Game Hunting

"Wildcat" Lynch poses with his namesake furbearer, the bobcat. Circa 1920s from *Thrilling Adventures* 1928.

Maine trapping legend Walter Arnold inspects the dryness of a red fox skin before turning the hide to fur side out.

WALTER ARNOLD

1894–1980

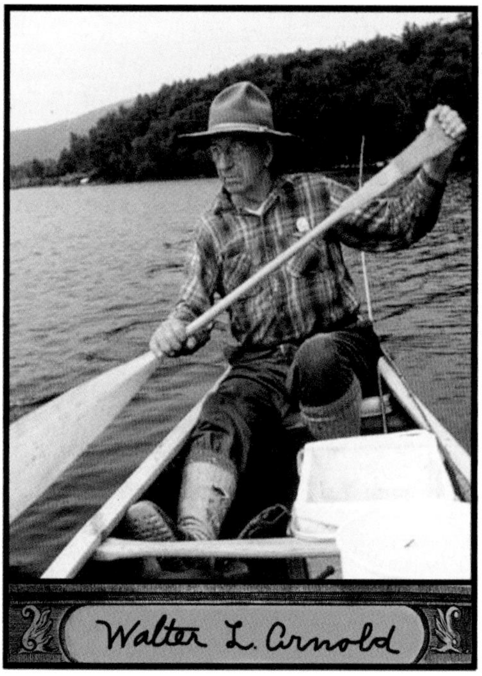

Photo by Jim Shaw

Walter Arnold was born in 1894 in Willimantic, Maine. His father was a market hunter in the 1870s, and as a young man Walter hunted, trapped and guided with him. Walter served in World War I and upon returning home he started a small mail order business, selling trapping supplies and animal trapping scents and lures, as well as running numerous traplines in Northern Maine.

He was the author of several books about trapping and preparing scents as well as numerous articles published in trapping and hunting magazines. Arnold's book, *Professional Trapping* which appeared in four editions between 1935 and 1947, was widely used by state and federal officials to train trappers to handle troublesome wild animals. Walter was one of the original founders of the Maine Trappers Association and served as its president, secretary, and treasurer, as well as the editor of its newsletter, *Maine Trapper*.

Walter Arnold sold his entire trapping supply business in 1959 to Oscar Cronk of Wiscasset, Maine and moved back to the woods, living by himself in a remote northern township of Maine until 1980. His life became the subject of many articles in various magazines and newspapers, and the book, *Goodbye Mountain Man* by Donald Anderson featured Arnold and his lifestyle.

Walter Arnold kept a daily diary from 1919 through 1976 in which he recorded his activities, the weather, and the wildlife he saw and hunted. Written in his vivid style, the diaries give a clear picture of his long and adventuresome life. Arnold remained active until his death in 1980. As he put it in a letter in 1971, "I am not like all these woods hermits you hear about that sit around, grow fat and pass on. I am 78 and still do probably more hard work summer and winter then nearly all the men in the state do at the age of 45."

Now the number of fur-bearing animals that you can induce to put their feet on the pans of your traps are not entirely ascertained by the kind of scent you use. Many successful trappers use no scent at all for coon, mink, fisher, muskrat, skunk, etc. However, I think a good scent is a help and about the best scent in most areas is the musk of the kind of animal you are trapping.

—Walter Arnold 1921 "Trapping"

Author's Collection

1921 First Edition of *Trapping* by Walter Arnold.

DICK WOOD

1895–1977

E.J. Dailey holds a pair of mink pelts while Dick Wood admires a dandy Adirondack red fox, circa 1930.

Richard K. Wood was born in Virginia on June 15, 1895. His father was a Methodist preacher in Scott County, Virginia. Growing up, Richard (referred to as Dick) enjoyed the outdoors and reading about life on the frontier in particular. Author George Canning Hill wrote the definitive biography of Daniel Boone in 1859 and once young Dick read the tales found in *The Life and Adventures of Daniel Boone, the Pioneer of Kentucky* he was hooked on outdoor adventures. Boone was a trapper and a fur trader and this sparked an interest in 14-year-old Dick Wood. With his parents moving to east Tennessee in 1909, young Wood was surrounded with wild places to plan his adventures. It was here on Pond Creek where Dick set his first trapline.

At the insistence of his parents to complete more than an eighth-grade education, Dick went to Madisonville, Tennessee for high school which he completed in 1916. During his school years, Dick met several Tennessee mountain men who helped him learn the ways of the wilds.

As fate would have it, Dick Wood won a photo contest in 1917 offered by the new Triumph Trap Company (founded 1913). First prize was $50. When Triumph offered a chance for the Wood to interview for a new position, a young Dick Wood was soon on the train to Oneida, New York. Dick was hired to his first "real job" as copywriter and photographer for Triumph Trap Company. This position allowed Dick to travel into the grandest of trapping areas and meet top trappers who were employed by Triumph to test or promote their traps. This included none other than E.J. Dailey.

Dick Wood married his hometown girlfriend Beulah Graham, in Tennessee the day after Christmas in 1917 and the two traveled back to New York together. Dick Wood would spend the next few years honing his skills as a writer, photographer and trapper-spending "on the line" trapping time with seasoned New York fox trapper Bill Randall and Raquette Lake fisher trapper Bill Wood (no relation). Dick's work included articles promoting Triumph traps and trapping in general for *Hunter-Trader-Trapper* and *Fur News and Outdoor World,* a magazine which would become *Fur-Fish-Game* in 1925.

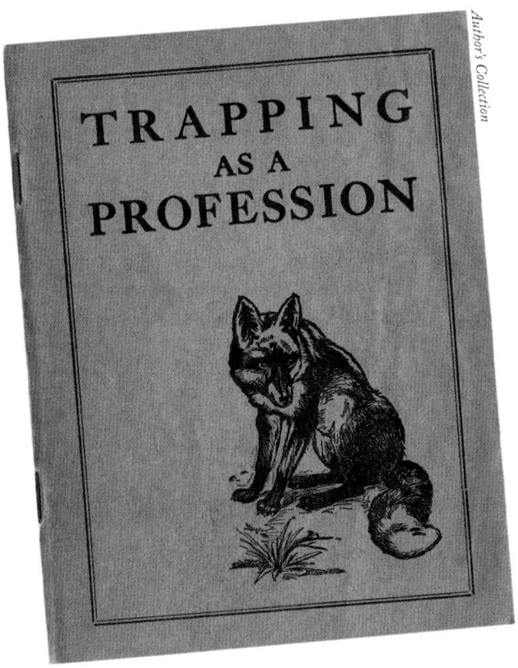

Author's Collection

1922 First Edition copy of *"Trapping as a Profession"* with alternate cover. Dick Wood was a contributor in this booklet of professional trapper stories.

By 1919 Dick was ready for anything the Adirondacks could dish out as he would partner with E.J. Dailey at Dailey's Cold River camp. Wood would be E.J.'s first partner on the wilderness line and by all accounts it was a grand success. Wood and Dailey ran the Cold River line together again in 1920.

Dick Wood especially liked what was called motor camping or essentially driving to a wilderness area and setting up a tent camp for a few days or longer. Much of Dick's writings would be done from a camp chair, taken from notes of a diary scribed on the trapline. Wood didn't like the stuffy surroundings of an office. He enjoyed the outdoors. Motor camping was the perfect escape and his wife Beulah could travel with him. Dick had always enjoyed motorsports owning a motorcycle as well and many automobiles. He also ran many auto-lines trapping foxes, raccoons, mink and skunks.

Dick Wood never gained the trapper fame of a Raymond Thompson, V.E. Lynch or E.J. Dailey. Likely it was because his job was to promote others and not himself. Yet he was an amazing trapper and like Robert Harding, was a pioneer in bringing the wilderness trapline experience to thc pages of so many articles and books. Like Raymond Thompson, Dick Wood was a master wordsmith and captivated me with his stories of the wild places and the romance of trapping I so craved as a youngster.

"The Upper Peninsular Country"

Undoubtedly the western end of the upper peninsular of Michigan and portions of Wisconsin and Minnesota remains to-day the best trapping grounds left east of the Mississippi river. Much of the country is a semi-wilderness with settlements far apart and trails few and dim.

A log cabin or well-built shack is the best form of shelter for the permanent trapper, in this country. A little farther west in the treeless sections, teepees or wiki-ups are used successfully by native trappers, but a greenhorn would freeze to death attempting to winter in one of them. The north woods trapper will need plenty of woolen and mackinaw clothing, traps of assorted sizes, a large portion which should be No. 3 and 4, besides several dozen small traps for marten, weasels and mink, about six bear traps and a rifle with low trajectory.

—*Dick Wood 1922*
Trapping as a Profession

Photo by Dick Wood

Dick Wood and partner E.J. Dailey snowshoe into Dailey's Adirondacks Duck Hole camp, circa1920.

ADIRONDACK DICK ENTERPRISES

Solid history about the men who pioneered our trapping industry is pretty scarce and disappearing every day. Trapper and author Scot Dahms has researched and written several treatises on some of the influential trapping and trap manufacturing pioneers, particularly Walter Gibbs, Dick Wood, E.J. Dailey and the Triumph Trap Company.

An Iowa native, Dahms resides in Indiana where he researches little-known facts about trapping and crafts them into delightful books and magazine fodder. Scot's interest in trapping expanded into antique trap collecting with a particular focus on the Triumph Trap Company. Coupled with an inquisitive nature and passion for history, Scot began a new journey which opened up legions of historical materials and information leading to Triumph founder Albert E. "Bob" Kinsley and progressing to Dailey and Wood, both of whom represented and worked with the Triumph brand. Gibbs would later buy the Triumph Trap Company.

This golden age of the trapping industry is well-described in Scot's biographies of these pioneers and company. Each volume is approximately 300 pages and chock full of turn-of-the-century photos and in-depth information that could only be mined by someone willing to look under every rock as would Sherlock Holmes himself. More information on obtaining these historical books can be found at www.adirondackdick.com.

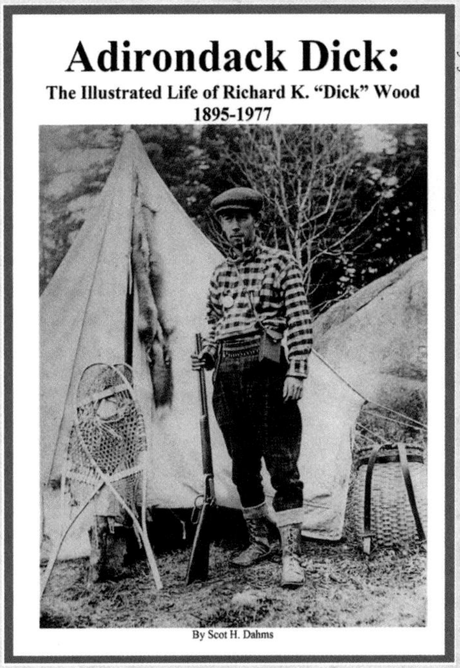

Courtesy of Scot Dahms

Adirondack Dick by Scot Dahms is a fantastic historical account of the life of Dick Wood.

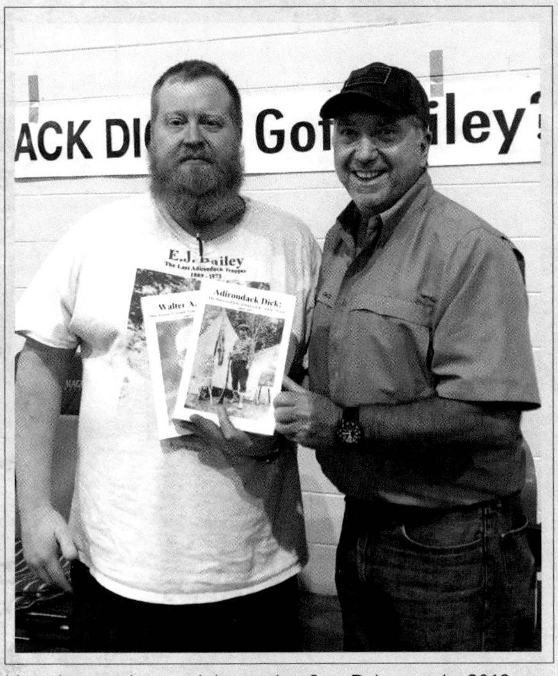

Author's Photo

Miranda poses here with biographer Scot Dahms at the 2019 National Trappers Association annual convention held in Springfield, Missouri.

AMERICAN WOODSMAN

JULY 1951 25 CENTS

Buster of Cottonwood Pool
See page 4

You Can Have More Shooting
See Page 6

CHAPTER 4

COTTAGE INDUSTRY TRAPPERS

The pioneer trappers paved the way for a wave of enterprising outdoorsmen to start their own cottage trapping businesses. Many of these entrepreneurial fur men grew up trapping and never stopped, making it their career. Others began as hobby trappers who eventually gained notoriety in their home area as a trapper and found a niche to make additional money in the trade. Some bought furs, some made and sold lures, some wrote books illustrating their methods. Some did it all. I refer to these years as the "Cottage Industry" because these small business trappers sprang up all across the country, utilizing their trapline fur shed as the home office.

TRAPPERS IN BUSINESS

1935–1970

There have been hundreds of trappers over the years who have started small businesses—some becoming quite well-known. My story continues with the trappers who inspired me first to become a trapper, then motivated me to hone my skills to excel as a fur harvester and eventually to begin my own cottage business in trapping. Many trappers influenced my career—both through books and personal instruction, and my trapping methods became a mixed influence of all of them.

> July 1951 was the first edition of *American Woodsman* magazine published by Stanley Hawbaker.

O.L. BUTCHER

1897–1967

Author's Collection

Born in December 6, 1897 Okey Butcher learned to trap as a youngster in rural West Virginia—hunting, fishing, trapping and digging roots was a way to make ends meet. Butcher enlisted in the Navy in 1917, touring the world and ended up being stationed in Europe where learned to speak several languages as a part of his military service. It's not well outlined what O.L. Butcher did immediately after the war but there's no doubt he was trapping and eventually settled near Shushan, New York. In 1938 he released a 36-page booklet titled *Trapline and the Trail* (A very similar title to Dailey's 1925 book *Traplines and Trails*). The book shows Butcher with several nice trapline catches and devotes much time to the natural bait hole set, obviously a variation of Dailey's dirt-hole set—only by terminology. O.L. Butcher's first trapline supply catalog was for the 1938–39 season. Butcher would produce several books and he gained quite a following with his trapping scents.

Butcher trapped the Adirondacks and like Dailey, was a master fox trapper. Butcher is often seen pictured with Dailey and this was likely because both were involved in the organized New York State Trappers Association as well as the American Trappers Association.

My introduction to O.L. Butcher was in the form of his trapping scents. I met a fur dealer named Harold Chapman in Pataskala, Ohio who was also a trapper and sold some supplies including Butcher's scent. I bought several bottles from Chapman and used the scent with good success especially Butcher 1 and 4 in combination. I eventually began buying in bulk direct from Butcher's Supply Shop. O.L. Butcher died in 1967 and his wife Alice carried on the lure business and eventually married Raymond Duntley who I dealt with at the time. In fact, my November Red lure is very similar to O.L. Butcher's Fox #4.

O.L. Butcher was inducted into the National Trappers Association Trappers Hall of Fame in 1993 along with Dailey, Harding and Negus and several other deserving trappers in the NTA's Hall of Fame's introductory first year.

From The Trapline and the Trail–first edition

O.L. Butcher poses with some furs in one of his earlier catch photos.

O.L. Butcher's first book, 1938.

Butcher's second book.

Author's Collection

Snow Sets

Around a frozen lake shore or open fields many good fox sets can be made by concealing a trap beside some object that stands out by itself like the end of a limb sticking up thru the ice. A burnt top of a stump or stick shows up a long ways. Set and conceal a trap beside the article and pour a few drops of fox urine on it, or a good scent. Stone cubbies are the greatest method known for all weather trapping.

Helpful Hints

A clean, dry scent bottle will make you a waterproof match box. Always carry dry matches. One prime pelt is worth a bale of unprimed stuff. Dress well and warmly in woolen clothing and avoid the rheumatism later in life. The Value of a winters catch for the professional trapper depends on the market value of raw furs, $500 to $3000 in the good old days so long ago I can hardly remember them.

—O.L. Butcher, The Trapline and the Trail, 1938

Author's Collection

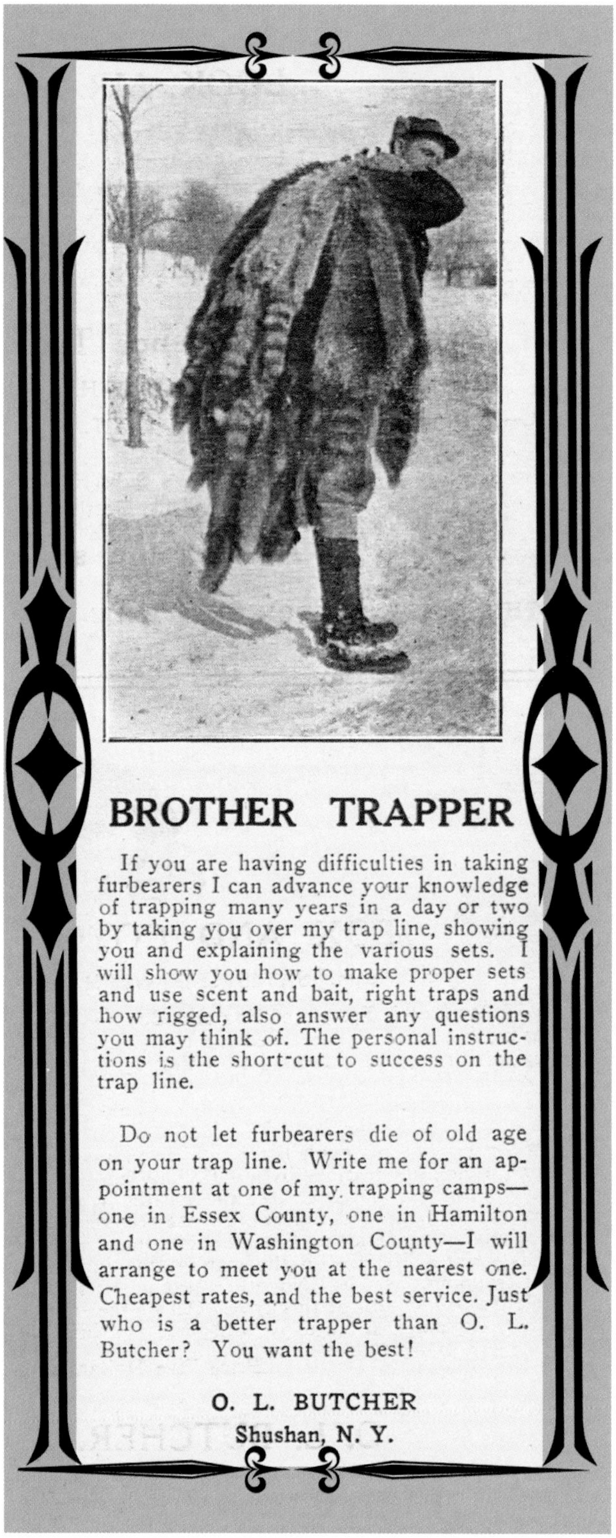

BROTHER TRAPPER
If you are having difficulties in taking furbearers I can advance your knowledge of trapping many years in a day or two by taking you over my trap line, showing you and explaining the various sets. I will show you how to make proper sets and use scent and bait, right traps and how rigged, also answer any questions you may think of. The personal instructions is the short-cut to success on the trap line.
Do not let furbearers die of old age on your trap line. Write me for an appointment at one of my trapping camps—one in Essex County, one in Hamilton and one in Washington County—I will arrange to meet you at the nearest one. Cheapest rates, and the best service. Just who is a better trapper than O. L. Butcher? You want the best!
O. L. BUTCHER
Shushan, N. Y.

O.L. Butcher offered trapping lessons in his 1939–40 catalog.

HERBERT LENON

1902–1979

Herb Lenon grew up in southern Michigan. His uncle was a part-time trapper and when Herb was 6 years old, began to teach him water-line trapping. It is said that Herbert's first catch was a mink and he wanted to be a professional trapper from that point forward. Herb began fox trapping at age 12 and by 16, he was more than proficient. Herb Lenon's first trapping lures were sold in 1924 and Herb used the money to move along with his wife Laura to Michigan's Upper Peninsula to run a semi-wilderness line. Lenon trapped the UP for 8 years and returned to Gulliver, Michigan to raise a family and continue his lure and trapping business, writing his first trapping book/pamphlet in 1933.

Courtesy of Lenon Lures

Likely the first trapping film ever produced was the 55 minute Michigan Department of Conservation film featuring Herb Lenon. This photo from 1938 is shown on the DVD sleeve cover.

Michigan instated a bounty on coyote and wolves in 1936—Lenon was so proficient in trapping them, the demand for his lures soared. In 1937 Michigan took off the bounty and Herb joined the ranks of Michigan Department of Conservation as a state trapper instructor from 1937–1939. The bounty system was reinstated in 1939 and Lenon stayed on with the

Department of Conservation as a conservation officer. From 1937 to 1940, Lenon ran his traplines using a film camera in cooperation with the Michigan Department of Conservation to document his trapline. The finished film was used as an instructional tool for predator trappers across the state. Herb Lenon's film is considered the first trapping instruction film and is still available today on DVD.

Herb left his Conservation Officer position in 1942 to continue his trapping, writing and lure business full-time Herb's articles in *Fur-Fish-Game* were always a welcome addition for readers and very informative. Herb also did the Question & Answers column in *Trappers World* magazine. Asa Lenon took over his father's lure business after his passing and Lenon's lures are now made under the ownership of John S. Chagnon. Herb Lenon was inducted into the NTA Trappers Hall of Fame in 1994.

Wind direction is a vital factor to success. Few trappers seem to recognize its extreme value. For the animal to detect the odor of the lure, the wind must be relied upon to carry the odor to them. To take advantage of the wind you must learn from which direction it prevails in your locality in the season you are going to trap. Here in northern Michigan 80% of the wind prevails from North, West, or Northwest during the late fall and winter trapping season. Using Northwest as the prevailing wind direction during this period, traps are set to the North or West of the road or trail where animals have been known to pass. If traps are set in an open area where no road or trail exist, they are placed Northwest of animals anticipated approach. he trap must be down wind from the lure, lure upwind from the trap which is always to be upwind from the anticipated approach of the animal.

—Herb Lenon Trappers Bible of Trapline Secrets

WILLIAM "BILL" NELSON

1908–1973

Born in Iowa and adopted as a child by Andrew and Hannah Nelson, young Bill grew up on a farm near the Des Moines River south of Croton, Iowa. Bill took to the woods as a youngster and only went to school through eighth grade. In the early 1920s pelts were valuable and the river abounded with mink, coon and 'rats. Bill took up boxing and after moving to Davenport in his early 20s, took a factory job and began boxing for sport. Boxing under the name of "Sailor Jones," Nelson fought some 200 amateur bouts before turning a "middle-weight" pro and he went 29–0. Bill contracted yellow fever which ended his sports career.

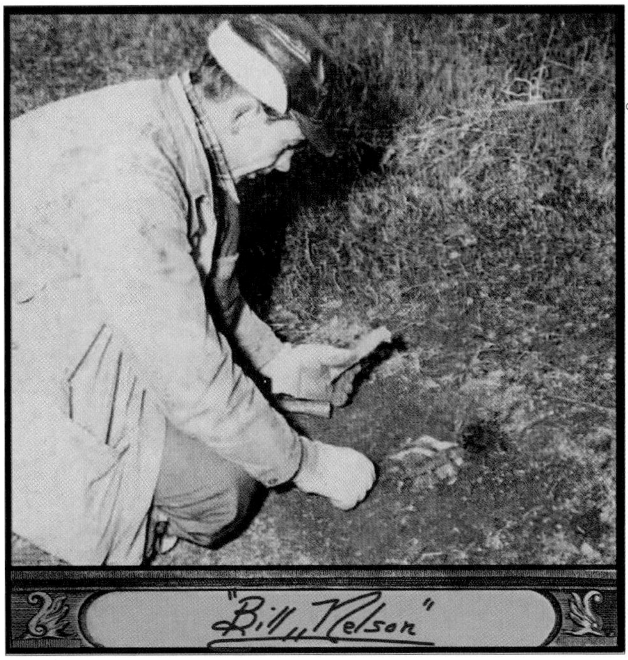

Des Moines Register, 1949

Bill Nelson shows his deadly dirt-hole set.

Bill Nelson moved to southern Minnesota in 1933 to fish and trap. In '34 he moved further north and out of the farm country to trap the wilds. Guiding musky fishermen in the summer and trapping the winter, Bill was learning to take coyotes and bobcats in the harsh snow and cold conditions of the north woods. Bill met and soon married Minnesota native Edith Peterson in 1935 and also ran an extensive trapline in northern Minnesota that year. Bill ran a small classified ad in 1935 offering his trapping methods and lure formulas.

Bill also started teaching Edith what he called "wild crafting" or making money on the side business of digging roots, gathering fishing bait, collecting wild nuts and berries as well as finding pearls. These skills helped them survive the heart of the Great Depression (1929–1939).

Bill and Edith went back to Iowa for the 1938–39 trapping season but because of the economy, trap thieves nearly robbed him blind. Bill made the decision to move west. He trapped in several areas of California from 1938 until 1946 and had many trapping partners while in California—trapping desert areas, costal mountains and the Sierras taking coyotes, gray foxes, raccoons, martens and other fur bearers. Bill worked as a forestry firefighter during his summers in California. This experience of trapping so many different species and area from Iowa to Minnesota and California gave Bill Nelson a huge skill set and perspective of wild animals, their habits and trapping techniques. Bill was honing his craft as when he returned to Iowa in 1946 and in August, he released his first big advertisement for Nelson's Formulas. The next year Bill started his lure business, trapping instructions and long auto traplines.

Des Moines Register 1949

A sneak peek into Nelson's skinning shed in 1949 with the days catch lying on the floor.

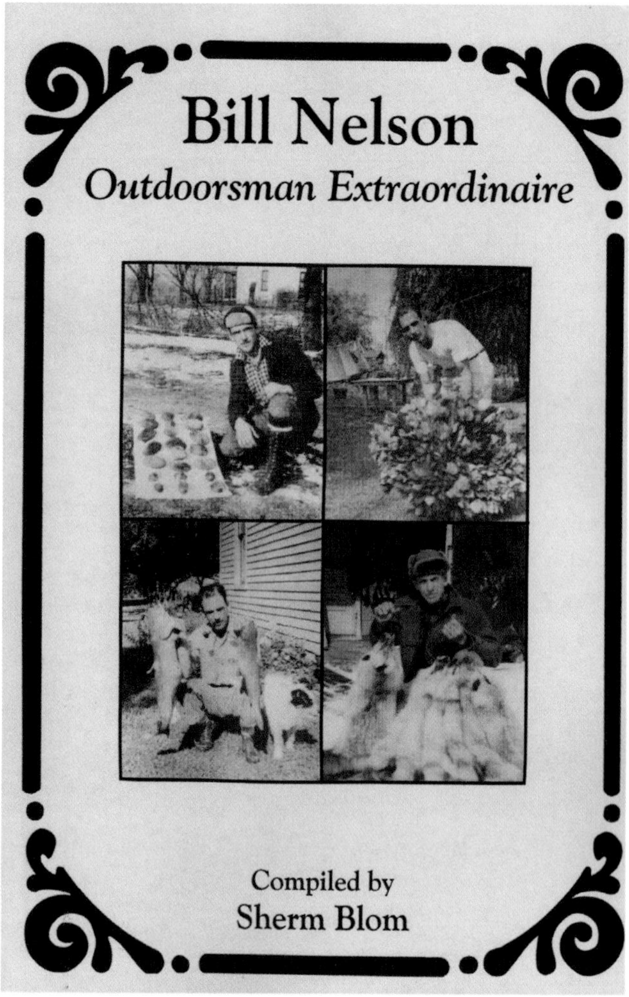

Author's Collection

Bill Nelson Outdoorsman Extraordinaire is a great biography of one of the best midwestern trappers ever known.

Nelson trapped what ever the fur market dictated. If fox pelts were selling at a high price, he ran predator lines, when mink were up he trapped mink— same goes for raccoons. When fur prices were low, there was often a bounty paid on predators and you can bet Bill Nelson was laying steel for coyotes and foxes.

Nelson gave trapping instructions for many years and taught some of the best fox trappers in the business including Craig O'Gorman. In fact O'Gorman was asked to take over Nelson's students in 1973 by Bill's wife Edith as Bill had fallen critically ill.

The real assets to trapping ability is the ability to be able to really think and analyze. After all, complete knowledge of the many strange habits of our fur animals and predators is of extreme importance in making good catches. The 'little tricks' of the game are far more important than the actual construction or generally- knowing standard sets or methods. Method application becomes far more important than knowing the method, itself. Proper set location can, in many cases, be as important as the set itself. Nothing under the sun in the way of fur-taking can replace a good working knowledge of all these important factors. There are no magic sets, no trapline wizardry, and no super-material that will do the impossible."

—Bill Nelson from the book Outdoorsman Extraordinaire

STANLEY HAWBAKER

1911–1983

From Trapping North American FurBearers

Trapping North American FurBearers by S. Stanley Hawbaker was no doubt most influential "practical knowledge" trapping book of my early years. Easy to read, well-illustrated and full of knowledge, Hawbaker's book helped me to catch more muskrats, more raccoons, my first fox, first mink, and many skunks and opossums. The first scents I bought were Hawbaker brand. Raccoon lure was the first, then muskrat. I remember making the floating log set for 'rats as described in Hawbaker's book. It didn't work with carrots. But if I covered the floating logs with vegetation and added a good glob of Hawbaker 'rat lure it worked!

I caught my first fox on Widow Maker 800. A gray taken in the woods along Big Walnut Creek. It would be 3 years before I caught a red fox, but it was also with Hawbaker's Lure. Wiley Red 500. My reynard trap was attached to a sapling drag as shown in Hawbaker's book and I'll never forget it. The dreams of wilderness adventures found in Hardings books never left my mind, but Hawbaker's methods put money in my pocket.

Raymond Thompson was right, there are two P's in trapping: pleasure and profit. I envisioned myself a wilderness trapper in training. Stanley Hawbaker was born July 11, 1911 near Greencastle, Pennsylvania. Young Stanley enjoyed the woods near his home and learned of trapping at a young age. At 25, Stanley opened Hawbaker Trading Post. By 1938 he had written his first book, *Trapping and Trailing.* By 1940 he released his first supply catalog and in 1941 *Trapping North American Furbearers.*

Author's Collection

This is the first edition of Trapping North American Furbearers by Stanley S. Hawbaker—the king of the "how to" trapping books at the start of the cottage industry. *Mink and Muskrat Trapping* was published in 1949. Also shown is Hawbaker's 1951 supply catalog.

Hawbaker modeled his business after E.J. Dailey and O.L. Butcher and improved upon it. The pioneer trappers—Dailey, Thompson, Wood, Lynch and Arnold romanticized wilderness trapline, the log cabin and snowshoe trail, however Hawbaker made a special effort to relate to farm boy trappers who didn't have wilderness at their doorstep.

In July 1951, Stanley Hawbaker took a page from A.R. Harding's playbook and released the premiere issue of *American Woodsman* magazine. In the first issue, Hawbaker mentions the *"policy and purpose"* of the publication as to "Build up a better understanding between sportsmen and game management." *American Woodsman* covered subjects like, fishing, hunting, trapping, camping and outdoor-related topics. Stanley did the trapping and fur report content and used his magazine extensively to market his books, lures and methods. *American Woodsman* magazine ran 54 issues from July 1951 to December 1955.

> *Trappers become the best self-made naturalists, in the world. They have to study habits, tracks, food, etc., and in doing this, they become well acquainted with all wildlife. The trapper is not the lazy sort of fellow. Most people think he is, but he is the most energetic of all persons. Trapping is hard work as one has to face all kinds of weather, long hard journeys everyday, with a heavy pack, and live lonely lives in the far back-woods and wilds. But with all this, the game is so fascinating that one follows the old trail year after year to get his share of the valuable furbearers.* —*S. Stanley Hawbaker Trapping North American Furbearers, 1941*

Looking back on it all, I'm convinced that there were better trappers afield than Hawbaker, yet likely there were no better trapping teachers at the time, and I would go as far to say that Hawbaker was the king of the cottage industry trappers. Hawbaker was a master salesman. *Trapping North American Furbearers* has been published in nearly 20 editions in soft and hardcover and today it's considered a classic. Stanley Hawbaker was inducted into the National Trappers Association Trappers Hall of Fame in 1994.

A Professional Method for Taking the Fox

THE ARTIFICIAL HOLE SET

A set that will enable you to take the most elusive fox on your trapline, as well as coyote, coon, skunk, etc.

Many times when we are out prospecting for fur in the fall months, we have noticed where some animal has dug out a bee nest. This occurence usually happens with the coming of August, September, or October. This digging has usually been done by fox and skunk. Look for these holes along old fence edges, stone fences, clearings, woods without undergrowth, edge of pine thickets, etc. If you can locate these diggings, you can immediately get a vision of what the artificial dirt hole set looks like. Once you have located these natural holes, make sets in the little mound of dirt that was removed in digging up the bee nest. Use for bait some old honey comb with a good fox lure. Have everything same as before you started making the set. Just in case you never located and have never seen just what these diggings look like, I will describe and illustrate one so you will have no trouble making an artificial set that will take the fox family — either red or grey.

The method of making the artificial dirt set has been cussed and discussed so many times that many trappers have come to the conclusion that some of

FINE LOCATION FOR ARTIFICAL DIRT SET

the ways that have been explained before are wrong and worthless. For me there is no definite way to make a dirt set. Make it a dozen different ways and it will take fox equally well. The location, the finished look of the set, and the lure arrangement are the three primary factors in making an artificial set that will click and produce fox.

Location of Set

Remember, never try to crowd a fox in a set. Pick out some location that fox uses in his natural haunts for food. These would include edge of wooden fences or stone fences, edge of pine woods, back pastures, clearings where a wood lot has been cut, or the edge or side of old woods roads.

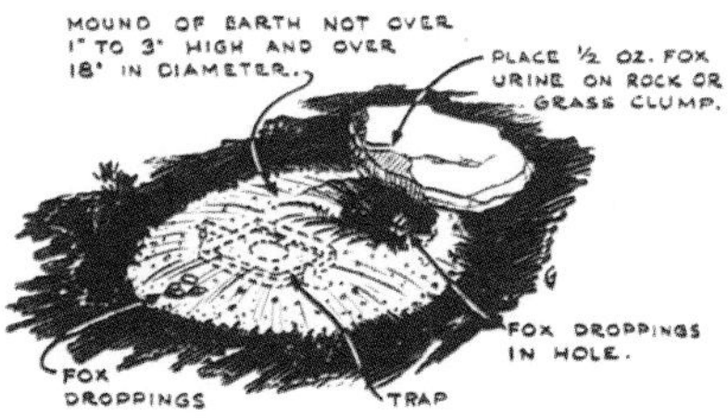

Dn't expect to find the fox down in a water ditch but up on the bank where he can look things over. Fox also come out to roam and hunt for food in pasture fields close by buildings as well as freshly plowed fields, stubble fields, hay fields, and almost any place where mice or other food will be found. In back sections, fox like to hunt on old abandoned farms, camp grounds, etc. Along the side of old trails very good set locations can be found and sets made. Always pick a location on some high point if possible or on ground that is nearly level. A fox will usually approach your set from the high side, so make it easy for him to walk into the set. Also in picking a location for your dirt set, be sure you make it when the grass or sod is short, or the ground is bare in spots. Under large pine trees are likely locations, especially at the edge of a pine thicket. If at all possible pick spots that are free of stones and roots, as the digging will be less difficult. If this kind of a location is used, advanced preparation should be made.

When you have spotted a location, which should be twenty-five to fifty yards away from the direct spot where set is to be made, set down your equipment container which should be a clean pack basket, grain or canvas

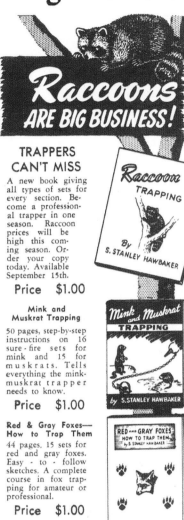

This instruction page appears in the first issue of Hawbaker's *American Woodsman* magazine.

A LITTLE HISTORY

My early trapping story starts in the suburbs. I grew up at 2202 Noe-Bixby Rd. Columbus, Ohio. Although my family no longer lives there, the house still stands today—albeit not as I remember it.

We lived near a railroad track that ran east and west and following the tracks west about 200 yards a trestle-crossed Big Walnut Creek. Our new neighbors were the Turners. Mr. Ken Turner was in the Air Force stationed at Rickenbacker air base. His wife Pat worked as a real estate agent. Their son Jeff was several years older than me and his sister Nina older still. One day in the late fall (likely November) I saw Jeff walking down the railroad tracks near our house and he was wearing a basket on his back. I watched him walk out of sight then followed him. I watched through the trees as he tended his traps along Big Walnut. A few days later, I was wearing Jeff's pack basket and helping him. Jeff had learned to trap where he originally grew up in Wilmington, Ohio. Jeff turned me on to *Fur-Fish-Game* magazine which was available at the magazine rack of a local drug store.

Young Tom Miranda- My first dog was named Candy as she came into the family about Easter time.

Author's Collection

This was my first trapping book. I would purchase many, many more over the years.

As a youngster, my first trapping book was A.R. Harding's *Trappers Companion.* It was a small book written in 1919 and described sets and skinning. I read it many times, then ordered another Harding title. *Trapping as a Profession* is likely the book dearest to my heart. This book brought out the romance of trapping and allowed me to enter a realm of make-believe. The woods and river near my home became a wild wilderness in my mind. These earliest books endeared me to the thought of being an outdoorsman, a trapper. I'm sure watching Daniel Boone on television also embellished the idea' of thrilling adventures. Both of the early Harding books I owned and my memories of reading them are still special to me today. Turner taught me how to make muskrat and raccoon sets and I caught my first 'rat and coon that first season trapping with Jeff. We became good pals despite our age difference and trapped together two seasons. Jeff graduated high school then went off to art school. I inherited the trapline.

I can remember buying traps back in the early 1970s at a chain store called Ontario. They sold 110 Conibear traps, and 1-1/2 Victor long springs. With out Jeff Turner to run the line with me, I remember thinking that trapping wasn't as rewarding without some one to share the adventure with. My parents were also a little concerned about me running traps alone at 4 o'clock in the morning before school. So, I talked my baseball pal Steve Blahnik into being

My grandfather Milton Miranda (left) with prize coon dogs Dot and Don and pal Harvey Frazier (right), circa 1933 New Albany, Ohio. I was very young when my grandfather passed away, but I'm sure his outdoor instincts and passion for the hunt were passed down to me.

my trapping partner. Steve was a great ball player and we had worked together at Walnut Creek Gun Club where his father was a part owner. Steve and I set clay targets on the Olin trap machines and were referred to as "trap boys." Blahnik was a great friend but only trapped with me about a month before deciding it wasn't for him.

Predator Control
Wildlife Management
TOM MIRANDA
Professional Trapper
P.O. Box 146 Channing, Michigan 49815
2202 Noe-Bixby Rd., Columbus, Ohio 43227
614-866-2764

Author's Photo

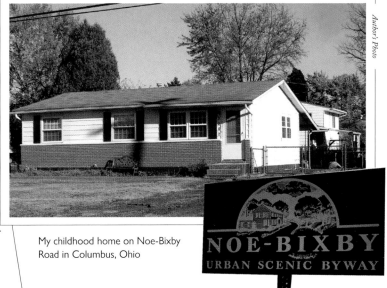

My childhood home on Noe-Bixby Road in Columbus, Ohio

One of a few photos of the Walnut Ridge high-school days. If you look closely, my parents can be seen, midway up the bleachers on the right.

I was a pretty energetic youngster and enjoyed playing ice hockey, baseball, football, ran track and loved music. I had a turntable, amp and speakers and spent some of my trapping money on rock albums. I worked several years as a substitute paperboy (delivering *Columbus Dispatch*) when the regular paper boys needed time off. (In our neighborhood the paper boys were all in one family, Rick, Ron, Joe and Chuck DeLille.) Dad let me use the lawn mower and I cared for several lawns in the summer, cutting grass for $5 a mow. I always kept busy and learned quite a bit about making money, saving money and spending money wisely when I was young. Lessons that would pay off later.

Fur-Fish-Game magazine kept me interested in trapping even after the season ended. It was with-in the pages of F-F-G where I read articles from other trappers in other parts of North America, learning new sets and theories. Trappers like O.L. Butcher, Herb Lenon, Bill Nelson, J. Curtis Grigg, James Mast, Vaughn Tingley and more. I learned about the concepts of long auto traplines, wilderness lines and many different types of sets. Today most of these men are legends in their own right, having contributed to trapping knowledge and organizations of which have helped to unite trappers in an attempt to educate the public as well as game departments in the conservation needs and efforts of trapping.

Author's Photos

This is the first trapping photo I have of one of my season catches taken in 1974 that includes; 79 muskrats, 7 raccoon, 3 opossum, 1 gray fox and 1 skunk. Sold for $255.

My third trapping partner was Paul Voz. Paul and I played ice hockey together. Voz was an outdoorsy kid from Minnesota and we got along great on the trapline and enjoyed each other's company. Paul could pull his weight with the traps and could make the sets and catches but he also lived several miles from my house where we skinned and dried the pelts. This meant that often the skinning fell on me. But Paul always made up for it. He was a great partner and we often talked about moving to the wilds and trapping. When we graduated high school in 1976, Paul and I made a pact that when we scraped up some coin, we would head north to run a wilderness trapline together. We called it "The Dream." But of course with jobs, girlfriends and maybe even college on the horizon, it seemed like "The Dream" would never materialize.

THE DREAM

"The Dream" was more than a dream to me. It was an obsession. After high school graduation, I bought my first car—a 1970 Kaiser Jeep CJ-5. I was immersing myself in trapping books, log cabin building books and wilderness survival books. I was also pretty interested in baseball and had gotten a letter before high school graduation from a University called Baldwin Wallace for a scholarship in baseball. However, I decided that if I were ever to play baseball in the big leagues, I'd need to go to a Division 1 school. So I walked on to Ohio State University as a freshman in late August 1976. I did well at the tryouts as I was a quick runner, which is something that can't be taught.

I played football, ran track and played baseball my senior year in high school and made the state finals in the 220-yard dash. Athletes born with speed are considered top candidates. In baseball having a strong throwing arm is essential. Players that can run like the wind and throw 95 MPH are the most desirable. I was eventually cut from the Buckeye team late in the process, mid-October 1976. Dejected, I focused on "The Dream."

School suddenly became an afterthought. I ran a trapline in November and December of 1976 and in the spring of '77 took a summer job making decent money at The Timken Company, a manufacturer of steel roller bearings. I drove a forklift stocking shelves and shipping orders. I trapped the fall and winter of 1977 while working and in early 1978, my father got me an "in" at Western Electric, a big factory where telephone parts were made. My position would be in the shop running a tap and die machine. My father worked at Western Electric as a tester of the big mainframe telephone switchboards. Dad was so good at his job the company offered to send him back to college to earn an associate engineering degree which he did in the evenings and weekends. We were all so very proud of dad when he graduated and became an engineer.

The years of 1977 and 1978 were my limbo years. I had quit college and was still trapping in the fall and winter but also working wage jobs that weren't really interesting to me. By late spring 1978 Paul Voz and I finally planned a trip north to Michigan's Upper Peninsula region. I was serious about finding some property in an area where we could build a cabin and run a trapline. At the time I was driving an old Jeep J-10 pickup and we loaded it with camping gear and headed out. It was a grand adventure. Paul and I looked at many pieces of land in several different areas, even-

Author's Photos

A view of the Michigamme River on the property Paul Voz and I purchased in 1978.

1. A view of the pier foundation and start of the A-frame trusses. 2. Setting the trusses. 3. Tom and Paul tie in rafters on second story. 4. Sheeting the roof. 5. Tom and Paul take a break—start of the second week. 6. Tom Sr. and Paul shingle the roof. 7. Finishing the steep pitch of roofing shingles. 8. Tom Miranda Sr. levels the window frame.

The finished A-frame cabin shell in July 1979.

tually settling on a 15-acre parcel at the end of the a trail fifteen miles from the hard top road. The property sat on the beautiful Michigamme River, south of a small town called Republic. We put down a deposit and bought the land "on contract" then returned home. Before we bought the property, it was decided that once the contract was paid in full, we would have the land surveyed into 2 parcels of seven and a half acres each. The cabin would sit on my half of the property and I would pay for the materials and all expenses to construct it.

For the rest of the year I worked the full-time job which my father helped me land at Western Electric Company "Manufacturing and Supply Unit of the Bell System" on East Broad Street in Columbus, which was located about six miles from my parents house. I was living at home and saving every dime toward "The Dream."

In late 1978 Paul and I made several trips to the property with plans to clear an area for building the cabin. We also hauled in needed supplies. The long, two-track road that led back to the property couldn't accommodate a large delivery truck so we took up loads of materials I purchased in Ohio. Materials like treated timbers and precast concrete footers. My father also brought a small travel camper and set it up so he and mom could stay in it as the cabin was being built.

Paul and I took a late winter trip to the property in early 1979. It was a snow camping adventure that turned into a misadventure. Paul and I parked along the highway and snowshoed the entire way back to the property towing sleds of supplies. We had brought a chain saw to girdle cabin logs and of course, food. The trip was long and the snow deep. When we arrived at the camper it was buried in snow. The temperature was minus 30 and getting the heater lit was a process with the cold. To add insult to injury, we both got food poisoning and were sick for a couple days. But we did manage to get some trees cut and some winter exploring. Late January in Michigan's Upper Peninsula region is nothing short of brutal!

I took two additional trips to the property in early 1979 again hauling up materials. Then in July my mother, father, Paul Voz and I went north to build the A-frame cabin. It was to be a 2-week project and I was prepared with plans, lumber, pretty much everything on the site. After just one long day of work we realized it was going to be a huge project. Because of the remoteness of the location, instead of having a footer dug with a backhoe and concrete poured, we dug piling holes, added precast cement foundations and set 10 x 10 treated posts as the foundation. Pairs of 2 x 12 treated girders would bolt to the pier foundation and support the structure off the ground. My mom did the cooking and was always there as need. Dad, Paul and I were the carpenters. I was pseudo foreman as I had been over and over the plans and had drawn up the foundation from a pole barn building book. We busted tail and got the shell up. We worked feverishly to seal up the house as I knew I wouldn't be back for nearly a year. The property was almost 800 miles north from Columbus, Ohio.

All in all, the cabin building was a grand time. We laughed, joked and together the four of us build a damned nice cabin. Those two weeks are some of my fondest memories of quality time with my father and mother. I think these two weeks were life changing for Paul Voz as well—as even though he had a good job back home, his destiny would eventually be rough carpentry, deck building and contracting, all things he had done and learned together with my father and me in Michigan.

debilitating eye disease made him legally blind around 1966. Grandpa was born and raised in the Kentucky hills and was very talented at many outdoor things like hunting, gardening, etc.

My grandfather used a forked willow branch to locate the best spot for the well. Known as dowsing, or water witching, it's sort of an unexplained or divine skill that some people have to locate water. Skeptics to dowsing say it's fake, but I will say watching my grandfather do the water witching was amazing as he was all but blind at that time. Once grandpa found the location we used a well point, pipe and hand driver to pound the well pipe into the ground 25 feet. The

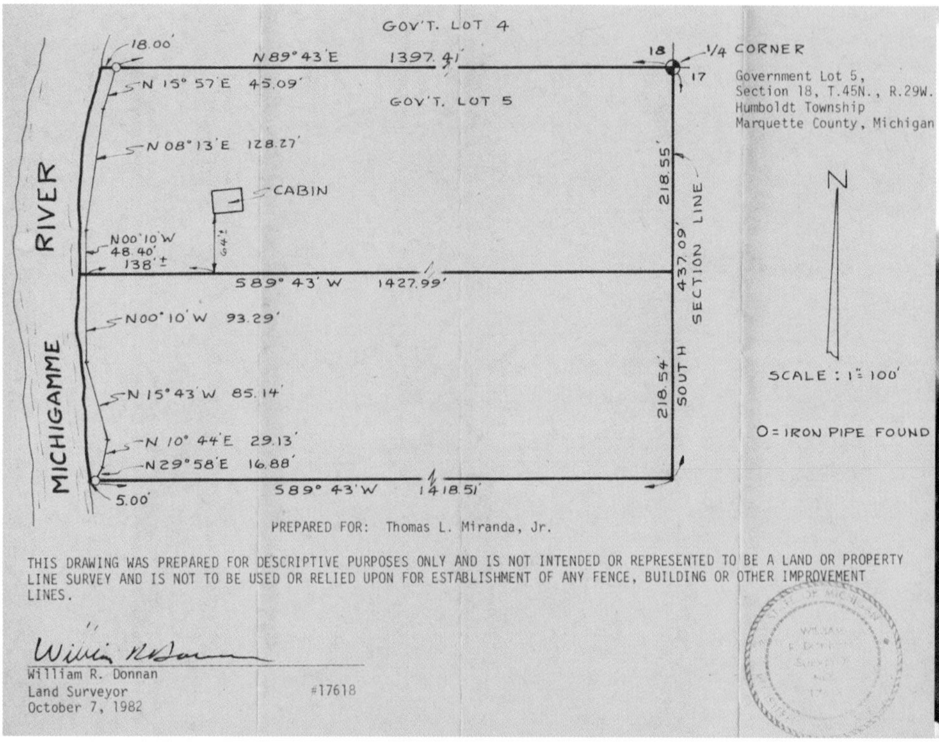

Lot Survey for Tom Miranda's Michigamme River cabin.

On the drive south back to Columbus, I remember talking with Paul that the next goal was to save up and buy our "grub stakes," then make the move north in the late summer of 1980.

I made a trip to the cabin in the spring of 1980 (without Paul) to haul up supplies, furniture and establish a well. My mother's father, Ben Blanton (my grandfather) came along to see the property and help with the water well. "Grandpa Blanton" as I called him had been a machinist for the large coal mining machine company Jeffrey Manufacturing. However, a

ground was soft sand, but large boulders were obstacles and we damaged two well points before digging down about 8 feet to find a seam in the rock. The well was eventually set and pumped good clear, cold water with a hand pump.

I can't express the gratitude and feelings I had for my grandfather—week I spent with him in Michigan was a huge influence on me. I was blessed to know all four of my grandparents and both my mother and my father's parents were all married 50-plus years. At this writing, my parents have been together 63 years.

I worked every ounce of overtime and trapped hard the fall and winter of 1979 and saved, saved,saved! I bought traps and gear, built a barrel stove, bought everything I could think of to outfit and finish the A-frame and be ready for trapping. But as the spring of 1980 came closer and closer, Paul showed less interest until one day he told me that moving north to trap really wasn't his dream at all. He had a good job at Commercial Lovelace motor freight company making serious money, a steady girlfriend and no plans on screwing up either with a move to the wilds of Michigan's UP.

I remember quitting my job at Western Electric. Even though my father was 100 percent supportive of me, when I tendered my resignation, he thought it was a huge mistake. How would I pay my bills, make my truck payment, insurance, food, and property taxes? Leaving a good-paying job to follow a career that until then had only been a hobby was making no sense to him. Yet, leaving for Michigan that fateful August day in 1980, my dad was there and supportive. I can remember my mother with tears in her eyes and my father both standing in the driveway when I keyed the truck starter. My dad leaned into the window of the truck and said "Tom, you watch your top knot," which is a famous line from the movie *Jeremiah Johnson.* I'm pretty emotional and did shed a tear or two as I drove away from 2202 Noe-Bixby Road, but I was determined to follow my dreams. I had made a plan and was following through. There was no turning back—no quitting. Come hell or high water I was going to learn to be the best trapper I could be. I had big plans.

Here's my Jeep CJ-7 sitting in the driveway on Noe Bixby Rd. It was my fourth Jeep and first brand new one. Trapping can be tough on a vehicle!

THE "OLD FOX" PETE RICKARD

1910 —2002

From the book *Legendary Fox* by Oscar Cronk

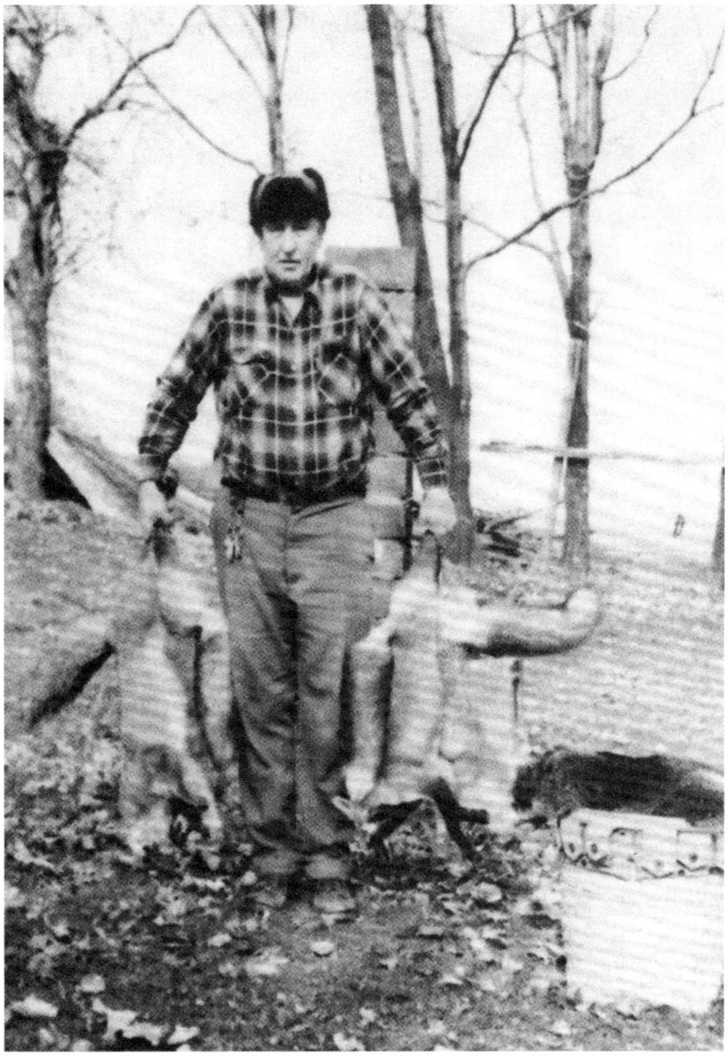

Pete Rickard with a morning's catch of foxes. 1970s.

Pete Rickard's name is now synonymous with his famous *Old Indian Buck Lure.* But Rickard wasn't nicknamed "the fox" for his deer hunting prowess. Born in 1910 young Pete enjoyed the outdoors. At a young age he started trapping skunks and in 1918 the fur prices were such that a skunk pelt was worth $8. Big money for an 8-year-old kid and Pete was hooked on trapping. Pete's first big job was with the Remington Arms Company where he spent his first two paychecks ($10 each) buying a 1923 Model T and a canoe—both for the trapline. At 18 years old, Pete was taking trapping lessons from the best-known fox-man in New York, Art Crane.

Pete and Art became friends and trapped together for a few years during the depression. Pete was more of an apprentice, yet he did well and kept all the fur he caught. In the early days of fox trapping, trappers often caught the animals early in the fall and kept them penned up until the pelts primed mid-winter, as the heavy Adirondack snows limited catches.

Pete became a fantastic trapper and by 1932 had begun making and selling his own trapping lures. Pete married Kathryn Hill in September of 1935 and the husband and wife team began to grow the Pete Rickard brand. By 1942 the Rickard family had multiplied to four with the addition of two boys Larry and Ivan, but the second world war would call Pete for service. Rickard was sent to the European theatre and fought in the *Battle of the Bulge.*

Returning from the war in late 1945, Pete endeavored to pick up where he left off. By 1947 the Rickard brand began branching into a new direction the deer scent business. While E.J. Dailey and Stanley Hawbaker were leading the way in the trapping business, Pete moved more forcefully into the deer hunting, developing not only deer attractants, but dog breaking scents, elk and bear lures for hunters. Big game scent was a new market and Pete's Original Indian Buck Lure was on the cusp of its infancy. By the 1960s he was still selling trapping scent and supplies, yet nearly the entirety of Rickard's business revolved around deer scent. In 1973 Pete's eldest son Larry came into the business and the timing was perfect as fur prices were rising. By 1980, Pete Rickard's was booming in the trapping business again.

The "Old Fox" was a nickname given Pete by his wife Kathryn and it stuck with Pete all the way to the end. Pete Rickard was inducted into the National Trappers Association Trappers Hall of Fame in 1999 a few short years before he passed. Pete Rickard is one of the few professional trappers who moved into the the sport hunting industry and succeeded. Pete Rickard Company still sells his Original Indian Buck Lure today.

From the book Legendary Fox by Oscar Cronk

Top N.Y. Fox Trapper Art Crane

Author's Collection

Oscar Cronk wrote the definitive Pete Rickard biography and it's a must-have for every trapping history buff.

CHAPTER 5

LONG-LINE TRAPPERS

Supply and demand has been the benchmark of commerce since the beginning of commercial trade. The fluctuation of fur prices has always been somewhat at the mercy of the market's demand. High prices for say muskrats, would encourage many trappers to trap muskrats and consequently a large muskrat catch. Typically when there is a high supply the price usually adjusts down—called a "buyer's market." Conversely, low prices for muskrats may lead to fewer trappers trapping 'rats and consequently a small muskrat catch. Typically when there is a low supply the price usually adjusts up—called a "seller's market."

Of course when supply is high and demand is low it's not good for trappers—period. However when supply is low and demand high, some trappers in the right locales can make good catches and profits. No matter the scenario, high prices paid for large catches will always be the trapper's dream.

For all trappers, the size of the catch was determined by the mode of transportation, density of animals and of course, weather conditions. The automobile industry allowed more mobility to the trappers of the "cottage industry" era, allowing a larger number of traps to be utilized in a wider range of territory and subsequently larger catches.

Author's Photo

Here's an enterprising trapper displaying his catch at the Winter Carnival in Saranac Lake, New York—circa 1915.

NUMBERS GAME

1950–1990

There have been long-line auto trappers since the assembly line made automobiles affordable. E.J. Dailey called it "spot trapping." However, as trappers and their businesses evolved, the1950s, 60s and 70s brought in a new age of the auto trap-line. Known as "long-liners," these trappers worked specifically on volume in an attempt to catch large numbers of specific animals. When fox prices were high, trappers would specialize in foxes, when mink were high—mink or

< *Justin Zuzak photo*

New York trapper Josh Stairs sent me this photo of his grandfather Douglas Stairs with a weeks, catch on the auto trapline—circa 1948.

cats or martens—you name it. If the fur price was up, the long-line trapper geared up and trapped "full throttle" in a commercial manner. During these times, "state hopping" also became very popular. Trappers could travel out of state, north to start earlier and south to extend the season. Focusing on one species allowed a uniform system. The same trap size, stake, lure, equipment, etc. could be used—streamlining the process. In this numbers game, making sets efficiently and covering ground put trappers into new territory and taking new animals.

Pennsylvania long-liner David Ziegler stands with great catch from his 2005–06 trapline.

The long-line principle involves what is called skimming. Trappers run through an area for maybe 10 days then off into a new area. The strategy is to skim off the surplus animals and then progress to a fresh area. Fox and coyote long-liners operating in areas dense with predators would generate large numbers because a typical pair of foxes may have 8–10 young and these fox are near maturity by October/November. Coyotes produce 4–8 young. Thus, long-liners are skimming a high percentage of younger animals because there are four times more younger animals than adults.

The primary motivation of the long-liner is average dollars per day. If a long–line trapper needs to make say $10 thousand in a season, the numbers would be figured on averages. Two hundred $50 foxes would make the goal. Four foxes a day on average would complete the goal in 50 days, 8 foxes a day in 25 days. Often longliners would look at non-target catches as covering their expenses. Four coon a day at $20 would buy a tank of gas, lure and lunch. Skunks would supply $10 each with the collection of pure quill essence and smart trappers piled their skunks in abandoned buildings to drain the essence once every week or so. In some farming areas, a mixed-species line makes more sense and trappers fortunate to have a bounty of different species do well to plan accordingly. Trappers targeting $10 thousand in a 60-day, mixed bag season—would need to average $167 a day. This might be 2—$50 fox, 3—$20 raccoons and 2—$5 muskrats to equal $170 each day. As most trappers know, the catches early in the season come easier than in the later season. Yet, earlier catches are less prime furs which grade out as less value. This is where the averages come into play. Also, fur value can fluctuate substantially. In the late 1970s fur boom red foxes in some areas were bringing $80–$100 and raccoons averaging $35–$45. In these times it took half as many animals to make the goal. I averaged $500 a day for weeks in several seasons, but I skinned pelts nightly and sold fur almost weekly for expenses to keep going. The negative in the fur boom years was the competition and theft with so many trappers afield and the opportunists who happened upon traps or catches.

Joe Kierl Photo

Nebraska trapper Joe Kierl poses with his children Addison and Thad and a mixed bag of ranch-land pelts taken in 2018–19.

BUSINESS SAVVY

Many of the most successful long-line trappers took the lead from the cottage industry trappers and developed trapping businesses, utilizing their knowledge and experience to write magazine articles and how-to books. They also made scent and lures, selling supplies and marketing with impressive catch photos. It was a successful recipe and many did exceedingly well financially. I was blessed to be in the middle of all this through the 1980s and early 1990s. The chart below assumes a trapper making $100 thousand gross and shows the potential income streams from various sources to achieve it.

PROFESSIONAL TRAPPERS INCOME CHART
(HYPOTHETICAL IN THOUSANDS OF DOLLARS)

CATEGORY	GROSS	NET	% OF INCOME
LURE	$35	$25	35%
BOOKS	$12	$10	12%
SUPPLIES	$23	$8	23%
LESSONS	$15	$10	15%
FUR TRAPPING	$15	$12	15%
TOTAL	$100K	$65K	100%

From this hypothetical income chart, it's easy to see that lure sales make up the lion's share of a professional trapper's income. Books and lessons have a high profit margin as well. Supplies are typically purchased and these have the lowest profitability. Many of the top names in the industry did many times these numbers, however few long-line trappers ever did more than $40,000 in furs alone unless they were also buying furs. It should also be recognized that not always the "highest volume" trappers made the most income. Typically the trappers who were keen at marketing and had a specific niche market did the best and achieved longevity in the industry.

There were also many successful long-line trappers who weren't well-known. These trappers operated under a cloak of secrecy, covering vast distances, trapping other states with different seasons relying on a substantial fur check to cover expenses and make a profit. Some did, but often these giant catches went unrewarded with low fur prices and high expenses. Even for these volume fur trappers, commercial trapping was only a part-time business and needed to be supplemented with other work, whether it be animal control, a seasonal job or another business altogether.

I was blessed to grow up in the 1960s and hit the "fur boom" in my prime as a trapper. I have been influenced by many long-liners, through their books and personal trapping instructions.

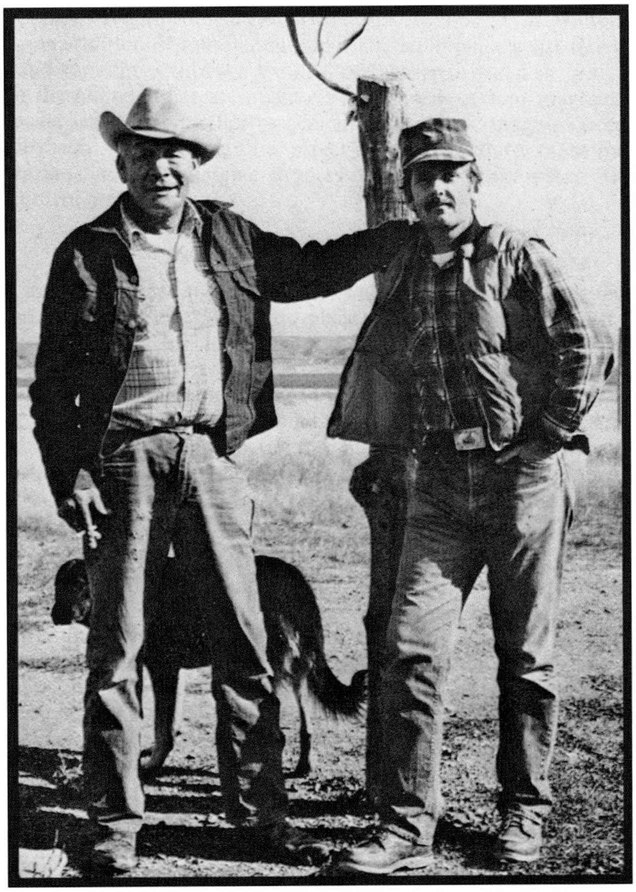

Garold Weiland poses with Lower Brule trapper Floyd Thompson around 1974. It's amazing to me that I read Weiland's books while in high school and ten years later I would be the government trapper for some of the areas Garold ran his line. I lived 20 miles from Lower Brule in 1984.

Author's Collection

GAROLD WEILAND

1932–

Just to hear his name puts a smile on my face. Garold Weiland's fox book hit me like a freight train. Wow! Every page made sense. Every set looked like it just had to work. Every location photo caught a fox, some doubles. And not just any fox, big Dakota prairie pales. There was no doubt in my mind—making a living at trapping was now absolutely possible, and there was no need to live in a cabin in the wilderness.

Weiland's 1974 treatise *Long Liner Fox Trapping* was like the first Betty Crocker cake recipe book for fox trapping. Yeah, sure—E.J. Dailey and Stanley Hawbaker showed the sets and a few locations, but Weiland's book was the list of ingredients, baking temperature, sweet icing with a cherry on top.

I can remember buying *Long Liner Fox Trapping* in Clarksburg, Ohio at Marvin Mallow Trap Company. Marvin was an icon in the fur business and had taken a liking to me and I him. My father would drive me to Mallow's place as I couldn't drive until mid-1974. And every time I went to visit Marvin it was a grand time. Marvin would show me the newest fur "lots" he had bought, or books and supplies that had come in since I'd been there last. Great memories—even as I thumb through my copy of Weiland's book today, I get excited to boil fox traps and start scouting.

The layout and premise of *Long Liner Fox Trapping* has been the template of literally *every* "how-to" trapping book to be released after it. Funny thing is by 1984, I was trapping some of Weiland's old areas as a government trapper.

Garold Weiland was born in 1932 in the early days of the depression. The Weilands moved east when Garold was just a boy so his father could find work in the timber business. Northern Wisconsin was a hunting and fishing paradise and Garold learned to trap in the north woods while living in a log cabin. Eventually his family returned to South Dakota and Garold began trapping the pothole region for the many mink and muskrats found there. As a professional trapper, Weiland also state hopped. Living in northern South Dakota offered access to Montana and North Dakota as well as heading south to extend the season in New Mexico, Arizona and Texas.

Garold Weiland also sold his own trapping lures. The success of his two fox books along with a coyote, mink and bobcat book had garnered him a sort of cult following. I know as I was in the cult. Long-liner Ray Milligan is also a Weiland fan and has fond memories of not only "the book that started it all," but of meeting and talking trapping with Garold. For us trappers, guys like Weiland, Butcher or Thompson were our heroes like Micky Mantle, Dick Butkus or Gretzky in the sports world. It's what dreams are made of.

"Determining fox density in strange new country can be difficult. Fox can be moving through a particular area and yet leave little sign of their existence. Test patches can be made in prospective areas. These patches are made by cutting up a three foot area of ground with a garden hoe. Cut out the sod and work the dirt up fine. In the center, a small piece of rabbit fur is fastened with a wire and stuck into the ground. Apply to the fur a generous run of good fox call lure. A few of these test spots made during September and early October will tell the story. Check them every 2–3 days for fox sign. You'll get tracks, digging, droppings and wet urine deposits. Many times the fur ball will be pulled free and carried off. These same locations if proven hot, can be locations for your traps later on."

—Garold Weiland, Long Liner Fox Trapping 1974

PETE AND RON LEGGETT

1925–2004 1945–

The Maryland father and son team of Pete and Ron Leggett rank right up at the top of the list as the best at what they do on the trapline. True eastern long-liners and role models for many. When Pete was alive, the team could roll into any trappers convention and immediately draw a crowd.

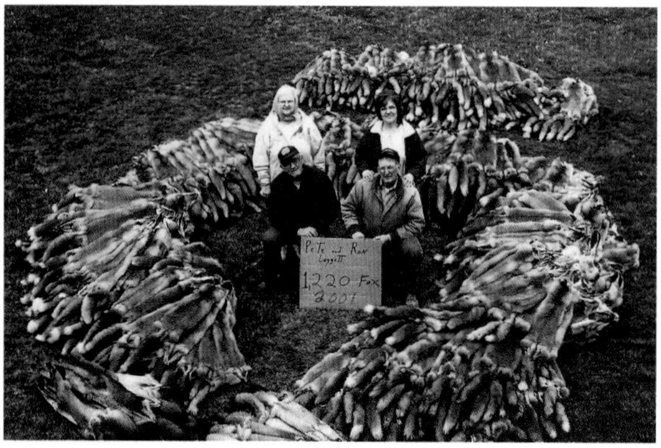

Ron Leggett Photo

Pete and Ron Leggett pose with their spouses and the 2001 record catch of 1,220 fox taken on their Maryland long-lines.

Pete learned to trap from his uncle and as a schoolboy trapped for spending money. Marrying his bride Charlotte at 19 years old put a halt to Pete's trapping and off to work to the dairy farm he went. Charlotte and Pete had 4 children, their firstborn was Ron. In 1964 (19 years old at the time), a fur buyer made a bet with Ron that he couldn't catch a fox. The story goes that both Ron and Pete ran six traps for nearly two months before Ron caught a fox. But the rest is history.

Being dairy farmers by trade allowed Leggett's access to many farms, but to catch more than 1,000 foxes in a two-month Maryland season, meant lots of ground needed covering. And both Pete and Ron were up to the challenge.

During their early years, the Leggetts pioneered what they called the "step-down" set, a set which not only has eye appeal, but puts the animal at a disadvantage when it must step down several inches to access the bait hole. Using the step-down for a couple seasons gave the Leggetts several variations of the set including the tapered step-down set. Both of the deadly sets are described in their books *Foxes by the Thousand*, printed in 1988 and *Coyote by the Thousand,* in 1999.

Ron Leggett Photo

Pete Leggett in action during a trapping convention seminar on fox trapping.

Ron Leggett Photo

Pete poses with 16 red foxes and 4 raccoons after a day's run over his Maryland trapline.

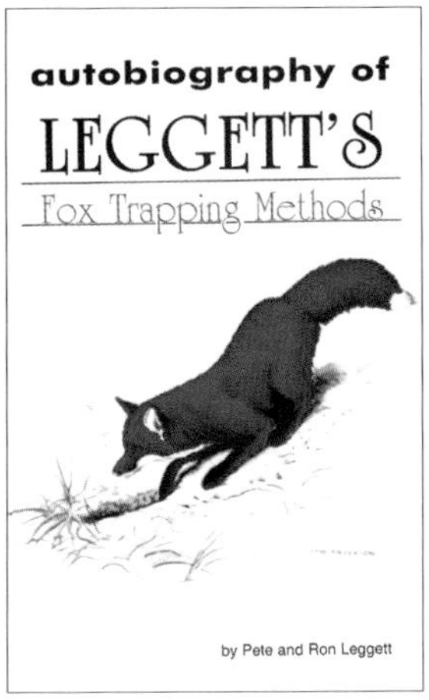

Author's Collection

Pete and Ron Leggett's *Autobiography of Leggett's Fox Trapping Methods* book in which illustrates their signature *step-down* set.

These books where revised and reprinted in 2008 as the *Autobiography of Leggett's Fox Trapping Methods* and *Autobiography of Leggett's Coyote Trapping Methods.*

Pete and Ron Leggett had harvested over 21,000 foxes together, however their best season was in 2001 when Pete caught 601 foxes and Ron caught 619 in about sixty days of trapping. If you put a pencil to their accomplishment, 600 foxes per man over a sixty-day season is a 10 fox per man, per day average. The 1,220 foxes' these trappers took between them stands as an amazing trappers catch for any state in any time period.

Since Pete's passing, Ron has continued to pile up foxes year after year trapping much of the same Maryland farms that he and his father did. Ron also does ADC work as well as running the family trapping business and is an instructor at the famed Fur Takers Professional Trappers College. Both Pete and Ron were inducted into the National Trappers Association Trappers Hall of Fame in 2003.

"The step-down dirt hole sets that were developed by us have been widely publicized throughout the U.S. and Canada. The reason for this wide spread publicity is the catch ratio per fox visit. We feel these two sets, the step-down and tapered step-down have made a large contribution to our catches. The deep dirt hole has been accredited with over 3,000 fox before we started using the tapered step-down dirt hole set. Our traplines are run using only the step-down sets. We don't use urine post sets, because without the dirt hole there is not enough curiosity created for the fox to further investigate the set."

—Pete and Ron Leggett Foxes by the Thousand, 1988.

JOHNNY THORPE

1933–2015

Johnny Thorpe became a legendary trapper because it was his destiny. I've placed Thorpe in the category of a long-liner as when I met him, he was running long-lines and basking in the highlight of his career. Growing up in the same small town and under the influence of Pete Rickard, Thorpe was catching muskrats as a youngster and learning that the outdoors was where he belonged. Thorpe's family lineage is tied to legendary olympian and football star Jim Thorpe, Johnny's grandfather—a native of the Sauk/Fox tribe and first cousin to the famous athlete.

Like every trapper who grew up after 1925, *Fur-Fish-Game* magazine played a big role in introducing them to trapping. Johnny was handed down some Diamond brand double jaw long spring traps and with 'rats bringing a buck twenty-five in the early 1940s, it was good money. By 1948, Johnny was catching good numbers of muskrats and mink and under the influence of Rickard's successful lifestyle, Johnny quit school and started his trapping career. Johnny lived in a tent and trapped wherever fur was found. Mink were bringing nearly $20 and 'rats $3. Johnny trapped all winter and did odd jobs for farmers or construction in the summer—then back on the trapline.

Like every trapper who grew up in upstate New York, the call of the Adirondacks lured them into the wilds. In the early 1950s New York had placed a bounty on predators, wolves—$75, bobcats—$50 and foxes—$3. With the stories of E.J. Dailey in his head, a 20-year-old Johnny Thorpe went into the wilds to learn the wilderness trapper mentality. It's a different ball game than the farmland trapline as I can attest!

Thorpe's life revolved around trapping, yet his character was defined by his passions after the season. Johnny was an eastern cowboy, a wrangler, guide, farrier, treasure hunter, artist—and the list goes on. Thorpe settled down for a time to get married and raise a family, but his passion for wild adventures never wained. In Johnny's book, *Fifty Years a Trapper and Treasure Hunter*—1995, he talks about some of his amazing long-line catches of mink. During the late 1950s and early 60s mink were king and Johnny was in full "pro-trapper" form, taking over 100 mink a season operating lines in the southern 'Dacks, one year he took 140. Johnny had come full circle in 1956 as his first article appeared in the magazine that started it all, *Fur-Fish-Game*.

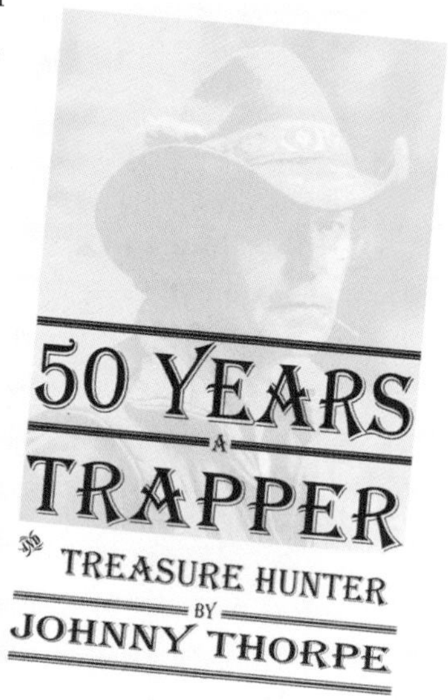

Johnny developed what he called the "Suicide Set" and in 1958 started selling his secret. The "Suicide Set" —as simple as it is, was a blind set along the concrete wing wall of a road bridge. The trap set against the wall and just below the stream's surface, takes advantage of a mink's tendency to "hug the edge" as they traverse along a stream. In the book *Fifty Years a Trapper and Treasure Hunter*, Johnny expresses some remorse for

stock for 8 seasons on out-of-state hops before and during the 1977–83 fur boom including doing beaver work for timber companies in the south. Boda and Thorpe trapped together on Thorpe's first trip to the desert southwest and Johnny liked the weather, trapping and treasure hunting so much he eventually made the area his second home. Thorpe was inducted into the National Trappers Association Trappers Hall of Fame in 1996.

John A. "Johnny" Thorpe, 82, a celebrated figure among trappers and die-hard outdoorsman, passed away peacefully, Tuesday, Oct. 27, 2015, at his home in Stony Creek, NY. His death coincided with the sixth super moon of the year, with the fifth being the ultra-rare "blood moon."

selling the secret as by the early 1960s "every bridge in the Adirondacks had a trap under it." Thorpe had mink catch numbers of 28, 31, 32 and 38 in a single day's run over the traps. Johnny also took 198 mink one season trapping in Canada.

Johnny's treasure hunting also defines his "boy-like" attitude to life. Just like checking traps, treasure hunting is that dive into the unknown, as you never know what you may find. Thorpe happened into the treasure hunting world by chance, as a "seeker" approached Johnny for his knowledge of the Adirondacks and especially cave and mine locations. Soon, stories were being bantered back and forth and Johnny knew when the "seeker" mentioned a story of a lost cannon that he might know the location. Johnny had found an old boat anchor years before in a small stream—in a totally out-of-the-way place. He knew it didn't belong there. Buying a metal detector and returning to the site, Johnny was able to locate parts of a fantastic 17th century treasure. I don't want to give away the complete story here as Johnny's book *Fifty Years a Trapper and Treasure Hunter* is fascinating reading and a book to add to your collection.

Johnny trapped with many partners over the years on different lines including New York trappers Jim Comstock and Bud Boda. Thorpe ran lines with Com-

"Big Jim Comstock is without a doubt the best trapping partner I ever worked with. He possesses the ability to improve on most any trapping method a feller can come up with. He is a real perfectionist and a top notch 'cat an' beaver trapper. He is also the fastest beaver skinner I have ever seen. I used to time him with a stop watch and he could skin a beaver in 2-1/2 minutes flat when he was really into it! An' I'm talkin' blankets! An' he could keep up that pace for a half an hour at a time! I have caught three thousand beaver an' better, but I'll be damned if I could ever get fast at skinning the things. About eight minutes was the best I could ever do."

—Johnny Thorpe, Fifty Years a Trapper and Treasure Hunter, 1995

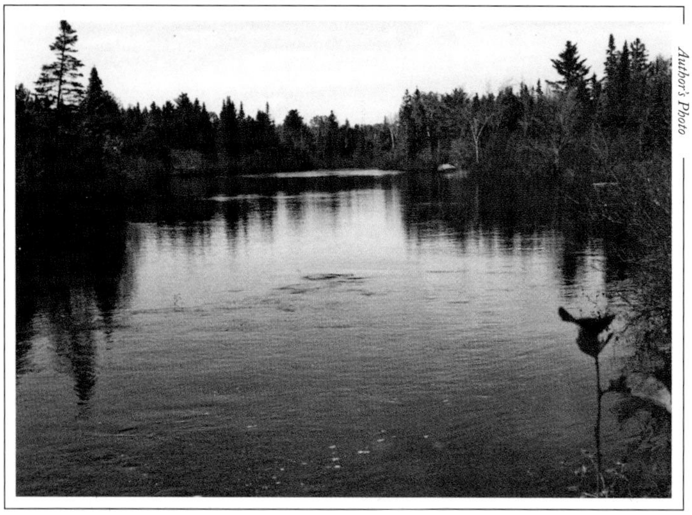

Michigamme River looking north to Witbeck Rapids, fall 1980

NORTH TO MICHIGAN

Leaving Columbus, Ohio for my wilderness trapping adventure the summer of 1980 was an exciting time for me. But there was plenty to do. The A-frame cabin needed additional work to be livable. I needed to build a woodshed and stock it with enough firewood to last the winter. I needed at the very least a shed to work on my traps, a place to skin and dry my catch. Plus my trapline needed scouting.

The first few weeks passed quickly as I immediately built a wood shed and began filling it with dry maple, poplar and spruce. Logging companies in the area allowed firewood collection as long as the pulp was cut, stacked and the crew moved on. In the clear cuts there were many downed trees and broken pieces that made great firewood. Maple and birch burned the best as it burns hot and the coals last. Second best is spruce as the sap burns hot. Poplar also burns well and was plentiful. Paper companies used the poplar to make paper. I built a shack over the well pump as here I would store supplies, traps and tools that needn't be in the house. My first season, I would skin and put up fur in the A-frame.

My 1980 Jeep I bought as part of my trapping outfit to bring north. Photo taken on the Floodwood plains along the Michigamme river.

I did my scouting with a Honda 185 dirt bike which was purchased as part of my trapping stake. The bike was good on gas and also had lights so it could be driven on the highway. I rode the bike and mapped nearly every road in a 50-mile circumference of my camp—scouting for fox and coyote tracks in the road, flowing culverts for mink as well as beaver dams for both mink as well as beaver and otter sign. The Michigamme River was deep and swift flowing and where there were muddy, grassy banks there was muskrat sign. I built some 'rat floats as well as mink cubbies and hauled them to areas with my Jeep preseason. I placed the mink boxes to allow the mink to get used to them but I hid the muskrat floats to be placed when seasoned opened with traps, lure and fresh grasses.

This was the first time I was ever away from home for any extended time. I went through bouts of loneliness and I reflected often about Paul Voz and how different it might have been if he would have been there to share in the adventure. But these times quickly passed

CRAIG O'GORMAN

1948–

Craig O'Gorman Photo

Craig O'Gorman accepts his induction into the North American Trappers Historical Society Trappers Hall of Fame, 2016.

If there was a trapper whose photo would appear in Webster's Dictionary next to the definition of a long-line trapper, it would likely be Craig O'Gorman. Craig undoubtedly redefined the term, image and attitude of a long-line professional trapper. O'Gorman cut his teeth trapping in Iowa amongst many talented auto-trappers who operated the Midwest in the 1940s–70s. Craig took lessons from legend Bill Nelson in 1969, and J.Curtis Grigg, Don Bolte and John Smith in the early 1970s. O'Gorman knew and shared knowledge with trapping experts like Bud Hall, Joe Reder, George Good, Slim Pedersen and others—all amazing, high-volume trappers. It was said in the 1970s that Hall was catching 20-plus foxes a day some seasons. Hall took over 10,000 foxes in his career and over 7,000 mink. John Smith caught more than 1,000 foxes in one season. Bolte took over 900 raccoons in one season, 60 bandits in one check over his line, Reder 400-plus beaver on the Missouri River, Slim Pedersen took over 200 bobcats in one of his mega seasons. Quite an impressive resumé.

Craig O'Gorman Photo

Here's 18-year-old Craig O'Gorman on the porch with some fox pelts in 1966.

Craig O'Gorman was born in Mason City, Iowa. For a short time during his childhood the family moved to Cody, Wyoming but Craig ended up back in northeastern Iowa catching his first fox at age 13. When Craig got his driver's license, he was unstoppable, taking 50-plus foxes a season while in school plus coon, mink and 'rats. Craig moved to Omaha, Nebraska at age 20 and trapped Iowa, Montana and Nebraska for seven seasons honing his craft.

When Bill Nelson fell ill early in 1973, Bill's wife Edith asked Craig to take over Bill's trapping students and the O'Gorman style began to take shape. That same year Craig began selling his own trapping lure formulations. Soon Craig was moving to Montana as a federal trapper with aspirations of putting down roots along the Powder River. The year was 1976, Craig was 28 years old and ready for anything. Southeastern Montana was the land of huge ranches where sheep and calves needed a guardian and young Craig was up for the task. Like any job, work is work—yet the politics of government predator control isn't the same as entrepreneurial fur trapping. Although public relations is a key aspect of fur trapping, in animal damage

Craig O'Gorman Photo

Craig with bundles of coyotes and foxes, circa 1973.

control work it takes on a completely different role. Where fur trappers skim surplus animals and move into new areas, ranchers want any and all predation removed. The government becomes an in-between. Craig soon learned that his federal trapping job was 70% public relations, 20% paperwork and 10% killing coyotes. O'Gorman knew this wouldn't be helping the livestock growers of Powder River County—in fact, the policy was costing Powder River County thousands of dead livestock per year.

Craig was determined to trap and certain he could provide a service to the ranchers of southeastern Montana. He resigned from his trapper job and began putting down roots for his new company, O'Gorman Enterprises. Craig would private contract the damage control trapping, make his lures, write books, give personal trapping lessons and trap fur when it was prime. It was a smart move and with Craig's work ethic and business savvy, the sky was the limit in "big sky" country. When Powder River County went to a private predator control program, O'Gorman would be on call working 365 days out of the year. Dedicating his time 8 months a year completely to predator control. The other 4 months Craig trapped for fur giving the area literally 12 months of full-time animal damage control. This work enabled Powder River County to boast a countywide 1% to 3% annual sheep loss, well below the state average. This has kept more sheep on the tax rolls than most counties in Montana. For a number of years Powder River County was the number three sheep producer in Montana.

Craig O'Gorman's private predator control business gave him vast experience with western coyotes and ample opportunity to experiment with effective lures and baits. O'Gorman had friendships with legends like Grigg, Nelson, Smith and Bolte. Their decades of lure-making knowledge and formulations undoubtedly gave Craig a sharp understanding of attractive smells, ingredients and effective combinations. Over several years of experimentation and aggressive

Craig O'Gorman Photo

Craig and Dana O'Gorman pose with part of Craig's massive 1988 season catch.

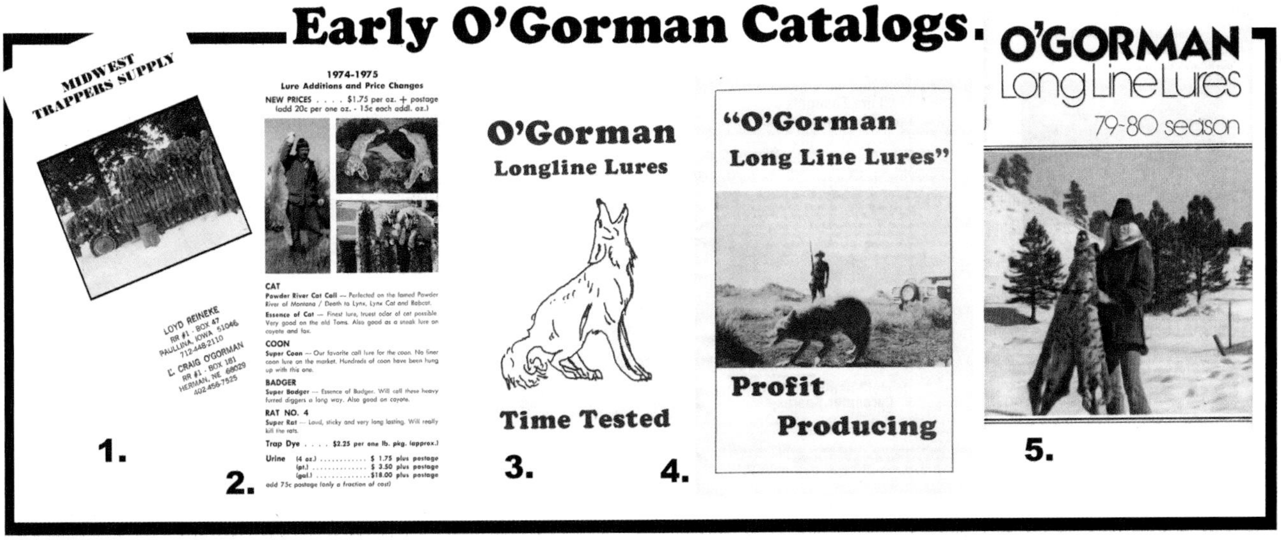

Craig O'Gorman Photo

1 -*Midwest Trappers Supply* 1973-74 is the first O'Gorman catalog, 2- *Midwest Trappers Supply* 1974-75 O'Gorman update, 3- *O'Gorman* 1976-77 with *Howling Coyote* art cover, 4- *O'Gorman* 1977-78 with *Coyote Lawman* cover, 5- *O'Gorman* 1979-80 with *Dana O'Gorman* cover.

year-round trapping, he developed several extremely effective lures and baits.

Craig's success in Powder River County had the caught the attention of the U.S. Fish and Wildlife Service. In the late 1970s O'Gorman was asked—along with two other commercial lure makers, Russ Carman and James Mast (Frank Terry)—to supply their absolute best coyote formulation for a government test of effective lures against the best government coyote formulas. After extensive "blind" testing of six different lures (three commercial formulations and three government), the final results were published in January 1980. The top three coyote lures in order were: 1. Montana Trap made by Craig O'Gorman, 2. Carman's Distant Call made by Pennsylvania trapper Russ Carman, and 3. Gov't Formula Synthetic Fermented Egg. Montana Trap is code for Powder River Paste bait which is still available today.

Besides being a talented trapper, Craig is a phenomenal businessman—he has always been ahead of the curve. It only takes about five minutes paging through his massive catalog to see O'Gorman is a marketer extraordinaire and has the trapping background, miles and resume to back it up. Craig was the first to offer trapping lures in pint, quart and mega-gallon volumes. To Craig, a one-ounce bottle was child's play. And his books were much more in-depth than the average, more about trapping business than hobby.

Craig O'Gorman Photo

Craig and his lovely wife Dana pose with a fantastic winter season's catch of coyotes and foxes from the 1980s. Craig trapped and skinned while Dana washed, fleshed, stretched and dried the pelts.

O'Gorman's literary library is also vast and among the best available trapping knowledge in print. Craig was co-author of *High Rolling Fox Trapping* released in September 1974. He also wrote works including *Wolfer Man* (1975), *The O'Gorman Style of Predator Trapping* (1977), *Open Water Beaver Snaring* and *Coon Snaring* (1978), *High Rolling Fox Trapping* and *High Rolling Coon Trapping* (1982), and *Hoofbeats of a Wolfer The O'Gorman Style of Coyote Trapping* (1990). Craig also updated his books many times, which is by far a more foresighted approach than just reprinting.

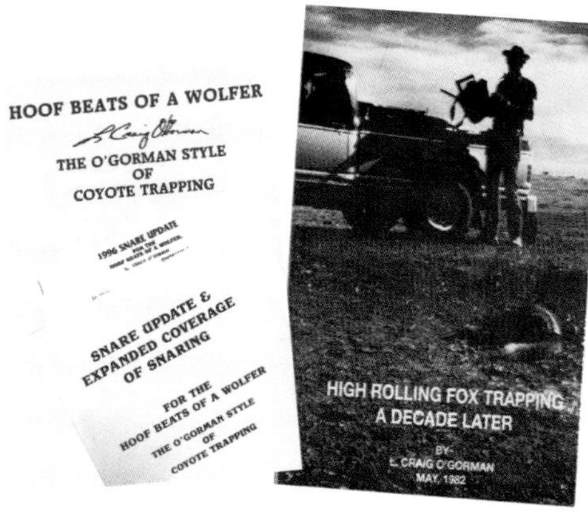

Author's Collection

Craig O'Gorman's original books can be hard to come by. Here is a copy of his well-known book, *Hoof Beats of a Wolfer,* 1990 with the 2 snaring updates issued 1995 and '96, *High Rolling Fox Trapping a Decade Later*—1982 is the updated version of Craig's first fox trapping book and is a must-read for a serious fox trapper.

Like most trappers, Craig also offers personal trapping lessons on his predator control line in Powder River County. Many O'Gorman students go on to start predator control programs of their own—some become well-known commercial trappers. In an attempt to stay on the cutting edge, Craig also released the first-ever trapping instruction video available to trappers. Made in the early days of camcorders and taped on VHS, the first O'Gorman trapping video was released in the late summer of 1984. The video allowed a trapper to visualize the making of the sets and locations much more than the black and white photos found in most trapping books. It was an awesome idea and today, how-to trapping DVDs are a staple for teaching trapping sets and locations.

Because Craig handles the trapping side of his business, his wife Dana covers the lure and supply side. Craig and Dana married in 1978 and they operate O'Gorman's as a team. With help in the office and shipping room from Nancy Kane, Dana can be found on the premises booking advertising and marketing, taking inventory, as well as organizing Craig's busy schedule. More often than not, Dana is actually in the lure shed, grinding, mixing and labeling the O'Gorman line of lures and baits.

Craig O'Gorman has supported nearly all trapping organizations over the years, some with life memberships. He's been sending numerous donations each season over the course of his nearly fifty-year trapping career. Owning it more to a difference of philosophy, Craig has been noticeably absent from the long list of demos given by many professional trappers at the national and state conventions. Often politics plays out in some of these organizations rewarding those of like thinking and demonizing those who dare to be different. Love him or hate him, Craig O'Gorman's list of trapping accomplishments speak for themselves. The job of an animal damage control trapper includes multiple methods of taking predators from steel traps, snares, M-44 cyanide, denning, calling and aerial hunting. O'Gorman mastered them all as a private business in an era during which the government controlled almost 99% of all the animal damage control industry. Naysayers would call O'Gorman an egomaniac, yet when you look at Craig's success over the years, it's easy to see his achievements have come from hard work, plain and simple.

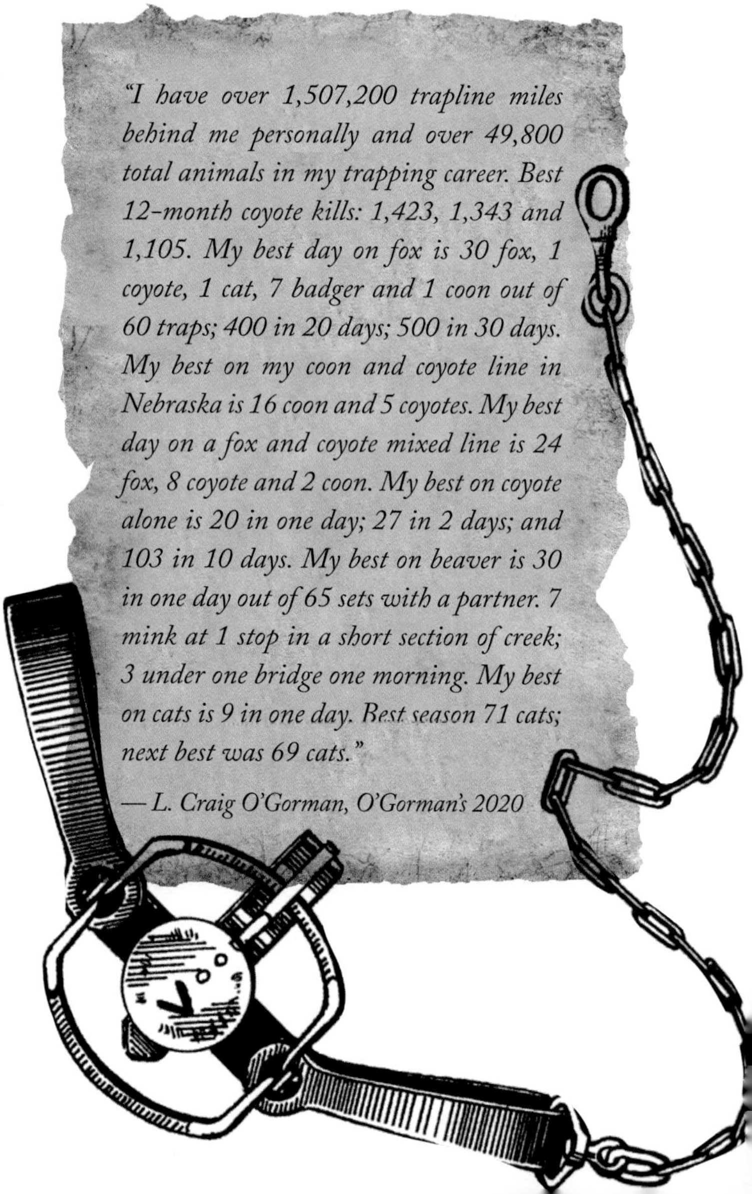

"I have over 1,507,200 trapline miles behind me personally and over 49,800 total animals in my trapping career. Best 12-month coyote kills: 1,423, 1,343 and 1,105. My best day on fox is 30 fox, 1 coyote, 1 cat, 7 badger and 1 coon out of 60 traps; 400 in 20 days; 500 in 30 days. My best on my coon and coyote line in Nebraska is 16 coon and 5 coyotes. My best day on a fox and coyote mixed line is 24 fox, 8 coyote and 2 coon. My best on coyote alone is 20 in one day; 27 in 2 days; and 103 in 10 days. My best on beaver is 30 in one day out of 65 sets with a partner. 7 mink at 1 stop in a short section of creek; 3 under one bridge one morning. My best on cats is 9 in one day. Best season 71 cats; next best was 69 cats."

— L. Craig O'Gorman, O'Gorman's 2020

RAY MILLIGAN

1950–

Ray was born in 1950 and by 4, yes I said 4 years old, young Ray had already set a small Victor trap and caught his first chipmunk. Inspecting the creature with the intrigue and wonder of a 4 year old, Ray became mesmerized by wild animals. Ray believes from that moment he was meant to be a trapper. Growing up in rural, western Pennsylvania allowed Ray Milligan the freedom to roam the woods, to have a dog, shoot a gun, hunt and trap—and that's what he did.

By 1968 Ray was an accomplished outdoorsman and headed off to college. Meeting his roommate for the first time, Ray noticed a gun leaning up in the corner and thought, "This is going to be a great season!" as Ray had also brought his shotgun to school with plans to hunt when possible. By 1974 Ray was off to Alaska with his two best pals. College was over and it was time for the new graduates to fulfill a dream and move north to Alaska. However, after 6 months reality set in and it was time to come back to the "real world" and launch a career.

While friends and schoolmates were taking "real jobs" Ray Milligan went full on into trapping. Page through an old December 1979 issue of *Fur-Fish-Game* to find one of Milligan's original magazine articles, "On the Road Fox Trapping." Ray had picked up a copy of Long Liner Fox Trapping

If one long-liner stands out as an influential trapper during the 1977–83 "fur boom" it would be Ray Milligan. Ray's career peaked in what he calls "the perfect storm," a time when fur prices were rising and trappers coming into the sport in droves. Milligan is a charismatic man who learned early in life that hard work can overcome many obstacles and this is certainly true on the long-line. Little has been published about Ray's beginnings as he's one who is always looking ahead, yet his story is fascinating.

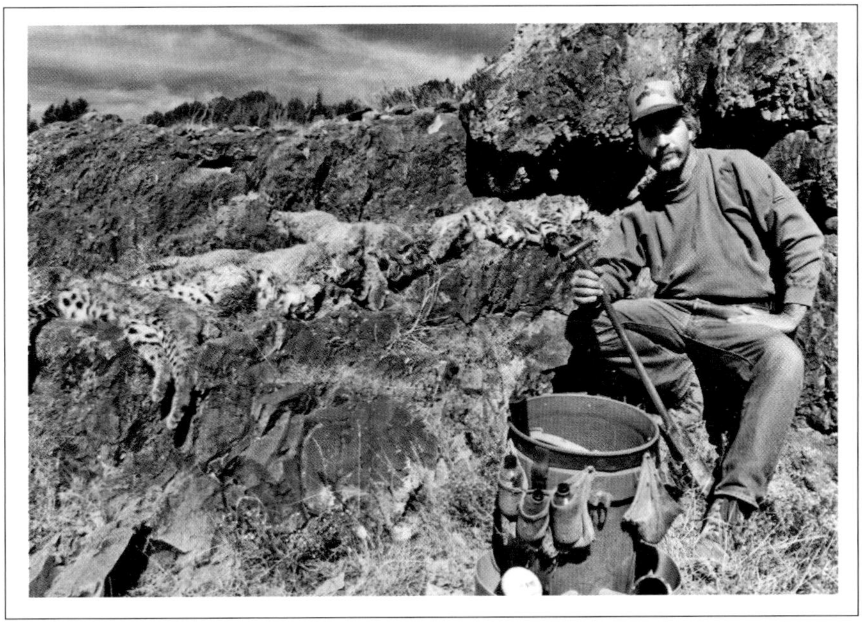

Ray Milligan may be a coyote man, but he can also put spotted bellies in the fur shed.

by Garold Weiland, mentioned earlier in this chapter. This book was the catalyst of Ray's dreams through the mid-to-late 1970s. Sound methods and hard work would get it done, and that's just what Ray Milligan was going to do.

Ray married his college sweetheart Colleen and the couple moved to Manhattan, Kansas. This would be home base for Ray's new company, Milligan Brand. Teaming up with Minnesota trapper and trapping supply guru Tim Caven, and *Trapper* magazine publisher Chuck Spearman would be Ray's recipe for success as Milligan launched his full on catalog business in 1979. The fur boom was full on and Ray was making the catches of his life. Spearman published Ray's catalog and books while Caven offered advice, friendship and blasted Milligan Brand in full page advertising and through Tim's network of dealers.

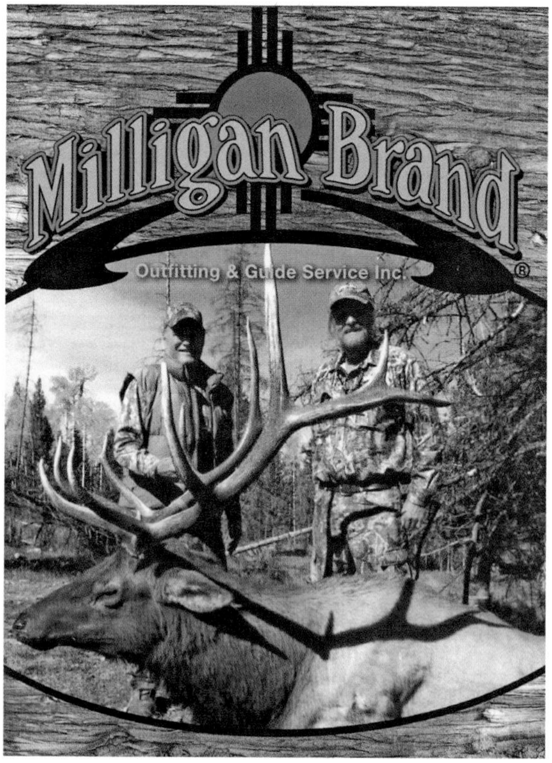

Author's Collection

After 15 years of long-line trapping, Ray Milligan reinvented himself as a New Mexico hunting guide and outfitter and now operates one of the most successful big game hunting guide services in the West.

Ray Milligan Photo

Ray Milligan incorporated his massive "Fur Barn" photo into his logo. Milligan Brand was one of the most successful lure makers during the 1977-83 "fur boom."

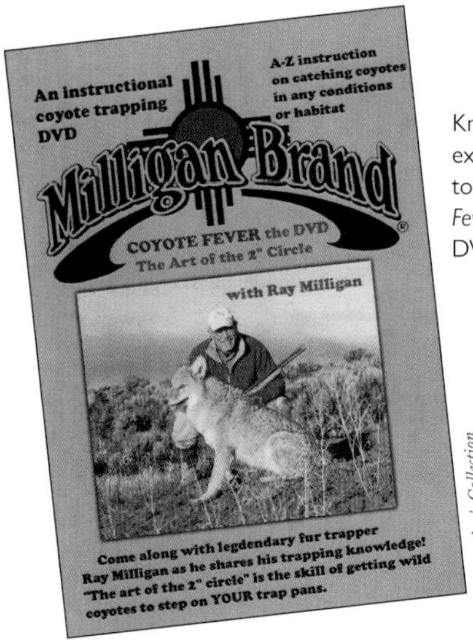

Author's Collection

Known as a coyote trapper extraordinaire Ray Milligan took his 1979 book *Coyote Fever* and re-released it as a DVD instruction video.

Ray Milligan operated his longlines with 80 percent dirt hole and flat sets and 20 percent snares. In the "hay-day" Ray started his season out of state early, transitioned home to Kansas for the "meat and potatoes" of his catch and as the weather deteriorated went south. This state-hopping strategy is well-known and used by many, however to make the catches Milligan was making in those days, you can bet he was covering long miles, running, setting and checking traps in 18-hour days, seven days a week. Ray often said, "St. Louis is not the Gateway to the West. Coyotes are the Gateway to accessing private land in the West."

If you ask Ray about his *best* season his response would be, "That kind of depends on whether you're talking number of pelts or dollars. I was fortunate to have several perfect storm seasons." Ray's two most memorable were the seasons of 1979–80 and 1982–83. These seasons were exceptional in every form of the word, in the fact that everything went to Milligan's favor. Ray says he never got weathered out, nothing broke down, he never got sick or wore down too far, and everywhere Ray trapped, the predators were at the peak of their population cycle.

Ray started his season in mid-September in the northern states. Usually Montana, Wyoming or the Dakotas, with red fox the target animal. By late October he was back in Kansas, where he had written permission to trap on 205 farms/ranches. On his home line, Ray targeted coyotes, coon and bobcats. After Thanksgiving, Milligan would take another road trip in search of prime fur, returning home for Christmas. After the holidays, he would head to Texas or New Mexico for a month in pursuit of coyotes. Ray froze most all of his catch and would hire help after trapping season to thaw, flesh, stretch and tumble the furs for market.

A wise man once said that "timing is everything" and Ray's 1979–80 season had it. With money short and the market hot, Ray sold a 47-day catch, for over $27 thousand. Remember, at that time you could buy an upscale house with a full basement for $25K. And after cashing out the first batch of fur, Ray still had more trapping to do. Ray says, "Dollarwise, the 1979–80 season was no doubt my best season."

Milligan's 1982–83 season was one of a 32-year-old trapper in his prime with all the tools and a driven purpose. It was Ray's best season for total animals, trapped and snared. The season started in New Mexico, then to Kansas and finished up in Texas, resulting in personal best season catches—365 coyotes, 43 bobcats and 262 raccoons. The "barn" photo Ray uses in his Milligan Brand logo shows 61 days of trapping from that magical season. And then BAM! In December 1982 the fur market crashes. Milligan immediately pulled all his fur together and and hit the road to find the best possible prices. After a few days in South Dakota with Melvin Fluth at M&M Furs, then to Minnesota and Tim Caven's Minnesota trapline, Ray finally headed to Iowa to eventually spend 2-plus days at Sheda's fur house. Ludy and Mary were fur buying legends and their shop was typically a wild place, with lots of fur buyers and trappers always coming and going. After two days of haggling with Ludy, Ray took $19 thousand for his furs, even though just 12 months earlier the same amount and quality would likely have fetched $35 thousand or more. Such is the life of a long-line trapper. In Ray's own words…

"Trapping teaches success, self-esteem and sense of worthiness. You need to learn about adapting the tool (a trap), sometimes re-manufacturing to make it better, then the formulation of baits and lures, catching the animals, skinning, fleshing and stretching the pelts. Then you market. It so clear to me that a complete trapper, must make all A's and B's in these basic understandings to succeed. Then, that person evolves complete in the realm of business. All this because he has learned how a business profile works, from start to finish. I personally feel that my trapping experiences in my 20's were the simplest most self-fulfilling learning experiences of my life, as I became self-reliant. I believe that the only ingredient a beginning or neophyte trapper needs is passion! Everything else will fall in place. I vividly remember when the "light" went on for me. I was a complete trapper and I recognized that it was my time. All this while spending day after day in my 20's, working alone. It did not matter that no one else knew – I knew. Several times I worked so long and hard, that mentally and physically I was done. That is when it happens. My truck turns into Luke Skywalker's hovercraft. I float above the rough road, riding a cloud of self-satisfaction. In what I can only explain as an out-of-body experience. I hope every person gets to take that extraordinary ride of passion someday."

— Ray Milligan, 2014

THE LOG CABIN

I started my lure and scent business in 1981. I bought some old formulas from a Canadian trapper through a classified ad in *F-F-G.* I remember spending a small fortune on the ingredients. As some of the formulas were wolf lures, I substituted coyote glands and urine. I was a big fan of O.L. Butcher lures and I formulated a scent I called November Red in an attempt to make a sweet lure similar to Butcher's Fox #4. I'll discuss more on my lure business later in this book.

In the summer of 1981, I built the now famous log cabin where the catch photos for Churchill's article were taken. The cabin was constructed to be my fur shed and as a backup residence if the A-frame were to ever catch fire and burn down, something that can happen when you heat and cook with wood. We used an LP gas refrigerator and oil lamps for light. Although my father had wired the A-frame for electric and we did have a small power plant, the unit was noisy. I set up a battery bank and some DC lights which were nice and also we had a DC-powered TV that got 2 channels with an antenna. I think Bernie liked the wilderness lifestyle but I wasn't home much and when I was, I was very busy. The plan was to trap five or six weeks in Michigan in the fall, return to Ohio where I could run my farmland line starting in November and return to Michigan to trap beavers and otters after the Christmas holidays.

Author's Photo

Author's Photo

Here's my log cabin after completion. It's a big job to build a cabin like this all by yourself. The cabin cost less than $800 in materials to build.

I had been a fan of James Churchill, the famous *Outdoor Life* magazine writer and I knew he lived near Iron Mountain, Michigan but across the state line in Florence, Wisconsin. Churchill had done many articles for *Fur-Fish-Game* and I found his phone number in the phone book, called him and went to visit. I was shocked to see that he lived in an A-Frame cabin almost identical to the one I had built. We chatted for a while, I told him my story and he asked if he could visit me sometime during trapping season. I agreed. Jim did come to the Michigamme and follow me on the trapline one day, went home and wrote an article—this was in the fall of 1981. The article wasn't published in *F-F-G* until March 1983, and was titled, "Home on the Trapline." When the issue was released, Jim's article was a hit and the catalyst which helped catapult my career. It was one of the biggest breaks I ever got handed to me.

TRAPPING SEASON

1981–82

I had one of my best seasons in 1981–82 and a few of my fur photos made the James Churchill article. Combining both the Michigan and Ohio traplines was the ticket and fur prices were as good as anyone could ask for. I caught 5 cross foxes that year and received $125 each. Also my lures had proven themselves and I would need to make enough to try and start a business selling them.

Home on the Trapline

A young trapper leaves the city behind to build a new life in the Michigan wilderness

By James E. Churchill

IT'S a big step from the security of an industrial job and the comforts of city living to the insecurity of full-time trapping and the rigors of homesteading. But there are still a few men who have the spirit of the mountain men in their veins and are willing to tackle such a challenge.

Young Tom Miranda, formerly of Columbus, Ohio, is just such a person. To find Tom, you have to travel to the backwoods of Michigan's Upper Peninsula. You then have to ramble over nine miles of jeep trail after you leave the highway. Finally, you reach the banks of the Michigamme River, where a well built A frame cabin blends into the pines surrounding it.

In the best tradition of homesteading, Tom built the cabin himself on land that he found by simply heading north from Ohio until he got deep into the woods. Although there were several trips back and forth while he was building, once the cabin was complete Tom settled into insulating it, installing the inside ammenities and prospecting his trapline.

His story is one of a young man who has the courage to live the life of his dreams. That's what makes him so facinating.

I found Tom puttering around his cabin. After I made my introductions and set my typewriter down on a handy tree stump, I began learning about his background. Tom decided he wanted to be a full-time back-to-nature type when he was about 12 years old, and he never forgot it. When he was 20 years old he started preparing himself by learning everything he could about trapping and homesteading. This involved purchasing about all of the available books and magazines on the subject, and also taking lessons from professional trappers. He ran an extensive trapline in Ohio catching fox, muskrats, raccoon and mink, thus honing his skills for the time when he would depend on them to make his living.

After attending college he found a high-paying industrial job. Moreover, he worked all the overtime possible, and even worked at a parttime job when the trapping season was closed. More importantly perhaps, he saved his money. Finally, the sugar bowl held enough capital so that he could start looking for

Fur Prices where outstanding. Between Michigan and Ohio I did nearly $9,400 in pelts total. That summer we stayed in Ohio. I worked at U-Haul as a mover and also in the hitch shop, plus delivered pizzas for Dominos at night. I had decided that working two or three jobs would allow me to invest in the materials to actually launch my scent business. My wife Bernie had a college degree in Elementary Education and wanted to use it. She applied as a substitute teacher and began working almost immediately. At the time we were living in the house she grew up in on Country Club Road near Walnut Ridge High School in East Columbus.

While working at U-Haul, I met a man named Steve Patton. He was an entrepreneur and was starting a new blacktop sealing business. He was at U-Haul getting some welding done and pitched me an offer to be the foreman of his sealing crew.. It would be the most money I had made at any job— an offer I couldn't refuse. During my time working for Steve, I told him of my dream to be a pro trapper and what I wanted to do. He asked me to compile all the magazines and info I had on the subject as he wanted to look into it. I gathered up trapping books, F-F-G and Trapper magazines and gave them to Steve. As the blacktop season was winding down and I was preparing to leave for trapping season, Steve invited me to his house and gave me some advice about my trapping business. Steve had a PhD in business and was a smart guy. I'll never forget what he told me. He said, "Tom, looking at all of these trappers and their businesses, one thing rings loud and clear. You'll need to build a huge resume of accomplishments in trapping and sell

Author's Photo

Here's my 1981 Michigan catch.

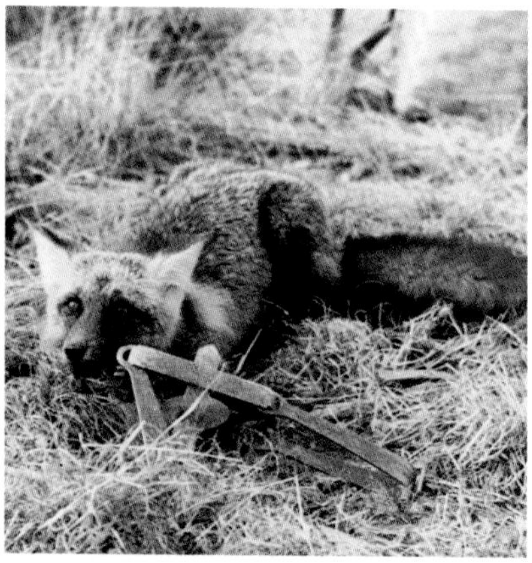

Author's Photo

I took 5 cross foxes out of 2 sets over a two-week period. I also caught my first triple on coyote but was so excited I didn't get a photo of it.

Author's Photo

Part of my Ohio catch with a few coyote, and the Michigan cross foxes not yet sold.

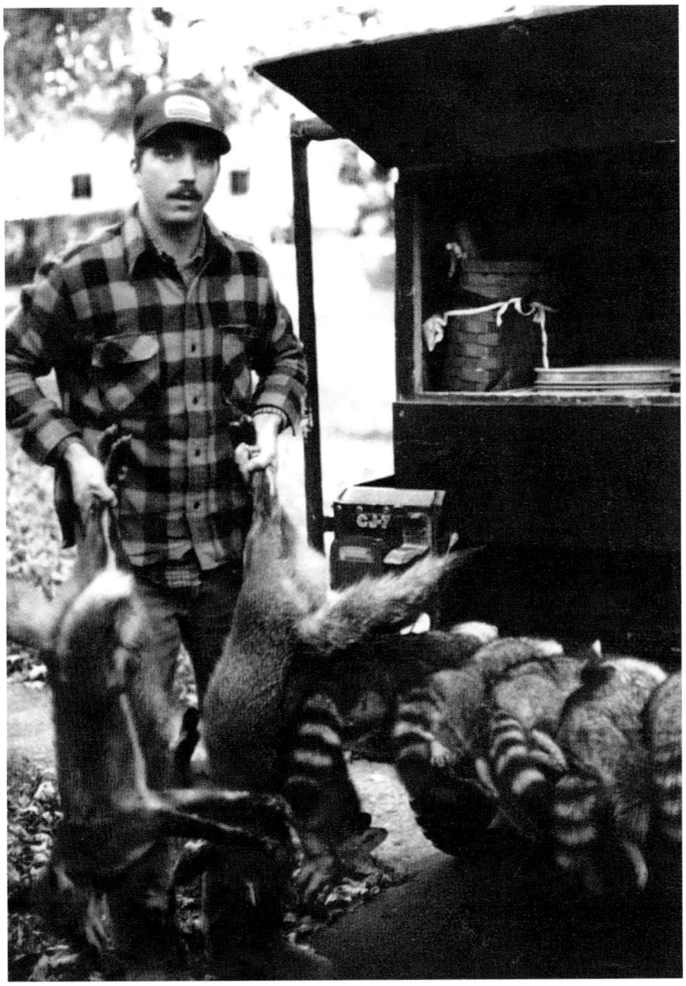
Author's Photo

Four foxes and 5 coon in the Boom was a $320 day, equivalent to $850 in todays value. I wasn't catching long-liner numbers, but I was staying on track with my average and building my resume.

your name. Tom Miranda is what you are selling. With the right resume and authentic accomplishments, your name will be gold."

TRAPPING SEASON

1982–83

It was fantastic advice. I had planned on calling my trapping lures Ohio Valley, They now would be called Tom Miranda's *Competition Line.* This was the height of the 1977–83 fur boom. I had half a dozen top trappers operating near and adjacent to my Ohio trapline including Jim Helfrich, Carrol Black and Chuck Mershon. This was why I called the lures *Competition Line.*

The 1982–83 season turned into my best to date. Because my wife was teaching, we didn't go north to Michigan that fall. Marvin Mallow had begun selling my lure and because of my 1981–82 cabin photos, the lure sold out. I had worked it hard as I knew that I needed to either make this trapping pay or end up getting a real job. I had good weather and and was able to keep above my average per day catch for the first full month. Some of the early fur I sold for expenses, and it sold for good money. But the bottom dropped out of the fur market in early 1983 and if you were holding pelts you were left "holding the bag." I had taken 146 foxes and a garage full of coon and possums which were sold for expenses throughout the season. I also had nearly 200 'rats I'd managed to catch, but ended up with less fur money than the previous year.

I took a job in March with a company in Columbus called M&D Blacktop Sealing. The blacktop job I had the year before had evaporated, Patton had sold the company and decided to enroll in Chiropractor school of all things. Then, in March 1983 Churchill's article hit in *F-F-G* and it was a home run. *Fur-Fish-Game's* main office is in Columbus, Ohio—about 10 miles from where I grew up, so I

Part of my 1982–83 Ohio fur catch taken in the driveway on Noe-Bixby Rd. Notice my lucky U-Haul cap.

Miranda
"Competition Line" Lures

Fellow Trappers

I trap fur for a living. I operate in Midwestern states which contain a high number of trappers using every type of lure imaginable. When you bank on your fur check like I do you can't afford to take chances by using the same lures your competitors use.

I developed my **Competition Line Lures** with a lot of testing and expense. I did it because I needed a different, effective lure to use in areas of heavy competition.

If you're looking for a lure that's not over used, different and super effective, I think you've found it. And I'd stake my reputation on it.

FARMLAND FOX #1 — My number one early season fox producer. Fox glands are used with special musks and oils to create a top notch fox lure.

FARMLAND FOX #2 — The cold weather relative to fox #1. Spiked with a mild odor of skunk.

NOVEMBER RED — This is my super sweet, non-meat food lure that predators crave. Fox, coyote and coon will dig this out and eat it.

FLOODWOOD FOX DOPE — A food based fox lure spiked with a strong foxy odor which gives confidence to trap shy-spooked fox.

FLOODWOOD 'YOTE DOPE — My coyote gland scent that stops old wiley in his tracks. A superior 'yote call at dirt holes and flat sets.

RINGTAILS CHOICE — Many special "sweet" ingredients are used in the "Choice" and the coons really love it. Wet or dry sets, the "Choice" produces.

CREEK BANK COON — A fish oil base lure but with many other added musks and oils to get Mr. Raccoon's nose twitching toward your set.

POCKET POPPER MINK SCENT — Mink and muskrat glands are used in proper combination to pull old light foot over the trap.

ALL LURES — 1 oz. $3.00, 4 oz. $10.00 ppd.
Orders under $20.00 add $2.00 postage and handling charge.

Tom Miranda
Box 175F, Brice, Ohio 43109
My lures are also available from
MARVIN MALLOW TRAP CO.
Clarksburg, OH 43115
PAULETTE FUR CO.
6210 Canton Rd., Malvern, OH 44644
NORTHERN FUR CO.
1720 W. 30th, Lorain, OH 44052
Dealer Inquiries Invited

went to the offices to buy a few extra copies of the March issue to give to my parents and grandparents. At the office, I met Ken Dunwoody, the magazine's editor, and sat with him talking about what I had been doing. Dunwoody was a great guy and for whatever reason took a liking to me. He asked if I had done any writing and I hadn't, but Ken told me to write about my experiences and he would correct the grammar and use the stories in *Fur-Fish-Game*. About a month Later, Dunwoody called me and asked that I come down to the office. When I arrived, Mrs. Adams (the granddaughter of A.R. Harding) who was running the magazine, handed me a shoe box completely stuffed with over a hundred letters from *F-F-G* readers who had seen the article. There were requests for trapping lessons, log cabin building lessons, marriage proposals, you name it. I immediately ran a small ad for trapping lessons in *F-F-G* and the *Trapper*. And I taught several students that late summer—these were my first trapping students.

JAMES CHURCHILL TRIBUTE 1934–2002

James Churchill was a well-published outdoor writer. I had read his many articles in *Fur-Fish-Game* and *Outdoor Life* magazine since I was a kid. I had one of his books, *The Complete Book of Tanning Skins and Furs.* It was actually sort of an amazing experience to meet him. Telephoning Jim was actually a bit unnerving but when he gave me directions to his home, I was excited to meet him. I can remember pulling into the driveway and seeing his A-frame house and smiling. It was just like my A-frame—actually I guess my A-frame was like his! I met Jim and his wife Joan and both were as nice as can be. Jim and I clicked immediately.

James Churchill drags his canoe ashore in the wilds of northern Wisconsin after a successful bow hunt.

Jim Churchill grew up near the rural town of Tomah, Wisconsin. He was a typical outdoorsy kid who learned to fish and hunt early in his life. As life does, it marches forward and Jim found himself living in Racine, Wisconsin married and with 2 children. Jim decided he'd had just about enough of the city life. His decision was firm and final, the family would move north. The year was 1974 and the Churchills settled on the outskirts of the small town of Florence, Wisconsin. They would build their home themselves and Jim would write about it. It would be a simpler life, laid back and striving to live off the land. The 1970s was a time in America when many felt the urge to get back to nature. A popular magazine of the era was the *Mother Earth News*, a bible for those people wanting to get back to the simpler life of self-sufficiency and eco-friendly living.

Jim Churchill wanted to live the lifestyle he wrote about. The self-sufficient life of the north woods hunter. There was no doubt that Churchill and I had much in common. In fact, I think when we met and talked, he saw so much of himself in me that he was compelled to write a story about my adventure. Even the byline of the *F-F-G* feature he wrote was, "A young trapper leaves the city behind to build a new life in the Michigan wilderness." This is exactly what Jim Churchill did.

I've often mentioned in my bowhunting seminars that I believe there are two types of people. *Givers* and *Takers*. *Takers* are the ones who are always looking out for number one, *Givers* are the ones who live by the golden rule, "Do unto others as you would have others do unto you." Important words to live by. James Churchill was a *Giver.*

I talked to Jim soon after his feature, "Home on the Trapline," published in 1983 to thank him again for doing it, and a few years after my TV show was airing on ESPN.

I remember him saying, "I'm happy that you have come so far Tom, I've been following your career and you've done very well for a trapper. I'm proud of you!"

I was proud too. Any outdoor writer could have written that article, but not any one did. James E. Churchill did.

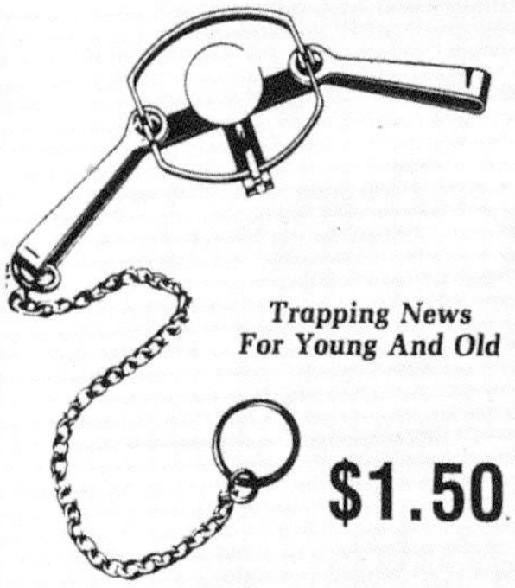

Trapping News
For Young And Old

$1.50

Vol. 9, No. 5 — January 1984©

the Trapper

FUR PRICE OUTLOOK

Prices being paid for raw furs across the country indicate that trappers may not fair as bad as expected. Although there is little or no market for early, low grade fur, buyers are showing increased interest in prime, well handled pelts. See Parker Dozhier's Fur Market Report for further details.

EXCISE TAX ON WILD FUR?

On October 28, 1983, eighteen sources of funds were proposed by the U.S. Fish and Wildlife Service to aid in providing grants to states for developing conservation plans. One item suggested is to levy an excise tax of 5 to 10 percent on wild furs, levied at the point of their purchase from trappers. Trappers across the country should oppose this measure. See Boynton's AFRI Report for more information.

COVER PHOTO

Tom Miranda of Channing, Michigan, is this month's cover photo winner. Tom displays some northern coyote and cross fox taken in the Upper Peninsula Region. The trapping cabin was built from scratch by this very talented young trapper.

The 2nd Annual Coyote Hunt (And Pig Out) — Gerry Blair

CHAPTER 6

EXPERT TRAPPERS

Einstein's theory of relativity is a description of physics phenomena in the absence of gravity and how the laws of gravity affect these forces of nature. This scientific concept actually has nothing to do with trapping, yet when one thinks about the many different levels of trappers and the trapping applications they are involved in, it doesn't take long to see that to make a good assessment of the "expert" all things *relative* must be considered.

The term "expert" might mean the "best" to some, yet wouldn't a professional trapper be an expert? Wouldn't a long-liner be an expert? What determines an expert? The truth of the matter is that there are many levels of success and expertise and every individual has their own gauge as to what does or doesn't qualify. From my experience, most experts don't look at themselves as such. In fact, those who claim to be experts often fall short of the mark.

That said, one concept that's often misunderstood is self-promotion. In the world of entrepreneurial enterprise, companies and individuals alike will toot their own horn as to services, value and expertise to get the job done. Salesmanship should not be confused with expertise. It's why the adage, "buyer beware" exists. True expert status is earned through years of learning, doing, teaching, understanding and excelling at one's craft. Being good at something doesn't make an expert—although experts are good at what they do. An expert typically has a long, detailed résumé covering years of practical knowledge and experience and continues to add to it.

MAJOR BODDICKER

1942–

Some people have a knack for making a positive impression. You meet them and remember them. They impress you with charisma, knowledge or in some way that makes you take notice, think and admire. Dr. Major Boddicker is one of those people. He doesn't look like a professor or talk like a professor, but smart comes in many forms—smart with a good dose of common sense is a rare trait in academia. Major could have grown up to be a surgeon or rocket scientist, but instead he chose wildlife science and education. It was a good day for trappers and trapping when he did.

Major Boddicker grew up in the hills and river breaks of Benton County, Iowa. In the 1950s, young Major focused on hunting, fishing and trapping. By age 10, he was trapping gophers and red foxes for bounties. By age 16, he and his shotgun were hunting

< *Author's Collection*

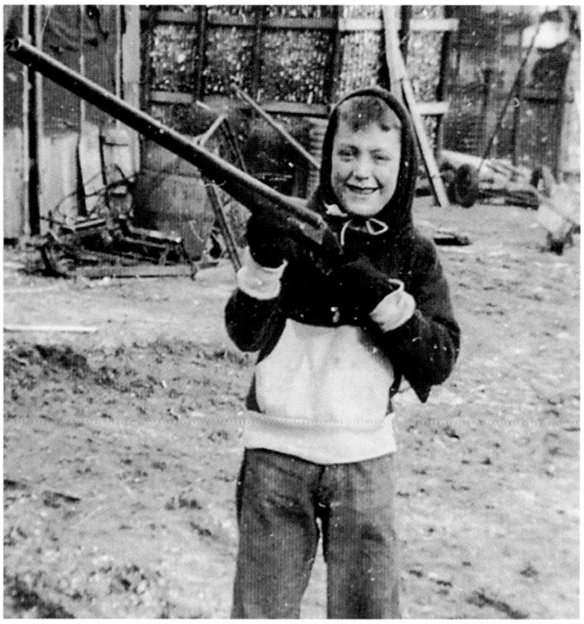

Major Boddicker Photo

A young Major Boddicker poses with a double-barrel shotgun.

both upland and waterfowl. Between hunting trips, he was an all-state football player, heavyweight-wrestling champion and president of his class. Boddicker played football at Minnesota St. John's University, yet decided the outdoors was more important to him than the gridiron and focused on a wildlife curriculum.

Boddicker chose to get three college degrees—a Bachelor of Science in biology, a Master of Science in zoology/wildlife, and a PhD studying diseases of sharp-tailed grouse.

Always keen for adventure, Major began working for the US Forest Service fighting fires during the summer fire season. Football-fit at the time, Boddicker enrolled at the prestigious Smoke Jumpers Academy and after training, fought fires in many western states and Alaska from 1963–69.

Major Boddicker enjoyed predator calling and came up with the concept and design of his now famous Crit'R•Call in 1968 while he was in graduate school at South Dakota State University. Major eventually worked as an outdoor education specialist in South Dakota, also for the Kansas 4-H program, and served as an Extension Wildlife Pest Control Specialist at Colorado State University for 10 years.

I met Major Boddicker at the 1983 Fur Takers Trappers College. Many may not know how the college came to be, but Major Boddicker was the catalyst and also wrote the curriculum. As the story goes, in 1978 Boddicker was the Conservation Director of Fur Takers of America. FTA president Joe Tennyson came to Major for ideas and programs for education. Major suggested to Joe that trappers needed a high-level education program and it would be best if it could be accredited by a university. The school would need to train teachers, leaders, scientists, and fur producers at the highest level of the modern trapping art. Joe agreed and asked Major to develop a course as a joint Fur Takers of America and Colorado Trappers Association project.

Major Boddicker Photo

Major Boddicker poses with a Colorado pale coyote, a lanyard of Crit'R•Calls and his trusty H&K 770 in .308 caliber.

Boddicker and Kansas State wildlife specialist Bob Henderson had developed a 4-H workshop in 1973–74 and Major's idea was that this curriculum could be expanded to a full-week, college-accredited course. The original premise was that different FTA chapters would host the college. Boddicker wrote,

Major Boddicker Photo

Boddicker poses with a nice catch of 65 coyotes taken on his Sandhills Colorado trapline, November 1980.

Authors Photo

Major giving field instruction at the 1983 Fur Takers Trappers College.

typed, researched, collected the photos, wrote the test and two books for the FTA college curriculum over an 18-month period with the help from his Colorado State University secretary, Darlene Bauhs.

As with all organizations there are politics. Major's proposal was originally vetoed by a small group of the FTA board who felt the college would impact private trappers who were active in selling trapline instruction. However, Boddicker persisted with help from Tennyson and others to finally establish the first western FTA Trappers College held at Colorado State University's Pingree Park Campus in early September 1980 and the eastern FTA Trappers College which was organized by Indiana Game Warden and Fur Taker member and champion, Charlie Park. The eastern college would be held close to Park's home at Limberlost Camp near LaGrange, Indiana during the last week of September 1980.

Three western colleges were held in Colorado 1980–82. After 1982 the western college was abandoned. The eastern college moved to several locations from Indiana to New York, Kentucky, Tennessee and back to Indiana where it's been held now consecutively since 1987. The eastern college has been administered

Author's Collection

Major Boddicker has authored many books, including *Trapping Rocky Mountain Furbearers*, the textbook used at the trappers college.

by Charlie and Pat Park, Gene Beeber and currently by Todd Lange. Major Boddicker played a major role in the FTA Trappers College through 1986 both as a lecturer and field instructor.

Major started Rocky Mountain Wildlife Enterprises in 1985. His Crit'R•Call brand wildlife calls continue to be the favorite open reed calls of many professional predator callers and government trappers. Boddicker became good friends with Tom Krause while working with the National Trappers Association and they both led trapper delegations to Russia in 1981 and to South Africa in 1991—furthering the knowledge of humane trapping and conservation worldwide.

Major Boddicker was inducted into the National Trappers Association Trappers Hall of Fame in 1997 and the Fur Takers of America Trappers Hall of Fame in 2008.

"My advice is to look at yourself in the mirror. What you'll see is your soul. If you see happy—then you like who you are. If you don't see happy—get busy to make things right. When a challenge presents itself, take up the challenge, say —Yes, I can do this! Then do it in the best way possible. Having ambition and confidence is a great habit that everyone can develop. If you want to be a great trapper and hunter, start now. Learn it and live it everyday. When you achieve knowledge worth passing on, share it. Telling someone that you are successful is never as rewarding as someone telling you that you are successful."

— Major Boddicker, 2014

CHARLES DOBBINS

1925–1997

Charlie Dobbins was a trap tinkerer. In the 1980s and early 90s, Charlie could be seen at many of the midwestern and national trappers conventions giving demonstrations, set up with a workbench modifying traps. Dobbins wrote a book about it. He was a kind man who dearly loved trapping and trappers.

Born in Martins Ferry, Ohio young Charles started trapping at age 9. As most youngsters, Charlie was primarily a water trapper and with Martins Ferry being a town on the Ohio River, young Charlie could be found each fall taking muskrats, mink and raccoons from many of the creeks and drainages that flowed into the mighty river.

Like most who were born in the 1920s, the onset of the second world war called Charlie to service. Charlie was inducted into the Army on August 3, 1943. He went to northern France in December 1944 attached to Company F 275th infantry. While fighting in France, Charlie was stuck in a foxhole during a prolonged battle and succumbed to a bad case of frostbite. After the battle, Dobbins was sent back to the states and Camp Butner, North Carolina where he remained until his discharge on September 6, 1945. Dobbins suffered issues with his feet for the remainder of his life.

Charlie married in 1948 and the couple had three children—Paul, Christine and Melanie. Paul Dobbins owns and operates trapperman.com, a trappers online forum and chat room. Paul also carries on his father's tradition of doing beaver damage control and still sells his father's trapping books and lures. Charlie Dobbins trapped fox for bounty in Ohio before moving to Virginia working for the Department of Health, hired to eliminate an outbreak of rabid foxes.

Dobbins ran traplines in Ohio, Maryland, Virginia, Indiana, Colorado, Kansas, Nebraska, Arkansas, Mississippi and Tennessee. His first book, *The Adjustment of Leghold Traps for Greater Profit* was his wheelhouse and Charlie was most recognized for his trap modification designs. His innovative approach to trap

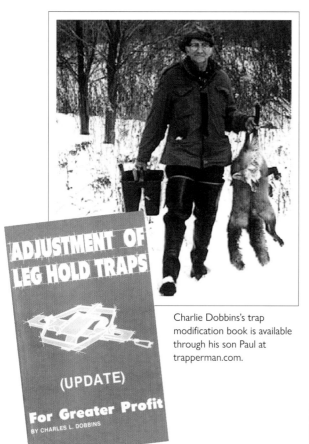

Charlie Dobbins's trap modification book is available through his son Paul at trapperman.com.

Charles Dobbins Photo

Charles Dobbins works late into the night to put up the day's catch.

Charles Dobbins Photo

Nice catch by Dobbins during the 1970s fur boom.

tuning and modification led to many standard practices today. Extra chain swivels, trap bottom swiveling, adding spacers to the pan bolt allowing the trap pan to fall more smoothly. Modifying the trap dog by crimping the eye to limit travel, then filing a bevel to make for a crisp firing trap were improvements Dobbins brought to light in the mid-70s. Dobbins went on to author eleven trapping books and six trapping DVDs during his career.

Here's an interesting Charlie Dobbins story relayed to me by his son Paul. Charlie was in Mississippi giving trapping instructions to some USDA trappers and ran across a man named Benny who wanted to learn how to trap beavers. Benny told Charlie that he couldn't afford to pay for the trapping lessons but Dobbins stayed a few extra days and taught Benny how to trap beaver at no charge. Charlie even gave Benny some traps to get him started. As Charlie loaded his pickup, Benny apologized that he couldn't pay for the lessons and Charlie said, "Don't worry about it. Pass it on."

About a year after Charles Dobbins's passing, Paul Dobbins met Benny in an online chat at a website called Otter Creek. Paul wasn't aware of his father's gift of trapping lessons to Benny at the time, however Benny relayed the story and offered Paul a gift to build him a new trappers internet forum. Paul knew little about computers at the time, but Benny insisted as he felt he owed it to Charlie and this was a way to "pass it on" as Charlie requested.

The long and short of it is that this was the start of trapperman.com. Paul Dobbins says Benny passed it on more than a thousand fold and I'm sure my father is looking down on Benny and Trapperman with pride.

Charles Dobbins was inducted into the National Trappers Association Trappers Hall of Fame in 1995 and the FTA Trappers Hall of Fame in 1998.

TOM KRAUSE

1940–

When opportunity knocks, it takes a certain type of person to capitalize on it. Someone who isn't afraid of trying something new, someone who is willing to adapt and change. Such is the story of expert trapper Tom Krause. His is one of hard work and passion, being at the right place at the right time and throwing in a huge dose of faith.

Tom Krause grew up west of Milwaukee in the small town of Elm Grove, Wisconsin. He began trapping at age 13 and caught his first mink that first season. In the early 1950s mink were a valuable furbearer and the incentive to catch more was a grand reason to spend more time trapping. Tom continued to trap and went to college, albeit his heart wasn't into academia. Tom married and took a job with the power company. Handy with a chain saw and not afraid of work, Krause topped trees, cleared power lines and worked as a lineman. Then in 1964, Tom felt the urge to move west, ending up in Iowa working the land as a farmer, trapping for added income and also started his own tree service business. The 1960s were a building time for Krause, his nose to the grindstone, saving and continually looking for that next big move up the ladder.

Tom Krause Photo

Wisconsin native Tom Krause sports his "lucky" Green Bay Packers cap and a pair of dandy western bobcats.

In 1970, Krause resettled in Nebraska. With fur prices on the rise, Tom would work seasonally and trap the winters. By 1975 Tom Krause considered himself a professional trapper. In 1977 publisher Chuck Spearman offered Tom a chance to edit his *Midwest Trapper* magazine. Krause was a trapper but knew nothing of the writing and editing. Even with formal journalism training, magazines are a ton of work. But Tom was good at work and said yes to this new job and looked at it as an opportunity.

Krause quickly adapted. He worked at his writing, and finessed the rest. After all, the path to the finish line may not always be a pretty one, but it's the end result that counts. The magazine was a hit and the timing a perfect storm as the fur prices between 1978 and 1980 exploded as did the numbers of trappers. Trappers buying subscriptions and suppliers buying

Tom Krause Photo

Tom Krause and his father Harvey pose with a great day's run over Tom's Nebraska trapline.

Tom Krause Photo

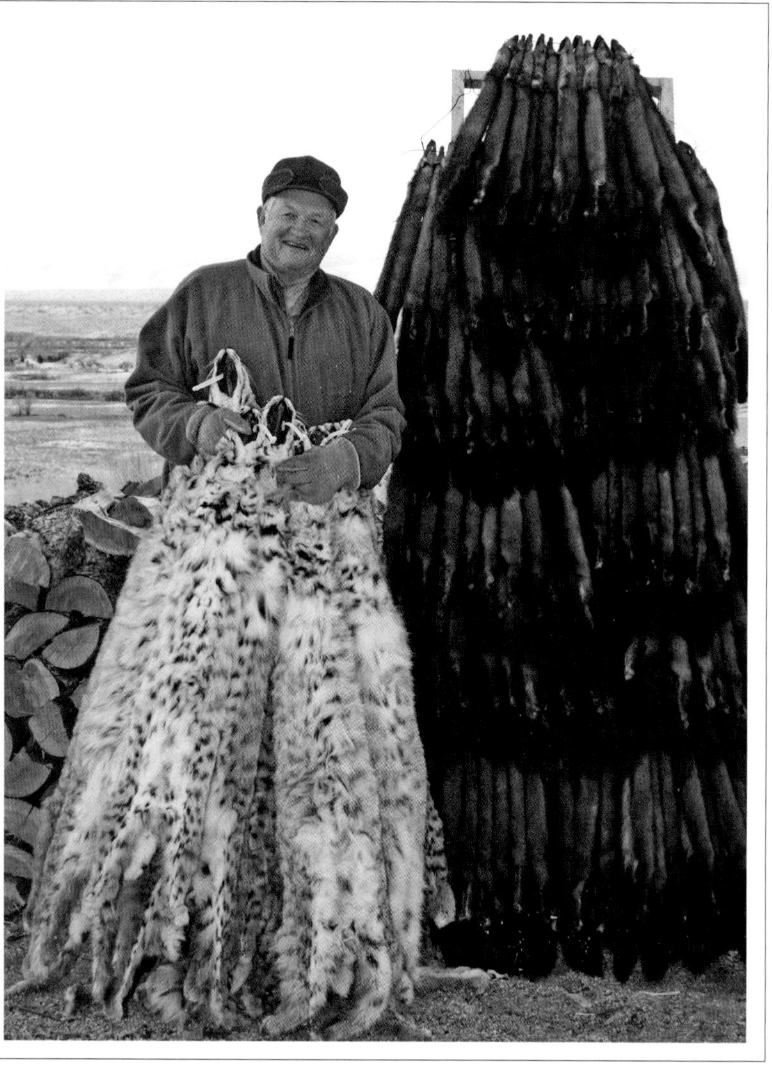

Expert trapper Tom Krause getting it done on his Wyoming mountain trapline. Krause learned many of his marten trapping secrets from western mountain trapper Wayne Negus.

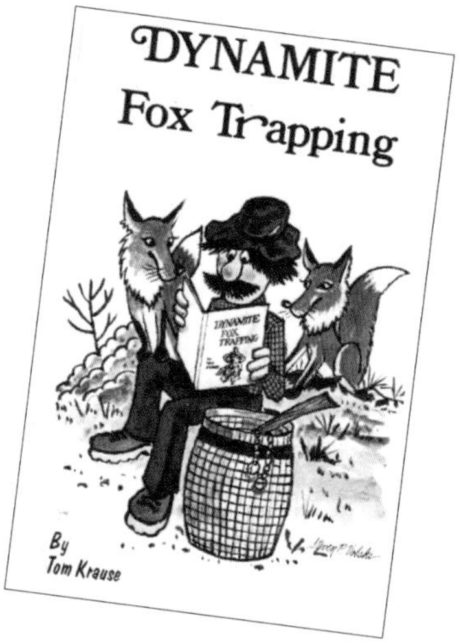

Dynamite Fox Trapping ,1978 is was the quintessential fox trappers manual during the 1977-83 fur boom.

advertising. Up-and-coming trappers were printing books and the publishing company was growing. All of trapping was growing. Soon *Midwest Trapper* became *Trapper* magazine and was now the trade publication of the trapping industry.

It wasn't long before the National Trappers Association took notice and offered Tom the prized editor's position of Voice of the Trapper. The association was growing and so were Tom Krause's skills. Part of his duties at the NTA included being a board member of the American Fur Institute (AFI). This was the arm of the NTA that fought the activists and their lobbies against trapping. AFI battled the federal government on discrepancies in their management of CITES Appendix II species, notably bobcats and river otters. Krause became involved and represented the trapping community at the first meeting of a U.S. Technical Advisory Group to represent the interests of the United States in international standards for mammal traps, including working groups to develop and draft international standards for humane killing and humane restraining traps. Tom also was elected to serve as U.S. chair of this important committee, and cast the American votes as head of the U.S. delegation at international meetings. The rest of the world at times did not like what the American Fur Institute had to report—especially since their not-so-hidden agenda was really to eliminate all use of foothold traps worldwide.

Tom Krause was instrumental in the National Trappers Association publications and fight for trappers rights for 23 years. In 1991, Krause led a delegation of American trappers to Russia with Major Boddicker at the request of the Russian government. Although Russia was in turmoil during their turn toward capitalism, and George H.W. Bush asked them not to go due to danger. Tom polled our delegation and we were unafraid. This was the trip of a lifetime. The entire delegation won the hearts of brother trappers in Siberia as well as other places in that land. Both Boddicker and Krause led another delegation of trappers to South Africa 10 years later. This was immediately after the fall of the twin towers in New York and a scary time to be flying.

Tom Krause was inducted into the National Trappers Association Trappers Hall of Fame in 1993.

"My trapping experiences have been terrific over the years. I will carry special memories to my grave trapping with T. C. Dawson in Alabama; Wayne Negus in the Oregon Cascades; Parker Dozhier in the Arkansas Ouachita Mountains; and Jim Masek in the Alaskan interior. If I have learned anything at all, it is I can learn from all others. It seems to me that my catches are not important. I have enjoyed great catches, and suffered lousy catches. We all have luck, good and bad. Creativity, innovation, and hard work pay dividends, and always will. The creativity and innovation learned is the stuff of method books and DVDs. I am particularly grateful to the trapping community for the excellent support of the books and DVDs I have created. The NTA Trapping Handbook was without royalties, and is my gift to novice trappers who may enjoy a shorter trapping learning curve than I did. If the right way in life is constant turns to the right, and following the crowd, expect a safe, average life. If you take left turns, and accept uncertainty, challenges, and rise to leadership roles, expect to suffer the insanity of politics. But do not let that deter you. Dare to not follow the crowd. Dare to serve others as a high priority. Dare to make a difference in the time you are given. Serve your nation. Serve your brothers. Just serve. My encouragement to you is 'hang a left' and enjoy the ride."

—Tom Krause, 2014

PETE ASKINS

1930–

Sod Sample gave 12-year-old Pete Askins a dozen traps in 1942 to start your him off on the right foot. It took those traps 33 years to come full circle into Pete's career as a trapper. Born in the depression era in southeastern Pennsylvania, Pete Askins learned that hard work meant survival. Knowing a trade and hard work, got you somewhere , but you needed a break to get an apprenticeship or schooling. So in 1946, Pete left home and traveled to Maryland to work at a dairy farm. When the trapping season was in—Pete set, checked and skinned at night.

Pete Askins got his break in 1950 when he landed a job at Fairchild Aircraft in Maryland. He would be a journeyman in training as a mechanic. Pete married his girlfriend Joy in 1951 and the two would become soulmates for life. For the next 24 years, Pete would hold a number of jobs with different companies work-

Pete Askins Photo

A young Pete Askins (Left) and trapping partner Don Lawson each hold a chissle-tooth while while smiling for the camera. Pete said Don was the best machinist he ever knew.

ing as a mechanic and machinist, building this and fixing that. All the while he was trapping when he could and using vacation and weekends if necessary. Pete co-founded the Maryland Fur Harvesters Association in 1961, a testament to his involvement in trapping throughout his career as a mechanic.

In 1975 the traps came back around when Pete was offered a job at Woodstream Corporation. Woodstream was actually the old Animal Trap Company, but with a newer fancy name. Woodstream owned the Victor trapline and a few other brands. Pete would be the research and development pro for Victor traps. Huge pressure from animal activist groups had started a wave of negative press toward trapping and the Cruel Steel Leg Hold Trap. Legislation was being drawn up to outlaw the steel trap and end trapping. The Bill H.R. 66 was real and Pete was now drawn into the battle to organize trappers, biologists and scientific testimony to go to the Senate floor and testify for conservation. The story of this epic battle is covered in the the book, *Mr. Pete*—an excellent biography of Pete Askins.

Pete immediately went to work in an attempt to begin to redesign traps—off-set jaws, padded jaws, chain swivels, cross plate swivels—Pete developed the Tin Cat, Woodstream's repeating mouse trap. R&D was in Askins's wheelhouse. Pete was a machinist and mechanic, so building prototypes was easy as he knew the science of building. And he was a hell of a trapper which meant he knew animals and how trappers caught them. Hiring Pete in R&D was like hiring Henry Ford to design your assembly line or Nicola Tesla to wire your house.

In Pete's first few years at Woodstream he would be asked to work on design mods and patents for the Frank Conibear trap. Canadian Frank Conibear patented his body-gripping trap in 1937 and Animal Trap Company purchased the trap from Conibear in 1958 for $15 thousand and a 4% royalty. Originally, the trap's design wasn't workable for mass manufacturing and sale. The design was reworked by Animal Trap Company design engineer John Laune. With the activists and anti-trapping legislation, Woodstream could see that the Conibear body-gripping trap could be a game changer. However the design needed reworking and parts of the trap patented to help prevent knock-offs and infringement. Pete Askins was the man for the job.

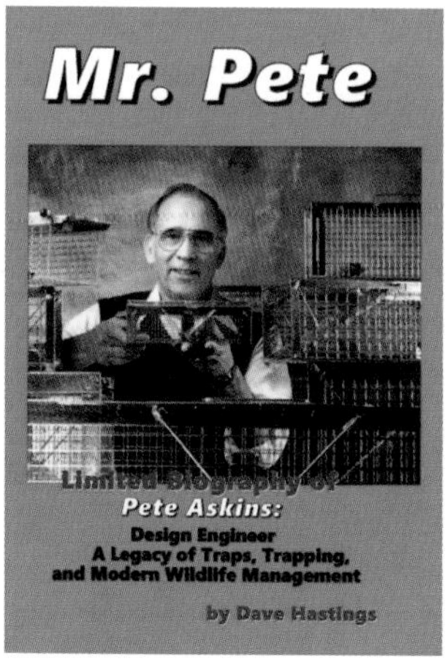

Pete Askins was a machinist and mechanic who became Woodstream Corporation's Research and Development pro. This book is a compilation of stories told by Pete and was organized as a biography of Askins by author Dave Hastings.

Pete started instructing at the Fur Takers Trappers College in 1981 and was my instructor in 1983 when I bought the course and attended. Pete was an excellent teacher. His no-nonsense approach to trapping had a sort of mechanical angle. Trapping was a process, like building an engine or designing a trap. A trapper needs to pay close attention to each and every step of that process. Askins and I got along right from the start. He called me Tommy (and nicknamed many of his students). Likely it was Pete who suggested to Charlie Park that I come back and instruct at the college. Tennessee trapper James Edgemon was a student of Pete Askins and became Pete's assistant instructor at Trappers College in 1985. Pete called James "Red" and James called Pete "Mr. Pete." Both nicknames stuck. Red passed away in 2003.

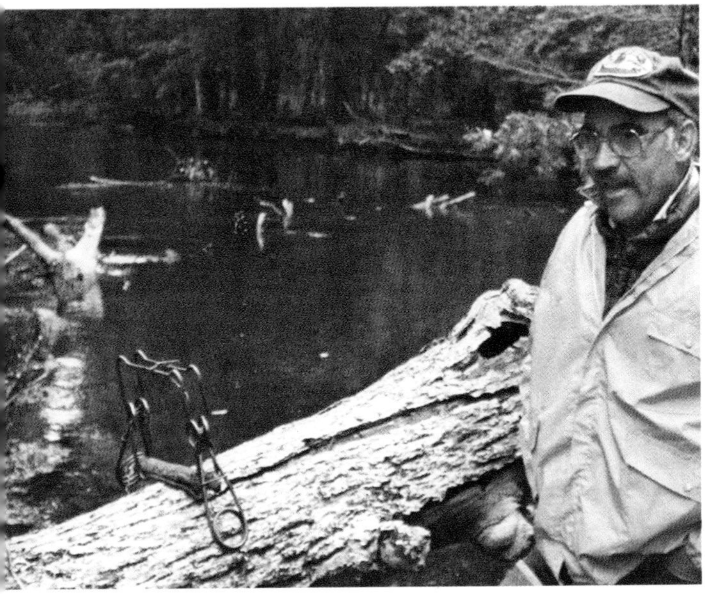

Author's Photo

Pete Askins was Tom Miranda's instructor at the 1983 Fur Takers Trappers College.

When Woodstream's parent company decided to break up the brand, one of the first things they did in 1992 was to stop making long-spring traps. It was at this time when Pete, along with his long-time pal and trapping partner Don Lawson, started Sleepy Creek traps. Pete was able to acquire some of the dies for the trap parts. Sleepy Creek started making the #11, #1, #1-1/2 and the #2 long-springs. Once these traps started selling well, the company tooled up to make coil-springs. Eventually the Victor coil-spring and Conibear brands were sold to Richard Butera of BMI.

Pete Askins's trapping history touched many aspects of the trade. His job with Woodstream opened doors into the lives and operations of many professional trappers and trapping businesses. Anybody who was anybody in the industry after 1975 knew Pete and the prototypes he built and the designs which were manufactured have influenced trapping for 45 years and will continue long into the future.

Pete Askins was inducted into the Fur Takers of America Trappers Hall of Fame in 1995 and the National Trappers Association Trappers Hall of Fame in 2011.

Author's Photo

89-year-old Pete Askins poses for a photo with Tom Miranda at the 2019 Fur Takers National Rendezvous in Harrisonburg, Virginia.

TRAPPING SEASON

1983–84

The first week of September 1983 I attended the Fur Takers of America Professional Trappers College. It was held in LaGrange, Indiana. Another home run!

I was assigned Woodstream Corp. pro, Pete Askins as an instructor and met Dr. Major Boddicker, mink-man Kermit Stearns, snare-man Keith Gregerson, mountain trapper George Stewart, Indiana coon and fox trapper Jerry Joe Barnett, Dakota trapper Odon Corr and College organizer Charlie Park. Obviously Odon had turned me on to the college and it was the best $700 bucks I'd ever spent.

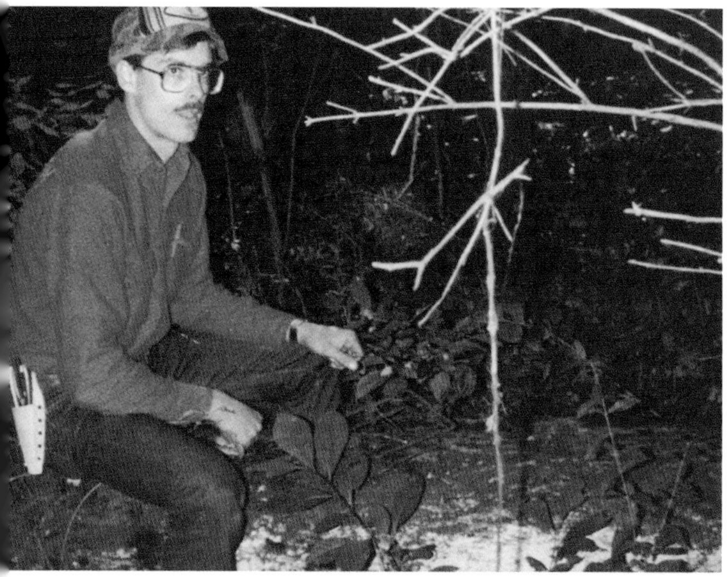

I met Mark June in 1983 at the Fur Takers Trappers College. Mark was an assistant instructor that year and we became pals.

Michigan trapper Mark June had taken the college in 1982 and was an assistant instructor in 1983. This is where Mark and I met. It was kind of interesting as I had my own lure line at the time and of course had just been featured in *Fur-Fish-Game*, so many of the students and instructors where interested in what I was about. I aced the week-long course, became pals with all the instructors and Mark as well. Charlie Park asked me back to be an assistant instructor for the 1984 college—I believe at the recommendation of Pete Askins—but it also may have been Major Boddicker. If you ever have a week open in September to attend the trappers college, I highly recommend it.

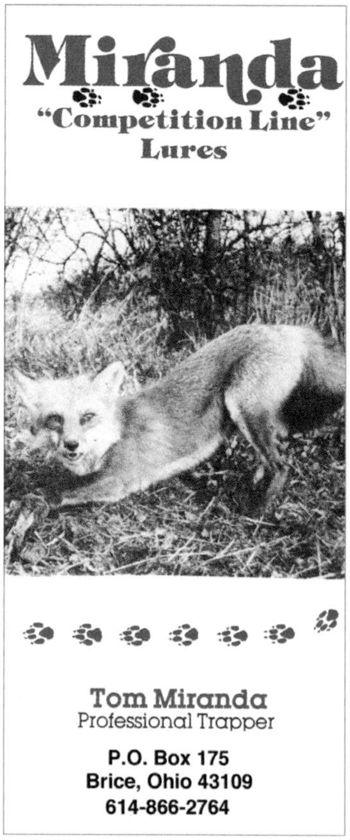

This is my first lure brochure for the 1983-84 season.

The 1983–84 trapping season was my best ever in Ohio. I worked it really hard as I knew I needed to either make this trapping pay or end up getting a real job. It was the first *big season* for my trapping lures as I used 90% my own lures with some O.L. Butcher and Carman's as backup on the line. I had made and bottled five times the amount I made in 1982 to sell as Mallow Trap Company came back for the second season, Paulette Fur and Ed Molnar both added the line. So now I had 3 dealers. Making lure with the proper ingredients is expensive and this was a huge investment for me. It needed it to pay off. Central Ohio had good weather that fall and and was able to keep above my average per day catch for the first full month. Some of the early fur I sold for expenses sold for good money. But the bottom dropped out of the fur market in early 1983 and if you were holding pelts you were left "holding the bag." My catch was 163 foxes, 147 raccoon, 212 'rats, 7 mink, 25 beaver and 1 otter. It sold for $9.7 thousand.

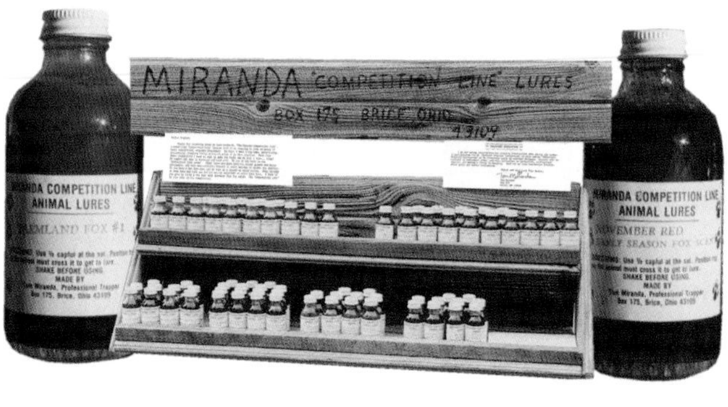

This was my first lure display I made for Marvin Mallow when he started selling my trapping lures in 1982.

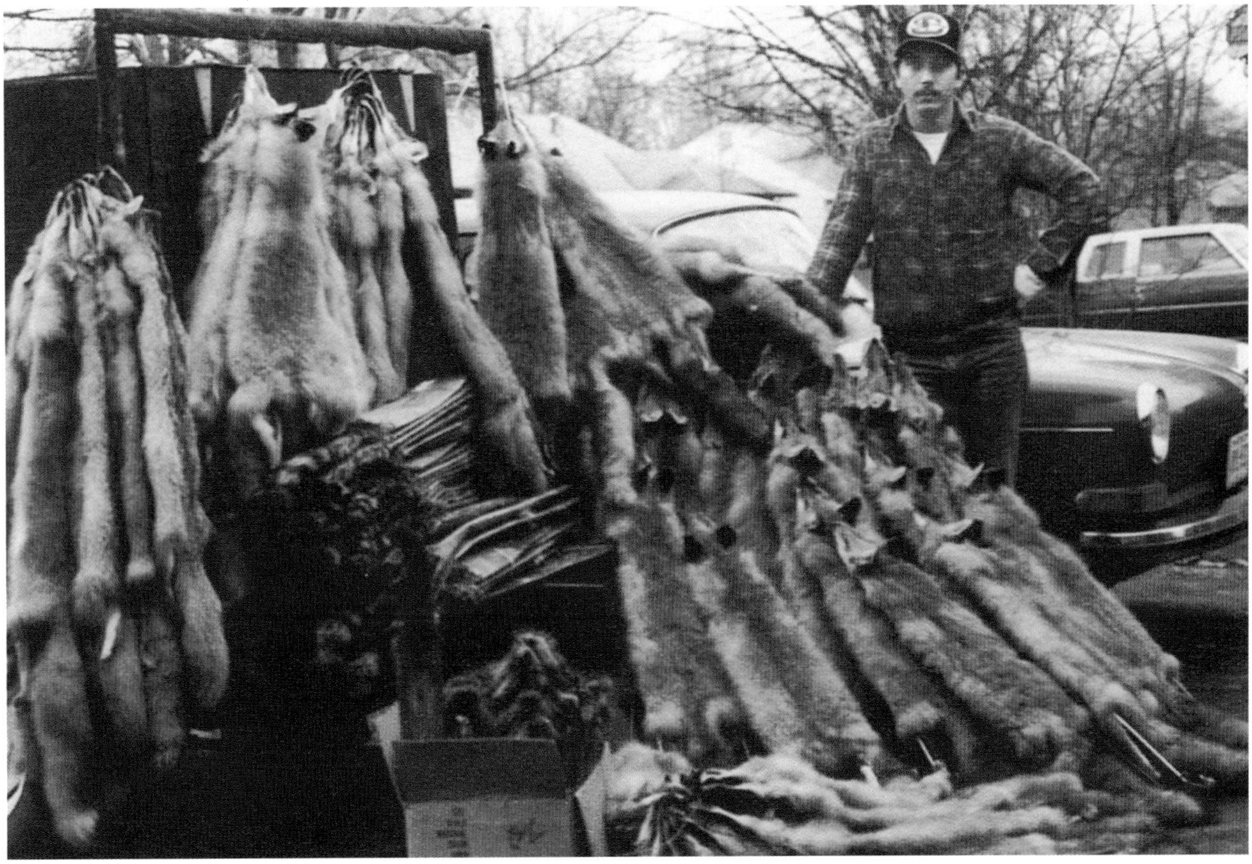

Author's Photo

Tom Miranda poses with the first part of his 1983–84 Ohio catch. Photo taken in the driveway on Country Club Road near Walnut Ridge High School.

Worn Levi's, flannel shirt, Herman Survivor boots, Woodstream Trappers cap and a day on the trapline—1983.

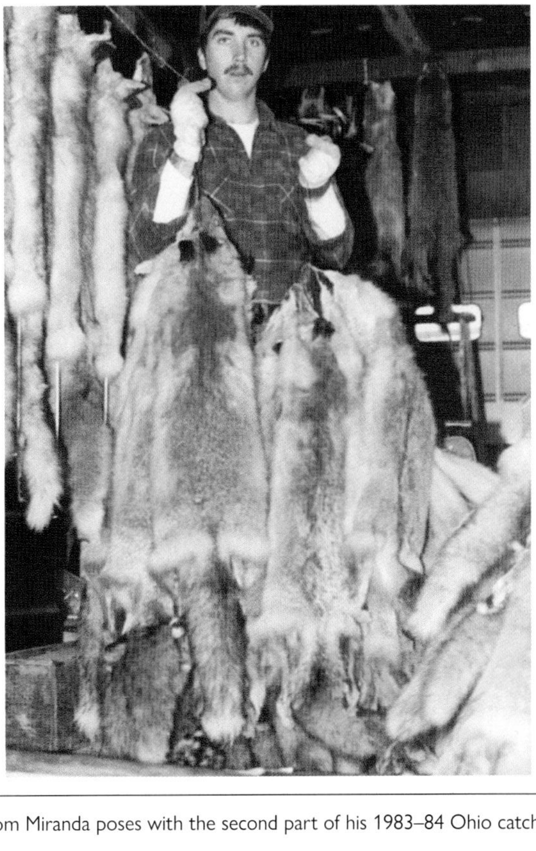

Tom Miranda poses with the second part of his 1983–84 Ohio catch.

Author's Photos

Tom with some under ice beaver and an otter, spring 1984.

My late-70s Skidoo and homemade dog sled trailer for beaver trapping. I bought the dog sled plans from Raymond Thompson Company

The only reason I did well financially on pelts in the winter of 1984 was I took about 70 foxes with me north to sell at a sale in lower Michigan. However, the sale was a bust and I kept my foxes, hauling them all the way to Michigan's Upper Peninsula and my cabin. Because the prices were so off, I had sold the top end of the catch in Ohio to Mallow. So the foxes I had were the lesser 2s and 3s. This usually isn't a good idea and I was holding hopes the market would bounce back in the spring. I was running some under ice beaver traps in February–March and preparing for some trapping students to come for lessons, when I heard that a fur buyer was stopping at Silver Lake Resort near Sagola, Michigan. I thought wow, why not? I took my foxes to Silver Lake on a Saturday and when they graded the bunch they offered me more than two, even three times the value. Graded every fox as #1 and $60 bucks per. I was shocked and said I'll take it. (I thought, wow—these guys don't know what the hell they are doing!)

Then the questions started to flow. Where did you catch these, how did you catch so many, do you have beavers, Can you get cats and otters? I told them I had a tagged otter at camp and about 15 flat-tails, but I wasn't ready to sell. In Michigan, the trapper limit at the time was twenty-five beavers and one otter. Then the shoe dropped. One of the buyers pulled me aside and said, "I have some extra tags. If you catch a few otter don't sweat it, just bring 'em buy and we'll tag them. We also have extra beaver tags and cat tags." RED FLAG. I knew this wasn't legit and now was worried that the check they gave me might bounce. However, I needed the coin, so I took the check straight to the bank on Monday and it cleared. Of course the check cleared— it was backed by the Mesabi Fur Company, a U.S. Fish & Wildlife Service sting operation. Spending tax payer money to catch outlaw trappers or as many trappers as the agents could entrap. No wonder I got so much money on those fox pelts. Many trappers got caught up in this mess. I honestly believe I was overpaid for my fox as a ploy that I might bite on the "extra tags" and sell them more fur or tell other local trappers of the high prices paid to attract Mesabi potential clients.

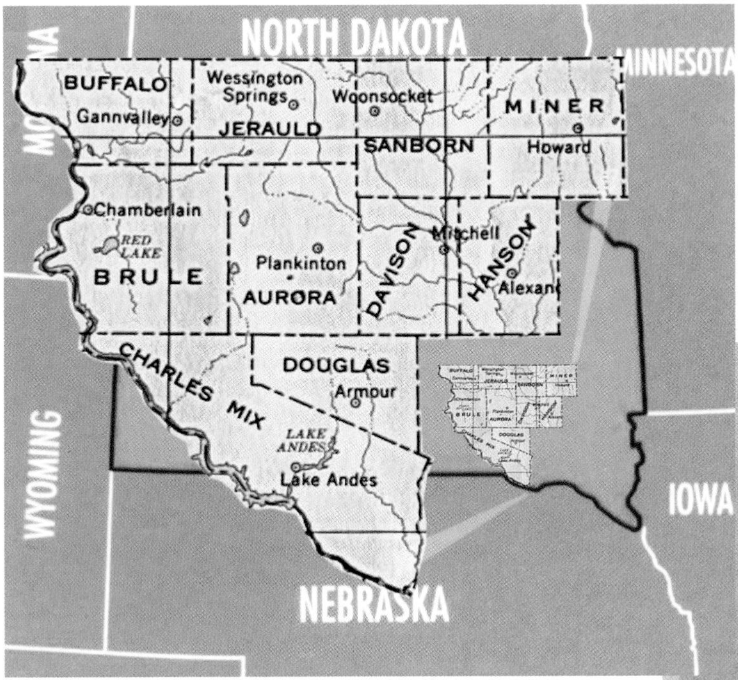

Home-based in Chamberlain, my trapline territory encompassed 52,106 square miles in south-central South Dakota.

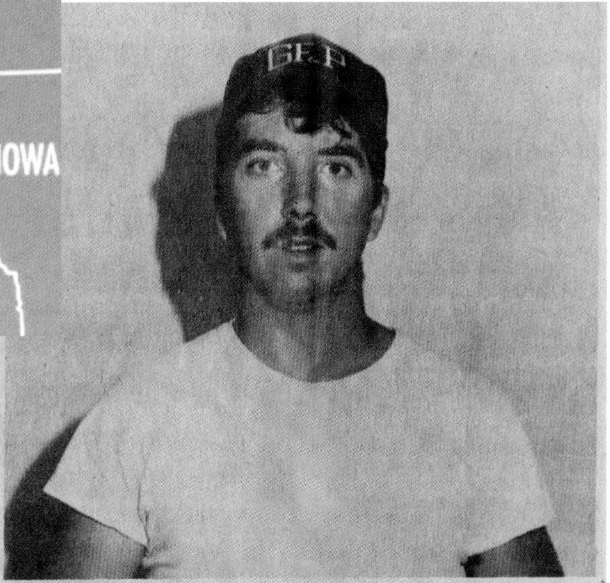

TRAPPER — Tom Miranda started his job as extension trapper specialist with the Department of Game, Fish and Parks office in Chamberlain on Aug. 13. The Columbus, Ohio, native will be working with landowners who request help in eliminating animals causing damage to their property.

My South Dakota Game, Fish, and Parks Trapper mug shot.

FULL-TIME TRAPPING

I was finally moving in the right direction. My lures were selling and I had as many trapping students as I could handle, giving lessons both at my Michigan cabin and on the farmland trapline in Ohio. At this point, the bottom had pretty much dropped out of fur prices. I had been working and making a living at trapping and building a name for myself for the last five years and now that I had gotten in a position to actually only do trapping and trapping-related jobs like writing, lure making, lessons and fur trapping, yet the industry was sliding in the wrong direction. The lessons of trapping have a tendency to bring out the reality of the situation. Hard work has a way of helping one muscle through-tough times. You learn that luck is a huge asset, yet it's about making your own luck.

Odon Corr phoned to tell me of a ADC trapper job opening with South Dakota Game Fish and Parks. It was late spring and at first I was totally uninterested. Yet, this could be a huge resume-builder and a chance to establish a new trapline in the Dakotas. I had to investigate it. I drove to Pierre, South Dakota to meet ADC Supervisor Alvin Miller in June 1984 for a job interview. I had heard that government trappers weren't allowed to make money in a trapping business and the more I thought about it, the more of a deal breaker it was. However when I got to Pierre and met with Miller, I laid out my *Fur-Fish-Game* articles, my lure brochure, and my ideas of possibly doing a trapping book. Alvin rolled his eyes as he looked at the materials then said, "The rules were set up to keep employees from personally profiting from the duties and credentials of their job. You already have this business established and if I were to hire you, you may continue it. However, you may not use your title of South Dakota Game, Fish, and Parks extension trapper in any of your advertisements, or materials. PERIOD."

I had the green light, but not the job. Alvin Miller did ask me when I would be available to start the job and I told him I would need until August to move to South Dakota. I also told him that I needed a week in early September to honor my invite to be an assistant instructor at the trappers college. I drove back to Columbus not knowing if I would be selected or not. It was my first application and interview for a trappers job. The next week, Miller called me and offered me the job. I accepted and headed north to Michigan. I had trapping students to instruct, plus I needed to button up the cabin and get some gear I thought I would need in South Dakota.

My trapping area would be ten counties east of the Missouri River. Brule, Buffalo, Jerauld, Sanborn, Miner, Hanson, Davidson, Aurora, Douglas and Charles Mix. Once I got to Chamberlain, I needed to find a place to live. I rented a room at the local hotel, but quickly found a house. Rather than rent, I offered a down payment and a land contract to buy it. I had no credit but I did have some money saved from furs checks and working. The center of my ADC area was actually closer to the small town of Plankinton, yet Chamberlain was larger, on the river and a nicer area to live, so my supervisor Alvin Miller allowed me to live in the river town. This was a big windfall for me, yet I had a long drive to the east end of the territory.

Steve Thompson was the trapper for my new area 13-5W and he was moving to west to Murdo to fill a vacant position. I would take his trapline. Steve was a great guy—in his spare time he trapped rattlesnakes from which he used the tanned hides to make snake skin belts, buckles and key fobs that he sold at the famous Wall Drug Store on the eastern edge of the badlands. Steve instructed me the correct use of M-44 cyanide getters, showed me some areas where he had done well catching coyotes, and introduced me to ranchers in areas where deprivation was a constant battle. I took all the tests to get the permits for the controlled substances as well as the rabies antibody titer vaccinations.

ODON CORR

1933–

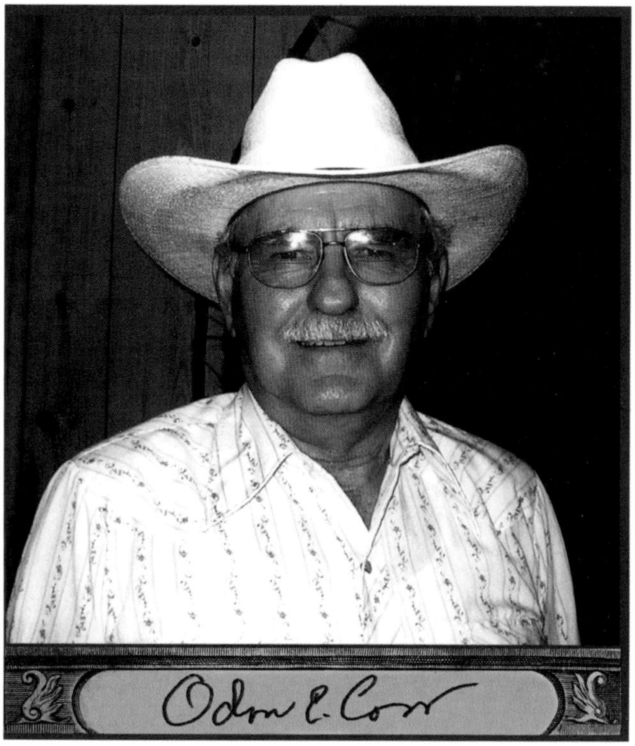

Odon Corr holds a very special place in my heart. Odon was the first professional trapper with whom I took "on the line" trapping instructions. Humble and a great teacher, Odon Corr was a South Dakota trapper who lived and trapped during the high fox and mink numbers of the 60s, 70s and early 80s. He was a government trapper, a lure maker and every trapper who knows him looks up to him.

Odon grew up trapping in the 30s and 40s starting with "flicker-tails" (ground squirrels) at age 5 and by age 12, he was catching mink. The mid-1940s was a good time to be catching mink as 12-year-old Odon sold three mink to Sears, Roebuck in Chicago for $120. In those days a good wage was $2 a day. After high school graduation, Odon was doing ranch work in South Dakota all summer and trapping in the winter.

With the start of the Korean War, Odon was drafted and soon on Army Ski Patrol in Alaska. When Odon returned, he studied at South Dakota State University in Brookings and afterward went to work with the U.S. Fish and Wildlife Service as a government trapper.

Odon Corr Photo

Odon Corr and a collection of prime winter-caught Dakota dawgs.

Author's Photo

Odon worked as a government trapper for 34 years. Corr would often exceed 500 coyotes taken in a single season—by all methods. These years and numbers build a wealth of knowledge few trappers ever reach. Odon also did wolf damage control in Minnesota, an assignment given to him because of his vast experience and expertise on canines.

Odon Corr shows me his Corr flat set in Buffalo County, South Dakota, June 1982

If you're interested in learning more about Odon Corr and his textbook flat set, the best way is watching his instructional DVD.

Author's Collection

Here's one of Odon's 3N gov't traps signed for me and in my trap collection.

I took lessons from Odon in 1982. Believe it or not, I answered his classified ad in *Fur-Fish-Game* magazine and wrote him. At the time he was living in Miller, South Dakota. When I arrived we primarily discussed western set location and his famous Corr flat set. Odon primarily used Victor 3N cast jaw traps and was meticulous in building his set. Bedding long-spring traps and blending is an art form in coyote trapping. Odon used a kneeling cloth not only to keep human odor off the ground, but to place dirt to keep the set area as original and blended as possible upon finishing the set.

The Corr flat set uses no little or backing so his locations are set to allow the animal to approach from any side. It was an interesting concept. Odon showed me many set locations where he took 20 or more foxes in a single season and one location on a ranch near Miller, South Dakota where he took 56 foxes in one season,"

Odon Corr Photo

Odon Corr and trapper extraordinaire Kenny Johnson get together to swap stories of the "good old days". 2019.

Yes, I said 56 foxes from one location. Five hundred plus fox seasons were not uncommon during the late 1960s and 1970s in South Dakota.

When you're a trapper for 70 years of your life you accumulate many stories. In 2018 at the National Trappers Association National Convention, Odon told me the story of a beaver hunt on the Cheyenne River in western South Dakota. So you must understand that hunting spring beaver is legal in South Dakota. Trappers will run a boat and shoot the beaver as they are swimming in the river, or sometimes the beavers are caught out on the bank. It is an exciting hunt and can be quite profitable as the beavers are plentiful and fairly easy to get if you know what you're doing and as long as you can net them before they go under in the current. Years ago, ace trapper Kenny Johnson and Odon were hunting a stretch of the Cheyenne at ice-out. The river was high and ice chunks were floating, making maneuvering the boat difficult. With a boat full of flattails the hunters were just about to take their load back to the truck when they spotted one more beaver. As they tried to turn the boat to get into position, the load shifted and the current caught them sideways. The boat swamped and capsized. Kenny escaped and quickly made shore but Odon was nowhere to be found. Kenny jumped back into the raging river, swam to the capsized boat which was lodged in a snag—and got under it and pulled Odon out—literally saving his life. To hear Kenny tell the story it was nothin'—to hear Odon tell it, Kenny Johnson is a hero. Such was the life of these professional trappers!

Odon also had his own lure business and made several good paste lures. Many government trappers and past students use Corr lures, paste lures that can be used easily on M-44 cyanide "getters." Another interesting story that involves Odon was that he called to tell me about a state trapper position open in South Dakota. I applied for it, interviewed, got the job and ended up living not more than 40 miles from where Odon gave me the trapping lessons in 1982.

"I like to tell young, up-and-coming trappers that the main thing is to be observant at all times. Study the habits of the animals around you. Get to know where they live, what they eat, when they mate and locate their main travel ways. I always tell the rancher, don't worry I'll catch the culprit, just some take longer! Always take trapping seriously and project a good image to the general public about trapping. Be honest and always level with people when questions are asked because you are representing all trappers."

—Odon Corr, 2014

GEORGE STEWART

1923–2004

Some trappers aren't interested in the limelight, even though they shine so brightly. George Stewart was one of those trappers. Don't get me wrong, George loved attention and enjoyed passing his vast trapping knowledge along to anyone who would listen, but George Stewart was not one to step in and take over a conversation. He was a grand listener and maybe that's what made him such a phenomenal teacher. Most who read this book will never know George Stewart and that is a shame, as likely you would feel the same way about him as we all do. With permission, I'm following here with a piece written about George by Dr. Major Boddicker.

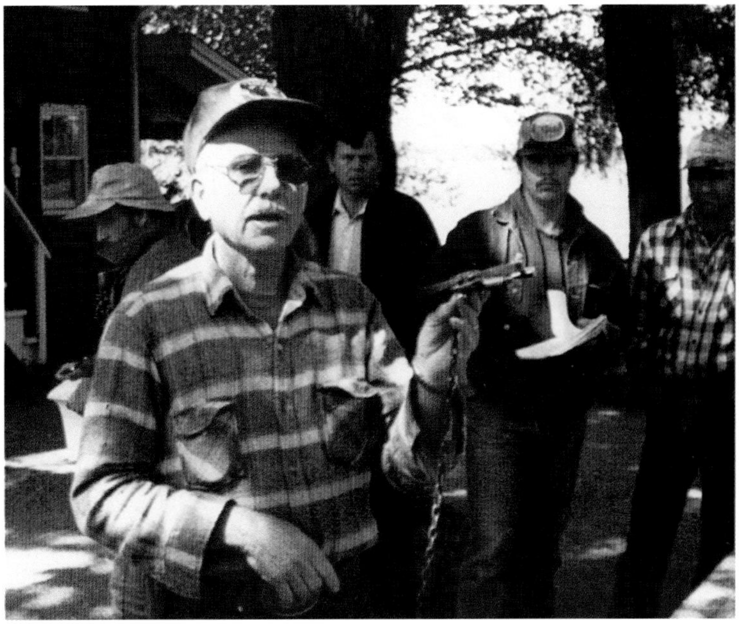

Author's Photo

George Stewart talks coyote traps and adjustment at the 1983 Fur Takers Trapper's College.

George was born in Windsor, Colorado on August 21, 1923. His ancestors originated in Oklahoma. His grandmother was a Cherokee a fact in which George took great pride.

George was an American classic. He volunteered for service in the Army Air Corp during WWII. He was a tail-gunner in a B-29 that was shot down on its first mission over Germany. George spent 18 months in a German prisoner-of-war camp. He was severely wounded and permanently disabled from his wounds. However, he managed to become a successful plumber after the war and through the 1950s and 60s. In the early 60s, he retired and devoted his life to trapping and doing odd jobs for the Rawah Dude Ranch, high in the Colorado Rockies.

I met George at the first Colorado Trappers Association Rendezvous at Fairplay in 1976. Everyone who knew George knew him as the *best of the best* trapper who unselfishly shared his knowledge with anyone who was interested in listening. He was an artist at trapping and everything else he did. He credited his early trapping knowledge to Warren Ewing, an old-time trapper from Windsor, Colorado.

Major Boddicker Photo

George Stewart instructs his class in the art of making the perfect coyote set at the 1981 Western Fur Takers Trappers College in Colorado.

George was instrumental in getting the Fur Takers of America Trappers College going. He was a star instructor for the FTA College from 1980 to 1987, teaching at Pingree Park, Colorado; LaGrange, Indiana; Land Between the Lakes, Kentucky and Tennessee; and Raquette Lake, New York. In my life of dealing with trappers from all over the world, he was hands-down the most skillful artist in the woods, plains, and mountains of all trappers I ever met. He did not catch the most, but he could catch anything, anywhere, at any time, with any trap, and tell you which foot he would have it by.

I went to college for 10 years and have been around many hundreds of teachers. George was the best teacher I ever had. There are many excellent trappers, alive and dead, who have had significant impacts on the trapping profession. George certainly was among the most influential. His knowledge, techniques, and tools are in nearly every trapper's basket whether they know it or not. He taught the trapping teachers of FTA, NTA, and many state trapper organizations.

George was a low-key guy. He enjoyed the spotlight when he got it, but he never sought it, never blew his own horn, and remained a quiet, unassuming man until the end. George had a coyote chiseled onto his tombstone of which he proudly showed me a photo ten days before he died. He was in good spirits laughing about his V.A. doctor who had given him 2 or 3 days to live, 4 days before. I asked him if he wanted me to quirt some coyote urine on the corner of his headstone so that coyotes would salute him for eternity. He laughed and said that would work just fine, and he and the coyotes would enjoy it. He earned their respect.

George was active and alert until a few days prior to his death, crafting arrowheads and Indian bows and tools within a few days of his passing. George Stewart was a friend that trappers cannot replace. There has been nobody like him, and there won't be anyone like him again. I will miss him.

—Major Boddicker March, 2004

It was a blessing to have been a trapping student of George Stewart. And to teach along side of him at the trappers college was a privilege. I have many fond memories of George, but my most special was the year we roomed together at the Limberlost Camp near Lagrange, Indiana. Limberlost was a 1920s era band camp built along Lake Oliver. I had gotten to the college early and selected my bunk in a room of beds at the end of the hallway. As I was getting situated, George walked in with his bag and said, "Tom is it OK if I bunk in with you?"

"Absolutely," I said. That first night, like guys sometimes do, we had a chat before falling off to sleep. It was a great chat as George opened up to me about his time as a prisoner of war. It was something he never talked about. George went into vivid detail about his plane being shot down and his experience. He talked about making traps to catch rats to eat and so many other unbelievable details. I can say that during the 10 years I taught at the college, instructors came and went, But George Stewart was irreplaceable.

George Stewart was inducted into the National Trappers Association Trappers Hall of Fame in 2002.

Major Boddicker Photo

GeorgeStewart accepts his National Trappers Association Trappers Hall of Fame award with best friend Major Boddicker in 2002.

Author's Photo

Instructors include *Top Row L-R:* Kermit Stearns, James Lee, Pete Askins, Red Edgemon, Major Boddicker, Tom Miranda. *Bottom Row L-R:* Dan DeZarn, Bill Neff, Jerry Joe Barnett, George Stewart, Bill Park, Charlie Park.

Class of 1985 Fur Takers Trappers College.

Instructing at the FTA Trappers College was one of the highlights of my trapping career.

ASSISTANT INSTRUCTOR

I had only been on the job a month when my first week of vacation was used. I had committed to being an assistant instructor at the Fur Takers Trappers College and I went back to Indiana to fulfill my obligation. It was an honor to be asked and I wasn't going to miss it. The full week of instruction was almost like taking the class again, a learning experience and fun. I was Pete Askins's assistant and gained even more respect for Pete that week than I did when he was my instructor in 1983. Pete was a fantastic trapper, but the way he talked to and respected his students, the way he handled himself, his quick wit and sense of humor allowed me to know the man, not the myth of the man. So many times in life we think we know somebody, yet in reality we don't really know them at all.

At the end of the 1984 college, Charlie moved me up to an instructor position as Odon Corr had taken a USFWS trapper job in North Dakota and couldn't get the time to continue his duties as an instructor. There were many other trappers more worthy than myself to fill this prestigious position. But saying "no" doesn't get you very far in life. "Hell yes. Thank You Charlie, It would be an honor," gets you the job and that's what I said. This meant I was going to be one of the seven main instructors at the college. At the time the field instructors were Pete Askins, George Stewart, Jerry Joe Barnett, Kermit Stearns and yours truly. Major Boddicker was the lecturer of the night classes and Dan DeZarn was the snaring instructor. I continued to instruct at the college until 1994.

The life of a government trapper is nothing like the independent fur trapper. My job was to kill coyotes that killed sheep, unclog culverts and trap the beaver that plugged them, get the skunk or raccoon out of the attic. I was on call and needed to file a work order with every complaint and follow through until it was solved. I was supplied a 4x4 truck, about 150 traps, 50 snares, M-44 equipment and shared a secretary with the wildlife biologist and game warden. It wasn't hard to put 1,500–2,000 miles on a truck per week. I could use traps, snares, M-44s, denning cartridges, and call in the plane to aerial hunt. The state owned 2 aircraft and most of the aerial hunting was done in the winter

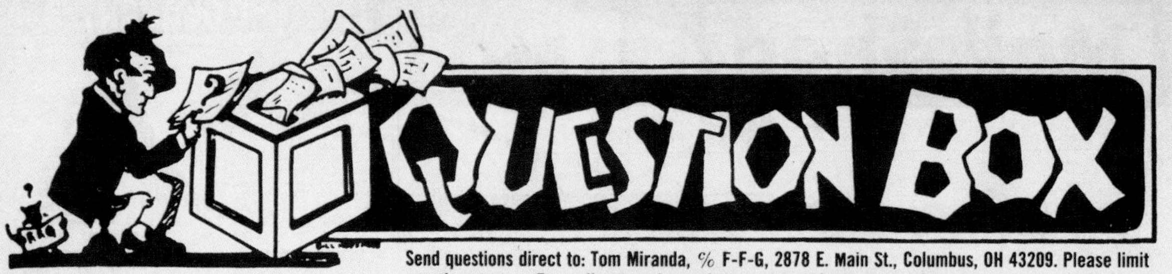

Send questions direct to: Tom Miranda, % F-F-G, 2878 E. Main St., Columbus, OH 43209. Please limit questions to two. For a direct reply, enclose a stamped, return envelope.

QUESTION—Where can I obtain information on hunting and trapping in North Dakota?—M. S., OH.
ANSWER—Write to: North Dakota State Game and Fish Dept., 2121 Lovett Ave., Bismarck, ND 58505.

QUESTION—Is bait or lure needed to trap fox? 2. Does bait or lure attract dogs and cats?—J. E., OH.
ANSWER—Foxes can be taken without bait or lures, but more will be taken using it. 2. Yes.

QUESTION—Where can I obtain a hunting and trapping regulation book for Michigan? T.M., WV.
ANSWER—Write to: Michigan DNR, Box 30028, Lansing, MI 48909.

QUESTION—Do crappie breed in farm ponds? 2. How deep do you fish for them?—L. B., OH.
ANSWER—Crappie are closely related to sunfish and black bass. They will breed in farm ponds of suitable size and habitat. 2. Look for crappie in sluggish, shallow waters. Depending on weather, fish at depths of two to eight feet.

QUESTION—Where can I obtain a net used for catching birds? 2. Where can I obtain a sparrow net trap?—D. I., NJ.
ANSWER—I believe the Nylon Net Co., 7 Vance Ave., Box 592, Memphis Tenn 38101 can help you. Netting birds requires special permits.

QUESTION—Which furbearers are found around Lawrence, PA.?—B. G., PA.
... grey fox, ... eaver and ... which fur- ... write your ... rden.)

Tom Miranda Joins F-F-G

TOM Miranda, a professional trapper and a frequent contributor to *FUR-FISH-GAME*, has been named as the new head of the Question & Answer Department. His responses appear in this month's issue.

Born and raised in Ohio, Miranda began trapping when he was 11 years old. After a stint in college, he moved to the wilderness of Michigan's Upper Peninsula where he built his own cabin and trapped fulltime. He has longlined for coyote, fox and raccoon in both Michigan and Ohio, and recently moved to South Dakota, where he has been hired as a professional state predator control trapper.

Miranda, who has had several trapping articles published in *F-F-G* in recent years, was an instructor at the Fur Takers of America Professional Trappers College and is an expert on survival skills and wilderness living. He has been making a living from trapping and related interests for the past five years.

F-F-G is proud to have Tom Miranda following in the steps of E. J. Dailey and other outdoorsmen who have made the Question & Answer Department such a vital part of this magazine since 1925. ■

QUESTION—Is it OK to use dog urine at a fox set? 2. What animals will come to a crawfish set near Yosemite?—M. Z., CA.
ANSWER—Dog urine is OK, but fox urine is better. 2. A crawfish set will attract raccoon and mink in that area. Locate sign of these animals along waterways and make sets.

QUESTION—Can you give me a recipe for fox gland lure? 2. Are mink common in southeast Pennsylvania, and if so, what is the most productive method of trapping them?—P. C., Pa.
ANSWER—Three ounces of broken down, preserved fox glands, two ounces urine, one-half ounce glycerine, one-quarter ounce tonquin musk, aged two months. 2. Mink are fairly common in your area. Blind and pocket sets are very productive. Large numbers of mink can only be taken by running a large number of traps over a large territory.

QUESTION—Do you have a recipe for jerky? 2. Where can I obtain Liquid Smoke?—O. D., OH.
ANSWER—There are many recipes for jerky. One is to marinate lean meat cut in strips in one-quarter cup steak sauce, one-half cup red wine, 1 tbsp. dijon mustard and salt and pepper to taste. Dry the marinated meat strips in an oven on low heat. Other jerky recipes are listed in "the book 3001 Questions and Answers" available through *F-F-G*. 2. Liquid Smoke is available at your local grocery or department store.

QUESTION—Where can I obtain the following chemicals—tonquin musk, oil of catnip, asafoetida, beaver castor, oil of roden and zinc valerate?—J. H., KS.
ANSWER—These are the common lure ingredients and are available through many dealers who advertise in *F-F-G*.

Competition Line Fox Trapping
First Edition 1985

with snow cover. We were allowed to trap fur on our vacation and the first year I did run a private line for foxes. It was only a week's worth of trapping, but I needed some photos for the lure business and I wasn't supposed to use any taken on the ADC job. If any of the ADC fur was prime, we did put up and the state sold the pelts to fund ATVs for us trappers. In those days there were 16 state trappers in South Dakota, 2 pilots, an assistant supervisor and supervisor.

In October 1984 I received a call from *Fur-Fish-Game* editor Ken Dunwoody asking if I would like to take over the magazine's Question Box column. I was flabbergasted as only 3 men had done the Question Box since *F-F-G* started in 1925. E.J. Dailey, Vaughn Tingley and Don Rouanzion. I would be the fourth. I couldn't believe it! I accepted, and took over in the December 1984 issue. It was a shock to the powers that

be in Pierre at the Animal Damage Control main office. This was all happening pretty quickly. Another shock would come in early 1985 when my first trapping book, *Competition Line Fox Trapping* would release. The bulk of my fox book had been conceived in Ohio and Michigan, but I did use some set and catch photos from my week-long line in Dakota, November of 1984.

TRAPPER WINGS

In the winter, when snow blanketed the area, we scheduled the state aircraft to aerial hunt areas that had a historical coyote problem. These aerial hunts reintroduced me to flying and this newfound association with trapping intrigued me, so here's the backstory. In my senior year of high school, I had opted not to enroll in the college prep chemistry class that many of my pals were taking. I instead took what was called Aviation Science. This course was essentially a ground school for students interested in an aviation career. When I had gotten my driver's license two years prior, this freedom gave me the chance to extend my trapline to a point where part of it was near the Columbus, Ohio International airport. Seeing the big jets land and take off as I ran my traps before school excited me—and in short, I was hooked on flying and knew I wanted to be a pilot. However, flying lessons where expensive and even though I was able to ace the ground school course in high school and take a few introductory flights, getting a private pilot license was financially out of the question. Reality set in—likely I would never own or fly my own airplane—fast forward to the spring of 1985.

With a little research, I located a Cessna pilot training center in the small 'berg of Wagner, South Dakota, about 100 miles from where I was living at Chamberlain. Roy Crisman of Crisman Aviation would be my instructor. Typically new pilots are trained in a Cessna 152, a small 2-seat tricycle gear aircraft that's easy on fuel and less expensive to rent. But my needs for a pilot's license were somewhat more specialized and at the advice of State ADC pilot Gary Hanson and instructor Roy Crisman, I made the decision to learn to fly a "tail wheel" or "tail dragger" aircraft. Tail Draggers are much more difficult to land than the more modern tricycle gear configuration, as the rear wheel sits far behind the main gear. This "dragger" configuration allows for rough field takeoff and landing, however when landing a "tail dragger," the pilot must be diligent with the controls and fly the

Author's Photo

Flight instructor Roy Crissman poses with Miranda's 1947 Cessna 140 before beginning Tom's first flying lesson in the spring of 1985.

plane even while it's on the ground until full stop. Tail Draggers have a ferocious tendency to "ground loop" which means the lighter tail of the fuselage wants to swing around on landing with a violent "loop" that can damage wings, propeller and worse. All that said, I was up for the task and I would buy my own "tail dragger" aircraft and learn to fly it.

EARNING MY WINGS

There are several types of small aircraft configurations.. The usual propeller in the front type, then turboprop, the pusher type (or propeller in the back), twin engine, high wing, low wing, tricycle gear and tail dragger. In the flat farm and ranch country of the Dakota's dictated that a high wing, tail dragger would be ideal.. My aircraft of choice was the Piper PA-18. Known as the Super Cub, this plane sported a 160 HP (some modify up to 180 HP) engine, light fabric skin and tundra tires perfect for bush flying. However, I quickly learned that this Cadillac of light planes was out of this trapper's price range, so I settled on buying a 1948 Cessna 140. I found the ex-mail plane (yes my first airplane was a plane that carried U.S. mail in western South Dakota) hangared in the small town of Lemmon and it's price, $6 thousand cash. With hopes that this Cessna wasn't a real "Lemon," I bought the 36-year-old plane with fur money that I had saved. The Cessna 140 has a metal fuselage and cloth wings with flaps, a 90 HP Continental O-190 engine and spring main gear. It was the basic of basic airplanes and a fantastic trainer, plus perfect for what I wanted it for—my trapline.

The plane was ferried to Wagner since I couldn't fly it yet and I began lessons in earnest. My high school aviation science came in handy for the ground school (although I had forgotten most of it), but it was easier the second time around. The flying was easy, very fun and soon I had made my solo flight. A young pilot's solo flight is pretty exciting—I'll never forget Crisman climbing out of the plane and saying, "Tom, you're ready. Take off, fly a pattern and land. I'll stand here on the runway and watch you. If it doesn't feel right, add power and go around!" It took me 3 attempts to land, but once I did it, I was set. Confidence in flying is just like trapping or bowhunting and comes from repetition and good experiences. After my solo, I started commuting by air to the flight lessons from Chamberlain which saved me 4 hours driving. The flight to Wagner was less than 40 minutes takeoff to touchdown, and I was building "Pilot in Command" hours. Upon completion of all the lessons, my FAA check ride was scheduled and completed at the state capital airport in Pierre. I'll never forget the day I received my Trapper Wings.

My "bird" opened up an entirely new trapping world to me—I could scout new trapping areas, I could locate coyote and fox dens, I could find hidden marshes and count the rat houses. I could use my plane to fly over ranches with coyote deprivation and see the whole picture. The aerial perspective immediately gave

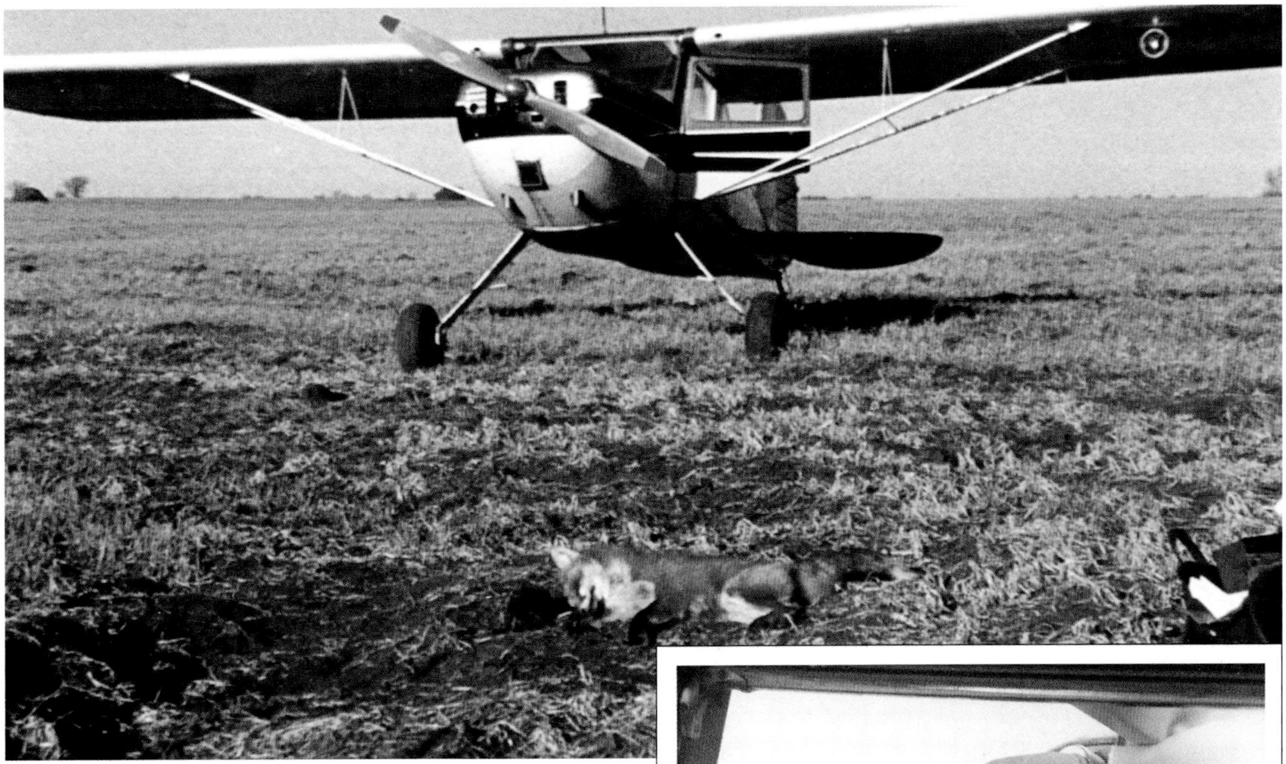

I ran my trapline with this airplane for 5 years. This is the first of many catches I landed to pick up over the years, 1985.

Tom Miranda poses in his trapline airplane after finishing his FAA check ride and earning his pilot's license.

Author's Photos

me a visual of the predator travel ways and best set locations, the easiest access into areas, etc.

My South Dakota trapline included a large part of the Missouri River from Fort Randall to Fort Thompson. This area of the Missouri which was traversed by Lewis and Clark was well documented in their travel diary. I ran extensive traplines in the "river hills" operating coyotes, foxes, mink, raccoons and beaver sets. I flew my airplane often along the river hills and up the White River thinking about what it must have been like to see this area as a trapper in the days of Lewis and Clark. In 1946 the Army Corps of Engineers began building a dam at Fort Randall and by 1954 the drainage was flooded and is known today as Lake Francis Case (named after a U.S. Senator from South Dakota) It was obvious to me, the benefits to having my own aircraft were endless. I remember thinking on one scouting flight, "This airplane is going to simplify my life."

Boy was I wrong! Things were about to change big time. . .

KERMIT STEARNS 1912–2004

I met Kermit Stearns at the 1983 Fur Takers Trappers College. Kermit was already a legend at this point in his career, authoring articles in *Trappers World* and *Fur-Fish-Game* since the 1930s. Doing the *Trapper* magazine Q&A column, numerous Trapping Association seminars and of course, the college. I spent time chatting with him at the first couple colleges but never really got to know Kermit well until the 1986 college after I had been an instructor for a few years. I think Kermit had seen his fair share of young whippersnappers come and go in the trapping biz and he wasn't too sure about me. Kermit was in his early 70s at the time, I was 25 years old. Kermit was the quiet type, not someone who started many conversations, but when asked he would quickly put his opinion forward. I remember the '86 college vividly as Kermit came up to me and asked jokingly how I could have gotten a better Q&A job at such a young age than he had. We both laughed. I had become the *Fur-Fish-Game* Question Box editor in December 1984—Kermit had been the *Trapper* magazine Questions & Answers editor since 1977.

With age comes wisdom and there's no doubt that Kermit had it. Trapping was fun to him and a challenge. Kermit was an expert trapper and made some fantastic catches, he didn't do it for the money. It was for the love of trapping. Kermit was in the automobile business and had been for years. I wish I would have written down some of what we talked about but I didn't. If I'm not mistaken, Kermit was one of the earlier motorcar dealers in Erie, Pennsylvania. He had property and raised Angus beef for sale. Kermit also owned horses and was a rider himself. He gave riding lessons. Kermit Stearns had been very successful in business.

Kermit had a way about him that exuded confidence. The kind of confidence that comes from years of doing something and knowing it works. He was the perfect instructor for the trappers college because he had the chops of a top trapper, the legacy and a gift to share it. Think about it, Kermit was born in 1912, ten years after the Wright Brothers flew at Kitty-Hawk, the same year the *Titanic* sank. When Kermit got his driver's license Ford was still making the Model T. He was a Navy Veteran in WWII, married his wife Juanita in 1941, had six children and even more grand children. And he still found time to teach the trappers college, answer hundreds of trapping questions a month for *Trapper* and run his own trapline.

Kermit was best known for his mink trapping prowess. That's because he liked trapping mink the best. It was easier and more fun than fox trapping, but make no mistake, Kermit was an ace fox trapper as well. Another interesting tidbit worth mentioning was that for years I was involved with the trappers college, Kermit was there every year and was always asked by students to sign their textbooks. Sure we all were asked to sign books and caps, but without question, Kermit was the rock star of the group when it came to autographs. I know firsthand—as I asked him to sign my *Trapping Rocky Mountain Furbearers* textbook in 1983 and that signature is included with his photo in this book.

Kermit Stearns was inducted into the Fur Takers of America Trappers Hall of Fame in 1991 and the National Trappers Association Trappers Hall of Fame in 1993.

Favorite Sets of Top Trappers

"To make a large catch of mink and other fur, a trapper has to have the ambition and health to work hard, setting a lot of traps over a large territory. Good weather and little competition often makes the difference between a large catch and a fair catch. Mark your sets and write down the locations. Support your conservation and trapping organizations. Respect the animals you trap, respect the rights of landowners, trappers and other recreational users."

— Kermit Stearns, 1997

Kermit Stearns's fox trapping gear was carried in this basket which is now displayed at Tom Parr's Trap History Museum in Galloway, Ohio.

Trap History Museum Photo

A younger Kermit Stearns with a great northwestern, Pennsylvania catch.

AMERICAN TRAPPER

NOV-DEC
2019
Vol. 59 No. 6

The Official Publication of the National Trappers Association

CHAPTER 7

LURE BUSINESS

Every trapper who pursues excellence in the craft eventually begins to tinker with lures. Typically a trapper will start out with using the glands and bladders of foxes, coyotes or bobcats. Then add essential oils, additional ingredients, aging, preservation and the formulation is complete. There is so much that goes into it. The lure business is one of the key income streams of most professional trappers. Yes, trapping skills and animals to trap are essential, but the trappers who make their own scent and catch good numbers of animals, will always have an industry no matter the fur value. When referring to the lure business a well-known trapper once said, "Trappers are often easier to catch than the animals."

SMELLS LIKE MONEY

Making concoctions that attract target animals isn't really that difficult. The difficulty arises with the consistency of the product year after year. And there is much that goes into it. Each ingredient in a formula must have a level of consistency that can be held up year after year. Any changes and the lure will not be the same. Glands loaded with fat will not render the same results if clean glands were used in the original formulation. And tainting or aging in the sun doesn't offer consistency as one year may be more sunny and hot while another year it's cloudy and cool.

I was blessed to be able to learn some key secrets from a few top lure makers. One essential trick is the utilization of a hot room. I built and used a metal room that was kept at 100 degrees inside year-round. I used it to taint meat, make fish oil, age glands, dry castor and for a number of other functions that require consistent temperature. Each lure formula required not only exact quantities of specific ingredients but exact times for the ingredients to age at temperature. For example, 4 gallons of clean, ground fox glands would get a gallon of fresh (yellow/sweet) fox urine added, mixed well and placed in a 40-gallon Rubbermaid trash can. Six 5-gallon buckets (30 gallons) of gland mixture per Rubbermaid. These batches would go into the hot room for 100 days, mixing two times a week. Then they were pulled out and preserved. This season's glands were next season's lure. So the glands would age a year before being put into the formulation. This is the process that is needed to make lures that stay consistent batch after batch.

Another key was tincturing. Tincturing is a fancy name for cutting, however the cutting is done over a

< *Author's Photo*

Author's Photo

Michigan pal Jerry Herbst came to South Dakota to trap and work with me in my supply business. Photo shows Jerry busy bottling lure with our makeshift lure dispenser complete with an electric mixing paddle.

long period. Say you have 16 ounces of pure quill skunk essence. If you pour it into a gallon glass jar and add 100 ounces of a medium like grain alcohol and mix it twice a week for six months—eventually you will have 116 ounces of very strong skunk liquid. This is tinctured skunk essence. And if it's tinctured in the hot room, the result will be different compared to tincturing in a cooler environment. Sixteen ounces of pure quill essence may have a value of $200. Add 100 ounces of grain alcohol ($10) which renders 116 ounces of tinctured skunk for a cost of $210 or $1.81 an ounce. Drop per drop, tinctured isn't a powerful as pure quill—yet 3 ounces of properly tinctured skunk could replace an ounce of pure quill in a scent formula, keeping costs down. Tincturing becomes even more important when very exotic civet and tonquin musks are purchased at hundreds of dollars an ounce. However, less expensive synthetic musks have pretty much replaced these authentic musks today.

Another issue that lure makers face is freezing weather. Lures must be made to be used in cold conditions. Frozen lure is not only impossible to get out of the bottle, but loses its potency. Lures must be made to function in cold and hot weather conditions with equal enthusiasm. Using bases that won't freeze are key. Some use propylene glycol, some salt, some alcohol, some use all three depending on the mixture. Cold affects a lure in two ways. First, the cold air is denser and thus heavier, so cold air pushes scent molecules down. Second, cold air slows molecules that may be in motion. The slowing of molecule movement in water is what eventually allows it to turn into a solid. This slowing of molecule motion limits the smell that can escape the lure. Conversely, in warm weather hot air is less dense, rises and causes more molecular movement allowing lure smells to escape and permeate the air.

Here is my lure formula for Perfect Partner Predator Bait as I sold in my catalog back in the 1980s.

PERFECT PARTNER PASTE BAIT

6 1/2 gallons	fermented egg (prepare by grinding raw eggs equally into two, 5-gallon buckets and bury in a shady place for 3 months—will turn to paste.
11 gallons	ground fresh bobcat meat (no taint); 3 cups sodium benzoate—to preserve
3 cups	ground powdered beaver castor
2 gallons	propylene glycol
1/2 gallon	clean, fresh red fox urine (golden, no ammonia)
5 gallons	ground rattlesnake carcasses—aged 100 days at 100 degrees to liquid

Mix all ingredients well. Add additional glycol if needed. The mixture spooned into 16-ounce jars and sold by the pint, quart and gallon.

Author's Collection

The cover and inside lure listings of my 1983–84 Trapping Lure Brochure. I actually used this brochure for two seasons by changing the address to 201 East Mott Street Chamberlain, South Dakota 57325 during the Government trapper days.

You can see the amount of work that would go into just one bait. I purchased my original lure formulas from a Canadian trapper in 1979 and started the 1980–81 season after I had saved some glands. I originally made my lures in gallon-sized mayonnaise/pickle jars. The bottled, labeled lures which I sold to Marvin Mallow in a wooden display for the 1982–83 season were Farmland Fox #1, Farmland Fox #2, November Red, Ringtails, Choice, Creek Bank Coon and Pocket Popper Mink. Fast forward to my 1987 catalog and I still made all of these *plus* Floodwood Fox Dope, Floodwood 'Yote Dope, 'Yote Dope SK (with skunk), High Plains Predator Call, Bobcat Supreme, Shellfish All-Call, Northern Plains Predator Bait and Perfect Partner Paste bait.

Once my lure business was kicking, I realized that the raw ingredients were the elephant in the room. Without quantities of glands, beaver meat, bobcat meat and snakes there was a limit to how much lure or bait you could make. I got on a kick and bought every gallon of raw glands I could find from every fur buyer who would collect them. I prepared them, aged them and put them up in 5-gallon buckets and cold stored them. I had glands coming out of my ears. And when other lure makers needed glands, I could supply them. And when I did—I made money. Plus this got me ahead on inven-

This is my first "real' Trapping Supply Catalog mailed with lure and book orders in 1985–86.

This book by Nick Wyshinski is a good starter course in learning about how to make your own trapping lures.

New lure bottle labels began in 1984. Address changed from Brice, Ohio to Chamberlain, South Dakota.

tory as by 1990 I had 6 predator lures in the marketplace and 50-plus, 40-gallon Rubbermaid cans of lure made, aged and ready to bottle when needed. I also had enough glands on hand to double that inventory, or sell at a substantial profit. I sold glands to most of the big name lure makers in these days and while they all liked the quality, they hated the price because I wouldn't give the glands away. The way I looked at it was that every bottle of lure these dealers sold, I made money because my glands were in it.

Having your own catalog and selling direct is awesome as it offers the highest profit margin. But having an army of dealers is how a lure maker truly gets established. You can tell everyone that you're the best trapper on the planet and your lures are the best, but it's so much better if word-of-mouth comes from satisfied customers. When supply dealers recommend your lures or books, its a home run and always worth their cut of the profits.

I've had some great relationships with trapping supply dealers over my career. As a kid, Marvin Mallow was my favorite and I sold him fur, traded fur for supplies and bought supplies from Marvin for years. Mallow was the first dealer to handle my trapping lures. I remember after Jim Churchill's article appeared in *Fur-Fish-Game*, Marvin used to call me famous. Marvin Mallow was a legend in the fur business, I was just too young to know it when I met him and after all the years we dealt and chatted and laughed together, he was a great old friend. Yep, he was a legend—and a hoot!

Another supply dealer I worked closely with after I got to South Dakota was Melvin Fluth. Melvin married his wife Irene in 1952 and she worked in the business the entire time I knew and dealt with Melvin. Back in the mid-1980s, used to fly my plane east, following Interstate 90 for about 100 miles and landing on the road where Melvin's fur shop was located on the outskirts of Bridgewater. Melvin thought I was crazy!

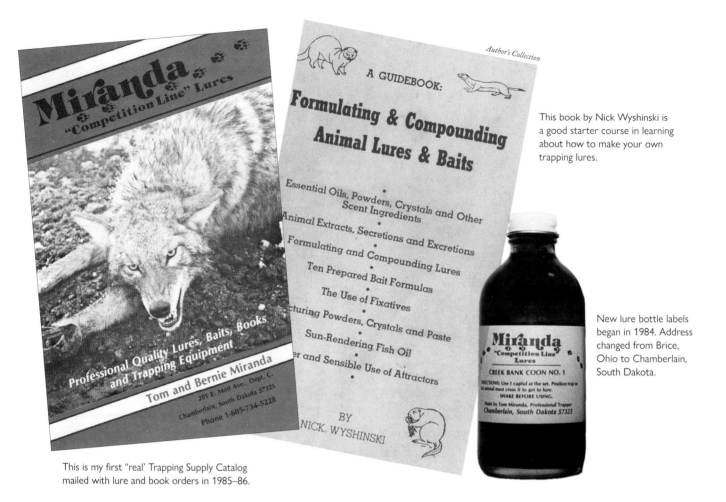

Melvin Fluth and I traveled the convention circuit together after my government trapper days and I spent many hours riding shotgun in his diesel truck as we drove pulling his trailer full of traps, lures and supplies to the trapping conventions. Melvin loved to eat sunflower seeds and would buy a 16-ounce Coke, dump half of it out, then fill the bottle up with salted sunflower seeds in the shell. Then as he drove, he would take a gulp and crack the shells with his teeth, eat the seeds and spit the shells on the floor. His truck was always a mess with sunflower seeds and I always gave him grief about it. Of course it was better than smoking. Melvin was a smart guy, he knew everyone in the trapping business and always gave me good advice. He also loved to come to Chamberlain and go walleye fishing in Lake Francis Case. Melvin Fluth was the real deal. He passed away in 2017 and will be missed by all who knew him.

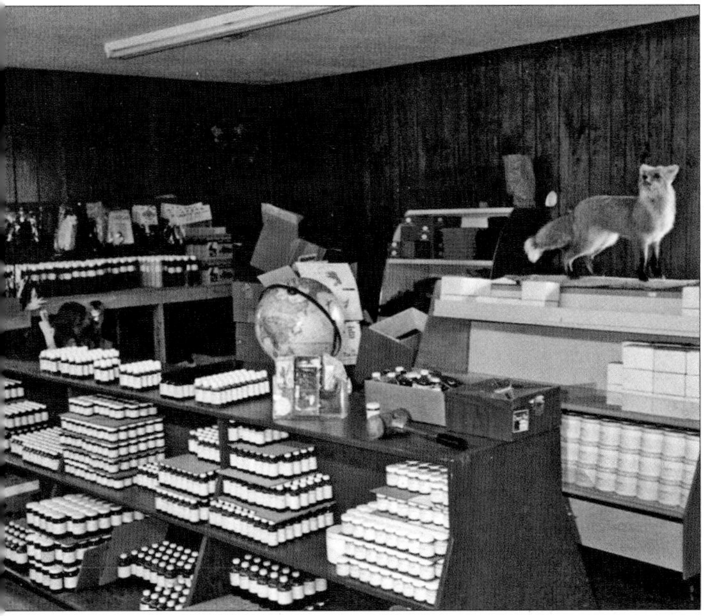

Author's Photo

This is an inside look at my trappers supply shop in Chamberlain, South Dakota- circa 1987.

Russ Carman

1942–

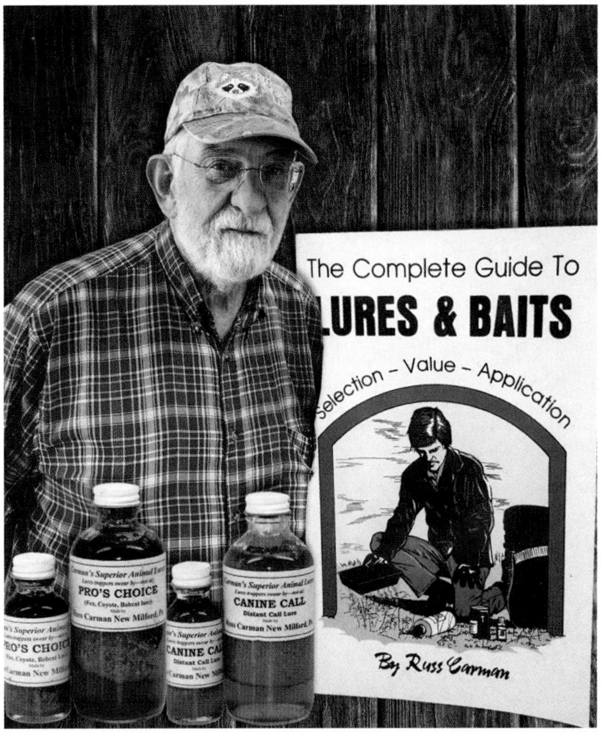

Russ Carman Photo

Russ Carman lure making prowess is a true success story of the "Cottage Industry" trappers.

New Milford, Pennsylvania's Russ Carman has raised the bar when it comes to trapping lures and scents. Wherever his formulas and ingredients came from only Russ knows, but in the fur boom of the late 1970s–early 80s and through today, Russ Carman's lures are held in high esteem and superior to most all of the other lures on the market. Hey, it's just the simple truth. I made and sold thousands of bottles of my Competition Line trapping lures and used them as my number one go-to. But I used other lures as well. Lures made by legends like Hawbaker, Butcher, O'Gorman, Corr, Milligan, Caven and Carman. But I have to say if I didn't have a bottle of Carman's Canine Call or Pro's Choice in my lure bucket—I was on the phone ordering some shipped via FedEx.

Born in 1942, Russ Carman grew up in northeast Pennsylvania. Speaking of his early trapping days Russ jokingly says, "In 1951 caught my first muskrat, I was nine years old and I only caught one that year. I caught 2 'rats total in 1952 so I doubled my catch!" This pretty much sums up Russ Carman, a quick-witted and down-to-earth trapper. By the time Russ was 13 he had begun tinkering with his own lure formulas (yes I said thirteen) and by the time he was 20, Carman has several very successful lures. Russ did many jobs over the years including excavating Pennsylvania Bluestone from a quarry for resale but he always trapped in the winter. Russ was a hardworking family man with a wife and kids to raise and in the early years, he needed the money that his fur catch brought in. But the word was out and trappers were discovering Carman lures. When Russ finally decided to take his lure business full time he was hit with tragedy. In 1975, the second year into his full-scale business, his lure building caught fire and burned to the ground, a total loss. Dejected but no quitter, Russ quickly rebuilt and thank goodness for that. His trapping lures have been the cornerstone of some of the biggest trapline catches across the country. During the trapping "heyday" Russ would put up 300-plus gallons of Carman's Pro's Choice and hire two men to help him bottle it. Think about it.. That's six 50-gallon drums of trapping lure, over 100,000 one ounce bottles. And he would sell out quickly.

Carman is also an expert trapper and has made some fantastic catches. One must keep in mind that during the fur season, the lure business is at its peak and there is always a battle to either execute the trapline to the fullest or to service the trappers ordering lure and supplies. Top lure makers like Russ Carman serviced their loyal customers and dealers.

Russ Carman's Professional Fox Trapping Methods

All lures can be classified into two different groups: (1) Call type lures which can be a food lure, a curiosity lure or a combination of the two. Call type lures typically have a powerful odor, and if made properly, will work with or without bait. A good call lure will make a fox scratch and dig at the set. (2) Natural gland lures can be a straight gland lure made from regular fox glands and urine, or a matrix lure made from glands and urine taken during the mating season. For a lure to be classed as a natural lure, it cannot contain ingredients other than would have a natural fox odor. The only exception would be the matrix lures which usually contain musks, oils or extracts that arouse the sexual instincts of the fox. I should add here that there is no sexual urge in either the male or female fox in the off season. I personally use 80% call lures in my fox sets with out using any additional bait. The remaining 20% of my sets are made with gland lures and bait or post sets using gland lures alone. During the early part of season I use three different lures almost exclusively. The gland lure and two different call lures. Then after a week to ten days I dig in a few new sets along the line with a different lure to take those fox that may have become shy of my other lures. In this was I am offering them something new and different. I will continue to alter my lures throughout the season.

—Russ Carman, 1978

Author's Collection

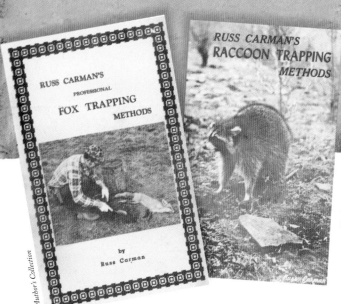

Carman's first two books were *Raccoon Trapping Methods*, 1976 and *Professional Fox Trapping Methods*, 1978.

U.S. FISH AND WILDLIFE SERVICE
LURE EFFECTIVENESS ON COYOTE, 1980

SAMPLE TRAPPERS	TRAPS	BAITED	COYOTE	OTHER	M44	COYOTE
1. MONTANA TRAP*	38	213	93	34	67	22
2. DISTANT CALL**	36	254	89	23	12	1
3. SYNTHETIC EGG	362	55	77	14	1	0

*Lure referred to as Montana Trap was made by Craig O'Gorman—Broadus, Montana
**Lure made by Russ Carman—New Milford, Pennsylvania
Synthetic Egg—Laboratory made synthetic

One little-known fact about Carman's lures is that the U.S. Fish and Wildlife Service did extensive testing on lure effectiveness for coyotes in the late 1970s and published their findings in January 1980. There were six lure formulas tested three were ADC Government Trapper Formulas and three were commercial lures. The top three coyote lures in order 1–Montana Trap made by Craig, O'Gorman 2–Carman's Distant Call. 3–Gov't Formula Synthetic Fermented Egg.

Russ Carman was inducted into the National Trappers Association Trappers Hall of Fame in 1997.

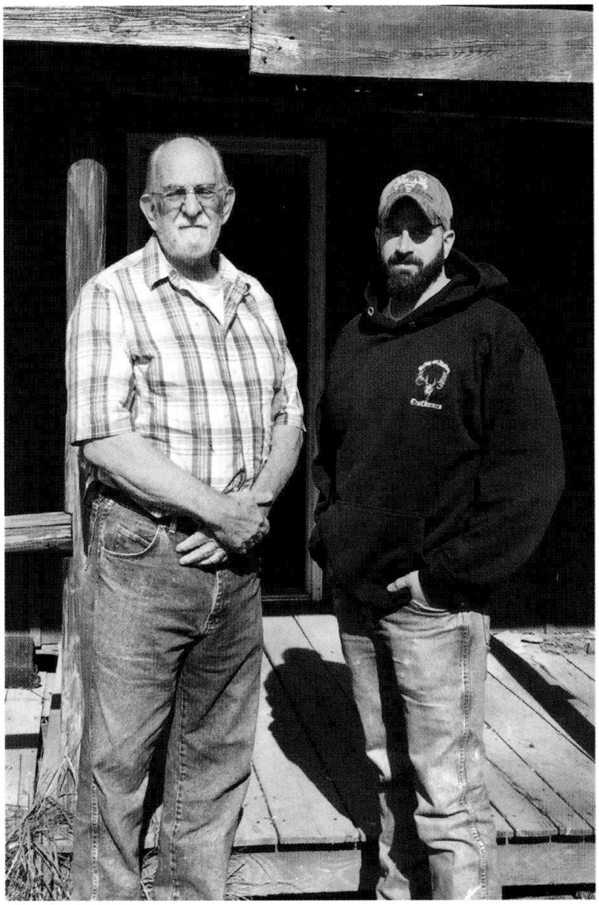

Frank Padula Photo

Russ Carman often greets visitors at his lure shop. Here Pennsylvania trapper Frank Padula gets a photo with the legendary lure maker.

The home offices of Fur-Fish-Game Magazine 2878 East Main Street Columbus, Ohio 43209.

KEITH WINKLER STERLING FUR COMPANY

1956–

Keith Winkler Photo

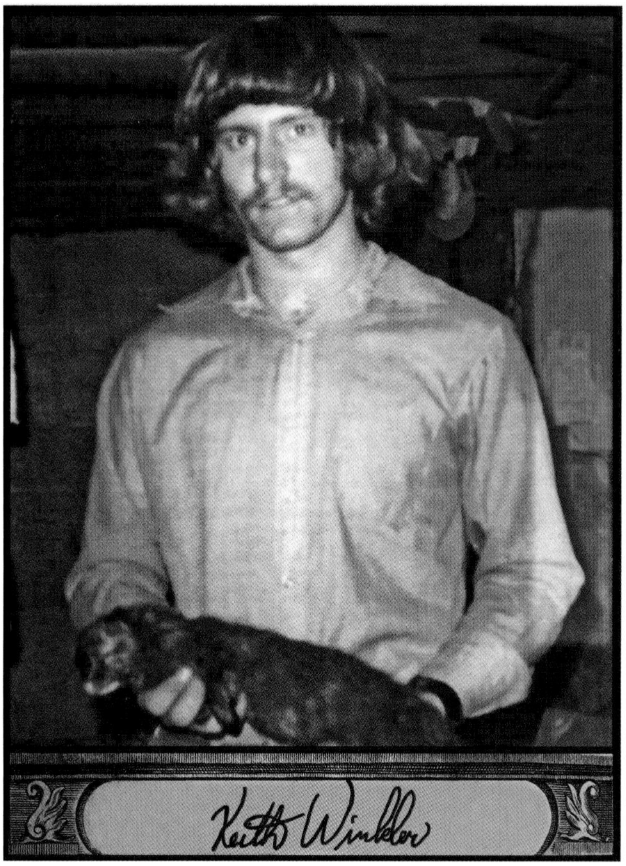

When I think of people in the trapping industry who truly made a mark with sheer ambition and drive, Ohio entrepreneur Keith Winkler quickly comes to mind. Where some may have gazed upon young Winkler at a trappers convention in the fur boom year of 1981 and thought he must have come from money—the true story is that Keith Winkler is self-made—a hardworking man with a passion for the trapping industry and a strong faith in God. Keith's Company Sterling Fur has outlasted most late 1970s trapping enterprises and continues to innovate today.

Keith Winkler grew up on a farm in Sterling, Ohio catching his first muskrats in 1966 along the muddy banks of a creek near his home. At 10 years old there was plenty to do around the farm, like cows to milk, chickens to feed, eggs to collect plus the normal chores of making your bed and taking out the trash. But Keith managed to keep it all going and run his trapline as well. Keith tells a story about an animal raiding the cow barn and his father buying a few traps. The animal was soon caught, a large black mink which had escaped from a mink ranch in the area. This mink led to buying more traps and more trapping. Keith was a tall, strong farm boy and the high school coaches were constantly after him do participate in athletics. Keith played football his junior year, and tried some wrestling but the trapline was calling. If you can imaging driving down a road and seeing a six-foot-tall, 16 year old standing by an orange Volkswagen Super Beetle in hip-boots with a raccoon in each hand, well that's Keith Winkler's senior photo.

Winkler took Ag Mechanics vocational classes while in school and quickly earned a job jockeying behind the parts counter at the local Massey Ferguson Implement Dealer. The pay was $1.65 an hour, however muskrats were $2.50 and Keith didn't need to be a college grad to see the difference. By 1977 Keith had started buying fur out of a small, unused building he and his father remodeled on the family farm. His new business would be called Sterling Fur and Tool Company. It was the perfect time to get into the

Here's the Sterling Fur antique trap room under construction with some of Keith's fantastic bear trap collection.

Keith Winkler Photo

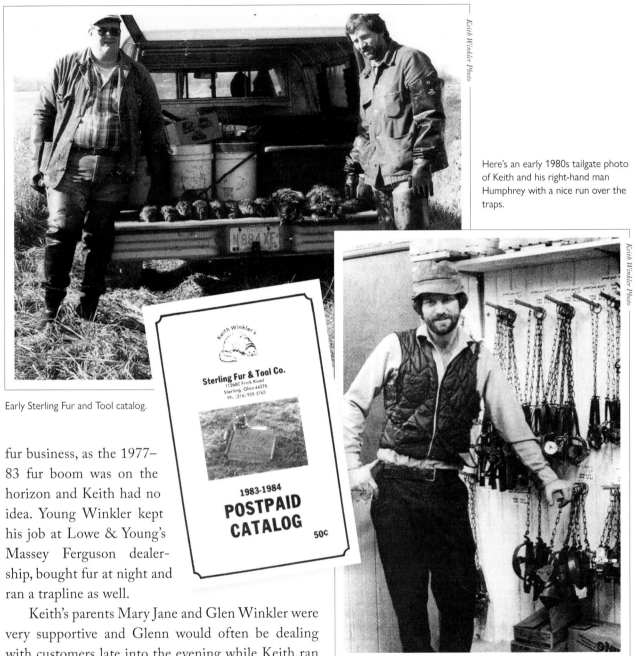

Here's an early 1980s tailgate photo of Keith and his right-hand man Humphrey with a nice run over the traps.

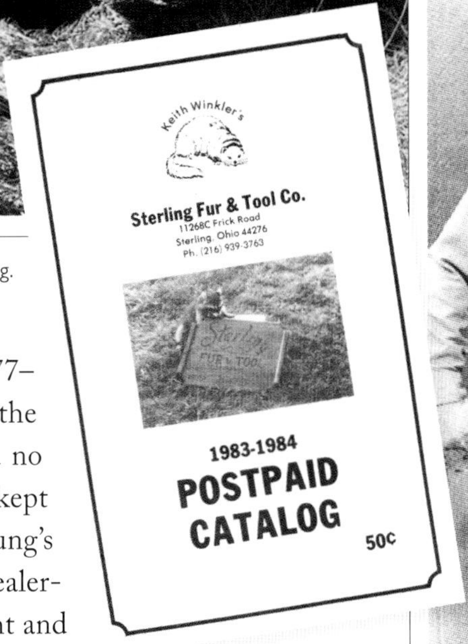

Early Sterling Fur and Tool catalog.

Keith Winkler Photo

Keith Winkler poses with traps in his original Sterling Fur and Tool Building, circa 1980.

fur business, as the 1977–83 fur boom was on the horizon and Keith had no idea. Young Winkler kept his job at Lowe & Young's Massey Ferguson dealership, bought fur at night and ran a trapline as well.

Keith's parents Mary Jane and Glen Winkler were very supportive and Glenn would often be dealing with customers late into the evening while Keith ran his traps. In 1978 Keith started selling trapping supplies he was able to buy at dealer prices from Midwestern fur buying legends Marvin Mallow and John Eby. Keith learned much from them as well as Indiana fur buyer Robert Phares. In fact, Keith gives Phares credit for teaching him the art of fur grading. Of course buying fur and selling fur for a profit is two totally different things. Keith talks about his first big fur buying purchase,"I bought 400 raccoons early in my career–it was a huge deal. I was driving a Chevy Nova at the time and it was all I could do to get the 'coon in the car. I immediately drove to New York to sell them and turn a profit. Upon arriving in New York, I was offered 25 cents less per pelt than I paid, no negotiation. So I lost $100, plus the time, gas money and risk. It was a huge lesson because it could have been much worse."

By 1981, Sterling fur and Tool Company was thriving to the point that Keith left the parts counter. He would take Sterling Fur and Tool on the road to the trappers conventions. With an outgoing personality, Winkler quickly made friends with other dealers in the industry. One person in particular was Minnesota trapper and supply dealer Tim Caven. They met at the National Trappers Convention held in Mason City, Iowa that year, and have become lifelong friends. There were other dealers at the convention, Iowa's Ludy Sheda, Ed Molnar's Northern Sport and Fur and others. Keith saw promise in networking with these companies and they with him. As an example in 1982, Keith and Ed Molnar started Chippewa Fur Company and both bought fur under that name until the early nineties when pelt prices were so low it wasn't profitable.

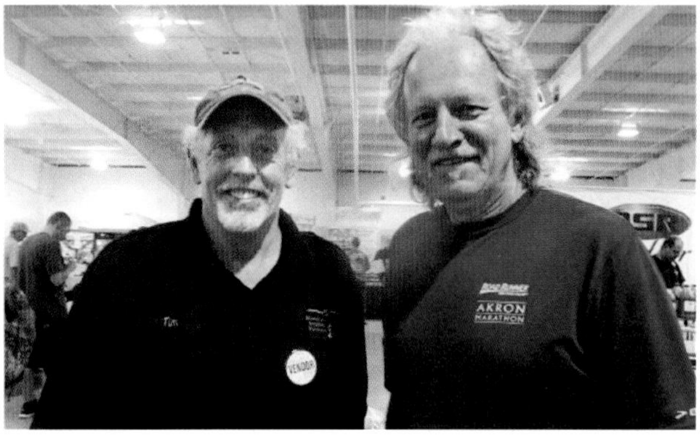

Author's Photo

Ohio's Keith Winkler and Minnesota's Tim Caven, two icon's of the trap supply business.

In the trapping industry, oftentimes the businesses are small operations making unique products. Keith, having built a huge network with other dealers, would take opportunities to expand his base both in manufacturing as well as ownership. A prime example is Necina fur company. Ron Necina sold his business to Keith in 1990. What many didn't know was Ron made a unique raccoon lure called Ultimate Raccoon Lure. Keith took it over and Sterling Fur has been the maker and distributor of Necina's Ultimate Raccoon lure ever since.

As some of the older supply dealers and pro trappers passed away or got out of business, Keith was quick to ante up and take over the reigns and rights of many books and lure formulas. This allowed these entities to continue. Many historic trappers, like Vaughn Tingley and his Northland Supply Company and legendary books, Ken Smythe's Bottom Edge Mink materials, Ken Elridge and his Maine pack baskets which Sterling Fur Company now makes under the Sterling name. Also, Nick Wyshinski's books, Berkshire stakes and swivels, Jim Helfrich and Don Nicely Books and lures, Andy Stoe's Speed Dip and Coverhulls, Necker fleshing knives, and the historic FC Taylor Fur Company. Keith also owns the Hawbaker legacy books and lures as well as Russ Carman's lure line, although Russ still formulates and blends and ages the lures personally in his Pennsylvania lure shop.

Keith believes he owes a lot to his success in the early years to his parents Mary Jane & Glenn. In the beginning both were very much supportive with his new business and both helped him in the shop and on the convention circuit. When Keith's father Glenn retired from farming in 1987, he started working full-time in the business. As the business grew, farm buildings went from housing cattle and tractors to traps and supplies. The family farm became the full-blown entity that is now Sterling Fur Company.

Keith's first love is trapping but he met the lovely Regina Boltz at a Christmas church event in 1990 and the couple married in June of 1991. Their first daughter Abigail was born in April of 1992 and second daughter Aliza Rose in August of 1994. The entire Winkler family would be trappers and eventually work in the family trapping business in some shape or form.

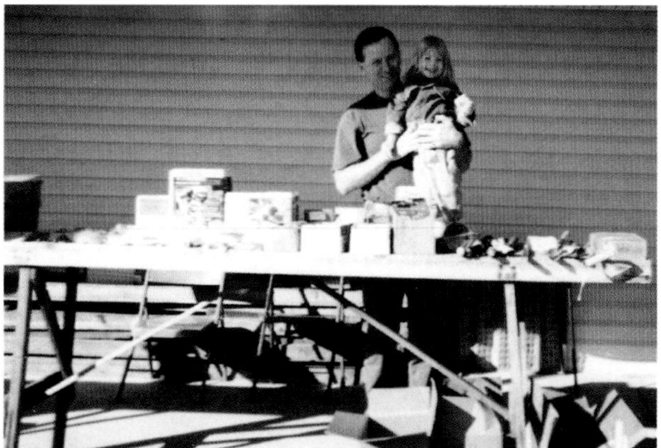

Keith Winkler Photo

Keith poses with his first daughter Abigail on the convention circuit, 1995.

Keith Winkler Photo

Keith presents Neil Olson with an award for promoting trapping at the New England Trappers Weekend for 39 years and counting. 2015.

Trappers World Magazine

"During the 1980s there was the Woodstream Victor Trap Company that bought the Northwoods Trap Company. Montgomery Trap Company was aggressively making and distributing their round jaw traps. The Pioneer Trap Company was on the way out and Bridger Trap Company was gearing up. Butera (BMI) was introducing their new line of coil spring traps. Blake and Lamb Trap Company was in the process of going out of business. The Duke Trap Company was coming on strong.

Also in the 1980s there were countless numbers of dealers, such as Necina Fur Company of Ohio, Marvin Mallow Fur Company of Ohio, P&B Fur Company of Ohio, Sheda Fur Company of Iowa, Sandstone Fur Company of Ohio, Lynder Fur Company of Illinois, Northwest Fur Company of Pennsylvania, Mowatt Fur Company of Maine and Ed Bauer Fur Company of Illinois, plus there were many more in business at this time. However the ones I just mentioned were all large dealers operating in the 1980s and all went out of business in the late 1980s or early 1990s."

—Keith Winkler 2009

In the mid-90s, the fur market had bottomed out. Keith had done well for himself but to this point his life had been 100% Sterling Fur Company. Wanting to get back into shape, Keith started jogging. He had always liked running, but had gotten away from it because of business. Soon Keith was running—and soon running marathons. By 1998, Winkler decided to take a weightlifting class at a local college. Looking into it more he decided to actually try and go back to school and get a degree. Keith enrolled at Wayne College, affiliated with Akron University. Here he quickly learned he needed some high school courses to freshen up his memory. For many, the thought of having to take refresher courses just to get into college would be too much, but Keith Winkler a quitter—"Fah gettah bout it." Keith knuckled down with some calculus tutoring and a few late-night study sessions and by 2003 he not only had his Bachelors degree from Malone University of Canton, but finished strong with an MBA from Tiffin University at the ripe old age of 47. Not too shabby.

Keith's father Glenn passed away in 2010 after a lengthy illness. It was a tough go for Keith, as he and his father were close. Yet it's an event we all must face in our lives and the strength of religious faith is what gets

Authors Photo

Here's Winkler and Tom at the 2019 National Trappers Convention in Springfield, Missouri.

one through it. Keith was raised in a faith-based family and has carried his faith forward, now more than ever.

Keith has continued to expand his Sterling Fur base by acquiring additional companies and working to keep the history of the fur business and trapping alive. Keith bought *Trappers World* magazine" with Tom Parr and Kyle Kaatz only to facilitate the sale then stepped out of it. Keith met Tom Parr in the antique trap collectors, world and knew he was the perfect fit as a historian of trapping to take over the magazine from the retiring owner, Virginia trapper Don Shumaker. Keith himself has a wonderful antique trap collection.

Keith Winkler was one dealer who had faith in the value of my trapping books, scents and videos. His salesmanship and honest approach to business allowed my brand to grow early in my career. It was a time when many trappers were pushing to make their mark in the business. Sterling Fur Company was a huge asset for me in those days and Keith's business savvy has stood the test of time making him an iconic supply dealer and fur buyer in the trapping industry. Like so many of the trapping legends mentioned in this book, Keith Winkler's trapping legacy will long outlast his days on planet earth.

PAUL GRIMSHAW

1941–2020

Paul Grimshaw is another icon of the Adirondacks. His story is one of a young boy growing up on a vegetable farm with his parents selling popcorn and raising chickens for the eggs. As a teenager, Paul saw a *Fur-Fish-Game* magazine and discovering trapping first doing it as a pastime, and then as his passion. Paul was a special person in my career as I bought many lure-making ingredients from Paul throughout the late 70s, 80s and early 90s. Paul was always available to help, answer questions and his service impeccable.

Paul Grimshaw Photo

Paul Grimshaw poses early in his career with a nice catch of muskrat.

Grimshaw was mentored by both E.J. Dailey and O.L. Butcher. I'm sure being in their presence and gleaning the years of knowledge gave Paul the confidence to build his own brand—and that he did. Like many trappers, Paul had a job; he delivered bottled gas for a hardware shop. Marrying Bernice Garrand in December 1962, Paul started a fishing bait, worms and minnow business which his wife Bernice took care of while he did the bottle gas deliveries. Paul started buying fur and selling outdoor supplies out of his house and soon decided to make a full-time go at the trapping business. Paul and Bernice rented a small storefront in 1965 and went to work. Grimshaw mailed his first catalog for the 1966–67 season and received more money in his first customer orders than he made in a week at the hardware store. He was off and running.

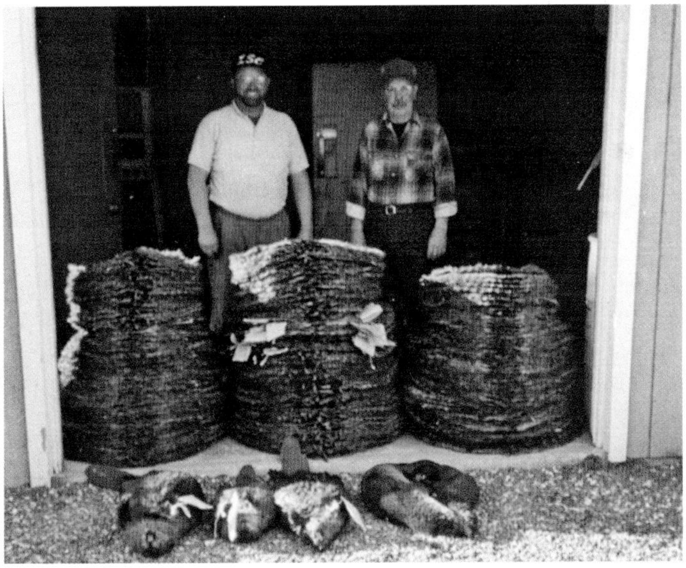

Paul Grimshaw Photo

Maine trapper Neil Olson (left) with Paul Grimshaw and a nice catch of prime and well "put up" beaver.

Paul Grimshaw operated in the heart of the old French fur traders region of the St. Lawerence River, Richelieu River and Lake Champlain. Where many trappers in this region went into the Adirondacks to trap foxes, martens and fisher, Paul specialized in the water dwelling fur-bearers, muskrats, mink, beavers and otters. These species were abundant and made sense to trap as Paul had a great market through his business for the valuable lure ingredients these animals supply. All lure makers use muskrat and mink glands in formulations. Beaver castor and oil are also valuable in lure making as well as the perfume trade.

Taking over 1,700 muskrats on a thirty-day line was one of the highlights of Paul's trapping career. Paul Grimshaw also couldn't resist the lure of the Adirondacks and ran lines into the mountains for predators and forest species. He also loved catching fisher. Of course what trapper wouldn't want to catch prime Adirondack fisher when in the late 1970's fur boom were worth well over $100 dollars.

Paul was good friends with Maine trapper Neil Olson and ran a line with Neil for 20 years. Neil Olson is a top trapper in his own right. In fact Neil was interviewed at his 43rd New England Trappers weekend in 2019 and read from his "trapping diary" that in his career he had harvested over 13,000 beavers, 700 river otters, 1,000 raccoons, 3,600 foxes, 1,600 coyote, plus numerous fisher, mink and other fur-bearers. Quite a career. Paul Grimshaw had a knack for hanging with top trappers. Paul passed away during the writing of this book and he will be early missed.

"The fur boom of the late 1970s was a wonderful time to be alive. We worked like hell, but it was great. I would trap during the day while Bernie ran the store and shipped mail orders. When I got home, people were waiting to sell fur. I barely had time to eat supper and unload my catch. We had one local boy working full-time skinning and scraping my catch and the raw furs I bought from trappers, and we had another boy doing the same part-time. Most nights we didn't leave the store until ten or eleven o'clock at night, and we had to get up early the next day to start all over again. During that time, we spent the summers traveling to several trappers conventions as dealers. We had a truck with a cap on it, and we packed it to the rafters. It was an effective way to meet other dealers and trappers. I was able to pick up some tips and get my name out. For many years, we had conventions — week after week. We would no sooner get home and unpack and we had to replenish the stock, pack and head out again."

—Paul Grimshaw 1995

Paul Grimshaw Photo

TIM CAVEN MINNESOTA TRAPLINE PRODUCTS

1958–

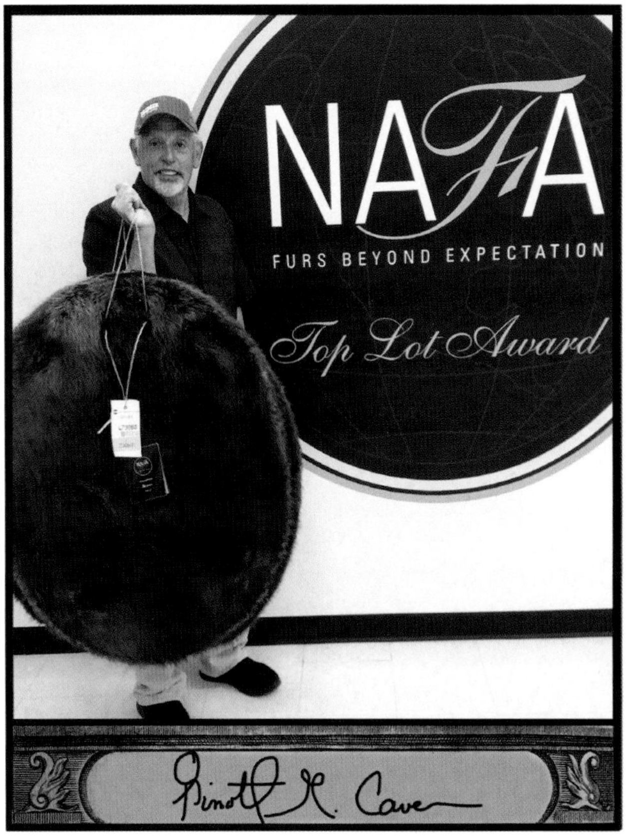

Minnesota's Tim Caven is a trapper's trapper. He grew up trapping, has run long-lines in several states and has the trapping skills most reading this book aspire to. His Caven Lures and Baits are top sellers in the industry, original formulas gleaned from miles of traplines and used by many of the best trappers in the United States and around the world. Tim's business savvy is second to none—his creed is to never let the customer down, to always over deliver. Tim gets his supply orders out the door faster than Dominos Pizza. Besides that—he's a great guy, fun to be around and about as sincere a gentleman as you would want to meet. Oh, and this wife Nancy is even better at all of this, *plus* she is the boss. Tim's close friends don't call him "Pellet Head" for nothing. Wait—you haven't heard of Pellet Head? Well this is his story.

Tim Caven was born in southwestern Minnesota in the small town of Sleepy Eye. Yes, one of those Laura Ingalls Wilder towns like Walnut Grove or De Smet, South Dakota. Raised on a farm in a loving, strict, faithful family, Tim's work ethic and faith were engrained at a young age. But a young Tim Caven still managed to get into mischief, his mother Dorothy pulling frogs, bugs, and shiny rocks from his pants pockets on a daily basis. Speaking of pockets, pocket gophers are a nuisance in southwestern Minnesota and by age 6, Tim was trapping them for bounty. At age 10, he made the jump to muskrats and the occasional raccoon or mink. By the time he reached 13, Tim had gotten his hands on two #3 Victor jump traps and he was ready to try his luck at beaver trapping. After catching his first flat tail and having to deal with it alive in the trap, Tim was ready for more water trapping. A stash of *Fur-Fish-Game* magazines hidden in the hay barn was a constant distraction from daily farm chores. Tim said it took many hours for him and his Dad to get the first beaver stretched into a shape that is still not recognized in any geometry book.

At age 15, Tim got his farm driver's permit and became obsessed with fox trapping. Now instead of his bike, he had four wheels and put on a lot of miles that first fox season but never caught a single fox. Needing advice, Tim talked with a local trapper who told him that foxes were very smart and would flip the trap upside down. So the best method was to set your trap upside down to fool them. Tim tried it on some of his sets. Reflecting back, Tim says he wasn't the brightest tool in the shed in those days. But seriously, Tim got it right and finally caught his first red fox and two gray foxes one late October morning. By the season's end in 1974 he had 40 foxes. At age 17 Tim broke the 100 mark and at age 18 took 200-plus foxes. Young Tim Caven had figured out the recipe. Hard work and long miles. Tim had a love for handling fur from a young age and worked for a local fur dealer part-time during his high school years honing his skills for the future.

After high school graduation in 1976, Tim moved north to Brainerd, and entered a 21-month intense natural resource program. It was while trapping in the fall in northern Minnesota, that he learned about coyotes

Tim Caven Photo

Tim poses with a fantastic day's catch of flat-tails.

and how totally inadequate his equipment was. While he caught and held some coyotes, the big dawgs often pulled out or pulled the jaws apart on his stock traps and escaped. The trap modifications which came in the late 1970s from forward-thinkers like Glen Sterling, J.C. Conner and Charles Dobbins allowed trappers to catch and hold these brush wolves of the north. Trap modifications such as baseplates, jaw lamination, and swivels became available to modify existing fox traps into acceptable quality coyote equipment.

Tim Caven Photo

New Mexico outfitter Ray Milligan and Tim pose with Caven's bow bull elk taken in southern Colorado.

Tim took three months off of school in 1977 to hire on with the Bureau of Land Management and was assigned to a project to catch wild horses near Rock Springs, Wyoming. Tim's adventure into the Red Desert will never be forgotten. By fall in 1977, Tim was back in northern Minnesota and better positioned to trap coyotes, bobcats, and fisher. Fur prices were good and Tim paid for his education, bought a brand new truck and 25 dozen new traps with his fur check that year. In the spring of 1978 in

Rob Caven following in his father's footsteps with great catch from the Bob Young / Caven Georgia trapline.

Tim Caven Photos

search of more adventure, Tim landed in an elite Helitack crew. Helitack is a team of wildfire fighters who utilize choppers to get into remote areas quickly to access hot spots and assess wildfires. Flying into remote fire locations in Sikorsky helicopters piloted by military veteran Bell UH-1 "Huey" pilots was never dull. Tim says, "It seemed these pilots lived to keep our hearts in our throats!" At 20 years old Tim Caven was enjoying his dream as the life of an outdoorsman, living in a tent on the shores of a lake fishing every night after work.

After the 1978 fire season Tim was approached by the owners of a fur company that were looking for a manager for the new facility that they were building along the Mississippi River in southeastern Minnesota. By late October, Tim was hiring a crew and gearing up as one of the lead buyers for Minnesota Hide and Fur. Tim soon began buying fur, processing pelts and traveling in search of prime collections of fur. It was a great job and learning experience. Tim not only bought collections, but was selling fur to big name German and Italian furriers that would come into the fur shop on a weekly basis. Tim was learning the fur business during the heyday from many of the top fur buyers of the 70s including Eddie Bauer, Max Belt, Tom Wiebke, Grant Groenewold, John Johnson, Ludy Sheda and others.

Trappers and hunters selling hides are often looking for supplies, but Minnesota Hide and Fur owners had no interest in trapping supplies or the headache of inventory. So when Tim inquired about possibly selling a few supplies, the owners said, "If you wanna sell supplies, go for it. Just don't let it get in the way of the fur buying." Tim had little capital but wanted to give the trap supply business a fair shot so he started off by selling 300 of his used fox traps and his truck. Tim repurposed the funds to buy a variety of trapping supplies for resale. These early transactions were the beginning of Tim's education in the trapping supply business. In February and March of 1979 when Tim was all of 21 years old, he was hired by a New York fur dealer to travel the western states to buy fur on a 2% commission. He would attend the Rocky Mountain Fur Exchange auctions in Montana and then work his way south to Texas. Tim mentions a story in which he bought fur from a trapper who was also the chief of police of a western town. Because of the value of all the fur and the possibility of being robbed, the police chief allowed Tim to store the pelts in the town jail and bunk in with his hoard. Over the next few years, Tim spent quite a few nights in small town jails guarding his valuable fur purchases.

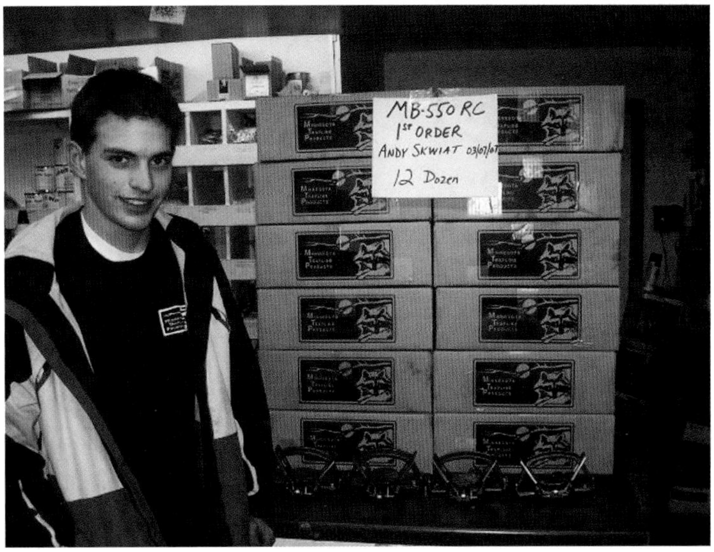

Tim Caven Photo

Rob Caven is head of operations at Minnesota Brand Trap Company.

Tim was working for the Minnesota Department of Natural Resources in the summer of 1979 where he met his wife to be. Nancy was on the tree planting crew and was soon to be promoted to a fire spotter. The summer of 1979 was tough season for wildfires and Tim got called into a bad fire in the mountains of Idaho. The Salmon River Fire, a hellish wildfire in the remote, rugged Idaho wilderness—was burning out of control. Tim dropped in with the crew and while fighting the fire in heavy smoke, Tim slipped and fell down an avalanche chute. Rescued by the crew and evacuated by chopper, Tim found himself at the hospital in Boise and on the national news. Of course Nancy was watching back in Minnesota with her parents. Tim was patched up and soon back in Minnesota. Nancy and Tim were becoming soul mates and for some reason, helicopters seemed to always be in the mix. But Tim says, "This is another story."

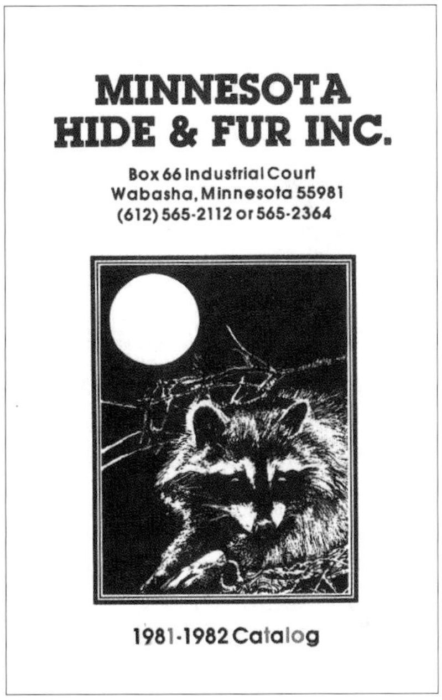

Tim Caven's first trapping supply catalog.

Three days before the start of the 1979 fall trapping season, a young man named Barry Meurer walked into Tim's shop with a proposition. Barry had suffered through a tough bout of bone cancer and at the age of 19 had one of his legs amputated. He had been trying to catch a fox for two years with no luck and had very few traps. What he had to offer was land—in fact more private land permissions than any one trapper could handle. As Barry said, "Who's going to turn down a guy who hops up to the door on one leg and asks to trap skunks?" Tim and Barry worked together the next three days to get their traps and gear in order. They caught 11 foxes the first run, 19 the second, and 20 the third. Needless to say, Tim and Barry made a great team. Tim trapped with Barry four seasons. Barry passed away six weeks before they were to enjoy their fifth trapping season together. Caven is still touched to this day by this young man's heart and attitude. "Many days Barry was so sick from chemotherapy that he needed to lie down in the trapping rig. But whenever we caught a fox, Barry was the first one out of the truck."

Author's Photo

Nancy and Tim Caven are not only business associates, but some of my best trapping pals on the planet. 2019 NTA Convention, Springfield, Missouri.

Tim sent out his first trapping supply catalog in 1981–82. Tim told me he sent out too many catalogs as he spent almost all of the money he could borrow on the catalog and postage and didn't have money enough to buy traps and supply inventory. The Minnesota Trappers Association convention of 1980 was the first of many great conventions at which Tim sold supplies. And if records are correct, he is the only supply dealer at that convention that is still alive today. The following August was Tim's first National Trappers Convention held at Marshalltown, Iowa and it was here where Tim met lifelong friends Keith Winkler and Ray Milligan. Caven recalls Ray Milligan coming up to him and introducing himself and stating that he had 3 lures—Steppenwolfe I, Steppenwolfe II and Coon Creek. Milligan went on to explain that the dealer price was $21 a dozen and that Tim would buy a dozen of each for a total of $63. When Caven asked Milligan how he knew that, Ray explained that he was broke and needed 60 bucks for gas money to get home! Tim scraped up the money and bought Ray's 36 bottles of lure. It was one of the best investments of Tim's early years as Ray Milligan and Tim have become lifelong friends.

In the 1980s Tim was often on the road at conventions trying to build and promote his Minnesota Trapline Products supply business, oftentimes, finishing a western state convention on a Sunday and being set up in New York or Pennsylvania the following Friday. "The early days were often a tough go," says Caven. "But they were fulfilling with friendships and memories that have lasted the past 40-plus years."

In 1983 Tim moved his fur buying and supply business from Wabasha, Minnesota 200 miles northwest to Pennock, MN. This put him back just north of where he grew up and in the thick of the red fox population at the time. Tim and Nancy were married in August of 1983. Nancy was a nurse at a local hospital but after work and on weekends she was highly involved in the business both answering the phone and packing orders. After daughter Erin was born, Nancy joined the business on a full-time basis and their final safety net of a salary was gone but they had their own home—albeit a rundown trailer house with polyester curtains and a redwood deck. Daughter Erin was born in 1985, sons Robert in 1989 and Samuel in 1991. Growing up in the business, all the kids helped out after homework was complete and always pitched in when needed. They started out putting tops on lure and urine bottles and worked their way up the ranks the hard way. Daughter Erin received a college degree in accounting after high school and has been the head of advertising, website development, and accounts receivable at Minnesota Trapline Products for the past 15 years. The Caven's youngest son Samuel lives in North Dakota and is in the construction business. He is a very talented designer, commercial and residential builder. He hit North Dakota at the perfect time and

Tim Caven Photo

Tim with a great catch of bobcats.

The first two Minnesota Trapline Supply Catalogs.

paid for much of his engineering college tuition with his muskrat catch.

Minnesota Trapline started manufacturing traps and hardware in 1994, working with Tim Sawatzky of Control Specialty Products and Lyle Bengtson of LFS Tool and Die Company, both of whom live near Caven's shop. In the beginning, the Minnesota Brand (MB) Trap Company had its share of aches and pains with suppliers as well as finding help and keeping quality control at a level that Tim expected. There were spring issues, pan issues and a whole host of hurdles to reconcile to make the system work. Today Minnesota Brand has evolved to be the Cadillac trap for most trappers operating long fur lines or doing Animal Damage Control. Minnesota Brand makes 4 different coil spring trap sizes and a body gripper. The coil spring MB450 for fox, MB550 fox/coyote combo, MB650 coyote and MB750 beaver/wolf. Some models come in multiple configurations like cast jaw and four coil. The MB-1216 Megabear body grip trap is for beaver and otter.

In 1996 I talked to Tim about him becoming my master distributor for all the Tom Miranda trapping DVDs, books and trapping scents. When my TV series began airing on ESPN in 1992, my full focus was ESPN and those TV episodes. Leveraged for time, I was struggling to to keep up with the trapping business side of things. Mark June agreed to take over distribution of my products in 1993 but he was also working a full-time job as a pharmaceutical salesman and trying to break big into the lure business in his own right. By 1996 it was too much for Mark and his wife Pat. Tim Caven and I hammered out an arrangement and in early 1997 I took all my remaining inventory from Swartz Creek, Michigan to Pennock, Minnesota and Minnesota Trapline Products. Tim and Nancy have both been stand-up partners in our joint venture which still exists today.

As the year Y2K rolled in, the month of May suddenly became somewhat of a jinx on the Caven family. In May 2000 the roof literally "fell in" on their

Tim and Nancy Caven, Minnesota Trapline Products.

major storage building. In May 2001, a tornado hit their house. In May 2002 the Caven's main warehouse burned to the ground. And in May 2003, Tim was shot in the head, neck and chest with No. 5 turkey shot pellets. No, I'm not kidding.

Tim was on a spring turkey hunt in southeastern Minnesota when the accident happened. Also on the hunt was family friend, Matt Schultz who was also the local chief of police. Immediately after the tragic gunshot accident, Matt jumped into action. Quick thinking and rapid response had Tim in a Medi-Vac chopper headed to the nearby and world-famous Mayo Clinic. Tim was immediately rushed into surgery in critical condition with brain surgery the end result. The quick thinking of Matt Schultz and world-class medical attention of the Mayo Clinic saved Tim's life. Tim Caven has had numerous surgeries since and has made a full recovery. Since that horrific day and jokingly—with much love and respect—Tim's nickname has become Pellet Head.

In 2006 Tim and Nancy's oldest son Rob began the development of the MB-550 and MB-450 traps with the assistance of Bob Young (Fox Hollow Lures) of Georgia. Tim and Nancy cosigned a loan for Rob for die costs and stepped out of the way. Rob was still in high school at the time but his parents thought this was a good time to learn how to sink or swim. Rob made his first sale of MB-550 traps in 2007 and first sale of MB-450 traps the following year. When many high school kids were enjoying their free time, Rob Caven was building and developing traps. In October of 2009 Tim and Rob traveled to Taiwan along with Terry and Nathan Montgomery of Montgomery Fur Company of Utah to meet the folks at the Bridger Trap Company. The Cavens were extremely impressed with the company's willingness to listen and to work on new ideas and upgrades. In January of 2010, Minnesota Trapline Products purchased the Bridger Trap Company from Montgomery Fur. Rob Caven had two of the Bridger family come and live with him and work at his shop in order to have a better understanding of the quality of work that was required and expected. Tim made it clear to Rob in 2009 that "One 17-hour flight to Taiwan was enough! And all things Bridger are your's Rob—period!"

Tim and Nancy continue to give back to the industry that has been their lives. You will always see their names as donors for any fundraiser having to do with trapping or fur. Tim continues to work with tanned fur on a daily basis—it is his first love outside of his family. He still attends the Canadian Fur auctions buying large amounts of fur for tanning and resale. He believes it is his responsibility as a member of the fur trade to promote what we produce.

In 2017 Nancy was diagnosed with cancer. Cancer comes in many forms and none are good. Nancy has had a tough go but she stayed strong and battled through fifteen grueling months of chemotherapy and radiation. At the time of this writing, Nancy says "There are good days and bad days, but at least there are days!"

Tim and Nancy Caven have ridden the ups and downs of the trapping industry for forty two years. They've survived the good times and the bad, the high points and tragedies. Raised three children to adults and done a damned good job. They've worked their fingers to the bone, and made their mark doing what they love. They also have interesting stories to share with their grandchildren—like back in the late 70s, Tim and Nancy would deliver fur to downtown Minneapolis after dark. Fur was worth a lot of money and robbery was always some concern. Guns for protection was part of the equation. Nancy would stand guard with the firearm while Tim loaded the bales of fur in the freight elevator. Tim says jokingly, "Grandma was packin' heat."

Tim has seen many come and go in the industry—"I've been blessed to work with most everyone in the trapping industry from the trappers, to the supply dealers and the fur buyers. There has been a bumpy road or two along the way, but overall I wouldn't change a thing. I will say that I do greatly miss Charlie Dobbins and Pete Leggett. Both were smart trappers and both as kind of gentleman as you could ever meet. Glen Sterling Sr. who recently passed was a trap building genius and way ahead of his time. I'd like to give a shout out to J.C. Conner, Mike Marsyada, Asa Lenon, and Bob Young as well. All are fantastic friends and have been mentors over the years."

While Tim Caven still enjoys some hard trapping and making a good catch, Tim says his trapping has come full circle. "Today a great day on the trapline is checking pocket gopher traps with 2-year-old grandson Wade. Oh—and putting things in Wade's pockets for his mother to find!" Yes, it seems that Tim Caven's life has definitely come full circle.

Trappers World Magazine

"To my parents Gene and Dorothy who had to do my chores at home for me when I didn't quite get back from checking traps when I said I would. For never discouraging me although it must have been hard not to when money was tight and I was using up more gas then I was getting for my fur. Thank you for the endless hours that you spent with me the spring and summer of 1976 stretching beaver. I think I'd still be at it if you hadn't helped. And most of all thank you for showing me how to treat people by the example you set, it has served me well.

To Nancy's folks Robert and Mary Newton, thank you for taking a chance on me. It had to look like a long shot betting on me the way I moved around and didn't have a "real" job. I told you I loved your daughter. That will never change and I will never let you down."

—Tim Caven, 2004

AIRPLANE TRAPLINE

My pilot's license was only a couple of months old when BAM! I get a call from my ADC Supervisor. "What's this I hear you now have your own airplane and you are using it for state ADC work?" Suddenly my plane was an issue in my job. Many of the ADC trappers had quads, snow machines, or argos, but a plane—well this was new territory. Supervisor Miller told me he wouldn't stand for any conflict of interest issues. He said you're a government employee, and using an aircraft while on the job was taboo.

I mentioned to him that I was using the plane at my own expense—fuel, insurance, maintenance. It was a 2-hour drive to the opposite corner of my trapline, but 25 minutes by plane. None of that mattered. The directive was clear, no private airplane use while on the job.

Needless to say my days as a government trapper were numbered. I had somewhat stepped over the line, albeit I hadn't intended it to be so. I had met some of the best trappers on the planet while working as a South Dakota state trapper. Guys like Kenny Johnson, Bob Curtis, Steve Thompson, Bob Lundquist, Joe Grimson, Blair Waite and many others whose names

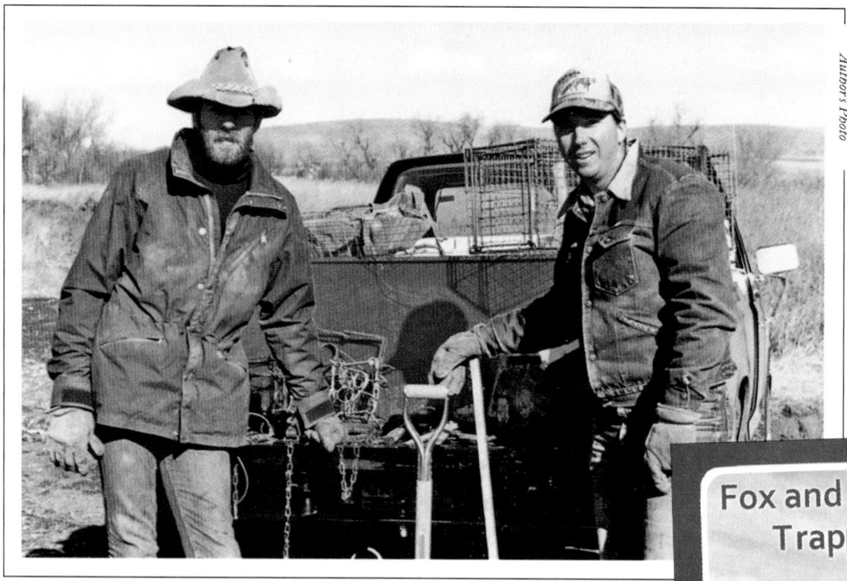

Author's Photo

Jeff Smith and I gearing up to talk "Production Line Water Trapping" on our first video shoot taping the East To West trapping VHS videos, 1985.

have escaped me after all these years. For now I would just buckle down, do my job and use my plane on the weekends, flying to scout my vacation trapline and build hours.

In September 1985 I was back in Indiana at the trappers college. I had taken copies of my "fresh off the press" *Competition Line Fox Trapping* book as a gift to students attending. One of the students was a Virginia trapper, by the name of Jeff Smith, who had recently moved to Montana. Right from the beginning of the college, Jeff befriended me and was interested in talking trapping, especially western trapping. He was a nice guy and it was a great week of trapping. Toward the end of the college, Jeff approached me and asked me point blank, "Why don't you turn your fox trapping book into a video?" Right here, let me say that I never even knew that someone could make a video to sell. Let alone a trapping video. I had just released my first book—and a trapping video was not on the horizon. But the more Jeff talked to me about it, the more sense it made. At the end of the college, Jeff asked if he could stop by my place on his way out to Montana. I was going straight home after the college but Smith was going to Virginia first, then back. I said "Yes, of course—stop by."

I had thought about his proposal the entire drive home. To my knowledge no one had ever done a trapping video before. Of course Craig O'Gorman had done one in 1984 but I didn't know of it at the time. It may have been where Jeff got the idea. When Jeff Smith arrived we sat down to talk. I agreed to do the video. Since we were both from the east and had moved west we would call the company East West Video Productions. The video would be titled *Fox and Coyote Trapping East to West.* The original deal was that we would film the video on my trapline in South Dakota in late October. I would be the host and do most of the sets, but Jeff would be in the video as well. Jeff would pay to have the video produced, I would write the material, do the majority of the instructions, design and print the packaging. We were off and running.

Original Video Sleeves for the *Fox and Coyote Trapping East to West* Instructional and Advanced Methods tapes, 1985.

Jeff brought cameraman Lex Hames from Missoula to do the taping. Lex would also do the editing of the original programs. I wrote the outline, however I had written much more into the scripts than we needed. Each set and explanation takes more time to do live "on camera" and by the third day of taping, we made the decision to make two videos, one as the instructional and one as the advanced program. We shot both videos in 4 days. Jeff suggested that with Lex there we spend another day or two and I would give

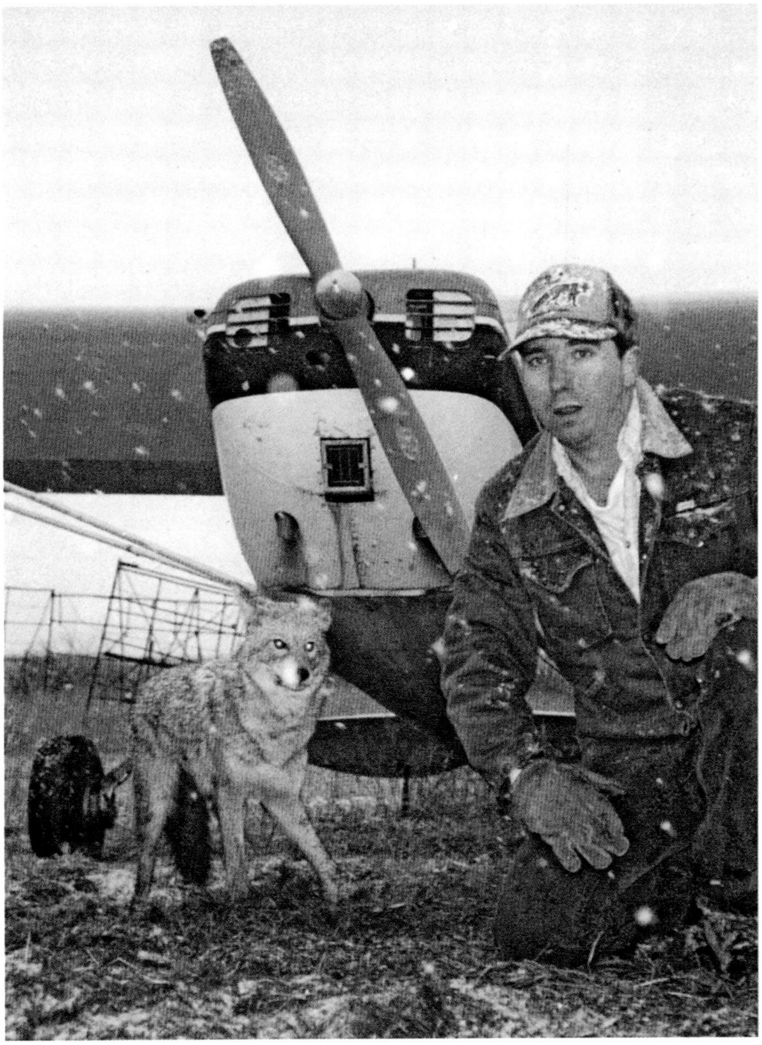

Author's Photo

I ran my traplines with the airplane after leaving my trappers job with South Dakota Game Fish and Parks, circa 1986.

a water trapping course and they would video tape it. He said if the fox and coyote videos go well we can edit and release the water trapping last. I agreed. So we actually made the three original trapping videos in a week's shooting. The editing is more involved, very tedious and it required several months to get the final Fox trapping 1 and 2 videos completed, so advertising and sales really didn't kick off until 1986. Soon after, we also had the water trapping video.

In my opinion, our business model wasn't well thought out, but the videos were a hit. Originally, East-West would own and sell the videos. But after some time I told Jeff that East-West should sell the videos to both of us at a wholesale price and we each could market separately. I was already running full-page ads in *Trapper Magazine*, so it was easy to add the videos into my advertising program. Initially I was worried that the videos would replace my lucrative trapping instruction business. Why would any students come and take my instruction class for $150 a day when they could watch a $50 video and get the lessons? Of course hindsight is 20-20, but I can tell you that in fact I had more student requests after the videos were released. My dealer network was growing, which was awesome as all the dealers took the videos. Looking back now, the video wasn't the best quality. But at this time in the trapping industry the only alternative was Craig O'Gorman's videos. The fact was that the people who watched the videos loved them. The videos were better than a book because the student could see the location and watch the sets being made. In the spring of 1986, I published my second book, *Competition Line Water Trapping*. It was also based on my Ohio line with some Dakota photos and tactics included. I also developed a couple of new lures and baits to add to the new catalog.

My first son Jeremy was born August 1, 1986. I was insistent we named him after Jeremiah Johnson. His birth was a huge deal for me, to the point that on the same day I called my supervisor Alvin Miller and put in my notice to resign from South Dakota Game, Fish, and Parks. SDGFP had been good to me, my best year as an ADC trapper in South Dakota was 1985. I took 212 coyotes that year using traps, snares, getters and calling and much of my area was nuisance beaver and skunk work. I had worked two full years of Animal damage Control, gained my pilot's license and now had a new son. My lure business was growing, I had two books and three trapping video lesson tapes and now needed to commit full-time to making my mark in the industry. It was time to go back out on my own.

OSCAR CRONK 1930–

Oscar Cronk Photo

Oscar Cronk was born in Aroostook County, Maine in 1930. Aroostook borders New Brunswick, Canada, is basically wilderness and is the largest county east of the Mississippi River. Oscar started trapping when he was ten and knew he would always be a trapper. After a stint in the military, Cronk returned to Maine in 1950 and began trapping in earnest. Oscar would dig worms to sell to fishermen in the off season and he raised hounds both to use on the hunt and to train and sell.

Oscar Cronk married his girlfriend Edie in 1960 and the couple as been together ever since. Edie loves the outdoors and was often a trapping partner with Oscar—pulling her own weight and then some. Oscar and Edie took over Wildcat Lynch's trapping lure business in 1961 purchasing Lynch's old formulas from Ed Howe. Oscar also knew famous woodsman and trapper Walter Arnold well and thought he would seek his advice on the lure business. Arnold had made trapping scent since 1918 and knew the ins and outs of lure making. So Oscar traveled north to meet with Walter in the bush and discuss lure making. After some chatting, Arnold offered Cronk his lure business as well.

By the mid 1960s, Oscar Cronk was busy trapping professionally and operating his lure businesses. Oscar's favorite animal to trap is the mink, however he had many seasons taking good numbers of marten, bobcats, fisher, foxes and coyotes.

In 1980, Oscar Cronk wrote his definitive biography about "Wildcat" Lynch and has authored several animal-specific, how-to books as well as a biography on the 'ole "Fox" Pete Rickard.

I met Oscar Cronk at his shop in Wiscasset in the mid 1980s. The Maine Department of Agriculture, Conservation and Forestry invited Dr. Major Boddicker and myself to do snaring instructions for 100 of Maine's top trappers.

Snaring was illegal in Maine but the coyote depredation on deer in their winter "yards" was so bad, they were opening up snaring that winter as a trial in an attempt to control the coyote population and save the deer. Oscar was a great host and the lobster feed we had was amazing. I think Major ate 6 lobsters!

Oscar Cronk was inducted into the Maine Trapper Associations Trappers Hall of fame in 1997. At this writing, Oscar and Edie are still together, active in the trapping business and living their lives in Wiscasset, Maine.

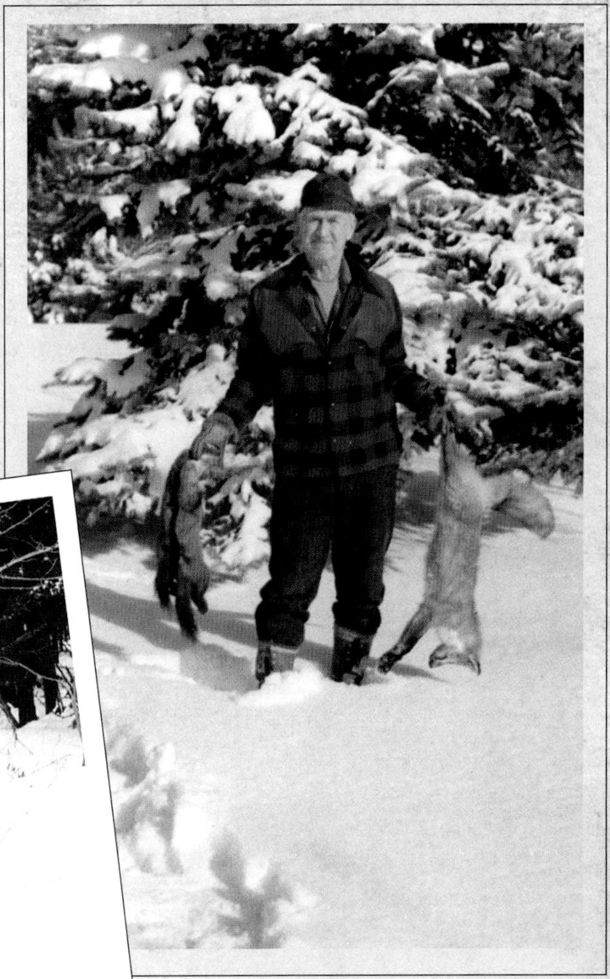

Oscar Cronk Photos

From An Interview with Oscar Cronk

"When I was long-lining, I was using 250-300 traps. Location and habits are the keys to success in trapping. I was a great blind setter for mink, but I found that I wasted a lot of time looking for that perfect blind set. After I learned the habits of the mink, I started using bait and lures, and my mink catch went up. The more traps you have out, the more animals you'll catch. Long-lining takes dedication and hard work. Weather can never be a factor when you're doing it. You have to go out no matter what. I always kept a log book of my sets, because when you have 250-300 sets, there's just no way to remember all of them. Keep it simple, put in long hours, and put out a lot of traps. I did mainly water trapping, but when I went North, then I had a mixed bag line consisting of bobcat, fox, coyote, fisher, and marten. When I was beaver trapping, it was pretty thick country, so I couldn't use a snowmobile. I used snowshoes. When you're long-lining, you can't waste time and along the way, you find little tricks that really save you time."

—Oscar Cronk, 2017 with Bill Falkowski

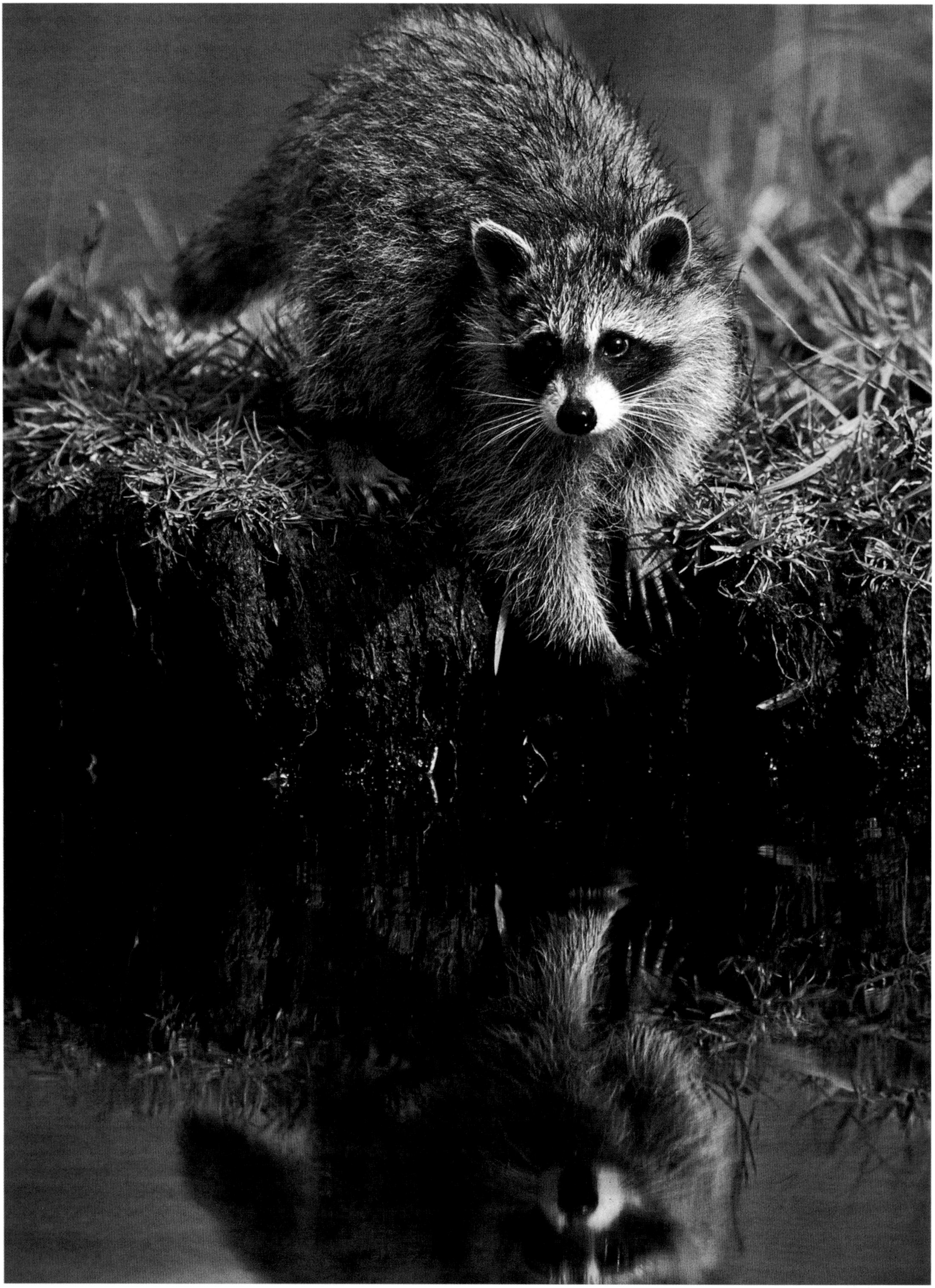

CHAPTER 8

COONMEN

Raccoons are prolific animals in midwest farm country. They're found along every creek, under every bridge, in woodlots adjacent to every cornfield. Add in the raccoons living in suburbia, raiding trash cans, and living in storm sewers, and the numbers of bandits available to the trapper climb exponentially. When pelt prices for raccoon rise, it doesn't take a calculator to do the math, they are worth going after. Raccoon catches, whether purposeful or incidental, add income to the trapper's pocket. During the fur boom, I can remember seeing guys pull over and pick up road killed coon knowing that carcass was a twenty-dollar bill lying on the highway. Heck, I did it.

RACCOON SPECIALISTS

Raccoons live in various densities almost everywhere —unless you trap arid desert, northern Canada or Alaska. A top mink trapper will catch incidental coon and muskrats. A fox-man will take coon, skunks and badgers. A wolfer will add a few fox, coon or cats to his catch as well. So for the average trapper, the raccoon plays a vital role on most traplines in helping make ends meet.

There are three key ingredients to large catches of any furbearer. First is recognizing the scope of the project. To catch large numbers you must think large numbers—large numbers of traps, sets, miles and hours. Second is to recognize the time and dollar investment required. The investment in four months work, two tanks of fuel each day, vehicle maintenance including new tires and upkeep, trap investment, stakes drags, wire, snares, lure and bait requirements, freezer space, and if needed, hired help and leases. Third is the execution of an organized plan. A plan that allows for scouting, permissions, and locating the animals over a large area. Plus the stamina and drive to see it through. It's easy to scratch out a plan on a sheet of paper. It's another exercise altogether to fill two or three spiral notebooks full of farmer names, phone numbers, set locations and a trapline that will keep fur coming for weeks on end.

Like any project, the trapline starts out exciting. However as long days limit sleep and combine with the day-to-day drama that comes with any job—the glamour of a full-time trapper trying to make a living becomes more of a ditch digging exercise.

Think about it, who is the more successful trapper—one who sets 10 traps opening day and catches 10 raccoons for 100% success? Or the trapper who sets 200 traps opening day and catches 50 raccoons

< *Len Rue Jr. Photo*

for 25% success? For the part-time trapper, 10 raccoons is a fantastic catch at a minimum investment. For the long-liner, 50 coon is a fantastic day with much more invested.

If one does a fair comparison of the success, it's easier to make a judgment.

Lets set up some basic guidelines to go by in our comparison. Both trappers trap in areas with the exact same raccoon density. Both trappers use identical methods, vehicles, and distance between traps are the same. The use the same amount of lure and all the raccoon are valued at the same price. We will leave out the pelt preparation to simplify the comparison.

	Part-time raccoon trapper:	Full-time raccoon trapper:
Initial investment	12 traps at $100 per dozen, hip boots, wire, supplies $200	200 traps at $100 per dozen, hip boots, wire, supplies $1,900
Fuel and lure cost	$2 per raccoon: $20	$2 per raccoon: $100
Time	10 traps set at 5 minutes per set: 50 minutes	200 traps set at 5 minutes per set: 1,000 minutes (16 hours 40 minutes)
Catches	10 raccoon/$20 each: $200	50 raccoon/$20 each: $1,000
Total Expenses	**$220**	**$2,000**
Total Income	**$200**	**$1,000**
Loss	**(-$20)**	**(-$1000)**

After adding in all the expenses and inventory costs—both trappers are at a loss after great opening days on the trapline. So hypothetically, let's now look at the risk/reward of a week's worth of checking the same sets with a gratuitous 15% reduction in catch per day for both the part-time and full-time trapper.

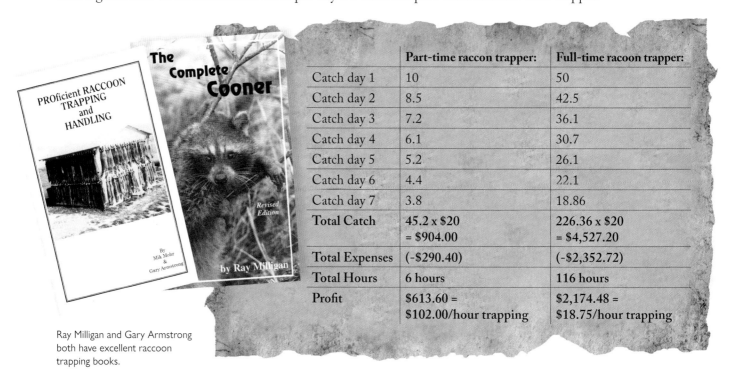

Ray Milligan and Gary Armstrong both have excellent raccoon trapping books.

	Part-time raccon trapper:	Full-time racoon trapper:
Catch day 1	10	50
Catch day 2	8.5	42.5
Catch day 3	7.2	36.1
Catch day 4	6.1	30.7
Catch day 5	5.2	26.1
Catch day 6	4.4	22.1
Catch day 7	3.8	18.86
Total Catch	45.2 x $20 = $904.00	226.36 x $20 = $4,527.20
Total Expenses	(-$290.40)	(-$2,352.72)
Total Hours	6 hours	116 hours
Profit	$613.60 = $102.00/hour trapping	$2,174.48 = $18.75/hour trapping

Three bandits taken in suburbia by avid trapper Nathan Roberts.

Although it looks like there is more money to be made per hour in part-time trapping it should be noted that this scenario gave the part-time trapper 100% success on opening day and the full-time trapper only 25% success. Typically, part-time trappers can be more selective in their sets and may have a somewhat higher catch percentage. That said, the full-time trapper bought and paid for 17 dozen traps out of his earnings and the part-timer only bought one dozen. Each trapper had the same expenses per animal. Note that even though the part-time trapper worked less than 10% of the hours per day as the full-time trapper, over the course of the week, the part-time trapper caught 80% fewer animals. It also should be noted that the full-time trapper would have had access to many more additional catches of mink and muskrats than the part-time trapper, variables that are not factored in here. And the actual bottom line is in order for the part-time trapper to have made the same weekly sum as the full-time trapper, he would have needed to also work a 40-hour job that paid $39 an hour.

If you decide to ponder this further, keep in mind that weather is a big factor in catches. Plus there are less raccoons to trap every day—the mortality of the raccoon population increases as trappers, vehicles and disease reduce numbers. Trapper motivation and stamina is also critical during a trapping season as most cannot keep up 16-18-20 hour days week-in and week-out. There are reasons why even only the best trappers, trapping in the best areas take 200-300-400 and maybe even more animals in fantastic circumstances.

Fur prices fluctuate as well. As little as a 20% increase in pelt value makes a huge difference to the trapper with larger catches. In our case, the part-timer would add $180 in his pocket and the full-timer a whopping $905 or $3,080 total profit for the week. A 20% decrease in pelt value devastates the profit with the part-time trapper making only $433 and the full-timer losing just over $900 and making $1,269.

THE RACCOON LINE

Both of my Victor 1 1/2 coils had connected and two masked bandits gazed from the culvert. It was 4 a.m. and traffic on Interstate 270 hadn't quite cranked up for the morning commute. Interstate 270 is known as the "outer-belt"—a ribbon of concrete that encircles Ohio's capital city and it was a fur rich corridor back in the mid-1970s when mink, rats, coon and foxes were all there for the taking.

My routine was systematic—as trapping along the usually busy highway was tricky business. Pulling my Jeep as far off the berm as I could, I hopped out and quickly bounced over the guardrail to tend the sets. I kept a tied white kerchief on the radio antenna which would indicate a distressed vehicle and usually kept the Ohio Highway Patrol from stopping. After tending sets, I would wait for a lull in traffic, scramble up the embankment, load up and move on down the road. Stops were recorded in miles and tenths in my notebook and clocked on the odometer, as in the darkness and with so many sets, it was impossible to keep track of everything without notes. Plus, a missed stop was a big deal on the freeway as you couldn't turn around easily. Road trapping as it's called is very productive as

Author's Photo

Aerial view of the White River. Raccoon and beaver heaven. Scouting beaver is pretty easy with the plane, but for bandits, not so much. Aerial view also helps show access into remote stretches as in the Dakotas you can spend a lot of time locating gates unless the rancher gives you a quick tour.

many traps can be tended quickly and much distance covered. I set every culvert, stream, bridge and wing wall of the hundred-plus-mile circuit.

Big catches are made by those who have everything laid out ahead of the season. One trick I've used with great success is to start setting raccoon traps at midnight—in the wee hours of opening day. I would set predetermined locations till 5 a.m. then go back over and run those sets quickly. Then I'd continue to set new sets all of opening day into the evening before turning around and then rechecking everything. My best was 54 bandits on opening day using this method and in areas where competition is keen, its a great way to bang out a few hundred coon in a week then get back to the fox line. In areas of heavy competition, the quicker the coon pelts are hanging in the fur shed—the better.

With every upside, there's a downside and road trapping is no different. Setting tiles, culverts and bridges along roadways is an open invitation for theft. The thought of losing expensive equipment often makes some trappers pass them up, even though tremendous numbers of water animals can be taken. Instead of passing up tiles and culverts, I decided to develop a system of sets and practices which would enable me to capitalize on this easy fur with minimal losses. On the larger culverts (4 feet in diameter or larger), I try never to set at the ends. Instead, I would crawl 15 to 20 feet in the culvert and set. This may sound unorthodox, but you'll be surprised how much fur and how many traps this saves you. Cubbies with conibears or body-gripper's work nicely in this type of situation and I have continued to harvest coon and mink in high-theft areas.

Live traps also work great in culverts and when you get in back under the road, throw some long grass cut from a road ditch over it. The big, bulky live trap suddenly looks like a pile of debris and again we're in business.

Author's Photo

Live traps can be used to take the place of body-gripper cubbies in states where dry land "conis" are illegal and depending on state game laws may not need to be checked every day. Culverts with running water can be narrowed with stones and blind set. If the water is too deep, build up the trap bed with an inverted piece of sod or if the water is really deep, use a concrete block with the inverted sod on top. Another plus to setting inside the culvert, is the water rarely freezes as the temperature is warner in the culvert. The trickling sound of running water is also an attractive call to animals moving up and down the drainage and it echoes from the culvert.

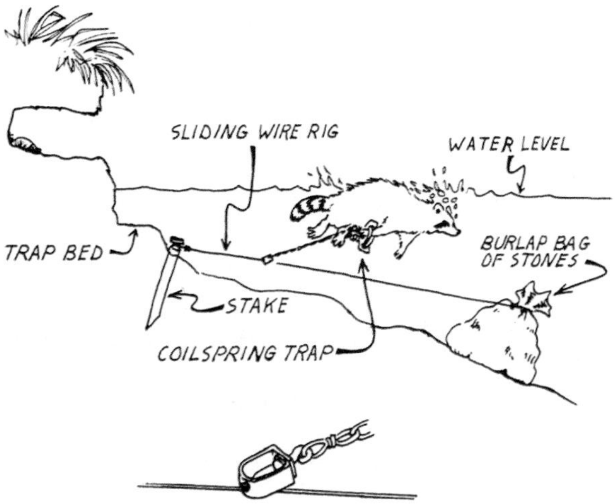

This is the "old school" method of setting up a drowning rig. However it's too tedious and slow for long-line use. Most commercial trappers anchor in deep water and weight the trap or use a DP which are the fastest methods.

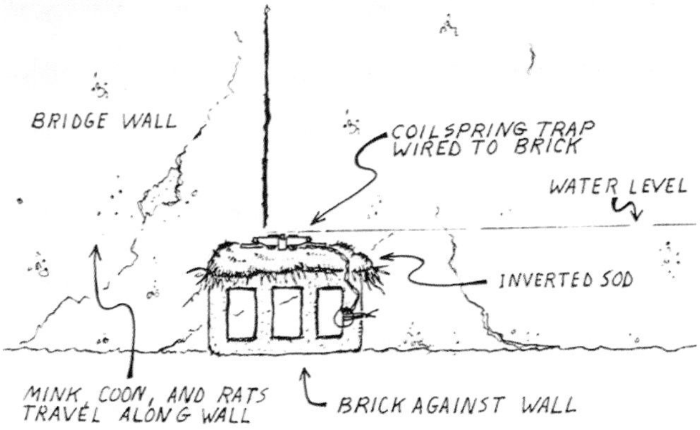

Smaller culverts must be set up on the ends. A good trick on small dry culverts is to use a sliding rod setup. The set can either be a blind set or rough dirt-hole at the culvert mouth. Use a 6-foot rod with a washer welded to one end and a one way slider to the opposite end where a weld bead can keep the trap and slider secure. Stake the rig securely at the mouth. When caught, the animal retreats into the culvert—the trap sliding down the rod and hidden out of sight. Once an animal is caught, the stake can be pulled and the animal retrieved by pulling the whole works out. Look for small culverts in out of the way places away from creeks and rivers. Dry culverts under roads near cornfields are excellent coon locations. Many times coon will move into cornfields away from streams to feed and just live in road culverts. Often these out of the way culverts are marked with a signpost and reflector so the mowing crew doesn't drive over the end of the culvert and damage the mower. Excellent, safe catches can be made in these places, so be on the look out for them. Remember, as fall turns to winter, some raccoons hibernate in these smaller culverts as they are warmer inside under the road. However in more northern locals, these locations often fade out as the coon will be moving back to the streams and rivers to prepare for denning.

If possible, most road sets should be tended in the dark. On heavy traffic roads, a hood up or white rag on the door knob, indicating vehicle trouble, may fool some potential thieves. Be discrete. Don't let everyone know what you're doing—in fact try not to let anyone know. If someone steals a catch or trap, try to determine who did it. A local youngster? A passerby? If you notice tennis or waking shoe prints near the set, the thief likely was a kid or passerby. Boot prints likely belong to a hunter with a case of "finders keepers" or an unethical trapper. If the catch or trap was a well-hidden set under the road, don't reset immediately. However, if you feel the theft was by chance, put another trap back in. Typically, someone who takes a trap knows they stole it and likely won't risk getting caught by returning to the scene of the crime. Sometimes moving 30 or 40 yards down the drainage and punching in a pocket set will let you take some fur without losing equipment. Another ruse I've used with success is to stake high theft areas—without traps—and leave them for a few days, then go back in after dark and set up. Pull all traps before first light—set at 10 p.m. and pull at 5 a.m. Oftentimes, the stakes will deter trappers from possibly setting on top of you, as they may think the area has already been trapped. Traps set in this manner take fur and keep equipment from being stolen. Using this method on muskrats, I have set a den entrance with a body-gripper and moved 15 feet down the stream to set another and heard the trap I just set go off taking a nice muskrat—SNAP! The important thing is to not get too paranoid about theft. In long-line trapping and especially road trapping, it's part of the game.

Author's Photo

Boat line bandit taken on the Scioto River in central Ohio— circa 1983.

BOAT TRAPPING

In some areas, there are stretches of river or marshes that will not permit a trapper to use a vehicle. They hold excellent habitat and fur populations, but there's no apparent way to get to the location without a boat. Float trapping has been around since the early French trappers and probably was used even before them. A boatload of traps, bait and the trapper can move along with the currents to excellent trapping in 1/10th of the time it would take a loaded down trapper to walk. Using a boat is just matching your trapping area to the mode of transportation which fits it.

Good boats for float trapping include a small john boat or flat back canoe. Marsh area trappers should not overlook the possibility of airboats. Whatever type of boat you feel would be best for your line, by all means, get a good one. I personally have used a 14-foot aluminum john boat with a 3.5 horsepower gasoline engine. Some trappers may prefer electric motors and ever smaller boats or canoes. This equipment choice really comes down to personal preference. All traps and gear should be loaded into the boat evenly. Traps should be wired together in dozens and each bundle wired to a flotation cushion if possible, especially if using a canoe. The traps may still sink, but they will be easier to locate and will keep a boat swamping from costing big bucks. Also, don't forget to wear a life jacket yourself.

When float trapping small river systems, use the put in and pick up method. Put the boat in at the bridge, run sets downstream until being picked up at another bridge at a predetermined time. By using this method, a tremendous amount of territory can be run in a short time, with no back tracking. If you can't get a family member or wife to pick you up, it would be better to find an individual who will pick you up and pay them $20 bucks a pickup. Larger rivers can be run without this extra "pickup man" as larger rivers are wide enough to support two separate fur populations—one on each bank. Put in at a bridge and run up stream on one side, cross over, and run the other side back downstream. This method will allow you to use the current to get back to your vehicle should the boat motor "shear a pin" or die on you—to leave you stranded.

Some trappers paint their DP traps so they are easier to locate. Nice boar bandit taken by trapper Luke Schwent.

HIGH-WATER POCKET SET

My "go-to" water set was always the high-water pocket. The way I made this set was somewhat discovered by accident. Sometimes you'll notice areas along streams in farm country where erosion has worked on a section of bank to the point that a 2- or a 3-foot chunk breaks away, leaving a shear cut mud wall and a sort of shallow water trail between the bank itself and the portion that has broken off. This trail makes a great mink set and will take every bandit that works the stream. I started making smaller versions of these with a tile spade or fast work with a long handled (yoho) trowel.

Cut a 3-foot long hefty chunk of bank and pull it toward the stream bed making your own sheer—cut bank. Quickly make a trail between and parallel to the bank but in 1 to 2 inches of water. Blind set the trap in the trail, then use the trowel handle to make a small round hole 8–10 inches up the sheer mud bank at the trap. Add lure into the hole and a squirt of fish oil up the bank. The set will have the eye appeal of a broken piece of bank yet won't look like a 'rat den. It will also

Bucket cubby hidden outside of dry culvert guarded with body-gripper. South Dakota.

handle a fluctuation of water rise and keep working. The pulled away bank also acts as a blocker, not only to force animals between but a person standing on the opposite bank likely won't see the trap as it's blocked from view. Five feet of chain and a drag on the trap will allow these sets to be made quickly. In the old days I used what was called an easy-stake—the precursor to the spade and super stake anchors used today.

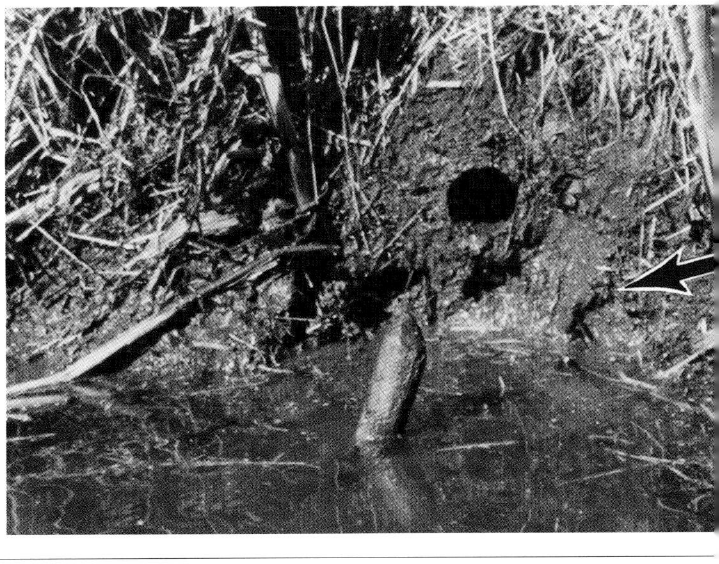

The shelf set is a variation of the high-water pocket. The bank soil that's cut down is used as the trap bed. The trowel handle again makes the hole. Arrow shows a trail quickly cut in that leads up the bank. Notice the driftwood jaw guard. Trap dog faces the hole so the 'coon walk between the jaws.

DOG-PROOF TRAPS

Tom Parr Museum Photo

Shown on the left is a Victor #2 square jaw with the DP conversion trigger. On the right, the original 1984 DP trap.

In my early days of long-lining, there was no such thing as a DP Trap. The concept started when California trapper Jack Isborn developed a kit in 1982 that would modify a #1-1/2 or #2 coil-spring trap to be "dog proof." The concept was to replace the pan with a trigger mechanism that needed to be pulled. To make a dog-proof set, the modified trap was set in a trap bed dug about 4 inches deep. Bait was placed in the split of the pull-trigger. A twelve inch square piece of 1/4 inch plywood would cover the trap and in the center of the plywood a small inch and a quarter hole was cut to allow access to the baited trigger—centered under the plywood hole. The entire set would then be covered and blended with the small bait access hole either exposed or plugged with sod. When a raccoon reached into the hole to secure the bait and pulled the trigger, the coil-spring trap fired catching the animal's front paw. The premise of course is that nimble fingered raccoon would work the trap whereas dogs and cats would likely not reach into the hole. Even if they could access the trigger they likely would not be able to pull the trigger mechanism. Although the kit worked, the plywood was often destroyed by the raccoon in his attempt to escape. The idea was sound, however, the mechanism needed refining.

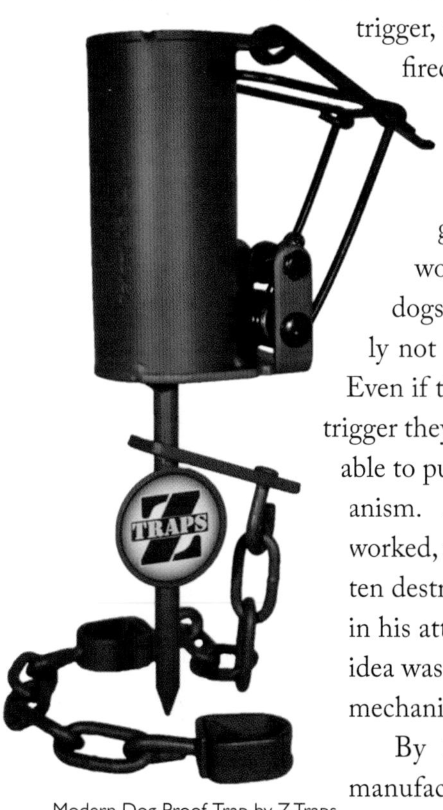

Modern Dog Proof Trap by Z-Traps

By 1984 the first DP manufactured traps hit the market. They were made of rectangular steel tubing, fully enclosed and designed to be buried flush with the ground.

The DP style traps answer many of the typical issues of trapping raccoons that all trappers faced before these ingenious traps were invented. First, raccoon have tapered and nimble paws which often are damaged by conventional traps, offering escape. Second, the urbanization of raccoon populations embed the bandits into areas where household pets are a concern. The DP traps solve both issues as the fully enclosed tube will not allow a raccoon access to his enclosed paw. Also, domestic pets can not operate the trap and thus don't get caught. In fact the DP concept eliminates most non-target animals. Only an occasion-

Tyson Andrews Photo

Trapper Tyson Andrews set ten DP traps and took nine bandits one night, proving the trap's effectiveness when the proper bait is used.

al, clever opossum or skunk will trip the device and oftentimes, these are traps in which the trigger was modified to fire easily. Newer models of the DP traps now incorporate push/pull triggers and these devices take more non-target species, yet offer a higher catch-to-visit ratio. Another key factor which advocates the use of DP traps is the education of non-trapping landowners. Demonstrating the discretionary and selective nature of a DP trap to a landowner will likely assist in a trapper gaining access to private land.

Tyson Andrews Surefire, Dog-Proof Trap Bait

10 Pounds Dry Cat Food
1 Quart Sun Rendered Fish Oil
1 Quart Salmon Oil
1 Ounce Vanilla Extract.
Mix Well

BERNIE BARRINGER

1959–

I met outdoor writer, trapper and long-liner Bernie Barringer during the late 1980s as one of the many trappers on the convention and seminar circuit. Bernie was an Iowa trapper specializing in waterline trapping and specifically, snaring raccoons. Of course he was adept at catching any furbearer he was after, but his knowledge intrigued me and when I began pulling a team together to do a video series for Krause Publications and the *Trapper & Predator Caller* magazine, Bernie was a great fit.

Bernie Barringer grew up in religious family, his father a minister who moved to different areas and started new churches. So at a young age Bernie lived in Montana, Washington, North Dakota and eventually Iowa in 1973. Bernie started trapping at age 14, however neither of his parents were hunters or fisherman. Throughout high school Bernie ran traplines and upon graduation went to work at the Winnebago motor home factory in Forest City, Iowa. It was a good job and Bernie's work ethic as a trapper allowed him to advance up the corporate ladder. But the outdoors was calling and by 1984 vacation traplines weren't enough. At 25, Bernie Barringer gave up six years seniority at Winnebago and went into full-time trapping.

Author's Photo

Bernie Barringer with a nice catch taken during the filming of the *Trapper and Predator Caller* magazine video, *The Professionals of Water Trapping, 1994*

Barringer had developed a system for catching raccoons in snares literally by the hundreds. He purchased a small travel trailer and began traveling all over Iowa living in the trailer while road trapping and bouncing fur pocket to fur pocket. Blind setting bridges and culverts with coil-springs also added mink to his raccoon snare catch and the nature of Iowa crop country led to many foxes snared in the tall grasses of section line road ditches. Barringer had some seasons where he took over 500 bandits and over 100 mink. Bernie did well enough on the line to also put himself through college—graduating with a degree in journalism at the age of 31.

Most top trappers rely on a system that allows them to be efficient. Bernie Barringer pre-made his snare setups, utilizing a hardwood stake with the support wire and snare attached. Barringer could bounce out of the truck with four snare rigs and stake the pre-made sets on coon trails in under 2 minutes. Gang setting the snares allowed multiple chances at traveling bandits often nailing them in the first or second night. Barringer says it wasn't uncommon to have a dozen snares set at one bridge stop and often 4 or more ringtails nailed on the first check.

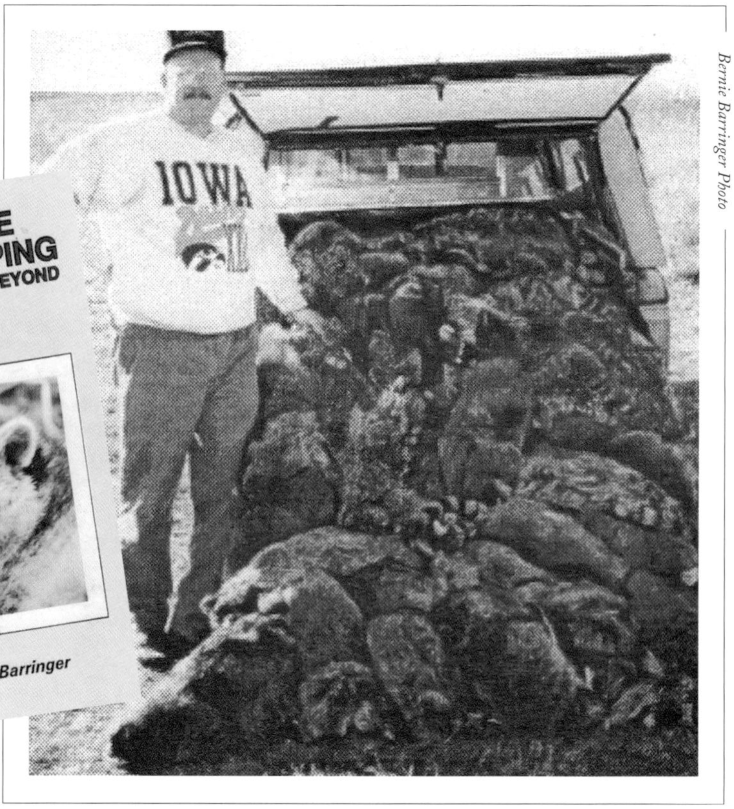

Bernie Barringer Photo

Bernie Barringer poses with over 60 raccoons taken in one day's check of his Iowa snare-line. Photo from *Space Age Coon Trapping*— 1991.

By the early 1990s the fur market had cooled some, but trappers were still hungry for information. Bernie authored *Space Age Coon Trapping*–1991, *Snaring in the Space Age* –1992. In the summer of 1994 I asked Bernie Barringer and Mark June to participate in a video project for *Trapper & Predator Caller* magazine. The videos were titled *Professionals of Water Trapping* and *Professionals of Predator Trapping*. The videos were a hit. Barringer continued to write many magazine articles about trapping as well as authored and published 2 more books, *Farmland Fur Trapping*–1996 and *The Numbers Game* –2001.

Bernie Barringer is one of the few professional trappers who went into the hunting industry. Moving to Brainerd, Minnesota in 2001, Barringer began writing more about fishing and hunting. Soon he was editing *Bear Hunting Magazine* among other pursuits. Barringer has taken more than 30 archery black bears and harvested the four primary color phases of bruins—cinnamon, blond, chocolate and black. Bernie contributes much of his time today giving back to young people and the less fortunate as well as continuing his freelance writing and media pursuits.

Bernie Barringer Photo

Barringer's hardwood stake rig includes stake, support wire and snare ready to hammer in and adjust.

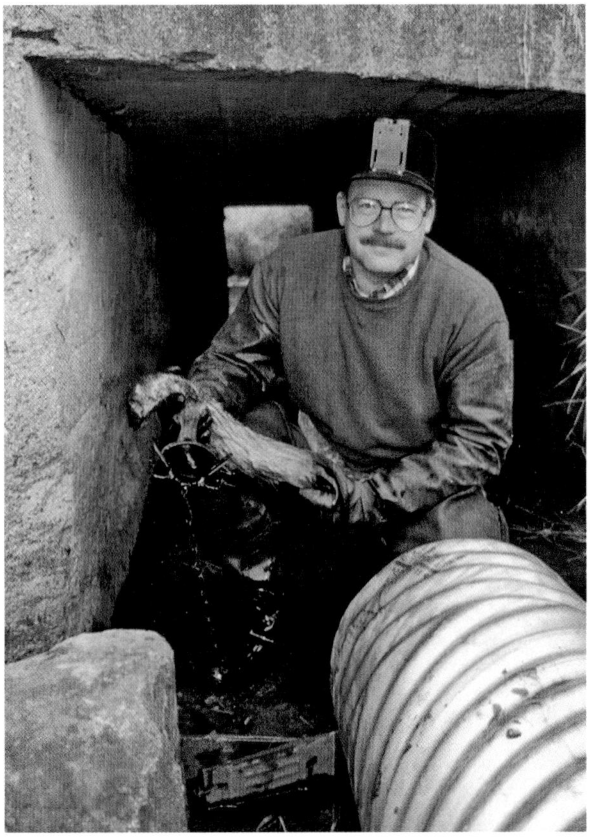

Barringer poses with a nice Iowa mink, Notice the railroad tie plates used to secure trap and block travel around culvert.

Bernie poses with a nice archery bruin.

"While some lures will work equally well for more than one species of furbearers, the same cannot be said for sets. Even the old standby dirt-hole set must be constructed differently based on whether the target is a fox or a coyote. A snare set for coon may miss the occasional fox. Yet, a snare set properly for fox will miss many coons. A hole in the bank of a stream will attract both mink and coon, but to catch one or the other with regularity, the hole must be constructed different based on which furbearer is the target. Trap placement and even the size and type of trap chosen will vary at these sets as well.

At each set, your mind must process a series of trade-offs to determine which is the best for the situation at hand. Understanding these subtle differences in methods will increase your effectiveness and your bottom line at the end of the season. Versatility, and the ability to make the right decision about the most effective method for each individual set scenario is what separates the run-of-the-mill trapper from the top-flight trapper."

—Bernie Barringer—Farmland Fur Trapping, 1996

TRAPPING VIDEOS

I don't think either Jeff Smith or I could have ever imagined the initial response to our trapping videos. It was a home run, end zone dance and hat trick all in one. We had set the price at $49.95 for the *Fox & Coyote Instructional* video, $34.95 for the *Advanced Methods* and $74.95 for both. *The Production Line Water* video sold for $49.95. At the time, I mailed out a FREE Tom Miranda red fox cap with every $50 dollar order and went through nearly three hundred caps a month. We sold so many videos that I couldn't keep the inventory in videos or caps. My cap supplier couldn't keep inventory either and we went from green camouflage caps to brown camouflage caps. Jeff Smith was dubbing the original videos and sending them to me and he couldn't keep up either. That August at the National Trappers Convention in Fond du Lac, Wisconsin, there was a sea of Tom Miranda red fox Competition Line caps.

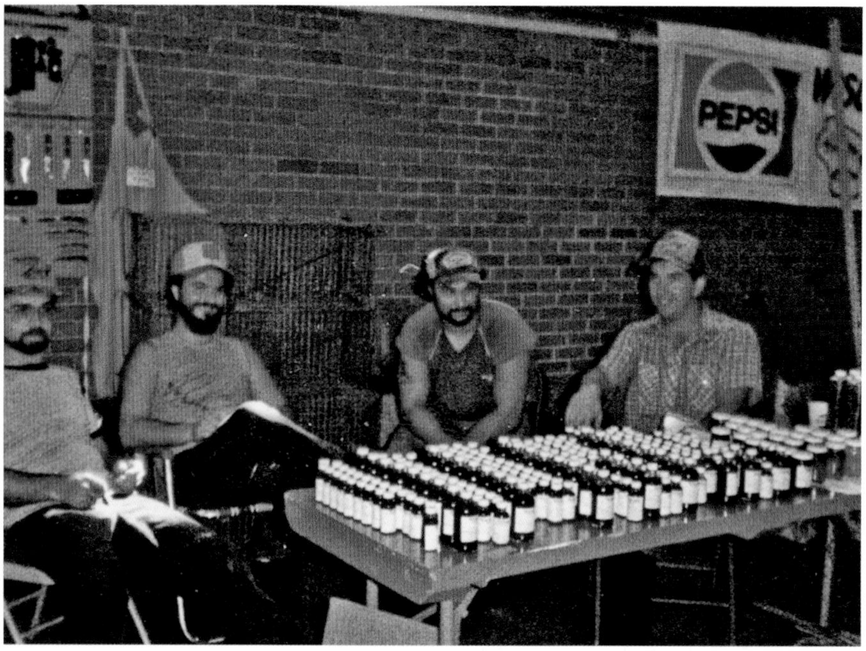

Author's Photo

Here's a photo of my booth in Fond du Lac at the 1986 NTA National. (L-R) Jerry Herbst, unidentified, Corry Dolbeer and yours truly. Corry bought my trappers cabin on the Michigamme in 1985 and still owns it today.

At the 1986 NTA Convention, besides selling every lure, book, cap and video I brought to the show, I had a meeting with *Fur-Fish-Game* magazine. On the agenda was the thought of me taking over the Fur Market Report. I had an idea to implement a simple chart into the fur market portion of the magazine. I had also pulled together some fur buyers who were willing to contribute to the information needed each month to make the report accurate. Keith Winkler of Sterling Fur & Tool was one of the fur buyers who helped me with this report. I also had an idea that *F-F-G* should upgrade the Harding "Pleasure and Profit" book line with some up-to-date trapping books and at the show we created the *Fur-Fish-Game* Book Market. The magazine would essentially become a book dealer, buying a select grouping of books to re-sell. But since the buzz of the convention was Tom Miranda and his trapping videos, *Fur Fish Game* was interested in the possibility of possibly making them their own set of "how to" trapping videos. It was a huge opportunity and I told them I was interested and would get back to them.

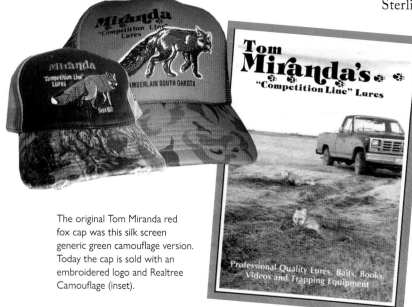

The original Tom Miranda red fox cap was this silk screen generic green camouflage version. Today the cap is sold with an embroidered logo and Realtree Camouflage (inset).

Author's Collection

Jeff Smith was also at the convention and set up in his own booth selling the videos. I went by his booth to discuss the *F-F-G* opportunity. At first he was excited, but then asked, "Why won't they just purchase our East-West videos and sell them?" Of course *Fur-Fish-Game's* goal was to own the videos and to make better ones. Peter Kirn was running the magazine and he insisted that the videos be shot on TV-quality equipment, which at the time was Sony Betacam. Eventually, Jeff agreed, but he also wanted Lex to be involved and Jeff himself wanted to be in the videos. Honestly, the demands didn't bother me as I would never have done a single video without Jeff coming up with the idea in the first place and pushing me into doing it. The way I was thinking about it, this opportunity would be a sort of "pay back" for Jeff. I agreed and began organizing the first four *Fur-Fish-Game* trapping videos.

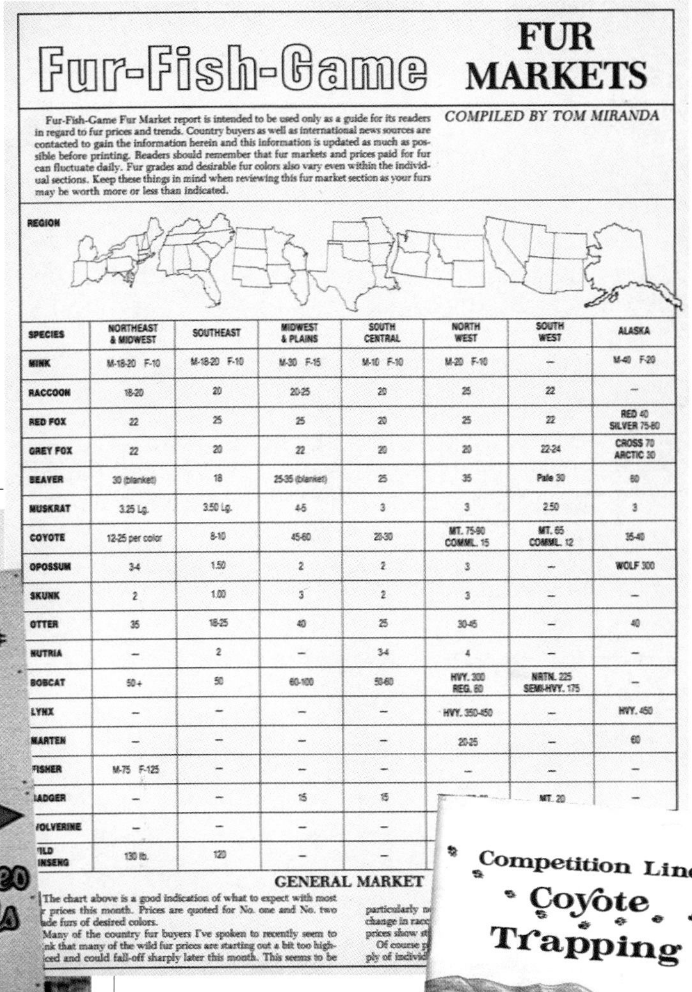

Fur-Fish-Game FUR MARKETS

COMPILED BY TOM MIRANDA

Fur-Fish-Game Fur Market report is intended to be used only as a guide for its readers in regard to fur prices and trends. Country buyers as well as international news sources are contacted to gain the information herein and this information is updated as much as possible before printing. Readers should remember that fur markets and prices paid for fur can fluctuate daily. Fur grades and desirable fur colors also vary even within the individual sections. Keep these things in mind when reviewing this fur market section as your furs may be worth more or less than indicated.

REGION

SPECIES	NORTHEAST & MIDWEST	SOUTHEAST	MIDWEST & PLAINS	SOUTH CENTRAL	NORTH WEST	SOUTH WEST	ALASKA
MINK	M-18-20 F-10	M-18-20 F-10	M-30 F-15	M-10 F-10	M-20 F-10	—	M-40 F-20
RACCOON	18-20	20	20-25	20	25	22	—
RED FOX	22	25	25	20	25	22	RED 40 SILVER 75-80
GREY FOX	22	20	22	20	20	22-24	CROSS 70 ARCTIC 30
BEAVER	30 (blanket)	18	25-35 (blanket)	25	35	Pale 30	60
MUSKRAT	3.25 Lg.	3.50 Lg.	4-5	3	3	2.50	3
COYOTE	12-25 per color	8-10	45-60	20-30	MT. 75-90 COMML. 15	MT. 65 COMML. 12	35-40
OPOSSUM	3-4	1.50	2	2	3	—	WOLF 300
SKUNK	2	1.00	3	2	3	—	—
OTTER	35	18-25	40	25	30-45	—	40
NUTRIA	—	2	—	3-4	4	—	—
BOBCAT	50+	50	60-100	50-60	HVY. 300 REG. 60	NRTN. 225 SEMI-HVY. 175	—
LYNX	—	—	—	—	HVY. 350-450	—	HVY. 450
MARTEN	—	—	—	—	20-25	—	60
FISHER	M-75 F-125	—	—	—	—	—	—
ADGER	—	—	15	15	[illegible]	MT. 20	—
OLVERINE	—	—	—	—	[illegible]	[illegible]	[illegible]
ILD INSENG	130 lb.	120	—	—	[illegible]	[illegible]	[illegible]

GENERAL MARKET

The chart above is a good indication of what to expect with most r prices this month. Prices are quoted for No. one and No. two ade furs of desired colors.

Many of the country fur buyers I've spoken to recently seem to nk that many of the wild fur prices are starting out a bit too high- ced and could fall-off sharply later this month. This seems to be particularly n change in racc prices show st

Of course p ply of individ

Author's Collection

Here is my old Trapping school sign on the road leading to my home and lure shop in Chamberlain, South Dakota, 1987.

Competition Line Coyote Trapping First Edition, 1987.

I had gathered quite a few South Dakota coyote catch photos in 1984-85-86 and wanted to do a coyote book to compliment the success of my fox and water trapping books. I had resigned from the South Dakota GFP trapper job, so any photos form my ADC job or even mentioning that I was an ADC trapper was now perfectly fine. As my resume was growing, it was the best time to finish the coyote book for release in early 1987. Having the three book manuscripts also made great material for the trapping videos and I relied on all three manuscripts when I put together the outlines for the *F-F-G* trapping series.

It was important to me that there would be a team of instructors in the *F-F-G* videos. The trappers college had made a huge influence on me—and the way different instructors taught, the different skill sets each instructor brought to the table, would make a much more interesting video. At the time, Bob Gilsvik was the trapline editor of the magazine and it was a must that he be in the original videos. When I discussed the project with Bob he was reluctant, but I told him that

FUR-FISH-GAME MAGAZINE PRESENTS . . .

PROFESSIONAL TRAPPING INSTRUCTION ON VIDEO!

Featuring —

TOM MIRANDA (South Dakota) — Pro trapper, trapping instructor, lure maker and our own Question Box editor

BOB GILSVIK (Minnesota) — Our top trapping editor

JEFF SMITH (Montana) — Pro trapper and instructor

JERRY HERBST (South Dakota) — Pro snarer and snare manufacturer

DAVE HEIB (South Dakota) — Pro fur handler and furrier

We selected these individuals to be in the videos, not only because they are professional trappers, but because of their ability to teach trapping.

Tom Miranda

We've pulled out all the stops and produced four (4) instructional videos featuring these expert trappers. All aspects of trapping Fox, Coyote, Mink and Raccoon are covered, including: favorite equipment; location for sets (in detail); best sets for each species; special sets; fur handling; and, most important — RESULTS — actual target animal catches!

Bob Gilsvik

Jeff Smith

Filmed in "Beta Cam" professional video format — unbelievable picture quality. No one else in the trapping industry has ever produced a "Broadcast Quality" video. Leave it to FUR-FISH-GAME magazine to put out the best trapping instruction videos available.

Dave Heib

Jerry Herbst

ORDER ALL FOUR VIDEOS AND SAVE 20%
(Buy all four for only $159.95!)

PROFESSIONAL FOX TRAPPING
* Equipment
* Fox Habits
* Location — General & Specific
* Our Instructors' Favorite Sets
* Special Sets
* Snaring
* Fur Handling
* RESULTS!
(One Hour of instruction)

PROFESSIONAL COYOTE TRAPPING
* Equipment
* Coyote Habits
* Location — East & West
* Sets
* Special Sets
* Snaring
* Fur Handling
* RESULTS!
(One Hour of instruction)

PROFESSIONAL MINK TRAPPING
* Equipment
* Mink Habits
* Location for Mink Sets
* Land & Water Sets
* Marsh & River Sets
* Fur Handling
* RESULTS!
(One Hour of instruction)

PROFESSIONAL RACCOON TRAPPING
* Equipment
* Raccoon Habits
* Coon Set Locations
* Special Drowning Techniques
* The Best Coon Sets
* Snaring
* Fur Handling
* RESULTS!
(One Hour of instruction)

it would be painless and I assured him that his parts would turn out well. Bob agreed to do it. I knew Jerry Herbst would be available to help me and I wanted his input, especially on the snaring as he had become quite the snare-man. We also wanted some fur handling tips and a local fur buyer Dave Heib was an additional asset, so and I added him to the mix. The cast of the original videos would be, Bob Gilsvik, Jerry Herbst, Jeff Smith, Dave Heib and myself. Lex Hames would direct the four films—Fox, Coyote, Raccoon and Mink. At this time Lex was working with a company called Sunrise Studios in Missoula, Montana. Sunrise would provide the cameras, lighting and production work.

We shot the first *F-F-G* videos in the fall of 1987 on my trapline in South Dakota. Sunrise Studios did a great job, they brought in lighting, dollies, lots of gear and a crew. It was my first "real" TV-style video shoot. I learned so much on that shoot about how to really make a video. Looking back on the experience now, at that time I had no idea where in the world this video business would take me—NO IDEA.

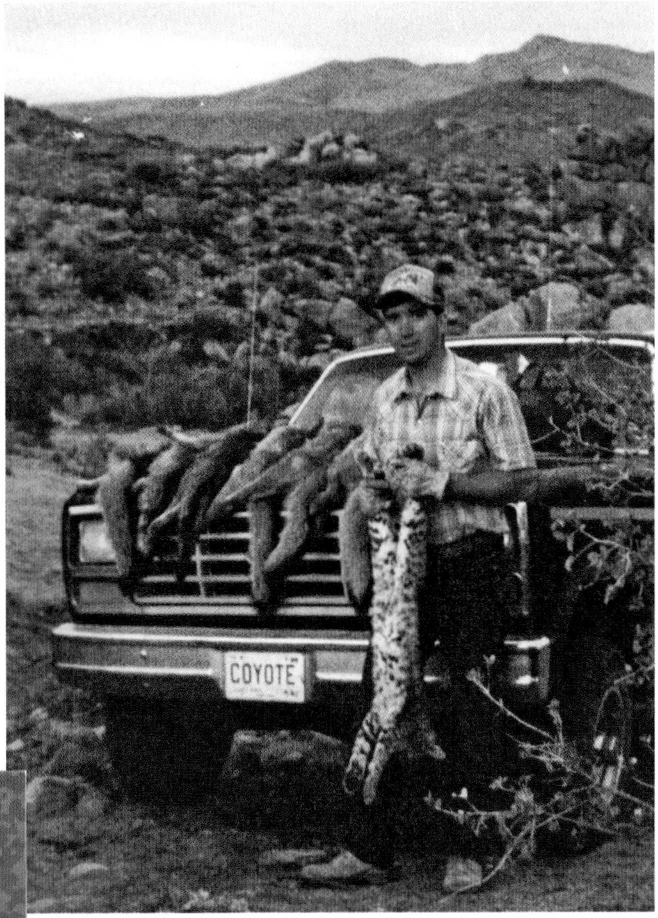

Author's Photo

Good day's catch near Congress, Arizona while taping the *Production Line Bobcat Trapping and Grey Fox Refresher* video.

Author's Photo

In early January of 1987 Jeff Smith & I went winter camping in the Bitterroot National Forest and shot a wilderness survival video. This video didn't sell well to trappers, but video stores bought many.

The *F-F-G* videos released in December 1987 with a back cover advertisement. Christmas season was the perfect release date. *F-F-G* sold their first run of trapping videos hand over fist. There's nothing like doing a business deal where everyone comes out ahead. Peter Kirn and *F-F-G* were more than happy, Bob Gilsvik enjoyed the whole process and had a good time in South Dakota, Jerry Herbst started his own snare supply business, Dave Heib enjoyed some local notoriety. Jeff Smith and I were basking in the limelight. Jerry had decided to go to Arizona and run a trapline for cats and left in December 1987. I was tied up and couldn't leave with Jerry, but asked Herbst to call me if he found a good place with

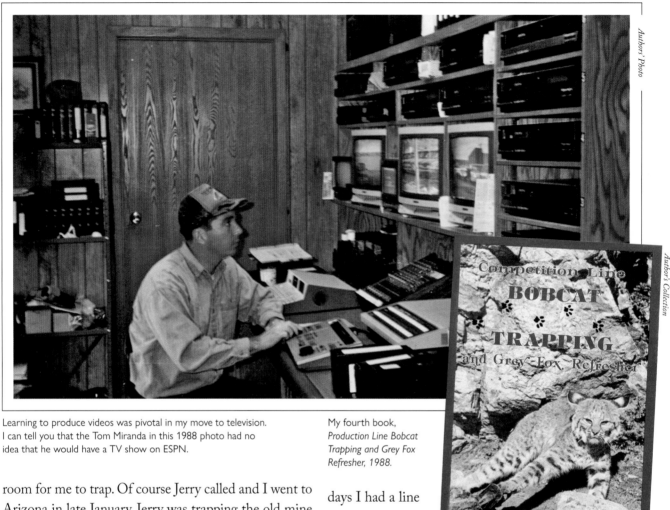

Authors' Photo

Learning to produce videos was pivotal in my move to television. I can tell you that the Tom Miranda in this 1988 photo had no idea that he would have a TV show on ESPN.

Author's Collection

My fourth book, *Production Line Bobcat Trapping and Grey Fox Refresher, 1988.*

room for me to trap. Of course Jerry called and I went to Arizona in late January. Jerry was trapping the old mine country near Wickenburg but said there was some good looking desert up near Congress, Arizona that I should be able to run. I left in mid-January Jeff was already in Congress and setting his line when I got in. Within 3 days I had a line operating so we used Jerry's line, Jeff's line and my line to shoot the new bobcat trapping video. I only trapped a few weeks in Arizona that year as I was excited to get home and begin work on upcoming projects. I bought a handheld cassette tape recorder in Arizona and dictated my bobcat book manuscript to it while making the 20-plus hour drive from Congress to Chamberlain, South Dakota. The dictation trick was actually a great use of time and once it was typed up, made a solid base for the bobcat book.

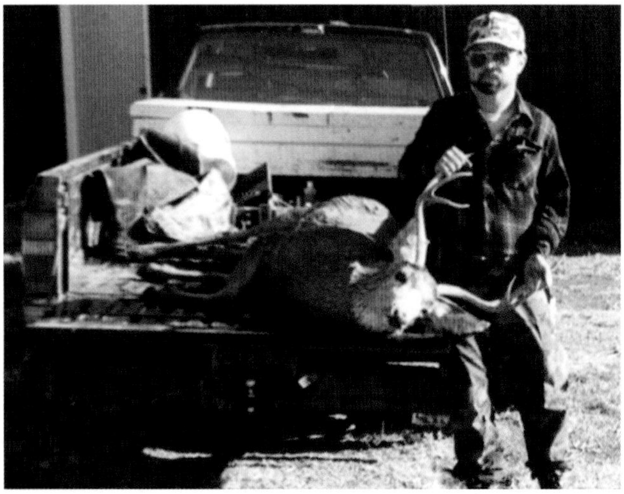

Jerry Herbst poses with an archery mule deer he took in South Dakota—circa 1989.

During the shooting of the *Bobcat Trapping* video and soon afterward, Jeff Smith and I hit some rocky times. I think there is rarely a perfect partnership and in my opinion, the way most partnerships stay together is how the tough times in a relationship get handled.

Author's Photo

Here's the Crew sans Jerry Herbst as he's taking the photo. (L-R) Tom Miranda, unknown, Lex Hames, James Echols and Bob Gilsvik. January 1989.

I have a tendency to want to work fast and progress toward the next stage of things. In many working partnerships, one person supplies the idea or the money and another performs the work. Workers almost always feel some discontent as to them, the idea or the money seemingly comes easy. It's the day-to-day work that is difficult. In Jeff and my situation, the reality was Lex and Jeff lived in Montana and they were controlling the editing and therefore I was somewhat out of the loop on how the final videos were put together. The other side was that my business was selling 90% of the video programs and the way we had East-West Video set up, with the full-page ads, shipping in videos from Jeff (as he held the Master tapes and all the inventory) and basically I was buying the programs from him. The long and short of it was that everything came to a head in the spring of 1988 with Jeff and Lex in my South Dakota shop. What started out as a negotiation to modify our arrangement turned into a power struggle. The bottom line was my name, likeness and reputation was all over the videos. My persona was plastered in *F-F-G* and the *Trapper Magazine.* I was selling 90% of all the videos we were making and absorbing the advertising, etc.

This is part of my personal instruction brochure from 1986. Once I updated the trapping videos, my private trapping lesson business exploded.

Tempers flared and Jeff walked out. The partnership was over. I paid Lex a day rate to stay behind a few days to teach me how to edit. New Sony Broadcast Video equipment was delivered and soon I was not only the writer and trapper, but the entire crew. Jeff and I eventually parted amicably.

VIDEO RESET

With East-West Productions no longer in business, I set out to update the trapping videos. My plan was to revamp them by dividing the lessons into 1- Location that would include A-maps of the trapline, B-Aerial views of the trapline using my airplane and C- location views from the ground; and 2- At the locations I would make the sets. Since I would be re-taping the lessons in the spring, the videos wouldn't be done during the actual trapping season. I was a little nervous about this, however all of my trapping instruction classes took place in the spring and summer. With Jerry Herbst running the camera, we set out to remake the original programs. I redesigned the video sleeves to say

The "All New" *Fox and Coyote Trapping* Instruction Video, 1988.

Author's Photo

Here's the crew of *Big Timber Bears*, my first video bowhunt. (L-R) Tom Miranda, Jerry Herbst, James Echols, Terry McGillicky and Paul Voz, May 1989.

ALL NEW and changed the photos used on the covers. It was a big project, but we collected the footage and I edited the programs. Adding the airplane was a big hit and soon I had students calling me wanting to take lessons and fly with me over my trapline. Of course there was an issue. I didn't have my commercial pilot's license. This meant I couldn't take students up in the airplane for hire. I could take them for a ride if I wanted, but the airplane ride over the trapline couldn't be sold as a paid portion of the trapping course. I got around it in my brochure by stating the disclaimers—however I was eventually challenged by the FAA. I received a call in the summer of 1988 from a guy wanting trapping lessons. But all he talked about was the airplane. He asked questions like, "How much would you charge to just to fly me over your trapline?" or "I'll pay for a day of lessons but they must include seeing your trapline in the airplane!"

I told the man that I wasn't a commercial pilot and we would do the ride only as a bonus, weather permitting. After a little more prodding, the caller came clean. He was with the FAA in Rapid City, South Dakota and a complaint had come in that I was flying paid clients in my trapping lessons. He was following up. I asked him who had submitted the complaint and he never said the name but did tell me the complaint was filed from Montana. Anyway, all was fine and my personal trapping instruction business became busier than ever.

No sooner than I finished my "All New" trapping programs on video, Peter Kirn from *Fur-Fish-Game* called me. Peter had told me back in 1987 when we did the original 4 trapping programs—"If these sell well enough to pay back the magazine's initial investment, I would commit to four more videos." In the late spring of 1988, he was ready. The *Fur-Fish-Game* video sales had outperformed all expectations. The response from trappers and mail from readers was, "When are the next videos coming out?" My thought initially was to do a combined fox and coyote tape, a combined mink and raccoon tape, a beaver tape and a muskrat tape. Taking the show on the road was also important, I wanted to get at least some north woods feel as kind of a tribute to my trapline in the Michigan wilderness. Bob Gilsvik lived in northern Minnesota which was perfect for the snow and ice trapping. Then we would go south to do the warmer weather sets and catches. Peter agreed.

Author's Photo

This 1989 Saskatchewan black bear was my first archery harvest on video.

My daughter Jennifer was born in the late spring of 1988. She was and is the apple of my eye. I now had a young son and new daughter. This drove me even more to succeed. One thing about being out on your own in the entrepreneur world is that sometimes you get this empty feeling like you don't know where your next dollar is coming from. I had to stay on top of my game.

I bought a used Itasca motor home the fall of '88 for us to operate out of. It would allow the whole crew to travel in comfort and have plenty of room for gear. In mid-January 1989 at the height of the winter season—Jerry and I headed northeast. We took my green John Deer snowmobile to Minnesota, and rented two Skidoos so Jerry and Bob would have machines. We taped 4 or 5 days in Minnesota and then drove south to Louisiana. We first stopped in the Northern part of the state for a few days to shoot some footage and instruction without snow, then headed south to the marshes on the Gulf of Mexico to finish. I can remember watching Super Bowl XXIII in one of the cabins we were staying in on the marsh.

ALL IN

In the spring of 1989 after returning from the *F-F-G* shoot, I wanted to start doing some hunting videos. Jerry Herbst was a bowhunter and had been practicing his archery shooting at the lure shop. He got me interested again and I picked up a McPherson compound and started shooting. I ended up doing a turkey calling video that spring with Missouri call maker Ike Ashby and his pal Bud Jones.

Right afterward, Paul Voz, Jerry Herbst, cameraman James Echols and I traveled north to Saskatchewan on a black bear hunt with pal Terry McGillicky. It was a great trip and a big change from the rigors of the trapline. The bowhunt was a success and my first bow harvest on video. On the drive home, I got this crazy idea to print a new catalog and bulk mail it to every trapper in North America. I could include my new trapping videos, all eight *Fur-Fish-Game* videos, my new hunting videos, all four books—plus new lures and other supplies. At this time *Trapper & Predator Caller* (TPC) magazine was very popular and had a circulation of about 55,000. The new owners were Krause Publications of Iola, Wisconsin. They had bought the magazine from Nebraska publisher Chuck Spearman in August of 1988. My original plan was to buy TPC's mailing list and bulk mail my catalog to all the subscribers. But I quickly learned when you start multiplying any number times fifty-five thousand it becomes a much, much bigger number. The bottom line was to print 65,000 catalogs (10,000 extra to include with mail orders), buy the mailing list and bulk mail 55,000 of the catalogs would cost roughly $60 thousand (that would be $120 thousand today). Having just bought new broadcast video equipment in 1988 and reprinted all the video sleeves, plus publishing the new bobcat book and two new hunting videos—well sixty grand was a stretch. And there was no guarantee I would get my money back in orders. Then the lightbulb went off—I telephoned Krause in Wisconsin and asked them if they would consider stapling my catalog inside the trapper magazine at the centerfold and if so what would the cost be. They said they would get back to me.

New York trapper Josh Stairs with a great end of the line photo and dandy boar bandit.

RICK HEMSATH

1956—

Iowa trapper Rick Hemsath likes it when the 'coon prices are up. Most Iowa trappers do, but for Rick catching bandits is an obsession. Sure, he likes catching fox and coyote & who would complain about a buck mink in a pocket set? But for a raccoon trapper, there's something about the masked bandit.

With grandpa's help, Rick started trapping pocket gophers in the mid-sixties and soon after graduated up to muskrats. Once a youngster gets trapping in his blood, the lure of the trapline often turns into an obsession. When Rick picked up his first Fur-Fish-Game magazine there was no turning back. He knew he would be a trapper.

"I think that first raccoon catch is special to every trapper. Hearing that chain rattle in the dark morning before school and seeing those glowing eyes, hearing that snarl— I will never forget it."

Rick trapped throughout his school years and and after graduation took many summer jobs, yet when the Iowa trapping season was approaching, Rick switched gears to trapping. In 1981 Rick and his trapping buddy Mike Mazur started R&M Lures (Rick & Mike's Lures). 1981 was smack in the middle of the fur boom when furs were bringing a premium and new trappers coming on the scene in droves. In these days, a trapper with good catch photos and a quality product could set up a booth at the trappers conventions and profit a month's wages on an average weekend. Rick and Mike jumped into the convention "circuit" with both feet and R&M lures quickly had a following. With conventions almost every weekend for 3 months, the travel was hectic, but it's how a trapper builds his brand.

After the fur boom, the trapping industry reset. Many fur dealers and supply businesses who found "quick money" in the trapping trade during the "boom" closed up after the fur markets tanked. It was at this time when Rick bought out Mike's half of their lure business. Rick was determined to see the business continue and despite the fur prices he was still planning on trapping. Rick's dedication to is trapping passion is evident as he's still operating R&M Lures today, now going on 40 years.

Rick told me that every season is his best season and he's had some good ones. Rick's best includes over 500 bandits, 92 mink, 255 'rats plus misc. fox, coyote and beaver. Rick says, *"I like to trap later in the season, because with the lure business I'm get pretty busy early keeping up with orders and shipments. My best trapping season financially, I ran 2 months hard— mainly mink but of course I'm a pocket set guy and a well placed pocket takes 'coon, mink, rats and beaver. I also buy fur and sell supplies so to take 92 mink and over 500 coon with everything else I had going on was a great run. Trapping is a business for me so I rely on lure & supply sales, fur check, Nuisance animal work and fur buying margins for my total income.*

Part of what makes up a Master Trapper is the dedication to educating youth and long time support of the trapping organizations. Rick has been an Iowa leader on both counts. Rick Hemsath has done how-to trapping demonstrations at the National Trappers Association Annual Conventions since 1981 and taught Iowa Fur Harvesters Trapper Education classes for 30 years. *"Part of being a trapper is giving back. Today with all the political correctness and pressure that's put against hunting and trapping— our sport is in real trouble. Conservation is being abandoned for preservation of animals and it will be the demise of not only our trapping and hunting, but wildlife in general. In my opinion, it's the youth that will save us and it's why I am so involved in the Fur Harvesters."*

Trapper Rick Hemsath remakes his set after taking a big Iowa boar 'coon.

Joe Kiel Photo

Rick started his own nuisance animal control business in 2004. With low fur prices, less trappers and more animals, Rick had been fielding animal complaints for years. Yet previously it was done for favors or permission to trap ground. With increased demand the nuisance complaints have now morphed into a separate business all its own.

Rick attributes much of his success to several fellow trappers. *"In my opinion many of the best trappers fly under the radar and nobody knows them. That's the way they like it. That said, my good friend Corey Meier has probably inspired me the most. His trapping drive and determination is infectious. Also Mike Mazur, Mike A., Kendall O., Brian Steines, Lee Steinmeyer for all support and friendship. And of course Keith Winkler for believing in me and my trapping lures from the start."*

Rick Hemsath is a trapper who isn't into the fame or glory of a famous name or bragging rights. He's a working trapper. A guy who grew up outdoors, dug in and worked himself into a niche to make a living as a trapper. During the lean times he didn't give up. Trapping is in his blood and true trappers know that the *lean* times make the *fat* times that much more grand. As furbearers go—the raccoon doesn't rate very high on the glamorous scale, and maybe being a raccoon trapper isn't the most glamorous occupation either. But if you ask Rick, he'll tell you— *"I don't do this for the glamor, I'm a proud trapper & hunter and if you ain't into that— I don't give a damn."*

Hummmm….. sounds like the lost verse of a famous Hank Jr. song.

Rick Hemsath Photo

Sun's just coming up. Nice morning run on Hemsath's predator line.

"Trapping is just like anything you do. To be good you have to just keep working at it. Experience is the best teacher. Get to know other trappers, listen to all ideas. You will develop your own style. Don't let the numbers game get in your head, you can't catch a 100 of something is you only have a population of 50. This took me a longtime to understand this. Also, there are a lot of variables, population, weather, competition and time you have to trap. If you really enjoy it, you just want to be out there doing it. Don't forget to stop and smell the roses along the way.I have been very fortunate to have been able to do what I do. A big thank you to my wife and kids for supporting me in this venture."

Rick Hemsath— In his own words, 2020

Rick Hemsath Photo

Trapper Rick Hemsath doing some nuisance animal control, 2020.

RAW FUR HANDLING
At Its Best
BY KEITH WINKLER
PROFITABLE 'coon trapping
"The Helfrich Professional System"
CRONK'S SCIENTIFIC RACCOON TRAPPING
by Oscar Cronk Jr.
HIGH ROLLING COON TRAPPING A DECADE LATER
BY
L. CRAIG O'GORMAN
MAY 1982
COON TRAPPING
BUD
COONS WITH CONIBEAR
trapping
MASKED BANDIT'
BY GERRY BARCELL
RUSS CARMAN'S RACCOON TRAPPING METHODS
SNARING in the SPACE AGE
by Bernie Barringer
You Can Make RECORD Coon Catches!
RACCOONS
Raccoon TRAPPING
By S.STANLEY HAWBAKER

KYLE KAATZ 1979–

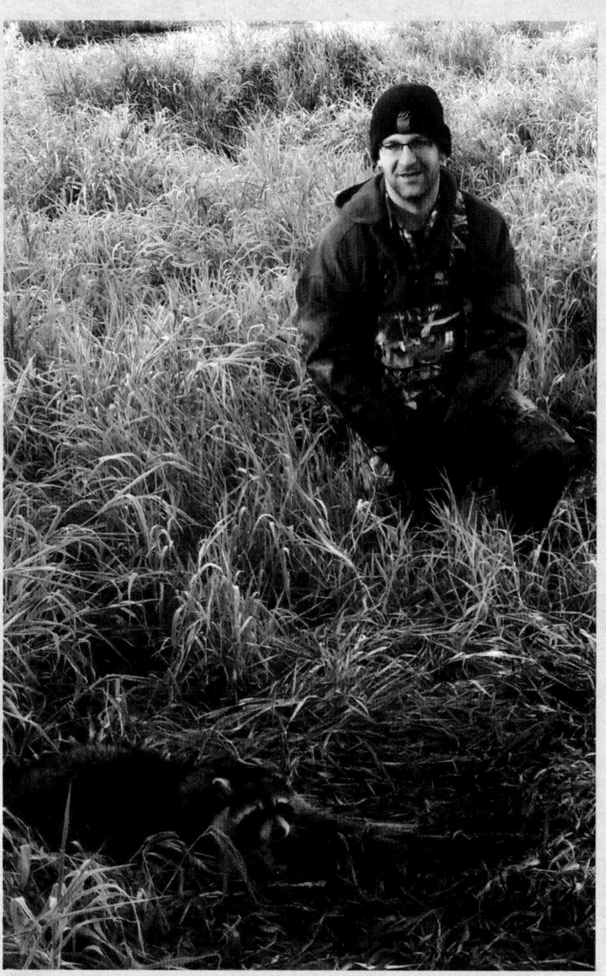

Kyle Kaatz poses with a bandit taken on a worn coon trail near a muskrat pond.

Kyle Kaatz grew up on Chicago's South Side and started trapping at age 13 with influence from his grandfather. A short three years later, Kyle and his brother Kellen started their own trapping business, Kaatz Brothers Lures. Kyle also authored his first book *Land Trapping Made Simple* in 1995. Kyle realized early on that he likely wouldn't be taken seriously as an experienced trapper because of his young age, but that didn't stop him from pursuing his dream. Two years later, Kyle was eighteen, had graduated high school a semester early, secured his Illinois nuisance wildlife control permit and was running his first Iowa long-line.

Kyle Kaatz had come a long way in a short time. Channeling his emphasis on raccoons, the youngster would refine his system until in 2001 at the age of just 22, he would take 416 raccoons and 30 mink on a 12-day sprint across the Iowa farmlands. Impressive numbers. Kyle says, "Those 12 days were grueling and I was skinning my coon every night. Operating on 2 hours of sleep a day."

Kyle primarily utilizes pocket sets but ultimately the location determines the set type. Kyle says, "There are only so many hours in a day, so maximizing efficiency is the key. I always felt I needed to work as a hard as I could. Ultimately I don't think I was doing anything that much different than other trappers."

Kaatz authored two more books, *Raccoon Trapping Made Simple* in 2001 and *Open Water Beaver Trapping Made Simple* in 2003 and attributes much of his success to hard work and trap supply dealers who took him in under their wing early in his career.

A prolific writer, Kaatz has done numerous trapping articles in his career and was also the editor of *Trappers World* magazine from 2000 to 2013.

Kyle and his brother continue to operate Kaatz Brothers Lures. Over the years they have established their own lines of trapping products including the TS-85 Beaver Trap, KBL Quick Dye and the Relax-A-Lock snare system, plus continue to make their own lures as well as custom private label.

Kyle Kaatz poses with a dandy mixed catch of muskrat and raccoons after a day on the trapline.

"There have been a ton of mentors and people who have had an impact on my trapping career. Charles Dobbins, Tom Miranda, and Ray Milligan books were my textbooks as a teenager. If I had to pick one person, I would say Keith Winkler, Keith was the first person to give me a wholesale catalog and extend me terms for buying lure bottles. And 25 years later, we still do tons of business with Sterling Fur. My advice to the up-and-coming trapper is to really focus. Hyper focus on trapping, and work insanely hard all the time and when other people are probably sleeping. Success comes at a cost, and you have to be willing to risk the time and money to pay for the success. Don't worry about the negative comments or the competition or the fear. If you believe in yourself, you really can will yourself into successful situations. Don't give up, Plan Bs are for losers, and success comes as a form of winning. I think every person that has the passion to pursue trapping, has a winning heart. Find motivation from within yourself to be the best version of yourself. Being motivated by money or 'fame' will not work. Success is an innate part of people, finding it is up to the individual who believes in themself."

—Kyle Kaatz, 2020

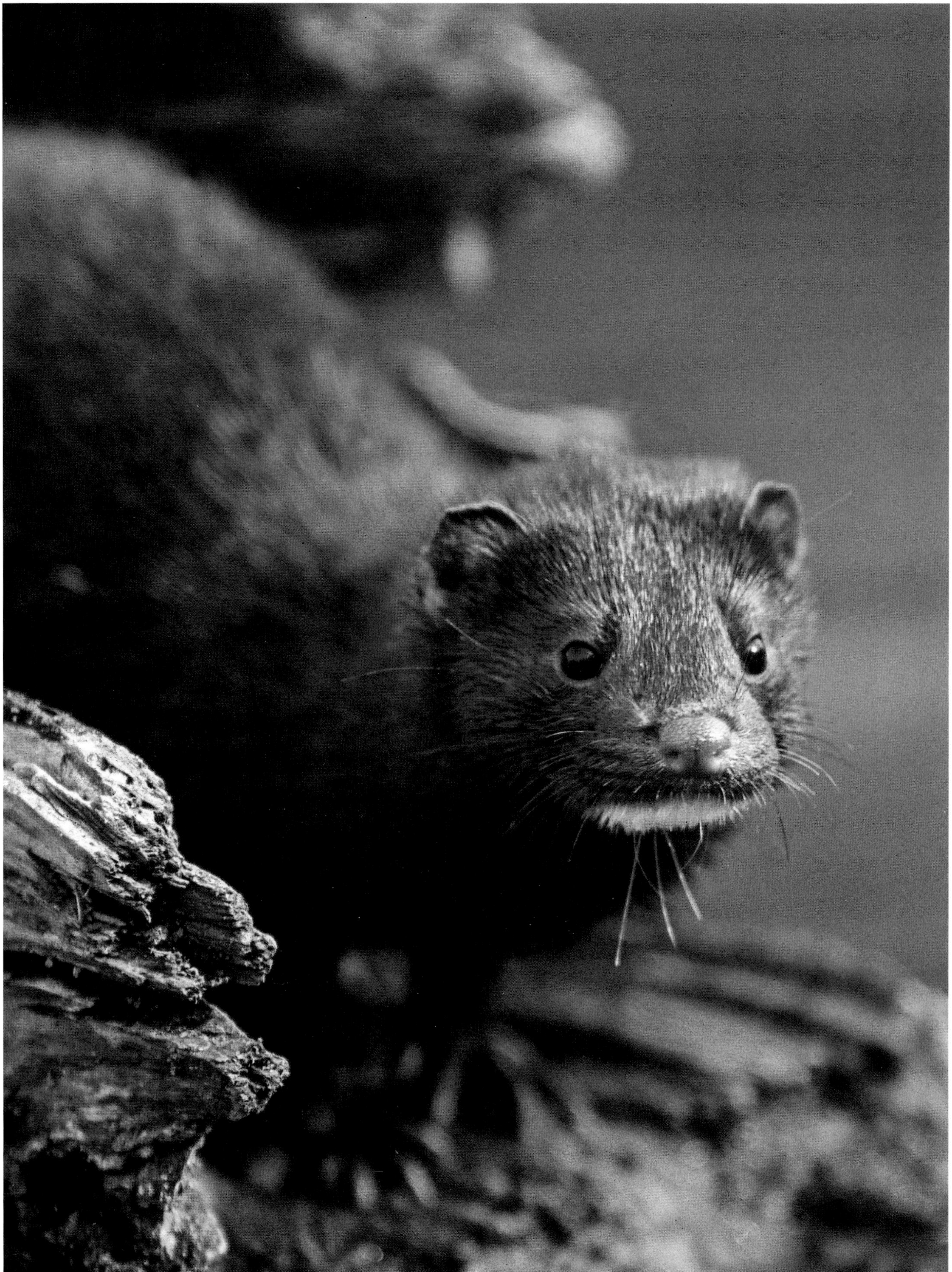

CHAPTER 9

MINKMEN

The mink might just be the most mysterious of all the furbearers. Where the raccoon will plaster a muddy bank with tracks, the "kitten-like" tracks of a mink are barely visible, seen by only the most observant woodsman. Muskrat dens and houses can be easily located, as are beaver dams and cuttings. But the mink operates from a hidden lair and runs a territory which keeps its movements concealed. At the turn of the century, mink were a valuable commodity yet as mink ranching came on the scene, fur buyers often went for the larger, even-colored and perfectly prime pelts a mink rancher could offer. Thus, mink prices never really went to the level of martens, fishers or foxes. Yet for the trappers who could catch numbers of these water weasels—there was money to be made.

WATER WEASEL

For most trappers, catching a mink is an incidental event. Because few trappers ever trapped them in numbers, the top minkers of yesteryear kept their trapping methods close to the vest. The mink is secretive in nature, leaving little sign and traveling a long, linear territory of creek banks, spring flows, riverbanks or the vast expanse of a marshland. Mink are always on the move looking for a meal, their darting and weaving movements inspecting every hole and crevasse along their route. Most muskrat trappers have witnessed a muskrat catch ravaged by an opportunistic water weasel who quickly kills the 'rat and leaves little behind for the trapper's efforts. Muskrat makes good bait for mink in areas were mink and rats are plenty, but the majority of mink prefer fish and crayfish. Typically, trappers who are adept at catching mink are also good otter trappers as these animals have many traits which are similar.

Where predator men operate with permission to trap many farms or ranches, mink and raccoon trappers often run road lines with little or no permission. Bridge trapping is popular as the waterway passes under the road and this stretch of land is considered in many states as public "right of way." Road trapping is always an iffy proposition when it comes to trap theft, but depending upon the fur prices some trappers do very well running road lines.

Mink are in the animal family of weasels, otters and ferrets. Known as the family of Mustelidae, a family of small animals that have a musky smell due to their glands. The strong musky glands of a mink are valuable and worthy of saving—as some predator lure formulas call for mink glands (as do many mink lures).

< *Len Rue Jr. Photo*

J. CURTIS GRIGG

1896–1995

Many of the early trappers in the northeast and Adirondacks gained notoriety. However, the midwestern trappers often operated in a clan of secrecy. Expert trappers like fox man Bud Hall who took over 10,000 foxes in his lifetime, cooner Don Bolte with a season catch of nearly 1,000 bandits and of course, J. Curtis Grigg the Iowa mink trapper extraordinaire. Recognized in Chuck Spearman's *The Trapper* magazine Hall of Fame in September 1982, J. Curtis Grigg was a trapper's trapper. Yes, he was a mink trapper, but also an expert at whatever animal he set out to trap.

J. Curtis Grigg Photo

Curt Grigg with a dandy catch of mink and skunk from his 1920 trapline.

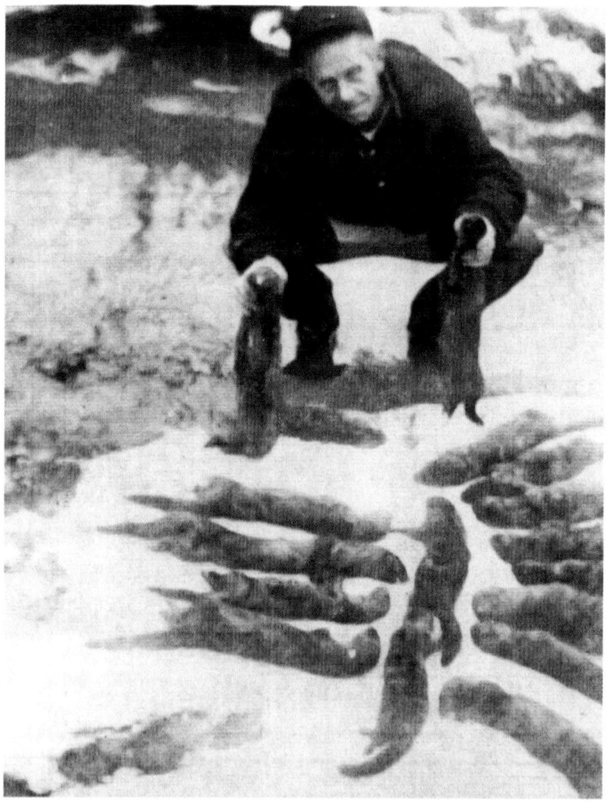
J. Curtis Grigg Photo

J. Curtis Grigg with 16 mink taken on a days run over his Iowa trapline.

Curt grew up in Hopkinton, Iowa and began trapping in 1908 at 12 years old. The story goes that Curt had 3 number 2 Newhouse traps (each with one spring removed so he could set them) and on his first check scored a muskrat and a raccoon. With a 66 percent catch rate, young Curt was hooked on trapping. Curt's season of 1909 was better with 67 muskrats, 5 raccoons and 3 mink—the total fur catch selling for a whopping $7 which in today's money equals $190. Not bad for a schoolboy trapline. Note that the average working man's wage in 1908 was $200–$400 per year.

Grigg was one of the first trappers to recognize the value of running a long auto trapline to catch animal's in numbers. Curt recalled that in the years when mink were valuable, he would use 3 different cars on his line as to not draw attention to trap and fur thieves. It's thought that Iowa long-liner Bill Nelson wore a white shirt and tie on the trapline to fool passersby of his trapping locations. Once the word got out about his mink prowess, Curtis Grigg was asked to contribute to *Hunter-Trader-Trapper* magazine as well as the *Fur News and Outdoor World* publication and eventually *Fur-Fish-Game.* J. Curtis Grigg wrote and released an 8-page booklet titled *Grigg's Mink Trapping Methods* in 1939, a difficult item to find nowadays if you're a collector. Griggs also dug ginseng in season and was known as an excellent fisherman.

Once Curt's son James got proficient with the traps, the two Griggs teamed up and through the late '40s and '50s stacked up some amazing catches of mink.

J. Curtis Grigg was one of the top "minkmen" to ever set a trap.

MARVIN "BUD" HALL

1919–2008

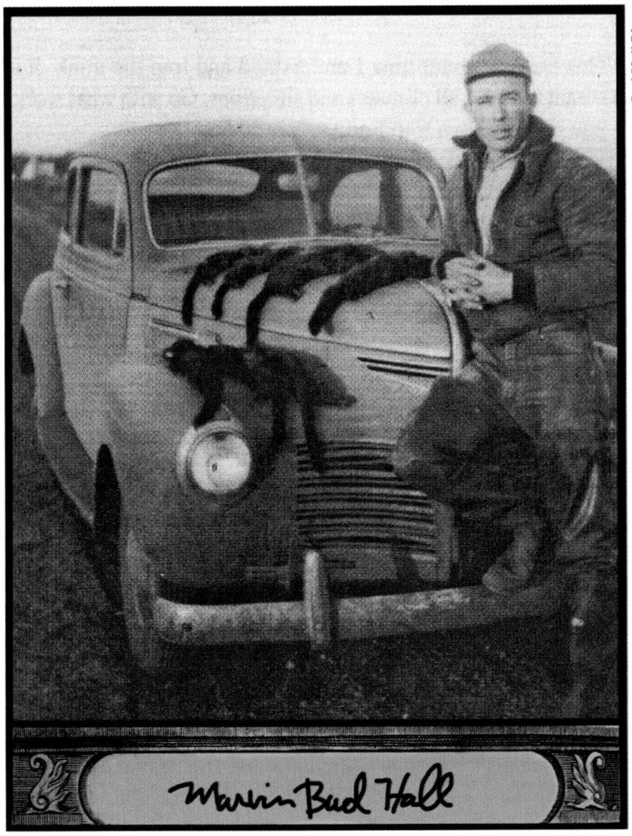

Bud Hall Photo

The early minkers were often as mysterious as the mink these trappers pursued. Marvin "Bud" Hall was born July 22, 1919, in Dexter, Minnesota to William and Edith Nichols Hall. Soon after, the Halls moved to Iowa where Bud's father took up farming. The Hall farm had a small river flowing through it—Bill Hall ran a small trapline. As a youngster, Bud would help his father check the traps and learned how to trap. Bud says he's pretty sure he caught his first mink during the 1927 trapping season.

Bud graduated from the Nashua, Iowa high school and eventually joined the military. He trained as an army pilot and flew the Douglas C-47 Skytrain, a transporter developed from the DC-3 airliner. After WWII, Bud married Norma Sours in May of 1946 and worked several jobs in the agricultural industry including Oliver Farm Equipment in Charles City and John Deere Tractor Plant and Foundry in Waterloo, Iowa. When Bud started his serious trapping he also got into commercial fishing during the spring and summer, a career that helped him secure his mink trapping bait.

Bud used carp for bait (and a lot of them), recommending nearly a pound of unsalted or preserved carp bait at each set for maximum odor. Operating several traplines in east central Iowa, Bud ran an area of approximately 16,000 square miles to make his massive mink catches. Bud preferred the smaller streams over the big rivers and would usually only make one set on the very small streams and make two sets on streams which were over 10 feet wide, making one set on each bank. Hall would run a particular line for two weeks and his rule of thumb was to pull 10 less productive sets each day and add 10 new sets to his line each day.

Bud gained much of his mink trapping knowledge by trailing mink tracks in the snow. By following a big set of buck mink tracks, a trapper can see the travel patterns, the objects that attract a mink's attention. Bud says in his book Mink Tales—The Essence of 67 Years as a Mink Trapper, that he has never trailed a mink more than a mile before he "holed" it. Oftentimes, mink that go into a hole will stay under for several days, especially in bad weather. A body-gripper guarding the hole and any close holes which may connect is almost a 100% successful set.

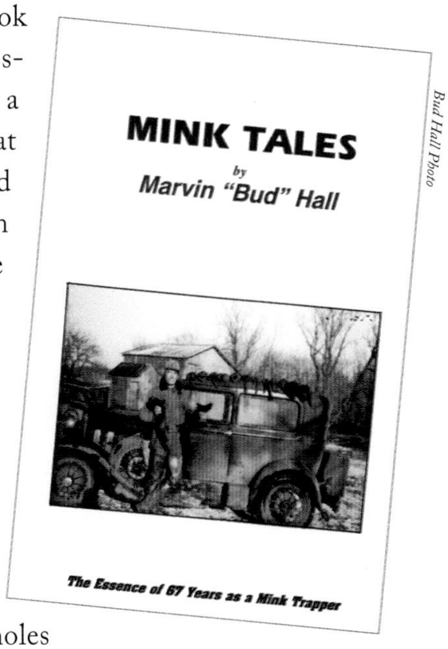

Bud Hall Photo

In my government trapper days, I can remember getting a call from a farmer in mid-winter who lost over 50 chickens one night in a small chicken coup. There was a fresh snow, and after circling the scene of the crime, I picked up a set of big mink tracks. I followed the bounding tracks across the pasture about 300 yards to a hole where the mink had entered. Upon further circling and looking, it was clear the mink was in the hole. I set a 120 conibear body-gripper over the hole. The mink came out three days later and the farmer's problem was solved.

Many bridge trappers use what Bud calls an invisible set. Basically, it's a pocket or shelf set which is covered and blended in such a way so as not to look like a set at all. There is no visual appeal and often the trap chain and drag are hidden in the silt bottom. These sets (when made correctly) help reduce trap theft and likely are only found by other trappers who know what to look for. Like all top Iowa trappers, when fox prices were up Bud trapped foxes and took over 10,000 of them in his trapping career and well over 4,000 mink.

"Some coon are caught no matter what you do to avoid them. I am plagued with them too. A trap placed one foot into a two foot deep pocket helps some. Use a snare cable or wire instead of the chain or they may rake the chain out with their paws. I avoid the big concentrations of coon when the season opens. Stay at least 1/2 mile from coon denning areas. One can come back later when coon are denned up. Try to place your pockets off of deep water. If a coon path is only one side of the waterway, set on the other side. Maybe 50% are not bothered by coon. My catch usually runs 3 mink to one coon. Some nights coon move well and not the mink or vice versa. I don't mind catching a few coon as they pay expenses."

—Marvin "Bud" Hall, Mink Tales, 1994

JIM SPENCER

1947–

Biologist and trapper Jim Spencer is passionate about the outdoors. Growing up in the flooded timber region of Stuttgart, Arkansas, Jim quickly learned that water trapping could be a fun, yet profitable enterprise. Jim started trapping in 1959 at 12 years old. Living around Stuttgart was a water trapper's paradise. Streams, rivers, swamps and ditches all were connected by culverts to control flooding in the area, and all were highways for raccoons, mink and muskrats. Jim quickly perfected his water trapping skills then put them to money-making use in Louisiana. The year was 1968 and while attending college at Louisiana State University, Jim helped pay his way through school by trapping nutria, muskrats, raccoons and mink.

Jim Spencer Photo

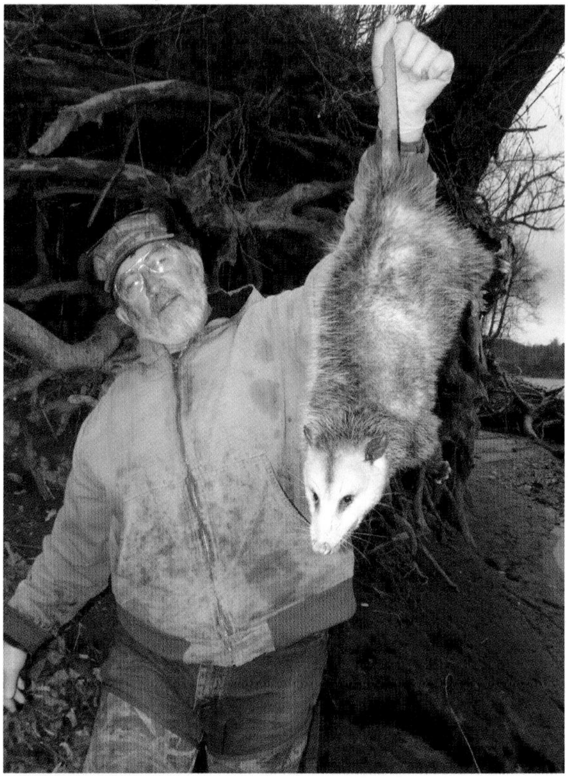

Minkman Jim Spencer jokingly holds up a Tennessee Cotton Mink

Jim graduated college and went back to Arkansas, this time working for the state's Game and Fish Commission. Jim's degree in wildlife biology would eventually land him the job as one of the agency's biologists. There he worked as a biologist and communications specialist. But Jim Spencer's passion was the trapping. And soon he would be taking vacation and weekends to set traps. A week of hard trapping can make a month's worth of extra wages which come in handy when raising a family. Maybe a few more dinners out or new shoes for the kids to wear to school, or even extra presents under the Christmas tree.

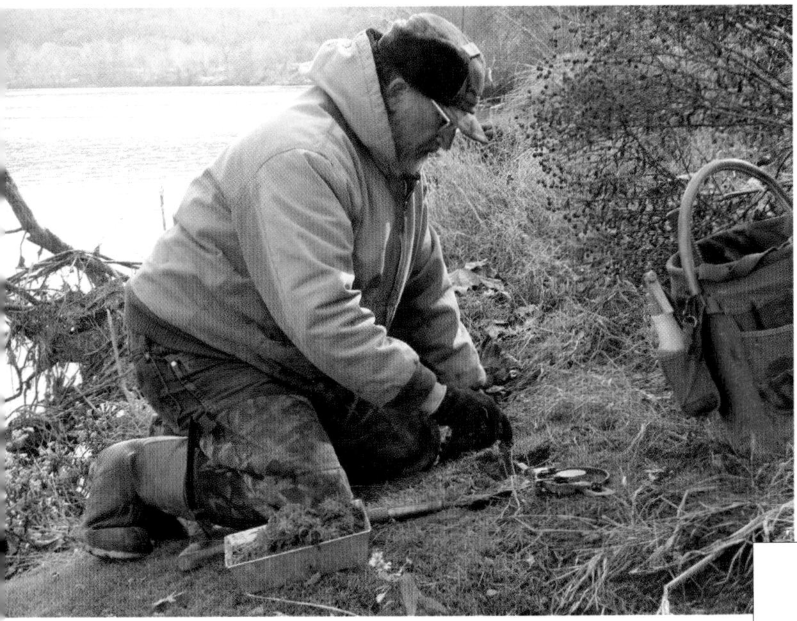

Jim Spencer Photo

Spencer incorporates both dry sets and water sets into his mink line.

Through the 1980s, Jim's trapping concentrated more and more on mink. By 1990 Spencer had published his first book, *The Mink Manual—A Common Sense Approach to Mink Trapping.* Jim then started recording his mink seasons in an effort to release a comprehensive video on mink trapping. Titled *The Mink Movies,* these instruction and "on the line" treatises were taped between 1991–1997.

Jim Spencer's The Mink Manual is a must read.

Jim Spencer utilizes a variety of blind sets and baited pocket sets on his mink line. Jim says for speed and effectiveness, Johnny Thorpe's suicide set is a tough one to beat. "My favorite set would be Thorpe's Suicide Set—a blind set at a vertical bridge wall or vertical bank, with the trap under half an inch or less of water at that magic spot where land and water come together at the vertical bank," says Spencer. He also advocates the use of sliding lock drowners on his sets, not so much for the mink catches, but the incidental raccoon catches. Like many trappers, Jim uses his raccoon and muskrat pelts to cover all his trapline expenses such as equipment, lures, vehicle wear and tear, fuel costs, licenses and more.

One of the interesting concepts in Jim Spencer's instructional materials includes his thoughts on habitat. Spencer refers to mink habitat as the "water level." This makes a lot of sense as the habitat at high water is much different than the habitat at low water. These variables effect not only the trapline itself but scouting, as well as mink population, density and survival rates. If you haven't read *The Mink Manual,* consider picking up a copy.

Jim Spencer Photo

Mink man Jim Spencer in his 'hey day" as a master Mink trapper. Nice days run in Arkansas.

Jim Spencer Photo

Author's Collection

Jim poses with a trapping partner and his mixed bag of Arkansas furs. Several bundles of mink hang from the far right eve

Jim's 1992–93 season was his best ever on the mink line. He took 332 mink, 120 raccoons and nearly a thousand muskrats. This was a seven-week run starting about December first. That's nearly a 7 mink per day average for almost fifty days. Wow!

Jim has retired from his Arkansas biologist position and is currently the Executive Editor for *Trapper and Predator Caller* magazine, following in the footsteps of another Master Trapper, Tom Krause—who's also mentioned in this book.

"I'm basically a lazy person, but when I'm on the trapline I work as hard as I've ever worked in my life. I suppose it's because I've always been absolutely fascinated by the notion that it's possible to place a mechanical device in such a way as to catch an animal you have never seen. I also have a personal belief that if you love something, it's your responsibility to become as good at it as you possibly can, in order to maximize the pleasure you get from that activity. Mediocrity is not much fun, no matter what you're doing. I also have a deep, pervading sense of peace and contentment when I'm out there all by myself, making every decision with no input from anybody else. I think a big part of my love for trapping comes from the fact that it's mostly a solitary activity, even if you're trapping with a partner. It's one-on-one, the trapper against a particular animal. That appeals to me. Finally, there is the financial incentive. First it was paying for my expenses at college. Later, it was putting shoes on my kids' feet. Nowadays, my trapline money is my "mad money." Last year I bought a pontoon boat with my trapline profits. This year, who knows?"

—Jim Spencer, 2014

Here's the big gamble. The 1989 August issue of *Trapper and Predator Caller* magazine inside cover advertisement and catalog insert.

THE BIG YEAR

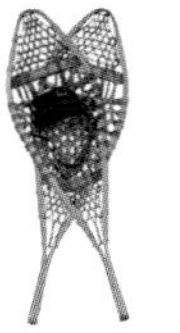

While waiting for Krause Publications and *Trapper & Predator Caller* (also known as *T&PC*) to get back to me on the bulk catalog mailing, I nearly backed out. It was a lot of money to spend on advertising and I had acquired many consumers with just running ads and doing trapping conventions. But when *T&PC* called and gave me the price, I couldn't say no. I had to go all in. I immediately ordered 65,000 of the new catalogs I had just designed for the 1989–90 season. Register Lakota printing in Chamberlain, South Dakota printed my catalog and books locally and were always the lowest price when I asked for printing bids.

I drove my pickup and trailer loaded full of trapping catalogs to Krause Publications in Iola, Wisconsin. There I met a young guy, Brad Rucks who helped me unload them. I mention him here as Brad worked himself up the ladder at Krause (and then F+W Media) to eventually start Media 360 LLC with several other outdoors enthusiasts, including fellow Krause coworker Dan Schmidt. Media 360 is now the owner and publisher of *T&PC,* as well as *Deer & Deer Hunting* and *Turkey & Turkey Hunting.* Wow!

My 1989 Catalog would be stapled in the middle of the *Trapper & Predator Caller* NTA Issue. The magazine was printed and mailed in July as to arrive in August about the time of The National Trappers Association's annual convention. I was on sitting pins and needles waiting for the response. When my magazine came, I opened it and sure enough the catalog was inside. But my excitement soon turned to worry when after two days, three days, four days of waiting—no orders. None. I was freaking out. Maybe trappers were turned off by this type of promotion? Maybe not every magazine had a catalog in it? Maybe all this good luck I was having was changing? On the fifth day I received 7 orders and all included the catalog order form. That's a good thing. On day six, the tsunami hit. I went out to the mailbox at the end of our 2-mile gravel road and the box was crammed full. Stuffed. And there was a note saying more mail was at the post office. On that fateful day I took in over $100 thousand of video, lure, book and supply orders. Each day the orders kept coming. The catalog mailing was a home run. I soon left for the National Trappers Association Convention in Richmond, Virginia. There I saw Jeff Smith for the first time in several years. He had flown in from Montana in his own airplane. My flying had motivated him to get his license—I thought that was really neat. We chatted and parted pals again. But I haven't heard from him since.

HUNTING VIDEOS

In 1989 I also was contacted by a video distributor who lived in Oklahoma City. His name was Sheen Rhea. Sheen was interested in being a distributor of my trapping videos. He sold hunting and outdoor videos to rental stores and was also recruiting a few producers to make hunting videos exclusively for him. I now had 2 hunting video programs—one on wild turkey hunting with Ike Ashby and the archery black bear video I did with Paul Voz and Terry McGillicky. Sheen invited me to his offices where I was shown Mark and Terry Drury's first video which Sheen was getting ready to market. Roger Raglin also had 2 videos that Sheen was distributing. I signed on to allow Sheen to market all my trapping videos, the survival video and both hunting videos. Within two months' time, I was shipping hundreds of copies of each video title to Oklahoma City. This was a totally new market and seemingly free money, so I began looking into more ideas to make hunting videos.

Paul Picciano Photo

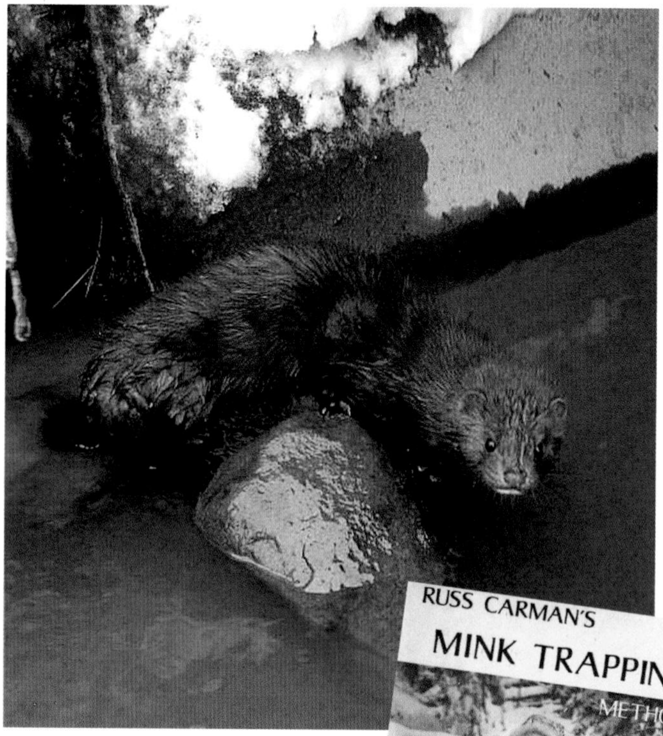

Nice mink nailed in Johnny Thorpes "Suicide Mink Set" by New York trapper Paul Picciano.

Living in South Dakota, there were many opportunities to do wing shooting, especially pheasants but also upland birds, ducks and geese. As luck would have it, a pheasant hunting outfitter named John Forester drove by my trappers school sign and saw that I made videos. He drove in and asked me what I would charge to make him a promotional video on his pheasant hunting operation. My mind was racing with ideas. I told John that I would like to make a full video on his hunting operation and then distribute it to rental stores. He need only pay me the price for a promo and he would have a full video. John was ecstatic and said yes. The video became *Wild Ringneck Bonanza*—it was a huge hit.

Authors Collection

On the pheasant production shoot one of John Forester's guides was a young guy from Reidsville, North Carolina. This is where I met Sandy Brady. We became pals as Sandy was very interested in the video business. During the filming of *Wild Ringneck Bonanza*, Sandy asked me if I had ever thought about doing a television series. I was only four years into the video business and busy as ever, I had no time for TV, nor did I even understand it. But it was an interesting idea and the more I thought about it, the more it made sense. John Forester was more than happy with his pheasant video and it was decided that we would do a sequel video on prairie chicken and sharp-tail grouse titled *Upland Game Bird Bonanza*, which would become a bigger hit than the pheasant video. Sandy Brady began coming by my shop always wanting to lend a hand and to learn more about the video business, how to run the camera and always wanting to talk about doing a TV series.

You must remember at this time I was rapidly expanding my lure business, running a trapline, teaching

Jimmy Houston Photo

Jimmy Houston helped me immensely in my start as a television producer by giving me perspective and direction

Author's Photo

Here's a snap during the early days of Outdoor Adventure Magazine. Pictured Top Row left: Pat Foy Brady with Sandy Brady. Bottom Row left: yours truly with North Carolina Turkey call maker J. Van Sharpe. Pat Foy passed away in November 2019, he was a fine and honest man and will be dearly missed.

at the Fur Takers Trappers College, writing for *F-F-G* as well as doing the *F-F-G* Question Box and Fur Markets. I was a busy guy. If I was to decide to get into TV, it would have to be a television series about trapping. Trapping was my first love—I was good at it. There were many stories to be told about the romance of the wilds and the trapper, about the animals and the renewable resource, about adventure and survival. But at this point, I didn't know how to make a television show, so I looked for advice from those who did. After numerous attempts to talk to several outdoor TV producers, I was able to reach well-known TV fisherman Jimmy Houston. Jimmy's show aired on the mega cable sports network ESPN, and if anyone knew outdoor TV it was Jimmy.

Jimmy Houston was very gracious and took the time from his busy schedule to talk to me about broadcast television. We spoke about needing a reason to have a show, audience expectations, potential sponsorship partners, different networks and finally—my idea.

Jimmy's advice to me was to rethink the idea of a trapping TV show and look for a hook that would excite the audience and endear them to me. He said

Author's Collection

that the goal of an outdoor host was to be a guy that the audience will stand up and root for.

It was great advice from a great guy. Several years later, I was a guest on Jimmy's ESPN fishing show and remember that Jimmy caught all the fish on that afternoon of taping. He was exactly the same in person as he was on TV—fun-loving, hardworking, God-fearing and a phenomenal fisherman.

Sandy Brady's father was Pat Foy Brady, his family one of the original oil distributors in North Carolina. Mr. Brady came to Chamberlain and made the proposition that he would invest in my talents if I incorporated, hired his son and started a TV company. Both Sandy and his father had big ideas. I was just a trapper. But fur prices were way off, and I was looking at doing more bowhunting videos.

Reflecting back on Jeff Smith and how that partnership turned out, I was skeptical to do it again. If I were to incorporate, I must have the controlling interest and call all the shots. It was agreed upon and soon Sandy Brady and his father were invested in my company, Tom Miranda Outdoors Incorporated. Sandy would work for me in sales and we would go forward making hunting videos until the time was right to try and produce a television series. Sheen Rhea at Telemark was hungry for titles, so Sandy and I started doing turkey hunting videos. Brady was a good caller and a bowhunter so it was a good fit.

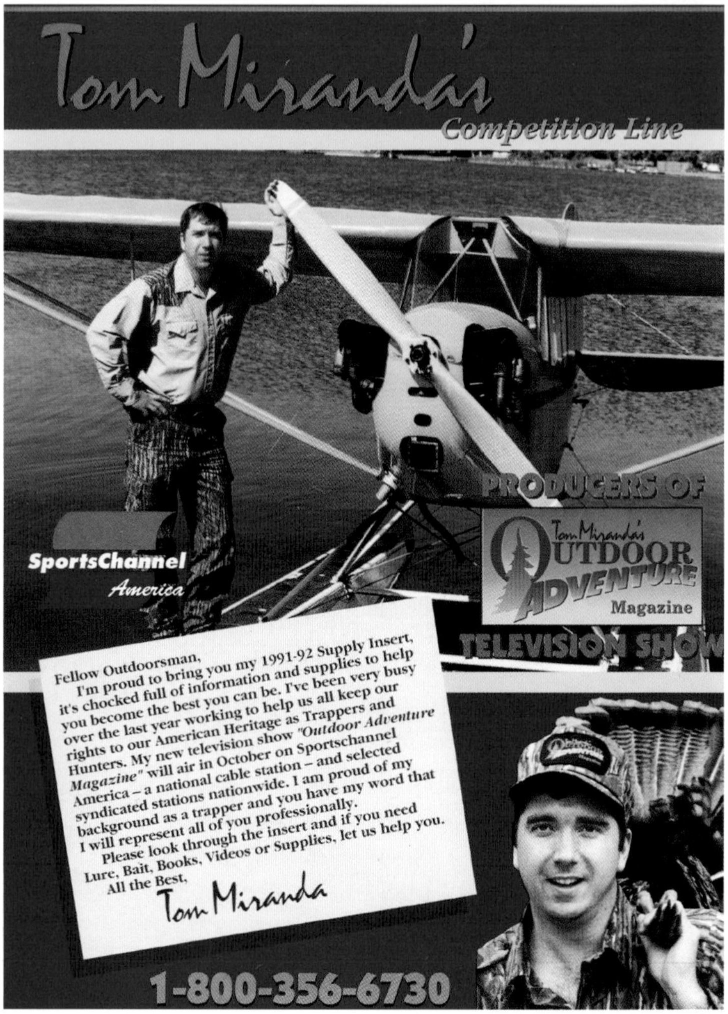

My 1991 supply catalog sported the SportsChannel America logo and had more video programs than trapping lures. This catalog folded open into a poster.

Over the course of 1990–91 we traveled and made videos. And Sheen took all we could make and sold thousands. Maybe you'll recognize some of these old titles—*Best of the Best, Professional Predator Calling with the Experts, System for Gobblers, System for Gobblers 2, Dynamite Ice Fishing, Gobbler Down, The Crowmen, and The Sign of Success.*

Some portions of the videos were done with the thought that they could possibly be used in a TV episode. Once we had amassed some substantial hunting and fishing footage, I thought maybe it would be a good idea to attempt make a pilot show. The series

Author's Photo

Tom Miranda in "original" Realtree camouflage and one of his archery whitetails taken on camera for an early episode of Outdoor Adventure Magazine.

would be called *Tom Miranda's Outdoor Adventure Magazine*. Each episode would include hunting, fishing and adventure segments taped around the globe. Originally, we had decided that Brady would primarily do the gun hunts, some bow hunts, some fishing and a few adventures. I would do bow hunts, some fishing and most of the adventures. In other words, we would co-host the show. We would hire freelance cameramen for field production. I would edit the series and Brady would sell the advertising.

It was a great plan—we immediately had chemistry. The road trips were a blast and we were doing really neat things. We hunted nonstop for big and small game, fished from Florida to New Zealand and did crazy adventures coast-to-coast. Our goal was to make 13 original hunting, fishing and adventure segments to complete a season of the show.

Because we were hunters first and I knew the video business, we started doing as much hunting as possible and making videos for resale through Sheen at Tele-Mark. These videos would make us money while we figured out the TV business. Plus, the wildlife footage we gathered would build a great library to enhance the hunting episodes when we went to broadcast.

In 1990 we finally landed a slot on SportsChannel America, a Minneapolis-based cable network, and captured Realtree, Martin Archery and Budweiser as major advertisers that first season.

DON POWELL

1963–

Pennsylvania trapper Don Powell is no stranger to trappers who live to trap mink. He has been obsessed by the water weasel since becoming a trapper and more obsessed with researching and discovering methods that would allow trappers to harvest mink on purpose, not just in accidental muskrat and raccoon sets. Don's thought process was that there must be a set for mink like the dirt-hole set is for fox, a set that can be made to catch a mink. Don's story of his pursuit is quite fascinating.

Don Powell Photo

Pennsylvania mink trapper Don Powell is all smiles as his mink set connects with a dandy buck mink.

Don Powell Photo

Master Trapper Russ Carman with Don Powell at Minktoberfest.

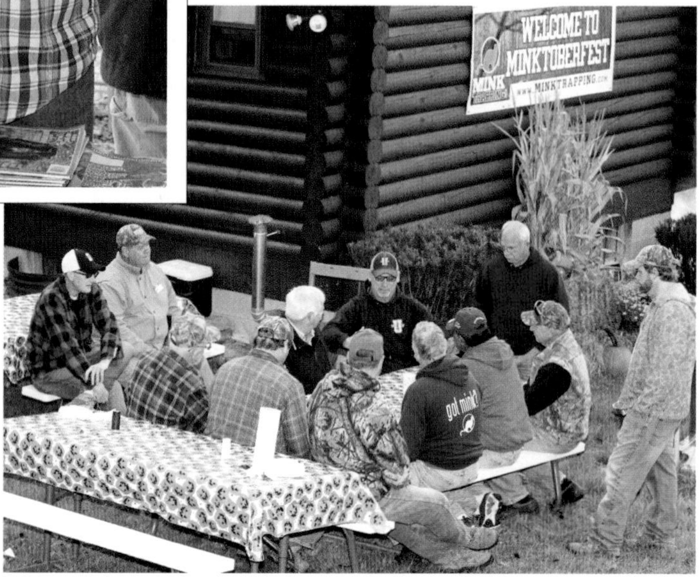

A group of trappers discuss mink trapping secrets at the 10th Anniversary of Minktoberfest, held in Punxsutawney, Pennsylvania.

Like most trappers Don started as a youngster trapping muskrat in west-central Pennsylvania. Beginning at age 9, using one of his grandpa's traps and following along with his older brother and pal, the trio learned trapping together on a small stream near their home. Don found a passion for trapping and by age 12, he was catching foxes—by age 16, his foxes were bringing 70 bucks apiece—a huge incentive to keep trapping. For Don, the trapping numbers weren't as important as the methods. Don Powell was intrigued by animal habits. A prime example was that Don could catch red foxes easily but struggled catching gray foxes. That is until he learned more about gray fox habits and preferences. Then grays were easy.

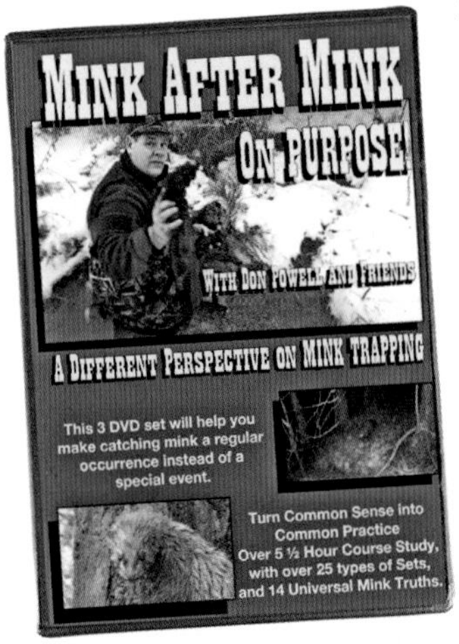

Author's Collection

Don Powell's 3-DVD treatise on mink trapping featuring Ruth the ruthless mink. It's a must watch.

One day Don met a trapper tending sets and the older gentleman had taken a mink while trapping muskrats. For Don, a mink was seemingly a mythical creature as he never saw a track, never saw a mink along his trapline, yet some of his muskrats would be eaten in the trap. Don knew that mink were there, but how could he catch one? Soon his desire became an obsession. First buying every mink book he could find, then every mink video. Yet seemingly the available lessons all revolved around blind sets. And to Don, a blind set was like a trail set for a fox relying somewhat on chance.

Sitting in a trapping seminar, Don listened to the late, great Paul Grimshaw talk about catching mink in 220 body-grippers set for otters at plunge pools. A plunge pool is a deeper place in a creek that's formed at the bottom of a riffle or rapids. Grimshaw was a beaver and otter trapper extraordinaire and these plunge pool sets were utilized for otters and set under water to keep sets working in cold weather. Fish often congregate in these plunge pools which is the attraction for otters. Then one day while walking a snowy creek looking for mink tracks, Don spotted mink prints in the snow on a hammock in the middle of the stream. Traps were set at the water's edge but frozen in. Don noticed minnows darting in the adjacent plunge pool—suddenly the light went on! This was the beginnings of Don's bottom baited mink setting method.

As technology advanced, Don started setting up deer scouting cameras along creeks, under bridges and near plunge pools to attempt to capture wild mink in their haunts. It was a difficult proposition, but he did log some footage. Then, another idea came to light. Don decided to set up a small captive mink ranch. The enclosure would allow additional filming of mink habits and bring Don even more insight on the habits of mink. One of his ranch mink was exceptionally active and was eventually referred to as Ruth when recognized in the video footage. Ruth was short for ruthless as Ruth was a savage hunter. Between the wild mink scouting camera footage and the ranch mink video taken in the enclosure, the mythical creature's habits were now being documented on video and lessons learned.

Don Powell's research evolved in his book *Mink Trapping—A Deep and Complete Long Lining System.* His treatise was critically acclaimed. The book was followed with an amazing 3-DVD set, *Mink After Mink on Purpose.* The video features footage of Ruth as well as many wild mink clips recorded by the scouting cameras. Don's premise (which is well outlined in his mink trapping methods) uses several different, but very effective sets including baited body-gripper traps, weighted and strategically placed on stream bottoms.

The success of Don's mink knowledge methods has spun into a unique event known as Minktoberfest. Originating in 2010, the event started with 4 trappers who came together to talk mink trapping. Ten years later, Minktoberfest attendance has grown to over 150 mink aficionados. Don attributes his success to the mentoring and friendships of legendary trappers Kermit Stearns, Major Boddicker, Russ Carman, Neil Olson and others. Don also has built an online forum at minktrapping.com where over 2,000 member followers have posted nearly 700 pages of mink trapping knowledge and discussions. It appears obvious to me that Don's hard work, passion and dedication to trapping has earned him a place as a Master Trapper.

"Everything I needed to know for business I learned on the trapline. From how to deal with people, understand their needs and show appreciation to the importance of getting up in the morning. If you want to know how to put up numbers of mink, look for small improvements that can lead to large incremental increases in catch. Understand the difference between ***Lead*** *measures and* ***Lag*** *measures.* ***Lead Measures*** *you can control such as the permissions you have, the sets you put out, the new traps placed each day. Understand the* ***Lag Measures*** *like time spent skinning pelts other distractions that take away from the focus or goal. Planning, preseason work, new sets each day and getting new permissions while retaining existing ones and postseason thank you's are all important. In Real Estate the motto is location, location, location, but the motto in mink trapping is Locations, Locations, Locations! In summary, remember, if you don't check your traps your line dies today—if you don't adjust your line, it dies tomorrow!"*

—Don Powell, Minktoberfest 2019

Ken Smythe's
BOTTOM EDGE
MINK SET
An new underwater mink
of mink to its credit, that
THE MINK
MANUAL
MINK MANIA
Trapping The
MINK
The Bank Runner
by
Leonard Pavel
PROF
mink t
"The Helfrich P
by
Jim Helfrich
MON SENSE APPRO
NK TRAPPING
MINK AFTER MINK
ON PURPOSE!
WITH DON POWELL AND FRIENDS
MINK TRAPPING
Mink and Muskrat
TRAPPING
by S. STANLEY HAWBAKER
Allweather
MINK
A Bodygripper Mink Trapping System that Functions Effectively with Little Maintenance During Flooding and Freezing Weather Conditions.
by Bob Noonan
MEGA MINK
METHODS
MINK TALE
by
Marvin "Bud" Hal
LURE
BANK
BUILD UP SMALL DAM OF SOD AND MUD IF NEED BE
WATER LEVEL
WIRE TO ROCK
SPRING COMING FROM OLD MUSKRAT DENS, BEAVER HOLES ETC.
THORPES SUICIDE MINK SETS

TODD HUMBERG

1969–

Todd Humberg is a name that may not come to mind when thinking about famous trappers. But some trappers keep a low profile. Todd hasn't written a trapping book or made a trapping DVD, but what he has done is learned to catch mink. Lots of mink. And his system is fascinating.

Todd started trapping muskrats at age 9 with his grandfather near Clear Lake, Iowa. Both Todd's grandfather and father were successful muskrat trappers in northern Iowa, also taking raccoons and an occasional mink. By age 12 Todd had his own trapline and trapped part-time throughout school. After high school graduation Todd got a real job like we all do, but he would spend his fall weekends scouting and his two weeks' vacation trapping. Todd learned much from his grandfather, father and from other trappers and what he did was put that information into a simple system and execute it over his allotted time to trap. In 1994, at age 25, Todd started his longline mink trapping education.

Like all mink trappers, Todd used blind sets. But his go-to set was the pocket set. Todd's variation was that he dug his pockets deep into the bank—a full 24 inches. Todd also made his pockets a little narrower than most, about as wide as the 1-1/2 coil traps he was using. Todd preferred the old-style Victor square pans on his mink traps as they provided a larger kill area.

Todd Humberg Photo

Todd Humberg poses in the basement with his 2000 season mink catch—108

What pans he couldn't locate and buy, Todd made himself. He also used carp for bait and liked to use a large bait the size of a large man's fist. His thought process was bigger is better as more fish in the hole would give off more smell—mink hunt with their nose. Todd's set philosophy was that a deep pocket allowed the mink to get all the way inside and gave him eight chances at a catch. Since mink have four paws, they would use four steps in and four steps out, thus eight chances.

Humberg's strategy was solely bridge trapping but on a massive scale. After years of successful mink catches in the 100-plus range, Todd figured in his area of Iowa that a trapper needed to run 100 bridges for two weeks to catch 50 mink. Thus 200 bridges equaled 100 mink and 300 bridges 150 mink. In his system, Humberg would also take upward of 250 raccoons and some seasons 400 raccoons—plus muskrats. Todd also started doing some Animal Damage Control work and was con-

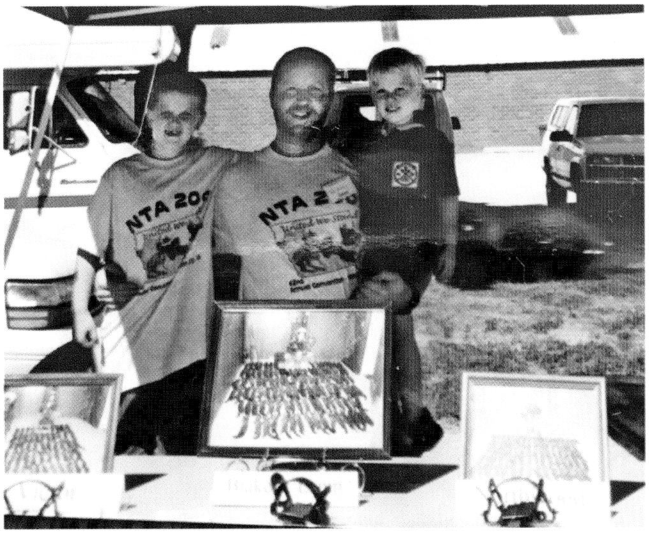

Todd Humberg Photo

Todd and his boys at the 2001 National Trappers Convention. Todd sold over 25,000 mink pans in the years he made them.

Todd Humberg Photo

Humberg with his growing boys and 120 Iowa mink.
Todd Humberg's massive northern Iowa catch of 160 mink in three weeks.

tracted by the Department of Natural Resources as one of three special trappers in Iowa to live trap and relocate river otters.

In August of 2001 the National Trappers Association National Convention was being held in Mason City, Iowa and by this time Todd already had several seasons of 100-plus mink under his belt. The convention was so close to home, Todd decided to make up some of his mink pans and tailgate the convention to try and sell them. Todd made up 3,000 of his special Humberg Pans and sold out to dealers the evening before the convention started. His massive catch photos and trapping conversation savvy made the pans an easy sell. In November that same year, Todd was blessed with three weeks' vacation. He was more prepared for this 2001 season than any previous season. Humberg had three traplines laid out—107 bridges on each line covering 140 to 200 miles. Three hundred and twenty bridges total. On a three-week, all-in, full-throttle run—Todd took 160 mink, 320 raccoons and enough rats for gas money. Pretty incredible. That's more than 7-1/2 mink a day average for 21 days. That famed season Todd used salmon for bait and said for him it definitely made a difference, but he offers, "It's expensive unless you have a source."

Todd knows that his hard work and KISS method (Keep It Simple Stupid) of running fast and keeping it simple was the real secret to his success, yet he gives his grandfather Carl and father Bob much of the credit. Today, Todd enjoys running the line with his oldest son Dylan. "My oldest boy Dylan Humberg is a fifth generation Humberg trapping in northern Iowa. He is currently my biggest motivation and with his drive, speed and knowledge of trapping it's been a lot of fun," Todd said.

"I was taught at a young age that if it's worth doing—it's worth doing right. If you put in the time and hard work, I believe you will be rewarded at the end of the line. It may not always be big numbers or dollars, but sometimes is the satisfaction that you gave it your all and did it right. Usually my trapping money in those days went toward Christmas presents for family. I was blessed to be able to concentrate on trapping mink and thus put up good numbers of those animals. Something that my father or grandfather never did. I feel a lot of pride in that."

—Todd Humberg, 2020

Todd Humberg Photo

Todd with 13 mink in a day's run over the traps.

FURBEARER NICK NAMES

MUSKRAT: 'rat, rudder tail, 'skrat, 'squatch, musquash

BEAVER: flat-tail, chipper, chisel tooth

RACCOON: bandit, ringtail, trash panda, masked bandit, rascal

OPOSSUM: grinner, slick tail, silver fox

SKUNK: polecat, stinker, striper, pepe

RED FOX: reynard, bushy tail, white-tip, red

COYOTE: 'yote, dawg, song dog, yellow-eye, butt sniffer, Wiley E, howler, yodel dog, yodeler

MINK: water weasel, bank runner

OTTER: torpedo, silver belly

BADGER: bulldozer

BOBCAT: bob, bobber, spots, spotted belly, 'cat

WOLF: lobo

LEAP TO THE TOP

In December 1990, my second son Joshua came into the world. Josh quickly became known as Mr. Touchdown. He was inquisitive, fun and always excited to be with dad. He was then and is now very special to me, as are all my children. Switching gears from being one of the most well-known trappers on the planet to being just another face on TV wasn't making much sense. But the hunting videos were selling and SportsChannel was a start. I put my nose to the grindstone.

SportsChannel America was great. It was the perfect entry network to cut our teeth in broadcast. But TV was hard work—expensive and airing on a small cable channel wasn't doing our show justice. We knew that a big network was required to bring big advertisers and at that time, the largest network carrying outdoor programming was ESPN.

So, in late 1990 as our first season was progressing on SportsChannel, I began sending tapes to ESPN. At the time, Bill Fitts was ESPN's programming genius. Bill had been a top producer at ABC under executive producer Roone Arledge of "Wide World of Sports" fame and had helped launch ESPN back in 1979. Fitts was a producer legend and the guy that I needed to help me move up to the big leagues.

The first tapes I sent to the network fell on deaf ears as I never heard back. Looking at those early shows, now I can see why! Then in the fall of 1991 I sent in another revised pilot episode that prompted a call from Fitts. Bill was polite, but firm and said that our shows lacked the drama and professionalism of an ESPN quality series. He said he liked the show concept, but we lacked professional training and the episodes needed to be produced differently. His suggestion was that I employ a freelance producer to train me as an ESPN quality producer—he recommended Kim Nye. Kim was a producer for MTV and had done the US Olympic athlete bio pieces for ABC. She also did limited freelance work—once I spoke to her on the phone she was eager to help us.

Sandy Brady, lead cameraman Mike Pellegatti and I did 3 short trips with Kim in March 1992, all in Florida. We shot an everglades wild hog hunt, largemouth bass fishing in Lake Okeechobee and a skydiving piece near Clewiston. Kim instructed us on pre-production techniques, interviewing skills and storytelling. The shoots went well and I remember Kim saying, "Tom, your hunting footage is great. It's the storyline that's lacking. Be true to the story and tell it completely. Your audience is smart and will appreciate a good story."

Pennsylvania trapper Nathan Roberts poses with an awesome mixed bag catch including a nice string of water weasels.

Several weeks later, Kim met me at Editek production studios in Omaha, Nebraska and we cut our first *professional* show. The show shipped to Bristol, Connecticut and ESPN home offices. Fitts liked it and with Kim touting our hunting expertise, we were soon approved to air on ESPN. Now all we needed was a time slot, something that is not easy to secure and often impossible to get on ESPN. Typically, a TV series must drop out or be cut to allow space for a new program. There are only so many half hours allotted for outdoor programming on ESPN.

When we got our chance, I'll never forget the phone call. I was speaking with Rich Caulfield, ESPN Outdoors' programming director. Programming directors are the individuals who say your show will air or not air, when it will air and how often.

Rich asked, "So Tom, if I give you 8 episodes in 3QTR can you deliver me top shows?"

"Yes sir," I replied.

He continued, "Third quarter starts in two months—that means in two months you will be providing me ESPN-quality, original programming. No episode shall be late, no mistakes in editing. Am I clear?"

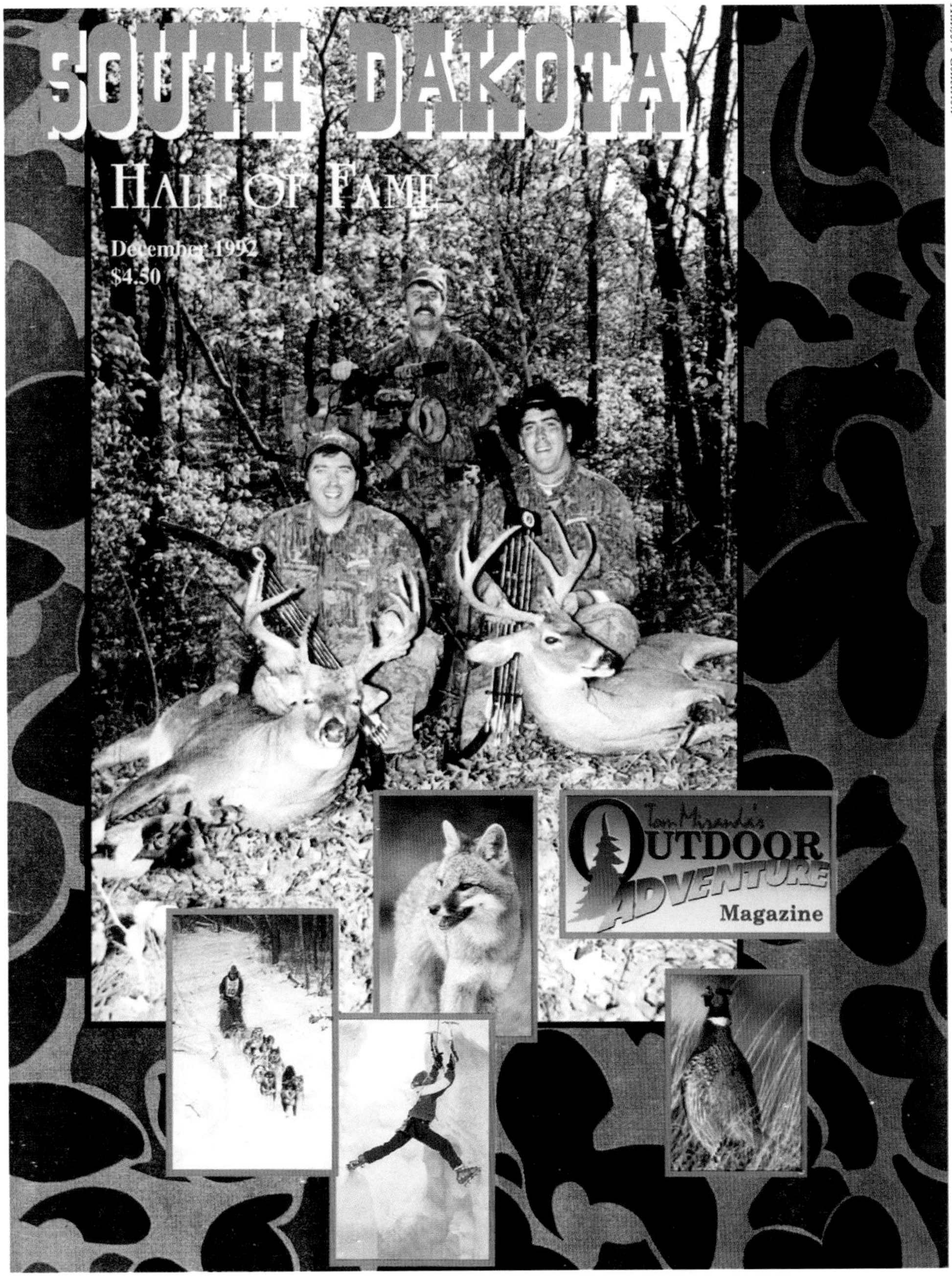

Author's Collection

Cameraman Mike Pellegatti, Sandy Brady and I make the cover of *South Dakota Hall of Fame* magazine, December 1992.

"Yes sir," I said.

"Mr. Miranda, welcome to ESPN. Legal will send you contracts within two weeks," he offered.

That was it. BAM! I was ecstatic. We had aired on SportsChannel America for two seasons, but now *Outdoor Adventure Magazine* would appear on ESPN. It was Little League to Major League—I had made it and I was scared to death.

Saturday July 4, 1992 at 8 a.m. eastern time, Tom Miranda debuted on ESPN. It was a milestone in my career. Who would have ever thought that a little kid from Columbus, Ohio with a passion for trapping could take that passion and build upon it to achieve at this level? How do you get from trapping to having your own outdoor TV series on ESPN?

SCHOOL OF HARD KNOCKS

You have to put this all into perspective. My show was airing alongside great Outdoor TV series like, *The Fishing Hole* with Jerry McKinnis, *Fly Fishing the World* with John Barrett, Mark Sosin's *Saltwater Journal* and *Jimmy Houston Outdoors*. All classic outdoor television shows. I couldn't believe it. But looking at the ESPN lineup, all of these series were about fishing. ESPN lacked hunting. Only Georgia's Wayne Pearson had cracked into the ESPN lineup with shooting sports. Tom Miranda's *Outdoor Adventure Magazine* promised viewers hunting, fishing and adventures each week. Rich Caulfield had given me a time slot. It was mine to keep it or lose it—I was bound and determined to deliver.

Of course, what's been left unsaid to this point is that the TV business was going to take me out of the trapping business. I could see that happing even in the videos we were doing. There was more hunting, especially bow hunting. I had worked so hard to get to the top in the trapping industry that I wasn't sure I wanted to switch careers. There was more financial upside to the TV gig, but was my heart in it for the long haul and ups and downs? At first, I just ignored the obvious but soon knew it was going to be the TV series winning out. I guess I made that decision when I signed the incorporation papers and took on investors.

The first ESPN season was a whirlwind. I was so busy traveling, taping, writing, editing, dubbing, etc. that I had no time to enjoy it. I watched a total of 2 episodes as they aired—what TV star luster there was quickly faded into 20-hour days and non-stop work. Something many viewers don't realize is that there are a great number of hours that go into producing a TV series. Also, TV deadlines are relentless. Once a season starts episodes must be submitted each week. That sounds easy except that an episode may take a week or two to shoot and two weeks to edit. Thus, you must be ahead of schedule and stay there or face the consequences of missing an episode deadline. Missing a deadline is akin to missing the last plane leaving Antarctica for the season. To the network, missing a deadline is like

Author's Photo

On location for rodeo clown school with Sandy Jessop, 1995.

forgetting your mom's birthday and Mother's Day all in the same week. Missing an ESPN deadline means you will never have an opportunity to miss another as you will no longer be airing on ESPN.

Then there are ratings. Nielsen Media Research rates TV dayparts to help equate a number of viewers to a cost basis or cost per thousand (CPM). TV ad time is based on CPM and TV networks constantly compare ratings of other networks during the same daypart—ratings before and after the same daypart and those between shows of similar genre. The bottom line is if you show isn't rating well, you will be cancelled, and your time slot will go to a more popular series.

Sponsors also add into the TV equation. Advertisers need to sell product—that's what they expect when they buy advertising. It's the producer's job to creatively blend product into the show to illustrate the product without being obvious or infomercial like. High ratings keep sponsors, mediocre ratings lose them and if your show is rating poorly, a good rule of thumb is "don't quit your day job."

I had learned all of this during SportsChannel America's two-year run, but the level of intensity and the dollars involved at the mega-network-level gave everything a new perspective. I was learning that even though it was difficult to get a series on ESPN it was going to be much more difficult to keep it. The cost of airtime was enormous. The workload for two guys—ridiculous. To coin a line from the movie *Top Gun*, "I was writing checks my body couldn't cash."

That said, just the mention of ESPN opened many doors for me. Few outdoor shows touted the huge universe and ratings that ESPN could provide. Sports celebrities all watched ESPN and a surprising number of these guys hunted. I rubbed elbows with the elite at ESPN. I met NFL, MLB, NHL, NBA and NASCAR personalities, rodeo cowboys, musicians, governors, other TV celebrities, actors and more. Guys like Dick Butkus, Joe Theisman, Ken Griffey Jr., Dale Earnhardt Sr., Ted Nugent, Gen. Norman Schwarzkoph, Gen. Chuck Yeager plus many more.

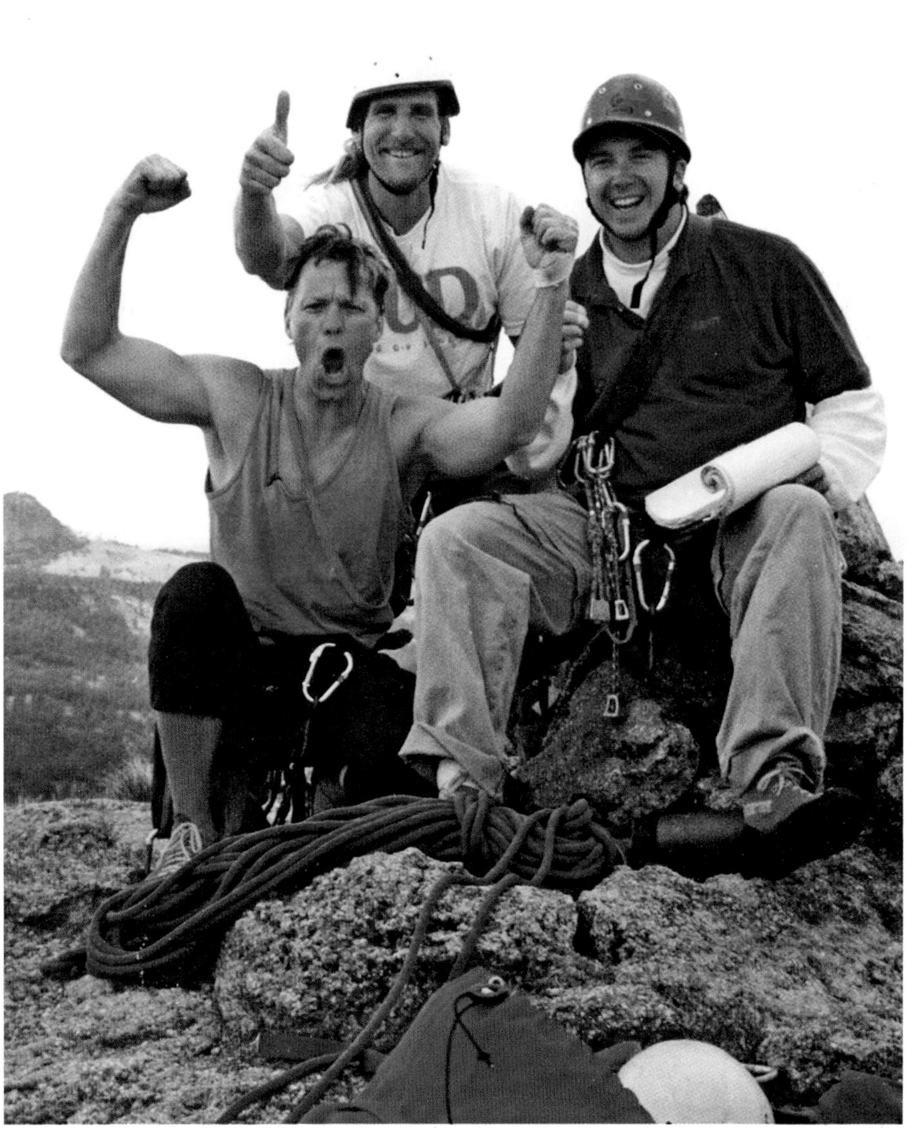

Author's Photo

At the top of Devils Tower National Monument. (L-R) Rollie Johnson, Paul T. Voz and Tom Miranda, ESPN Outdoors, 1993.

Outdoor Adventure Magazine was a fun show to do and became a huge success. I loved doing the bowhunting episodes, but my favorites were the adventure segments. During the six seasons of the show, I bungee jumped 4 bridges, skydived 6 times, walked on fire, rode a bull (with lessons from rodeo champion Ty Murray), was a rodeo clown, trained the Navy F-14 fighter syllabus, flew or co-piloted B-25, P-51, glider planes, hang gliders, helicopters, did cave diving, cave crawling, climbed Devils Tower National Monument, took batting lessons from Seattle Mariner pros Jay Buhner and Ken Griffey Jr., trained in a SWAT team, drove a NASCAR, a top fuel dragster, Ferrari race car, dove with sharks and had many more adventures. When it becomes my time to travel to the "Great Beyond," I think I will go out knowing that I lived life to the fullest.

KEN SMYTHE 1956–2014

Author's Collection

Have you ever noticed that mink trappers give mink sets all the cool names? Fox trappers have the dirt-hole and the flat set. Blah-blah names. Coon trappers get stuck with the pocket set or cubbie set. Blah-blah-blah. But mink trappers have the suicide set. BAM! That's a great set name. And then there's the blind set. Face it, even blind set sounds better than dirt-hole. And of course, there's the bottom-edge set. Bottom-edge, a mysterious, descriptive name. Most trappers have heard of the bottom-edge set but many have no idea what it is or how to make one.

When trappers gather and talk about mink trapping the name Ken Smythe seems to always come up. Ken was a Michigan trapper who like most of us started trapping at a young age and had a passion for it. Ken caught his first fox at age 16 and in his area of Michigan could catch about 70 foxes a season. During the late 1970s and early '80s, fox prices were at their peak and Ken would catch as many as he could. But as the mid-'80s rolled around the fur prices fell and Ken became interested in mink trapping.

Ken repurposed his 1-1/2 coil-spring fox traps as mink traps and made baited sets at the water's edge, but water fluctuation either had his sets high and dry or too deep. Ken trapped muskrats as well and would take a dozen or so every year in body-gripper traps in 'rat runs. Ken decided to try and use more body-grippers for mink and fashioned 150 - inch PVC pockets for the next season. These were set up above water or at the water's edge. But the mink were refusing them. Ken took only 2 mink in his PVC pocket sets that season and both were in flooding conditions with the PVC pipes and traps submerged.

Ken also would set body-grippers for 'rats in deeper creeks where there were no runs. Instead he set the traps on steep bank side and on the bottom. These sets took 'rats but also took mink. The next season Ken took 20 mink in these blind bottom sets.

Smythe also received some expert advice from Michigan trapper Steve Redman. Redman was a good mink trapper and had taken 27 mink in one day's run over the traps. When Ken asked Steve for some advice, Steve wouldn't give up his methods but he instead said, "Use the set that you caught 20 mink with this season and duplicate those sets. Then you'll catch numbers." Ken pondered Steve's message. The weather had turned cold and it was all Ken could do to keep his 40 pocket sets from freezing in. So, he decided to pull that line and set in 70 of his new bottom-edge sets. Ken let the body-grippers set six days then went through and pulled the works. Ken took 8 mink. This got Ken's mind spinning—if he could take 8 mink in a week with 70 traps, what could he do with three months and 200 traps?

The next season Ken went all in. No foothold traps. All body-grippers and bottom-edge sets. He kept 180 sets working for most of the three-month season and took 113 mink. The season was not only his best ever on mink up to that time, but the exercise gave him a better idea as to in what locations the sets worked best. In the 1991–92 trapping season, Ken ran 180 sets for two months and took 149 mink and more than 400 muskrats.

When it gets cold enough so that ice starts forming on the edges of the stream, mink can't get in and out of the water as easily as they could before. So, they spend more time down there and travel longer distances. The ground on the banks is frozen hard and so is the mud at the water's edge. There's usually some snow on the ground. The bank top food, mice and other rodents, are pretty much cleaned up, or hibernating or hard to get at. And the frogs and little fish at the water's edge are gone. Now mink have to get into the water almost full-time to eat. Six inches of snow or an inch of ice will really drive them down there.

Now the bottom edge set really starts to work. You might not make the big catches you did after the first few storms, because the mink population has been cut back somewhat. But after the weather gets really nasty in December, with ice and snow and deep cold, I start making regular catches of a half a dozen or so mink per run. It's the steady, consistent, smaller catches over a period of time that make up a big catch total.

— Ken Smythe, Bottom-Edge Mink Set as told to Bob Noonan

Bob Noonan Photo

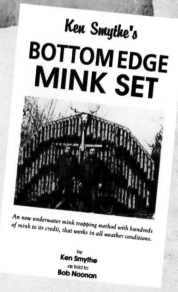

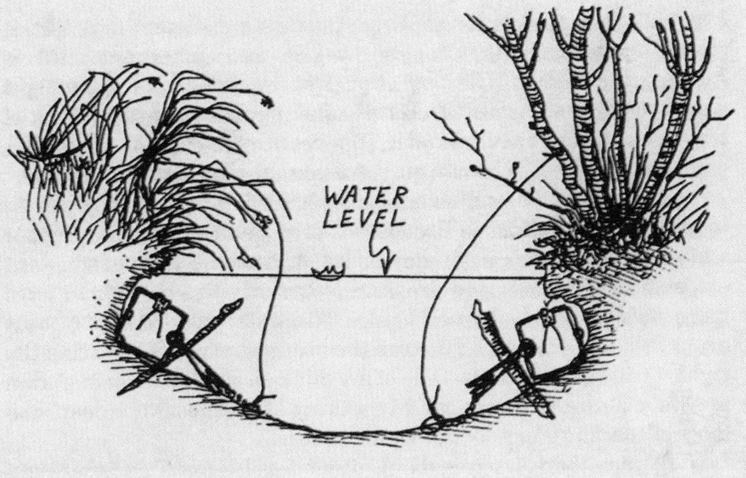

Ken Smythe's
BOTTOM EDGE
MINK SET
An new underwater mink trapping method with hundreds of mink to its credit, that works in all weather conditions.
by
Ken Smythe
as told to
Bob Noonan

I highly recommend this book if you want to up your mink trapping game.

Here's the Bob Noonan artist's rendition of Ken's Bottom Edge set. However, you'll need to study Ken's location photos and diagrams closely for location.

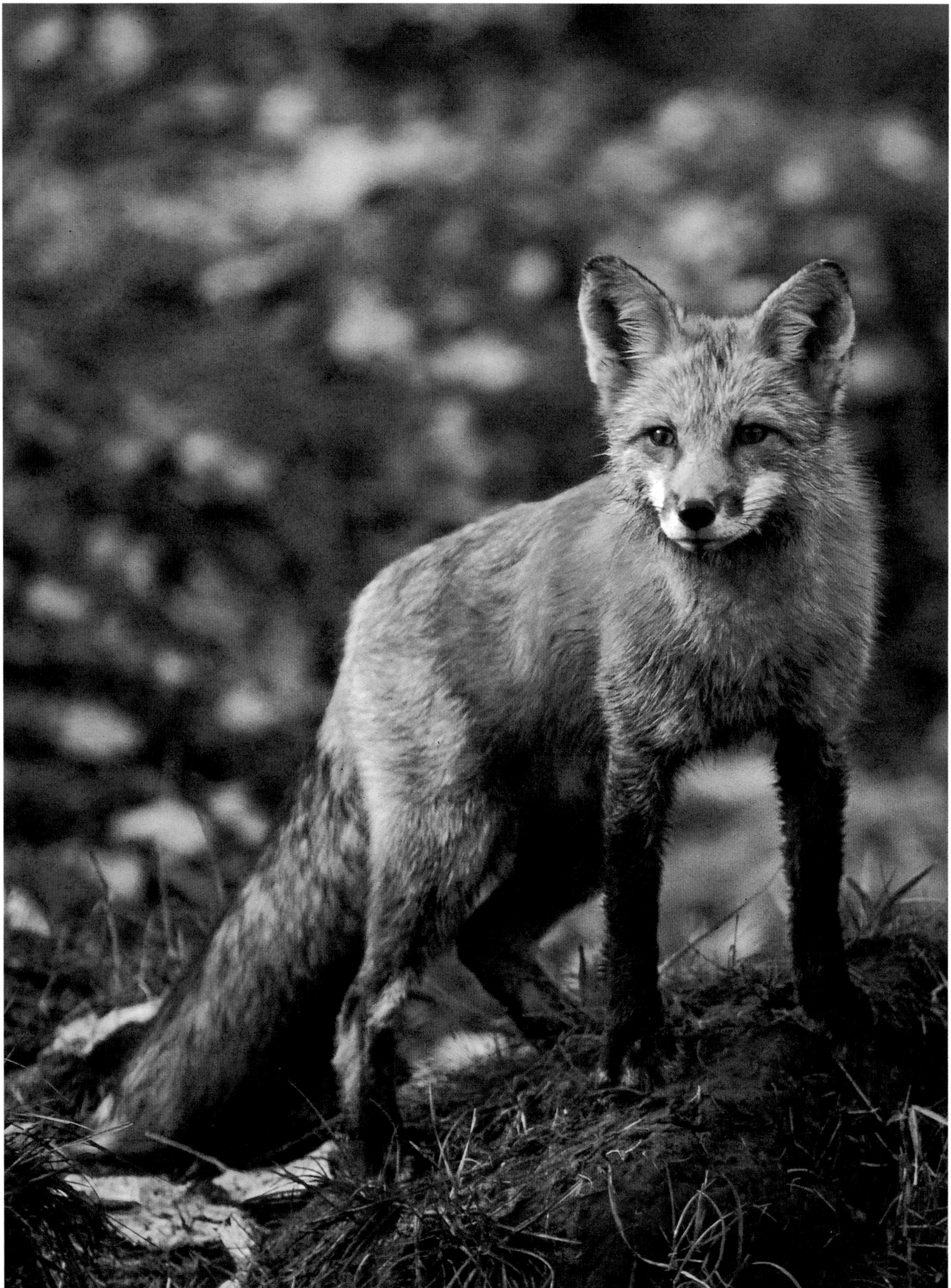

CHAPTER 10

FOXMEN

Josh Stairs Photo

Leslie Stairs poses with a great fox catch taken in New York state, 1940s.

The fox is one of nature's most revered creatures. One of its most charming animals. One of nature's most beautiful specimens. There's a reason why phrases like "sly as a fox," "outfoxed," or even "bright-eyed and bushy-tailed" are used. Or descriptive words like "foxy" or "vixen." Foxes have captivated humankind for centuries—and they still captivate trappers. I know many fox trappers and without exception they all love the fox. Red, gray, cross, silver, arctic—it doesn't matter. The attractive, nimble and sometimes shy reynard is a valuable furbearer and a joy to outwit on the trapline.

Like deer, rabbits, mice and many animals, foxes have enjoyed increased populations due to farming. As land was cleared and crops planted, the ecosystem changed from a forested habitat to agriculture. Agriculture inflates the land's carrying capacity for animals as the increased food available per acre is expanded exponentially.

FOX SPECIALISTS

Over the years there have been many trappers who were considered the best-of-the-best at catching foxes. Many of the early trappers did little to bed their traps and pan covers were non-existent. The water set was considered one of the most effective early fox sets. The water set utilized a trap hidden in shallow water. The trapper would place a small sod on the pan, resembling a dry place for the fox to step to as it investigated bait placed on an island farther out in the stream. The submerged trap gave off no scent, the set looked natural and the pan placement was perfect every time. It was all up to the bait or scent to attract the fox across the stream. These early fox trappers also trapped water animals like mink, beavers and muskrats, so these sets were easy to make along their walking traplines.

< *Leonard Lee Rue III Photo*

New York trapper Art Crane was one of the earliest to be recognized as a master fox man because he not only made large catches but is thought to be the inventor of the dirt-hole set. E.J. Dailey gets some credit in books about being the originator, yet it's known that early in E.J.'s career he spoke with Crane and likely watched Art make at least one dirt-hole set. E.J. had a large sounding board with his early magazine articles and no doubt made the dirt-hole set popular. Because much of Art's trapping area was in or near the Adirondacks, wintertime trapping was brutal. Many of Crane's late-season dirt-hole sets were made near rotting stumps where the dry-rotted wood could be used as a covering. A large maple leaf was used for the pan cover when Art used soil. It should be stated that the biggest "secret" of the old-time trappers was that they trapped their foxes in the early fall and kept them penned up until their pelts became prime. It's known that all the old-timers did this in the early days of game laws. Foxes were often on a bounty and could be trapped year 'round. So, what they did was legal, albeit maybe in today's way of thinking not so ethical. I mention this info in no way to take away from these trappers, it's just how it was in those days. History is history—we learn and move on.

Other fox specialists over the years include of course Dailey, Rickard, Butcher, Thorpe, Lenon and many of the aforementioned legends in the earlier pages of this book. Arguably Stanley Hawbaker's book, *Trapping North American Furbearers* taught more new trappers how to catch a fox than any other book between the 1940s–1960s. I would be amiss if I also didn't mention Dakota fox man Garold Weiland. I realize he was also mentioned earlier in this book as

Stanley Hawbaker Photo

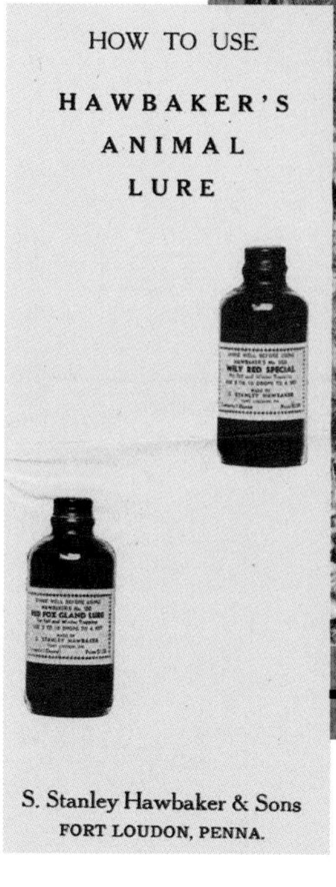

Here's Stanley Hawbaker in his later years. I caught my first fox with Hawbaker lure and many other trappers did as well.

well, but the influence that his long-liner books had over me, pal Ray Milligan and so many of us who held a copy at such a vulnerable and perfect time in our lives cannot be overstated. It was a perfect storm when one was graduating from school, in love with the outdoors, fur prices rising and the pages of Garold's book making it all look so glamorous, so doable. So adventurous. It's so exciting for me to type these words now and remember those days like they were yesterday. Wishing all those dreams could come true back then and knowing the outcome now will put a tear in the eye of anyone who felt the same and experienced the same—whether they acted on their dreams or not. Craig O'Gorman's fox-trapping prowess should also be restated here—his fox book is a must for any serious fox trapper.

And as I think of it, another name more than worthy of mentioning is expert fox trapper Bob Wendt.

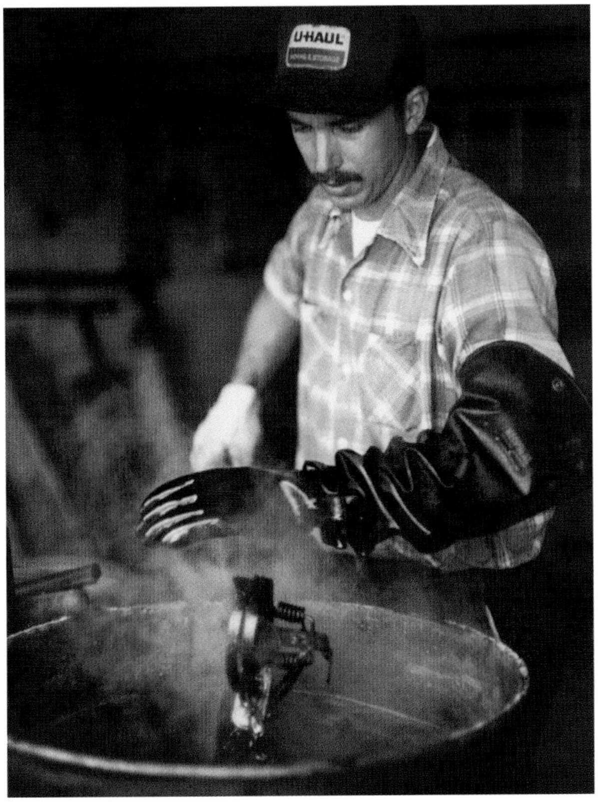

Dying traps in 1982 Columbus, Ohio

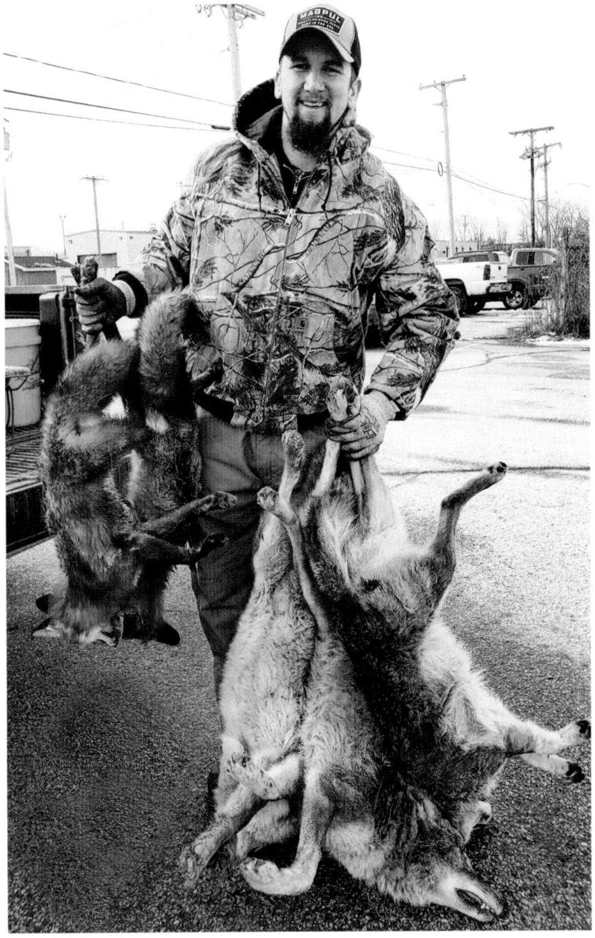

Ryan Reay Photo

Predator trapper Ryan Reay poses with a great morning's run over the trap line.

FOX MENTALITY

The stumbling block for most trappers as they increase their skill set is understanding the sheer magnitude of what's required in property and permission to keep active traps in fresh areas and average catch numbers up throughout the season. As youngsters we were lucky to have one or two farms to trap. Or one good stretch of creek or river. Two or three weeks of trapping and the areas were played out. Most youngsters over-trapped their small territories because they didn't know any better and likely had nowhere else to go. The thought that 100 (or 200 or even 300) farm permissions is required is almost unfathomable to most. Or the fact that one would tend traps from 4 a.m. until 8 p.m. every day for several months and use at minimum a tank full of fuel each day for the truck as well as six to ten 4-ounce bottles of lure each day.

Planning a production fox line includes thinking through all the variables. One of the things I did that was valuable to me was first putting up massive amounts of dry dirt. Found under bridges or during mid-summer dry spells, twenty or so 30-gallon trash cans full of dry dirt is a blessing during a rainy fall. Setting up your gear so sets are quick and easy involves preseason planning. Required are stakes long enough not to get pulled by an overzealous coyote, good trap swivels and a firm plan of the number of sets and locations that would be placed on each line. I had a rule of thumb that I set a minimum of ten new trap locations every day on a new farm or area. Also, in some fox areas there are many "trash" species and setting heavily in these areas helped to weed out the opossums and skunks to allow the foxes time to find my traps.

I also used two different sets of gear—I had a set to make all fresh trap sets—new sets in new dirt. My second equipment bag was for remakes and I only used this gear and gloves on a remake. Whether the trap held a fox, coyote, possum, skunk, badger, coon—it didn't matter. This remake bag and the tools it held—my gloves, sifter, trowel and kneeling pad always smelled like animals. The theory was simple, don't contaminate clean traps or a clean location with dirty gloves and equipment.

Author's Photo

Classic double catch on reds. The "walk thru" set is amazingly effective on foxes and coyotes.

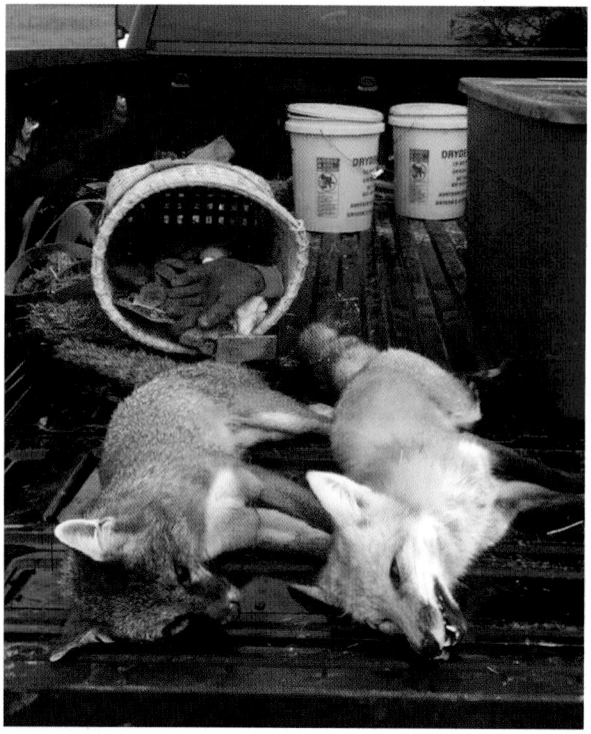

Josh Stairs Photo

In some areas of the East and Midwest, both red and gray foxes can be taken on the same trapline.

Another big help was a 30-gallon can of logwood always at the ready. Inevitably every day there are dirty traps that get pulled. I would hold them until I had about three dozen or so then wire them together and throw 'em in a creek riffle or river rapids for a few days. Often, I would pull out the clean traps from the riffle and add more dirty traps at the same time, so this was a twice a week stop. The water action would clean them thoroughly. I would then throw the traps into the logwood barrel for a few days, hang to dry and then reuse. If I had time, I waxed them—but not always. I suppose I could have purchased another 300 traps to have an ample amount for the full season, but I didn't. Loading your truck in the evenings with fresh traps, lure, fox urine and overall getting ready for the next day always gave me an early start.

PRINCIPLES OF LOCATION

Every fox trapping book and DVD covers locations in detail. But there is a theory behind location that most don't discuss. Experienced hunters and trappers know that 90% of the game lives in 10% of the habitat. Locating that habitat and getting permission to trap it is the secret ingredient to having the animals at one's disposal. Sure, there is dispersion of fox pup litters, but when your permissions are in the best habitat the animals come to you first.

The strategy is to start big and work down. In a perfect scenario, you would select the best state to trap foxes, then look for the best county in that state, followed by the best township to trap foxes in that county. Then the best section in that township, the best quarter section, and finally, the best location. If you follow this method exactly, you'll end up at Ron Leggett's house in Maryland! No, I'm joking. But you see where I'm coming from. Top trophy whitetail hunters use the record book entries to find the states and counties where more giant bucks are taken and concentrate their efforts in these counties and adjacent areas.

So how do we find this magic 10% of the habitat where 90% of the game are located? Here is an easy way. Take a map of one of the counties in which you want to trap foxes. Lay it out: using a set of magic markers, look at one township at a time. Begin to color all the rivers with a blue marker, all the creeks blue and all of the lakes and marshes blue. Then look for the major travel corridors. Mark the freeways, the railroad right-of-ways and the four-lane highways—mark all of these areas in orange. Look further for habitat areas like state parks, industrial parks, retention ponds, gravel pits, feed lots, hog confinements and similar spots and color these with a red marker. Now look to see where all the colors on your map begin to touch, cross or connect.

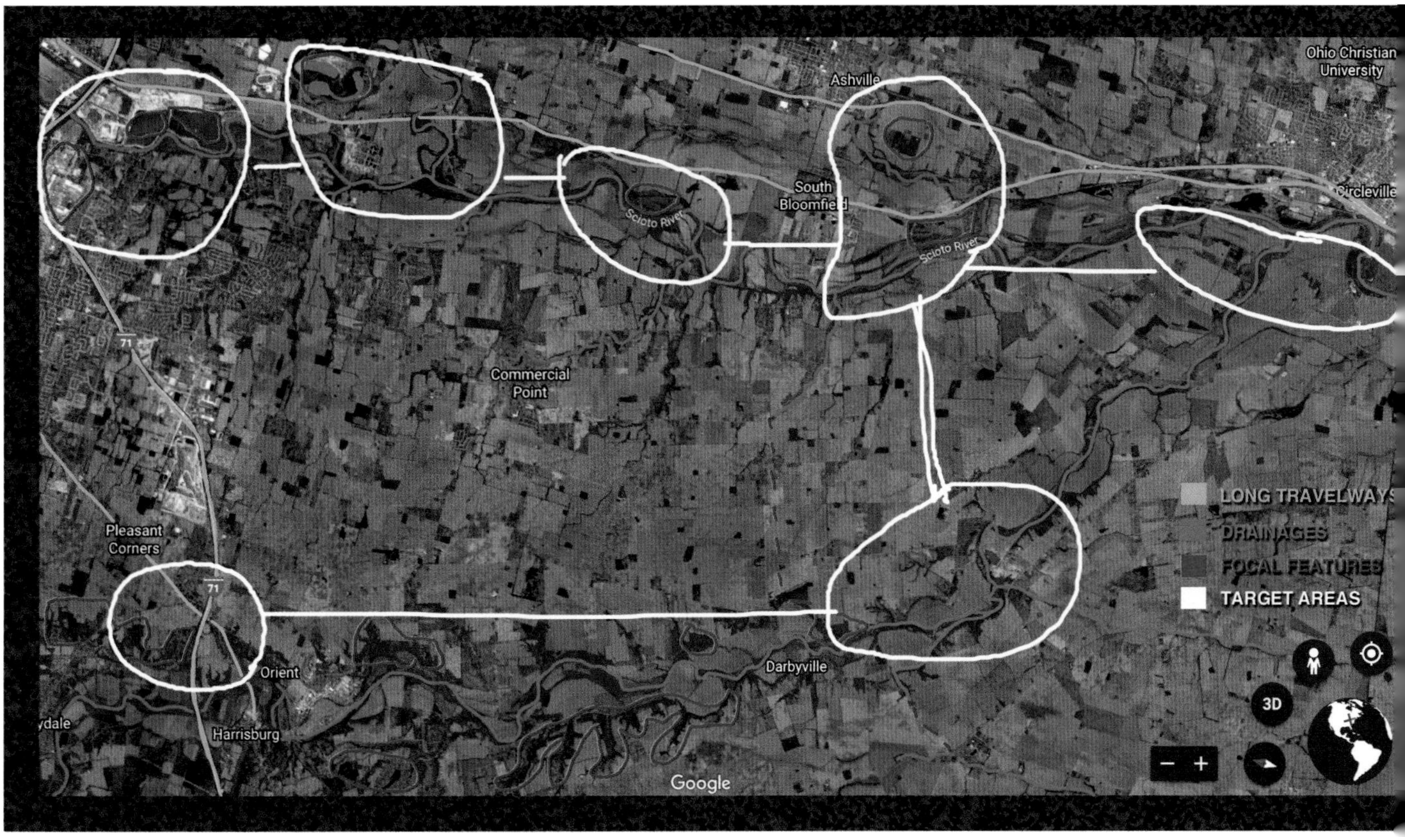

Using Google Earth is a great way to map potential areas for scouting and permission. I used paper maps years ago, but the theory is still the same and electronic maps are more detailed and up-to-date. The white circles on the map are the areas to concentrate on. The area shown is of a small part of my Ohio trapline circa 1980–83.

These areas where all the colors come together are "target areas" (circled in white on my map) and places where you need to gain permission. What we are actually doing is creating an organized way to begin to lay out areas that likely have crossing long-running barriers and habitat change. Wildlife prefer to live in what's called interspersion or places that include many types of habitat situated closely together. These interspersion areas have a higher interest to animals and higher carrying capacity for numbers of animals. Where creeks meet rivers, rivers meet rivers and interstate highways meet rivers, are bottle necks and areas that naturally funnel all game which may be traveling through an area.

Here's a late 1970s photo of young Ray Milligan on the fox line. This photo was use in one of his first articles in F-F-G Magazine, December 1979.

Here's Dakota long liner Garold Weiland in his famous tailgate photo which appeared in his first book, *Long Liner Fox Trapping*.

Of course, the above is the old-school way I used to do it. Today with a laptop, Google Earth and a little GPS knowledge, a trapper can electronically lay out a probable line without the paper map or markers.

These same methods can be used in any state and commercial trappers who know that the weather late season affects catch numbers will play the weather factor by state hopping. Starting a month early in the North, trapping at home in the prime of the season and then trapping in the south late season. Of course, the thought process is easy. It's the logistics that deter most who would seek such an adventure and added trapping edge. Considerations include scouting and permissions in three states and a huge outlay of traps and gear: travel trailer, and generator, multiple freezers. The list is endless, and all includes overhead as well as maintenance year to year. Full time trapping is not only a business but a risky one when fur prices become unpredictable. And they seemingly always are. It's why most trappers trap for the challenge as well as their passion for the animals and preference for an outdoor lifestyle.

EFFECTIVE FOX SETS

Stanley Hawbaker's original 1941 first edition of *Trapping North American Furbearers* chronicled more than a dozen fox sets. Today, a few variations of the dirt-hole and flat set are primarily used. Because of game laws, some states only allow live traps, others snares or body grippers. Using these types of traps requires specialized methods.

When I took trapping lessons from Odon Corr back in 1982, he taught me his signature flat set. As a government trapper Odon primarily used long spring Victor 3N traps making a banana-shaped trap bed. I liked Odon's approach to having the pan close to the attractor. His philosophy was, the closer the trap to the attractor the less chance of a miss. Corr also always guarded the loose trap jaw in an attempt to elim-

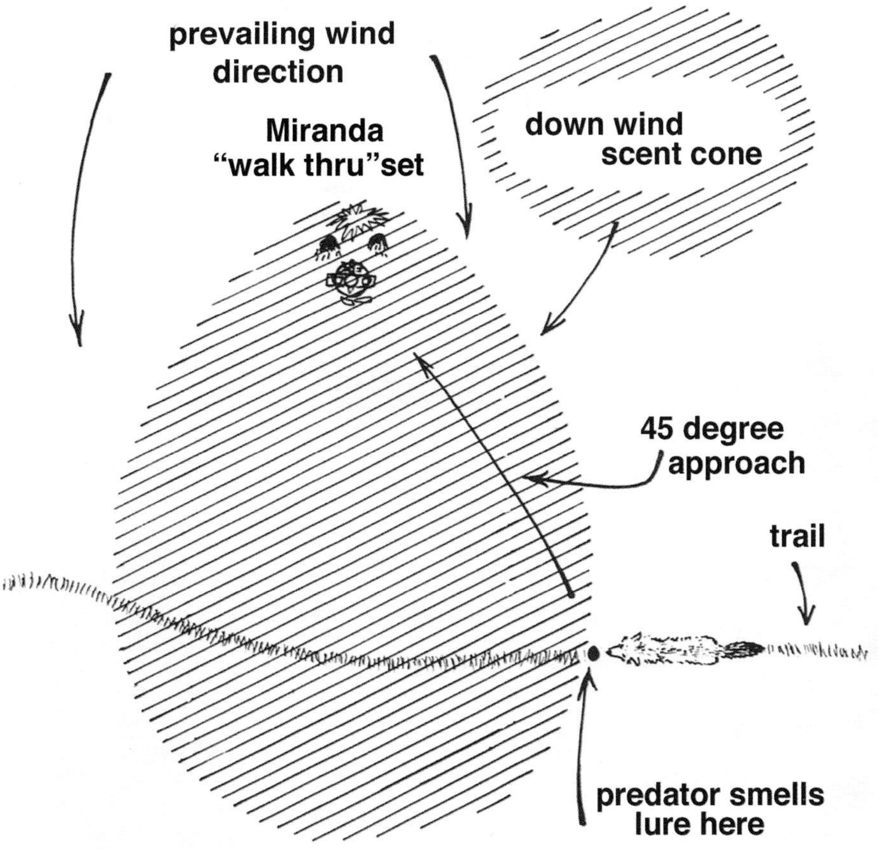

4 out of 5 animals (80%) will approach from downwind of the set. When the animal hits the scent dispersion cone, they will bird dog into the set at about a 45- degree angle. In my "walk thru" set the conical bait holes are both angled toward the center of the trap, the fox (or coyote) must walk through to the center to access the scent or bait in either hole.

inate toe catches from a predator's paw stepping on the loose jaw and pan at the same time.

When I attended the FTA Trappers College in 1983, I learned much more about the animal's reaction at the set. College lead instructor Dr. Major Boddicker was a stickler about taking notes on the trapline and had worked closely with George Stewart on many aspects of how predators worked a set. In the late 1970s during the USFWS lure effectiveness testing, the trappers involved in the study also took notes about the type of set used, wind direction at the set and other variables. These variables may or may not have been scientifically applied in all cases, but the observations which were recorded, charted trends like spacing from the attractor (4 inches back, offset 3 inches for foxes, or 9 inches back, offset 4 inches for coyotes). They also tracked data that showed eight of ten predators located the lure from downwind. This meant knowing the wind direction at the set and placing the trap downwind of the attractor increased set effectiveness as much as 80%. Understanding the way scent molecules disperse downwind and the fact that foxes (and coyotes) have such acute olfactory senses, it was clear to see that by offsetting the trap left or right took into account the predator's likely 45-degree approach to the set. Furthermore, if two traps were used, the catch per visit increased as much as 50%.

Now this is all fantastic info, but how does one apply it in the real world of the trapline?

What I did to create my "walk thru" set, was combine the information of both Boddicker and Stewart's Trappers College data and Odon Corr's 40-plus years of trapping experience. My "walk-thru" set incorporated the best of it. First, I would always make my sets facing the prevailing wind direction and tried to keep all sets upwind of the predator's line of travel. Second, I crowded my trap as close to the attractor as possible and guarded my loose jaw (as Odon did). Then, instead of using one hole and two spaced traps, I used one trap with two spaced holes. I made the holes as Odon did with a smooth-rod trap stake. Instead of making both holes straight away, I angled the holes at 45 degrees. If you picture both stakes in the bait holes, the stakes would cross over the pan of my trap. I used lure in one hole and bait in the other.

I called the set the "walk thru" because if a fox (or coyote) approached the set from the right he would be

Author's Photos

Face into the prevailing wind direction with the animal's travel ways preferably downwind. Cut the trap bed to fit the trap.

Position the trap with the dog facing twelve o'clock into the prevailing wind direction. Stake at six o'clock and rest the loose jaw on the stake head.

Rather than dig a bait hole, Drive a trap stake in at ten o'clock and then two o'clock. Ream out each bait hole in a conical shape about 10 inches deep. These holes will face the pan. If you place 2 trap stakes in the holes—they will cross over the pan. This is how you know you have the right angle and the true "walk thru" set.

Use a pan pad or pan cover, pack dirt inside the jaws and finish the set level. Your sifter should be able to rest over the trap, with some pressure applied—without setting the trap off.

Lure in one hole bait in the other. Cotton is left exposed here to help illustrate the triangle shape of the set.

Add the Jaw guard and blend the set. This is the finished Tom Miranda "Walk Thru" set. Excellent for foxes and coyotes.

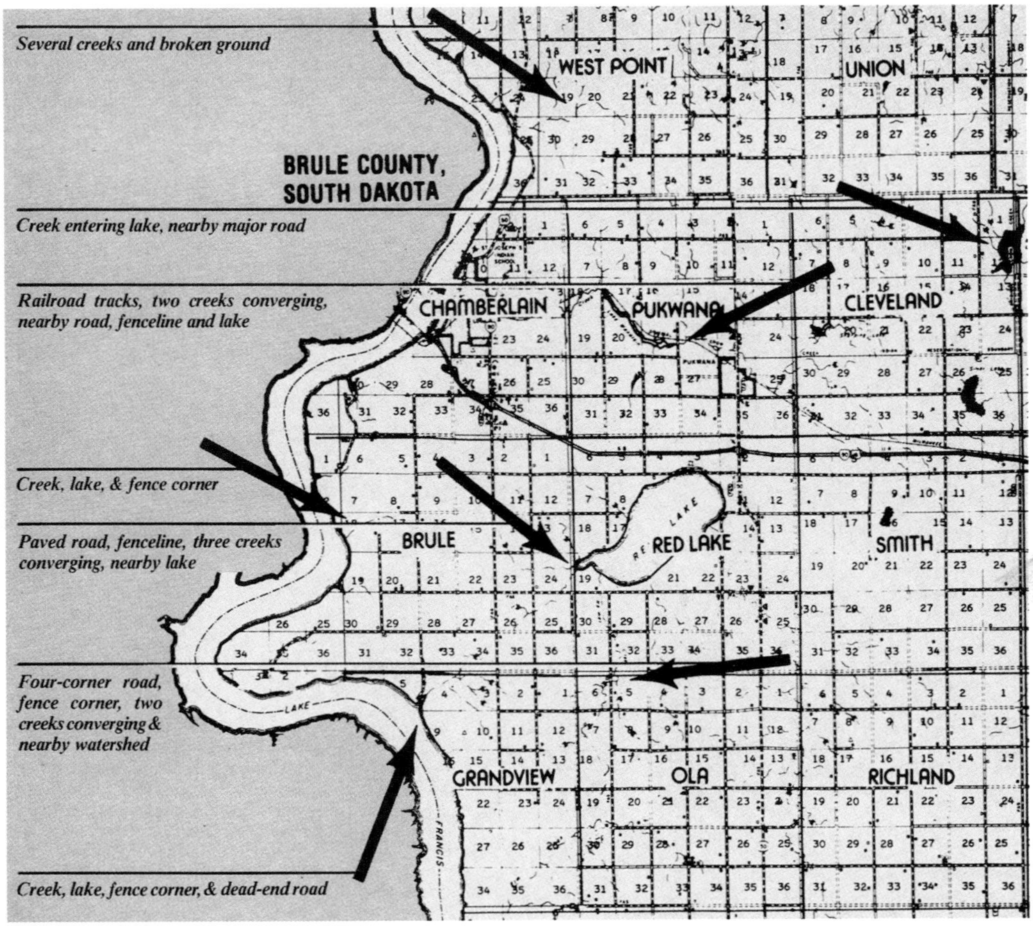

Pete Rickard

This map was used in a three-part article on fox trapping location which appeared in the October, November and December 1987 issues of *Fur-Fish-Game* magazine.

E. J. Dailey

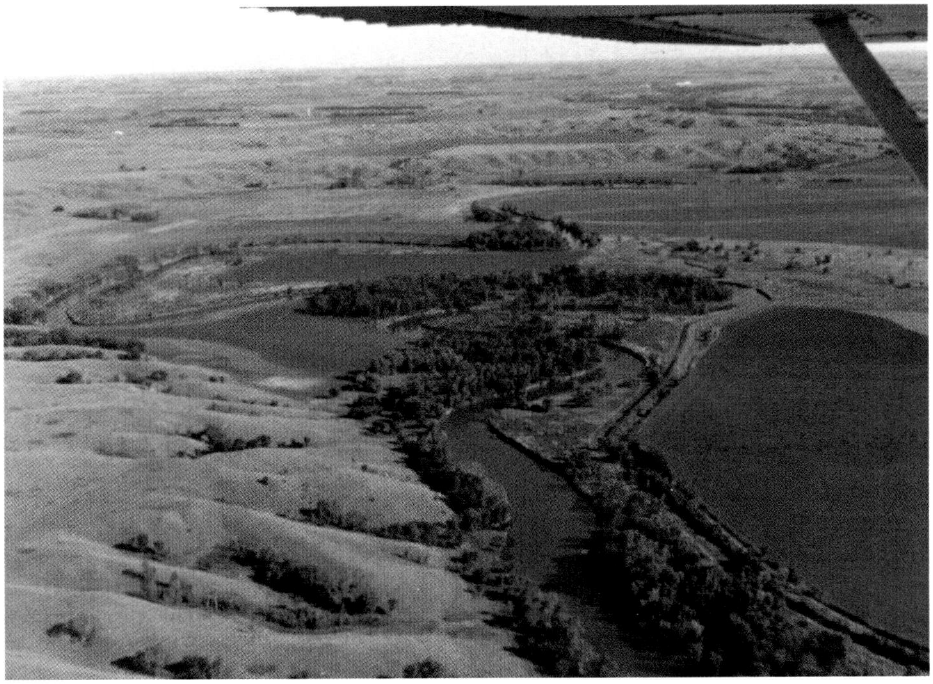

Author's Photos

Here's an aerial view of one of the target areas shown on this map of part of Brule County, South Dakota. It's easy to see the locations from the air.

caught when walking between the holes and jaw guard to access the opposite hole. The same was true for a fox approaching from the left. The set was incredibly effective for me and I taught over 400-plus students the "walk thru" set at nine of the ten FTA Trappers Colleges where I was an instructor. And about 300 private lessons, plus untold thousands through the videos and DVDs I made and sold personally as well as the *Fur-Fish-Game* and *Trapper & Predator Caller* videos and DVDs.

ANIMAL MOVEMENT

Top buck hunters know that mature whitetails live in a different place in the spring and summer and transition to more comfortable habitats as the seasons change. There are many reasons for this, which include availability of food and water, access to females during breeding season (rut) and other influences. All land animals travel to varying degrees. Some species like caribou take it to the extreme with an actual migration. Of course, all animals themselves are unique and there are some whitetail bucks who are born raised and live in a 4-square-mile area their entire lives in the right circumstances.

Author's Photo

Reynard taken in 3N on ranch trail in coyote country.

Where a doe whitetail will have a fawn or possibly twins, foxes are small animals and often have litters of six to ten pups. Each pup is different. One may be a runt—two pups may become pals and travel together. One may be a loner. As pups become young adults

Author's Photo

Red taken at round bale near interstate.

Author's Photo

Fox nailed at weedy patch in stubble. Used weeds to hide catch.

(they do so in about six months), they disperse and move to find their own territories and eventual mates.

Trappers looking to catch numbers of foxes are well-advised to locate their traps in areas that are conducive to these dispersion travel routes. To understand dispersion better, one must look at percentages of probable behavior. This sounds complicated, but it's really common sense. Here's an analogy. Ten different red foxes come to a river. Which way do they go? The laws of probability tell us that one fox will cross the river immediately. One will *never* cross the river. The other eight foxes will disperse up or down the river. Five of these foxes will likely travel the direction into the wind. The other three with the wind. Eventually, other foxes may cross the river, but what is happening is that the barrier of the river has created a long running travel way for foxes. And most foxes that encounter the river it will follow it. This river creates a dispersion route. The same is true with lake edges, interstate highways, railroad right-aways and other long-barrier features.

Author's Photo

Red taken at draw head in stubble, Missouri Breaks.

SPECIFIC LOCATION

Set locations for foxes are best found by following three simple guidelines. #1- Locate fox sets near as many *intersecting* travel features as possible. #2- Build the sets to utilize the benefits of the prevailing wind direction. #3- Gang set to ensure lure disperses to cover all avenues of predator travel through the area.

If a field corner creates a crossing into three different agriculture fields and a woods, that's a minimum of four travel ways and two habitat types. If locations can include long barriers like a creek, river or railroad track, the location is typically better. The best trappers look for locations in three dimensions, which means they are also looking for high and low points along with travel ways. Look for swales or shallow ravines that cross agriculture fields and meet the edge of the woods. Interspersion locations are also killer. An example would be a corner that transitions from agriculture to woody river bottom with adjacent CRP—three vastly different habitats all coming together. Predators also follow the path of least resistance so plan on foxes "cutting the corner." Outside elbows, saddles and rocky or steep land features funnel animals naturally and all are good bets for sets. There are many good trapping books and DVDs available which cover location in detail, and many done by the master trappers mentioned in this book.

Author's Photo

Corrals in cattle country are often great locations. This spring pasture is free of cattle in November

Author's Photo

Bulldozer taken in prairie country. This fresh dug soil will attract foxes and coyotes, so the remake will be a hot location.

Author's Photo

Gravel Pits are excellent set locations.

Triple on reds. Often fresh combined crops are fox magnets.

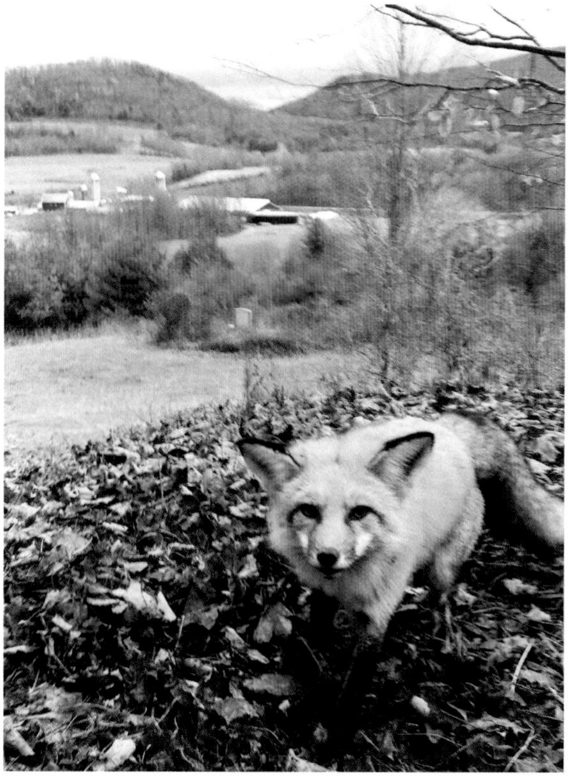

Tyler Brown Photo

Red taken on a knoll in pasture lands by Tyler Brown.

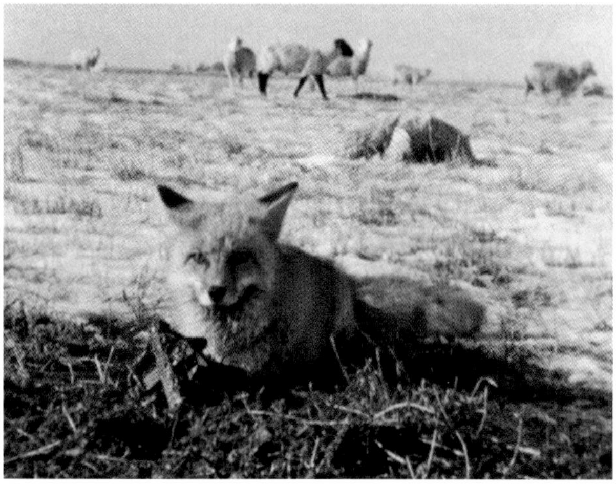

Fox nailed in with the groceries.

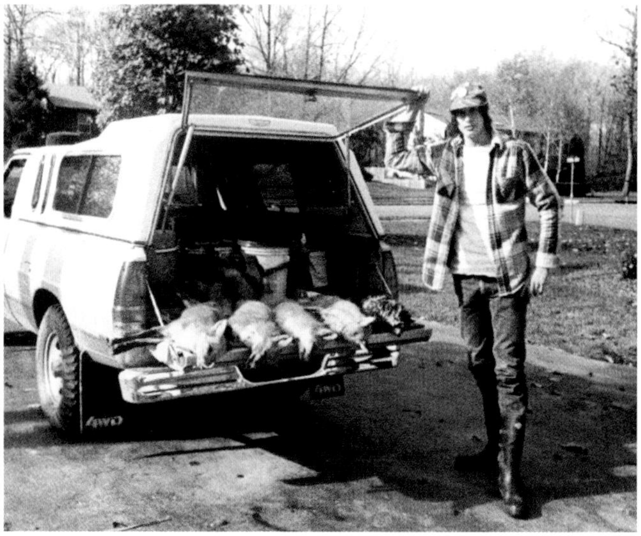

Craig Elms Photo

New Jersey trapper Craig Elms was a young trapping student of mine and a quick learner. Photo circa 1986

O. L. Butcher

MARK JUNE

1957–

Recognized as one of several notable trappers of the modern era, Mark June is one of a few fur boom trappers who have withstood the test of time. Coming to prominence in the early 1990s, Mark continues to trap commercially and educate both young and old with his tried-and-proven trapping techniques. Growing up in the Chevy Truck capitol of the world, Flint, Michigan, young Mark and his family experienced a tragedy which would eventually set him on a course toward his destiny. In 1967 Mark's childhood home burned to the ground. Thankfully, no one was injured. Needing a home and with no time to rebuild, the June family relocated south of Flint, along the shores of Lake Fenton. It was here, where 10-year-old Mark June set up his first trapline.

Author's Photo

Here's Mark with a dandy whitetail buck. Notice Mark's ESPN jacket. This buck hunt was videotaped as a segment for my ESPN show to promote "Make a Scrape," 1995.

Equipped with a canoe and a basket of traps, Mark would strap on his life jacket and paddle the lake's edge before school, tending his line. Muskrats were plentiful along the muddy banks and among the cattails where he made his sets. Young Mark did well, learning on his own and advancing his knowledge from the pages of *Fur-Fish-Game* magazine. Mark eventually expanded his line to a creek that flowed through a nearby golf course and it was here he that he would catch his first raccoon and mink. Mark mowed lawns in the summers, trapping in the fall—more importantly, he learned the value of hard work and saving his money.

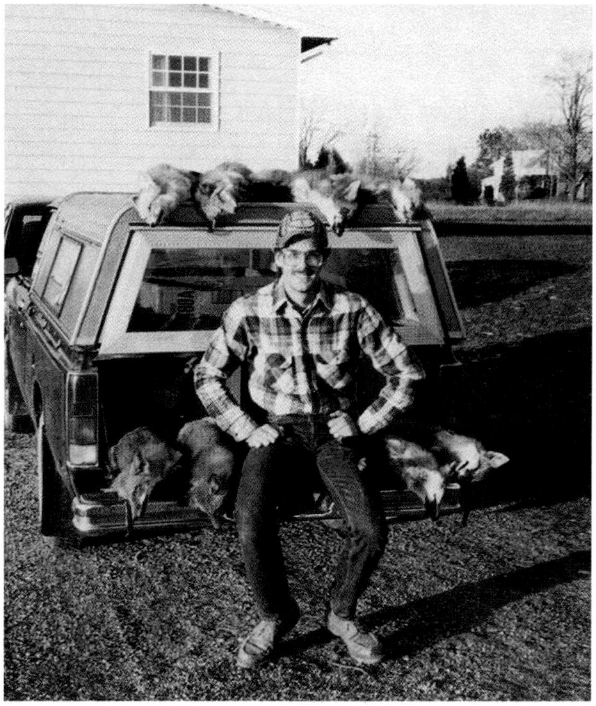

Mark June Photo

Trapper Mark June with a nice days catch of southern Michigan fox. Circa 1982

Mark continued to trap throughout his school years, eventually graduating up to foxes and mink. By high school he was making some excellent catches and once old enough to obtain his driver's license, Mark was off to the races. After high school graduation, he enrolled in college at the University of Michigan yet continued his trapping as time would allow. Mark's big season came in 1981 when he took 167 foxes and nearly 90 mink. I can remember him telling me when we first met that he made over $11 thousand that mega season and walked into the registrar's office at University of Michigan with cash in hand to pay off his last two years of college loans. That big payday was actually $11,700 and a testament to Mark's early

Mark poses with 23 bandits and 8 water weasels—a grand day's run over the water line.

Here's Mark with a nice catch of reynard and mink sporting one of my Good Luck Fox Caps, circa 1985.

Mark June with a dandy catch early in his fox trapping career.

Mark June with a great catch of Michigan foxes, 1982.

Mark June's *Fox Trapping in and Around Suburbia*—First Edition, 1989

Mark June, Paul Voz and your's truly circa 1995. Mark June's "Make-A-Scrape" inset.

trapping skills as well the fantastic prices at the peak of the fur boom.

Mark attended the Fur Takers of America (FTA) Professional Trappers College in 1982. Smart and quick-witted, he was immediately liked (and obviously knew his trapping). The college was looking for new instructor talent and FTA College founder Major Boddicker was quick to notice Mark and asked him to come back as an instructor's assistant in 1983. Mark quickly agreed. It was at that 1983 Trapper's College in LaGrange, Indiana where I first met Mark. We were nearly the same age and immediately hit it off, becoming pals. Soon after the end of that college Mark took a full-time pharmaceutical sales job. With the responsibility of a wife and children, steady income would be his priority. A responsibility which left no time for Mark to continue forward as an FTA College instructor.

Working at building his career in Big Pharma, Mark June continued to trap when he could. He also began dabbling in the lure and scent business with advice and help from Ray Milligan's pal Make Marasyada, Nick Wyshinski and of course myself. With ambitions of promoting his trapping scents and continuing to juggle trapping with full-time employment, Mark released his first book, *Fox Trapping in and Around Suburbia*, in 1989 to help promote his new scent line. I can remember Mark talking to me about naming his scent brand Michigander Blend and my advice to him was to use his name. Mark took my advice and Mark June's Lures started out with six scent varieties. Today Mark markets fifteen different formulations.

Mark along with Bernie Barringer, worked with me on one of my last trapping video projects in 1994 for *Trapper & Predator Caller* magazine. Mark and I also worked together on several deer hunting video projects as well as deer scent products for one of my TV sponsors, Hunters Specialties. One of Mark's products utilized waxed dirt impregnated with deer scent which he called "Make a Scrape." It was a unique product and as friends often do, I invited Mark as a guest on my ESPN TV series with hopes of helping him sell his new Make-a-Scrape deer scent. However, like many products in the commercial world, promotion is important but there are no guarantees. Mark's forte was trapping, not deer hunting and although both Mark and I felt that Make a Scrape had merit, it didn't stand the test of time.

COYOTE TRAPPING
WITH MARK JUNE
Ride along with one of America's Top Coyote Trappers
Complete course on catching coyotes in all fur zones
Mark June's Coyote DVD, 2008.

Mark moved from Michigan to Nebraska in 2004 after advancing to a pharmaceutical sales manager position. This move introduced Mark to western trapping and gave him access to more coyote work. In 2007 Mark wrote his coyote book and followed up with his best coyote season taking 231 dawgs in a 6-week run. Mark's go-to set for predators is the dirt hole and he adds several droppings in a triangular pattern when setting for coyote. The droppings found along the line or pulled from intestine in the skinning shed. In 2008 Mark made his first June's lures trapping DVD on the coyote.

Retiring from Pfizer Pharmaceutical in 2012, Mark and his wife Donna live south of San Antonio, Texas. Mark continues to operate a trapline in both Nebraska and Texas, and curates a week-long trappers academy in the spring. In 2018 mark put a push on bobcats and took 105 spotted bellies trapping his old Nebraska trapline and in south Texas proving that he not only knows his fox trapping but can outsmart a clever dawg or light-footed spotted belly.

"I am currently enrolled as a full-time student in a 4-year Master of Theology and am finishing up my first year of studies. I have no plan for this studying but feel led to this calling, trusting that God will have us all do what He wishes. It's a very tough curriculum, but it's very wondrous. Great sacrifice of time and effort of course, but my wife, my family and many friends are very intrigued why a successful retiree with a full-time side biz would possibly think to do this. My answer. You only live on this earth once. I've always felt a religious inkling, but only lately has it sparked into a passion.

I've just always worked hard and smart. I'm an achiever by nature and that can be a good or a bad thing at separate times. I was a top 200 of all time at Pfizer, the world's largest pharma company, in sales results, so somewhere in Manhattan, NY is a bronze bust of me, taken during an award ceremony. That's how I roll. Give me a task, and I'll get it done, but I'll out work ya to get it done correctly. Staying in balance with wife, family, and work. . . . That's not easy, but I reflect on it often!"

–Mark June in his own words, May 2020

Michael DiSalvo Photo

The trapping tradition is one that's often passed down from father to son. Michael DiSalvo's grandfather was a Pennsylvania fox trapper and his father a fox trapper. Michael would grow up with the love of fox trapping all around him. Pictured center top is Mike's grandfather and his trapline Ford Maverick. Left and center bottom a very young Mike with his father during the molding years. The photo on the right is Mike as a high school student and his dandy Pennsylvania fox catch.

Michael DiSalvo Photo

Fox trapper Michael DiSalvo with a day's work from his nuisance wildlife business,- Iowa Wildlife Control.

Here's a day's run on my South Dakota fox line, 1986.

TRACY TRUMAN

1960–

Likely when trappers think of foxes they think of reds and primarily eastern or midwestern trapping. However, the gray fox has a wide range encompassing many areas of the desert southwest along with its brushy haunts of the east. Nevada trapper Tracy Truman is a gray fox man and to hear him tell it, the little gray fox is by far his favorite. *Grays are plentiful, predictable, bold, and beautiful. Each one has its own unique colorful array of gray, chestnut, cream and black."*

Tracy Truman Photo

Tracy with a nice run of gray foxes ready for market.

Tracy was born on the outskirts of Las Vegas but grew up in Enterprise, Utah. Trapping squirrels at age 7, he eventually turned to furbearers and the lessons of fooling western coyotes in ranch country. Tracy's first inspiration to become a trapper came from his great uncle, Clifford Hall. Clifford was a trapping legend in his small Utah community and especially known for tracking coyotes to their dens. Rumor had it that Cliff could track a fish under water and young Tracy believed it. In the early summer months when Tracy was but 10 years old, his uncle Cliff always had several litters of coyote pups at the house waiting to be sold. Tracy looked forward to the times he could visit his great uncle and help him bottle feed the hungry pups with a big lambing bottle with a nipple on it. Feeding the pups gave Tracy lots of time to ask questions. Tracy says, *"Clifford was a kind and patient man. He never seemed irritated with all those questions."*

Years later, Tracy had a coyote set in an area where Cliff was hunting coyote dens. Cliff found the trap and snapped it off. When Tracy confronted him later about it, Cliff said, "You had zero chance of ever catching a coyote in a set like that." When Cliff told Tracy he was essentially a failed coyote trapper, he was devastated. Tracy had held his great uncle in such high esteem that hearing the honest opinion motivated him to learn to be not only as good a trapper as Clifford but to be good enough to make his uncle proud. And it's a life lesson that continues to this day.

When Tracy got into college, he had substantially upped his game trapping fur in the fall-winter, and predator control trapping for area sheep ranchers in the summer. Tracy says, "Every animal I caught during my college days translated directly in my eyes, into tuition, books, lodging or meals. A "dry spell" wasn't just something to shrug off—I had to pick up, move traps, improve sets, find new locations, learn a new technique, find new fur pockets and keep working. Failure wasn't an option, and by then I had learned to enjoy my independence from a boss or supervisor, so I was too proud to quit and go to work at a 9-to-5 job."

Tracy Truman and his dog "Foxsized" pose with a day's catch of 38 gray foxes.

Gray foxes are beautiful animals and add value to traplines in areas where they are found. This one is sporting a white-tipped tail common for red foxes but not often seen in grays.

them and leave them for 2 weeks and you can have 14 days' worth of activity recorded. On the ground scouting only shows a few nights tracks at best. Once an area is a proven producer, it will likely continue to produce year after year, and the scouting cams can be used to prove out new territory.

Nevada trapper Tracy Truman lines 'em up.

And his hard work paid off. A degree in law eventually took Tracy Truman back to Las Vegas and his education in desert trapping began. As many of the trappers chronicled in this book are career trappers, some have made a name for themselves while holding down a professional career. Tracy is one such trapper. Desert trappers typically specialize in trapping bobcat with gray foxes "paying the gas." It's no different than eastern fox trappers who use incidental raccoon catches as their "gas money" or mink long-liners who do the same. However, with many states restricting traps, trapping methods are changing.

Tracy uses 99% dirt holes on gray fox. He uses an auger so the holes are a standard 3" size and about 8 inches deep. Pretty standard. Tracy shines in his pre-season work and set blocking. First, in new areas Tracy uses scouting cameras to get an idea of both fox density and travel. Keep in mind that in dry, rocky desert, there's little sign as gray foxes are light-footed and often—even in sand—their paw prints are not discernible. Plus javelina, coyote and other animals using a wash often eliminate the tracks. The cameras are also watching for 'cats which financially are a more desirable target. A bonus with scouting cams is that you set

Tracy also pre-baits, doing so a few weeks prior to the season opener. His bait and method of use is one of the keys to Tracy's fantastic catches. He uses two homemade baits. One is ground bacon with a bit of honey, castor, muskrat and mink glands in it. The other is a fish-based bait made from jack mackerel, smoked salmon or trout with a bit of castor, muskrat and mink glands added. Both baits are made in a fashion that whips them into a pourable slurry. Tracy drills holes 1 inch in diameter at selected locations and pours them full of slurry. He then sets a pin on his GPS to mark the location. A week later, the holes that have been "hit" look like a bomb went off. These locations get at minimum, a double set on opening day. This takes the guesswork out of locations. It is not uncommon for Tracy to take 40–45 gray foxes on his first check—and his pre-baiting sequence has a large part to do with that.

The use of scouting cameras with actual traps set has also modified Tracy's approach to his set placements. Noticing a number of foxes visiting sets and not getting caught, Tracy now uses a system of blocking the sets down to force the grays over his approach.

"I don't believe most trappers realize how many foxes visit their sets and never get caught because they are too open, or because the fox approaches the set from the side or the rear. Using a few dirt clods or twigs is not going to cut it. You have to forcibly block a gray fox away from the approach you don't want him to have. And if you use blocking or backing that is too large, the fox will walk on it or use it to climb over the set. They can climb trees like a cat so they can climb on and use your large backing objects if you let them. Until I started using trail cameras extensively, I didn't realize how many foxes I missed."

Tracy Truman's book, *Modern Grey Fox Trapping* was first published in 2007 and that year, he also released a DVD of the same name. In 2009 Tracy teamed up with California trapper Jeff Yancy to produce the DVD, *Cage Trapping Bobcats and Gray Fox*. Yancy specializes in live trapping 'cats and Tracy's portion of the production illustrated live trap techniques for gray foxes. Tracy Truman has had some fantastic seasons trapping gray foxes however he thinks his best season is yet to come.

"Young trappers should get into trapping for the same reasons one gets into marriage—for love, not money. Oh, the money isn't all bad and I certainly allow money to motivate me, but if you really love trapping, you will not only stay with it longer, you will be a better trapper. You will be a more ethical trapper. You will also be in the trapping game longer than others who are only trapping to make a quick buck. If you are only interested in trapping because you want to make a bunch of money, there are lots of other, more likely ways of accomplishing that goal. If the sight of a big tom bobcat hunkered down under a boulder, hoping that you won't see him—or the thought of a coyote on a frosty morning bouncing around on the edge of pasture—or a pair of gray fox doing somersaults at the end of a chain doesn't excite you, then I would recommend another hobby. People who are successful at something usually have a passion for it. Motivation which drives their success. The money part usually catches up later. If you don't already love trapping, then nothing I can say will truly help you get much better at it. On the other hand, if you love trapping, nothing I can say will ever stop you from being a great trapper."

–Tracy Truman in his own words, 2014

ADVENTURES ABOUND

The first years of my ESPN series were exciting. I was living the dream, having fantastic adventures and bowhunting all over the place. Flying, climbing, diving, jumping, crawling, riding—you name it, I was doing it. This included lots of whitetail bowhunting as these type episodes always rated well. I had some exotic adventures too—like bowhunting red stag in New Zealand and shotgunning doves and ducks in Argentina. Every episode needed to be different, and the more adventurous, the better. I did segments on bobcat telemetry studies, game warden sting operations, beaver damage removal and the Bailey live trap, the Fur Takers Trappers College, and a segment on the National Trappers Convention—all airing on ESPN. My *Outdoor Adventure Magazine* series enjoyed grand popularity and great ratings in the early 1990s. ESPN was happy, and they would offer me more time slots and opportunities to do additional series. My TV business and notoriety were skyrocketing.

Author's Photo

Tom Miranda on location for ESPN in New Zealand, 1993.

TRAPPER & PREDATOR CALLER VIDEOS

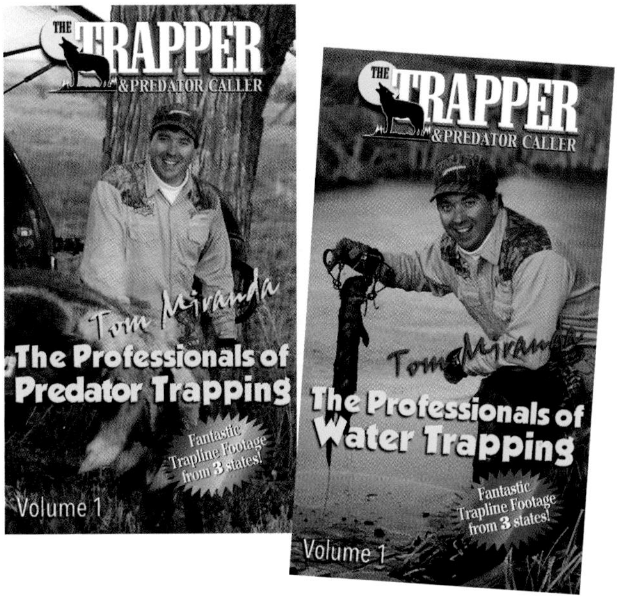

In 1994 I decided to put together another set of trapping videos. I could see that this might be my last chance to actually run a trapline for a while. After the success of the *Fur-Fish-Game* trapping programs I knew the door was open to do a set for *Trapper & Predator Caller* magazine (TPC). I called the powers to be at

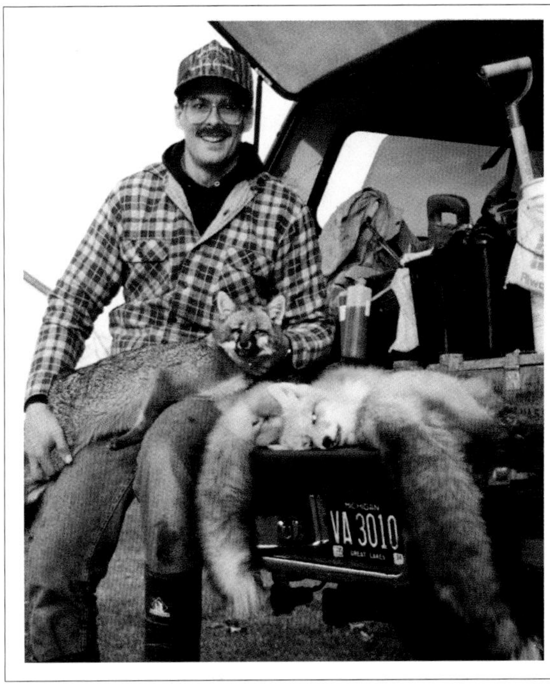

Author's Photo

Here's a photo of a day's catch with Mark June during the filming of Trapper & Predator Caller Magazine's Professionals of Predator Trapping, 1994.

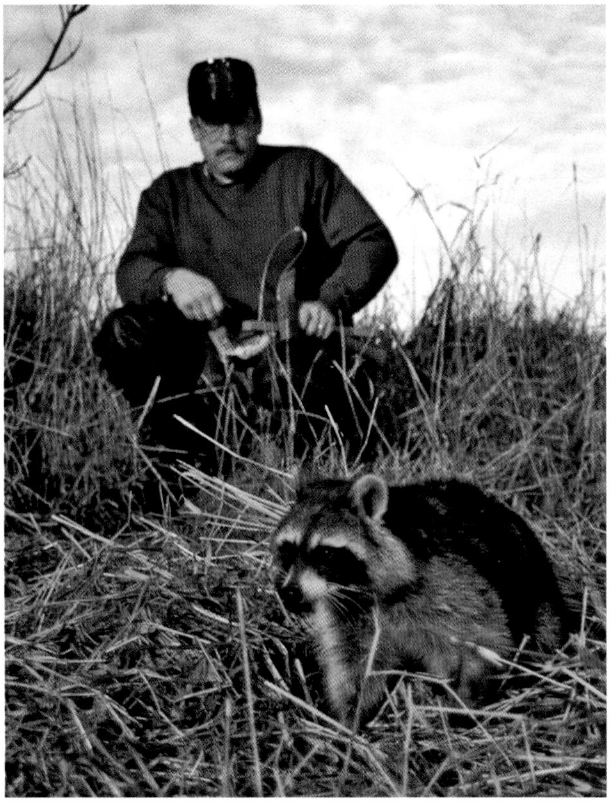

Bernie Barringer poses with a raccoon snared during the filming of *Trapper & Predator Caller* magazine's Professionals of Predator Trapping, 1994.

Krause Publications and made them a "godfather offer" (an offer they couldn't refuse). The deal was that I would do a special 2-video set hosted by myself and with two additional professional trappers. I would tape it in the Midwest during trapping season "on the trap line."

I would write, produce, edit and package the programs. All TPC needed to do was sign an agreement to buy a certain minimum inventory of tapes. They would run the ads in their publications and ship their inventory from the TPC warehouse in Wisconsin as they also sold caps and books etc. I would push the videos as *Trapper & Predator Caller* videos packaged with their logo, into my massive distribution channel. Krause Publications execs were excited and all-in.

I then needed to find two trappers who knew their trapping yet needed some publicity. Of course, Mark June came to mind—once he heard of the project there was no keeping him out of it. Mark had put out his first trapping book in 1989 and this would be a big boost on the national scale for him, requiring only a time investment. We both discussed a third trapper—ultimately, I chose Iowa trapper Bernie Barringer. Barringer was a good trapper, honest, sincere, and eager to be involved. He was a snare man and specialized in the water animals although he did trap foxes as well. Barringer had released books in 1991 and 1992 so he was progressive and keen on promotions and networking. Both Mark and Bernie could also buy the videos from me at a special wholesale price and market them through their individual networks. Neither Barringer nor June had their own videos at the time, so there was no conflict. The TPC videos were shot in the late fall of 1994 in lower Michigan, Iowa and South Dakota. I edited them and they were out by the Christmas season. They were a hit not only for TPC, but the programs boosted both Mark and Bernie's careers at a time when they both were expanding their trapping businesses. At the time I was transitioning more and more into bowhunting, so in essence the project was sort of a last hoorah for my trapping promotions.

PERSONAL ISSUES

Of course, with ESPN TV work, trapping and bowhunting, I was extremely busy. And it wasn't helping my relations at home. In fact, my first marriage was crumbling. Every time I left for a trip there was a fight. Nothing I did was right. My first wife wanted me to stop traveling, return to fur trapping, writing, giving trapping lessons and being home. Period. A janitor or garbage collector—anything but an ESPN producer. There was no negotiation. My argument was my career was going places and I'd worked too hard to give it all up now. It wasn't like I was never home or didn't have a relationship with my kids. Yes, I was opting for quality time over quantity, but I was being presented an ultimatum with no flexibility whatsoever. The handwriting was on the wall. Divorce was imminent.

Let me say right here that getting a divorce was the lowest point of my life. It's not something that I look at with a smile or something I'm proud of. For those who have experienced it, you know that there is plenty of blame to go around. And of course, with children involved it's never a best-case scenario. Marriage can be awesome. But it can also be horrible. The deterioration of a loving relationship is wrought with distrust, deceit and anger. Divorce is neither pretty, nor fun, nor a badge of honor. In fact, it would likely have been so much easier for me to stay married. Damn sure less expensive. My first wife and I divorced after fifteen years of marriage, so no decision was made lightly. One picks up the pieces and puts their life back together.

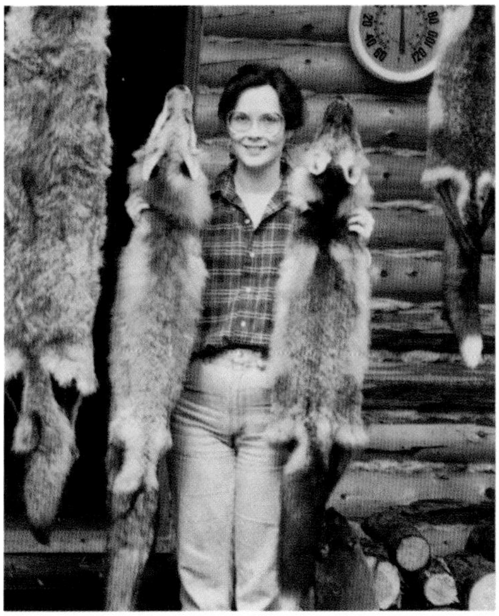

This is my first wife Bernie at the Michigan log cabin, 1981.

With me moving out of the house, my lure business needed moving as well. I had built up a fantastic trapping business and with the two new TPC trapping videos it was only going to grow. If you reflect back, my trapping videos were available at thousands of video rental stores back in the late 1980s.

Mark and I did several catalogs together. This was the first one in 1993.

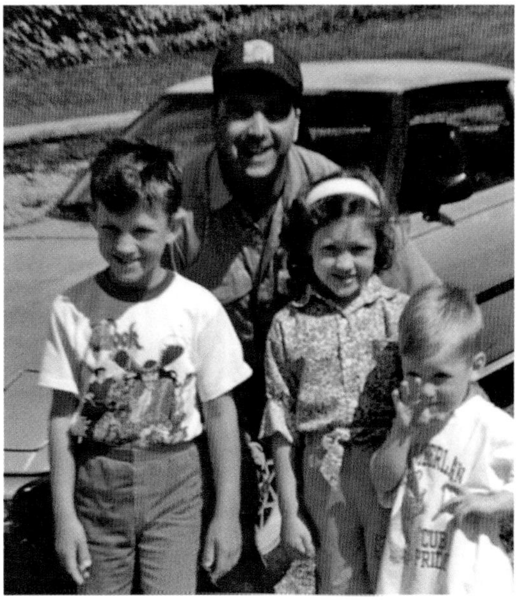

Here's a photo of my three children with dad at a very tough time in our lives.

Add in the forty-thousand-plus reach of *Trapper & Predator Caller* and the latest new batch of *Fur-Fish-Game* trapping videos that released in 1989—I had 14 trapping-specific videos being marketed in multiple outlets. Ten of which were titled and backed by the trapping industry's leading magazines. I had built a dynamic sales machine.

Since Mark June and I had become such close friends, I talked to him about taking over the sales for my

Author's Photo

Pictured are producer Jeff Murray and cameraman Mike Baker with yours truly and a nice black bear I arrowed for Cabela's Sportsman's Quest TV series on ESPN.

entire trapping business. I would move the full inventory to his facility. We made a deal that he would pay me dealer price on all my products and market them as Tom Miranda Competition Line, yet Mark would be the master distributor, and everything would ship from Michigan. He agreed and I moved a huge U-Haul truck and trailer of product to Michigan. You must understand that at the time, I was making lures in 40-gallon Rubbermaid trash cans and had lure made and aged to last for several years of sales. Mark and I did three catalogs together, which included the trapping and hunting videos, trapping lures, deer scents and supplies.

This was a huge financial windfall for Mark, and actually a windfall for me, as I could now concentrate 100% on my ESPN TV work. The years of 1994 and 1995 were grand years for ESPN adventure episodes. The shows were highly rated and the sponsors were happy. One of my biggest sponsors at the time was Virginia Tourism. The board was so excited about the show and what we were doing that they basically let me do whatever I wanted to do in Virginia. I did cave spelunking, shipwreck diving, the Navy F-14 Tomcat flight syllabus, Six Flags roller coaster marathon, hot air balloon—I could go on and on.

In late 1994 my TV partner Sandy Brady came to me looking to do something else. Sandy enjoyed the limelight of television, but the daily grind and constant travel had taken its toll. Brady's relationship with a girlfriend had grown deeply—she would soon be his wife. So, Sandy slipped quietly out of his TV hosting roles and I began a schedule to buy out his family's shares of the corporation. Now the burden of the show was all on me—the financial side, the production, writing, editing, sales—my plate was full. To be successful, I needed to work harder than ever.

A NEW BEGINNING

In May of 1995 my phone rang. It was Jim Wilburn, CEO of Winnercomm. Winnercomm was ESPN's largest purveyor of TV programs. They produced the National Finals Rodeo, soccer, horse racing and several other genres of outdoor sports. Mr. Wilburn asked if I had time to host a TV series for him that his company was working on. The series would be titled *Under Wild Skies* and would be a hunting show that would begin airing on ESPN in 1996. Jim offered me $100 thousand to be the host and assume some camera duties on location as he knew I could run the big Sony Digital Betacam cameras. The call was unexpected and a huge windfall. I agreed. I was living in Sioux Falls, South Dakota at the time. Mark June was running my lure business and my TV studio was set up at an ad agency known as Nichols Media. I had a small studio apartment with a fold-down Murphy bed.

Two weeks later Jim Wilburn called me again. This time he apologized and told me that the National Rifle Association had taken the title sponsorship of the *Under Wild Skies* series and that they wanted a host who was a rifle and shotgun hunter not a bowhunter. So as quick as I was in, I was out. Tony Makris would be host. OK. Easy come, easy go, right? Well only a month later Jim Wilburn called me again and this time asked me to host Cabela's *Sportsman's Quest* for ESPN. I accepted under the previous terms of the Wild Skies proposal. Now I would be seen in two ESPN series each weekend. I had my first paid TV hosting gig!

Here's my wife Sandy and three children Jeremy, Jennifer and Joshua at our little beach house in Florida.

In July 1996 I married Sandy Jessop, a Florida gal whom I met at Cypress Gardens in Winter Haven, Florida. Sandy worked in the marketing department and we met when I was in town to do an ESPN episode on flying hang gliders at the famous Cypress Gardens ski show. Sandy was not only beautiful, but smart with plenty of business and street savvy. We would make a good team. We decided that I would go to court to ask that I get summer visitation with my kids with alternating Christmas and Thanksgiving because we had plans of moving to Florida as soon as the TV editing season ended. To explain how busy I was at the time, I rented a tux in Duluth, Minnesota while on a walleye tournament shoot for Winnercomm, flew to Las Vegas where Sandy and I got married, flew from Vegas to home, then a few days later to Alaska on another shoot.

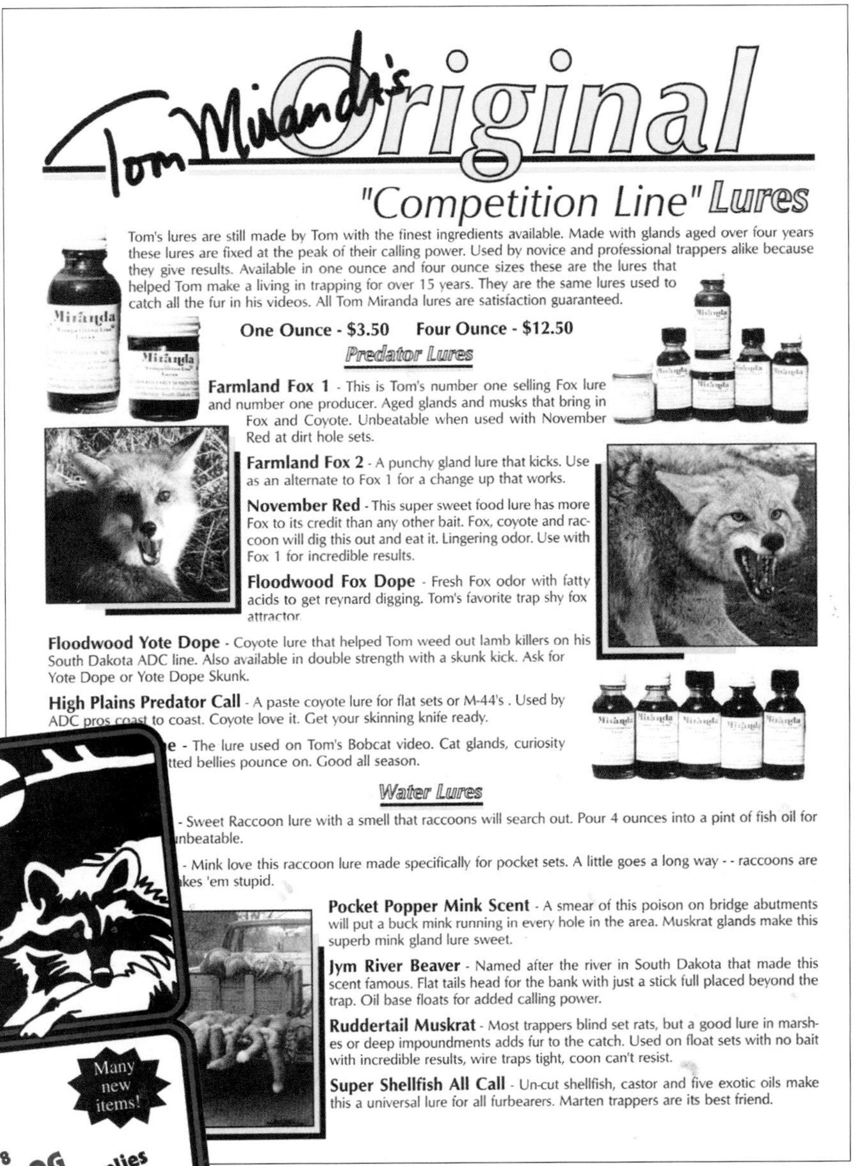

Tom Miranda's Original
"Competition Line" Lures
Tom's lures are still made by Tom with the finest ingredients available. Made with glands aged over four years these lures are fixed at the peak of their calling power. Used by novice and professional trappers alike because they give results. Available in one ounce and four ounce sizes these are the lures that helped Tom make a living in trapping for over 15 years. They are the same lures used to catch all the fur in his videos. All Tom Miranda lures are satisfaction guaranteed.
One Ounce - $3.50 Four Ounce - $12.50
Predator Lures
Farmland Fox 1 - This is Tom's number one selling Fox lure and number one producer. Aged glands and musks that bring in Fox and Coyote. Unbeatable when used with November Red at dirt hole sets.
Farmland Fox 2 - A punchy gland lure that kicks. Use as an alternate to Fox 1 for a change up that works.
November Red - This super sweet food lure has more Fox to its credit than any other bait. Fox, coyote and raccoon will dig this out and eat it. Lingering odor. Use with Fox 1 for incredible results.
Floodwood Fox Dope - Fresh Fox odor with fatty acids to get reynard digging. Tom's favorite trap shy fox attractor.
Floodwood Yote Dope - Coyote lure that helped Tom weed out lamb killers on his South Dakota ADC line. Also available in double strength with a skunk kick. Ask for Yote Dope or Yote Dope Skunk.
High Plains Predator Call - A paste coyote lure for flat sets or M-44's . Used by ADC pros coast to coast. Coyote love it. Get your skinning knife ready.
e - The lure used on Tom's Bobcat video. Cat glands, curiosity
tted bellies pounce on. Good all season.
Water Lures
- Sweet Raccoon lure with a smell that raccoons will search out. Pour 4 ounces into a pint of fish oil for
nbeatable.
- Mink love this raccoon lure made specifically for pocket sets. A little goes a long way - - raccoons are
kes 'em stupid.
Pocket Popper Mink Scent - A smear of this poison on bridge abutments will put a buck mink running in every hole in the area. Muskrat glands make this superb mink gland lure sweet.
Jym River Beaver - Named after the river in South Dakota that made this scent famous. Flat tails head for the bank with just a stick full placed beyond the trap. Oil base floats for added calling power.
Ruddertail Muskrat - Most trappers blind set rats, but a good lure in marshes or deep impoundments adds fur to the catch. Used on float sets with no bait with incredible results, wire traps tight, coon can't resist.
Super Shellfish All Call - Un-cut shellfish, castor and five exotic oils make this a universal lure for all furbearers. Marten trappers are its best friend.

Here's the Tom Miranda lure insert used in Tim Caven's 1997–98 Minnesota Trapline catalog. -Authors Collection

MINNESOTA
TRAPLINE
PRODUCTS
Tim and Nancy Caven
Minnesota Trapline Products
6699 156th Ave. N.W.
Pennock, Minnesota 56279
(320) 599-4176 (Telephone)
(320) 599-4314 (FAX Only)
Many new items!
1997-98
CATALOG
of Quality Trapping Supplies
"We Set the Standard for Others to Follow."

At this same time, Mark June had grown tired of being under my overshadowing TV persona. Mark was also still working full-time in the pharmaceutical industry and wanted to put what time he did have into his lure brand, not mine. I totally understood but needed to find a new home for my lures, books and videos. I contacted one of my largest dealers at the time, Tim Caven of Minnesota Trapline Products. Tim agreed to take over my brand on the same terms I had with Mark. Even though I had offers to buy my scent business, I just couldn't part with it. So, I went to Mark's place in Michigan, loaded up a U-Haul truck and headed to Tim and Nancy's shop in Pennock, Minnesota. The Cavens are salt of the earth people—hard workers and likely the best friends I have in the trapping industry. Here's what Tim said about our arrangement in his 1997 catalog.

"Last month we entered into an agreement with Tom Miranda to be his exclusive marketing agent. With Tom's ESPN show and video productions he has found it very difficult to conduct a mail-order business with being out of state and the country a high percentage of the time. We are pleased that out of all the trapping dealers to choose from, he picked Minnesota Trapline Products based on our ability to service his customers in the fastest and most accurate manner. Tom will continue to make his lures here on his periodical visits, so the only thing that will change is where you purchase his lures, videos and books. Please find the Tom Miranda Outdoor Products flyer inserted in this catalog." —Tim Caven

Tom & Sandy Miranda's first home on Manasota Key, Florida 1996.

Once my child visitation arrangement was secured, Sandy and I moved to the Gulf Coast of Florida. We put down some money on a little beach house and remodeled it, turning the garage into a TV studio so I could edit my ESPN programs. Now let me say right here that a TV bowhunter moving to the beach during the building years of his career might sound a bit foolish. But I'll confess that I do love the warm weather. Plus, with my schedule and frequent travel, as long as I have a good airport nearby, I can pretty much live anywhere.

DAVID ZIEGLER

1962–

Ask any ten trappers to tell you their favorite fox set and nine out of ten will say the dirt-hole. Yet likely all ten will make it differently, adding a nuance here, a change there and fashioning a signature style set that gives each trapper their own edge. Pennsylvania long-liner David Ziegler is a dirt-hole man and he would be the first to tell you that his set may be important, but it isn't the set itself that contributes most to his large catches. David's secret is his trapline management, a systematic approach to every detail of the trapline. Here's an analogy. Take a screwdriver. A carpenter can use one and set a screw straight and solid in a few turns of the handle. However, setting 100 screws by hand is a different story. A power driver will do the first screw a little quicker, but it will finish the following 99 screws much, much faster than using a screwdriver. This is how David Ziegler approaches his fox trapping.

David grew up near Eddystone, Pennsylvania and started trapping when he was 14 years old. Like most trappers David began with muskrats and progressed to raccoons, mink and eventually, foxes. Most trappers who were trapping during the late 1970s fur boom experienced the mega prices for red foxes. The excitement of watching a red bounce in the set is something that few can ever forget. Red foxes are typically clean animals, easy to skin, and their pelts a joy to work with. The fascination with eastern trappers and their red foxes is a relationship that lasts a lifetime. When it comes to a trapping mentor, David quickly mentions Charlie Dobbins which no doubt means that Ziegler's traps are likely adjusted and tweaked out to the nines.

Utilizing 85% dirt-hole sets and 15% flat-sets, David's philosophy is to manage is trap-line in as streamlined a manner as possible. David believes that being consistent even on the smallest details will make you a more efficient trapper. Load your truck the same way every time. Approach a trap-bed, lay your equipment down and make every set the same way *every time.* Consistency creates efficiency and saves time. In trapping, time is valuable. More time allows you to make more sets, travel more miles and catch more fur. Since a trapper cannot create time, one must be efficient and not waste it. Think of it like this—one extra minute needed for each set when you are running 120 traps equals two hours. David says, "Time equals value. Value equals money."

David Ziegler Photo

Here's a 19-fox day on the Ziegler line. Amazing! My best was 15 reds in one day on the South Dakota line. But I had 2 coyotes, 12 coon and 4 badgers as well.

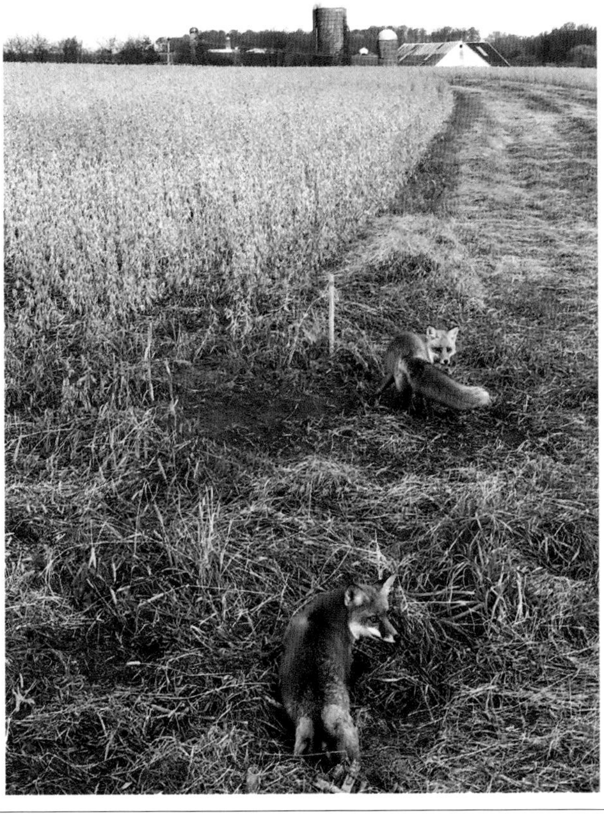

David Ziegler Photo

Nice Pennsylvania double nailed by David Ziegler.

One of the key aspects of large catches of foxes is the local fox population. Uniquely, in some areas of the country, the coyote hasn't found as strong a hold as in other areas. It's in these pockets where fox numbers can climb allowing trappers access to larger numbers.

Ron Leggett knows this firsthand as in his area of Maryland are primarily foxes. David Ziegler's area is similar. In the 2017–18 Pennsylvania trapping season, David caught 230 foxes yet only 7 coyotes. Trappers in Ohio, Michigan, Kentucky, West Virginia and New York—all states that surround Pennsylvania would never see this imbalance of foxes over coyotes in their fur shed. Unique areas create special circumstances and allow golden opportunities.

David Ziegler Photo

David Ziegler's personal best of 325 Pennsylvania reds.

David also mentions that he has switched to a more innovative pipe set. Some years back he tested a new style "pipe--set" for a fellow trapper friend and set 50% dirt-holes and 50% pipe sets. David found no drop in his success rate on catches. David says that utilizing the pipes to contain the attractor works better in nasty weather by allowing the scent to stay dry and protected from water which can fill up a dirt-hole. David Ziegler has consistently taken 100 to 150 foxes a season for the last 18 years and over the last two seasons has upped his game taking 230 foxes in the 2017–18 season (as previously stated) and a whopping 325 foxes in 2018–19.

Like many long-liners, David makes his own gland lure for personal use and has used some of fox pro Bob Jamison's lures as well. Ziegler says Bob's Fox Cream and Red Devil are tops. Of course, David's catch photos have been used on the cover of Jamison's Supply catalog the last four seasons. Such is the life of a Master Trapper! As Life Member #424 of the Pennsylvania Trappers Association, David does his share of trapper promotion and support especially in the schools of his District 12 Chapter. Like many top trappers today, David also operates his own Nuisance Animal Control business, Ziegler Wildlife and Pest Control LLC.

David Ziegler Photo

Here's David's 2017–2018 catch of 230 foxes and 7 coyotes. Phenomenal catch in PA.

LEONARD LEE RUE III 1926–

Every outdoorsman who's ever read a hunting, trapping or fishing magazine has seen the photos of famous wildlife photographer Leonard Lee Rue III. But what many don't know is that when Lenny was 16 years old, he was well on his way to becoming one of the top trappers in his home state of New Jersey. At 18, Leonard Rue took 61 foxes and at age 20, he took 93 foxes on a six-week trapline while working a full-time job at night. Lenny says in 1952, for the first time in 100 years, New Jersey allowed three beavers to be taken as the beaver population was finally increasing to the point where they had to be controlled. Lenny bought his permit and caught his three beavers the same day. Lenny and I have been good friends for many years. We met at a sport show when Lenny walked up to me to chat as he recognized me as a fox trapper.

During the height of Lenny's career—the 1960s, 70s, and 80s—he was the most published wildlife photographer in North America (and likely the world). Rue's staff turned out over 100,000 black and white photographs a year. Leonard Lee Rue III had both black and white, and color wildlife files publishing in 87 magazines and 28 state game agencies, plus 17 photographic companies marketed Rue images all over the world.

Lenny has been credited with over 1,800 magazine covers and has presented over 4,000 lectures on wildlife and photography for schools, clubs and organizations. Rue has written monthly columns for several magazines, including *American Hunter* (15 years), *Outdoor Photographer* (16 years), *Deer and Deer Hunting* (30 years) and *Whitetail Times* (12 years).

> *"Being a trapper helped me to become a successful wildlife photographer. Learning about the behavior, habitat and habits of wildlife, I was able to apply that integrate knowledge throughout my photography field excursions around the world."*
>
> –Leonard Lee Rue III in his own words, 2020

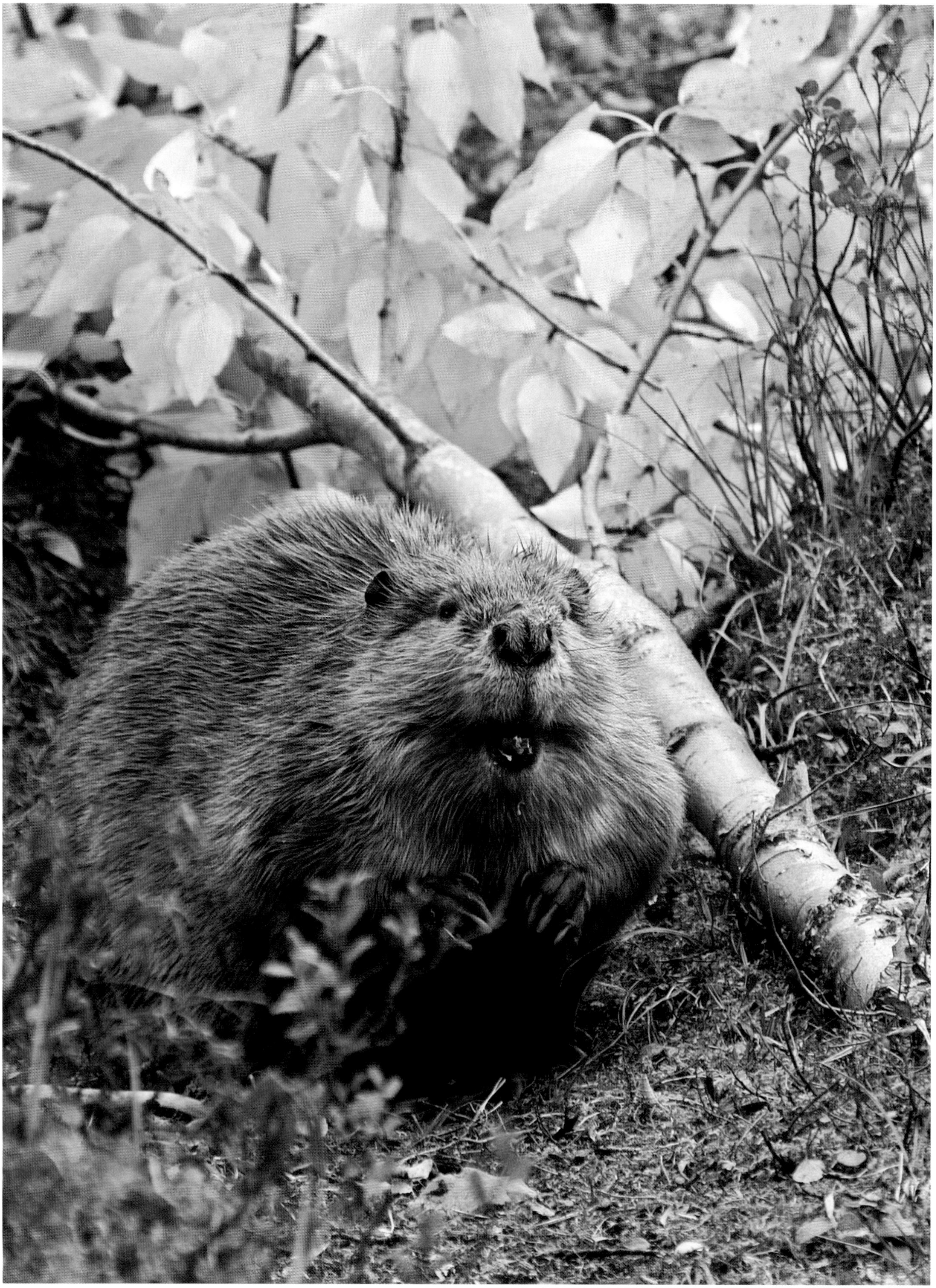

CHAPTER 11

BEAVERMEN

The beaver is a unique animal. In fact, the beaver is the only animal that can modify its habitat. The ingenious method in which beavers construct their water impoundments offers these large rodents a way to regulate the water depth of their pond during drought as well as in preparation for winter ice. This water sanctuary protects the beaver from natural predators and provides habitat for a variety of mammals, birds, reptiles, amphibians and fish. Stockpiling green limbs and twigs in the bottom of their pond allows a colony of beavers to survive a long winter under thick ice.

North America's fur industry was built around the fur of a beaver. Early French traders bartered goods with native trappers in exchange for pelts. These beaver pelts were never tanned, but the underfur was sheared off and used make felt. In turn, the felt was used by European hatters to make fashionable hats. Beavers were nearly wiped out by the mid-1800s—until the game laws and stiff penalties of the early 1900s, the only thing that saved the beaver was that hat felt could be made less expensive using other materials.

CONSERVATION

Many books have been written about the success of the North American Model of Wildlife Conservation. The premise of conservation started in the old world in the mid-1600s after many of their forests were depleted. Unfortunately, it didn't carry over to America. The North American continent experienced an expanding population of settlers who saw the New World as an endless bounty of land, trees and animals. Conservation did eventually come to America—albeit 200 years late. In 1854 philosopher and author Henry David Thoreau penned a book titled *Walden,* which included Thoreau's experiences of being one with nature, praising the wilds and wild places as sacred sanctuaries. This romance for wild places started a movement.

Thoreau's philosophy spread through the fields of botany and forestry with the help of men like forestry educator Carl Schenck. Trees were recognized as a reusable resource by this time in both the United Kingdom and Germany, two areas whose forests had been decimated by uncontrolled timber cutting. As America recognized the need for conservation of timber, the thought of conserving wildlife had also become a necessity. With the railroad expansion into the west, market hunting of bison, elk and deer had become big

< Len Rue Jr. Photo

Wikimedia Commons

Theodore Roosevelt in 1885. Roosevelt's badlands ranch near Madora, North Dakota allowed him to live, work and hunt in the wide-open spaces of the west. This gave Roosevelt a unique perspective of nature and a common sense view of wildlife conservation.

business as the meat could be transported to Chicago quickly by rail. Support for wildlife conservation grew from the likes of Theodore Roosevelt, George Grinnell, Aldo Leopold and John Muir. Roosevelt founded the Boone and Crockett Club in 1887 with a goal that hunting be regulated. That wild meat was for individual and his family, not commercial gain. When Roosevelt became president in 1901, he took action, embarking in major conservation efforts that would include creating the US Forest Service and the National Park Service, along with setting aside many landmarks and large land tracts for wildlife.

Roosevelt was also instrumental in helping states regulate hunting and trapping. He believed that open access to hunting would result in many benefits to society—that hunting supported both access to firearms and the hunting industry, where most conservation funding is derived. The North American Model of Wildlife Conservation offers two basic principles. Fish and wildlife are for the non-commercial use of citizens and should be managed so they are available at optimum population levels—forever.

BIOLOGICAL CARRYING CAPACITY

In the wild, different habitats grow at different rates. Desert plants grow much slower than rainforest plants. High alpine grows slower than the lower mountain sides. Since wildlife species gravitate to preferred habitats, nature balances between available food and the number of animals the land can sustain. This is called the biological carrying capacity. Unfortunately, nature handles this number in an erratic fashion. In years of bountiful food, animal populations flourish, mortality rates fall, and animal populations rise. When the number of animals rises to a point that stresses the habitat, plant life can't replenish fast enough, and the animals become malnourished and susceptible to disease and increased mortality. Outside factors also play a role—

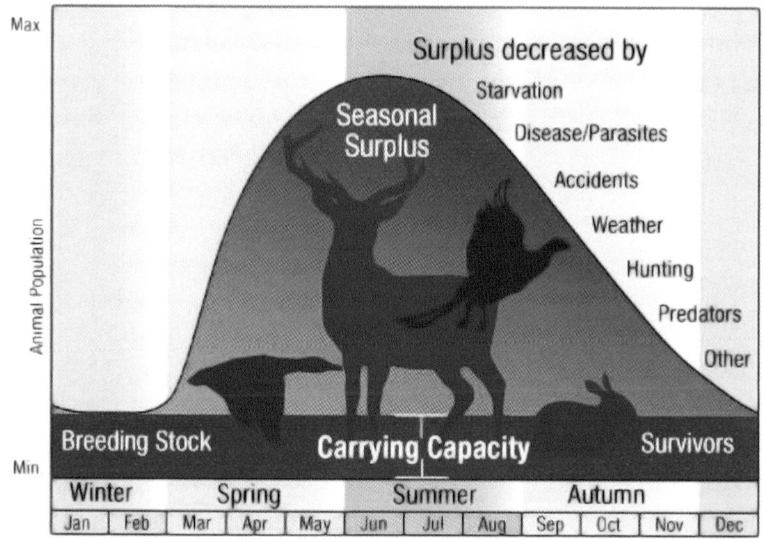

Author's Collection

drought, floods, range fires, unusually brutal winters and other factors often punish both the flora and fauna. Thus, in the process of natural selection, animal pop-

Len Rue Jr. Photo

ulations often experience dramatic swings in numbers from boom years of population growth to bust years of disease and starvation.

As humans look to be caretakers of the land and wild creatures, there are two schools of thought—preservation and conservation. Preservationists want the wild spaces to remain as they always were. This is more of a hands-off approach where wild lands and animals are designated as parks and hunting is prohibited.

Conservationists incorporate a "wise use" mentality in which the land and wildlife are managed for sustainable use. Trees are selectively cut, and the wood utilized. The animals are harvested by individuals for meat, fur and leather. For example, realizing that a herd of 100 deer is perfect for a piece of land, when the population becomes 150, 50 deer can be harvested for food and leather, supplementing the food supply and sustaining the residents of the area who harvested them. The remaining 100 deer will create less impact on the habitat and have a much higher survival rate into the next growing season. This wise use philosophy gives both wild lands and the wildlife a value. Money that is generated from these resources in the form of hunting licenses, hunting gear, ammunition, firearms and traps can be channeled back into the resource to help sustain it.

CULTURAL CARRYING CAPACITY

Where biological carrying capacity involves all the natural processes that affect plants and animals, cultural carrying capacity adds the human element. As human populations expand, wildlands shrink as cities and suburbs expand. Less habitat means less living space for animals. Farming destroys woodland habitat and artificially increases carrying capacity as row crops increase the land's sustainable food value per acre. This bounty of food is eventually harvested, eliminating most of its initial value to wildlife. Residual crops provide some nutrition, however, 100 acres of mature corn sustains more animals than 100 acres of plowed soil.

Cultural carrying capacity includes man's tolerance for certain species. Wolf packs in cattle country kill livestock which affects ranchers. Grizzly bears kill deer and elk which affects sportsmen. Beavers clogging culverts floods roads, affecting travelers. Even a skunk under a family's front porch affects homeowners. The carrying capacity of the land may sustain these animals, however the individuals being affected by this wildlife will not. The culture of humans will always dictate wildlife acceptance. Wildlife departments are constantly working to balance the scales to not only keep wildlife populations healthy, but to keep them in wild places.

JUDGING THE BEAVER POPULATION

Fur trapping is much different than damage control trapping. On the fur line, we skim the surplus animals and move to new areas. Since the number of beavers is limited by their habitat and because they are fairly easy to catch—it can be easy to over trap a colony. Understanding the dynamics of the beaver colony is essential to judging the population and thus trapping only the surplus. Trappers who operate along limited stretches of rivers and flowages will rely on migrating beaver

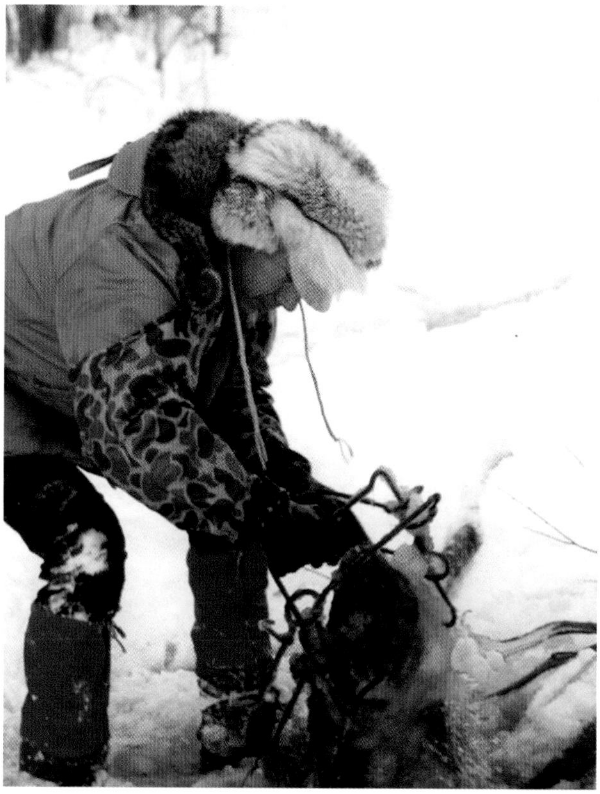

Tom Miranda pulls a beaver through the ice hole taken in a baited conibear set.

to fill the void created by removing the local animals. However, on a remote wilderness lake with three beaver houses, a trapper needs to gauge the population and take only a surplus number of animals.

Beavers mate for life and a lodge can contain 10 or more of them, including the breeding pair, 2-year-olds and kits. Three active lodges on a small lake could mean 30 beavers, yet conservatively there are likely two adults. Two 2-year-olds and two 4 kits per house. Beavers can live over 20 years in the wild and sometimes there are bachelor beavers in some impoundments. The age of a beaver can somewhat be judged by the height of the tree cuttings. Younger beavers will cut the trees closer to the ground than adults who sit on their haunches, cutting trees 12–16 inches off the ground. Also, a few beavers can cut an enormous amount of wood, so it's easy to overestimate the number of beavers from a quick look around their pond.

As a rule of thumb for harvesting beavers, look at 20–30% of the area's population. If you think there are 10 beavers, take 2 or 3 adults.

UNDER ICE BEAVER TRAPPING

There are two disciplines within the world of beaver trapping. They include open water trapping and under ice trapping. Under ice trapping is an art which involves baited sets that are lowered through a hole in the ice. Alternatively, are channel sets made where runways can be located either by locating bubble trails through clear ice or setting channels which were marked before freezing up. Most trappers in the cold climates of the north trap beavers through the ice once the snow is deep and catches of other furbearers have slowed.

When setting beaver lodges, always be uncertain of the ice. I've seen 36 inches of ice 50 feet from the lodge and open water around the lodge. Usually at the lodge openings and runways, the ice will be thinner. This can be found by tapping on the ice around the lodge. The tone will change when you're over thinner ice and likely that's a runway or channel.

Because the beaver's cache of food is buried in the pond bottom near the house or den, it sours in the midwinter—fresh bait cut when traps are set is often preferred. When I was ice trapping beaver, I used a chain saw and ice spud to make the ice hole. Pond ice was typically 2–3 feet thick in January in Michigan's Upper Peninsula. Usually, I cut a 2-1/2 foot square hole in the ice, and on the first run I would pre-bait with fresh willow.

A week later I would return with traps and areas where the willow was eaten, and set up a pole set and at least one or two baited conibear traps. The actual under ice sets are too bulky to build at camp and bring along, so they must be built right at the site. Nails, hatchet, axe, wire and some scrap lumber pieces really help get these pole sets together fast. Usually all the dry poles you need will be found nearby as well as the green poplar or willow baits. Small dry sticks for fencing and constructing the platforms can be taken right off the lodge. Be sure when building any under ice sets to use dry poles and not green ones. Only the bait should be green, or the beaver will eat your set.

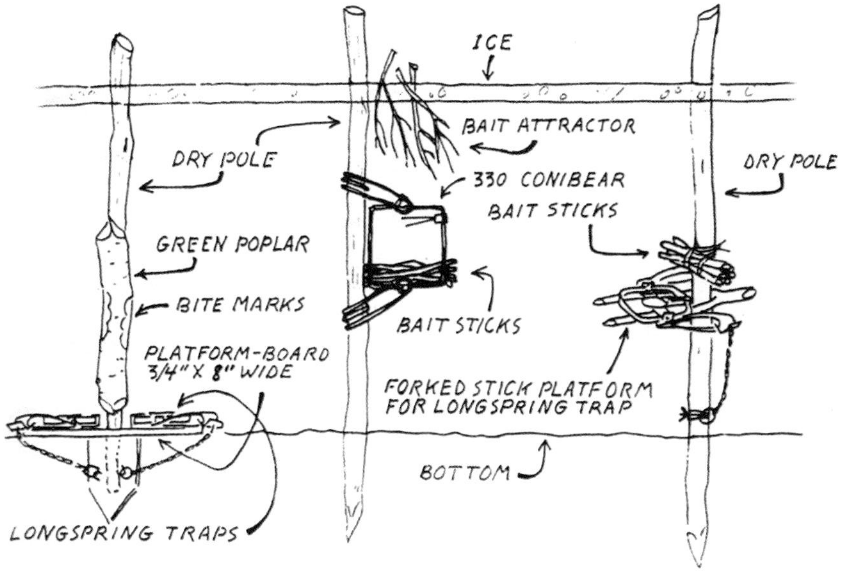

Sketch by Bob Noonan

el below the ice is 4 feet or less, put the set on the bottom. If the water level is deeper but you still touch bottom, make the set so it's up near the top, just below the bottom of the ice. If you don't touch bottom, a suspended set must be made so the set hangs just below the bottom of the ice. Often the water was deep on the lakes I ice trapped in Michigan. I hung the sets off the ice so the traps were 2–3 feet below the bottom of the ice.

Here's a trick! Use a 3-foot, square piccc of corrugated cardboard to cover the ice hole and pack snow over the top about 12–18 inches deep once the trap is set. This seals the ice hole and will allow the ice to freeze clear. The cardboard and snow will act as some insulation and help keep the water in the hole from freezing back so quickly. When I came back a week later to check sets, the hole was frozen with 2–3 inches of clear ice. If clear ice was full of air bubbles, I most likely had a catch.

I found in deeper water, more bait was needed to attract beavers to the set. So, if you're working in deep water, don't skimp on bait. Four or 5 "green" willow trees stuffed in the ice hole is a good bait. I would also shovel the snow off the ice around the bait hole to allow the sun to shine through the ice, helping the beavers find the new bait. All traps set under ice should have a double strand of wire leading up the dry pole and should be tied off above the ice. Also, if trap tags are required in your state—they should be connected to this wire and visible above the ice. When I was living and trapping full time in Michigan's Upper Peninsula, the limit was 25 beavers and 2 otters per licensed trapper so once I had 20 beavers or so, I needed to be careful not to have too many sets out and go over my limit.

Safety is important on the beaver line. One time after a fresh snow, I was building some fresh under ice sets. I snowmobiled out onto a big lake and headed to one of several beaver houses. I stopped about

Here's a funny story that happened to me. On one of my snowmobile trails in the bush, I had to cross a creek that flowed into the larger Michigamme River. It was spring-fed so it never froze over very thick. I spent a full day building a bridge across the flowage. The trees I used were poplar, about 4 to 6 inches in diameter. When spring breakup came, the ice went out and the water rose. The bridge was anchored in well, so it didn't float away—but when the beavers found it—they chewed it up and hauled off the entire bridge! Needless to say, the next bridge was built from dry spruce and hemlock.

It's a good practice to score your bait bundles to make them look like a beaver has cut them. This also exposes the light wood under the bark and gives more sight attraction to the bait. Bait should be wired about 6 inches above the trap or so. Be sure the sticks won't get in the way of the trap action. On the 330 conibears, never wire the bait directly to the trigger. Conibears are baited in between the jaws. The bait should be down and the trigger up high, so the beaver hits the trigger with his head, not his front paws. The depth of your under ice sets depends on the depth of the water you're working in. After the ice hole is made, test the water depth with a pole. Remember to note the ice thickness as well as the soft mud on the bottom. The set must be placed below all surrounding ice and above this mud. If the water lev-

When I returned to Michigan after state hopping to Ohio there was always plenty of snow to shovel. Time for under ice beaver trapping.

30 yards shy of the house, got off the sled grabbed by spud and was walking to the house when BAM! I went straight through the ice and in over my head. I scrambled to get out of the lake, as the ice that broke free was about a half-inch thick and slick. I was finally able to push the broken ice aside and climb out. The temperature was about minus 30. I was about 10 feet from the house when I went through. The snow had drifted over the thin ice above where the beaver was coming and going to the lodge and the air bubbles and insulation from the snow kept the ice thin. I was soaked. So, I stripped down, rung the water out of my clothes and put them back on and they quickly froze solid—my pants legs were stove pipes. I did have a survival kit with me and built a fire under a spruce tree, but by this time was shivering uncontrollably. Once I warmed up enough, I got on the sled and headed back to camp. It was 20 miles by sled. I think I was colder when I got to camp than I was when I fell in. It took me half an hour just to get out of the ice suit I was wearing. The crazy thing was that I was sawing 34 inches of ice on another house on that same lake just before I fell through.

Another crazy story on the beaver line was a time when I pulled up to a baited conibear set, scooped off the snow, pulled my cardboard and saw nothing but air bubbles in the hole. "Beaver," I thought. I grabbed the axe and chopped out the hole, put on my gauntlet gloves and started to pull up the entire pole set and flat tail. It would come up about a foot but then stop. It felt heavy and I thought the beaver was sideways and caught in the hole. The ice around the hole was about 30 inches thick. So, I laid down on the ice with my body wedged against the pole holding it up and reached down as far as I could to grab the beaver and flip him around to come up through the hole. It was all I could do lying down with my arm fully extended in the water to reach the conibear spring. Then all at once. Snap! There was no beaver. I had just put my hand in a 330 that was lodged under 30 inches of ice. My thumb was broken.

Fond memories of trapping beavers through the ice, 1984.

As I laid on the ice I thought, "How 'effin stupid is this? How in the hell am I gonna get out of this mess?" Well I laid there for about 15 minutes pondering the situation. During this time my arm numbed to the cold. My problem was that I really couldn't move as I was flat on the ice and my arm was fully extended straight down and held in place. I tried and tried to pull the entire set out. My axe and spud bar were both out of reach. More than an hour later I'm still there and still stuck. I finally decided that I would just "bite the bullet" and try to pull my hand out of the trap. At first it seemed impossible, and hurt like hell, yet slowly by wiggling and pulling—little by little, my hand pulled free. Once I got the gauntlet glove off, I could see how the thumb was broken and the swelling which made the hand larger and more difficult to pull free. Moral of the story—treat the big conibear traps like a gun. They are always loaded.

Because of the difficulty of trapping through the ice and the limited success rate, most game departments offer a spring beaver season. After breaking up, the beavers are very active, and the open water offers much easier access.

CENTER OF THE UNIVERSE

The beaver dam is the center of the universe to a beaver. Many colonies will not exist without it. The maternal instinct of the female beaver is to protect her young, keeping the water level up to protect den entrances and facilitate access to fresh willow at the water's edge. This is why the female monitors and fixes the dam every night. If she notices a change in water level, she immediately leaves the lodge and inspects the dam. The male will help patch breaches as will the 2-year-old colony members, but the female is in charge.

Where legal, breaking the dam becomes a "black hole" in the beaver's universe. As the water rushes out of the pond it's like the strong pull of gravity—pulling the beaver to the location to fix it. Trappers know that traps set along the dam will catch animals fixing and patrolling it.

OPEN WATER BEAVER TRAPPING

An enterprising trapper can catch more beavers in a week of open water trapping than a month of under ice trapping. Most beavermen who aren't doing damage work, or operating in the south, trap the spring season. Sets used can consist of channel sets with 330s, castor mound sets, trail sets and baited sets.

Castor mounds are scent mounds made of mud, which beavers construct along the bank. Beavers will make these little mud pies and mark them with their

Author's Photo

Dig a false den entrance with a tile spade then a trail up the bank to the mock mud pie castor mound at arrow. Trap is in front of both hole and trail in 8 inches of water in front of the light brown root protruding from the water.

Author's Photo

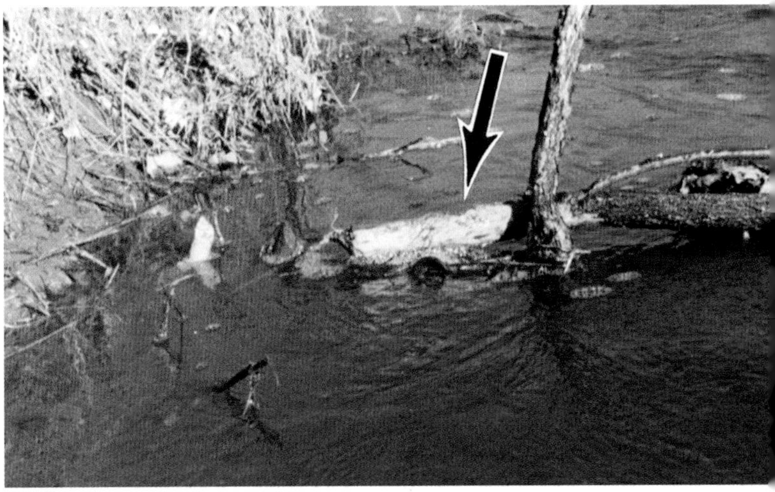

Using a freshly chewed dive pole attracts beavers to your fenced conibears when there is no defined channel.

A beaver snared on dry land makes one heck of a mess. Reset is best made up the trail and out of the catch circle.

castor scent, staking out their territory. These mounds attract migrating beavers and thus attract mates. Traps can be set at actual castor mounds or replicas of the real mud pies can be quickly made and lured with a glob of good beaver lure.

When setting foot traps for beavers consider placing the trap to make a back-foot catch. Beavers have small nimble front feet and because of their strength and weight, the beaver can twist out if not quickly drowned. The large back feet of a beaver give a much surer hold and most expert beaver trappers today prefer the large, strong MB750. Traps should be set fairly deep in 8–10 inches of water. A beaver swims with his front paws pulled back under him until his chest bumps the bank. As the beaver approaches the set, he will grip the bank with his front paws and place a back foot in the trap. If you've rigged a good slide wire set up, the flat tail will quickly drown.

All body gripper traps set for beavers should be completely submerged, if possible. A 2-inch diameter dive-stick should be placed on the coni to force the beaver down under and into the trap. Keeping your beaver underwater will keep the direct sun off of him and keep a 2- or 3-day old beaver from slipping due to the warm spring sun. In areas where creeks and rivers are apt to rise and fall more than a few inches overnight, use a gauge to keep track of the water level. Use a stake driven in the water near the bank with the water level marked when the traps are set. Place this stake in a convenient place such as where you put your boat in on the river. Check the stake each day you run the river and note the water level—Is it the same? Higher? Lower? This gauge will help you guess the tendencies of the water fluctuation and let you adjust the trap placement accordingly.

Snares can be used effectively for beavers and have a few advantages over steel traps. If you miss a beaver in a snare, he won't be trap shy and can easily take in another snare. Pinch a beaver in a steel trap and I can assure you he won't be taken again so readily. Snares are also more portable and can be packed in long distances to remote colonies much easier than large MB750s and 330s. Beavers taken in snares will usually be very much alive and believe me, they will cut every inch of vegetation down as far as the snare will reach. Keep this in mind when rigging beaver snares and especially anchoring them. Use 3/32" 7x7 cable snares for flat tails and metal stakes when possible or be sure wooden stakes are driven in below the ground level.

Everyone has their own techniques of snaring, some snare beavers on dry land, some go out in the water. In my experience, beavers are easier to snare if you can get the snare out in the water, several feet from the bank. Beavers have more confidence and feel more secure in the water and they will readily swim though the loop. Also, if you can keep them in the water after capture, they are less likely to ruin the set location, and more beavers can be taken at the same set replaced with a new snare. However, spring flooding often brings debris downstream and water rises making snares on the bank more effective. When setting beaver snares on dry land, most snare men place the bottom of the loop on the ground.

Author's Photo

Here a string of castors drying in my lure room greenhouse on Mott St. in Chamberlain, South Dakota, circa 1985.

Author's Photo

Miranda on the set of the *Fur-Fish-Game* Beaver trapping video, 1989. I think I had a half dozen of these red flannel shirts and wore one almost every day on the trapline.

SKINNING BEAVERS

Putting up beavers is a laborious process. Beavers are skinned open and stretched round. Rough skinning beavers is pretty easy but fleshing them by hand is a monumental task. Learning to clean skin beavers is an art form and trappers who can do it usually have the best-looking pelts for market. That said, trappers who catch lots of beavers have little time to clean skin as it can take more than an hour per beaver to clean skin a blanket beaver and a full 20 minutes for even the best-of-the-best skinner. Colorado beaver trapper and NTA Trapper Hall of Fame member, George Stewart was one of the best clean skinners I've ever watched peel a flat tail. Keep in mind that High-volume beaver trapping is like any other species and the trapper who spends time in the field trapping will catch more animals than the trapper who is putting up fur every night.

All parts of a beaver are valuable. Of course, the pelt is valuable, however beaver meat is often sold. Trappers with access to a cold locker can sell gutted, carcass beavers to butchers who have a market for the meat, also fox ranches buy carcass beavers as do lure makers. One hundred beaver carcasses might average 20 pounds each, which at 25 cents a pound makes 500 bucks.

Beavers have a pair of scent glands which are called castors. Connected to each castor is an oil sack. These are found in the beaver's pelvic region, positioned on both sides of the vent. Beaver castors and oil are very valuable and should be saved. Price per pound varies depending upon whether the castors are wet or have been dried. If the oil sacs are drained into clean glass, it is worth more than just the sacks sold as a whole. Warming the sacks by the fire will aid in getting the oil from them. Lure makers use beaver castor in many formulations. It takes about 10 adult beavers to yield a pound of dry castor. With an average price of $50 per pound, the average beaver has $5 worth of castor. I have seen castor markets in the $80 per pound range which means that a decent 100 beaver season would net $800 in castor alone. Only the skunk can outdo the beaver in value for its glands as skunk essence often trades over $1,200 a gallon for pure quill.

NEIL OLSON

1948–

Neil Olson was born in Maine January 28, 1948 to Nellie and Haakon Olson. Neil's father was a self-employed logger in the summer months and did carpentry in the winter. Haakon also enjoyed trapping, and this is where Neil picked up his interest in animals, furs and traps. Neil's mother stayed at home and raised young Neil while his father was out earning a living.

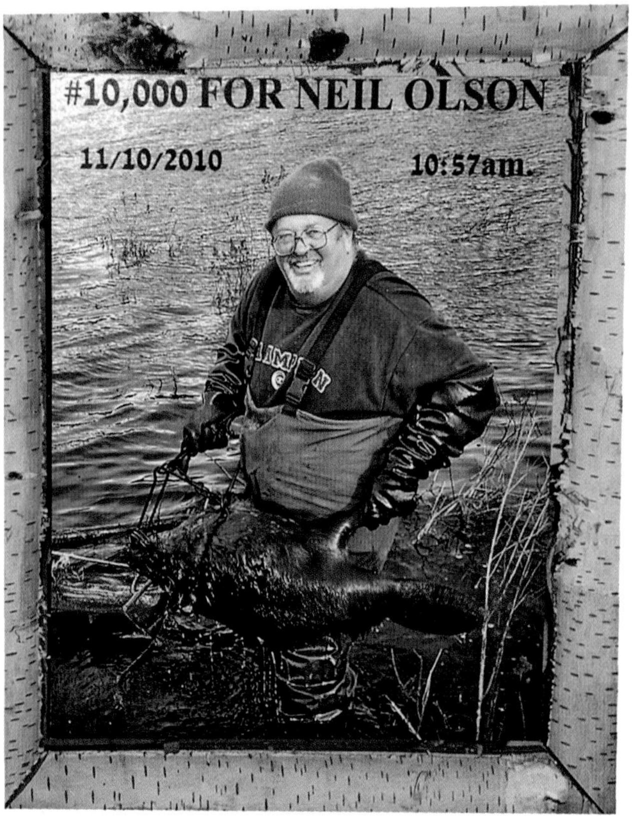

Neil Olson with beaver #10,000 taken in November 2010. Olson has harvested over 13,650 beavers in his career.

Neil Olson Photo

Neil Olson caught 27 foxes and 24 foxes in separate days on his Maryland trapline. Here's a dandy day's catch of reds.

Besides trapping, Neil loved baseball and dreamed of one day being a major league player. Of course, every kid dreams of the glamour of professional sports, but Neil was actually a talented athlete. Neil was 100% baseball, sleeping with his mitt and throwing the ball in his parents' basement fielding grounders and playing make-believe pitching games. Neil was good enough to attend the Ted Williams baseball camp in Lakeville, Massachusetts and did well enough to be asked back as a counselor, eventually meeting Ted Williams himself.

In high school, Neil played shortstop and pitched, two highly skilled positions. Often in high school pitchers who were good hitters played two positions. Neil went to New Haven College in Connecticut and played third base for his four-year degree. Olson led the team in hitting for two of the four years as well. Often it takes more than pure talent to make the big leagues. As with so many players pursuing so few available positions—timing as well as influence play a major role in who actually makes it into the dugout of a pro baseball team. Neil never did make the big leagues, but he was involved as a part-owner of both the Mill City All-Americans baseball team in Lowell, Massachusetts

Neil Olson Photo

Neil Olson New Mexico catch of 132 coyote and 5 bobcats in three weeks.

and the Sanford, Maine Mariners. Neil's baseball legacy continues as his grandsons play college baseball. There are some amazing stories about Neil and his life in his 2019 book, *My Lifestyle is my Pay.*

Neil moved to Connecticut to attend college and after graduating, married Linda Sullivan. Together Linda and Neil moved back to Maine and had two daughters, Carrie and Jill. It was around 1972 when Neil was in his mid-20s that he got serious about trapping. In 1973, Neil decided to supplement his trapper income and became a fur buyer. His story is interesting.

"I went to a local fur buyer by the name of Merritt Kimball to sell my fur. Merritt quoted me $320 for the pelts I had. I told him I was hoping for $400. Merritt said he'd split the difference with me, and I agreed. Merritt was the largest country fur buyer in New England back then. I used to call him 'The King.' On the way home from Merritt's place that day I decided to buy fur. I bought my license and put up a sign. I had no idea what to pay for anything. So, I bought a fisher cat that had been shot. It had a hole in its neck. I took it to Merritt's to ask him what it was worth. Merritt said that I was a buyer now—I'm supposed to know what it's worth. I lost money on that fisher."

Fur buying intrigued Neil and if he learned the business—it was possible he could earn 10% on the pelts he bought. Neil was up for the challenge.

The fur business is a curious trade and most trappers who at least dabbled in it learned much about the industry and how all the pieces of the puzzle fit. Neil talks about buying $50 thousand in fur on a weekend like it was small change. Of course, his banker called him the following Monday telling Neil he was overdrawn. In the fur boom Neil says that in New England, *"Fisher hit $200-plus, fox—$70, coyote—$50, mink—$40 for males, $20 for females, bobcats—$200 and beaver was selling for about a dollar an inch!"*

Neil Olson Photo

Neil Olson (left) stands with famous NY trapper Paul Grimshaw and their 1990–91 catch of 432 beavers.

Neil Olson is known for his beaver numbers but was actually an incredibly well-rounded trapper. And he was meticulous in keeping records. So much so that Neil has a chart he's kept since 1973. And through

An Adirondacks Adventure

Veteran trappers enjoy an extraordinary winter season of beaver trapping in New York's famed semi-wilderness area.

By Neil Olson

THE NEW YEAR found me, as usual, opening the beaver season in my home state of Maine. The area really didn't hold an over-abundance of beaver. They'd been pushed rather hard the last few years. Knowing this, I was only making a half-hearted attempt.

This, along with not wanting to call it quits, was eating away at me.

I had harvested quite a bit of fur earlier in the season. Trapping in Maryland, where there is an incredible amount of fox, I caught 400-plus canines. You'd think after catching 27 fox one day and 24 the next I'd be a satisfied trapper. I had proven to myself I could catch fox with the best of 'em. But, my life-long goal of spending each season learning as much as possible about all aspects of trapping was not being fulfilled. Or maybe it was just that I felt I hadn't punished myself enough yet.

Gene Lane, from New York, invited me to go back to North Carolina to trap beaver and otter with him as we had the year before. My truck was packed and ready to go when the 100,000 miles I put on it the previous four years caught up. A vehicle, in a lot of ways, is the biggest expense on any trapline. Now, mine was costing more than money. I was watching my season slip away.

It was already January 27 and the truck was still in the shop when my good friend Paul Grimshaw called. He wanted me to join him trapping beaver in the Adirondacks of New York State. The area he had in mind was about an hour's drive from where he lived—the same area legendary outdoorsmen Johnny Thorpe and E. J. Daily had trapped in years gone by.

With only a short time of the North Carolina season left, I decided to forego the trip south and headed over to New York to take a look. Bill Sweinen, a Massachusetts trapper who had lived in the Adirondacks, offered to help us. When we reached the region, we were greeted by a bitter winter storm. On one snowmobile excursion, Bill's ear turned completely white. I was concerned, but luckily it turned out okay. With Bill's help, we located 20 colonies in two days, enough to get us started.

Photo by Bob Noonan

Paul Grimshaw (left) and Neil Olson get ready to set up a big, active beaver house. Trapping in the semi-wilderness of the Adirondacks region, the pair encountered little competition for such choice locations.

Trading open-water in North Carolina for under-the-ice trapping in New York was a bit of a mental battle. But, I went home, packed my gear, and back to Paul and Bernice Grimshaw's I went. By the time I was actually on my way, I felt like I'd been let out of jail and was a free man again. As soon as I reached the Grimshaw home, I knew Paul felt the same way.

Right here, I should explain Paul and Bernice a little. Bernice? What a sweetheart. Every night a four-course meal was waiting for us, and during the day we ate a packed lunch any gourmet chef would be proud to serve. It got so bad both Paul and I were afraid to leave the other guy alone in the truck. Some days "lunch" was eaten by 10 a.m.

Paul? He's a little bit harder to explain. A trapper who truly loves his trapping, the only real disagreement we had was over who was enjoying himself the most. Seeing how stubborn he was, I decided to let him think he was. A local trapper who didn't like us teaming up summed it up best when he said: "Those two deserve each other."

How two so-called adults could put in the hours we did and enjoy ourselves so much I'll never know. One day we were checking sets on a big lake that had three or four flowages on it. There was a regular blizzard blowing snow level to the ground. It was cold, cold, cold

Paul Grimshaw, his wife Bernice and Neil Olson with some of the harvest from their trapline in the Adirondacks.

Continued on page 56

DECEMBER, 1991 13

Here's part of Neil Olson's 1991 *Fur- Fish-Game* article about his Adirondack trapping with Paul Grimshaw.

Neil's home state of Maine is his bread and butter trapline. It's the area he enjoys trapping most and where he's spent the majority of his trapping seasons. However, to make a living trapping you need to trap as long and hard as you can, so when winter had a firm grip on Maine, Neil was looking for greener pastures and fur pockets. Neil has traveled out of Maine to trap almost every year of his career. He's trapped in 12 states plus Maine. Neil has also enjoyed 23 trapping partners in his career. Trapping out of state can be a lonely game and with a partner you can watch out for one another. Partners share expenses for food as well as lodging. Plus getting a hand skinning in the evening is always a bonus.

New York trapping legend Paul Grimshaw was Neil's trapping partner for over 20 seasons. The team primarily trapped winter and spring muskrats, beavers and otters together. In Neil's book, *My Lifestyle is my Pay*—he shares many funny stories about his times with Paul Grimshaw. It's obvious the two became friends and enjoyed the trapline together. Neil talks of a story in which Paul and his good friend Ron Pfleger were trapping together. Neil wasn't with them at the time. They came to a location heavy with sign and Paul told Ron to make a set. Ron said, *"We can't set a trap here—it's sure to be stolen!"* Grimshaw replied, "*Use one of Neil's traps. . .*"

2018 Neil has taken 3,540 foxes, 1,678 coyote, 1,481 raccoons, 13,650 beavers, 2,541 muskrats, 85 mink, 724 otters, 115 fisher, 1,117 skunks, 53 bobcats, 343 opossum and 12 badgers. To see his chart, you'd realize it's authentic and as I have looked it over and the first thing that came to mind was, "Why I wasn't smart enough to keep track of my numbers?" I can tell you that they wouldn't compare to what Neil has accomplished.

Neil Olson Photo

Here's a group photo from an early Neil Olson New England Trappers Weekend. Pictured: 1. Bill Bailey, 2. Bob Jenny, 3. Louie Venetz, 4. Andy Stoe, 5. Dianne Kent, 6. Willis Kent, 7. Bud Boda, 8. Spoony the Clown, 9. Neil Olson, 10. Paul Grimshaw, 11. Joe Baldwin, 12. Pete Askins, 13. Kernit Stearns, 14. Herb Lyons, 15. Dennis Theriault, 16. Daryl Stevens, 17. Charlie Dobbins, 18. John Lisenby, 19. Norn Gray, 20. Steve Plummer.

Over the 20 years that Paul Grimshaw and Neil trapped together they took over 4,000 beavers. Neil says their best season was 400 beavers and 58 otters and a lifetime of grand memories. A short time before Paul passed away, he gave Neil the old lunch box they had shared during all those years of trapping together. Written on the lunch box was an inscription, "To my little buddy Neil from Paul." Both men cried. Few relationships in life attain the level of trust and friendship as Neil Olson and Paul Grimshaw had while trapping beaver in upstate New York.

Neil describes his beaver trapping technique as "nothing special." Catching beavers in numbers requires numbers of beavers to trap, big traps and lots of hard work. Neil tells of a time when he and Paul were trapping an area they had trapped for years. One day they returned to check the sets and nineteen 330 conibear traps had been stolen. Neil looked at Paul and asked, *"What are we going to do now?"* Paul said, *"Reset!"* This is the dedication and work ethic it takes to make big catches. No trapper catches 400 beavers. Beavers are caught one at a time. If you take into account the effort to catch just one beaver then multiply it times 400, it's easy to see the amount of work required. Just carrying four hundred, 40-pound beavers back to the truck is quite a chore!

Neil also experienced some amazing fox trapping while trapping with Dale Quillan in Maryland. Neil says that he used the same set and lure in Maryland as he used in Maine yet caught many more foxes in Maryland. On Neil's third year trapping in Maryland, Dale had commitments, so Neil went it alone and had an amazing run taking 27 reds in one day, 24 in another. Neil said he was through checking traps by 1 p.m. nearly every day and spent the rest of the day skinning!

Although Neil is a fantastic trapper, he's probably best known for his New England Trappers Weekend Rendezvous which has been held every year since 1976. Conceived by Neil and his friend Alvin Yates, over the years the event has seen trappers from across the country travel to both Pennsylvania (held in the Keystone state 5 years) and Bethel, Maine for the remaining 38 years. The weekend is a carnival-like event that showcases unique demonstrations of outdoor interest.

Attendees not only see the usual convention-style trapping demos but interesting seminars and displays of outdoor pursuits from log cabin building, to using a winch to get a vehicle unstuck, and how to survive in the woods. Neil thinks that the success of his yearly weekend has been the result of both unique events and loyal trappers who have made friends at the Trappers Weekend and pledged to make the pilgrimage to Bethel every year.

Neil Olson has authored three books. His *Active Trappers Method of Fox and Coyote Trapping*—1979, *Trapline Adventure Stories*—1995, and *My Lifestyle is my Pay—2019*. All are interesting reading.

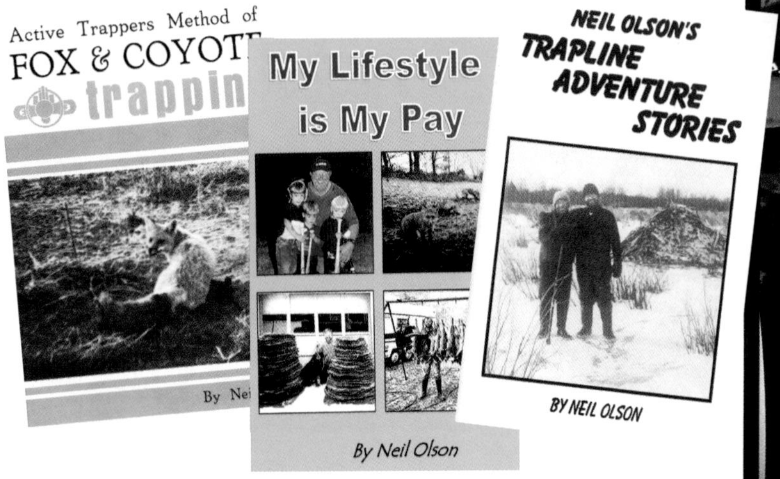

Neil Olson's 13,650 beavers over his career is nothing short of major league numbers. Think about it, Ty Cobb led the American league in hitting, batting a whopping .378 over 12 seasons. Neil's pal Ted Williams won 6 batting titles with an average of .365. If you take Neil Olson's number of 13,650 beavers and the 45 years it took him to catch them, Neil would average 303 beavers each season. That's batting over 300 for 45 seasons!

I'd call that an "ALL STAR" trapping career if there ever was one.

JEFF DUNNIER

1954–

Jeff Dunnier catches so many beavers his truck smells like the castor room at a perfume factory. No, I'm not kidding. Jeff makes a living trapping flat tails for numerous coal corporations, timber companies and private landowners in east Texas, Arkansas and points south. Through trial and error and what Jeff calls "necessity" he's developed and perfected a rather unique system to trap the culvert clogging chippers.

Dunnier is an Ohio boy who started trapping muskrats and raccoons in 1972 and caught his first gray fox that same year. After graduating high school, Jeff went into the Army, first stationed in Colorado and then Kentucky. When he could, Dunnier ran a line near both of his Army posts as a sideline to his military duties. After his service, Jeff returned to Ohio and worked construction, trapping in the winter. In 1977 fur prices made trapping a lucrative enterprise and Jeff went at it

Jeff Dunnier Photo

Here's Jeff with a day's catch of otters.

hard, starting off with a fox line in Indiana, then his old Ohio stomping grounds and south to trap in Tennessee. By 1979 the fur boom was in full swing and Jeff went to Arizona as well.

Over the course of his state hopping, Jeff Dunnier ended up trapping in the east Texas swamps in 1980 and soon decided to settle in Texas. Jeff found a good-paying job that allowed him to continue to trap and there was plenty of trapping to be done. With low fur prices beaver populations had exploded and Dunnier built quite a side business over the next ten years. By 1993 he had so much damage control work scheduled, he pulled the plug on his 9 to 5 job and started East Texas Wildlife Damage Control as his full-time occupation. And Jeff has had his foot on the gas ever since—logging 95,000 miles and trapping nearly 2,000 beavers and 200 otters in his first two years of full-time trapping.

I know Jeff personally, as he was a student in my 1988 class at the Fur Takers Trappers College. A solid trapper then and an obvious go-getter, Jeff found his niche with the beaver work and quickly excelled at it. Like all trapping systems, simple is best. In predator trapping we use steel stakes, short chains and lots of swivels. This system anchors the trap and holds the animal. This is much better than trying to wire a trap to a tree or wooden clog. Or using a wooden stake that may split. Jeff recognized early in his beaver trapping if he could force the beaver to swim through his sets utilizing fencing, he could gang set and solve his beaver problems faster. But using sticks and brush found onsite to fence the beaver was time consuming and often ineffective. Jeff needed a barrier that was heavy duty, but light enough to use efficiently. Manufactured hog confinement panels were the answer. Hog panels are made 16 feet long by 34 inches high. Jeff cuts the 16-foot panels into six equal sections. and bundles them together for easy transport in his truck and for carrying to the site. These heavy-duty wire panels are then arranged to prevent beavers from accessing their dam or culvert. Conibear traps are set in the access channels which Jeff leaves between the panels. Jeff sent me the following photos to illustrate his deadly system.

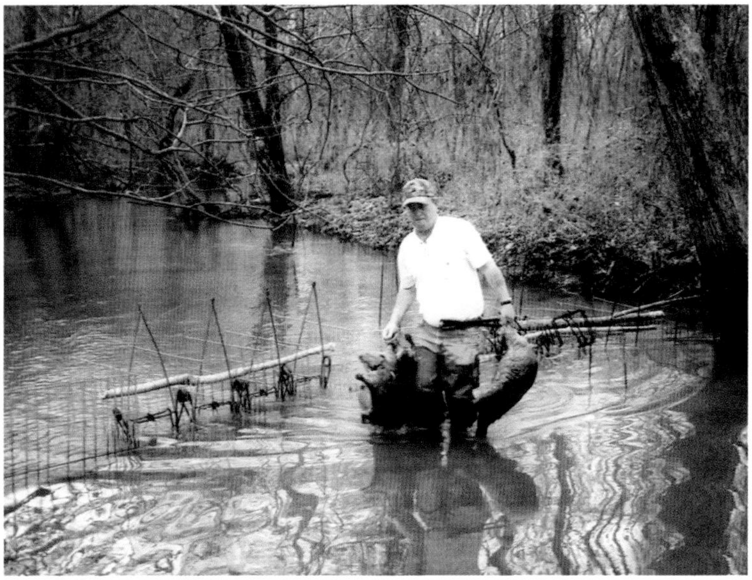

Jeff Dunnier Photo

Here Jeff Dunnier shows the effectiveness of his panel system on a wide flowage with Dunnier's signature "gang set."

By blocking every avenue to the dam spillway, den, channel or culvert with panels and guarding a select few openings with traps forces beavers into the traps. And by using multiple traps, Jeff often catches 3–5 or more beavers at one location in one check cycle. His system is rather ingenious and the heavy metal

panels are beaver-proof, as there's no chewing or going around. Because of the method Jeff uses to position and anchor the traps, when a beaver is caught, it pretty much blocks that channel from others passing and helps in his multiple catches. Jeff also posts custom made signs which warn passersby. **DANGER** TRAPS IN THE AREA. This business approach helps limit liability from the public as well as giving a would-be thief a second thought before taking the traps. When using this panel system there is no way to hide the sets. However, Jeff creatively arranges the panels in such a way that traps are set out and beyond reach from the bank, in deeper water where theft is less likely.

Beaver Business
by Jeff Dunnier
East Texas Wildlife Damage Control
A Guide to Beginning the Business of Trapping
Beaver for Fur and Animal Damage Control.
Including the Dunnier Panel System,
an extremely efficient method for
Damage Control and Fur Harvesting
Beaver and Otter.

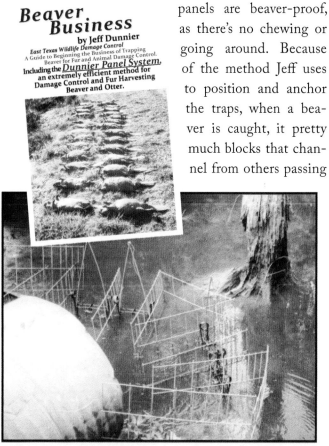

Different setup with panel system on a culvert. Notice the panels all the way around the culvert.

Small drainage with 8" pipe. I surrounded the area with panels and two traps. The results were an adult male and female. Notice the warning sign to protect you and the public.

Beaver Business • 41

Jeff Dunnier's book, *Beaver Business* is a must for the serious beaver trapper. The book is well-illustrated with various scenarios and how the panel system is set up for maximum effectiveness. This is only page 41 of many, many pages of sets and results.

Trappers who are using this system adjacent to public right-of-ways might consider not only using the signage as mentioned above but also hiding an infrared deer scouting camera nearby. If trap or fur theft were to occur, photos and potential license plate numbers would aid wardens in the apprehension and prosecution of those responsible.

Beaver trapping is often described as the *"hardest-easiest"* trapping there is. It's hard because it's so laborious. Often, beavers live in muddy swamps with fallen trees crisscrossing in all directions. Big traps are tough to set and once the beaver is caught it's often a chore just to get one to the truck. A big beaver easily weighs 50-plus pounds. Beavers are also difficult to skin and stretch properly. Beaver trapping is easy because most landowners quickly give permission to trap them. Beaver sign is unmistakable and set locations are often very obvious. Their travel ways are easy to find and sets easy to make. What Jeff has done is developed a fool-proof system of taking beavers in numbers. In beaver damage work, the essence of the job is to eliminate the colony so the culvert and road can be repaired or the land drained. And Jeff is a pro at it. Businesses like this can offer an enterprising trapper a six-figure income once contracts are in place.

Jeff Dunnier is the quintessential professional trapper and has risen through the ranks with hard work and a don't quit attitude. Jeff took his schoolboy trapping hobby and carried it through as an adult. No matter his occupation, Jeff found time for trapping until he eventually put himself into a position to follow his passion as a full-time trapper. Jeff gives credit to those he's learned from and shares his experiences and methods so others can utilize what he's learned.

Jeff Dunnier Photo

Dunnier catches a few otters along the line as well. Here's nearly fifty torpedoes spread out for a photo.

His book, *Beaver Business* is a testament to his success, and I would suggest any reader interested in full-time trapping get a copy. Jeff Dunnier was inducted into the North American Trappers Historical Society Trappers Hall of Fame in 2019.

My *Outdoor Adventure Magazin*e (OAM) series on ESPN was in its fifth season when the *Cabela's Sportsman's Quest* TV series debuted. This gave me one hour of exposure on ESPN every weekend. At the time I was producing 13 original OAM episodes and hosting 26 originals for Cabela's. This 39-episode schedule involved a rigorous travel schedule. I was flying everywhere and gone for weeks at a time. I did manage to get July and most of August at home to bond with my three children. Summers were always special and once the kids got old enough to travel easily, we took some amazing vacations. Cayman Islands, Italy, Hawaii, California, Washington DC and more. I will say that kids grow up much faster than one would think and reflecting back—I remember them little, then grown up. There is no in between.

The Cabela's TV gig was lucrative, and I did a lot of neat hunts. My first mule deer, first caribou and first muskox were taken with Cabela's. However, there were trying times. One issue was the gun and bullet sponsors. Producers wanted me to use a rifle on many of the hunts so the manufacturers would get their products used on the show. I was a bowhunter and rifle hunting in my opinion wasn't really a challenge. It is a challenge—but not nearly as challenging as bowhunting. Successful bowhunting demands the hunter to work to get into range and 100 yards isn't close enough. Rifle hunters often take big game at 300 yards. My effective archery range is inside 60 yards.

I did do some bow hunts for Cabela's including black bear, muskox and whitetail, but I also did some rifle hunts. I eventually told the producers to bring Cabela's execs on the trips and let them hunt with the rifle. I would run camera and host as needed. The full second season was almost entirely Cabela's executives as guest hunters, except for two bowhunting shows where I did the hunting.

Here's the Miranda family during a Christmas visit. Bush Garden's and Disney were always favorites while the kids were growing up. L–R Tom, Sandy, Jennifer, Joshua and Jeremy, circa 1997.

If you can believe it, I was nearly killed on two separate Cabela's TV shoots and no, I'm not kidding. Cabela's ran what they called Walleye Trail fishing tournaments. Several of the Sportsman Quest TV episodes would feature these walleye events. I host-

Winnercomm Producer Jeff Murray and I on location for Cabela's *Sportsman's Quest.*

ed these shows but also ran camera during the day. Typically, I went out with a pro angler favored to win and as the tournament progressed, I would videotape in the boat with the leader in hopes that we would have footage of the winner catching his fish. The first incident was on the first day of a Duluth, Minnesota event on Lake Superior. I was sitting in the bow of a pro's boat, videotaping him as he drove the boat out for the day's competition. The 18-foot Lund-style boat had a big 80 HP motor but used a tiller for steering, not the usual console and steering wheel. The boat was "on step" and we were moving fast to an area the fisherman had scouted and caught fish the day before. All of a sudden—BAM! The front of the boat hits a large steel marker buoy and I mean at full throttle. The impact nearly rips the huge TV camera from my arm and shoulder and almost threw me out of the boat. As the boat pushed past the buoy, it ripped the aluminum hull open, substantially wrecking the boat. And then the angler had a nervous breakdown, sobbing and apologizing for nearly killing me. He said afterward that a steel collar on the huge marker buoy missed my head by only inches and in the instant he saw it, he thought he had killed me.

The second Cabela's TV "near death" experience was during season two at a tournament held in Toledo, Ohio on Lake Erie. It was the last day of the event and I was going out with the pro leading the tournament and he had asked me the night before to be at the dock early. He told me it was a 90-minute ride to the area where he was catching all the fish. The weather was iffy with rain and wind. I had my TV camera in two plastic bags and was wearing a full commercial fisherman rain suit with bibs and a parka. As we loaded the boat, started the motor and idled out into the marina, the tournament officials were undecided as whether to call the event. As "go time"

Author's Photo

This was one of the most exciting bow hunts in my early TV career.

came they were still undecided but because my pro was leading the event and we had such a long run, they let us and a few other boats go. They'd indicated they would radio us if they canceled the tourney. Once out

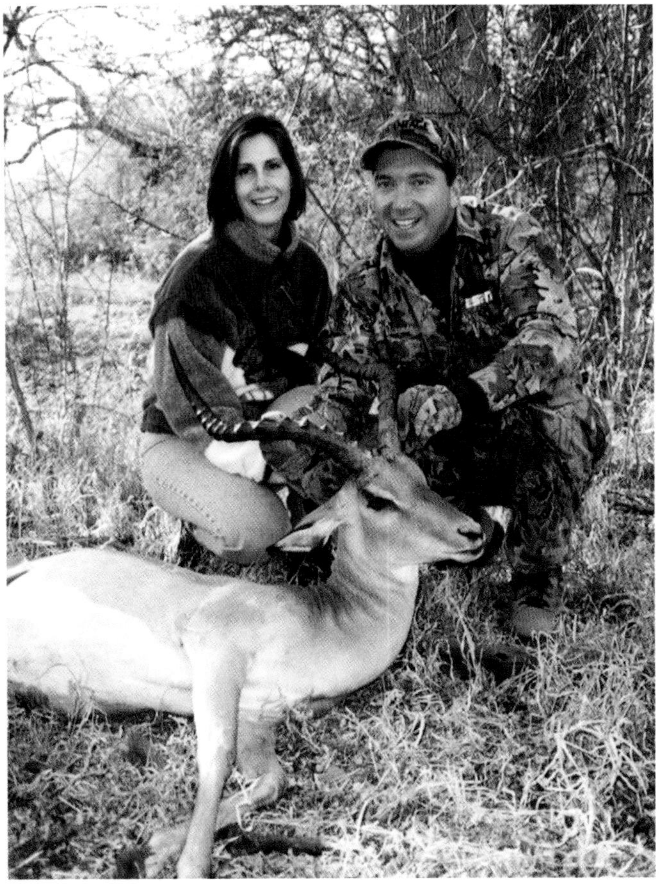

Author's Photo

An impala taken on my first trip to Africa. My wife Sandy was in the blind running the camera when I arrowed him.

of the marina and on the lake, the full force of the storm was evident. Lake Erie is shallow and when the wind gets the water rolling, the waves can be 6–8–10 feet in swells and in a Ranger bass boat with low sides, it's like a carnival ride. We were taking the waves head on, bam, bam, bam and it was a rough, choppy trip. The tournament was a pro-am and the amateur in the boat quickly got seasick from the rough conditions. About an hour out of the marina we hit a wave unusually hard and believe this or not, the boat split in half. The fiberglass hull cracked and broke behind the console from port to starboard. The captain shut the motor down and the boat filled with water to the gunnels. Anything that wasn't strapped in washed out of the boat. And we couldn't raise anyone on the radio. No land in sight and waves crashing. The boat was floating because the hull was filled with Styrofoam. The pro, amateur and yours truly standing in knee deep water trying to ride the waves.

Since we had been driving into waves on the way out, we now had the waves pushing us back to shore. The captain had gotten the trolling motor battery up out of the water and set it in one of the pedestal seats so we could use the trolling motor to keep the boat oriented with the waves. Seven hours later we finally reached the lake shore. While the captain and amateur stayed with the boat at the shore, I hiked across several farm fields to a road where I hitchhiked back to the marina for help. My cellphone was soaked and useless. Soon the coast guard located the boat and then they knew we were all OK. I mean, really you can't make this stuff up!

Needless to say, after two seasons of the Cabela's show, I was ready for a change. I just couldn't keep the schedule of doing my own show and Cabela's. Dallas Cowboy's tight end Jay Novacek took over my hosting duties for the third season. No sooner than I left the Cabela's show, Realtree founder Bill Jordan called me and asked if I would consider doing an ESPN series for him. His new Advantage camouflage pattern needed more national exposure and ESPN was the place to showcase it. Realtree was my first big TV sponsor and I couldn't say no to Bill. That said, I didn't want to do two TV series. My kids were at the age where I needed to spend time with them. I had been thinking about revamping my own series, giving it a facelift and doing more adventurous bow hunts.

ADVANTAGE
ADVENTURES

I had an idea. I called the network in Bristol, Connecticut and asked them if I could change the name of my show to *Advantage Adventures with Tom Miranda*. They pushed back some as *Outdoor Adventure Magazine* continued to do well. But eventually they agreed.

I called Bill Jordan back and told him I would change the name of my show to *Advantage Adventures* and we would concentrate on hunting. He agreed. So, 1997 was the last season for *Outdoor Adventure Magazine* and in 1998 *Advantage Adventures with Tom Miranda* debuted on ESPN.

This began what would be the origins of my nickname, Adventure Bowhunter. In 1998 I went to Africa for the first time taking my first 4 African species—a warthog, impala, kudu and red hartebeest. I arrowed my third black bear in Alberta, an Alaskan mountain goat and I continued my quest to do adventurous bow hunts. The next year I stepped it up going after Africa's black death—the cape buffalo. Also, in 1999 I arrowed my first Alaskan brown bear. White-tailed deer were always on the schedule and by 2000 I had taken more than 45 bucks on camera for TV episodes and videos like *Buckin' the System, Legends of Whitetail, Hidden Treasure Bucks* and more since 1989.

Author's Photo

This is the first animal which began the quest toward my North American Super Slam, 1998.

I think everyone knows where they were on September 11, 2001. I was in elk camp in New Mexico. I can remember returning to camp that morning and the guys saying that New York was attacked. We had no TV, no cell reception. We listened to the radio in one of the trucks at camp. I had a satellite phone so I could call home and see how my family was doing. It was a crazy time. The next day, September 12, I arrowed my first bull elk.

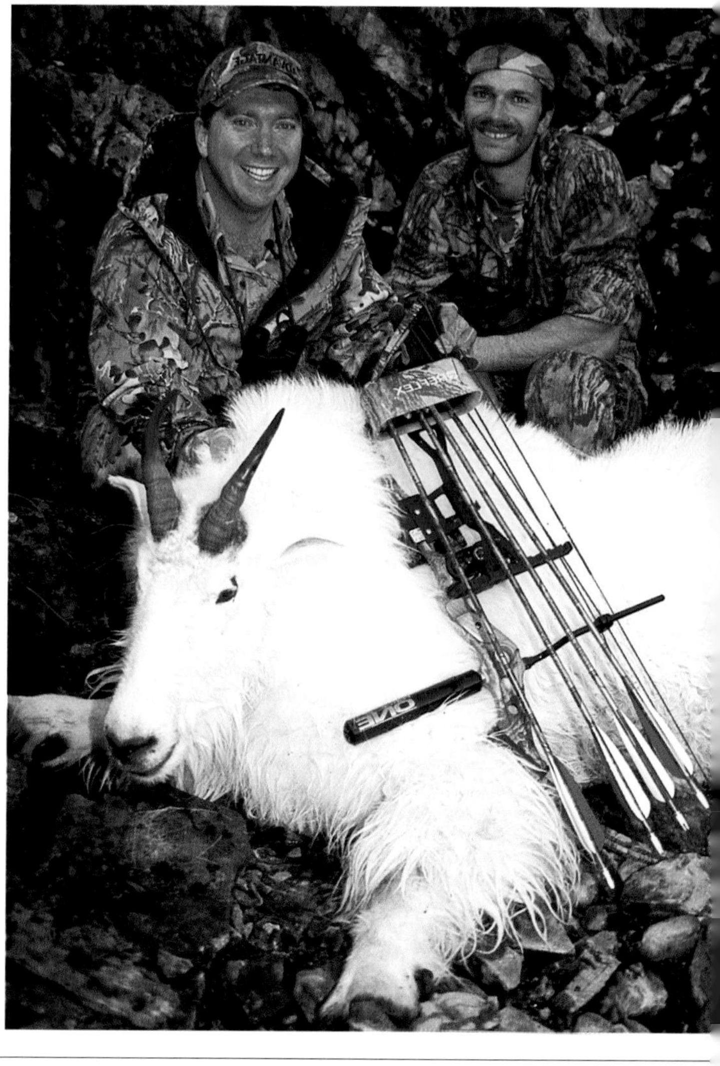

Author's Photo

Alaskan guide Dennis Zadra and yours truly with my first mountain goat taken in 1998.

During the late 1990s and early 2000s my adventures had allowed me to start quite a collection of animal species. It started out totally by accident. My goal was to visit new places and bow hunt. Different kinds of big game animals lived in these areas, species I'd never seen or hunted before. My analogy for a trapper would be an Ohio trapper wanting to trap in different areas like Maine, Alaska and Arizona. With success this trapper might catch many new species, North American furbearers—marten, fisher, lynx, otters, wolves, bobcats, etc.—adding to species this trapper already had taken in Ohio would lead to quite a collection of unique furs, mounts and experiences. My job was to make the best outdoor TV shows I could, and the adventurous aspect of the locations made the job interesting and always a challenge.

Author's Photo

This is my first cape buffalo taken in 1999 for an ESPN TV episode.

In the late 1990s I learned of an organization called Safari Club International and discovered their convention. Outfitters from around the globe exhibit at the SCI show and for a hunter attending the show is like Christmas shopping on Amazon— anything you can think of is available. The SCI show set me on a kick where I was traveling to Africa to hunt 2–3 times a year. The seasons are opposite in Africa, so April, May and June are good bow hunting months. In 2002

My first bull elk taken the day after 9-11-2001 on the Floyd Lee Ranch in New Mexico.

African PH Zak Grobler and I decided to set up a Tom Miranda bowhunting camp in South Africa's Northern Province. And I began collecting the African species in earnest, along with trips to New Zealand, Australia and across the North American continent.

Author's Photo

This is the TV frame before the shot of my African cape buffalo.

This rhino is still alive! Darted with a sedative tipped arrow. Called a "green hunt" it's an exciting challenge. For a bowhunter this is the only path to taking Africa's Big Five as rhinoceros cannot be legally killed with an arrow.

My first dangerous hunts were real learning experiences. Like Africa's cape buffalo. I had to train to be able to draw an 85-pound bow. It's not to draw the bow once, but 50 times while practicing. Often on a tough bow hunt, a hunter may hike 8–10 miles then hide in a cramped clump of bush for an hour before getting a shot. When shot time comes, getting the bow back is essential and you must be able to do it standing, kneeling, sitting or even after running. Hunters in pursuit of cape buffalo in those days were required to take a dangerous game course which was given by the National Bowhunters Education Foundation. The thick-skinned animals of Africa require heavy poundage and heavy arrows with cut on impact broad heads. On my first cape adventure I used a specially made Golden Eagle bow with 85-pound limbs and shot an arrow shaft sleeved with a smaller shaft and filled with silica sand. The shaft was tipped with a 210 grain Magnus broad head. This rig was high-tech in the late 1990s but by today's archery standards it's archaic. But I got it done with one arrow and the hunt was captured on video and seen on ESPN.

I actually used the same bow on my brown bear hunt that fall, however I used a lighter arrow and Muzzy 3 blade Trocar-tipped broad head. The arrow zipped through the bruin like a knife through hot butter. At that time, the brown bear hunt was the most exciting experience of my bowhunting career. But the hunts got even more exciting.

Author's Photos

Here's a TV frame of the brown bear just after the arrow blew through both lungs. Will he charge or flee? He ran. Well-placed arrows kill quickly.

In Africa there are several hunting achievements that hunters can attempt to accomplish. The most revered and difficult is called the Big Five. Africa's Big Five animals include the elephant, rhino, cape buffalo, lion and leopard. In 2004 I did what is called a "green hunt" for white rhinoceros. Rhino are protected in the wild, but inhabit many of the large private estates and parks in Southern Africa. The rhino's hide is so thick that only the heaviest arrow shot with a high poundage bow can penetrate only certain areas of the hide like the softer underbelly. However, because rhino need to be fitted with tracking devices to prevent poaching, Safari Club International in cooperation with wildlife biologists and veterinarians created the

Author's Photo

My Colorado pronghorn, August 2001

"green hunt." In a green hunt, the bowhunter uses a needle-tipped arrow with a syringe that when injected into the rhino, sedates him so a transmitter can be placed, blood drawn, and antibiotics given. The hunter works with the biologist and veterinarian on the hunt. Once the rhino is sedated, the hunter can get a photo with the rhinoceros while the medical team tends the beast. Then an antidote is given and the rhino wakes and walks away. It's actually a pretty amazing hunt and I did it in 2004 for an ESPN episode.

OTTER TRAPPING

Like a mink is a prize to a muskrat trapper, the river otter is a prize for the beaverman. Where they are legal to trap, otters are a challenge. Their fur is short dense and durable. They are truly a unique species of furbearer whose population is expanding more and more into the Midwest. The river otter is a somewhat nomadic creature, traveling waterways in a constant search for food. Although the otter has a specific territory, it can cover a fairly large area. Sign of the otter may look fresh and yet none are taken for a week for even two weeks. However, if there is fresh sign, likely the animals will be back. Just like a good coyote trapper, the otter trapper places his best sets in the best locations and leaves them hoping for the torpedo to return on his rounds.

The same blind sets that take beavers will also take an otter including, runs, channels and spillways. Although many otters are taken in 330s which are set for beavers—otters are known to pass through these same traps without getting caught. Many otter trappers prefer to fence the otter into a tighter space and use the smaller 280 and even 220-sized body grippers.

LenRue Jr. Photo

Otters are often found living in beaver impoundments. Fish that live in streams which are damed congregate in the pond than forms and these areas are attractive to otter. Otters also make use of abandoned beaver dens and houses to raise young and get out of the elements during certain times of the year.

Otter toilets are places where they visit often on their rounds. These locations make good set locations for snares, conibears and foothold traps. Droppings at toilets often contain fish bones, scales, even frog or salamander parts which will tell the observant trapper their local diet. Otters are very strong and can be savage in the trap so it's essential to try and drown them when using footholds. Snared otters are almost always alive, and it takes perfect cable placement to catch one and a tuff cable to hold 'em.

BRANDON JOHNSON

1991–2020

Ohio trapper Brandon Johnson has taken his passion for trapping and the outdoors into the stratosphere. When Brandon was 10 years old, he began watching his father's old *Fur-Fish-Game* trapping videos. Brandon was mesmerized by the animals and thoughts of being a trapper. Together with his father, they would start a small trapline that same year. Little did they know that not only would Brandon's passion grow for trapping, but he had a knack for it.

Brandon Johnson Photos

Brandon Johnson and his father Steve pose for a tailgate hero with Carolina beavers and otters.

Even as a youngster, it seemed Brandon could pick the set locations. It was like he had a four-leaf clover and rabbit's foot in his pocket. Animals would find his traps. What may have started as beginner's luck has turned into what most of his friends say is a sixth sense in understanding animal habits.

Brandon's schoolboy catches were better than most. But like all schoolboy traplines, school is top priority. And of course, growing up near Cleveland, Ohio meant raccoons and muskrats were the go-to animals. Plus, when you don't have a driver's license, options are limited. Once Brandon passed his driver's license test, he was bent to get himself a long-line territory set up in Ohio. He also saw an opportunity to start his own nuisance animal control business. Fur prices weren't all that great, but he had gotten into a position where there was an opportunity to make a buck trapping animals which found their way into being a nuisance.

Growing up as fur trappers, most who read this book may define nuisance animals as beavers plugging a culvert or raccoons in the corn crib. And although nuisance animal control does involve homeowners, farmers and trapping skunks, coons and beavers—it also involves corporations like Walmart, Kroger, Fed-Ex, municipal airports, golf courses and many, many other clients who need help with rogue animals on multiple, large properties. And the guilty animals make up quite a unique list. Like bats and birds, snakes and alligators, rats, mice, bees and wasps. Also

Brandon Johnson's one day Iowa catch included a pick-up full of raccoons and 13 mink.

armadillos, cane toads and iguanas. Plus, the normal raccoons, skunks, badgers, even wild hogs, deer, and the list goes on.

Imagine a Super Walmart—you know the ones with a grocery store and everything else under one roof. These buildings are gigantic and have daily deliveries by semi-trailers. Semi-trailers need a loading dock and that means 3, 4, 5 or more large garage doors. When these doors are open, birds fly in. During night deliveries, bats fly in. Imagine birds flying over the produce section—chirping, diving, eating, crapping on everything. The county health

Brandon Johnson's 2013 catch of 59 otters and other pelts.

Brandon Johnson Photos

Brandon Johnson on his home line in NE Ohio. Full-day's run over the traps.

department won't stand for it. The ceilings in these buildings are 30-feet, some 40-feet-tall. Who's going to get the birds out? A trapper. And also keep in mind that some animals that fly in are protected species—so you can't just string nets and throw away the culprits. Large corporations have budgets for animal control on their properties. Trappers eager to learn the techniques required to provide services can work their way into a pretty lucrative business.

By the time Brandon Johnson was 18 years old, his nuisance wildlife business was almost too big to handle alone. Plus, he was figuring out the corporate world of nuisance wildlife and had established an extensive Ohio long-line for fur. Brandon's business grew leaps and bounds. He was trapping every day and his expertise received rave reviews. Word-of-mouth endorsements travel fast and soon Brandon was hiring and training trappers to help him. Brandon took a

Brandon Johnson poses with his final catch of the 2013 season to take 59 otter.

month in 2010 and went to North Carolina in the winter to trap. Timber companies are always looking for help with beaver control in the south. When fur value is down, animal populations can explode and beavers flood roads which halts logging operations. What first started as a trip for possible timber company beaver work turned into Brandon's obsession with otters.

Catching an otter on a beaver line is like catching a mink on a muskrat line. It's a prize. Yet few trappers graduate to be top minkers. The same is true for otter trappers. Brandon's obsession with otters turned into a love affair that continues to this day. Brandon had some early successes on the trapline that even seasoned pro trappers would give the nod. Like 59 beavers in one day, 85 'coon in one day taken in Ohio, 59 otters in 14 days in North Carolina—25 beavers, 7 otters and 4 'coon in one day. Impressive fur catches.

Over the next few years Brandon expanded his trap-lines in Ohio, North Carolina and also traveled to Alabama. During this time Brandon also met trappers Scott Adams and Clint Locklear. Locklear had started a new TV show called *Trapping TV* and Clint proposed that Brandon be featured in several of his TV episodes. Brandon thought it would be fun and used the promotional opportunity as motivation to go all in and full throttle on otters. In 2014, teaming up with his father Steve and Scott Adams, the trio would run traplines as partners for ten weeks in Pennsylvania, Ohio, Alabama and North Carolina.

Raccoons, foxes, mink and 'rats were on the list in the Midwest and the team was off to a good start. For Brandon, he was hammering the coon taking his personal best of 85 in a one day run, but his

Awesome day on the water line—25 beavers and 7 otters.

focus this season was otters. Brandon had made some decent otter catches including his 2013 season where he took 59. North Carolina Hall of Fame otter trapper Claudie Taylor had taken over 200 otters in a season. Brandon set his sights on that goal. Could he more than triple his catch in a single season? If there ever was a chance, the timber swamps of North Carolina were the place to make it happen. After running lines in both Pennsylvania and Ohio, the trappers went south to Alabama specifically to trap predators. After 2 weeks in 'Bama the team moved east to North Carolina.

Once in "tar-heel state" Brandon went to work on otters. His strategy would include using 330 body-gripper traps—setting crossovers, channels and where sign was heavy utilizing gang sets as otters often travel in small groups. Brandon would locate prime locations and run the line on a 72-hour check. Because otters are travelers, it's not uncommon for them to pass through an area once every 7–10 days. And traps need to be operating and in the right places when these animals come through. To approach Taylor's otter record, it was going to take a herculean effort. Brandon kept busy setting beaver traps and scouting more territory between his otter checks. It seems the population was up, and the weather was staying stable.

Brandon told me the secret to his success is hard work plain and simple. *"Yes, you need the ground and to have access through permissions or damage contracts, but the drive and determination not to quit is in my mind the key to large catches."*

There is so much effort involved in spinning up a trapping season and often only a few short weeks or a month to operate the line at full capacity. Anyone who has trapped the south knows it's a world away from the Midwest. Pine forests, thick kudzu, swamps, snakes and more. But in some areas, the density of fur is incredible. The price per pelt of southern fur doesn't approach the value of prime northern, "snow county" furs—yet the numbers a hustling trapper can amass in the south can help make up for it. Brandon dug in for a push to his goal. He had taken more otters than ever so far that season and the areas he had set were all active with animals. His numbers climbed. Days quickly turned to weeks and soon Brandon pulled the plug. Exhausted and tapped out, he pulled the traps, gathered up ten chest freezers of fur and headed back to Ohio.

And there was another month of work left. Thawing and fleshing the hides, stretching fur and drying. The final tally was nothing short amazing. In rounded numbers, the catch included 1,500 raccoons, 1,200 muskrats, 900 beavers, 150 coyotes, 70 foxes, 50 mink, 30 bobcats and 198 otter pelts. Just an incredible season.

Brandon and his wife have two young sons, Killian and Carter and Brandon looks forward to the day when he can take them trapping. I think it's pretty awesome that this master trapper found his trapping passion in a set of Tom Miranda *Fur-Fish-Game* trapping programs.

Brandon Johnson's 2014 mega season included 1,500 raccoons, 1,200 muskrats, 900 beavers, 150 coyotes, 70 foxes, 50 mink, 30 bobcats and 198 otter pelts.

It is with a heavy heart that I relay the news that Master Trapper Brandon Johnson passed away in late December, 2020 with a sudden, tragic medical condition. Brandon was not only a phenomenal trapper but a great son, husband and father. Brandon will be dearly missed in the lives of his friends and family.

MUSKRAT TRAPPING

Pennsylvania trapper Nick Wyshinski wrote a book on muskrat trapping titled, *Muskrats: The Trappers Meal Ticket,* in 1963 and boy did he get it right. Most young trappers "cut their teeth" in the world of fur trapping pursuing muskrats. Easy to catch and prolific, rudder-tails have beautiful dark fur and long silky guard hairs. Depending on the fur market, their value may be but a few

dollars each, yet 'rats are easy to skin and add up quickly.

Walking a small mud-banked stream in hip waders, wearing a basket of traps and seeing den after den, trails up the bank, and droppings every rock or log above the water line are memories of my childhood that will keep a smile on my face the rest of my life. A 110 conibear set at an active den was my introduction to instant gratification, as there was always a 'rat waiting in the morning. In a book of this magnitude, discussing muskrat sets and methods isn't necessary, however some strategies used by mega muskrat trappers is in order.

The 'rat trappers who take thousands of rudder-tails first have access to them. There are areas of isolated, yet large populations of muskrats in tidal areas along the Atlantic and Gulf coasts. In the upper Midwest around the Great Lakes as well as western Minnesota and the eastern Dakotas, potholes and large marshes are found full of 'rats. Large catches have also been made by enterprising trappers in farming areas where behind private fences, muskrats have overrun ponds and creeks as well as on the Ohio, Missouri and Mississippi River watersheds.

Like beavers, many muskrat areas have a spring season. This is ideal trapping as the fur is prime, the 'rats are active after ice out and the muskrat glands are valuable this time of year.

It's almost unfathomable, but there are large marshes where trappers set and check traps continuously. Thousands of 'rats moving all day and night.

Often where legal, colony traps are used with great success. A colony trap is a homemade wire trap (approx. 6"x6"x30") with flipper doors on the ends. Set in runs, these traps can take between 2 and 4 'rats in one night. I personally caught 7 'rats in a colony trap one night on my Ohio line and needed to take one door off the trap to get the 'rats out. Twenty well-placed colony traps can produce 50 muskrats a night. Smart trappers rotate these traps nightly and trappers with access to larges marshes tow trailers full of colony traps. With the right tools and some ingenuity, a trapper can make a colony trap to fold flat and these traps are much easier to transport, carry in the marsh and store after season.

Besides being a mecca for muskrats, marshes also handle rainy weather much better than streams and rivers. A full day of rain can bring streams over their banks and make 'rat trapping impossible. Marshes might rise an inch or two. One year while I was running a mixed bag line in Ohio, we got a tremendous amount of rain and the forecast was more of the same. Rivers were out of their banks, fields so sloppy that dirt trapping was out of the question. So, switching gears I trapped several small 'rat marshes I had permission on. I only averaged 55 'rats a day for the week, but I stayed productive and 'rats averaged almost 6 bucks a piece. Almost $2,000 for a week's work.

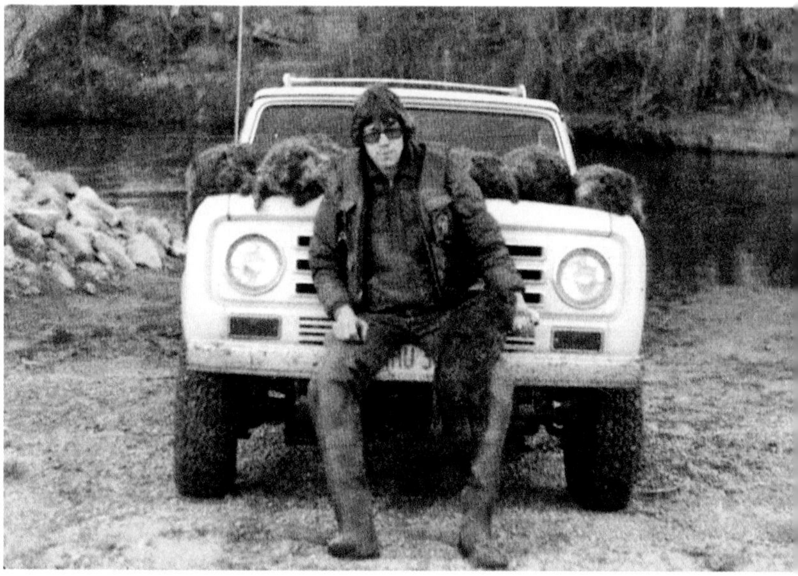

Ron Hauser Photo

A young Ron Hauser with his International Scout and a dandy run of flat-tails.

RON HAUSER

1959–

Minnesota trapper Ron Hauser took nearly 6,000 muskrats in six weeks. His video *Muskrat Frenzy* made in 2001 shows 5,000 of those 'rats taken in 25 days. It's a phenomenal catch of muskrats by a self-made outdoorsman who has followed his passion for trapping since the early days. Ron got involved in all aspects of the outdoors to keep his dream alive.

Ron was raised on the north outskirts of Mankato, Minnesota. Ron started trapping barn 'rats when he was just 8 years old. By 12 he was running a trapline with his bicycle. Ron told me, *"My brother and I would bike 14 miles before school to run traps. We would leave the catch hidden in the road ditch and Dad would drive by and pick everything up. After school, we would ride 18 miles going the other way tending the rest of our line. And every time I tell that story today my knees hurt!"* The year Ron got his driver's license he took 71 red foxes on his Minnesota trapline, a grand catch for a 16-year-old trapper.

After high school graduation, Ron's goal was to be a full-time trapper. Ron worked odd jobs when needed. One day he heard there was good money in picking morel mushrooms, so he began a small business. Selling some morels, the buyer asked him if he ever saw any ginseng while he was 'shroom picking. Ron didn't know what ginseng was, but he soon learned and was digging more root than anyone in the county. Turtle trapping was also a way to make money as were fishing bait and other outdoor pursuits.

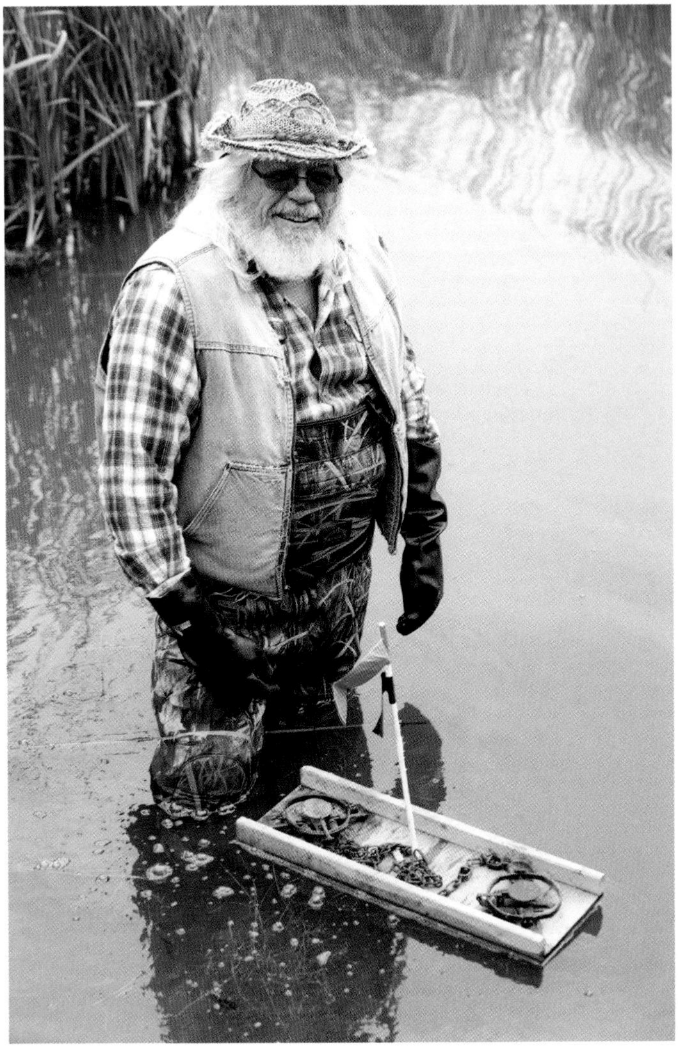

This is the float set up Ron Hauser used to take over 5000 muskrats in South Dakota.

Hauser with a great day on the water line.

Ron Hauser did a little bit of everything when he wasn't trapping.

"I was working a job in August 1983 and my buddy pulled up in his truck and said, 'We're headed to Kansas for the National Trappers Convention. Let's go!' Well, I was seriously broke at the time. So I went home and got a box of old Fur-Fish-Game magazines that I had gotten from an old trapper years before—some of the magazines were from the 1930s and 40s. I took them to the Hutchinson, Kansas Convention and sold them one at a time to fund my trip. It was at this time that I realized I needed to get something going in the trapping business to sell."

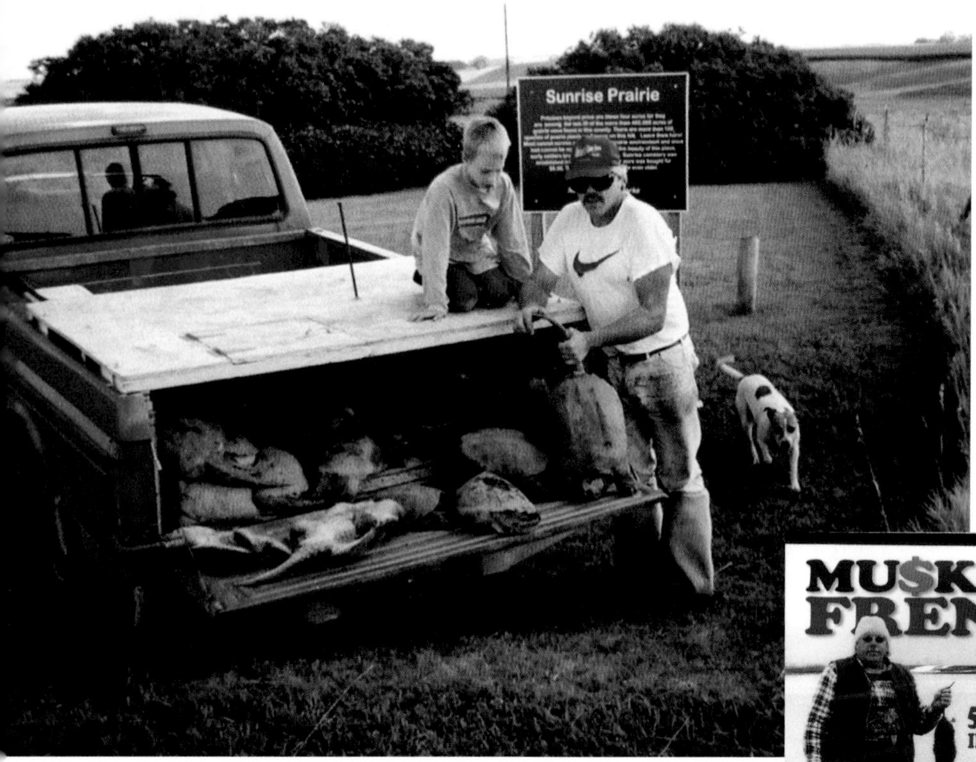

Ron Hauser Photo

Ron Hauser also trapped and sold turtles to support his family.

Ron Hauser started selling farm produce in 1984 and it's a business he still does today. "*Yeah, I operate 5 and sometimes more roadside produce trucks. I'm coming up on 37 years in the business. It's surprising how well the produce business has done. We actually get quite a few people who look for us year after year. Sweet corn, tomatoes and watermelon are roadside staples, but we sell other produce as well. The produce is fresh, grown locally and less expensive than the grocery!*"

In 2002 Ron made his first DVD program on trapping. *Full Time Trapping* covered the Ron Hauser style of trapping raccoons, mink, muskrats, beavers and snapping turtles. Since that program, Ron has done several additional outdoor DVDs. *Longlining Raccoon's & Conibears 2004, Marshland Muskrats 2004, Morel Hunting 2004, The Pocket Set 2005, Full Time Shang'un 2005, Full Time Beaver Trapping 2006, Winter coon Trapping 2011, Raccoon's Coil Springs & Blind Sets 2012, and Muskrat Frenzy 2011.*

Muskrat Frenzy is an interesting video. Ron Hauser traveled to Clark, South Dakota with his wife (who also is his trapping partner) in late March 2011 for the spring muskrat season. His goal was to spend a month and try to capitalize on the 4 dollar a pelt muskrat prices. When the team arrived, the ice was just starting to melt and the trapping was slow going, but after about a week as the water opened up, things started to click. One of the unique aspects to Ron's massive catch was that he used foothold traps and float sets almost exclusively.

The floats consisted of half-inch plywood and 1x2 furring strips with Styrofoam glued on the bottom. The floats were 2 feet long and 12 inches wide. The furring strips were cut and attached to help hold the trap in place. Ron used two 1–1/2 coil spring traps, one on each end of the float on long chains. The floats were staked with a white 3/8-inch x 48-inch fiberglass electric fence post. Grass and bottom debris would cover the floats and traps lightly and Ron would squeeze some sweet lure to the middle of the float for added attraction.

South Dakota had an unusually wet year on 2010 and there was not only plenty of water, but plenty of 'rats. Ron was catching over 100 muskrats a day and finishing his trap checks in early afternoon, so he ordered more traps and added more floats. By the end of his second week in South Dakota, he was running 230-plus float sets with 460 traps. Ron had several 300 'rat days when the line was in full swing. Ron and his wife sold their muskrat catch for nearly $18 thousand. Not bad for a month's wages on the trapline.

ZACHARY CORRADI 1990–

Michigan trapper Zachary Corradi likes to trap muskrats. Sure, there are plenty of raccoons, foxes and mink to trap near his hometown of Caro, yet Zach says, "Muskrats put me in my happy place." The thumb of Michigan is surrounded on three sides by the waters of Lake Huron and Saginaw Bay, creating a large freshwater marsh habitat along its shores. These oceans of cattails provide refuge for many types of birds, waterfowl and yes, muskrats. These huge marshes offer grand potential for the trapper willing to put a system together to trap the thousands of acres of vast, waist-deep water and reed entanglements.

Zachary Corradi with a day's catch of muskrats during his 2019–20 mega season.

Zach began trapping at age 16, a bit later than most trappers chronicled in this book, yet in the decade-plus he's been trapping, Zach has concentrated on a system that has catapulted him into the top 1% of muskrat trappers in North America. Marsh trapping is one of the most difficult habitats to master because if the intense amount of work involved. Zach says, *"We have lots of water and thus lots of muskrats, but to catch numbers of them you must have lots of traps and work through the full season."*

Zach and partner Brent Tribble pose with about 1,700 of their 2,000 'rats taken on their 2013–14 muskrat line.

Moving the quantities of traps and stakes required to catch the numbers of 'rats Zach is taking is not an easy proposition. Walking in the soft bottom of a slough is difficult as is using a pram or canoe. Two hours in the marsh can be quite a workout, let alone checking sets for 8 hours. And the catch can weigh more than the traps. Michigan also has a fairly short open water season which means much of the season is tedious trapping through ice. Zachary Corradi operates his own landscaping business, a seasonal entrepreneurship that allows for time in the winter for trapping.

Zach uses 1-1/2 coil spring traps, 110 conibears and colony traps. In Michigan it's legal to set feed beds and the outside of muskrat houses. Zach stakes his sets with white, 3/8-inch x 48-inch fiberglass electric fence posts which can be purchased at most Tractor Supply stores. Like most 'rat trappers, Zach sets runs and channels with the colony traps and 110 conis. However, foothold traps are his go-to. In fact, when there's open water he uses 100% foothold traps. Zach utilizes a special stabilizer bracket he calls "Zach's Improved Stabilizer," which he designed with help from Keith Winkler. The bracket stabilizes his coil spring foothold traps to the 3/8-inch diameter stakes. One of the difficulties in marsh trapping is finding a solid place to set a trap. And under ice it's even more difficult. The use of a stabilizer offers a quick method to anchor and stabilize the trap with one stake.

Zach organizes his trapline to take advantage of the weather conditions. When there's open water, he is running full bore as many traps as he can which is about 350 sets. After the ice comes however, this number drops to about 200. Zach says, *"One thing I've learned that really helps on the catch numbers is that in the transition from open water to ice, I try and run more ditches and set bank dens with colony traps. And once we have 2 inches of clear ice, I take a day to scout and mark at least 500 dens, channels and bubble trails in the marsh. It's easy to see where the 'rats are going with clear ice, but once we get snow it's almost impossible to find the best locations."* Zach also says that he thinks muskrats get trap shy of colony traps. *"Colony traps are great for a day or two, but I'll replace them with 110 conis after that. Muskrats are smarter than many give them credit for, and an empty colony trap doesn't mean that there aren't 'rats still using a channel."*

Zachary Corradi took 4,569 muskrats in the 2019–20 season between November 10 and March 1 which is the Michigan trapping season dates for Zone 3. If you add up the days and do the math, that's a 112-day season or almost 41 muskrats a day for the full season.

Corradi can skin a 'rat in 45 seconds once he gets rolling, but when you have an average of 41 rats a day to skin, the time adds up. And skinning is the easy part. Muskrats need dry fur to be put up which means heat and air circulation, then skinning, flesh-

Zach Corradi lining 'em up in 2019–20 season.

ing and stretching. Even if you can put up one 'rat every 3 minutes that's 2 hours of fur work every day for 112 days. Zach had a 300 'rat day which at 3 minutes per is 900 minutes or a whopping 15 hours of fur prep.

Trapping at this level is like two full-time jobs, one as a trapper and the other as a skinner.

Zach says his biggest motivator is himself. *"When I first started trapping it was always competition driving me to catch more and be better. The more years I trap I find myself just trying to beat me. If you've got the animals and basic knowledge, it's all in your head to just push yourself that much harder."*

Zachary Corradi trapped a few weeks with Michigan 'rat trapper Trent Masterson and the team took 300 rudder-tails in a single check of their marsh line.

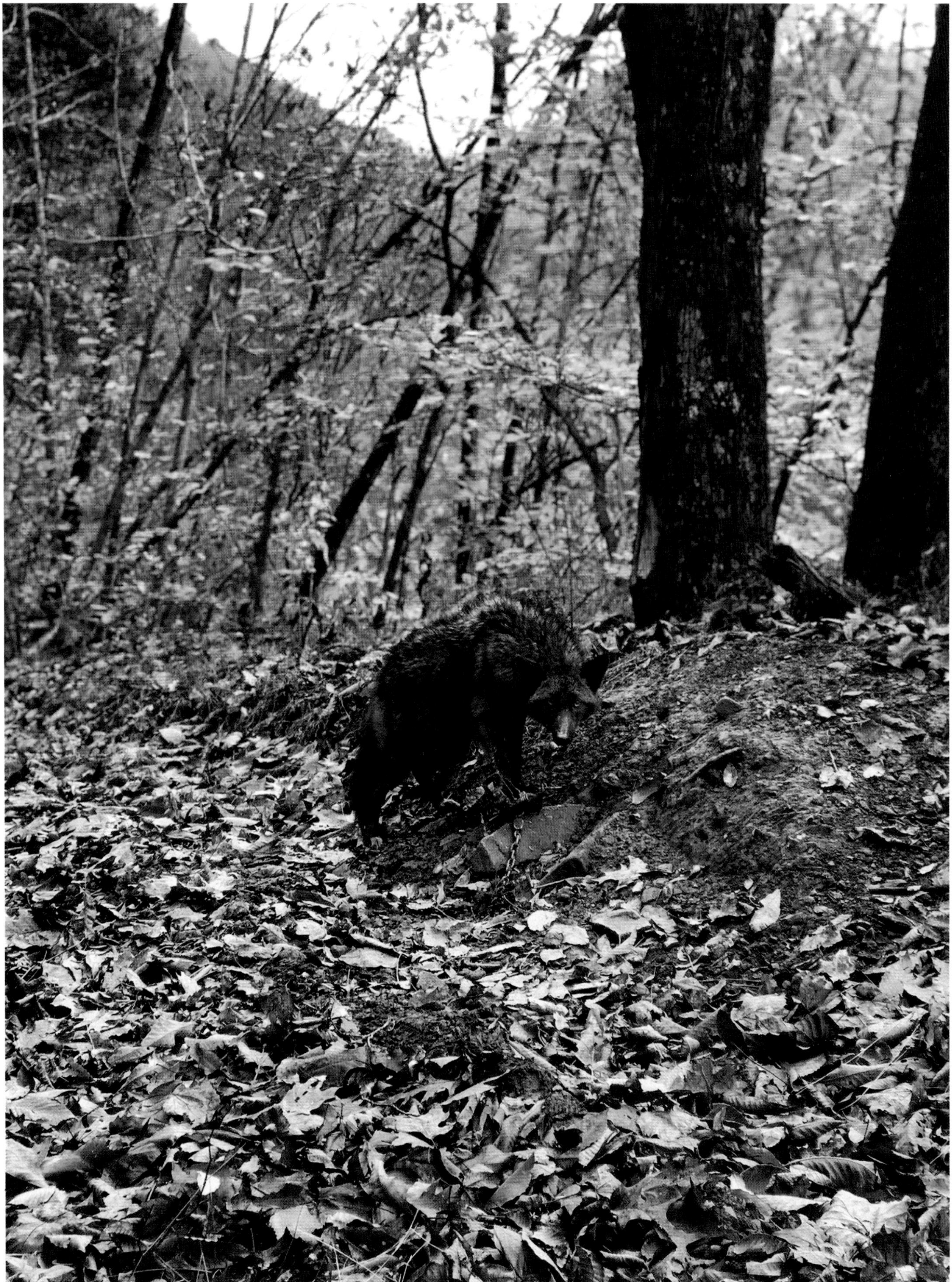

CHAPTER 12

WOLFERS

Mike Golich Photo

The best test for a hidden bowhunting stand is the coyote test. If a bowhunter is set up on a stand and a coyote comes into range where the archer can get a shot, the setup is more than adequate for deer, elk, bear or any big game animal. Coyote senses are tack sharp. The slightest hunter movement, hint of scent, or rustle of clothing, and Wile E. is on it. Animal scientists believe the coyote has 50 power vision, over 100 times more olfactory sensors than a human, and hearing so acute that can identify a mouse squeak at a distance of 200 yards.

When a trapper plants a trap next to an attractor and the coyote approaches it, all of these keen senses are focused on the set. It's no wonder the coyote is considered one of the most difficult animals to take consistently. Think about it. Google recognizes just over 3,600 practicing brain surgeons in the USA. I would bet there are less than 300 top coyote trappers.

TOP COYOTE MEN

The best trappers often stay out of the limelight. Government trappers for example, run huge areas, trap coyotes year-round for 30, 40, some 50 years, and are well-known in their home areas, yet unknown in the grand scheme of the fur trade and trapping business. Ethics rules within the federal trapper arena prohibit these trappers from advertising and selling lures, lessons and books as a conflict of interest, thus these men have taken thousands of coyotes as a job for a paycheck.

My experience in the realm of South Dakota's ADC program brought me in touch with 16 phenomenal coyote trappers—99.9% of readers would not recognize one name. Yet this doesn't take away from their abilities, dawg numbers or savviness as experts. Kenny Johnson is a name few would recognize, yet

< *Eric Eversole Photo*

he is a legend in Newell, South Dakota. As are Joe Grimson, Bob Curtis, Blair Waite, Chris McAllister and many more top coyote men in their particular locales.

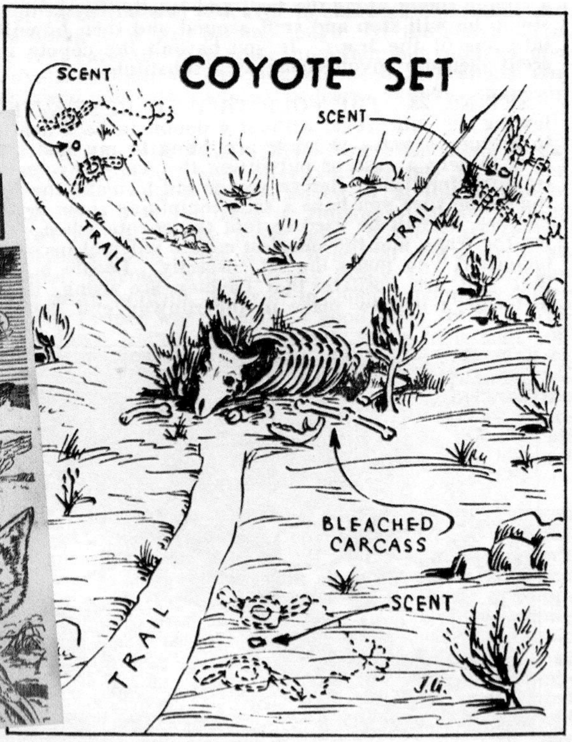

James Mast illustration from his book, *Coyote, Wildcat, Gray Fox Trapping*, 1943.

James Mast was a California predator man who wrote a groundbreaking trapping book back in 1943. Mast also made coyote scent which was used by many top government trappers for 50-plus years. Mast's friend Frank Terry eventually took over James's lure business and was a fantastic coyote trapper in his own right.

Nebraska trapper, Ivan White wasn't nicknamed Mr. Coyote for his muskrat trapping skills. Ivan was a legend in western Nebraska and his skills became nationally known once he joined the Fur Takers of America and began telling his stories.

Wyoming trapper and master dawg caller, Bill Austin was one of the first predator men to discuss and use coyote vocalizations for use in coyote hunting. Austin would use an open reed call and imitate some 12 different coyote sounds which he mimicked to trick coyotes into coming into range. Manipulating the call and adding a horn to amplify the sound, allowed Austin to bellow out howls, barks and combinations similar to how elk are bugled in today. Because of his impressive coyote vocabulary and his realistic call sounds, Austin is often referred to as the father of modern coyote calling.

Western predator man Roy Kuykendall wrote the book, *Fur Harvesting and Predator Control* in 1975 and was an expert coyote trapper, yet few know of him. Often a small classified ad in *Fur-Fish-Game* is all the print you will find of some trappers or an obscure article in *Trapper's World*. A good example is Bob Wendt, an expert trapper who ran a classified ad in *F-F-G* for offering trapping instructions for years yet avoided the limelight until releasing some very educational DVDs illustrating his long-line success some years later. Other coyote trappers who have come on the scene in the last couple of decades would include Jeff Dunlap, Clint Locklear, Andy Weiser, Jeff Hagerty, Robert Waddell and of course, others.

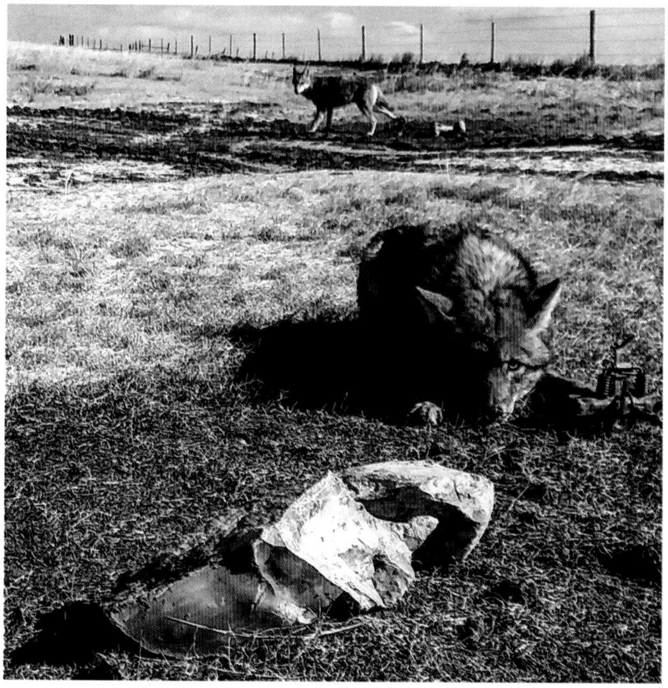

Joe Kierl Photo

PREDATOR TRAPPING THEORY

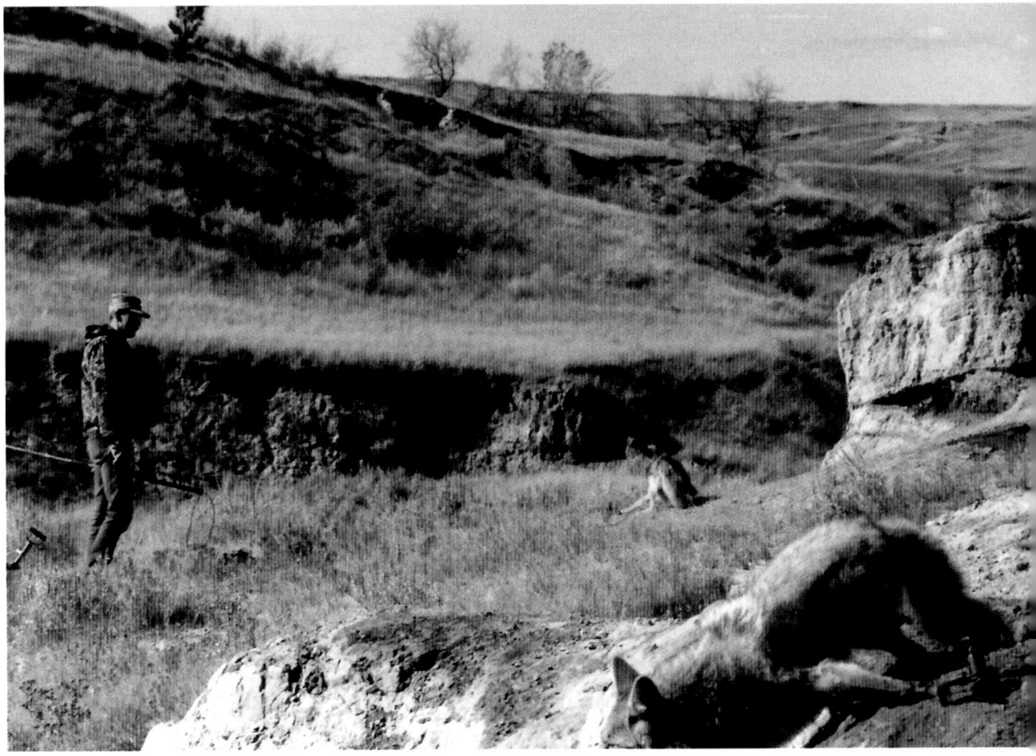

Slim Pedersen Photo

Montana long-liner and Hall of Fame trapper Larry (Slim) Pedersen with a pair of nice Montana Pales.

The best predator trappers learn to think like a coyote. Of course, if one is to talk with a wildlife biologist or zoologist, they would quickly tell you that a coyote's brain isn't capable of reasoning. Yet trappers who work and live with the yellow-eyes know differently. There is no magical lure or location that brings a coyote into a set blindly. In fact, it's quite the opposite. Most top coyote men know that it's not the common cockroach which will be the last living thing on our planet. The last coyote will eat the last cockroach and likely mark the spot with a well-placed turd on the rock where the dawg found the hiding roach.

I was blessed to spend some quality time with Montana trapper Keith Gregerson. Gregerson is a Hall of Fame trapper and expert snareman. I asked Keith if he could put a finger on the one thing he did to consistently make large catches of coyote. His response was this, *"Take a location where you usually catch 2 or 3 coyotes and look at the area closely. Note the habitat, the travel lanes, the features that make this location a good coyote location. Then look at your set, the way you make it, the lure used, the trap placement, the location in relation to the coyote travel ways and the wind direction. Once you have absorbed these details, go out and find 100 more locations exactly like it and repeat the process. The best coyote trappers are like copy machines, they make the same sets in like areas over and over and over again."*

I'll admit I was expecting a much more technical answer and was somewhat amazed at his response—that is until I thought about it a while and realized it was genius. Gregerson's advice is about as simple a recipe for coyote trapping success as one could give.

There is much more to successful coyote trapping, of course, with clean traps being very near the top of the list. And among the best trappers there are various schools of thought regarding clean traps—some trappers will err on the side of very clean, dyed, waxed traps and stakes, others may only wax traps—some only dip traps. Climate affects many of these choices as dry desert allows success through one approach compared to very wet or humid climates which may require something altogether different.

One of the key points in successful predator trapping that I've always tried to stress in my trapping books and videos is consistency in the basics. One of the biggest factors in learning anything is understanding and perfecting the basics required for success. Often the novice coyote trapper will experience a miss, a dug up trap, or sets that are refused. In the frustration of these experiences, often these trappers start making changes to their sets and locations. Changes which can make matters worse—not better. Here's an exam-

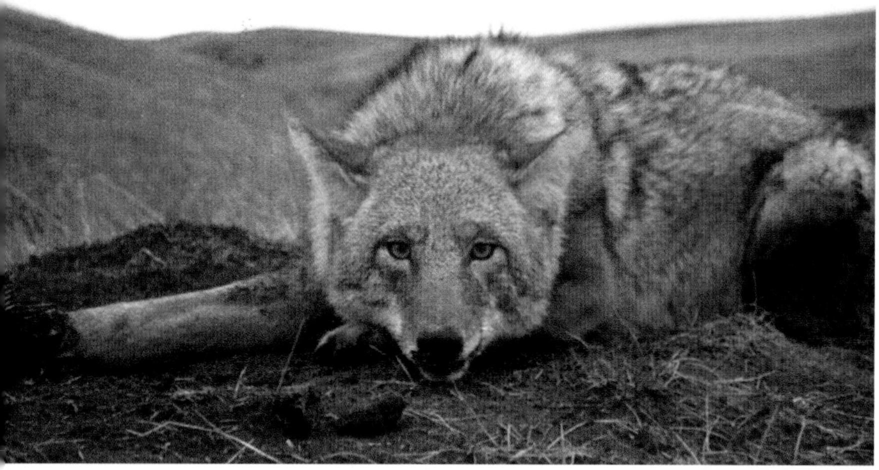

"Walk-thru" yellow-eye with textbook right front catch.

Narrowing It Down

In my opinion, one of the biggest differences in bowhunters and gun hunters are the nuances of tracking and recognizing sign. Rifle hunters need a shot inside 300 yards. Bowhunters require the animal at say 30 yards. This is 10 times closer.

Thus, a bowhunter must do 10 times the work to accomplish the same result to harvest the animal. Within the parameters of success, much of how a bowhunter accomplishes the feat comes with reading sign and setting up in range of where the animal will pass. Trappers in turn need the animal to step into a 4-inch circle. And the best trappers realize that setting up sign like tracks or droppings utilizes an animal's habit of following the same path through the area. Most often the sign isn't obvious. Sometimes it isn't fresh and sometimes the animal takes a different path through the area.

ple. Your truck won't start. It could be a loose battery cable connection, dead battery, a solenoid or starter failure, or something else. If you try a remedy and it doesn't work, typically you will try something else. If you don't understand how the system works in the first place, one thought might be to swap the battery cables. To a mechanic this is a foolhardy solution and will do more harm than good. The same is true with troubleshooting on the coyote line. If a trapper changes what he is doing right, he is not fixing the problem but is actually complicating the problem further.

Good trap placement and they wade right in. Reynard by both front feet.

Remake using droppings as a sight attractor. Punch holes are covered in duff. Arrow locates trap pan.

The difficulty in applying this to the coyote is their large range and infrequency of passing the location. Top coyote trappers know that the trap-set must be

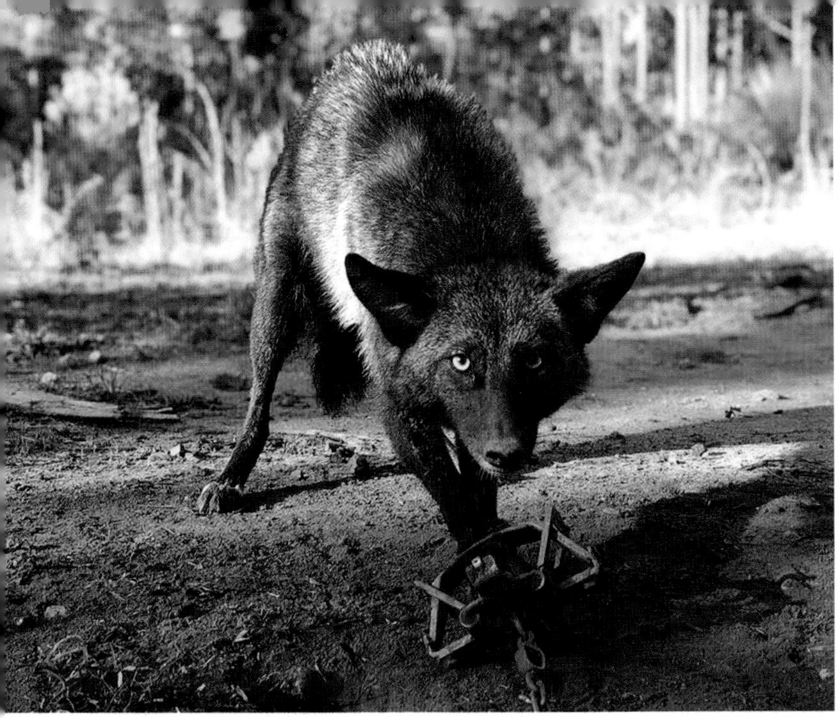

Mark Wooley Photo

Nice black coyote taken by predator trapper Mark Wooley. MB550.

"yellow-eyes" will amass the biggest trapping territories. The fact is that the coyote himself has been the salvation of the steel foothold trap as well as opening up areas to legal snaring where it was once prohibited. The effect that coyote populations have on ranchers and the deprivation of their livestock is well-documented, as are their brutal effects on the yearly whitetail

Nebraska trapper Joe Kierl uses a livestock skull for eye appeal and nails this prime winter dawg. Sets with large bones used for eye appeal are often called Flintstone sets.

operational when the dawg visits the set. Many of the trails coyotes use are also used by other animals and livestock. Animals like badgers, skunks and foxes that clog sets meant for coyotes. Provisions must be made for these variables.

Utilizing the target area principles discussed in Chapter 10 will really aid a trapper in finding the best ranches to trap. By combining the principals of long-running barriers and habitat changes, features that funnel dispersing coyotes will be found in these areas. Here's an interesting principal that's not discussed in many trapping books: The Familiarity Principal states that an animal **in his home area** may or may not investigate something new. Something new could be a Coke can, a work glove, a trap set or anything new to the area. However, on the edge of the animal's territory, that same animal is 2.5 times more likely to investigate something new. And animals traveling outside their home range become 10 times more likely to investigate. A trapper's interpretation of this principal would be that dispersing animals are seeking out their own kind and are much more likely to work sets with foreign odors while traveling in new areas. Food for thought.

Coyote trapping skills are a huge asset to every trapper. Often these skills are noticed by landowners and word quickly spreads to other farmers and ranchers who want fewer coyotes. Private land trapping permission for a serious coyote man isn't difficult to obtain and those who learn to consistently catch

and mule deer fawn crop. Access to private land in trade for helping farmers and ranchers with coyote control is a win-win scenario.

Textbook right front catch with an MB550 on a nice "yellow-eye" nailed by Kentucky Trapper Neil Triplett.

Some trappers will argue that a coyote is a larger animal than a fox and therefore requires trap spacing from the attractor to accommodate the size difference. There are two schools of thought at play. The first is "crowd the attractor." This mentality suggests that if the animal wants to get at the scent—the closer the trap is to what he's after—the higher percentage of a paw on the pan. The second is "matching the anatomy." And this mentality suggests that traps be spaced back and offset to accommodate the animal's size. A typical spacing would be 4 inches offset 3 inches from the attractor to the pan center for foxes. Coyote spacing would be 9 inches offset 4 inches.

The unique quality of my "walk-thru" set which utilizes the twin punch holes with the trap crowded and centered—is that when using the appropriate sized trap, say a MB550—the center of the pan is 4 inches offset 4 from the left hole (and 4 inches offset 4 from the right hole). Using a larger MB650 trap will set the trap back even further because of the size of the trap itself, not the size of the animal. Thus, this system takes into account spacing and offset, even though we are crowding the trap (see illustration).

River breaks dawg taken on my South Dakota line, 1985.

HAMMERING THE BASICS

When a trapper learns to dig a precise trap bed, stake, pack, level, guard the loose jaw, and cover the trap exactly the same way every time (and do it quickly), the basic set mechanics have been mastered. The differences between sets from this point are how the attractors are displayed, their orientation to the prevailing wind direction and the animal's approach. Almost 100 percent of my dawg sets are made as shown in Chapter 10.

𝖂ILEY CARROLL

1921–2003

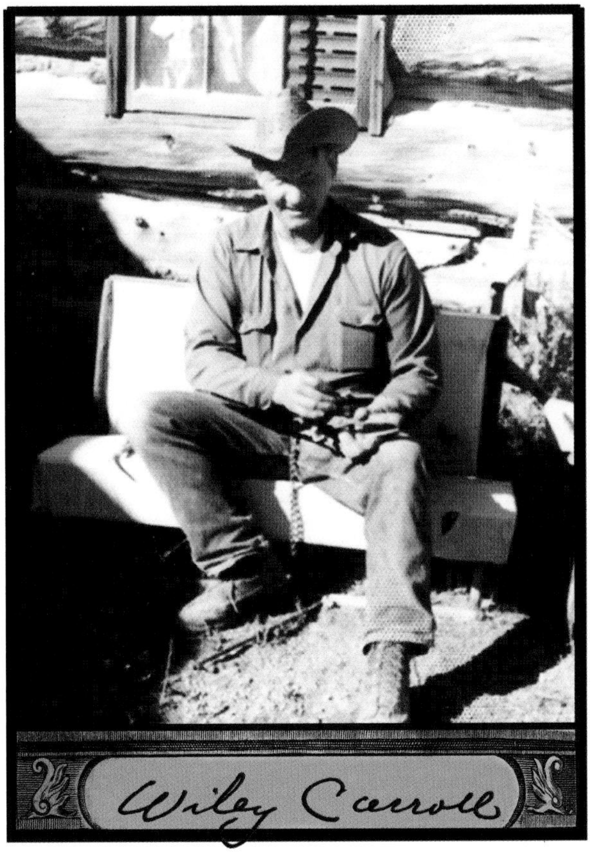

There are many "old-time" western trappers who cut their teeth trapping coyotes, cougars and wolves from the Sonoran Desert up the Continental Divide and west to the Pacific. Most never read a trapping book, let alone wrote one. They were rugged, tight-lipped individuals who lived the life of a bounty hunter, a predator control agent, a hired gun. Not much is written about most of them and the few that are known were brought to prominence by the few who witnessed their talents and left their midst influenced enough to tell the story.

Wiley Carroll was one of these rugged, predator men. Born in Oregon, Wiley ran his first mountain lion at the age of 16 near the Deschutes River in central Oregon. Wiley's passion from an early age was trapping and running dogs.

Before long, the Army drafted Wiley into the 85th Infantry 10th Mountain Division where he worked as a mule packer. The 10th Infantry was a special unit trained for harsh, remote-terrain deployments. The 10th Infantry was in fact, one of the first units entering Germany during WWII.

After Wiley returned home, he went to work for the Lee Brothers of Arizona. Ernest, Vince, Clell and Dale Lee operated a guiding and big game hunting business out of Tucson, Arizona through the 1940s and 50s. It's thought that by 1957 the brothers had taken more than 1,000 bears and 1,000 lions in that 17-year period and Wiley Carroll was a big part of those numbers for nearly eight of those years. Carroll would run his hounds for cougars, bears and jaguar south into old Mexico.

Wiley Carroll Photo

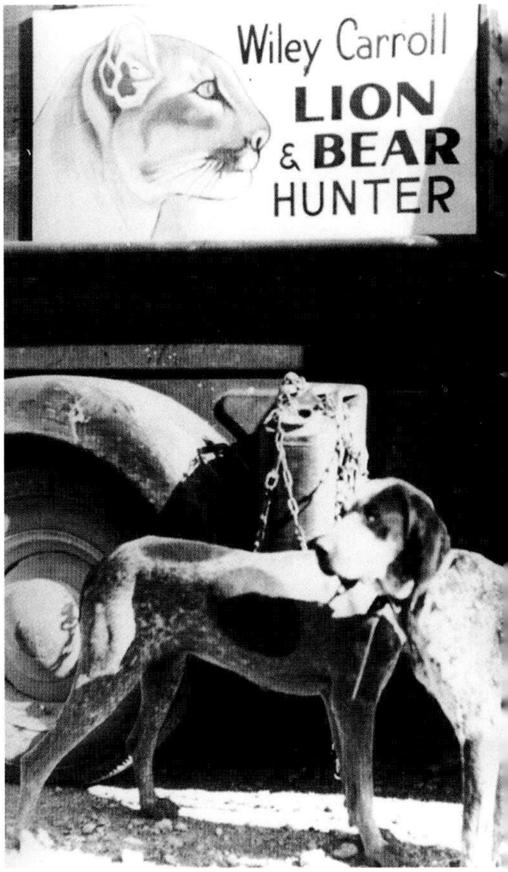

Wiley Carroll's pickup which he used for transporting his horse and dogs, circa 1950s

By 1951 the Nevada Game & Fish Department offered Wiley a job and the 30-year-old trapper and dog man took on the new state predator trapper position. When Wiley wasn't chasing lions, he was trapping coyotes. Wiley worked for 30 years as a Nevada hunter and trapper. It's thought that Wiley Carroll caught over 800 mountain lions and 500 bears during his work for the state of Nevada, protecting livestock from deprivation.

Nevada wildlife biologist Mike Laughlin spent quite a bit of time with Wiley and had this to say about the wise government hunter. *"Wiley hauled his horse and dogs in a flatbed pickup with a horse rack and*

Wiley Carroll Photo

Wiley with his hounds and a recent cougar catch.

did all his hunting by horseback or on foot. He camped out on the sheep and cattle ranges of Nevada with sheepherders and cowboys and laid out many nights under a tree with his dogs for warmth on an old lion track in order to be able to start out early the next day, trailing the cat. Like the majority of the old-time lion hunters, Wiley stuck on a track like glue until the job was done. No one I know today lays out on a lion track anymore. Most of today's hunters give up, go home to their warm beds, and look for another fresh track the following day. Wiley Carroll was a true Nevada legend."

Nearing his retirement with Nevada Game & Fish, Wiley began working with Tom Krause and *Trapper Magazine* publisher Chuck Spearman, doing a monthly column of "ramblings." This exposure is where most trappers learned of Wiley Carroll, his coyote trapping skills and lion hunting exploits. Spearman printed a small book which included Wiley's ramblings, circa 1986. Here's Wiley Carroll in his own words.

"Now a coyote likes to die from old age and his life span usually depends on how clever and smart he is or maybe how dumb the trapper in his area is. Coyotes breed in January and February. The largest pack I saw was thirteen. They do not follow regular runways during mating time and are difficult to trap, even with possum scent or bitch in heat scent which is about all that might attract their attention. One trapper I knew cut up chunks of hemp rope in pieces to resemble coyote droppings, then used these pieces of hemp rope soaked in coyote urine at his sets. These looked like coyote droppings and retained the odor well."

—Wiley Carroll in his own words, circa 1980s

ARDELL GRAWE

1942–

Ardell Grawe Photo

Ardell Grawe poses with a pair of Dakota foxes taken in the early 1970s.

North Dakota trapping icon Ardell Grawe could have been placed in nearly any chapter of this book. Growing up in southeastern North Dakota, Ardell started trapping muskrats in the early 1950s when he bought four 'rat traps for $2. Extra-large muskrats at the time were bringing 50 cents each. Ardell's father passed away when young Ardell was just 12 years old and his mother faced the hardships of raising a family under difficult financial circumstances. Ardell remembers his mother taking and selling his 50-plus muskrat catch to buy him school clothes. Grawe continued to trap throughout his school years as it not only helped the family income but gave him spending money as well. In the mid-1950s, big buck mink could bring $40, at a time when the average worker's wage was but a buck forty an hour.

When Ardell graduated high school, he did many different odd jobs until becoming a house painter. Painting houses and commercial buildings during the hot Dakota summers and trapping in the late fall and winter made a good combination.

Ardell Grawe took trapping lessons from Iowa legend Bill Nelson in the early 1960s and it was this experience that got him interested in the lure business. Nelson showed Grawe his dirt-hole set and several fox set locations and Ardell went back to North Dakota with a new outlook on predator trapping as well as Nelson's lure formula pamphlet. Then, 20-year-old Ardell went to work.

As the fox population of western Minnesota and the Dakotas expanded in the late 1960s and early 70s, so did Ardell's fur catch—taking as high as 38 foxes with one check of the traps. The animal numbers were phenomenal and a

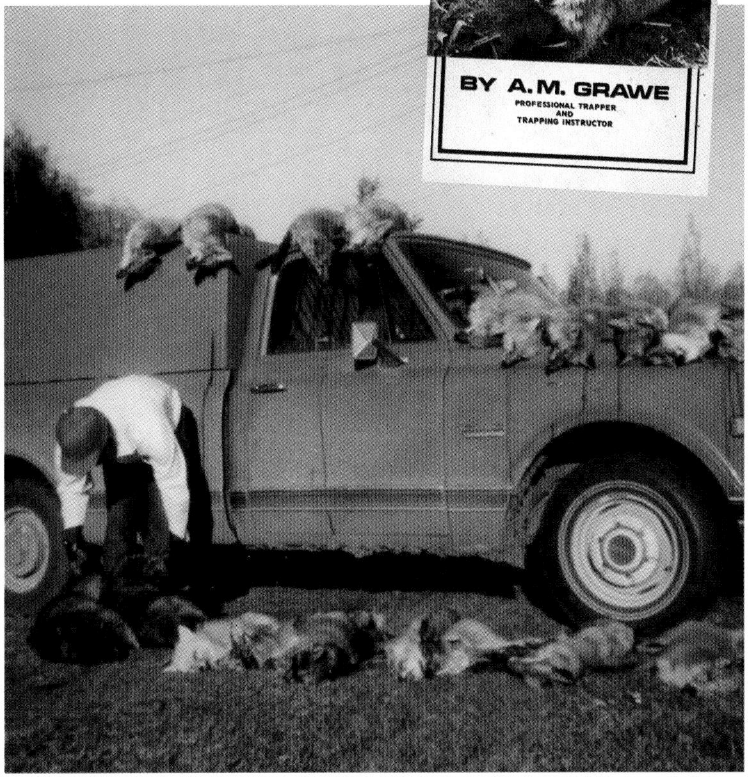

Ardell Grawe Photo

Grawe with a day's catch of Dakota reds and a few bandits.

fantastic learning ground. By 1970 Ardell would begin to send out flyers for his lures and in 1977 released his first book titled, *Grawe's Fox Trapping Methods.* Ardell was a prolific trapping instructor during the 1970s and early 80s and said in his 1977 first edition fox book, *"I don't claim to be a writer. In fact, I am far from it and I find it very difficult to put actions down on paper. I do profess to be a professional trapper and trapping instructor and have instructed more students in the field of trapping than any other living man at the time of this writing."*

Ardell Grawe Photo

Whether this is a true statement is up for debate as Stanley Hawbaker was alive in 1977 yet gave few personal lessons. Bill Nelson and E.J. Dailey both passed in 1973. There's no doubt that Ardell Grawe would become a major force in the trapping community and build his empire and legacy as a trapper and lure maker. Grawe went on to write mink, raccoon, coyote and snaring books.

Ardell Grawe was a versatile trapper and changed his trapline species as fur prices warranted, running long lines for mink as well as foxes, cats and coyotes. Typically, throughout the 1970s and 1980s, Grawe would trap North Dakota for 12 weeks or so, then state hop into new areas. Over his career, Ardell trapped some 16 different states plus his home Dakota line.

Ardell Grawe attributes much of his early success to Bill Nelson as well as Gene Carpenter and "Badlands" Bill Jaborski. Carpenter was a mink trapper who opened a young Ardell Grawe's eyes to some of his mink trapping tactics. "Badlands" Bill was a western Dakota coyote trapper who took Ardell under his wing. This passage taken from A.M. Grawe's *Fox Trapping Methods,* 1977. *"A man I ran into by chance was a fellow by the name of Gene Carpenter. We met while working on a large commercial job together, Gene as a carpenter foreman and myself as a painter. Gene is the type of fellow who can talk about trapping and make you feel like you are actually out on the trapline. I found him to be an excellent fox, coyote and cat man and an unbelievable mink trapper.*

"Another man that I must give a bit of credit to is "Badlands' Bill Jaborski of North Dakota. I found Bill to be a very modest, quiet, soft spoken man who could take fox, mink and especially coyote in unbelievable numbers. Of the many things I learned from Bill was the ability to study the small details and turn them into great trapline assets. He was a master at set construction and had an uncanny ability at using whatever materials were at hand."

Ardell Grawe was inducted into the Fur Takers of America Trappers Hall of Fame in 2014 and the North American Trappers Historical Society Trappers Hall of Fame in 2017.

GLEN STERLING

1942–2019

Most known for the Sterling MJ600 coyote trap, Glen Sterling was a man of many talents. Born in Colorado Springs in 1942, Young Glen grew up a cowboy. As a youngster he learned to ride and rope and was a bull rider in high school. Glen continued to rodeo after graduation for nearly 10 years.

Dave Hastings / Fur Takers Photo

Glen and his wife Connie with a nice batch of bobcat pelts.

Dave Hastings / Fur Takers Photo

Glen Sterling holds a "Wyoming Big Iron" trap which he manufactured for Craig O'Gorman and his classic MJ600. Circa 2015

In 1970, 28-year-old Glen Sterling moved to Schuyler, Nebraska where he began making trophy saddles and running a line of coyote traps in the winter. Always a tinkerer and with an excellent mechanical mind, Glen started experimenting with a trap design which had similar characteristics of the popular Victor Government 3N long spring trap jaws, but was a four-coil wire spring mechanism. The result after much work and testing was the Sterling MJ600, a coyote trap which was years ahead of its time. In fact, most coil traps today borrow from many features of Glen's original trap and some designs might be considered outright copies.

Glen cut his teeth trapping coyotes in Nebraska from the Sandhills and west. His trapline was the original testing ground for his new trap, however once he was sure the design was solid, Glen pushed out traps to top trappers across the west for additional testing. It didn't take long for the MJ600 to command the attention of all coyote trappers nationwide. And although the price point was more than most trappers we're accustomed to, Glen sold traps—all the traps he could make, in fact. Glen's best season fur trapping coyotes was right at 400. Proof that Glen knew coyotes and his trap could get it done.

After the fur boom, Glen looked to transition into the world of Animal Damage Control and in 1986 took a job with the South Dakota GFP ADC Division, the

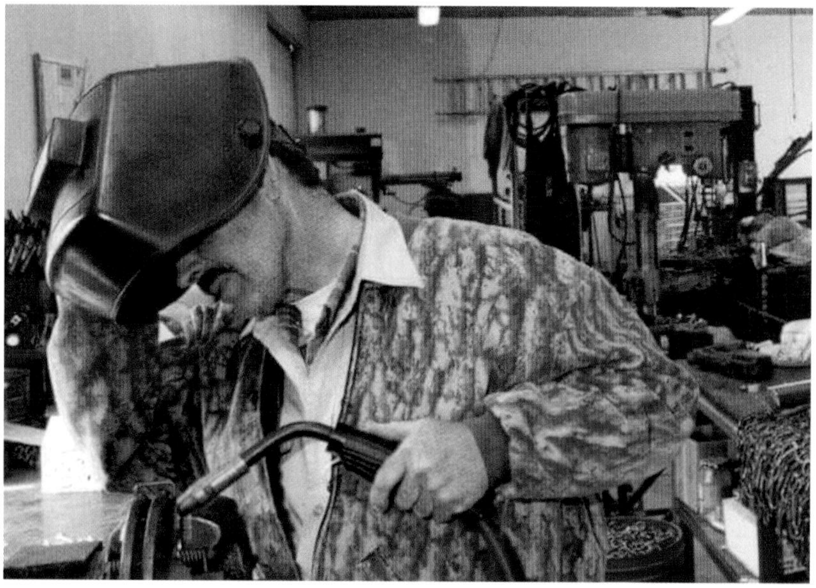

Glen Sterling Photo

Glen Sterling was a hands on kind of guy. Here he add's the finishing welds to his popular MJ600 coyote trap.

very same unit of ADC trappers I resigned from in August of 1986. Glen worked out of Huron, South Dakota until 1989 then transferred to the western town of Faith, South Dakota and a new territory closer to his western roots. Since one of the state's ADC aircraft is located in Faith, this move allowed Glen to also assume some aerial gunner responsibilities. Since pilot/gunner teams are used during aerial hunting missions, having a top gunner and pilot living in the same area allowed for better damage complaint logistics.

Glen's son took over trap manufacturing in 1995 and carries on the trap maker's tradition in Huron. Glen Jr. is also a South Dakota ADC trapper and works his father's old area in Huron. He is also an aerial gunner—following in his famous father's footsteps. It's estimated that Glen Sterling made and sold some 30,000 MJ600 coyote traps in his career. Twenty-five hundred dozen is a pile of MJ600s when you look at the craftsmanship of how these traps were made and are still made today. Quite impressive. Glen Jr. makes 3 sizes: MJ500, MJ600 and MJ800 sold exclusively through Keith Winkler and Sterling Fur Company.

Glen married Connie Erie in 2003 and soon after retired from his job as a South Dakota predator trapper and aerial gunner with nearly 20 years of service. They moved to Hulett, Wyoming so that Glen could turn a page in his industrious life to build kit airplanes. Glen always enjoyed working with his hands and the tedious job of building airplanes was a perfect fit for the twilight of his life. Before Glen took ill, he had built some 12 kit planes for resale and was still doing some trapping.

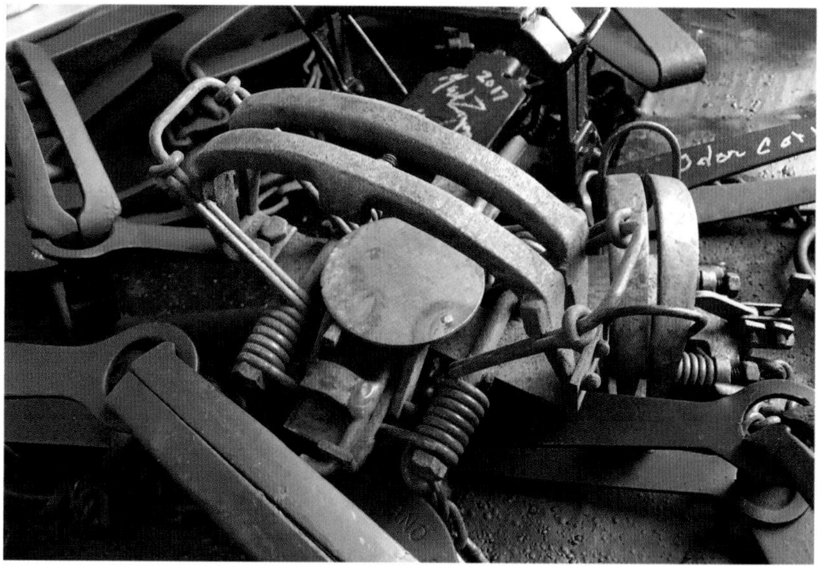

Author's Collections

Here's an early model of the MJ600 that Glen Sterling gave to me back in the mid 1980s. When I asked Glen to sign it, he gave me his cowboy grin and in his western drawl said, "Ha! I ain't nobody." Then turned and walked off. That my friends is the Glen Sterling I knew. His MJ600 is a cherished part of my trap collection.

Glen Sterling was a superstar at everything he did. He was a cowboy, a trapper, an entrepreneur and a straightforward, to-the-point kind of guy. Everyone who knew him, knew where he stood. In the last year of his life, Glen Sterling was honored as an inductee of the Fur Takers of America Trappers Hall of Fame.

Mark Zagger

1965–

New York trapper Mark Zagger has taken western coyote methods and modified them for eastern canine trapping. A business executive professional who runs his mega coyote line on his three weeks' vacation, Mark has harvested an average of 130 dawgs a year over the last ten seasons—in upstate New York, no less. Quick math puts Zagger's average catch at 6.2 coyotes a day, every day for three weeks. Pretty impressive.

Mark Zagger Photo

New York predator man Mark Zagger poses with his coyote dogs and a nice days catch of "yellow-eyes."

Mark grew up in Cortland, Ohio and began trapping at age 10. The farming areas of Northeastern Ohio are rich in raccoons, mink, muskrats and foxes. The perfect learning ground.

At the start of the fur boom in 1978 Mark was 13 and quickly found that trapping was a great way to make a little money. As fur prices climbed, so did the number of trappers, yet young Zagger loved the challenge. In fact, today Mark says, *"I always thought the money was a bonus."*

By 1989 and Mark was gaining notoriety as a coyote trapper. And he had all the tools. An excellent student throughout school and a tremendously hard worker by upbringing, Mark had indeed gotten serious about his predator trapping. Serious enough to invest both the time and money to take trapping lessons from some of the top predator men in the country—master trappers like Craig O'Gorman, Ray Milligan, Ron and Pete Leggett, and Johnny Thorpe. Mark had read all of these mega trappers' books and watched their DVDs, but meeting his mentors in person and seeing them build the sets, talk location and noticing every nuance about them made him a better trapper. Seeded with this knowledge, Mark had all the confidence and drive to succeed.

"I am one of the few Eastern' trappers that utilize trap line dogs, big traps and big grapples on my coyote line. Equipment typically reserved for western trappers," Zagger says. *"My dogs can locate coyote sign largely invisible to man. I am pretty good at picking locations, and the dogs validate that for me. Then, traditional dirt holes come into play, coupled with scent station sets which are constructed with grass tufts marked by coyotes that my dogs find. I also use flat sets but more and more I am turning to what I call the Pipe Dream set, designed to keep lure working for longer periods in the nastiest of weather. The pipes are 9-inch pieces of electrical conduit which are driven 6 inches into the ground and used as a lure/bait holder. To keep the trap operating in rain and snow, instead of using sifted dirt, I cover with dry grass clippings or hay. My wire screen pan cover holds this material in place and allows excess water to drain through the grass and pan cover. With so much rain and snow here in upstate New York, I had to come up with a weather-resistant system for these conditions."*

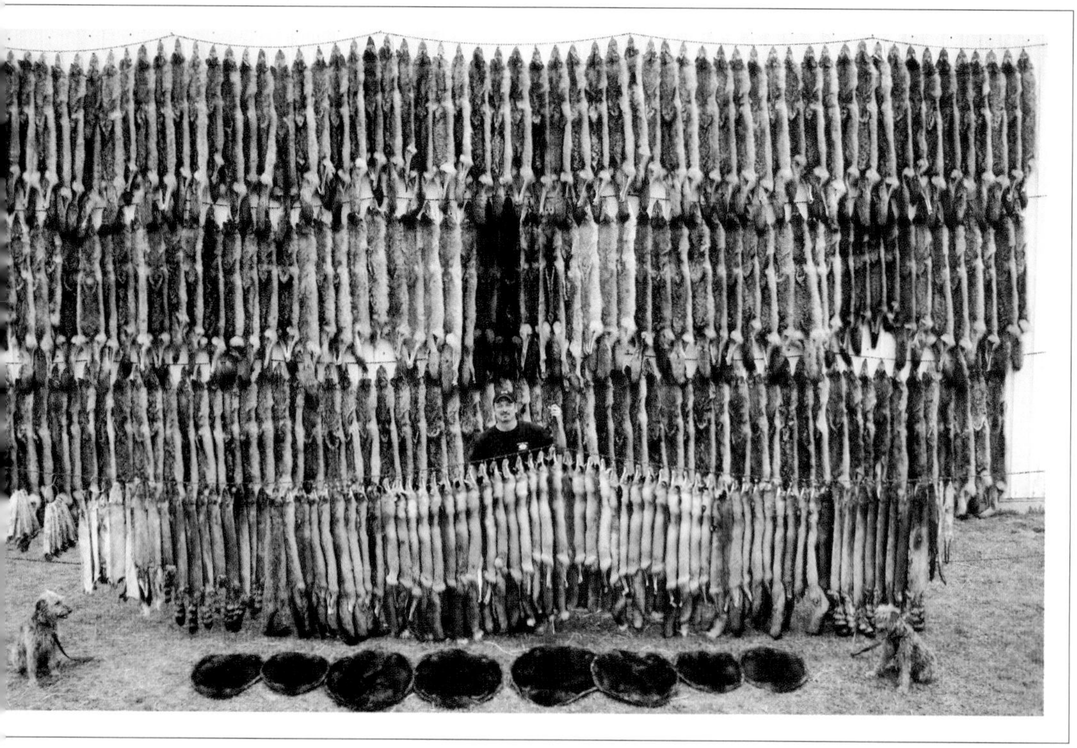

Mark Zagger poses with his best season of 183 dawgs, 47 foxes and other furbearers taken in upstate New York.

Mark's best season netted him 135 coyotes during a three-week hiatus from work. And at the end of his vacation, the usual heavy snows of upstate NY had held off. Mark decided to keep a small line operating which he could run before work, eventually skinning 183 coyotes and 47 foxes. An incredible catch for his area. *"I think most really good canine trappers also have strong personalities and egos. Certainly, my catches have brought me notoriety. The value of that is intrinsic to me, and certainly not financially motivated. Barn wall shots at the end of my season generate lots of oohs and ahhs, however few understand the year-round commitment to prepare for that catch. Or the long hours needed to properly "put up" the fur for market. Big catches of any animal are not made of luck. A rank amateur can kill a Boone and Crockett whitetail on any given day. This is not the case with large catches of fur, regardless of species."*

Mark Zagger has operated his own trapping school for several years. Coyote U is a 2-1/2 day intense class in eastern coyote trapping theory, sets and location as well as fur handling.

Mark Zagger Photo

Mark Zagger poses with a dandy display of his 2013 catch.

Mark Zagger Photo

Mark with 14 coyotes on a day's run over the traps.

"I think being a straight-A student in elementary, high school, and college started me down of path of attempting to achieve excellence. From a very early age, I began to appreciate the opportunities that came from excelling in my studies. Later, my successes as an eastern coyote trapper brought me respect outside of New York. My biggest competitor has always been me, and I drive myself to improve on my numbers annually. Additionally, I have an open mind and am always willing to try new ideas, methods, hardware, etc. I think many good canine trappers are also successful businessmen, and that's no coincidence.

"Tom Krause once said, 'The harder you work, the luckier you get!' and it's so true. My advice for beginners and up-and-coming trappers is to take trapping lessons. Personal instruction will cut years off of the learning curve. It's a rare combination for young trappers to make large catches. Those of us that began trapping during the fur boom did not have the opportunities afforded to us that a new trapper does. Tools like the internet, YouTube and trapping DVDs provide a flood of information. Still, that information can be both contradicting and confusing. Taking lessons from a top trapper can help to focus one much more quickly on what does doesn't work. The knowledge can be taught, however the work and drive required to succeed cannot be taught. Trapping is a game of percentages. Everything else being equal, 100 traps is better than 50 traps. Traps and miles are what lead to most great catches."

—Mark Zagger in his own words, 2014.

In the mid 1990s I had famous bowhunter guest appear in several of my ESPN episodes. His name was Chuck Adams and his claim to fame was that he was the first archer to take all 27 North American big game animals with a bow and arrow. Chuck completed his feat in 1990. At this time the Pope and Young Club only recognized 27 big game animals. Today P&Y recognizes 29 animals, adding the central Canadian barren-ground caribou in 1993 and California's tule elk in 2008. I met Chuck through Hunters Specialties Company who also supported my show and wanted to get Chuck out in front of a large audience using their products. When we did the taping for his deer hunting tips which were called, "Quest for the Big Buck," Chuck and I spent hours talking about his bowhunting accomplishments and stories. I can remember thinking that I likely could never achieve such a goal as it was not only a very expensive undertaking, but some of the mountain species like sheep and goats as well as the arctic species of muskoxen and polar bear would be extremely difficult to videotape.

Here's a great photo of Chuck Adams and "yours truly" with a Texas buck I arrowed for an ESPN episode.

WHITETAIL COUNTRY

In 2002 ESPN came to me and asked if I would be interested in doing a whitetail series for the network. Wow—that was a big undertaking! At first, I didn't think I could pull it off as whitetails are not slam dunk hunts (no bow hunts are) and 12 deer hunting episodes a year were a tall order on top of my already busy schedule. But I thought about it and came up with an idea. Instead of me doing all the buck hunts, the show would feature deer hunters who I knew in the industry. Each episode would include a biography of the hunter's life, how they started hunting and would also include a hunt with the person. I named the show *Whitetail Country*. Then I went to Realtree with the idea and they loved it. In fact, the first season I did biographies on Bill Jordan, Michael Waddell and David Blanton as well as other Realtree pro-staff hunters including Tiffany and Lee Lakosky, Greg Miller, Stan Potts, Jim Shockey and other top hunters. The best part was that I could share some of the ESPN limelight with these friends as they only had exposure on the smaller outdoor networks like Outdoor Channel.

Bill Jordan's *Realtree Outdoors* aired on The Nashville Network (TNN), a solid network but it was not the size of ESPN. For most of my guests on *Whitetail Country*, it was a big deal and I was blessed to have so many industry friends. Needless to say, *Realtree's Whitetail Country* was a hit, airing from 2003–2010.

This is the original season of Realtree's Whitetail Country on DVD.

Realtree's Whitetail Country is approved and is issued a time slot, say 9:30 a.m. on Saturday. ESPN's fee for this time slot is $250 thousand per quarter (13 weeks). Contracts are done for two quarters minimum. First and second quarter is January through June. Third and fourth quarter is July through December. So, the cost for eight, 30-second commercial units for two quarters is $500 thousand. Now the producer (Tom Miranda) must go sell these commercials to make the income to pay ESPN, the cameramen, travel, hunts, editing, music, narration, closed captions. What's left over is the profit. It's a tremendous undertaking. Of course with my trapper background, I'm a "do it yourself" kind of guy and I learned to be a cameraman and editor to limit my overhead. In the height of my TV production career I had five cameramen and six full-time editors—plus myself doing both camera work and editing.

This is the editing studio built in my Florida home where I edited *Advantage Adventures, Realtree's Whitetail Country* and eventually, *Mathews Territories Wild.*

THE OUTDOOR TV BIZ

A misconception about outdoor television is the incorrect assumption that the network buys the TV programs. In fact, it's the opposite—outdoor TV producers purchase the airtime from the network. The way the system works is that once your TV series is approved for air on a network and once a time slot is available, the network offers it to you at a price. This time slot can come with anywhere from two to eight commercial placements. The producer buys the "airtime" and then sells the commercial placements to pay the network as well as for the taping, editing and profit. This is how all my series contracts began as what the industry calls "time buys," *Outdoor Adventure Magazine* and *Advantage Adventures* included. Here's an example:

TV cameras and editing gear is never cheap and in these early days it was very expensive. I had five TV cameras that cost $80 thousand each. A full-blown A-B roll editing studio to ESPN standards was a million dollars. I learned quickly that you have to pay to play. TV networks like ESPN required a level of quality that only could be achieved with the higher-end broadcast cameras and equipment. *Whitetail Country* advertisers like Realtree paid large amounts (such as $150 thousand) to advertise in my shows. Some advertisers paid $300 thousand to be considered title sponsors. *Whitetail Country* had Realtree Camouflage, Mathews Archery, Summit Tree Stands and Thompson Center Firearms as big-time sponsors. And there were many smaller companies involved for billboard recognition or product use or shorter advertising campaigns.

I offer this information to the reader not to flash large dollar signs or to discuss financials. The fact is that TV production at the ESPN level is very expensive and risky. I was blessed that most all my advertising partners paid their bills. Some seasons I barely got my bills paid. Other seasons I made a killing. It sounds a lot like fur trapping, doesn't it? Risk equals reward.

Rocky Mountain Elk, 2004—New Mexico

More Big Game Hunts

By 2003 and I had taken many big game animals with a bow. However, in North America I had only a handful of different species. Yes, I had taken many whitetails and several black bears, but only one white-tailed deer and one black bear count toward a Super Slam. Other species I had taken with archery tackle included the mountain goat, elk, pronghorn, muskox and Quebec-Labrador caribou. That was six species and basically one-fifth of the Super Slam accomplishment. In my mind at the time, the archery Super Slam was still out of my reach, but I pledged to keep chipping away at it, one animal at a time. Completing any goal requires the successful completion of smaller goals. Hunters taking one species a year would take 29 years, two species—15 years to complete.

In 2004 my oldest son Jeremy graduated high school. He seemingly grew up so quickly. His mother had made a mural of childhood photos of him taken throughout his young life. Attending his graduation and afterparty, I took some time to look at the photos. Soon my eyes began to tear up. I was grief-stricken that I could not remember even one of the events portrayed in the photos. I had been so focused on my career that I had missed so much of his life. I went out to my rental car and sobbed. Was it all worth it? I was overcome with remorse and a feeling that I had missed out on so much of his life by pursuing my dream. I regained my composure and finished the graduation ceremonies. However, I vowed that I would re-engage with my children even more than I had been. Jeremy would attend University of Nebraska in the fall as a member of the Big Red marching band.

In September of that year, I traveled to the Rio Costilla in northeastern New Mexico to hunt with Lee Vigil during the elk bugling season. Vigil ran Ute Creek Outfitting service and had contacted me by email as a fan of my show and offered an opportunity to hunt elk. I took my second Rocky Mountain elk on that trip, this one a better bull and much better footage. One must remember that my job was producing television episodes for ESPN, not collecting species of animals.

Whitetail, 2004—Illinois

Combining interesting locations with solid animal footage and great hunting experiences made for the best TV programs. A bugling bull elk screaming to the call and closing the distance is a hunt that always rates well on TV. That same year I also had a great whitetail hunt in Pike County, Illinois hunting with Dale Carter of Carter's Pike County Hunting Lodge. In 2005 I went to the arctic for my second muskox. My first muskox bowhunt was taped for Cabela's *Sportsman's Quest* and the mega-hunting store chain owned the footage. So, I needed to do the hunt again for my own footage. It's a fantastic adventure to the arctic and I knew the bow hunt would make a great *Advantage Adventures* ESPN episode.

The reader might remember seeing this hunt on TV as it included the infamous "mock charge" where the muskoxen lunges toward me on the attack. My shot was taken at a very close 10 yards. I can remember the Inuit guide yelling at me in the distance, "That bull will kill you!" Even today many people mention this episode as one of the best TV bow hunts ever produced. Sometimes it's better to be lucky than good. After the successful arctic trip, I edited my newest video release Tom Miranda's *Bowhunters Encyclopedia.* This video was to be the precursor to my upcoming Super Slam video if I was to ever finish the feat. At least this was my plan. The *Bowhunters Encyclopedia* 2-DVD set included 100 bowhunting tips, along with 15 whitetail hunts and 15 world hunts, as well as bonus footage of missed shots and bloopers. As soon as the DVD was released, Stoney-Wolf contacted me about releasing the set under their label. I agreed, and sold tens of thousands of this DVD set.

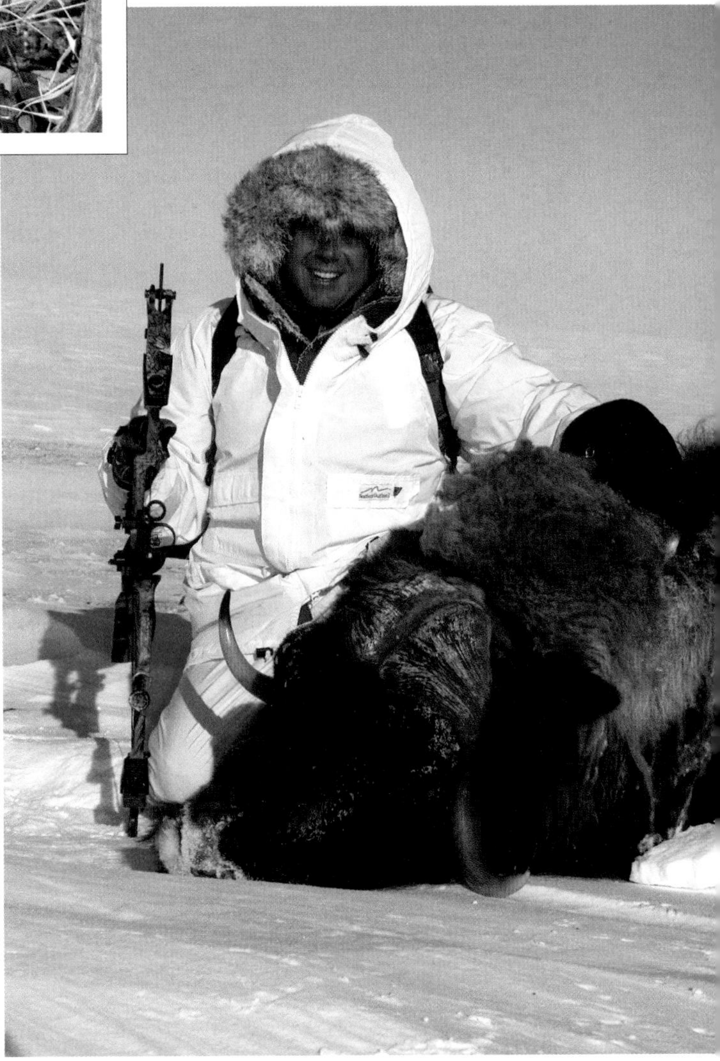

Greenland Muskox, 2005—Nunavut

In September I traveled to Zambia to hunt leopard and hippopotamus. I shot a great hippo on the famous Luangwa River. The hippo isn't a part of Africa's Big Five but is considered part of Africa's Big Six, added to the list in the early 1980s. Crocodile also counts toward what's known as the Dangerous 7. Unfortunately, had no luck on the trip for leopard.

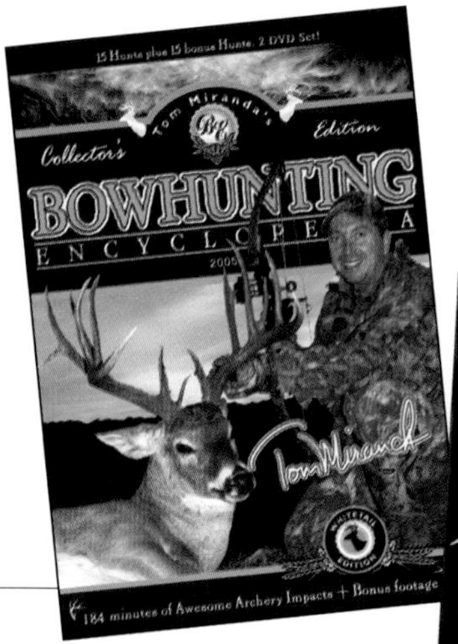

This video set released in 2005 is the precursor to my Adventure Bowhunter Super Slam DVD set.

I did a contract with the big video distributor Stoney-Wolf and this is the video sleeve they used to sell tens of thousands of the DVD Bowhunting Encyclopedia.

By the fall of 2005 I had been on four moose hunts in the last six years and not connected. The moose was becoming my nemesis. However, in January 2005 I met a Canadian outfitter at the Mathews Archery booth at the Safari Club Convention. His name was Chad Lenz. I had told him of my moose hunting "challenges," and he said, "Come up and hunt with me—we will get you on a moose." So, in September 2005 I went to Alberta and "Savage Encounters" for a chance at the Canadian moose. It was a memorable hunt. Chad was an excellent moose hunter. Chad had cut his teeth guiding hunters for moose in the original Macmillan River Yukon Camp operated by Dave Coleman back in the 1980s. Made famous in those days by their moose hunting video series which included giant bull moose taken with bow and rifle in close quarters. I took a great moose with

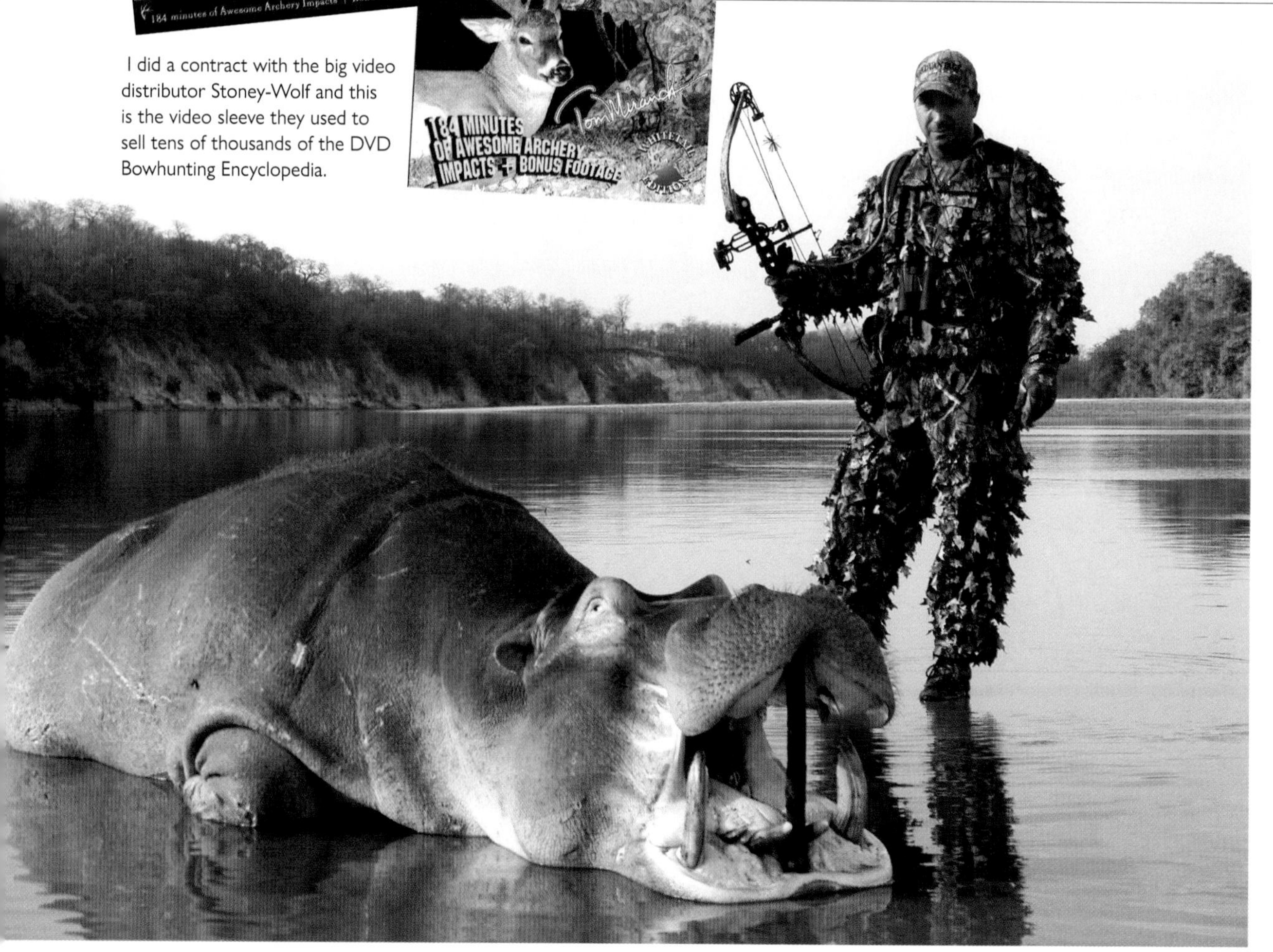

Hippopotamus 2005 — Zambia

Canadian Moose, 2005—Alberta

Chad and we got fantastic footage, so my moose jinx was finally broken. I didn't know it at the time, but I would forge a lasting friendship with Chad Lenz. We did many hunts together toward my Super Slam.

In 2005 I drew a tag to hunt a coveted trophy unit in Utah for cougar. I would do that hunt in February 2006 and connected with a huge lion. I was off to a good start. In fact, the spring of 2006 my daughter Jennifer graduated high school—this would be a big year for my bowhunting. Jennifer was to attend the University of Nebraska, the same school her brother was attending. She is my only daughter—a daddy's girl. Thankfully, I was able to "slay the demons" that ravaged my brain during my oldest son's graduation. After a year in Nebraska, Jennifer would eventually come to Florida to live with Sandy and I to attend the Ringling College of Art and Design.

Mountain Lion, 2006—Utah

Alaskan/Yukon moose, 2006—Alaska

That same spring I drew another tag—this one for the Shiras moose subspecies. I already had an Alaskan moose hunt booked, so in September I went to Alaska, then to Wyoming in October. BAM! BAM! I arrowed two moose in two trips and now had taken all three moose subspecies. The nemesis was definitely off my back. In November 2006 I returned to Alberta to hunt with Chad Lenz for bighorn sheep. This was a big hunt for me—my first sheep hunt. The hunt would take place in the Canmore bow zone, an archery-only unit and season which takes place the full month of November. Chad told me the last two weeks were best, so we were on the mountain November 15.

Shiras moose, 2006—Wyoming

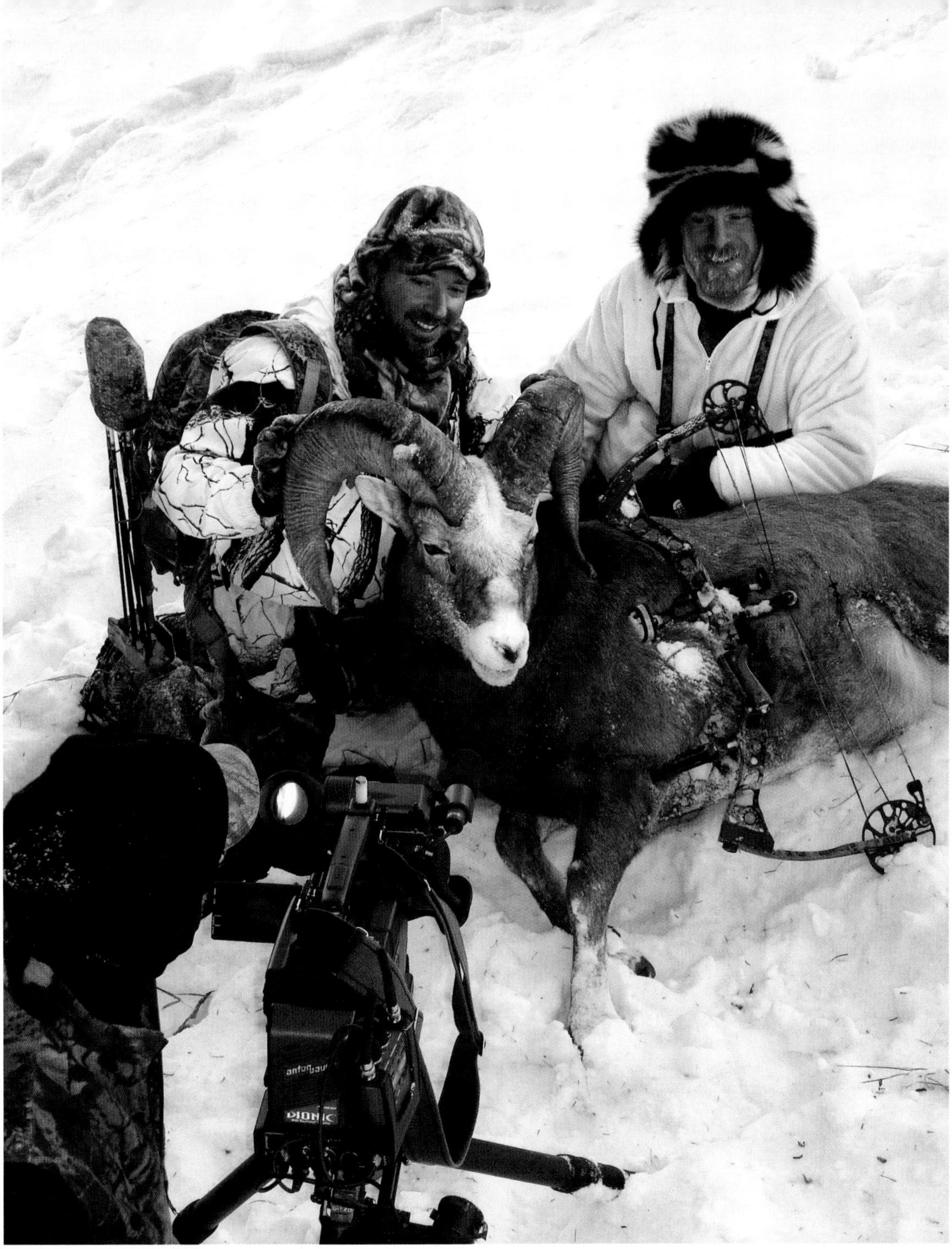

Bighorn sheep, 2006—Alberta

Mid-November in the Canadian Rockies is an unforgiving time to be in the mountains. Operating out of a tent, using horses with two feet of snow and minus 20 sometimes minus 30 temperatures and bow hunting at 10,000 feet. The hunt was brutal and the toughest I had done up to that time. It was cold, slippery and always windy. I slipped and fell many times a day, so much so that most of the pins were broken in my bow sight. I replaced them with toothpicks. I missed 7 rams— yes 7, before finally scoring with a 60-plus yard shot on a great Canmore bighorn. Eleven hunting days in that steep, frozen ice box. I was exhausted, but I had done it. I now had 13 species toward my Super Slam 29 and all the arrow impacts on video. It was at this moment that I knew it would be possible for me to complete the archery Super Slam of North American big game. My goal would be to continue the quest capturing all 16 remaining bow hunts on video for TV episodes to be seen on ESPN.

SCOTT WELCH 1973–

Ohio outdoorsman Scott Welch is a successful trapper who grew up in the midst of fur boom trappers Jim Helfrich and Carrol Black. Born in Lakeville, Ohio Scott started trapping when was eleven and ran a line throughout school for 'rats and 'coon. During his school years, well-known Ohio trapper Carrol Black and Scott became friends. By high school graduation Scott was already into fox trapping and coyotes were finding their way into Holmes county. In 1992 Scott began traveling with "Blackie" helping Carroll sell his popular Blackie's Blend lures at the National and state trappers conventions.

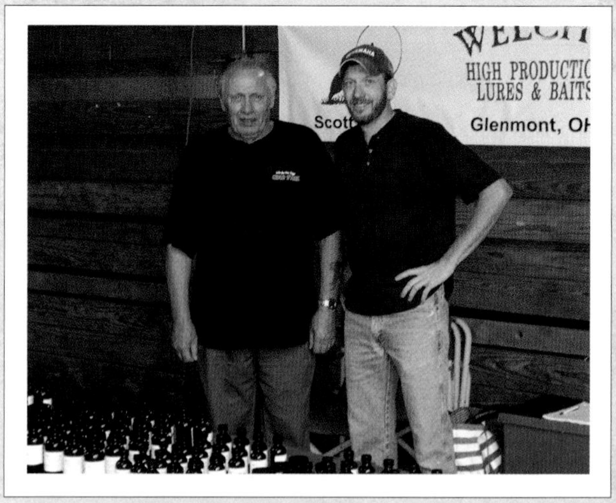

Scott Welch with Carroll "Blackie" Black at the 2007 Ohio State Trappers Association Convention.

Ohio trapper Scott Welch poses with a nice double on Buckeye State "yellow-eyes."

Scott started long-lining that same year and although he was remodeling houses, Scott still found time to connect with "Blackie" and began a pseudo apprenticeship into lures, baits and the trapping trade. One of Carrol's friends was a young Wisconsin trapper who also came to prominence during the fur boom. Jeff "Coon" Richter had written some trapping material and was selling trapping lures in the 1980s. Hearing from "Blackie" that Richter was getting out of the business, Scott decided to buy Richter's lure formulas in 2005 and added a few of Jeff's more popular formulations into his new Welch's High Production Lures and Baits lineup. Scott recalls, *"Growing up, I trapped a lot with my grandfather and he would never think to spend money on bait. So, I learned a lot about how to make baits very early in my trapping career."*

With his new business, Scott Welch was now trapping more aggressively than ever, taking 38 bandits in one trip over the traps and 11 coyotes in a day as his personal bests. Scott also began state hopping for fur and lure testing. In Mississippi, Welch averaged 8 furbearers a day on one 26-day trip—taking beavers, otters, gray foxes, raccoons, bobcats, and his favorite animal, the coyote. With over 18 years of long-lining under his belt and five years operating his own lure business, Scott penned his book, *"Predator Trapping Theories and Techniques»* released as a first edition in 2010.

In the book, Welch describes his land trapping style as *"a big, showy dirt-hole guy." "I am not afraid to make big holes, small holes, use natural holes, whatever it takes to make a set look rough and natural. I have even buried bobcat carcass' in washed-out culverts and caught coyotes and bobcats that way. I am always more interested in letting a set look natural instead of trying to make it into something I think it should be. That rough and natural philosophy has always helped me catch fur."*

Welch is a big fan of Bill Nelson's writings and trapline concepts. One key element in Nelson's dirt-hole theory was never making the bait hole larger in diameter than the trap. Thus, sets with fox traps would have smaller holes than sets for coyotes using larger traps. Holes can be smaller than the trap diameter, but not larger. Often in midwestern farm country, dirt-hole trappers are apt to catch anything from a light-footed gray fox to a coyote. Using traps that will hold whatever steps in is essential in Welch's system. Offset and laminated jaw traps are top choices for Scott.

Scott poses with a nice run of dawgs.

Ohio predator man Scott Welch in his lucky "John Deere Cap" peeling one of three bobcats taken on his Mississippi long-line.

Scott has three DVD trapping instructional programs: *Trapline Techniques: Mud, Snow and Predators*—2011, *Trapline Techniques : Raccoons and Cornfields*—2013, and *Trapline Techniques: Canine Fundamentals*—2014.

In 2013 Carroll Black fell ill and Scott bought Blackie's Blend lures in 2015 shortly before Carroll's death. Carroll Black was a well-respected trapper and lure maker.

If you read Scott's predator book, you'll see quite a bit of the influence of Slim Pedersen. Often trappers who learn from others pick up traits and styles similar to their mentors. I know pal Ray Milligan followed long-liner Garold Weiland closely and was greatly influenced by him. My experiences with Odon Corr, the FTA Trapper's College and many others greatly affected my trapline motivations as well as style of trapping. It's natural to take a tip, technique or idea from many trappers and blend each into your own style of trapping. Unlike the trappers of yesteryear who held their trapline methods secret, the trappers who began our cottage industry and those fur men who have followed in their footsteps had proliferated trapping methods.

Scott Welch is a trapper who grew up reading about famous trappers. Met famous trappers. And longed to be a professional trapper himself. While many men wrestle with life, career and family—only dreaming of traps and trapping—others take a different path, following the romance of the trapline and their dreams to fruition. Scott Welch carries on where his friend and mentor Carroll "Blackie" Black left off.

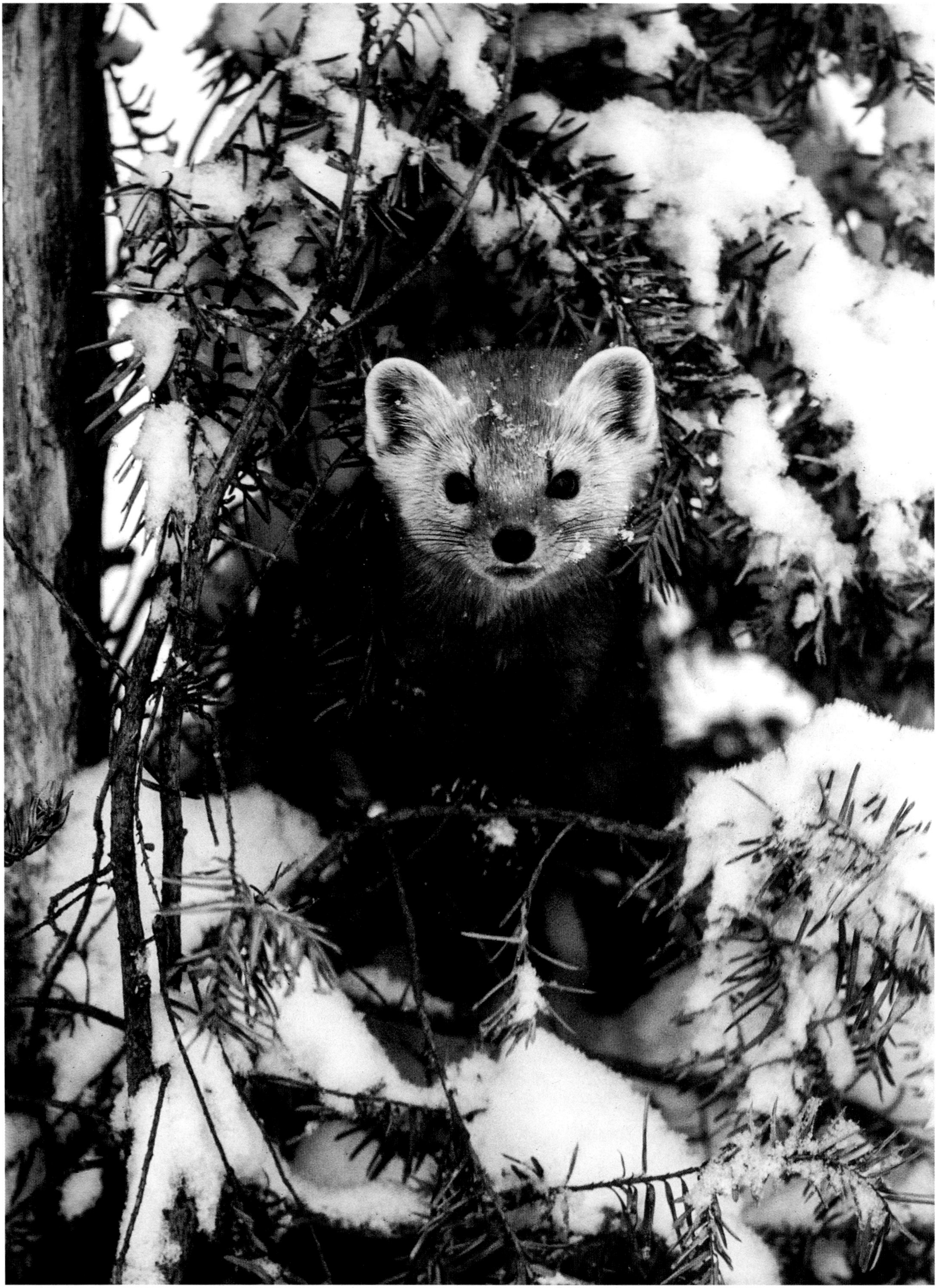

CHAPTER 13

WILDERNESS TRAPPERS

Every trapper has a warm place in his heart for the wild places back and beyond. Wilderness where the forests are deep and dark, where the streams flow as clear as crystal. The romantic notion of a handmade log cabin adorned with moose antlers, built along a wild river where beavers and otters frolic, and pine marten dance in the treetops. The cry of the loon, howl of the wolf, and the golden leaves of aspen rattling in the wind.

Of course, there are varying degrees of true wilderness. Some wish to quantify it as "semi" wilderness. The reality is wilderness comes in many forms from desert expanse, to mountain peaks, trackless tundra, barren coastline, swamp and wetlands, as well as forests. To think that 30 miles east of Miami, Florida, a metroplex with a population of over 2.7 million people—that one could find wilderness seems mind-blowing. Yet, if you have actually been to the Everglades you would know this place is about as unforgiving wilderness as you can find. So are areas 30 miles outside of Las Vegas, Salt Lake City, Portland, Oregon or Maine, and I could go on and on. So, the thought that wilderness is only in the outer reaches of Alaska or some other remote place just isn't accurate.

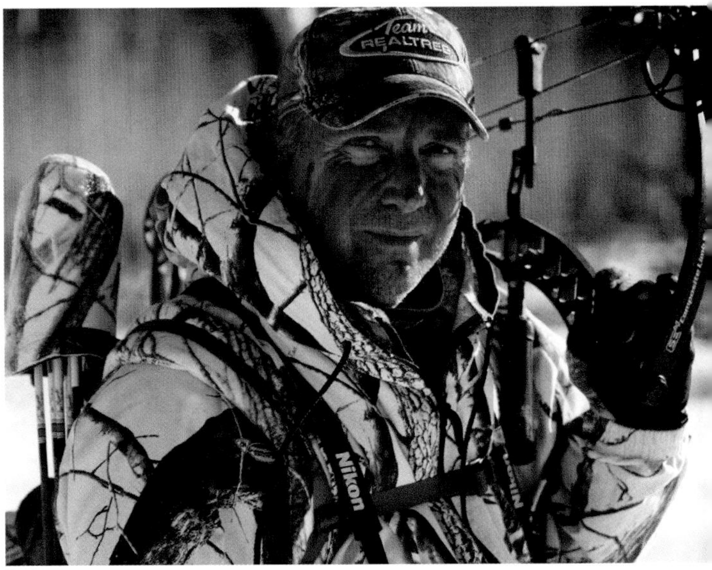

ADVENTUROUS BREED

I have been blessed to experience many wilderness places around the world. In my bowhunting quests into far reaching lands, the goal has been adventure—the wilder and more remote the destination, the bigger the adventure. Whether it was hunting amongst the jungles of northern Mozambique, the flood plains of Australia's Northern Territory, France's rugged Pyrenees, the Kalahari, Andes, High Arctic, central Turkey, the Urals, Caucasus and many other places, one central fact rings true—an outdoorsman knows true wilderness when he's in it. Another fact: just because it's wilderness

< Leonard Lee Rue III Photo

doesn't mean that animals abound. Often, I have found animals scarcer in the wildest places.

My passion to trek north from Columbus, Ohio into the wilds of Michigan's Upper Peninsula region was a powerful motivator to my future as an outdoorsman. Once one steps outside of their comfort zone, perspective changes. For some the wilderness is a grand opportunity, for others it's a prison. One fact that looms large in the wilderness is that tasks become more difficult. Those who venture into the "back and beyond" are left to only what is at hand. There is no hardware store around the corner. No electricity to light the night, no place to come in out of the rain, sun, heat or cold. No texting or cell coverage. Necessity becomes abstract. Forgetting to add a blanket to the bed on a cold night may be an inconvenience at home. Forgetting your sleeping bag in remote country may be life-threatening.

I'm of the opinion that wild places are fantastic learning grounds for good old-fashioned common sense. As without it, one cannot survive in the wilderness.

ANIMALS EVERYWHERE

One of the biggest misconceptions about wilderness areas is that animal populations are extremely high. The thought that unmolested wildlife living in virgin habitat thrive in an endless bounty just isn't the case. Nature manages itself in brutal ways and animals will thrive in pockets of rich habitat, yet vast areas are often void of wild creatures. I've sat in caribou camps where tens of thousands of caribou should be living and never seen a caribou. Other camps 50 miles away had thousands of 'bou. There are places in the Rockies where elk herds fill the valleys and other areas where one is hard-pressed to find a track. On a moose hunt in the Yukon I returned from just recently, we were operating with a jet boat and headed up a small tributary looking for a good bull. I looked the better part of an hour for furbearer sign as we motored up the drainage and saw very little. Animals are where you find them, hence the statement, *"Ninety percent of the wildlife lives in 10 percent of the habitat."*

Often tracts of mature timber create such a canopy that sunlight never penetrates, thus the forest floor is void of smaller plants that provide food for animals. In dense evergreen forests, the centuries of pine nee-

dles dropping to the ground change the pH of the soil to be slightly more acidic. This deters growth of some understory plants as well. Beavers in far northern habitats have been known to eat themselves out of house and home in some areas because willow growing cycles in these harsh climes can't keep up with what the beavers are cutting.

Mode of transportation is always key in taking numbers of animals for any trapper, yet on a wilderness line, it's even more important. For a trapper operating on foot, it's difficult to travel much distance before ice up unless a well-established trail system is in place. Once rivers are frozen, these become highways for expanding territory and reaching pockets of fur. Areas that include trails which can be run with motorized vehicles allow much more flexibility. Some trappers will live on highways adjacent to wilderness tracts and operate off the highway, fingering into the back country from the road. Boats are also used in coastal areas and on large lakes with trappers accessing the beaches and tributaries. Some Alaskan and Canadian trappers use an airplane to bounce from remote lake to lake, running sets around them. During the high lynx prices of the late 1970s through the 1980s, some of these resourceful trappers made enough money trapping lynx in one season to buy a new aircraft.

WILDERNESS SPECIES

The uniqueness of some of the wilderness furbearers is a big part of their allure. Trappers who operate in areas of northern wilderness have access to a wide variety of some very special animals—pine marten, fisher, bobcats, lynx, beavers, otters, ermine, mink, wolverine, wolves, foxes and coyotes. In the northern areas where these animals live, the pelts become very prime. Tough weather along with remote habitat limits catch numbers keeping supply low and prices up. Often in the north, color phases give additional value to pelts like fox. Red foxes have several melanistic color phases such as black, silver and cross—all of which can bring a higher pelt value. In the far north, pure white arctic foxes are also taken.

In many wilderness areas, trap check laws allow for sets to be tended every three days, in some places once a week. Many animals like marten, fisher, beavers and otters are taken with body-gripper traps, which kill quickly, and the brutal cold temperatures preserve the hide until the trapper can retrieve the animal, thaw and skin the pelt. This allows for several lines to be run, allowing for more sets and better chances for a larger catch.

Master Trapper Tom Krause poses with his "newspaper box" marten cubby and a dandy Wyoming marten.

MARTEN TRAPPING

The small, agile pine marten is a prize for many wilderness trappers. The marten is a tree climber that lives in the dark pine forest fringes eating squirrels, mice, voles—any small rodent it can catch. Trappers typically take marten in baited tree sets, utilizing a box cubby with bait, lure, or both placed inside and a 120 body-gripping trap guarding the entrance. When the marten tries to investigate, it must pass through the trap and is caught. Typically, these sets are made on poles leaning up to a tree or on the tree trunk itself. Marten trappers typically set to catch the marten up in the tree and often staple the trap so that when caught, the marten dangles 4–5 feet off the ground. This helps to prevent small animals like foxes or wolverine from finding the animal and damaging its pelt.

Back in the fur boom of the 1920s, 20 marten pelts were valued at $1,000 dollars. This was one third of the average yearly wage earned in 1920.

WOLF TRAPPING

The wolf is one animal that conflicts with man's existence. Once wolves were prevalent west of the Mississippi River and across the entire northern tier of the United States. However, because of their blood-thirsty nature and lack of regard for livestock, wolves have been all but eliminated in the lower 48 states except for the Rocky Mountains of Yellowstone and north, as well as areas of northern Minnesota, Wisconsin and Michigan where they have been irresponsibly transplanted.

The wolf also is a poster child for animal activists and protectionists. Whether it's because of their kinship with modern-day dogs or the fact that the story of their eradication from farming and ranching areas in the late 1800s–1940s plays well to naive donors, the wolf gets much attention. In areas of Canada and Alaska, wolves must be managed—since their pelt is valuable, it only makes sense to allow trappers to help control their numbers.

Wolves are effectively taken with steel foothold traps or snares by trappers trained in predator trapping. Large traps like the MB 750 are required to hold a wolf, as a large alpha male can weigh well over 100 pounds, yet the average wolf is 65–80 pounds. Wolves, like their smaller cousin the coyote, have very keen senses and an innate sense for staying out of trouble. Wolves have a hierarchy in their clan or pack and will often travel with 5 to 12 animals. These wolf packs can easily kill livestock including cattle and wreak havoc with wild populations of deer, elk, moose and caribou.

Chad Lenz Photo

Alberta guide and trapper Chad Lenz poses with a dandy wolf.

Trappers make dirt-hole and flat sets for wolves and often will use wolf droppings found in other areas, added to their sets as a fear eliminator. Wolves are very territorial—if another wolf is thought to be trespassing—these foreign wolf smells will attract alphas to the traps. There are networks among trappers in Canada that actually collect wolf feces and trade to trappers in other areas to use this ruse as a decoy.

In winter snow conditions, trappers often place a large bait in a thicket and after the wolves have found the bait, hang 20–30 snares on every conceivable trail the wolves can use. A unique concept often added to this strategy is for the trapper to go into a thicket area and hang the snares first, covering every trail that will lead into the thicket. Once there is a fresh snowfall and the scent dissipated from the snares, the trapper returns to set the bait. Top wolf trappers respect a wolf's senses that much. Like a coyote, a wolf that is pinched or escapes a trap learns very quickly and becomes much harder to catch.

WOLVERINE

The wolverine is a relative of the mink and weasel and the largest member of the family Mustelidae. The wolverine's scientific name is *Gulo gulo* which means *glutton,* but they are also called a "devil bear" or a "woods devil." Wolverine hunt and kill small mammals for food but they are better at scavenging. Any large carcass bait like moose or bear will quickly be found by a wolverine if one is in the area. Wolverine prefer remote wilderness and roam widely covering vast distances in search of food. Thus, sets for wolverine need be made on sign or at trail crossings along drainages where the animals will pass. Wolverine trappers know they must remain patient and await their return. Sets made for wolves or lynx often catch a trap-robbing wolverine.

Trappers in the north use leg hold traps, body grippers and snares to catch wolverine. MB750, 330 conibear, and 1/8", 7x7 cable snares. Some trappers even utilize the 4-1/2 Newhouse. Wolverine are fierce in the trap so only heavy traps, grapples and drags should be considered. Traps and snares can be set on trails leading to large baits or used to guard the entrance of a large wolverine cubby. The 330 conibears are typically used by trappers in wolverine cubby sets as they kill quickly and leave the cubby undamaged so the trap can be reset.

Wolverine fur is thick, durable and typically used as a fur trim on parka hoods. The unique hairs of a wolverine don't soak up moisture and freeze solid ice like other fur types, but instead form rime ice with the condensing moisture as each breath passes over the guard hairs. Rime ice is easily brushed away. Wolverine pelts properly skinned for mounting are also sold into the taxidermy trade where legal.

LYNX

The lynx is similar to the bobcat, yet has much longer legs, big furry paws and tufted ears. Lynx are never really abundant, although their populations fluctuate with the populations of small mammals they hunt. The primary prey of lynx in most areas is the snowshoe hare, which undergoes an 8- to 11-year cycle of abundance. Lynx numbers fluctuate as the population of hares and other small game fluctuate but lag one or so years behind. When a hare population declines, lynx numbers soon decline. Lynx tend to be the most valuable fur-bearing species in the areas where they are found. This makes them prized to the trapper who can locate their haunts and catch them.

Lynx are taken in baited and flagged sets similar to those used for bobcats. Since these cats like to kill their prey, they're attracted to contrasting fur, feathers

or ribbons waving in the breeze. Large holes, small caves, crevices, rock or snow cubbies all create interest to lynx on the hunt when eye appeal is combined with an attractive lure or bait. Lynx can be caught in somewhat smaller traps like MB650s yet most trappers who pursue lynx also plan for the possibility of a wolverine or a lucky wolf catch, usually using the larger foothold traps. Well-made cubbies can be guarded with 220 or 330 conibears with good results.

Lynx fur is luxurious, light, soft and attractive. Coats made from lynx pelts are highly desirable fashions demanding an equally high price.

WAYNE NEGUS

1907–1991

Wayne Negus Photo

Wayne Negus was born in Davis, South Dakota. His family moved to the North Dakota prairies before Wayne was of school age. Wayne's uncles taught him basic trapping skills when he was young—this along with the spending money he earned, enamored young Wayne Negus with trapping. The family eventually moved from the Dakotas into northeastern Wyoming where Wayne continued to trap, fish and hunt.

As youngsters, Wayne and his brother Tom learned to shoot white-tailed jack rabbits with a .22 rimfire in winter and sell the carcasses for meat. Traveling buyers would pay 50 cents a carcass during the 1920s and these traveling "meat" buyers would ship boxcar loads of frozen "jacks" back east for table fare. It was these early years of trapping and hunting that molded young Wayne Negus into an outdoorsman. Wayne said, *"Since my childhood days, I had longed to emulate the exploits of the mountain men and fur trappers."*

Wikimedia Commons

A dozer works on the Alaska Highway, circa 1942.

Just before his 20th birthday in January 1927, Negus took a train to Oregon to visit relatives. Wayne recalls three feet of fresh snow when he arrived in Bend. That summer Wayne took a job with Brooks-Scranton Lumber Company and began working in a long log logging camp. It was here that he met his first trapping partner. Negus struck a deal to stake their first venture together by paying for provisions and traps in exchange for the know-how of wilderness trapping skills for pine marten, foxes, mink and otters. Wayne's story includes five weeks of hiking in the grubstake and traps over nine miles on winding trails to a quaint two-room cabin which would be base camp for his first wilderness trapline experience. Over the next month the trappers scouted the area and built cubbies in preparation for the trapping season. However, about the middle of October, Wayne's trapping partner borrowed $20 and said he needed to go to town for necessities before the trapping commenced. Wayne's partner never returned.

North Dakota Rabbit hunt, circa 1926.

So that first winter in Oregon, Negus was on his own and began to set up his trapline on November 16, 1927. The first snows arrived November 21 and Negus had traps set along 42 miles of wilderness—a trapline he checked on snowshoes. By the end of the trapping season Wayne had turned 21 years old and his catch was 50 marten, 7 otters, 20 mink and several foxes, two of which were silvers. Wayne said the snow reached a depth that year of 22 feet actual measurement and he had to tunnel into his cabin.

Wayne Negus poses with trapping partner Charlie Mock holding some dandy Cascade mountain marten and a cross fox, circa 1978.

Willamette National Forest as well as Mount Bailey and Mount Thielsen traplines in the Umpqua National Forest north of Crater Lake National Park. Some of the trappers' cabins Wayne used still exist in these areas today.

Wayne utilized small lean-to shelters on his marten lines. Built with the leaning logs often times placed against a deadfall or a tree that was partially blown over, these small camps were constructed where convenient and utilized materials at hand. Negus could stretch a tarp over the leaning logs to keep water from melting and dripping from the fires he would build under the lean-to. Because of the latitude and proximity to the Pacific, winter temperatures in the Cascades aren't as extreme as in the Rockies or points north in Canada

Wayne Negus soon took a job with the railroad that allowed him to travel into different parts of the Cascades and across Oregon. This enabled him to scout new areas and expand his winter trapping haunts. Working on one section of track near several waterways allowed Negus to gain permission in a fur pocket that netted him over 900 muskrats and several mink. Wayne also trapped bobcats in the eastern Oregon desert one winter when marten prices were low.

Negus married Anona Hinshaw in 1934 in Payette, Idaho and the couple had two sons, Gary in 1936 and Lyle in 1939. Marriage is a big responsibility and trappers know all about responsibility. Wayne worked hard all summer and trapped hard all winter to provide for his family. His wilderness traplines in the Cascades were his passion. Negus ran lines in several areas of the Cascade Range including his Vogel Lake trapline west of Bend in the

Wayne Negus Photo

Negus with a day's catch of muskrats on the frozen Klamath Marsh, 1956.

Tom Krause Photo

Master Trapper Tom Krause knew Wayne Negus well and it looks like some of Wayne's marten trapping savvy wore off on him.

and Alaska. Operating from a main cabin, these lean-to shelters were often set up at the halfway point of a "trail loop" which would allow Negus to leave his base cabin and check a line of sets until reaching the shelter. At the lean-to, Wayne would eat lunch, skin his catch and even camp for the night if weather was tough. Otherwise he would continue checking the line until reaching his line cabin. The next day he could loop back checking a different line stopping at another shelter at the halfway point, then continue his trapline to return to his base cabin. These halfway shelters were safety nets for a lone trapper who must be prepared to take care of himself if trouble arises. It should be noted that it takes a fit trapper to snowshoe deep snow at altitude day in and day out. Snow depths in the Cascade mountains are incredible, as the area receives more annual snowfall than anywhere in the continental United States.

These long treks into the wilderness were tough on a marriage. By the early 1940s Wayne and Anona's marriage was over. It's unfortunate that these things occur and it's the case more often when a spouse must be gone for long periods and the other spouse is left to raise the children.

Over the ensuing years, Wayne Negus worked on construction of the Alcan Highway, in the Aleutian Islands of Alaska, in numerous grocery stores, as a cook in restaurants, and as a logger or a logging camp cook in many remote areas. But when winter came around, Wayne would find himself in one of his remote cabins or on his wilderness trapline trails.

Oregon closed the marten season for nine years from 1941 through 1949 and although Wayne was trapping, he was also romancing. Wayne met his wife-to-be Roberta "Bobby" Engle in Wyoming back in 1932 when she was still in high school, however Wayne's parents moved to Oregon and Wayne's life didn't take him back to Wyoming often. With the marten season closed in Oregon, he went back to Wyoming to trap and looked up Bobby. The couple rekindled their earlier relationship. Wayne and Bobby Negus married December 7, 1944. Wayne and his new bride would live in Oregon and start a family. Daughter Toni would be born in 1946 and Susan in 1950. By 1950 Wayne's sons were now 14 and 11.

Once the girls were old enough, Bobby, Toni and Susan would go with Wayne on his wilderness trapline. The young girls helped collect kindling and did chores around camp while Bobby would dig in skinning and preparing pelts as well as cooking and even doing some trapping. Wayne Negus continued to trap when the fur prices were good and even when they weren't so good.

Wayne also got involved with the National Trappers Association as he had a talent for writing about his exploits and adventures on his wilderness traplines, which was much appreciated by many readers of trapping publications throughout the years. His knowledge of pine marten was extraordinary. Wayne Negus wrote one book, *Wilderness Tales and Trails* published by Chuck Spearman in 1980 and another collection of his stories, *A Man to Match the Mountains: 70 Years of Trapping* was organized and printed by his family following his death.

Wayne was most deservingly inducted into the National Trappers Association Trappers Hall of Fame posthumously in 1993 (two years after his passing). Without a doubt, Wayne Negus was a legendary trapper for the better part of the 20th century.

DEAN WILSON

1941–2010

Dean Wilson was born in Walla Walla, Washington on January 14, 1941. Soon after, his family returned to Alaska. Dean's father Dale had trapped in Alaska in the late 1930s for pine marten with his trapping partner, Oscar Albert. Dean recalls his father telling him that in the season of 1930–40 trappers caught 18 marten and received $75 each or about $650 for each trapper. In 1940 the minimum wage was 30 cents and the average man earned $950 a year.

Dean Wilson Photo

Dean Wilson poses in his fur shed with some prime Alaskan furs taken on his wilderness trapline.

During World War II, Dean's father Dale served in the Army, stationed in Alaska working construction on the Alaska Highway. In the late 1940s the family moved to Northway, an area of Alaska between Tok and the Yukon border. It's here that Dean began following his father's footsteps along the trapline. Dean recalls the favorite times of his childhood were running traps with his father and the excitement when they would catch a lynx. *"My father was an excellent lynx trapper. In fact, I'm sure it was his favorite animal to trap. Dad always said that a good trapper learns to use traps first and when you get good with traps, learn snares. The best trappers use both because each have their own applications."*

Dean's outings with his father helped him learn how to hunt, fish and trap. Dean recalls that Walter Northway, the chief of the village was the absolute best hunter in the area. Dean learned much from him and his younger brother Stephen. Both Walter and Stephen were kind, generous men who did much for the village and they both influenced a young Dean Wilson to pursue a life outdoors. After finishing Northway grade school, Dean attended Sheldon Jackson High School in Sitka for three years, then completed high school in Homer. In 1963, Dean married Ada Tega of Tanacross,

Alaska. In 1966 they acquired land along the Edgerton Highway near Kenny Lake, where they built a home and raised three sons, Dell, Rick and Dean Jr.

Dean Wilson Photo

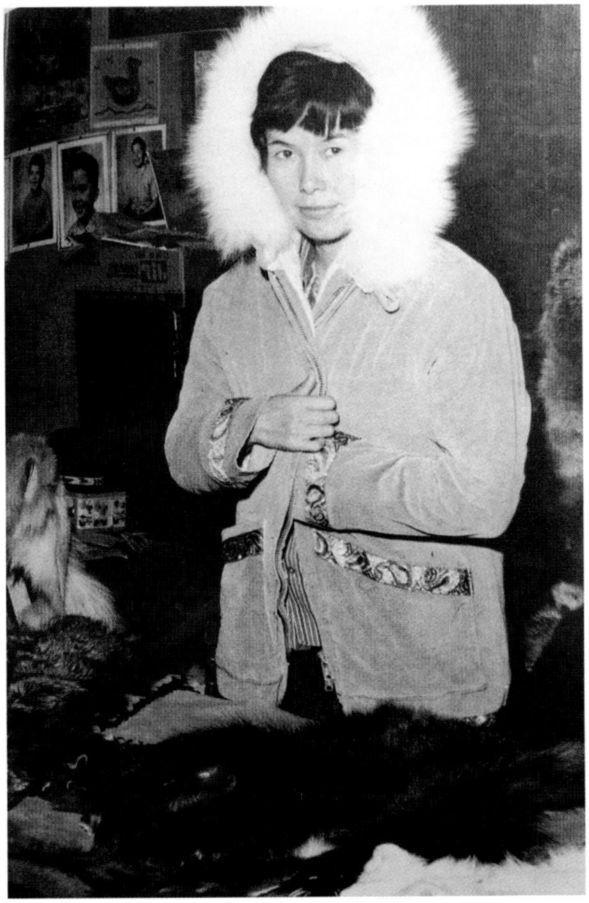

Dean's wife Ada Tega Wilson in the early years of the Klondike Fur Company.

Even as a young man, Dean considered trapping to be his primary livelihood although he supplemented his income by taking jobs in construction, firefighting and oil exploration. About 1967 Dean got his first snow machine and became serious about his trapping. By the mid-1970s Dean was long-lining 300 traps through the wilderness. He concentrated on the animals whose pelts were demanding the highest price—typically lynx. In the early 1970s lynx were bringing $40–50 dollars per pelt. By the late 1970s lynx were averaging $500 and higher. Dean used cubby sets and typically didn't use bait. Instead to save weight on the trail, he used Laugeman's Big Sky lures made by Fuller Laugemen of Winnet, Montana. Laugeman purchased Bill Nelson's lures from Bill's wife after his death in 1973. Dean also likes to trap wolverine saying, *"If you have a big bait you can hardly keep a wolverine off of it!"*

After several years of increasingly successful trapping, Dean began to buy fur and sell it at the major markets. Soon he and his wife Ada started Klondike Furs which they operated for many years. To buy furs, Dean traveled throughout Alaska, especially to many small villages where he made many friends and became highly respected for his business ethics and personable manner. To develop markets for their Alaska furs, Dean and Ada took several interesting and enjoyable trips to the eastern US, eastern Canada, Europe and Asia.

In the 1980s, Dean wrote a very successful how-to book titled, *The Alaskan Trapper's Handbook*. The book was based on Dean's decades of experience as well things he had learned from many older trappers, including his father. The book has been reprinted many times. Dean was also involved in both the National Trappers Association and the Alaska Trappers Association. Over the years he held various leadership positions, attended many annual meetings and wrote occasional pieces for the publications of both organizations. Dean Wilson was a prominent trapper and fur buyer for more than 30 years in the Interior, and is considered the patriarch of trapping in Alaska. He was sometimes called the "Father of Fur" and developed a reputation over the years for treating trappers fairly and honestly.

Dean Wilson with his plaque and induction into the Alaska Trappers Hall of Fame.

Wilson was the Alaska Trappers Association "Trapper of the Year" in 1985, and when the Alaska Trappers Hall of Fame was established in 1997, Dean was the first person selected for the honor. He was a lifetime member of the Pioneers of Alaska and Igloo 35 in Delta. Dean was accepted into the Kluti Kaah tribe of Copper Center in a ceremony by the late Chief Jim McKinley in the 1980s, and he considered it a great honor. Wilson was also inducted into the National Trappers Association Trappers Hall of Fame in 1998.

In 1990, Dean was diagnosed with Parkinson's disease and began treatment for it. After a few years Dean found it necessary to severely limit his activities—later he was unable to continue operating Klondike Furs, and as the disease progressed it became increasingly difficult to walk or perform simple tasks. Dean passed from complications of his illness in 2010.

Dean Wilson gives a grand tribute to native hunter Walter Northway in his oral trappers history recording available from the Alaskan Trappers Association. A must-listen.

"Walter Northway was an incredible man. He was without any question, a man of great wisdom within the things of living off the country. I remember when Walter turned a hundred years old—a local pilot took him up in an airplane to see some of his old hunting and trapping areas and Walter came back just amazed and said, 'In just one hour I saw all the country it took me 100 years to learn.'" "He was a real good teacher, no matter what we would be doing around the village, maybe shooting at a squirrel with slingshots or maybe making a bow and arrow or making another arrow, maybe skinning muskrats. Walter would come by, he would always stop, see what you were doing and try to help you. Show you a better way of doing that. He was a very kind, gentle man. He really liked to interact with the kids. He always was good at passing on things. He was the best bow maker, without question the best snowshoe maker, he was a leader by example. He was an idol for many, many people and a highly respected man, particularly for his hunting ability and he trained a lot of people throughout the years on hunting."

PAUL TREPUS

1963–

Paul Trepus is a modern-day mountain man. A professional trapper and big game outfitter, Paul grew up in Fort Saint John, British Columbia, a small community located on the Alaska Highway. Paul began trapping at 9 years old and throughout his school years he trapped the farms and ranches located on the outskirts of Fort St. John. After graduating from high school, Paul embarked on an adventure to move to the wilds and trap full time. Paul trapped three winters alone in the wilderness where he says he learned bushcraft and made a good living as a professional trapper.

Paul Trepus Photo

Paul Trepus poses with a fine catch of British Columbia furbearers, 2009.

Paul Trepus Photo

British Columbia trapper Paul Trepus poses with a wolf taken in a dirt-hole set on his wilderness trapline.

In 1990 Paul purchased a registered trapline near Prince George, British Columbia and in turn bought some property to build a log home to accommodate his growing family. In Canada, formal trapping territories assigned by the province are typically called "registered traplines" though each province administers its own system. The registered trapline system is a commercial furbearer harvest management system whereby the "line-holder," is granted the exclusive opportunity to harvest furbearing animals in the area designated as registered. The system ensures sustainable furbearer populations by controlling the number of trappers in that area and making the line-holder the steward of the resource. In British Columbia where Paul's trapline is located, the registered trapline system continues to be the primary system for setting harvest guidelines and managing fur-bearing animals. In fact, in British Columbia it is illegal to trap an animal on a registered trapline that does not belong to the trapper.

Paul says, *"In my desire to be the very best at trapping canines, I took private trapping instruction from Craig O'Gorman, Dan Lay, Carl Gitcheff's Advanced Trapping Course and snaring canines with Marty Senneker. These investments in my education allowed me to quickly increase my success and subsequently my catch numbers increased as well."*

Paul Trepus Photo

British Columbia trapper and outfitter Paul Trepus and the first half of his 2012–13 catch.

Paul prefers to use dirt-hole sets on his wolves and his expertise has gained him recognition with the Ministry of the Environment as a top wolf trapper for research projects as well as trapping wolves, which are doing depredation on ranches and community pastures that border the wilderness areas. Paul says that the only difference between a coyote set and a wolf set is the size of the trap and the anchoring system, as wolves are hard to hold. Trepus's best season on canines included a combined 350 coyotes, foxes and wolves. His best season on Lynx was 65 and pine marten, 120.

Paul has several trapping DVD programs including *Wolf Trapping Training*—2008, *Wolf Snaring Training*—2009, *Beaver Trapping Training*—2009, *Wolverine Trapper Training*—2010 and *Survival Snaring*—2016.

INZANA
OUTFITTERS

In 1999 Paul purchased a guiding area known as Inzana Outfitters, a 2,000 square mile territory rich in moose, grizzly and mountain goats. Paul's wife Marilyn and their 2 children, Julienne and Aaron help with the family business.

Here's an interesting story Paul related to me.

"At 7:30 a.m. my phone rang, and a rancher friend was whispering into the phone, 'I am looking out my window and I can see 11 wolves in my pasture with the cattle. They've killed my two big guardian dogs and 5 calves. Can you come down here?'" "This same rancher had bought 2 guardian dogs to keep the predators away a couple of years earlier and had decided not to allow me to trap any more, as he didn't want his dogs caught in the traps.

I went to the ranch the next day and found that his 2 guardian dogs had engaged the wolves but were no match for the pack. The dogs were torn to pieces and died in the battle. The rancher showed me where a bull had died earlier in the season and I made my sets near what was remaining of the carcass. A few bones and a bit of hide marked the location of the bull. I promptly made a few dirt-hole sets around the perimeter 25 to 50 yards apart; the wolves had fed on the carcass as indicated by wolf scat and I knew the pack would check out this location on their next pass through the area. I also set a few snares on well-defined livestock trails to capture milling wolves (the livestock had been moved out of the pasture). I like to set at least 6 or more wolf traps on a setup like this as I am trying to catch the whole pack at once and hopefully the most dominant wolves first. The best opportunity to catch a wolf is the first trap visit as wolves learn fast.

I promptly captured 7 of the wolves. The remaining wolves left the area. All cattle killing stopped for the remainder of the year. Here in British Columbia I use the BC Wolf Trap built by Tom Skuratow. It has a 9 in jaw spread and it is very powerful. Since Tom is no longer building wolf traps so I also use the new Bridger Brawn #9 also has a 9-in jaw spread, has lots of power and is swiveled, rubber padded and ready to go right out of the box. I have a little saying about wolves, they are easy to catch the first time around, but they are always hard to hold. Typically, I take about 20 wolves a winter on my trapline and guiding area."

-Paul Trepus in his own words, 2014.

MEGA ADVENTURE BOWHUNTING

In 2006 I decided to re-release my original trapping videos on DVD. I had gotten many requests over the years from trappers who wanted to replace the VHS with a DVD, but with so many expert trappers doing new DVDs, I thought, why bother re-releasing the old ones? Then Tim Caven called me and said he was doing a package for Cabela's and wanted use one of my trapping videos in it—If I would put the program on DVD. So, I ended up converting all seven videos into four DVDs. It actually was a great move and Tim sold many trapper packages with my DVD included. Stoney-Wolf also sold the trapping DVDs and it was sort of a revitalization of my early trapping days all over again. Advantage Adventures was the name of my TV series at the time, so I used that logo on the DVD packaging.

Fur-Fish-Game also re-released the old trapping videos on DVD and still sell the programs today—some 30-plus years after their initial releases.

In late February 2007 I got a call from Jerome Knapp of Canada North Outfitting. In 2006 had put in a $1,000 deposit to get on a 3-year waiting list to go polar bear hunting. I was just starting my second year on the list when Jerome called and told me that a scenario had arisen where there was an opening in May 2007. I quickly jumped at the opening and said yes. At the time, animal activists were trying to get polar bear hunting banned and the U.S. Fish and Wildlife Service (USFWS) was seriously looking at listing white bears as a threatened species to appease activists as well as some scientists focused on global warming and a reduction of sea ice in the Arctic. This would mean that any bears legally taken would not be able to be imported into the United States. The opportunity to hunt in 2007 was a huge windfall as the available tag was also in a CITES approved area. CITES stands for Convention on International Trade in Endangered Species. Since polar bears are covered under the Marine Mammal Protection Act as well as CITES, only bears taken in CITES-approved units of the Arctic can be imported. And if the bears were to be listed as threatened, none will be importable.

The crazy thing was that I had just been called to go to Zimbabwe for a chance to bowhunt elephant on a damage complaint. So just a few days after agreeing to do the polar bear hunt, I was on a jet to Africa. Elephant hunting is the pinnacle of African big game hunting (and likely big game hunting in the world). As mammals go on our planet, only a whale is larger than an elephant—to take an adult bull elephant

Author's Photos

Tom Miranda poses with his African bull elephant taken with bow and arrow in Zimbabwe's Omay Concession, 2007.

Elephant tracks are like fingerprints and we followed this marauding bull 8 kilometers before a bow chance.

with a bow is a terrific undertaking. The bow I would use was a Mathews Black Max model, fitted with 100-pound limbs. My arrows were sleeved (arrow inside an arrow), filled with silica sand and tipped with 180-grain cut on impact broad heads. My comfortable shooting range was 30 yards.

Elephant do a tremendous amount of damage in Africa as an adult elephant will eat 300 pounds of foliage a day. This particular pachyderm was walking from a mountainous area to a village where he would pull banana trees out of the ground with his trunk and eat them like a stalk of celery. By the time I arrived he had decimated a large banana grove near a native village. It took us nine days to find the bull. Local native trackers knew the bull's track. So, every evening we would drag a mopane tree behind the land cruiser to rub the sign off the road and cruise the road at daybreak looking for the marauder's tracks. Once the bull tracks showed up, we followed him approximately 8 kilometers up into the mountain where we found the bull sleeping under a tree. When he awoke, he walked a trail where I was hiding in some boulders and I arrowed the brute in the heart at 12 yards. It is exciting video footage to be sure. The hunt was absolutely all the excitement any "adventure bowhunter" could ever ask for.

Author's Photo

POLAR BEAR

When I got back from Africa, my two bow cases and four bows didn't make it on the jet. In fact, I waited five days for them to come and the bow cases never showed up. So, I lost four bows, lots of arrows, two pairs of binoculars, two range finders, camouflage gear, broad heads—it was a nightmare as my white bear hunt was fast approaching. I called the Mathews bow factory and they quickly sent me two new bows of which I quickly set up and started shooting for the trip north. You can imagine that since I hunt on television, I'm constantly changing and using new or different equipment. Manufacturers of hunting gear expect to see their newest creations on TV, so you would think that I would be familiar with quickly sighting a new bow and turning around on another hunt. Yet, like most bowhunters, I like to have a relationship with my bow. I want to shoot it and get to know it. Confidence is a huge aspect of successful bowhunting and I was being forced to go to the Arctic, on the adventure hunt of a lifetime with completely new, one-week-old everything.

Tom Miranda poses with his massive polar bear taken with bow and arrow in 2007.

Author's Photo

Here's our camp on the ice during the big storm.

The trip north is always an adventure—my two trips to Cambridge Bay for muskoxen had always been four flights. This trip into the upper reaches of nowhere took five flights and was one of just two small Inuit villages in the far north. Resolute Bay and Grise Fiord are the end of the line for adventure hunters, as far north as you can book a flight on our continent.

Arriving in Resolute Bay, I soon learned that because of the weather we would be traveling and hunting at night. So close to the North Pole, days in May have 20 hours of daylight—the night is really only twilight, not dark. In fact, the sun never dipped below the horizon. Polar bear hunts are done from dogsled and the entire hunt was amazing. I arrowed a great bear and experienced a severe storm with minus 80 wind chills. A polar bear hunt is absolutely the biggest adventure found on the North American continent.

As a postscript, I was able to get my polar bear out of Canada and into the United States just weeks before the USFWS classified the polar bear as a threatened species and closed imports of their hide and skull. My amazing ice bear is mounted life-size and displayed in my Florida game room.

RAM TIME

Author's Photo

One of only two Super Slam animals of which I arrow on the first day of the hunt. Beautiful Stone ram, 2007.

At the end of July 2007 I headed to northern British Columbia. This would be my second sheep hunt. Stone's sheep are thought by many bowhunters to be the hardest of the four rams required for the Grand Slam of wild sheep. I thought, *"If anything is tougher than the Canmore bighorn hunt, I'm in trouble."* I was hunting again with Chad Lenz and we had decided to go in on horseback four days before the season opened to set up camp and hopefully locate a legal ram to make maximum use of our time. Sheep hunting is expensive, and we not only needed to hunt with archery equipment, I needed the kill on video.

Chad and I set camp and soon found a good ram—we watched him for two days. On the morning the season opened, August 1—we hiked to the top, got on the back side of the mountain and began making our way to our ram's position. We needed to hike about a mile in cliffy terrain and shale slides. En route, we bumped two rams we hadn't seen before and eventually I had a shot at one of them. With camera rolling, I drilled the ram and BAM! The hunt was over just like that. I shot my Stone sheep on the first day of the hunt.

In early summer 2007 I caught wind that Realtree was planning on releasing a DVD titled, *Advantage Adventures with Jay Gregory*. Gregory is a whitetail hunter from Missouri and at the time had some notoriety of shooting big whitetails. The DVD would be about whitetail hunts and sold in Walmart. I called Realtree and ended up speaking with the company boss at the time, Rod Hinton, as owner and founder Bill Jordan was not available. I was furious. I had been branding *Advantage Adventures* on ESPN for Realtree since 1998. Rod was very nice and politely told me that Realtree owned the name Advantage Adventures and they could use it as they wished. I told Rod if they released the video with Gregory, I would change the name of my series. Of course, this is how business works. You roll with the punches. Realtree felt they were doing what they needed to do to promote their brand, I was doing what I needed to do to protect mine. Realtree was my first big TV partner and when I get a cut—I bleed Realtree camo.

Hinton threatened to cancel my contract if I changed the series name. Realtree released the video and I finished the season as *Advantage Adventures*. However, in 2008 my series name would change to *Mathews Territories Wild with Tom Miranda*. John Skrabo was one of the top licensing men at Realtree and he along with Bill Jordan kept me on the Realtree staff. As I type this, I am still on the Realtree pro staff—now some 32 years. Only Jackie Bushman of Buck Masters has been with Realtree longer. The lesson is there are a lot of things in life that money can buy, but some things you can't—one being true loyalty.

Television production had been good to me. By this time, I was a staple on ESPN and in my 17th season on the network. In 2008 I was producing *Territories Wild*, *ProHunters Journal*, *Whitetail Country* and *Strategies in the Wild*, all on ESPN. Plus, I produced *Game Trails* and *Beyond the Lodge* for the Outdoor Channel. I had a staff of editors and cameramen, and I was focused on big game bowhunting.

During July 2008 I went to Canada again for sheep, this time to the Northwest Territories. I didn't have the luck I had in 2007, but I did arrow my Dall ram on the eighth day of the hunt. On the same trip I hunted mountain caribou, taking a great bull. Reflecting as I boarded the plane home, it had been a great trip. I now had three of the four sheep and a total of 17 species. In September I traveled to Alberta and arrowed a Rocky Mountain mule deer. In November, a Columbia black-tailed deer in Oregon.

Author's Photo

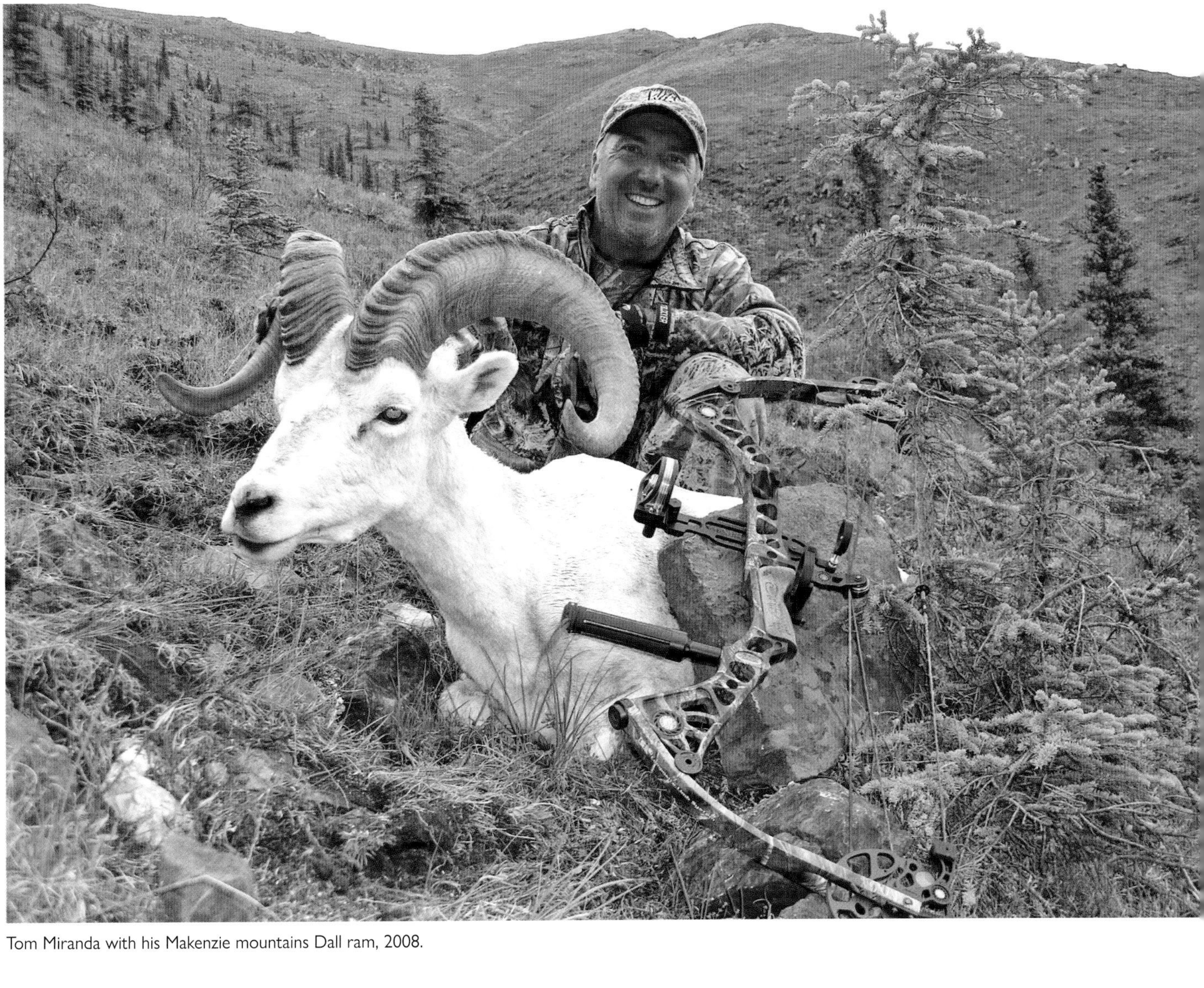

Tom Miranda with his Makenzie mountains Dall ram, 2008.

Three in College

In 2009 my youngest boy Joshua graduated from high school. Josh was quite the athlete, playing basketball, running track and being quarterback for his high school football team. He would go on to South Dakota State University as a football player.

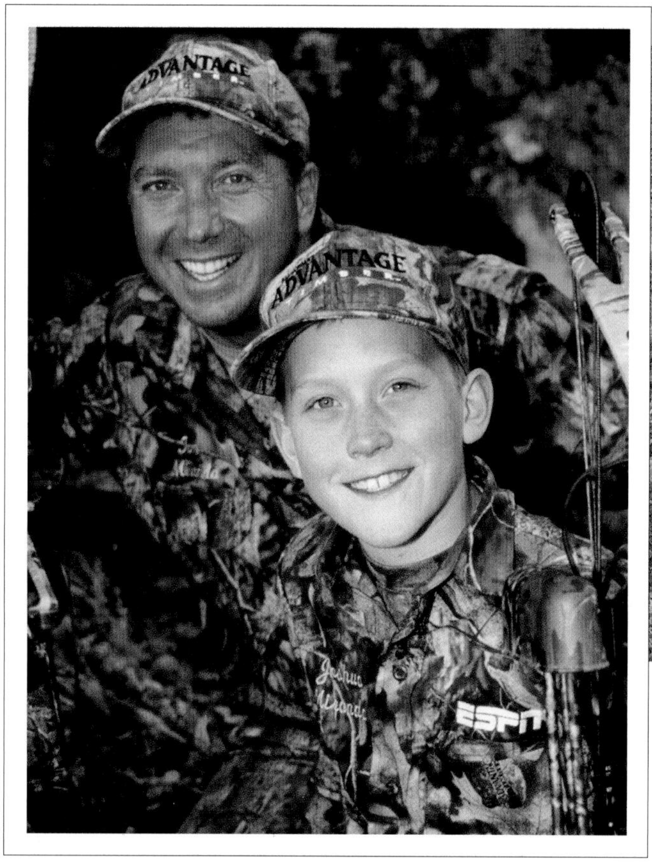

I took my youngest son Josh on several hunts. Here we pose together for a photo in 2001. They sure grow up quickly.

Josh's brother Jeremy had decided to transfer from Nebraska to University of Florida in 2007 and Jennifer transferred to Ringling School of Art & Design in Sarasota that same year so both Jeremy and my daughter Jennifer were going to college in Florida. You can bet with three kids in college, I was glad to have put some money away for their education.

In April 2009 I went to Zimbabwe to try for another leopard. This was my third attempt as I had tried in Zambia in 2005 on my Hippo hunt and Zimbabwe in 2007 during my elephant hunt. Leopard is known as the most difficult of Africa's Big Five. Again on at-

Here's the crew: Guide Chad Lenz and Cameraman Martin Teeter with Miranda and his mountain caribou.

Author's Photos

Miranda poses with one of his three African cape buffalo. The first taken in 1999, one in 2009 and this one taken in 2016.

Tom's Alberta mule deer buck.

Tom Miranda poses with his whopper Columbia Blacktail arrowed in Oregon.

The first two seasons of Mathews *Territories Wild* on DVD.

Cameraman Martin Teeter poses with Miranda and his beautiful woodland caribou taken in Newfoundland.

Author's Photos

tempt number three, I was skunked on leopard. However I did take a cape buffalo.

In early September I was hunting with famed bear guide Jordy McAuley. Bears rut in the spring, so in the fall bears are usually found and hunted near food. It's illegal to bait grizzly in British Columbia (at the time of this book's publication, grizzly hunting is illegal in British Columbia), so we would be glassing timber slashes, meadows and berry patches for a feeding boar. We looked for six days before finding a good bear and I stalked into range with a cameraman behind and arrowed the brute.

October found me again on the road, this time in Newfoundland on the hunt for a woodland caribou. It was a great hunt and for the trapper interested in a caribou hunt, I highly recommend Newfoundland. There is also great black bear and moose hunting on the Viking island. Oh . . . and fantastic codfish and chips with malt vinegar. One of my favorites!

Tom Miranda poses with his first mountain grizzly taken in British Columbia in 2009.

Author's Photos

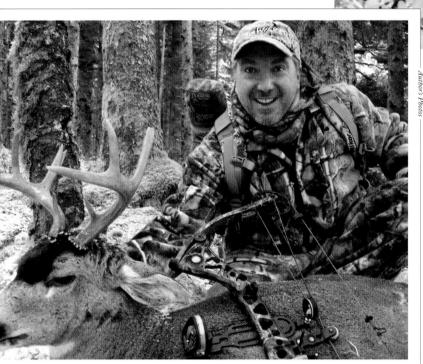

Tom Miranda and his Alaskan Sitka black-tailed deer.

Early December is prime time for hunting the Sitka black-tailed deer. These deer live in the Queen Charlotte Islands of British Columbia and north along Alaska's coastal islands. My hunt was on Afognak Island off the north coast of Kodiak Island. The islands are thickly forested and mountainous. Snowfall pushes the deer out of the high country to the beaches to eat kelp. My hunt was exciting—I took a nice buck. This hunt is one of the most popular hunts seen on my *Adventure Bowhunter* DVD.

NEWTON STERLING

1951–

Newt Sterling Photos

Newt with a Mississippi otter taken in a cable restraint.

Newton Sterling is an authentic outdoorsman. Although Newt lives and traps in New Jersey, much of his trapping is done alone, offshore on barrier Islands and in tidal marshes. One needn't be too far offshore to be totally alone and the sea is actually a wilderness all its own. An avid hunter, trapper and commercial fisherman, Newt does it all with a passion for life that few men will ever have. If a venture pays decent money and is outdoors, Newt is always ready to dig in. He learned early in his life to adapt and roll with what's working, and this flexibility has led him to become a "jack of all trades," making a good living from his broad skill-set.

Newt was born in Falsington, Pennsylvania in 1951. Trapping with his father as a youngster Newt recalls, "In the early 1960s the muskrat money was as fun to spend as the 'rats were fun to catch." When he was 14, Newt's parents bought a motel and moved to Absecon, New Jersey. The inn was situated on Route 30, one of three major roads leading into Atlantic City. Once settled in New Jersey, young Newt quickly learned that trapping was a big deal—everyone trapped muskrats. In fact, Newt recalls that even the old-timers hardly ever caught a raccoon, let alone a fox. Newt caught his fair share of muskrats but also learned to catch clams and soon had a boat. He was too young to drive, and the boat was actually much better. Newt could fish and trap from his boat, and the neighborhood girls liked Newt's boat. He says, *"The girls were a bonus."*

Newt Sterling gives the "thumbs up" for his catch on the South Jersey snare line.

In 1973, 22-year-old Newt Sterling bought his first house in Port Republic, New Jersey. Captain Kenny Wilson, a commercial fisherman, turtle and muskrat trapper, lived nearby. During the summer, Newt would mate on Captain Wilson's charter boat. When the boat wasn't chartered, they trapped snapping turtle in season. During the winter, the team would trap muskrats. Newt says, *"Captain Kenny taught me that there was money to be made if you worked it like a job—not as a sport. And he was right. In 1978 at the start of the fur boom, I bought a new F-150 4x4 pick-up with my fur check."* By this time Newt had learned how to catch raccoons and foxes and expanded his trapline.

Newt Sterling Photo

Newt Sterling "getting it done" in North Carolina.

Self-employed and raising a family, Newt says, *"Times were sometimes rough . . . but we made it."*

In 1984 New Jersey voted to ban the steel "leghold" trap. Newt was essentially out of business when it came to trapping—that is, unless he could learn to use snares. Newt remembers it as a rough transition. *"I bought book after book about snaring. Most were western methods and I just couldn't grasp locations. Where I trapped looked so different. Nothing worked for me. So, I signed up for the Fur Takers Professional Trappers College in 1984 to learn how to snare."* Both the 1984 and '85 trapping seasons were learning years for Newt and his snares. Then, Newt went back to the Trappers College for a second time in 1986. He now had a grasp of snaring and knew what questions to ask. At that 1986 college—BAM! The light went on. Newt's 1986–87 trapping season was special. He was finding trails and setting locations on his line he had walked past before. He was becoming a snare man.

Soon after the 1986 college, Newt became a contractor for the USFWS as a predator control specialist. Newt says, *"That was a big title for just being a trapper. But it was mine!"* Newt was hired to snare red foxes on the barrier islands on the Edwin B. Forsythe Wildlife Refuge. The foxes were killing the endangered piping plovers. *"You had to know your seamanship even to get out there. Lots of shallow water and sandbars. Only experienced bay men could get out there and back at low tide. Plus, there were few safe anchorages. The question was often, Was your boat gonna be high and dry, or sunk when you got back to it? Getting to the fox was more difficult than catch'n the fox. I contracted with the Feds off and on for over 30 years and their contracts always paid well,"* Sterling adds.

Newt married his wife Sally in 1991 and he had her full support to go into the trapping business full speed, which he did. Soon, trappers started asking him for snares, snare parts and snaring lessons. The time had come to form his own snare shop and supply business. Newt Sterling's Snare One trapping business became a reality in 1992 and soon Newt was making and selling more snares than he had time to make.

Newt Sterling's first book, *Master Land Snaring*—First Edition, 1999.

Newt Sterling Photo

Newt Sterling commercial fishing white perch with his teammate.

Sterling authored three books: *Master Land Snaring*—1999, *Master Otter Snaring*—2004, and his newest book released in 2020, *Snaring for Survival*—a treatise on using snares to survive not only the wilds, but for doomsday preparedness. Newt Sterling's Snaring DVD library includes eight titles, *Master Raccoon Snaring*—2000, *Master Mink and Muskrat Snaring*—2002, *Master Beaver Snaring*—2004, *Otterly Simple*—2004, *River'n*—2006, *Turtles by the Ton*—2006, *Cable Restraints*—2007, and *Master Wild Hog Snaring*—2008.

His personal bests on the snare line are pretty amazing and include 22 red foxes snared on one check, 12 raccoons out of 18 snare sets, 5 feral hogs and 2 coyotes from 28 snares on his Texas line. Newt took 10 predators a day for two months in South Jersey back when furs were worth the effort. Sterling also caught 500 pounds of snapping turtles a day for five consecutive days—selling most of the snappers live.

Snaring otters, bobcats and feral hogs are what Newt enjoys best. Of course, bobcats are protected in New Jersey, so Newt's out-of-state trapping gets him his share of the spotted bellies. According to him, *"The otter is a fighter and you need strong cable and lots of swivels to hold them. Feral hogs are by far the most dangerous in a snare. They never give up and charge until the death."*

Newt builds all of his Snare One brand snares himself. Tens of thousands of snares. From 1/32" 1x19 squirrel snares to 1/8" 1x19 large wolf and hog snares. Black bear foot snares, 3/16" 7x19 and 1/4" 7x19. Then the biggest bear foot snare for polar bear and grizzly, 5/16" 7x19. These snares require a five-ton press to make them strong enough. Sterling says he builds every snare as if he was going to use it. *"My end stops won't come off are stronger than the cable itself. I use the world's best cable and have in stock the largest assortment of snaring supplies east of the Mississippi."* Newt's

Newt Sterling Photo

Newt Sterling on the snare line in East Texas doing feral hog control.

Newt Sterling Photo

Skipper Newt Sterling and a dandy day's run on his South Jersey snare line.

master lock is small, made to fit only one size of cable and comes in four sizes: 3/64", 1/16", 5/64", and 3/32". It's also made of non-polished stainless steel. Newt Sterling has his own line of trapping lures which are also in demand as well as his Formula One Instant Trap & Snare Kote. Many top trappers use the coating to rehab dirty traps during the rigors of a long season. All are available at SnareOne.com.

When teaching others, Newt's philosophy on the art of snaring is to keep it simple. There's no need for a packed basket full of gimmicks and tools to set a snare. All one needs is the right size snare, a roll of 14-gauge wire and a pair of slip joint pliers.

Newt credits his success to a "don't quit" attitude and his soulmate of 40-plus years, Sally. *"Without Sally supporting me in the lean times, I couldn't have done it. It takes one hell of a women to be a full-time trapper's wife. She puts up with me gone weeks at a time on the road and the dangers of commercial fishing and trapping offshore. Commercial fishing has picked up lately using Fyke nets from November 1 to April 30 for Atlantic white perch. It can be iffy at times on the water, but I love it. And Sally puts up with it. Oh, how I love her. Thank you, Sally."*

On January 6, 2004 Newt Sterling along with Pennsylvania trapper Bob Jameson, his Labrador retriever Max, and taxidermist John Skagline were headed out to check snares in Sterling's homebuilt garvey bay boat. The team had a canoe lashed on a carrier rack and were headed for the barrier islands. The wind was kicking from the northwest and waves were pushing the boat. Newt felt like it was going to be a rough morning's ride, but this wasn't out of the ordinary for January. Off the west shore of Egg Island, Newt's garvey hit an unusually deep trough followed by a rogue wave which capsized the boat. The water temperature was hovering at 38 degrees. With wet cell phones, hip boots, heavy clothing, wind and waves pounding, the three trappers were in peril. It's a mariner's rule to stay with the boat, yet Newt knew no one would be passing by for a rescue. Hypothermia was certain to set in and all would succumb to the ice water and the Atlantic.

For three hours the group held on, attempting to talk each other through the grim ordeal. Like all stories with a happy ending, Captain Al Kurtz— a duck guide from the area happened by seeing the white canoe at a distance. As Kurtz's curiosity rose, he maneuvered his boat toward the canoe to investigate, discovering the accident and rescuing the trappers. The complete and harrowing tale written by Bob Noonan can be read in the January 2005 issue of *Trapper and Predator Caller* magazine.

Newt Sterling Photo

Newt poses with a nice North Carolina 'cat and mixed bag of beavers, otters and rats.

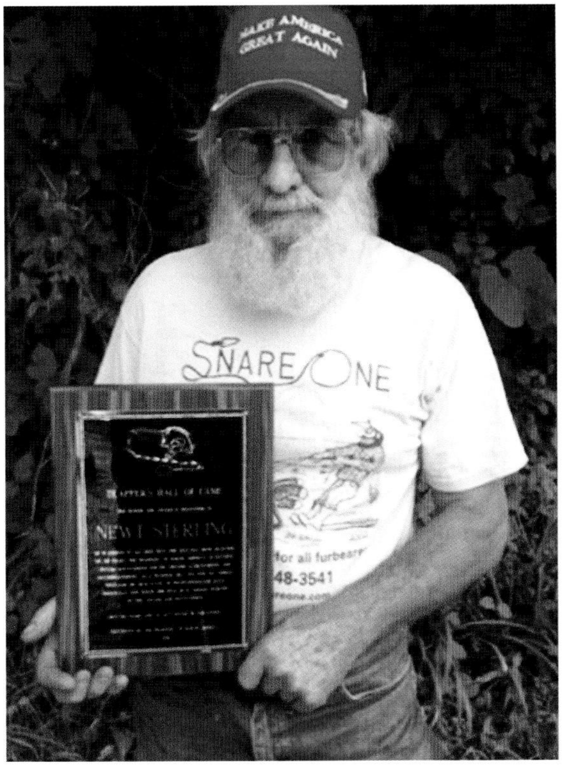

Newt Sterling Photo

Newt Sterling with his prestigious North American Trappers Historical Society Trappers Hall of Fame plaque.

Sterling enjoys his trapping life. His freedom and independence. Sure, he's made mistakes but he owns them and moves on. Like a miner searching for silver and gold, Newt lives for that next nugget—finding a rich fur pocket and making the big catch. When money's flowing all is good. Newt knows the truck will need fixing sooner than later—likely his boat too. Money's always been "easy come, easy go." There's a comfort that goes beyond finances when you're living life on your own terms. Work isn't work when it's a passion. Fishing and trapping is a good life. Sleeping in a wilderness cabin with wood heat and no running water might be considered "roughing it" to some, but to a trapper it's a blessing. On the ocean, the thin hull of a boat is often the difference between dying today or living tomorrow. Risk comes with the job. Except it's not really a job if you live to wake up in the morning and do it all over again. Today, Newt finds himself spending more and more time with his grandson Keith Dow, teaching him the ways of a New Jersey Piney-man, living his outdoor lifestyle in the Pine Barrens and adjacent salt marsh.

Newt Sterling was inducted into the North American Trappers Historical Society Trappers Hall of Fame in 2016 with the likes of Craig O'Gorman and Paul Grimshaw.

"And while I'm thinking of it, for all the young guys thinking they missed the 'hay day,' well I did too. Remember that other things will always open up. When good coyotes are bringing 100 bucks or more, you're a free American—get in your truck and go chase that dream.

Ole' Swamper Swartz told me this a long time ago. I'll never forget it. 'This is it— it ain't no dress rehearsal, there's no second chances in life.'" "I've worked for other people and had a real job. I don't like it. Don't put in 20 years for the boss man. He'll take the best part your youth. Take trapping instructions, go to the FTA College. Keep your mouth shut and listen. Some of us old farts know what we're talking about."

—Newt Sterling In his own words, 2020

North American Trappers
Historical Society Trappers Hall of Fame

2016
*Paul Grimshaw
Craig O'Gorman
Newt Sterling
John Graham
Oscar Cronk
Don Shumaker

2017
Kent & Linda Eanes
Mike Marsyada
Russ Carman
Morris Fenner
Jim Comstock
Ardell Grawe

2018
Wayne Derrick
Keith Gregerson
Bud Jenkins
David Tobey
Rob Erickson
George Wacha
Ken Peck
Slim Pedersen

2019
Jeff Dunnier
Tom Beaudette
Paul Dobbins
Gary Bussen
Gary Jepson

Cornerstone Award:
Tom Parr
Major Boddicker
Tom Krause
*Chuck Spearman

*Denotes Deceased

North American
Trap Collectors Association Hall of Fame

2000
*Richard Gerstell
*Bob Carlson

2001
Tom Parr

2002
*RonMurno

2003
*Willis Brettmann

2004
*Jim Gipe

2005
*Warren "Butch" Rogers
*Chuck Clift

2006
Dennis Helman
*Donald Whitley

2007
No Inductees

2008
Jack Lay
*Orville Lawrence

2009
No Inductees

2010
Rex E. Marsh
David Drummond

2011
*Jane Parr

2012
Bob White

2013
*Bud Lindsay
Jim Stewart

2014
Dennis & Dianne Fuse'

2015
*Ed Myers
Ed Knobloch

2016
Tony Diebold
Henry Struchtemeyer

2017
Sam & Margaret Delavan

2018
Terry "Swamper" Swartz
*John Barbee

2019
Dick Dennison

*Denotes Deceased

Author's Photos

I visited my Michigamme River wilderness cabin in July 2018 to chat with owner Corry Dolbeer and reminisce the old days. He has done a fantastic job of caring for my trappers homestead over the last 36 years. Thank You Corry.

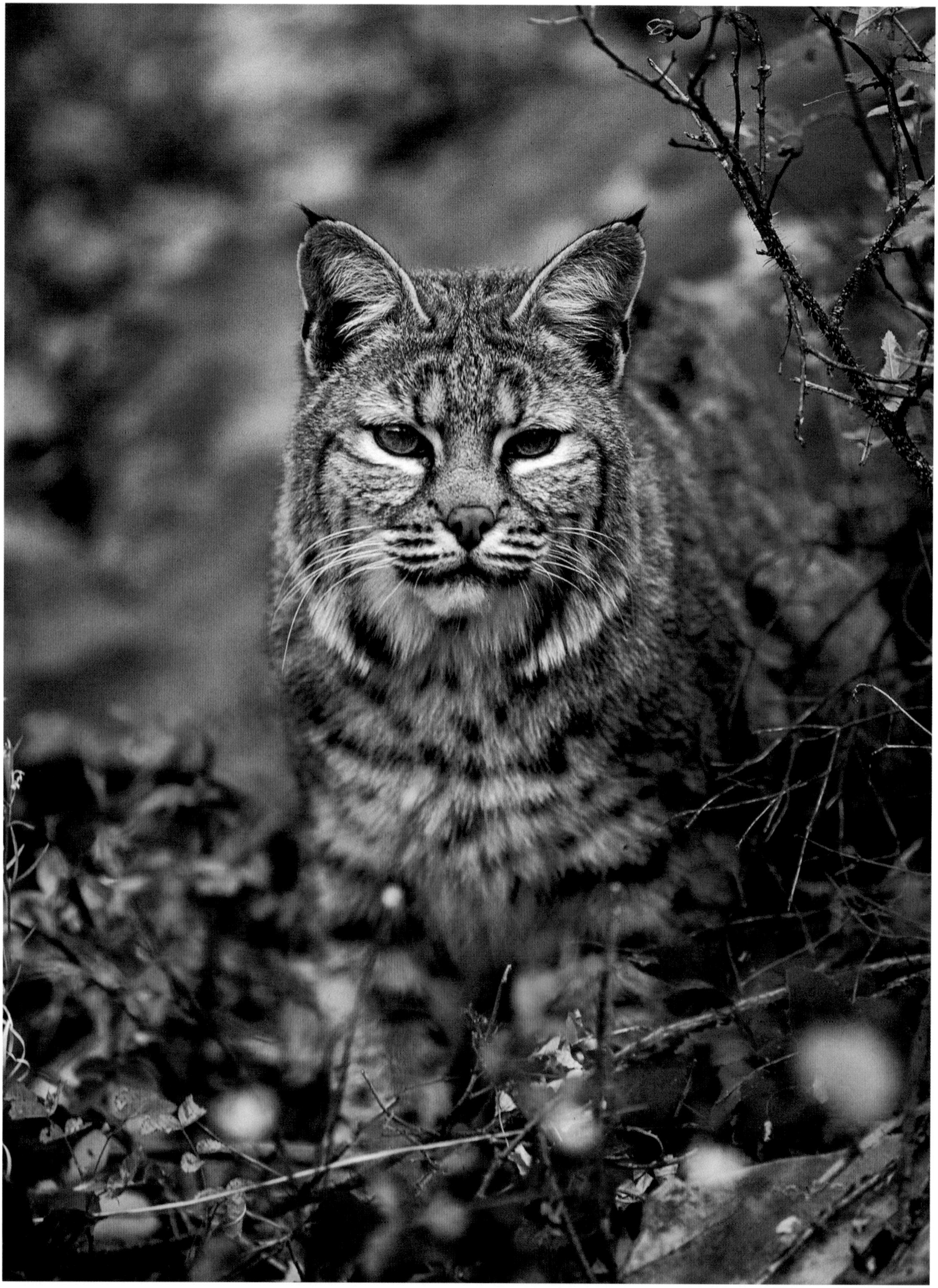

CHAPTER 14

CATMEN

If a 'cat trapper was an artist in a rock band, he would be the lead guitarist. All predator trappers can catch bobcats, yet the top cat trappers have that little something extra that allows them to pick the ideal riff, improvise a creative chorus and have the patience to put it all together. The best cat trappers pick "spot-on" locations, make sets that catch on the "first visit," and have the confidence to wait out a finicky tom.

Bobcats are fairly plentiful, yet they rarely overpopulate an area. Most importantly, bobcats are particular about the areas in which they inhabit. Bobcat habitat is very diverse from southern swamps, to western rimrock and northern beaver dams. Like a fox trapper who can stand on a farm trail and point out the best locations to catch a sly reynard, the best 'cat trappers are magicians at locating physical bobcat sign and planting traps at the feet of the finicky felines.

Some cat trappers own house cats and save the dirty cat litter for trap coverings. Some make their own scent from glands, bladders and intestines of the 'cats they catch. Still others utilize electronic squeaker units at or near sets. Top catmen are as unique in their methods as they are successful—thus the old saying, "There's more than one way to skin a cat."

< Len Rue Jr. Photo

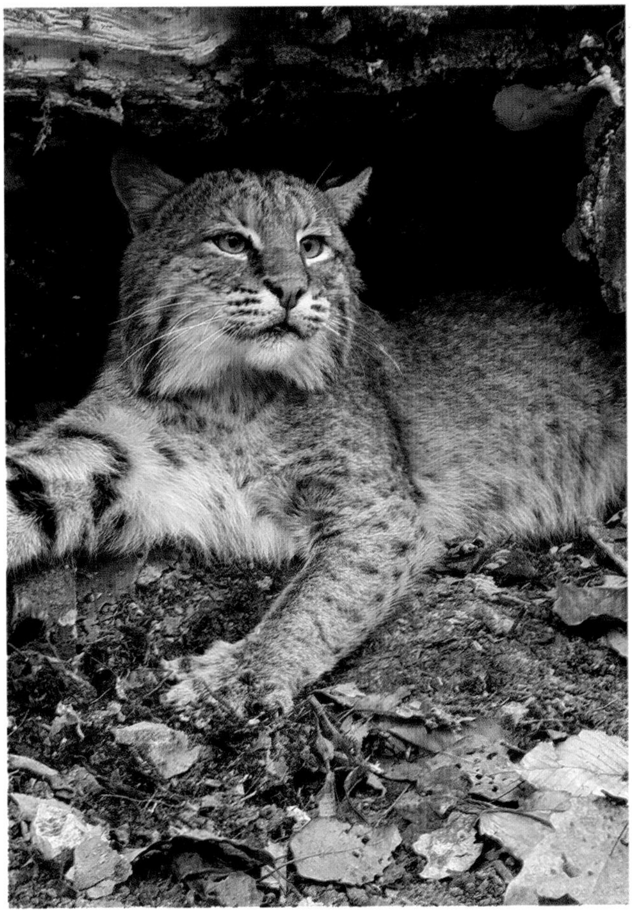

Greg Sulfridge Photo

FINDING THE SPOTS

Bobcats like rough terrain, yet "rough terrain" means different things in different parts of the country. Rough terrain to a Maine trapper may be cedar bogs and marshy swamps. In northern Michigan, it could be beaver flowages or edges of cut timber sections. To a bobcat trapper in Georgia, perhaps pine plantations, swamps and beaver dams. In mountainous sections of the Blue Ridge, Black Hills or Rockies, rough country is rocky outcrops or logging trails leading back to nowhere. Bobcats in badlands country hunt dry washes and rocky mesas. A southwestern trapper looks for rimrock and dry washes winding from rock-strewn mountains into the flat desert.

Top 'catmen are always looking for prey species habitat. Areas where rabbits and mice are abundant, historic bird roosts and reliable water sources in dry areas are good bets to find bobcats. Bobcats are attracted to areas that have spotty, dense ground cover as it allows prey species some security yet gives the 'cats room to sneak and stalk. A bobcat's home territory may run 10 or 12 sections but there may be two sections of rock that are frequented nearly nightly and then foray trips off this rock into different sections of the territory may happen in a more random timetable.

Author's Photo

Each arrow shows a trail with bobcat tracks. These are the terrace trails.

Author's Photo

More terrace trails. Bobcat tracks on both. In these terrace type sets lean a dead tree branch with some flagging attached and hook the trap grapple to it. This way the sets can be checked with binoculars. If the tree branch is knocked over the trap has been drug off.

UNIQUE SPOTS

Land structure dictates how animals will traverse through different areas. Bowhunters who look to ambush game animals are always looking for an advantage—often the terrain will supply it. Looking at areas in three dimensions is always advantageous because animals often use elevation to their advantage. Elevation allows animals with sharp eyes to spot opportunity or danger at a distance. Low areas allow animals to travel while being hidden by terrain. These terrain types give bowhunters the same advantages. However, elevation creates additional benefits. The dynamics of the sun heating the earth creates wind currents. In areas of elevation, thermals become columns of air that animals with sharp noses can rely upon. Where animals use these thermals to be on the right side of the wind to smell danger, hunters use them to keep from being detected.

Here's an example. Elk often bed on south-facing mountainside during the day. A herd bull and his cows can find security in a small patch of quaking aspen lining a bench. The elk will use the elevation to put them above the meadow and the thermals to stay safe. Before sunup, cool air is falling down the mountain. Elk use these "falling thermals" to smell for danger as they climb to their beds in the morning. Once the sun is up and heating the valley, the thermals switch and draft up the mountain allowing the elk to smell any predator which would be below them. Smart bowhunters use their senses, the lay of the land and the wind direction to get on the right side of elk.

Here's another example. A whitetail buck is cruising for does during the rut. The buck knows there is a bedding thicket within a 20-acre woodlot. This buck doesn't need to explore the entire woodlot to find the

Author's Photo

There is a set in the foreground (no arrow) and one in the draw. arrow on the bank denotes squeaker location.

estrus doe. All he needs to do is cruise the downwind side of the woodlot, as his sense of smell is so refined, he will be able to smell any estrus doe in the woodlot. Smart bowhunters often set up downwind of historic doe bedding areas to catch trolling bucks.

Often trails will run at different levels along the sides of a hill or mountain. I call it the terrace effect. These terrace trails are travel ways around the circumference of the hill or mountain. Big game use these terrace trails and bobcats do too. Set the trail in the valley and then climb up to the terrace trails to also set high. A trapper may walk up 50 steps and there will be a trail. Walk another 50 steps and there will be another trail. These terrace trails are often overlooked but are the key to thinking about set locations in three dimensions.

Bobcat trappers also look low for set locations—dry culverts are excellent places to catch 'cats. Just like a culvert necks a stream down to force mink into a narrow travel way, bobcats are also susceptible in dry culverts. Because of the bobcat's value, most trappers tend to stay away from culverts which are susceptible to trap and fur theft, yet in some areas or behind the locked gates of large ranches, these locations can be killer.

GETTING SOME ATTENTION

Understanding how animals survive gives bowhunters an edge. The best bobcat trappers also think with this "predator" mentality. I've sat for hours (on some hunts for days), with a pair of binoculars watching an area for a glimpse of movement. I know that a grizzly will come down the creek somewhere below me and I just need to be patient. Sometimes when glassing, I may notice something out of place or spot some slight movement, but I don't see a bear. So, I'll watch this area closer. Eventually it may be a branch swaying in the wind, or the reflection of the sun on a shiny branch, or a bird roosting and flapping a wing from time to time. The point is that I'm hunting, and the goal is to see the animal before it sees me. Bobcats hunt the same way. They're patient and look for movement. Bobcats move slowly, deliberately and spend lots of time crouched and looking for opportunity. This is why 'cat trappers use flagging.

Ray Milligan Photo

Ray Milligan poses with a mixed bag on the 'cat line including 5 spotted bellies in a days run over the traps.

Imagine a bobcat lying on a bolder overlooking a valley and seeing the sun's reflection on a CD disc

Randy Birdsong Photo

twisting in the breeze above your bobcat set. The reflection disappears, then flashes again. Soon curiosity for the object has the bobcat up and slowly moving to inspect the anomaly. This same bobcat may be working up a dry wash and spot the movement of another well-placed flag. Curious, the 'cat crouches and begins to close the distance. Along the edge of the wash is an area of boulders and a trail guarded with traps. Visual appeal is very important in specific location. Visible rock outcrops attract 'cats. Dead falls lying over in the woods near a bobcat's line of travel are excellent set locations. Flagging is always effective in 'cat trapping because 'cats hunt on sight and have a curious nature. Domestic goose, duck or chicken feathers if legal, will really spruce up a bobcat set. As on any visual flagging, look for contrast. Trappers who learn to select locations where 'cats are frequenting will always improve the set with the use of flagging that can be seen at a distance.

SELLING THE ILLUSION

When digital technology allowed sound to be recorded onto small chips, 'cat trappers started making and using squeaker units. The original squeaker units only used an electronic chirp. But as tech improved, many sounds were digitized, and squeaker units today include mice, bird and rabbit distress sounds. Adding realistic distress cries in an area where visual flagging and big hole sets are located, along with attractive odors allows a third dimension of emitting the sounds of wounded prey.

Most trappers use the units up and away from traps with opinions on how far to place the squeakers away from sets varying from a few feet to 50 yards. 'Cat trappers forced to use live traps often bury the unit under the cage trap's pan with the sound emitting up and out at low volume. Like any calling device, it's worthless if the animal doesn't hear it, so vol-

Tom Whiting has manufactured quality squeakers for years and his units have called many bobcats to the traps.

ume is important. Typically, the closer the unit is set to the traps, the lower the volume setting.

Utah trapper Tom Whiting has been making bobcat and mountain lion squeaker units for game departments and ADC trappers for years. Tom builds both a standard and a custom unit with several authentic distress cries available as well as volume control.

SETS A BLIND BOBCAT CAN FIND

The most widely used predator set is the dirt-hole set. And it's the most widely used bobcat set, all areas of the country considered. What makes the dirt-hole set attractive to 'cats is the curiosity about what is in the hole. The deeper the hole and larger its size, the more curiosity it holds. The object is to fence the cat down tight while making the attractor as big as possible. Bobcat dirt-holes should be four inches diameter minimum and deep enough or shaped in such a way that the 'cat cannot see the bottom. One option is to dig the hole at more of a right angle. This way the 'cat cannot see into the hole from a distance which will cause him to work in closer. Note that when using a large attractor, it can be difficult to naturally fence it down, so in some instances it may be wise to use two traps to cover the kill area.

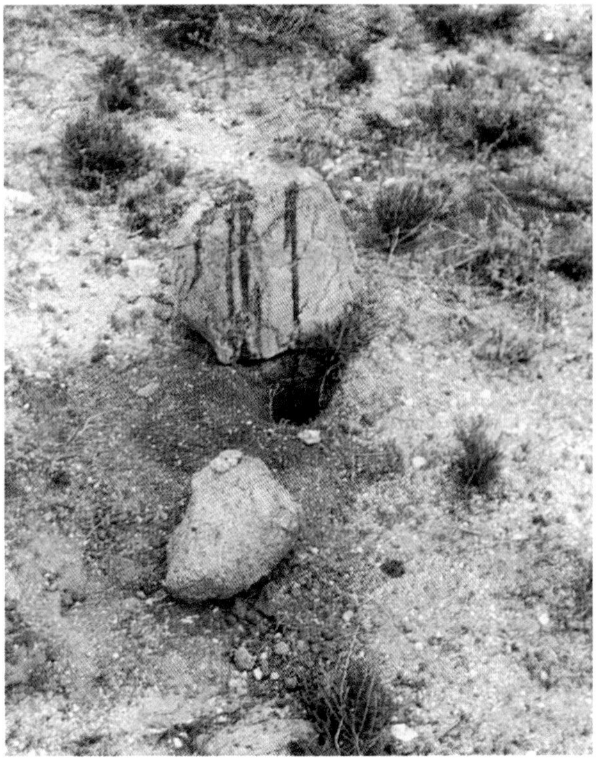

Miranda bobcat dirt hole with near vertical bait hole and walk — thru concept.

Miranda dirt- hole with jaw guard and white stone guides.

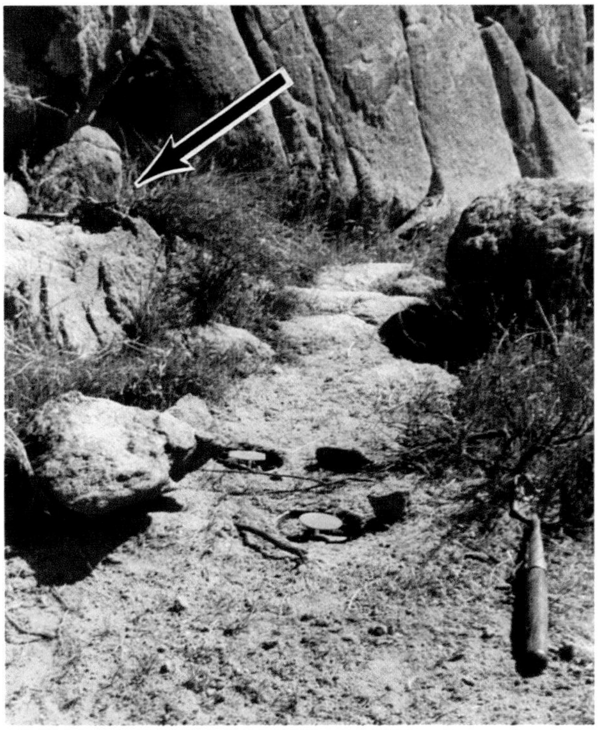

Miranda two trap trail set before covering. Arrow denotes squeaker location.

Some trappers collect bobcat droppings to use at sets and some cage 'cats for fresh urine. As mentioned previously, trappers with pet domestic cats often bag used litter box material to place at sets and this ruse will catch bobcats. Today with so many feral cats in the wild population, bobcats often seek out these domestic wanderers to kill them. Strong cat litter near a set—combined with a good gland lure and fresh urine is often better than any bait.

Here's my standard "walk — through" set made in a dry wash. A little white sand or dirty domestic cat litter over the pan can be a variant to this killer set when used for bobcats. 2 different lures will be used at arrows and bobcat urine on the 2 jaw guarding rocks.

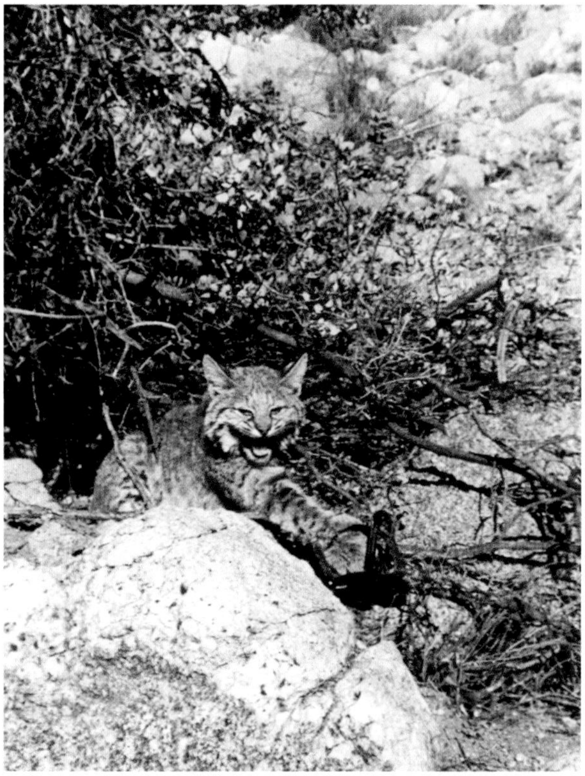

Arizona bobcat nailed in a dirt- hole set.

Grey fox taken in a walk thru set made at the arrow. The area isn't disturbed as the trap was on a 5 foot chain with a grapple.

Another popular bobcat set is the exposed trap trail set, which is an exposed trap set on a trail. This set was a well-kept secret for years, designed by top 'cat trappers to keep non-target animals—specifically coyotes—out of the traps. In the desert southwest, coyotes are plentiful and not anywhere near the value of a bobcat. Trappers leave the trap exposed and fence down the trail to make the pan as inviting as possible for a bobcat, yet obvious enough to keep any self-respecting coyote from stepping in such a place. 'Cat trappers prefer large jaw spreads and offset or padded jaw traps and typically use enlarged pans. Bobcats have soft paws and although a large catch area and lightning fast trap is desirable, it also must be somewhat gentle on the paw, holding and not cutting skin or breaking bone. There are several ways to enlarge pans including tac-welding a larger square or round sheet metal extension. Some temporarily attach a heavy wire mesh to the standard pan.

One trick to use in an exposed trap trail set is to use stark white "play" sand on the enlarged pan of the trap. At night when the 'cat is hunting up the trail, everything is dark and then all of a sudden there's a

Mark June stands with his personal best 105 spotted bellies taken on his combined Nebraska and Texas bobcat lines.

white "bulls-eye" laying on the trail—more often than not they will just have to step on it. Don't laugh—it works! Usually when you catch 'cats in an exposed trap trail set, you have a nice pad catch because they will put their foot right on that pan and are caught just perfectly. If you've ever seen trappers come in with four or five 'cats in a day's run (and no coyotes) and you really want to know how they can catch numbers of 'cats without picking up non-targets, the exposed trap trail set is how they do it.

CAT IN A BOX

Some states in the west have outlawed steel traps and thus trappers have learned to be creative with live traps. Live traps are bulky to handle and require more work to conceal but will take bobcats consistently when set properly. Most trappers who use live traps as their main method of catching bobcats set out the traps and build the sets in advance of the season, often pre-baiting the cages and wiring the doors open so the traps will not hold 'cats. It's essential to cover the bottom wire with dirt to keep a 'cat's soft paws from walking on the wire as this will cause suspicion and often refusal. When the season opens, baits are refreshed, lured and the traps readied.

Getting most any animal to commit to the tight quarters of a live trap is an art and even more of an art for shy animals like foxes, coyotes and bobcats. Larger cages can help take away the claustrophobia yet are bulkier and even more expensive. Cages should be wide enough so a bobcat feels like he can turn around easily. Visual decoys can be placed inside traps as well. Fake fur with a cottontail can look like a rabbit and help entice a cat to pounce into a cage. Some trappers use double door traps to allow a tunnel effect and this can help. Old timers often used live bait at 'cat sets like caged chickens or pigeons. These noisy and smelly birds were often placed about four feet off the ground on a fashioned log table with traps placed un-

Nick Burri Photo

der. Squeaker units are used today by some with fantastic results.

Cubbies are another method commonly used to take 'cats in areas where snowfall is heavy or body gripper traps can be used on dry land. Typically used for lynx in Northern Canada and Alaska, cubbies when made correctly, are effective anywhere bobcats travel. A cubby is a constructed "house" to secure the bait with a trap guarding the entrance. In big snow country, the best cubbies have long porches on them to keep snow off the trap area. Generally, the cubbies are built along known bobcat travel areas and are constructed with the eye appeal of a cave or dark deadfall—a place where prey could hide or where the 'cat might find shelter. Cubbies are enticing to bobcats and their construction keeps the bait out of the weather as well as away from the watchful eyes of birds of prey. Cubbies are very effective sets and when built in good crossing locations and in good bobcat country, can take several bobcats per location.

The best bait for cubbies is usually beaver meat. Some trappers will hang half of a carcass in a tree 20 feet or so away to attract birds into the area and use the remaining half in the cubby. Flags should also be used at or near the cubby to catch the eye of any 'cat sifting through the area. Cubbies built pre-season will be frequented by 'cats. To make these sets more effective, rub some good catnip oil on the cubby front and add 'cat lure inside. These prebaits will make for a sure fire set when traps are put in.

Brian Fish Photo

Surprise coyote catch in a bobcat cage set by Arizona Trapper Brian Fish.

Building cubbies is a lot of work, which is their major drawback. Some trappers feel that in the time it takes to build a cubby, they'd be better off to punch in 3–4 quick sets and move on, maybe looking in anoth-

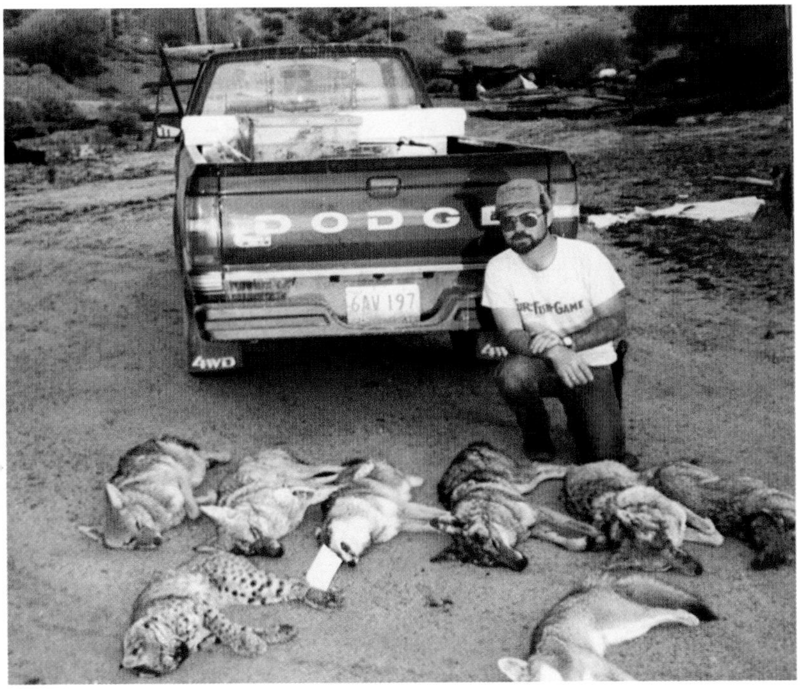

Jerry Herbst Photo

My longtime friend Jerry Herbst poses with a days run over his Wickenburg, Arizona trapline.

When Keith Gregerson was an instructor at the FTA Trappers College in the early 1980s, he showed the students a portable snare cubby he would make using a 4-foot section of woven sheep wire. Gregerson would pre-make these with a snare attached and stack them in his pick-up bed. On site, Keith would take a section of wire fence and bend it in the shape of a Quonset, cover it with grass and sticks and hang his snare on the end, guarding the entrance. The cubby looked like a tunnel in the grass. Of course, lure and bait were used inside and Keith touted it as an all-weather set he had much success within Montana.

er canyon or another place for more bobcat sign and spreading out the line even farther. This is a good argument and one that can't be disputed.

SNARING SPOTS

Catching bobcats in snares requires some finesse. Where coyotes and foxes are focused down the trail and often push through a set, the bobcat tends to walk with a more calculated step and will often refuse a snare. Wiremen use a lighter cable on 'cats and tend to use smaller loops setting 8–10 inches off the ground with a 6-to-8-inch loop. Some catmen use a larger loop of 12 inches and 12 inches off the ground. Typically, these larger loops are set on trails where 'cats must maneuver over a short obstacle like a 4-inch log lying over the trail in a tight area. These sets will also allow raccoons to pass under which is desirable in areas where coon and 'cats coexist.

Craig O'Gorman Photo

Craig O'Gorman caught this string of Wyoming bobcats in the late 1980's during a high rabbit population cycle.

LARRY SLIM PEDERSEN

1944–

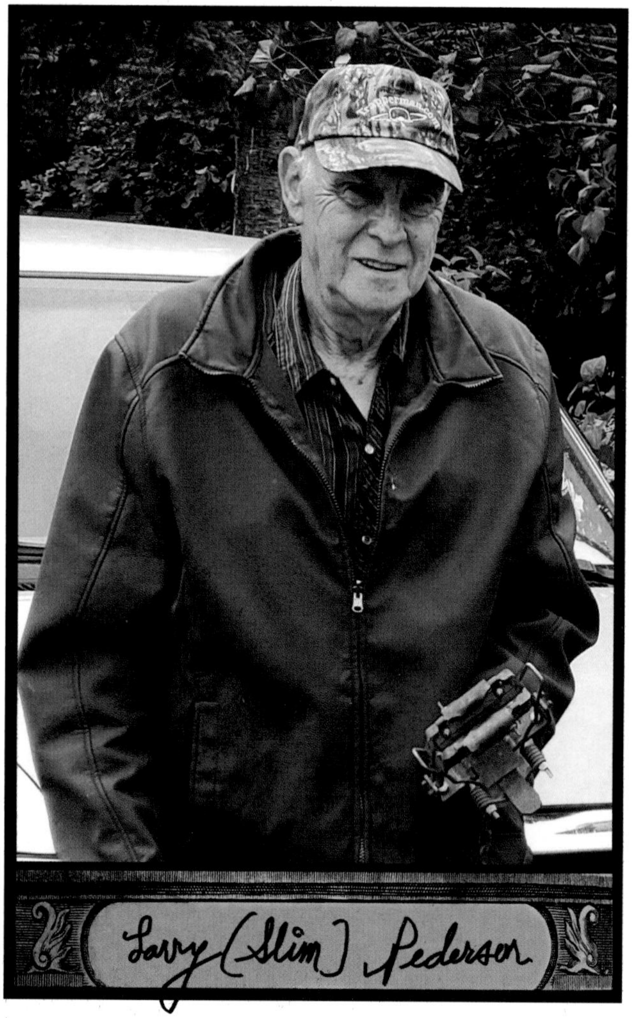

If you're known as one of the best trappers of all time, it would figure that you would live in a town named after a famous mountain man. Larry "Slim" Pedersen is and does. Pedersen's accomplishments as a trapper are revered by America's top predator men. And living in Bridger, Montana suits 'ole Slim right down to his druthers. A tall, lanky man, Larry was often referred to as Slim—and his nickname has stuck with him.

Growing up in Absarokee, Montana Slim was raised by his grandmother. The Rosebud River flows to Absarokee where it branches into the Stillwater River which runs into the Yellowstone River. Absarokee is in the heart of Crow lands and the native meaning of Absarokee is thought to be, "our people." However, in the Crow language it's interpreted as "large-beaked bird children." The culture of our American west is fascinating if one takes the time to learn it. Eastern Montana was a different place 100 years ago and the events that settled the west can be spun by historians and politicians alike, yet the land was untamed, wild and considered God's country by those who lived there. In all respects, it still is.

Slim Pedersen add's another dawg to his pickup during the trapping "hey day."

Slim's grandmother lived on the outskirts of town. Saddled to a wheelchair, Grandma Steffans kept Slim busy when he wasn't attending school. Slim recalls his first time setting a trap. "A skunk had gotten into Grandma's chicken house and she had me fetch an old trap to catch the pole-cat. It was a 'chore needing done' for Grandma, but for me it was a brand-new adventure." Slim caught the skunk a few days later and when walking home from school, Slim was asked if he had a run into a skunk. When Slim answered yes, the man—questioning Slim's smelly predicament—offered to buy the striper and any more that Slim could catch.

Soon skunk trapping turned to other critters. In the mid-1950s, fur paid decent money and few places in North America have better quality fur than the Yellowstone basin. After high school Slim held several jobs and like many trappers, once the first frost came in the fall, thoughts turned to trapping.

Slim eventually ended up in Billings Montana, where he married and started a family. Needing a steady income, he took on a position as a salesman, selling Kenworth semi-trucks. Interstate 90 ran through Billings and this area of eastern Montana is a major trucking route to the West Coast. Slim quickly rose within the ranks of the dealer sales staff. He was young and outgoing. His voice was one that the truckers listened to and trusted. Maybe it was his Montana drawl. Selling the big trucks was a good job and Slim settled into it for a few years.

After a long day at work Slim came home to find his wife upset and son asleep on the couch. Slim had been so involved in work that he'd totally forgotten his son's birthday. With his wife upset and a load of guilt on his shoulders, Slim was disappointed in himself. "*I'm not much for this city life,*" he thought. Two weeks later Slim took off his tie and said, "I'm going trapping." Quitting his sales job, he moved the family—lock, stock, and barrel—to Jordan, Montana.

Slim opened up a tire shop in the small town of Jordan to have a steady income and went to work trapping when he could. The day-to-day feel of Jordan, was a slower pace than Billings and offered opportunities for trapping. As ranchers visited the tire shop, the conversation often turned to ranching and trapping. Slim started helping ranchers with coyote trouble and began building his reputation as a trapper who could catch coyotes. As word spread, Slim was asked more and more to help the sheep and cattlemen of Garfield county. Eventually his trapping expertise would pay off.

Slim took his first real trapping job in 1966 as the federal trapper for Garfield County, Montana. It was a summer job and he enjoyed it. Slim quickly got into the federal trapper mentality. His relationship with ranchers was caring and down-to-earth. He was a damn good trapper so most predation was put to a halt when Slim got in the field and got his traps set. Public relations is a big part of animal damage control. And Slim was as good at PR as he was a trapper. It's a winning combination when you're a federal trapper.

In Slim's mind the top trapper in the area was Frank Morgan who lived in Jordan and worked for Garfield County. George Good was another respected trapper who lived close by in Richie, Montana, and worked McComb County. Also, a young Iowa trapper had moved to Montana and was living with George Good for a while. This is where Slim met Craig O'Gorman. Later on, Craig would start his own predator control business in Powder River County. Slim Pedersen would get to know all these men well and they would get to know him. Through conversations, chats, lunches and a few excursions over many years, a tremendous amount of information was exchanged between these four trappers. As fate would have it, all of these men would eventually become some of the best trappers and predator control men on the planet.

Slim Pedersen in camping mode as he "State hops" south to the desert for an extended predator season.

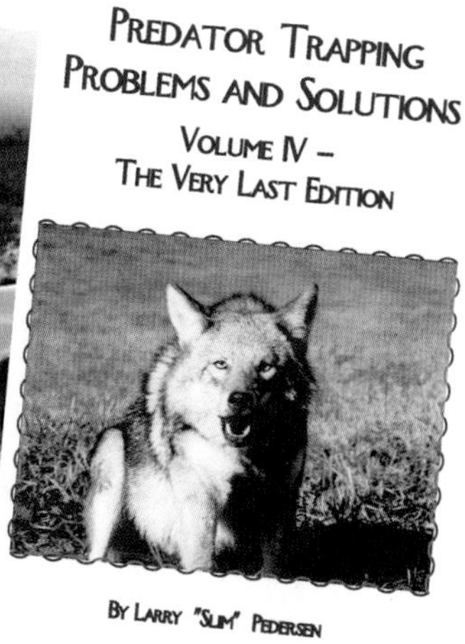

The 4th edition of Slim Pedersen's *Predator Trapping Problems and Solutions* — 2007 is an excellent book… as is his Complete Bobcat Methods — 1986.

Slim Pedersen's Garfield County trapline lies on the southern edge of the Missouri River which in 1940 was flood controlled by the U.S. Army Corps of Engineers with Fort Peck Dam. The massive lake that ensued, created opportunities for crop irrigation and increased the potential for ranchers to operate livestock. Garfield

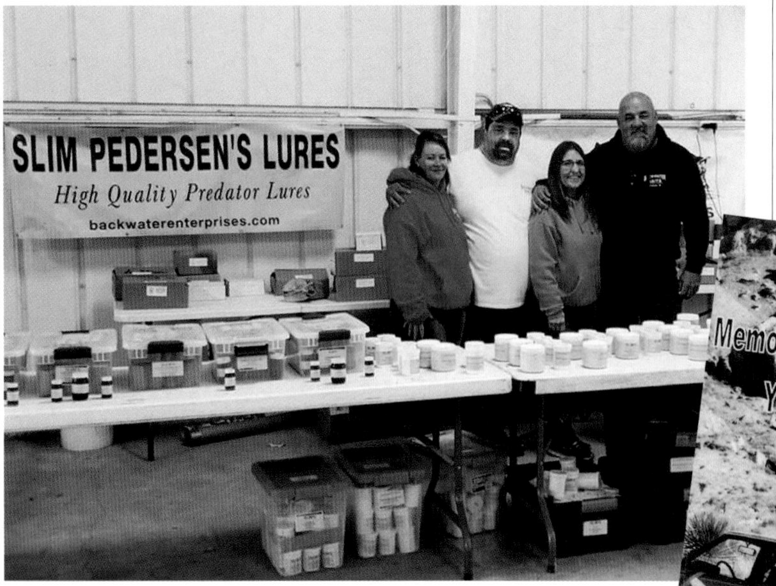

Slim Pedersen Photo

Slim Pedersen's lures are now owned and distributed by Iowa trapper Bruce Rhoades of Backwater Lures and Baits. Slim tells me his best sellers are GH3 and Kitty Curiosity.

County is located in the northeast agricultural section of Montana, one of the top sheep-producing regions in the state. This is the area where Slim Pedersen cut his teeth on predator trapping.

The job of a predator control trapper is different than a fur trapper in many ways. First and foremost, control trappers—government or private—serve the farming and ranching community as kind of a "Sheep Sheriff." Livestock depredation is a problem in the west, particularly in areas where ewes lamb in the pasture. Animals are opportunists and although the predation may be caused by a coyote, it also could be lion, bear or even a fox. Birthing in the pasture with three or four foxes nipping at the mothers' heels may not kill the ewe, but the stress of it and the easy pickings of the afterbirth and sometimes biting at the newborn lamb causes death. And dead lambs are bad business for sheep ranchers. Lions and bears also attack birthing cows and even a pair of coyotes can cause havoc on a ranch once the female has pups to feed and has figured out that warm meat is easy pickings. Predators educate quickly and thus most ranchers who attempt to handle the issue themselves give up after the dawgs are educated. Federal control trappers also have more measures at their disposal than the fur trapper, such as M-44 sodium cyanide "coyote getters." Also snares, steel traps, denning cartridges and predator calling. In some instances, aerial hunting is used as well. County control trappers can use some of these methods but not all of them.

Predator calling is a popular tool often used in animal damage control. It's awesome when it works as the problem is solved quickly rather than scouting, setting and tending traps. Top western trappers get good at calling and some have innovated the techniques used to help with the success rate. Top predator callers like the late Bill Austin and Glen Sterling along with Odon Corr, Craig O'Gorman and of course Slim Pedersen, utilize locator sirens, mouth calls and dogs to give them the edge. A loud siren will often trigger coyotes to howl. This allows the hunter to locate animals. Using live dogs to decoy or troll coyotes, the hunter will move into a closer position, hide, then use the predator call sounds of a wounded rabbit to entice the coyote into shooting distance. When a coyote hears the call, it often approaches—seeing the dogs offers live decoys to entice the coyote further. Once the dogs see the coyote, they run to it and agitate it to a point where aggressive coyotes will chase the dog, inevitably closing the distance to the caller. As for the best breed of dog to use in coyote hunting, typically cur breeds like the mountain cur or black-mouth cur and crosses of same are used, but each hunter has his own preference including Airedales and Lurchers.

It was during the early 1970s when Slim was operating full time that his trapping was hitting on all cylinders. Combining effective predator calling with surgical trapping of problem animals gave Slim Pedersen the reputation of a top predator man. It was during these years that Slim and began making the trapping

Slim Pedersen Photo

Jordan Montana's Slim Pedersen poses with a nice catch of bobcats.

lures that would bear his name. He had ample opportunities to test his lures in all temperatures and weather conditions. When food for animals is plentiful or scarce, when breeding is important and when it's ignored. This is why many of the top lure formulas come from trappers who are in the field 24-7-365.

When fall came around Slim would switch gears to fur trapping. Often, he would travel out of state to trap first either in North Dakota or Wyoming, and back to Montana for the main season. When the snow got deep and the prices were good, Slim would head south to Arizona, New Mexico or Texas. From the mid-1970s through the mid-1980s bobcats were a top commodity and Slim concentrated on them especially in Montana and down south.

Slim Pedersen's go-to trap sets include the standard dirt-hole and flat set. Like many "old-school" long-liners, Slim relies heavily on his locations as well as the natural appearance and small nuances of his set to steer the predator over the trap. Slim says,

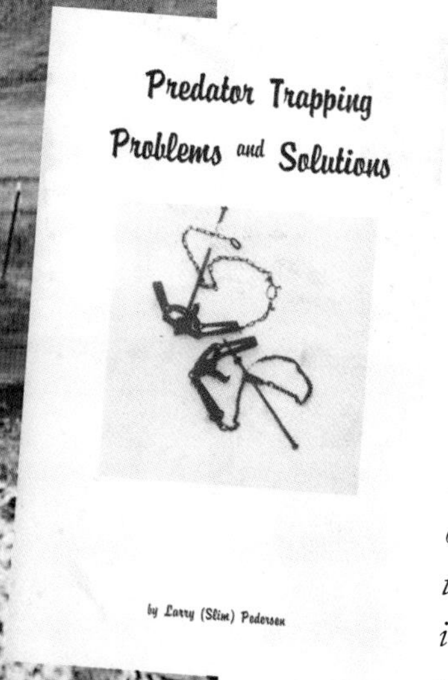

Hard to find First Edition of Slim Pedersen's first book *Predator Trapping Problems and Solutions* — 1976.

"As far as what I do differently than maybe other trappers do at these type sets, is pay attention to small details, such as eliminating the visual 'line' around the sets, or any other reason for animals to temporarily stall before approaching the set. I could write volumes on the important small details such as some sort of eye attraction to stimulate curiosity, and trap placements in relation to these curiosity items."

And Pedersen has written volumes. His first book titled, *Predator Trapping Problems & Solutions 1*—1976, is a classic and difficult to find in its first edition. Other books include *Practical Snare Methods*—1977, *Improved Bobcat Trapping*—1978, *Predator Trapping Problems & Solutions 2*—1978, *Efficient New Snare Methods*—1981, *Predator Trapping Problems & Solutions 3*—1985, *Complete Bobcat Trapping—1986, Life of Coyotes and Its Survival in the Wild—2001, Next Generation Life of Coyotes*—2003, *Predator Trapping Problems & Solutions 4*—2007, *An Old Trappers Lifetime in the Outdoors*—2008, *A Life Cycle of Predators*—2012, and *Looking Back Memories from Trapping Years Gone By*—2019.

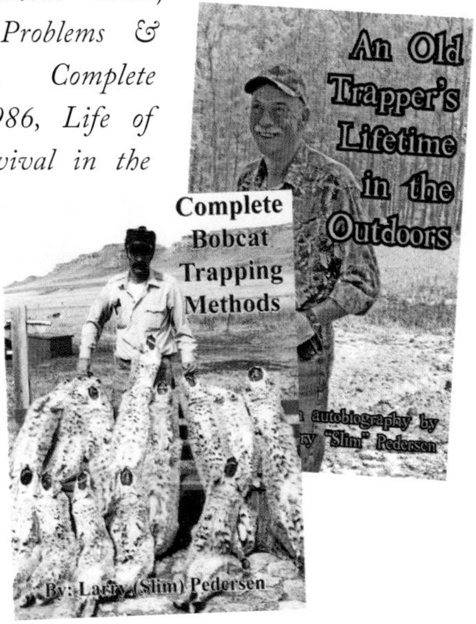

Although all these books are interesting reading, I highly recommend Slim's *Predator Trapping Problems & Solutions* books as well as his *Complete Bobcat Trapping Methods.*

Slim's DVDs are also very instructional. They include *Predator Trapping Problems & Solutions*—1994, *Productive Snaring Techniques*—2002, *Complete Bobcat Trapping*—2003, and *Predator Trapping Problems & Solutions Advanced*—2004.

Slim Pedersen has also been an innovator in the art of snaring, popularizing the use of snares with long tails. *"I never use less than five feet of cable for my snares. More of them are probably eight feet in length and a few are ten or twelve feet in length. I use longer snares for several reasons, not the least of which is that often the extra length is needed to reach something to fasten the snare solid from where it is actually set. At other times, I may use a stake to fasten the snare into the ground when nothing heavy enough to fasten off is close. The longer snares give the animal room to struggle, as well as get entangled into brush as well as tall heavy grass. The longer snares give the animals additional vegetation to chew upon, and not concentrate all their chewing efforts on the snare cable. Also, the additional length gives them a chance to hit the end of the snare harder, making the lock fasten tighter."*

Pedersen's book, *Practical Snare Methods* permanently changed the snaring industry. Before the book came out, trappers could only purchase short snares and had to attach them with wire. Slim's idea of longer snares was the biggest reason he won the Pioneer Award that year—for the longer snares and the famous Pedersen Snare Knot.

Craig O'Gorman praises Slim Pedersen for his trapping ability and mega seasons. Slim has not only had fantastic catches of coyotes and foxes but took over 200 bobcats in a season during the fur boom. A tremendous accomplishment! Slim was known to use miniature electronic "squeaker" units developed by Ed Courtney as part of his 'cat trapping bag of tricks. Pedersen initially tested Courtney's squeaker units and the two became friends. Texas Ed Courtney was known to use a lot of cotton ball flagging on his 'cat-line and make his sets under mesquite trees that had so many cotton balls in them Slim called them Texas cotton trees. Slim doesn't use cotton as Montana is too wet and the moisture renders the cotton ineffective. Also, the cat flagging Slim uses in Montana is darker to contrast against the snow.

Slim Pedersen was awarded the National Trappers Association Pioneer Award in 2003, inducted into the National Trappers Association Trappers Hall of Fame in 2006, and the North American Trappers Historical Society Trappers Hall of Fame in 2015. In 2019 Slim was honored with the National Trappers Association Lifetime Achievement Award. These four awards make Slim one of the most decorated, living professional trappers honored by his peers. I'd say old Jim Bridger is looking down with a nod and a smile at the predator trapping legend who is Larry "Slim" Pedersen of Bridger, Montana.

Slim Pedersen Photo

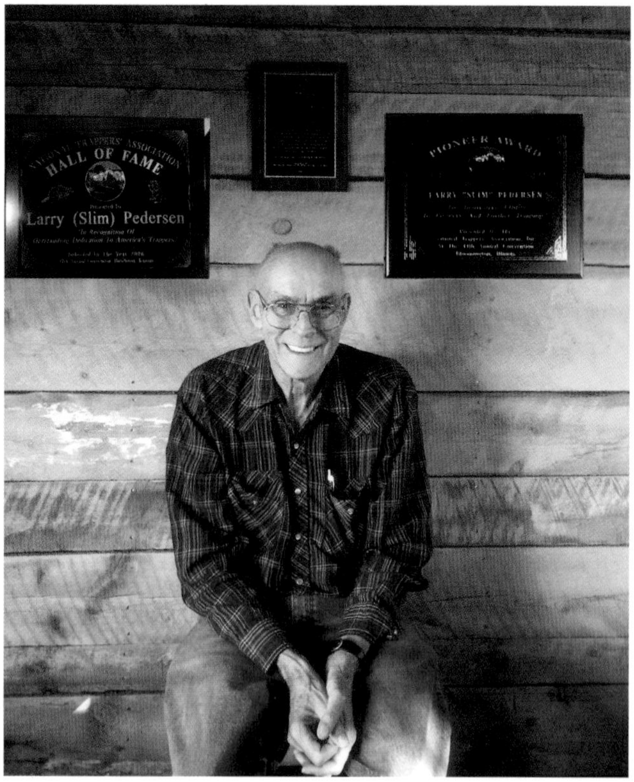

Larry (Slim) Pedersen poses with three of his four major trapping awards. Shown (Right) is Slim's National Trappers Association Trappers Hall of Fame award. (Center) The North American Trappers Historical Society Trappers Hall of Fame Award and (Left) the National Trappers Association Pioneer Award in 2003. Missing is his 2019 National Trappers Association Lifetime Achievement Award.

Slim recalls, *"In my earliest years I can remember hundreds of rocks on our porch. My mother called herself a 'rock hound' and she would bring every interesting rock she saw home to her collection. One day I asked her what a rock hound was and she said, 'Slim, you take a bag of marbles with you and for every rock you pick up, you replace it with a marble. You become a rock hound once you've lost all your marbles!'" "I suspect her curiosity with nature and rocks combined with my grandmother's love for animals is what eventually led me to the life of a trapper.*

"Young trappers today have so much information at their disposal, that information overload could be a problem for the first time in trapping history. To separate themselves from the crowd, a young trapper should learn patience—so he will slow himself down to study what the animals are doing and why. Also, paying attention to times of the year, and where they step in their daily travels, will enable the young trapper to utilize some of this information he has been handed."

—Slim Pedersen in his own words, 2020

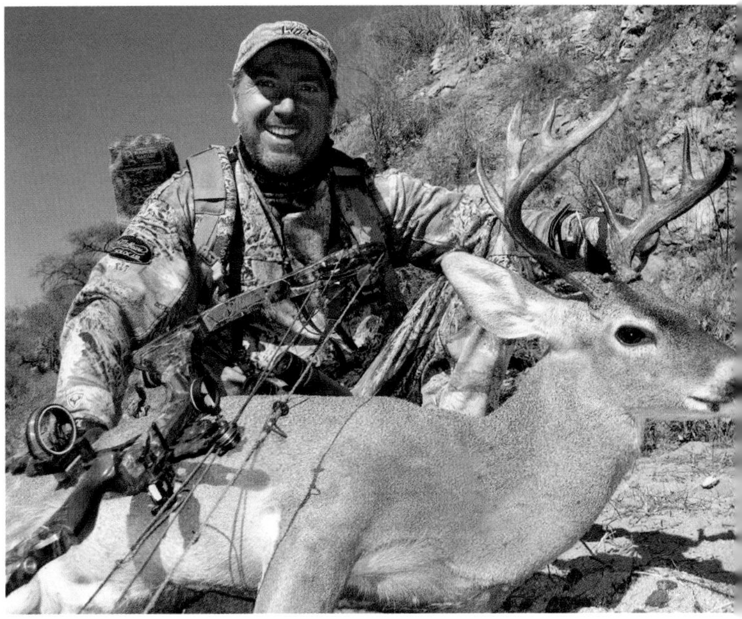

Author's Photo

The desert Coues whitetail is the toughest bowhunt of the 5 deer species required for the Super Slam. This buck is a rare 10 pointer, as 95 percent of desert bucks sport 6 or 8 point antler configurations.

By the start of 2010 I had arrowed 22 unique animals in my quest for the North American Super Slam. At this point my secret of being the first bowhunter to capture all the hunts on video was starting to unravel, as many TV viewers were watching my successful hunts on ESPN and counting the species. Thus, I began to get emails from prominent bowhunters and other hunters pursuing the Slam with a camera and bow. I would plan the last seven species and finish as soon as possible. In 2008 after I arrowed my Dall sheep, the third ram toward my Grand Slam—I booked a desert sheep hunt in Mexico. These hunts always come with a waiting list, are difficult and very costly. My goal was to finish the Grand Slam first, knowing it would be more of a downhill push toward the end goal. The hunt was scheduled for mid-January 2010. I needed a desert bighorn, desert Coues deer, Roosevelt elk, tule elk, bison, barren ground caribou and central Canadian barren ground caribou. None of the hunts were a slam dunk.

SOUTH OF THE BORDER THEN NORTH

I decided to hunt the desert Coues whitetail first so after New Year's Day 2010 I was in Mexico. These hunts are fun and pretty laid back. Coues deer can be very spooky and are by far the most difficult of the five deer needed for the Super Slam. Rather than stalk, I decided to hunt waterholes as it would be much easier to document the hunt on video from the confines of a pop-up blind. I arrowed a fantastic Coues buck and was rolling.

The desert bighorn was another story. The hunting area was on the Baja coast of the Sea of Cortez in the Santa Domingo area—very steep rugged mountain cliffs. Cameraman Martin Teeter, my Canadian pal Chad Lenz and I hiked, hunted and camped in a tent for 19 days in search of a shooter desert ram and came up empty. The hunt was going to be a do-over. That spring and summer I didn't go to Africa. Typically, I was doing two, sometimes three trips to the

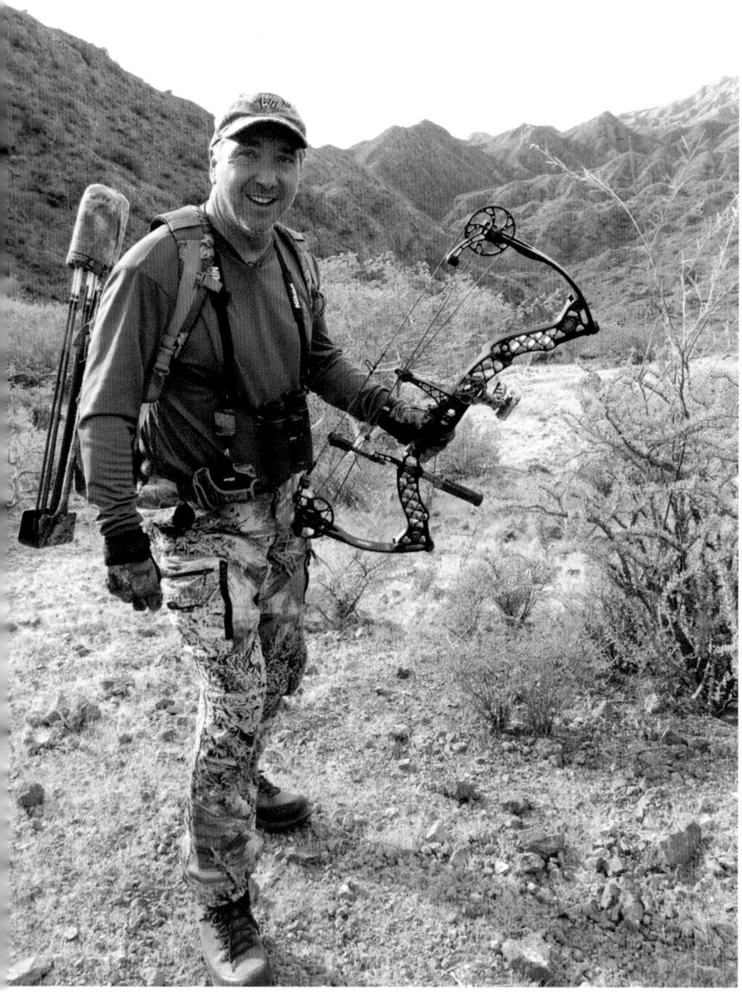

Tom geared up and ready for the days hunt on Mexico's Baja.

Author's Photos

dark continent every year for TV bowhunts, but my hunting budget was maxed out and I had pushed all the chips into the Super Slam game.

In August I booked another back-to-back trip, first to Alaska's north slope for barren ground caribou. The porcupine herd at the time was the best bet for a decent bull in Alaska as the Mulchatna herd in the south was disappearing. This was my third trip for barren ground as I had taken Will Woller from Summit Treestands to Alaska as well as SCUBA pal Mitch Skaggs. Both had taken caribou on our self-guided hunts, but I was busy helping their success and never shot out myself. In 2010 I arrowed a nice velvet 'bou then headed to Canada's Nunavut territory.

In Nunavut we hit the migration of the central Canadian barren ground caribou perfectly. Thousands of caribou were streaming around the many cobalt blue lakes. This species was added to the Super Slam in 1993 which took the number of animals required for a Super Slam from 27 to 28. In Nunavut you can take two caribou bulls per hunter and the Inuit guides pushed hunters to do it as the guides get to keep the meat. Caribou is good meat but too expensive to fly home anyway. I arrowed two whopper bulls in just a couple of days. Of course, only one counted towards the Slam. My bull was number 25 leaving me only four more species to complete the milestone.

ON A ROLL

Home from northern Canada for only a couple of weeks, I headed to California to hunt tule elk. The tule elk was added to the Super Slam in 2008. With the tule being a "new species" the hunt costs were quite high as tags for the unique bulls are limited. The hunting area was a working cattle ranch north of San Francisco and after several foiled stalks and some spooky bulls, we coaxed a dandy bull into range with cow calls and I throttled him with a 35-yard shot. Three left.

Early October found me in central British Columbia hunting Plains bison. You wouldn't think that Plains

This Alaskan "north slope" 'bou helped me close in on my archery Super Slam.

bison would be found there, but there is a large herd dispersed along the Sikanni River in the Pink Mountains. Since this herd doesn't require a draw tag like Arizona's Kiabab Plateau or Utah's Henry Mountains, British Columbia draws many bowhunters to this area to hunt the free-range bison which will qualify for the Pope and Young (P&Y) record book. Bison are huge animals and actually quite cunning. I had taken a bison previously on the Oglala Sioux Pine Ridge Reservation in South Dakota and it was quite a difficult hunt. That bison was in a very large herd fenced in a 16,000-acre pasture and thus wasn't considered fair chase by P&Y.

Author's Photos

A caribou hunters dream come true. A whopper central Canadian BG caribou. We called this one droopy when we saw him as the bull's antler tops kind of "droop" inward which made him easy to spot in a large group of migrating animals.

In my opinion, California may be the most beautiful state in the union. One thing's for sure, this fantastic tule elk was a great animal to take on my first hunt for the elusive species.

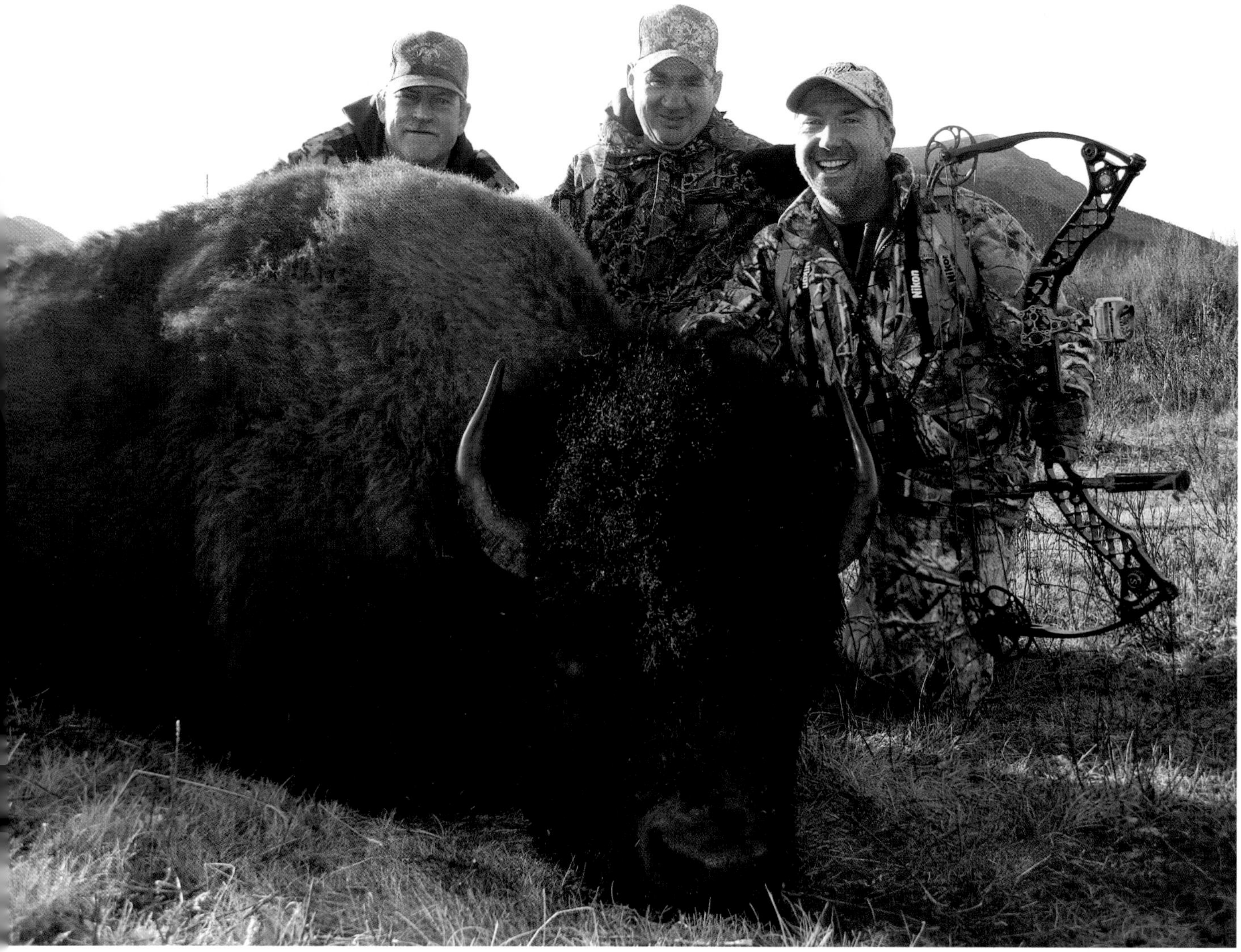

Sikanni River's Mike Hammett, guide Don Harris and I pose with the huge Pink Mountain bull. Don't under estimate the difficulty of a hunt like this. Bison is often a hard won trophy. Both Mike and Don have now passed on.

In 2009 I had come to the "Pinks" and struck out. Never drew my bow on a bison. So, I was back and more determined than ever. After several days of seeing nothing we finally got on some bison. They were very spooky and would run at the sight of the vehicle. These animals can be a tough rifle hunt, so I was up against it. On day six I got into a good position where bison were coming to wallow and lick salt and a good bull walked into range. Two animals left.

ESPN NO MORE

When I got back from the bison hunt, I received a call from ESPN. It was bad news. The execs at the network had made a business decision to go back to ESPN's roots of a stick-and-ball network. This meant they were no longer going to carry outdoor programming. ESPN Outdoors would be no more—December 31, 2010 would be the last of it. I was devastated.

I had been on the network for 19 years and POOF! It was all over. You must understand that replacing the incredible reach of ESPN was tantamount to impossible. ESPN was a universe of 115 million households. The next closest network which carried outdoor programming was Versus (NBC Sports Network) at 50 Million. I quickly called them . They recognized me and my show immediately and we negotiated a time slot for 2011. I then called Sportsman Channel which had approximately 22 million households and negotiated a deal with them as well. So, in 2011 my *Territories Wild* series would be on two networks, reaching approximately 72 million households. It wasn't ESPN but it was something. I could only hope my sponsorship partners would follow me.

My next trip was to Vancouver, British Columbia and then north up the "Sunshine Coast" in pursuit of the Roosevelt elk. I had attempted to bowhunt Roosevelt elk three previous times, the first time, I passed on a branch bull in Oregon. My second hunt was in Washington near Mount St. Helens. No luck. Never saw a bull. During the third hunt I saw bulls, but never drew my bow—also in Oregon.

I had heard of an area in British Columbia where there was only one bow tag—I asked around and got on the list for it in 2009. The area had plenty of elk and nice bulls, but the season was late (after the rut and the elk lived in small private tracts around town), so the issue was finding a bull on property we could hunt. Roosevelt elk are tricky animals—they live in dark timber and they're not very vocal. Finding a good bull and getting within range with a bow and getting the hunt on video is very difficult. You won't see many archery Rosie hunts on TV or DVD.

On my hunt we found elk every day, but seemingly they knew where they were protected and places we couldn't access. At sunup they were always either moving back in the dark or already in their safe haven. Finally, we caught a bull one morning on a power line with cows. He got to dark timber before we did, but after several days of cat and mouse we caught him on the power line at first shooting light. It was my chance and although not my best shot of the Super Slam, I connected and three hours later we found the bull.

It took me 4 hunts on 4 trips to nail down a Roosevelt elk bull. When the chips are down, it's time to make the doughnuts. Awesome archery Rosie bull.

GRAND SLAM CLUB/ OVIS

Because I had been keeping my video Super Slam quest somewhat of a secret, by October 2010 I had 28 of the 29 and was down to just needing the desert sheep. I decided to go public by registering my Super Ten® of North American Big Game with Grand Slam Club/ Ovis (GSCO) and flew up to Birmingham to talk with Dennis Campbell.

Because I had all 28 animals on video and was doing TV episodes on the hunts, Dennis and I came to an agreement to promote the new Super Slam milestone on television. The deal needed approval from the GSCO board of directors, but the idea was a hit and was passed by the board. I had become the new face of GSCO in their promotions of the Super Slam—and I didn't even have a Slam.

For me personally, I didn't feel worthy. I needed a desert sheep which would complete my Grand Slam of four wild rams and the Super Slam 29 big game animals. It was a must. How can I represent the Slam's without either?

I was bent to find a desert sheep hunt in 2010 and finish out, even if it meant mortgaging my house. I contacted pal and expert bowhunter Ricardo Longoria about desert sheep opportunities for bowhunters and he told me that the place to get my desert

Rugged but beautiful Carmen Island, the cobalt blue Sea of Cortes and the jagged peaks of Santa Domingo on the Baja.

ram was Carmen Island, Mexico. The island had been established as a desert sheep sanctuary, with limited hunts available and all monies going toward the proliferation of wild desert sheep. The issue was Isla de Carmen only took three bowhunters a year and was booked four years out. I got on the list and asked Sergio Jimenez, the curator of Carmen Island, to please call me if anything opened up.

DESERT SHEEP SAGA

In late November I received a call from Sergio. He could now accommodate me in early December. The cost was $58 thousand and because of my association with GSCO, he would make an exception to allow a fourth bowhunter, as the three bow hunts for 2010 had been filled earlier in the year. This was a huge windfall and I accepted the terms. I know that price sounds insane (and it is), but I knew that if I could be the first bowhunter to document the Super Slam on video, it would mean a windfall of DVD sales and a book. Likely I would easily recoup my expense and make money from the entire Super Slam aftermarket sales. Plus, I was using the footage for hunts on TV, so I had to go all in.

I got to Carmen Island in early December 2010 with cameraman Chris Douglas. The first evening we were on a ram at close yardage, but the situation wasn't right and the video footage poor, so I didn't shoot. Yes, this is the life of a TV bowhunter. We live for the video footage. Three days later we are on a ram below us about 45 yards, but it's somewhat windy and I shoot over him. Strike two. The last day of the hunt I miss another ram at 45 yards, this time under him. Strike three, the hunt is over. I'm devastated.

In February 2011 I went back with the outfitter on the Baja mainland where I hunted desert sheep the first time. The area we would hunt was called Agua Verde. For seven days of a 10-day hunt we hunted like crazy and found no legal rams. On day seven the guide fell in the rocks and hurt his back. The remainder of the hunt went south. My brain was a shambles. Three desert

The A Team. (L-R) Cameraman Chris Douglas, guide assistant Abundis, head guide Gaspar Figueroa and yours truly with the Super Slam desert ram that stepped in front of my arrow and took one for the team.

sheep hunts and no ram. No Slam.

I knew I could return to Carmen and hunt when they had availability. That time came in March and I was ready. In sheep shape, shooting great and like Elwood Blues once said, "We're on a mission from God." I almost changed my cameraman for good luck, nothing personal—I was grabbing at straws. However, I decided to stay with cinematographer Chris Douglas as we had become a team in this saga. On the first morning, about 90 minutes into our hike, we spotted two shooter rams. In the course of about five minutes, I slipped into range and arrowed the largest one. It was done. The monkey was off my back. That one arrow and the subsequent video footage cemented me as the first bowhunter to take all 29 North American big game animals on camera to complete a Super Slam.

It had taken me 13 years to complete the archery Super Slam on video. I released the full 3-DVD video set in January of 2012 and a book the following year. My desert sheep TV episode won "Moment of the Year" at the Sportsman Channel TV Network Awards in 2012, one of their highest honors. To date I've sold over 30,000 *Adventure Bowhunter* Super Slam DVD sets and nearly 10,000 Adventure Bowhunter books.

MICK DeROCCO

1960–

Some men are set on a course of destiny from an early age. Born in Ilion, New York along the banks of the Mohawk River, young Mickey DeRocco came into the world. The son of a trapper, Mick's hometown was the birthplace of Remington Firearms. To the north are the famous Adirondacks. To the west, the Oneida Community and the original Newhouse trap factory. Mick's father wanted his son to be a trapper and at the young age of 7, dad would set the traps and Mick would place them, under the watchful eye and critique of a loving father. Soon Mick was trapping on his own and interested in everything outdoors.

Mick DeRocco Photo

Nevada long — line 'cat man Mick DeRocco poses with a portion of his 2020 catch.

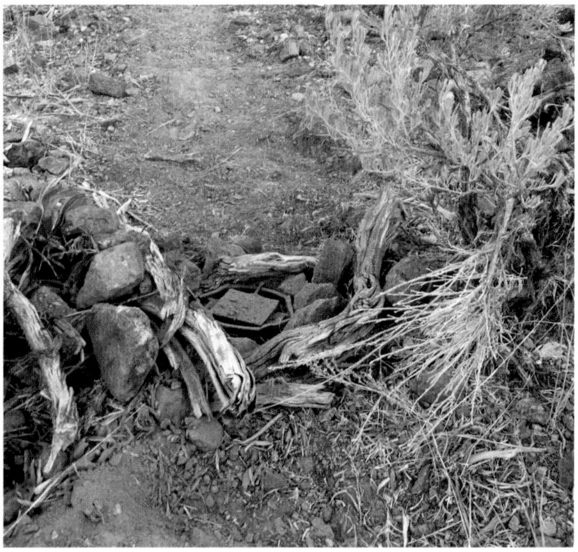

Mick DeRocco Photo

DeRocco exposed trap trail set.

Mick says, *"When I was a young boy my mom and dad had a camp in the Adirondacks. Each year my dad and I would go to the annual trappers rendezvous held back in the late 1960s in Piseco Lake, NY. Guys like E.J. Dailey and O.L. Butcher would attend. I will always remember Mister Butcher teasing me as I tried to talk my dad into buying me his bobcat trapping book, asking if I was gearing up to trap house cats. I think that was a sign of things to eventually come for me."*

Mick also had a copy of Hawbaker's *Trapping North American Furbearers*, of course. *"I remember my first copy of Trapping North American Furbearers which over the years I've lost count how many times I've read though the different copies I've owned. It might sound crazy, but I recently purchased another copy just for nostalgia's sake."*

Like many youngsters, hunting, fishing and trapping turned to an interest in taxidermy. After graduation, many different jobs and some formal taxidermy training, Mick opened his own taxidermy shop. *"Even though I was making a living as a taxidermist, I never quit trapping and thought about trapping constantly. I used to promote my taxidermy business with a booth at the New York State Trappers Association conventions and always chatted with Paul Grimshaw as well Charlie Dobbins and his son Paul. Once trapping is in your blood, I think you're a trapper for life."*

Mick DeRocco had some great seasons trapping New York along some of the same areas that his mentors and idols trapped. Through the late 1970s and '80s, Mick trapped mink, 'rats, raccoons, foxes and bobcats with a passion. After spending over 20 years

These three photos illustrate Mick DeRocco's trap — line location strategy with the brushy ravine & rimrock, necked down location and results,

in the taxidermy business Mick sold his shop and moved west to fulfill his trapline dreams.

DeRocco landed in Reno, Nevada where he took a job as a retail sales manager and quickly began laying out his trapline. The high desert around Reno is a 'cat trapper's Eden and although Mick knew he needed to work a "real job" for a few more years, his goal was retirement and a full-time 'cat line. During his part-time trapping in Nevada, Mick refined his locations and sets.

Mick DeRocco uses a variety of necked down exposed trap trail sets and double and triple dirt-holes. Mick prefers rimrock country and woody draws that hold the prey species that 'cats hunt. *"I use a lot of walk through sets in areas that cats frequent. I look for rimrock locations, or brushy draws that hold lots of cottontails. I use multiple scents at my walk throughs in opposite corners, hoping to get the 'cat to stay at the set and step around while he investigates. I use multiple man-made materials and objects, some homemade and some store bought as flagging."*

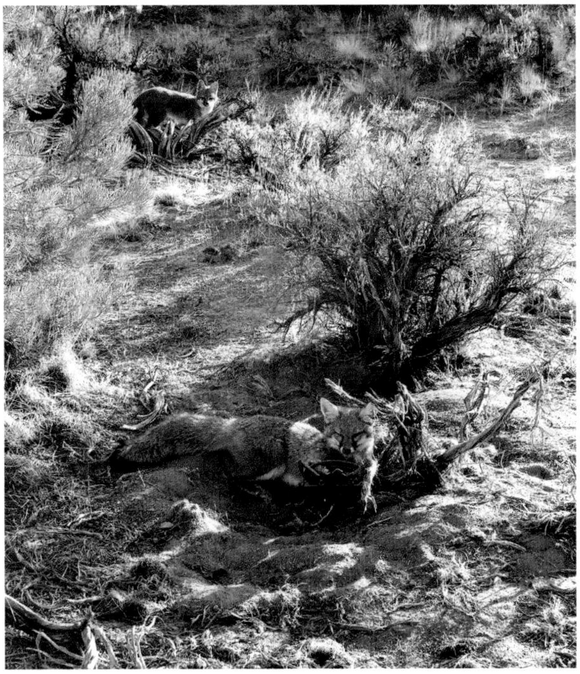

Nice double on gray fox in a gang set location for spotted bellies.

Nevada doesn't allow any natural fur or feathers within 30 feet of a trap or snare set. Mick's 'cat flagging is quite ingenious—strips of indestructible Tyvek cut into strips, rubber pet and baby toys with reflective eyes, and CD discs are just a few of his fantastic ideas. *"Bobcats are my passion and my wheelhouse, but I catch a surprising number of gray fox in the cat sets. I set heavy so even when I catch a pair of fox there's still at least two 'cat sets guarding my location. Location is key, but success comes with patience as cats cover ground and it can take time to get back around if a tom slips through a location. Refining 'cat set locations on a long-line is a constant process."*

Mick typically makes two "fenced off" trail sets—one on each side of at least pair of dirt-hole sets. Flagging near the "walk-throughs." He makes his own bobcat lure and runs 50 percent commercial lure and 50 percent homemade. Mick also makes all his own baits and enjoys the process saying that there's an extra special feeling that comes with a catch knowing it was your own lure and bait that got it done.

Mick DeRocco Photo

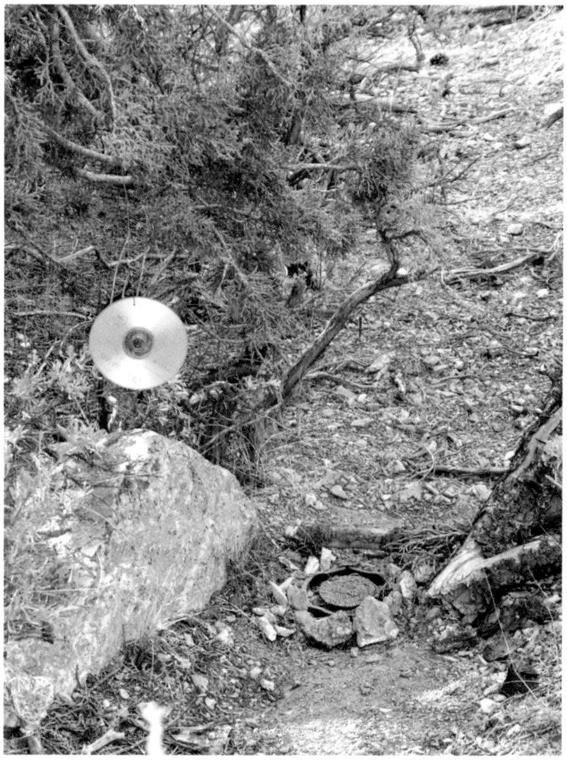

Exposed trap trap set with creative flagging.

Mick DeRocco Photo

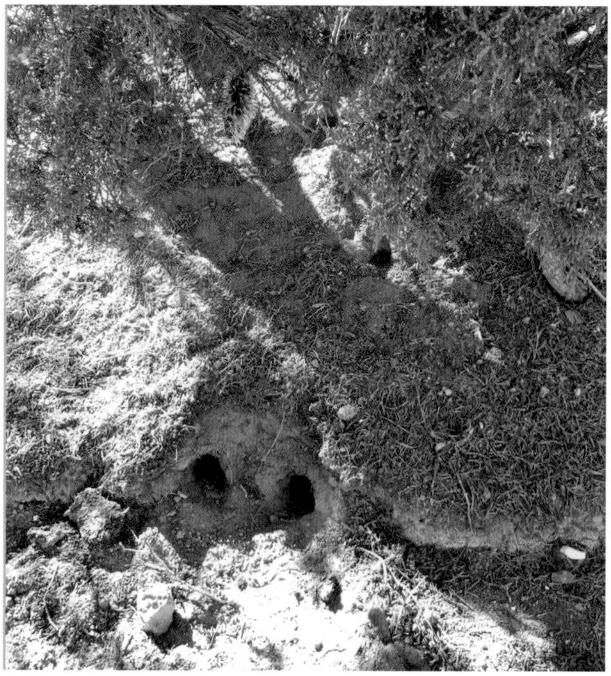

Mick DeRocco twin hole set with flagging.

Keep at it and never give up. Trapping is not something that's going to make you rich anymore, so allow it to enrich your heart and soul. As a trapper, you're no longer just an armchair observer of nature, but a genuine participant. So, embrace your inner predator and learn as much as you can from the animals you pursue. Keep your eyes open, observe, observe, observe and never stop learning. It's essential that one never thinks that they have reached their peak and have nothing else to learn. Because even if it were true, when you stop learning, the fun and excitement leaves with it."

—Mick DeRocco in his own words, 2020

Mick DeRocco Photo

DeRocco necked down trail and electric fence rods with creative flagging.

Lance Stizel Photo

Western predator man Lance Stitzel with a great 3 bobcat day.

Lance Stizel Photo

Mick DeRocco rock wall set. Notice large pan trap in the center.

Mick DeRocco Photo

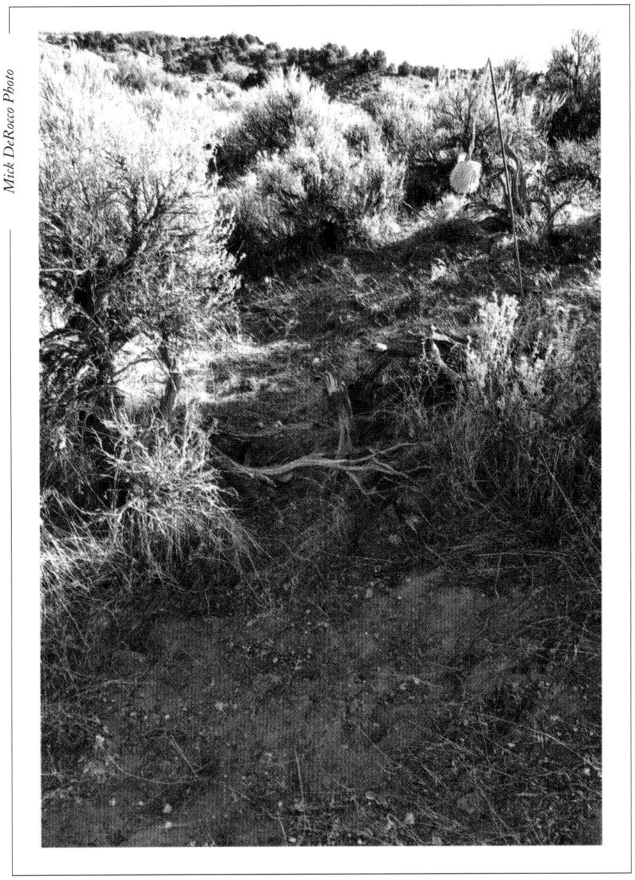

DeRocco trail set with creative flagging.

JAMES LORD

1972–

Tennessee trapper James Lord grew up in southeastern Oklahoma and began trapping at age 12. James says, *"A local landowner gave me two traps but no tips on how to use them. So, I learned the hard way by trial and error."* James eventually bought more traps and kept a line running off and on during his school years. Once out of college he moved to Tennessee for work. It was here that James got serious about his trapping.

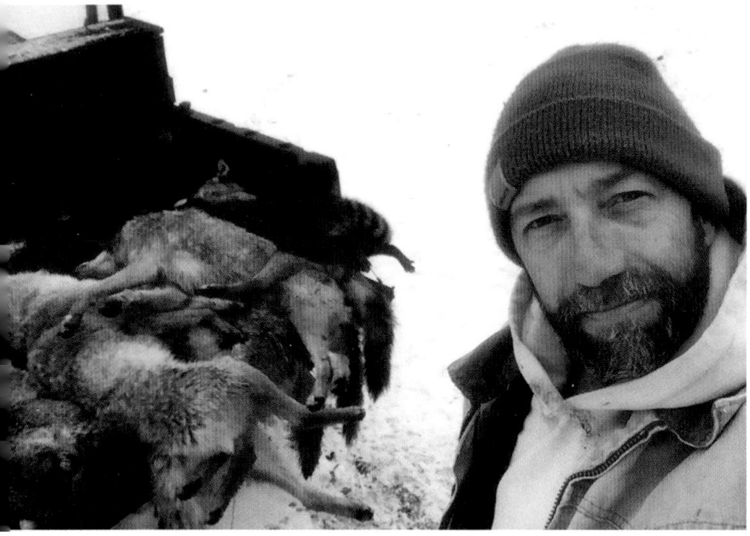

Master Trapper James Lord poses with a days catch on a Tennessee ADC landowner complaint.

Tennessee isn't known for high-volume trapping, however James Lord is doing what he can to change that notion. Living in Lexington, TN which is about half-way between Memphis and Nashville, when James isn't working at his career in the restaurant business, he's doing animal damage control work or operating a fur line in season. James's favorite animal to trap is the bobcat and he's become quite the Tennessee bobcat specialist.

"My favorite set for bobcats would be a variation of a dirt-hole set. A regular dirt hole somewhat centered, with up to two more smaller dirt holes or punch holes strategically set to make the 'cat move its feet just enough to get caught. I pay more attention to lure placement than pan placement."

Even though James pretty much runs a mixed bag line while balancing a full-time career, he's had some great seasons trapping 'cats. His personal best: 41 bobcats, 42 otters, 74 coyotes, 28 foxes, and 87 beavers.

James Lord Photo

Nice mid-winter double on Tennessee dawgs taken by James Lord.

A pretty amazing run for the Volunteer State. James also says, *"Several years before that, I targeted beaver and otter one season, with a few 'cat sets thrown in around the swamps, I caught 197 beaver, 39 otter and 27 bobcats. All this while working a full-time 'regular' job."* James began doing ADC work in 2004—that continues today.

When asked what trappers influenced him, James quickly says, *"No doubt that Larry 'Slim' Pedersen and Charles Dobbins were my biggest influences. Slim for the cat and canine trapping and Charles for the water trapping. I have a good work ethic, which drives me to do my best at everything I do. I think like most trappers, I've learned many pointers, methods and sets from the great trappers and I hope that maybe someday I would be known or even just mentioned in the same paragraph as some of the all-time great trappers. I don't think I'm there yet though."* Of course, modesty is a trait of all Master Trappers.

James Lord has made four how-to trapping DVDs: *Runnin' With Lord 1*—2008, *Bobcat Trapping*—2009, *Canine Trapping*—2010, and *Runnin' With Lord 2*—2010. James has also put plenty of time into the protection of trapping as vice president and president of the Tennessee Trappers Association.

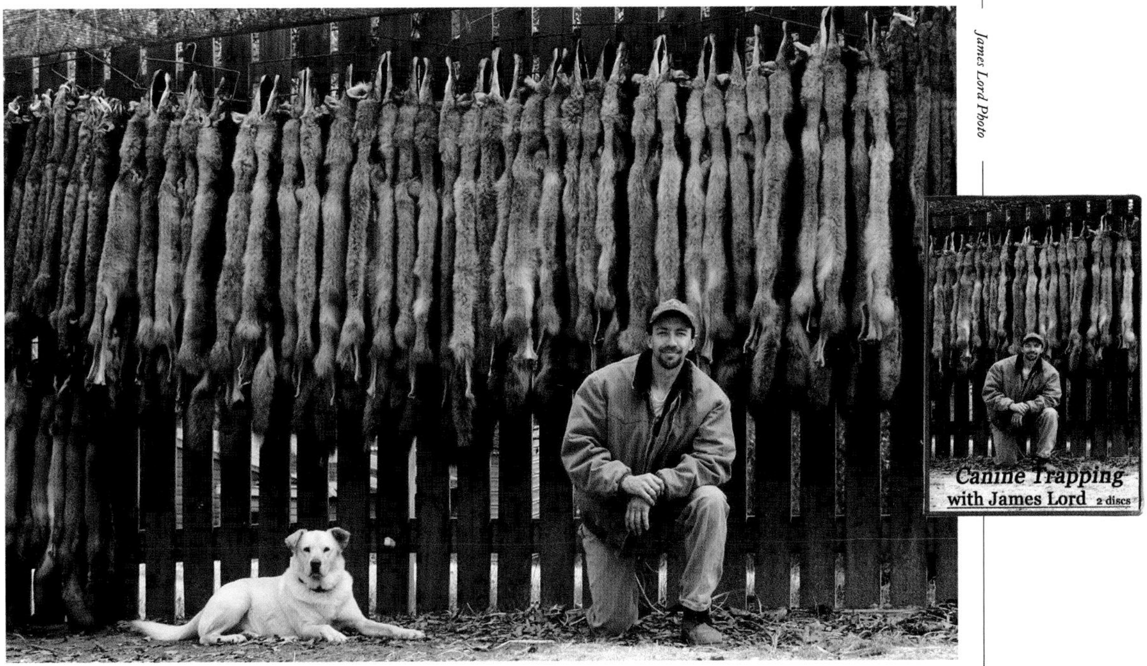

James Lord Photo

James with a dandy catch of predators taken during the taping of his Canine Trapping DVD 2010

James Lord Photo

James Lord poses with part of a seasons catch of Volunteer State spotted bellies 2009.

"The time I spent in the organization helped me engage quite a few youngsters into the sport of trapping, by helping in organizing as well as teaching in the Trapper Training Camps we held annually. Also, in Tennessee I was involved in helping get the snaring regulations passed through the State Legislature statewide. At the time, trappers were not allowed to snare in 18 counties, while the rest of the trappers in the state were allowed to.

I usually tell upcoming trappers, to read and learn as much as possible about the animals you're targeting. It may be a slow process out there with weather conditions, learning from mistakes, and other unforeseen mishaps, but to always keep your head up, keep trying different ideas and of course if you really want to be great you have to keep at it and never give up."

—James Lord in his own words, 2014

JERRY HERBST 1954–

Jerry Herbst Photo

Jerry moved from Michigan's upper Peninsula to White, South Dakota to continue his career as a trapper for South Dakota Game Fish & Parks. As the photo shows, Jerry is a fantastic mink trapper. circa 1986

Jerry grew up in the Chicago suburbs and got interested in the outdoors at a young age. Near his childhood home, Jerry had access to a small wildlife area. It was in this preserve where Jerry found his passion for the outdoors. Jerry especially enjoyed bowhunting, fishing and trapping. He also had close relatives who were sportsmen and they owned property in Michigan's Upper Peninsula. Traveling north on these childhood adventures enamored him to the Michigan wilds.

In 1980 Jerry decided to move to Michigan's Upper Peninsula to run a trapline and it was here where I met him. We coincidentally had moved to Michigan the same year, living only 20 miles apart and we learned the ways of wilderness trapping together. When I moved to South Dakota in 1984 to take my animal damage control trapping job, Corry Dolbeer, one of Jerry's close friends from Illinois, bought my Michigan property and cabins. Jerry eventually came to South Dakota, also working for Game, Fish and Parks. Jerry was instrumental in helping me with my lure business from the mid-1980s to the mid-1990s. Jerry also started his own pro-line snare shop and sold thousands of snares in the '80s and '90s.

Author's Photo

Master Trapper Jerry Herbst on location for Fur-Fish-Game Magazine 1989

Known for his snaring expertise and his extreme attention to detail, Jerry Herbst is most recognized as one of the featured trappers in the *Fur-Fish-Game* magazine trapping video series along with Bob Gilsvik, Jeff Smith and Dave Heib. Jerry actually made his video debut in my revised *Fox and Coyote Trapping, East to West: Advanced Methods* video where he discussed building and setting snares. Jerry is an excellent trapper and we worked together in the trapping trade for over a decade.

What many people don't know is that Jerry Herbst got me back into bowhunting. As a kid, I had a Fred Bear recurve and shot targets in the yard, but Jerry would bring his bow to the lure shop and shoot in the late summer, preparing for bow season. Watching him shoot rekindled my interest in bows and bowhunting. So, I secured a new McPherson bow and we began to shoot together. Jerry was the cameraman on my Saskatchewan black bear hunt, documenting my first big game bowhunt on video. He and I also traveled extensively, doing many trappers conventions together. Jerry was the life of the party on many of those trips, always having something funny to add to every conversation.

Herbst helped hundreds of trappers, answering questions one-on-one and showing his snaring methods at the conventions we attended, not to mention the hundreds of thousands of trappers who learned from Jerry in the very popular *Fur-Fish-Game* videos. Jerry is also fond of skunks and has had several of them as pets. Herbst enjoys the reaction people have when they see his pet polecats climbing around in the truck and they are clearly a window into the humous side of this talented trapper.

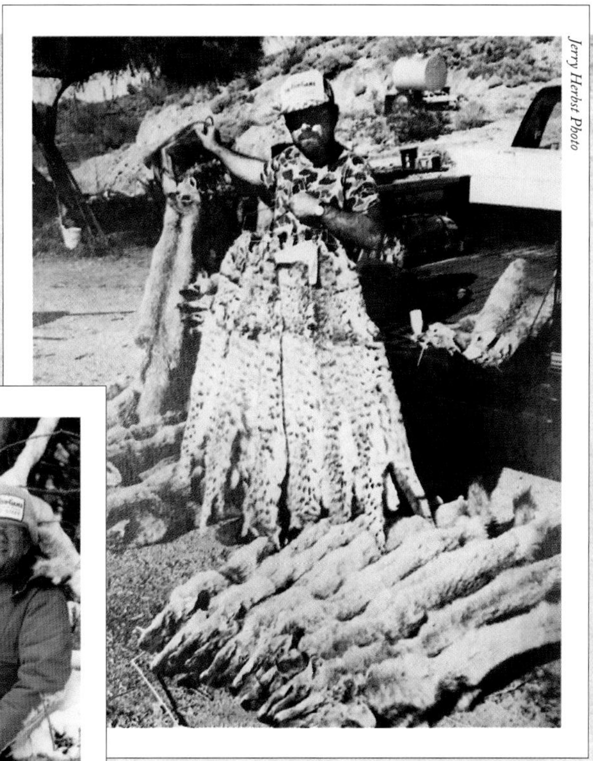

Jerry Herbst poses with part of his 1988 Arizona winter trapline catch.

Jerry and F-F-G Trapline editor Bob Gilsvik pose with a coyote Jerry snared for the F-F-G Pro Predator Trapping video.

Jerry Herbst went on to become a Deputy Sheriff in Brule County, South Dakota. His career as a lawman allows him time to trap on weekends and vacation. With his retirement coming soon, you can bet Jerry will be back on the trapline, as no matter the prices paid for pelts, Jerry will never lose his passion for trapping.

Tough enough to catch one bobcat in a live trap let alone two. Nice job Jerry.

National Trappers Association

Trappers Hall of Fame

1993
*Authur Robert Harding
*E.J. Dailey
*O.L. Butcher
*Wayne Negus
Ed Danko
*Kermit Stearns
Tom Krause
Scott Hartman
*Jake Korell

1994
*Stanley Hawbaker
*Herbert Lenon
*Joe Brescia

1995
*Norman Gray
*Charles Dobbins

1996
*Johnny Thorpe

1997
Major Boddicker
Russ Carman
Art Scott

1998
*Dean Wilson
*Don Hoyt Sr
*Omar Shipley

1999
*Gerald Walkup
*Pete Rickard
George Wacha Jr.

2000
*Jim Campbell
*Al Perry

2001
*William Kindervater
*David Reed

2002
*George Stewart
Jin & Mary Ann Connor

2003
*Ray Bruedigam
*Pete Leggett
Ron Leggett

2004
*William Jones

2005
*Bernie Serafin
*Marvin D. Miller

2006
Francis Hutton Riggs
Larry "Slim" Pedersen

2007
*George Scalf
Anna Marie Scalf

2008
No Inductees

2009
*Joseph Raymond Alcorn
Cynthia Ann Seff

2010
No Inductees

2011
Jim Curran
Pete Askins

2012
Gary Meis

2013
Paul John Dobbins
Tonnie Elwood Davis

2014
Gordon "Gordy" Berndt

2015
No Inductees

2016
Craig Spores

2017
*Theron C. "TC" Dawson
*Paul Grimshaw

2018
Robert Colona
*Eugene Purdy

2019
Jim & Fran Buell
Russ & Susan Voelker

2020
Ron Harder
Tom Miranda

*Denotes Deceased

Fur Takers of America
Trappers Hall of Fame

1974
*John Parker

1975
*George Liljestrand

1976
*Raymond Thompson

1977
*Ed Marks

1978
*Frank Terry

1979
*Ben Sudul

1980
*Joe Tennyson

1981
*J.C. Woodard

1982
*Wilbert Pierce

1983
*Tom Landers

1984
Louis Krumwiede

1985
*Wilt Wernsman

1986
*Red Edgemon

1987
*Omar Shipley

1988
Don Nichols

1989
*Ivan & Connie White

1990
*Charles Park

1991
*Kermit Stearns

1992
*Pete Rickard

1993
*Tom Wright Sr

1994
*Red Edgemon

1995
Pete Askins

1996
Gary Jepson

1997
Charles Andres

1998
*Charles Dobbins

1999
*Tom Hammond
Dean Mitchell

2000
Ron Cauble
*Robert "Hawk" Hassfuther

2001
*James Lee
Roy Greenfield

2002
Jerry Hall Sr.
Jerry Joe Barnett

2003
*Wally Schmieg
*Pete & Ron Leggett

2004
Dave Hastings
*Kenneth Jones

2005
Garry Armstrong
Dorothy Lee

2006
Ed Murdock
*Ed & Mary Helterbrand

2007
John Wilson
Dave Plueger
Robert Wilson

2008
Major Boddicker
*Paul Brown
*Ken & Elaine Schwar-zhoff

2009
*Irv Schirmer
Jim Mahoney

2010
Tom Fisher
Joe Papa

2011
*Larry "Doc" Green
Bernie Bailey

2012
Gary Isbell
*Carol Krumwiede

2013
Gene Beeber
Charlie Masheck

2014
Ardell Grawe
Owen Hall

2015
Art Scott
*Tom Dearmont

2016
Don Hoyle
*Joe Griffith

2017
Gene Purdy
Jim Julien

2018
Robert Himmel
Gayle & Arlene Kirchner

2019
*Glen Sterling
Nancy Mahoney

*Denotes Deceased

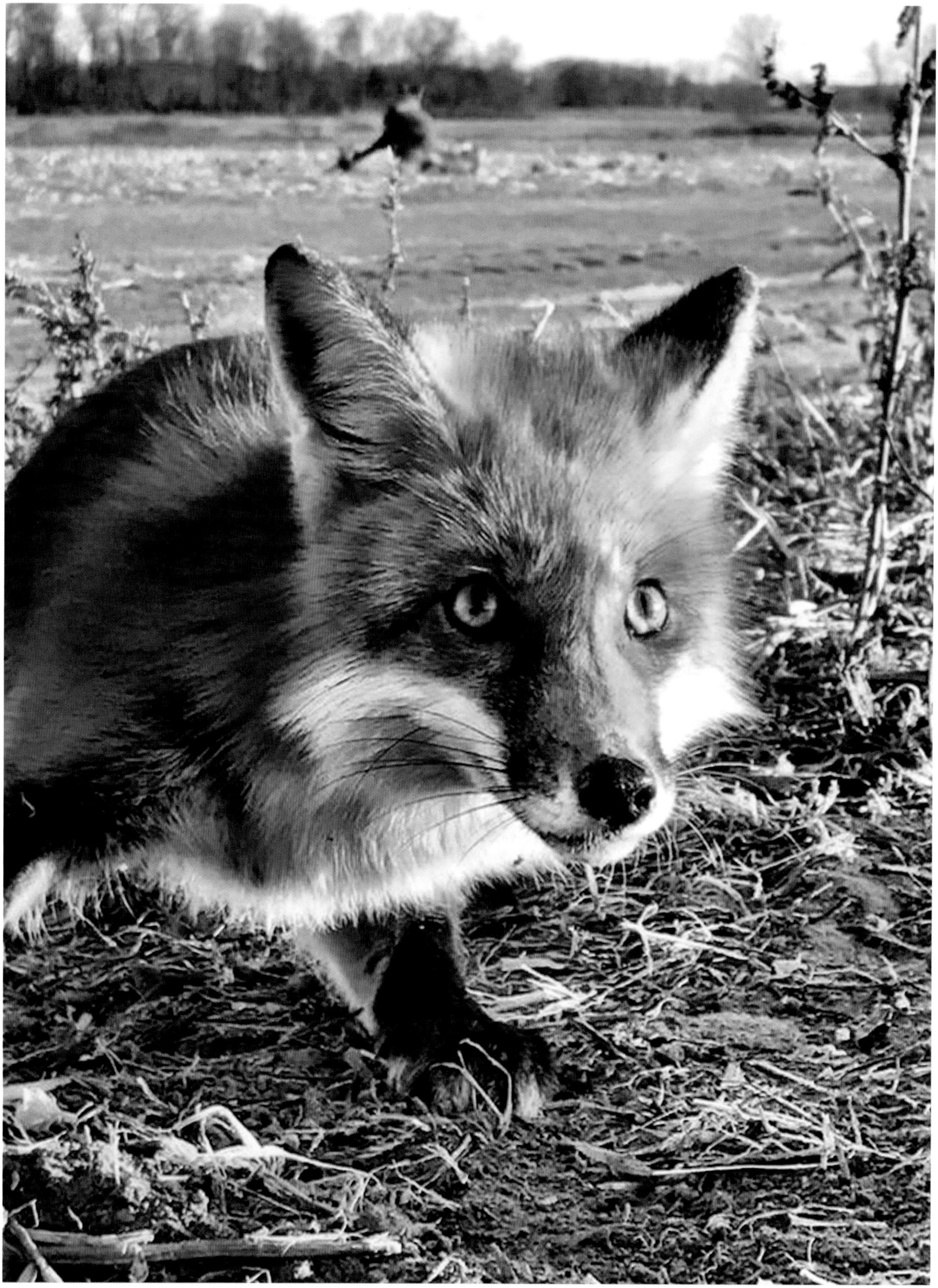

CHAPTER 15

LESSONS LEARNED

The paradox of writing a book like this is that it expands the notoriety and fame of the trappers within but leaves out many trappers worthy of inclusion. Writing a treatise inclusive of every trapper who has contributed to the history of trapping would never be completed, as young trappers are graduating up the ranks every day. Plus, because of the nature of trapping, many expert trappers never became well-known outside their circle of acquaintances and therefore many of these trappers' methods and accomplishments passed with them.

The body of record on effective trapping techniques available today in print and on video is mind-blowing in comparison to 100 years ago. In today's connected world, it's not difficult to find solid information on how to trap. However, solid history about historical trappers, their methods and careers are more elusive. The trappers outlined within the pages of this book provide a look at the men who influenced and molded my career in the outdoors and its roots of trapping.

PLANETS ALIGNED

When I became a trapper in 1969 at 11 years old, I had no idea the home offices of *Fur-Fish-Game* magazine were a mere 10 miles from my home. When purchasing my property in Michigan's Upper Peninsula and while building my cabin, I didn't realize famous author James Churchill would eventually write that fateful article. As I took trapping lessons from Odon Corr in South Dakota, I never dreamed that I would eventually become a government trapper in the same area where famed long-liner Garold Weiland trapped and wrote his famous books. When I took that job, I never realized that I would live only two miles from the foundations of famous Fort Kiowa on the banks of the Missouri River. Yes, the same Fort Kiowa where all the infamous

< *Martin Baker Photo*

mountain men would stage up before starting their trapping expeditions.

Who would have thought I would earn my trapper wings over the Missouri River breaks and eventually run my trapline with an airplane? Or be selected as the editor of *Fur-Fish-Game* magazine's "Question Box" column, the same column that E.J. Dailey did for so many years? Why did I make one of the very first "how-to-trap" videos in 1985? In 1989 when I put my trapping catalog in the pages of *Trapper & Predator Caller* magazine I never dreamed I would have a TV show in 1990 and debut on ESPN in 1992. When I interviewed famed bowhunter Chuck Adams in 1996, I had no idea I would ever complete a Super Slam, let alone be the first to capture all the hunts on video.

Author's Photo

Tom Miranda's signed "relic" traps which he used on his 1980s Ohio, Michigan and South Dakota longlines adorn many a man cave, trophy room or trap collection.

Brian Briggs Photo

Trapper Jeff Briggs poses with a dandy catch he and his brother Brian took on their Ohio trapline. The brothers are fire fighters and excellent trappers.

In retrospect, how the planets aligned for me is quite amazing. None of it was planned in advance, but when opportunities came along, I was more than eager to jump in and accept the risks in exchange for a chance at something better. Maybe it was my destiny. I learned a long time ago that there were trappers who were much better at trapping than I am. And bowhunters who were much better at bowhunting than I am. In fact, there are many people who are much better than I am at doing most everything. However, one thing I can do is work. I'll outwork most people. I won't quit. My philosophy on achievements and goals is that I worry about what I need to do, and I don't worry about what others are doing.

BUILDS CHARACTER

Some pick up the trap, make a few bucks and leave it to pursue other interests. Thank goodness, since there is only room in the world for so many trappers. I will say the outdoorsmen I have met who actually ran a trapline, all have fond memories of it. Trapping is hard work and I am sure it was my early years on the trapline that molded my "don't quit" work ethic which has al-

Author's Photo

My father running traps with me in South Dakota circa 1988

ways steered me toward success. Lugging heavy traps and furbearers up and down muddy riverbanks, through cattail swamps, over hill and dale—in hip boots no less, is real work. Add to all that, skinning the catch, fleshing the pelt and drying the hide for sale. In a nutshell, hard-working trappers make great employees, management leaders and entrepreneurs.

A clear advantage I had early in my trapping days was support from my parents. Neither my father nor mother were trappers, nor did they know much about it, but they encouraged me because they saw the passion I had for the outdoors. My parents' flexibility contributed to my early success—they weren't as strict with me as they could have been. Dad and Mom trusted me without question. This allowed a wide latitude when it came to house rules, giving me the freedom to leave home in the wee hours of the morning to amble down a dark riverbank and to stay out well after dark stomping in the woods to set new traps or spend late nights in the garage skinning my catch. As parents do, mine worried about my hours in the woods and its dangers. Their love and understanding of me and my work as a trapper required flexibility and they entrusted me with this latitude—a privilege I never abused. I'm not sure in today's society that it would be as easy to allow an 11-year-old to leave the house with a flashlight to run traps in "out of the way" places like I did in the early 1970s.

Thomas Gradowski Photo

Illinois Trapper Thomas Gradowski poses with a days catch on his "deer patrol" trapline circa 2015.

Glen Bruette Photo

Nice coyote taken by avid trapper Glen Bruette.

Trapping teaches more than hard work. It teaches responsibility, ethics, the value of money, the value of life, the benefits of trial and error, as well as the relationships between risk and reward. In the early days, few kids had money they'd earned on their own other than allowance. There weren't many opportunities for an 11-year-old to make spending money. There are only so many newspapers needing delivery or lawns needing to be mowed. But as a trapper, I had days where I made a month's worth of summer mowing money and trapping was much more adventurous. I'll admit that the money was a huge incentive, but even when furs became less valuable, I couldn't see myself not trapping. Having a passion for what you're doing can make hard work seem like fun. This feeling of self-satisfaction goes a long way to motivate and compartmentalize difficult tasks. It's more difficult to run a mile than walk a mile, however a runner would consider walking as lazy. And after the run, most runners feel invigorated, satisfied and with self-esteem. I have always looked at trapping like that.

Many who were trappers as youngsters have gone on to become successful businessmen and in my career as a TV bowhunter, I'm not alone. Well-known outdoorsmen and TV hunters Bob Foulkrod, Rob Keck, Stan Potts and famous photographer Leonard Lee Rue III were all accomplished trappers.

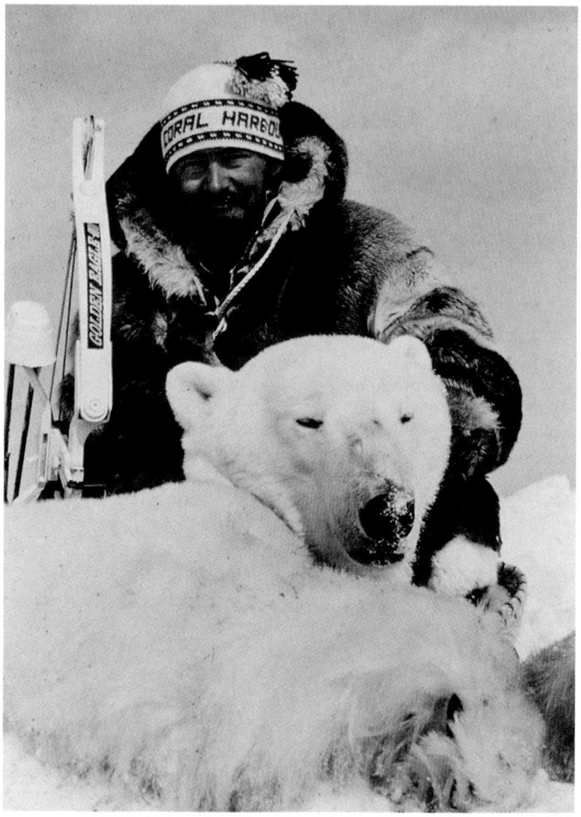

Bob Foulkrod Photo

TV hunter Bob Foulkrod poses with his archery polar bear.

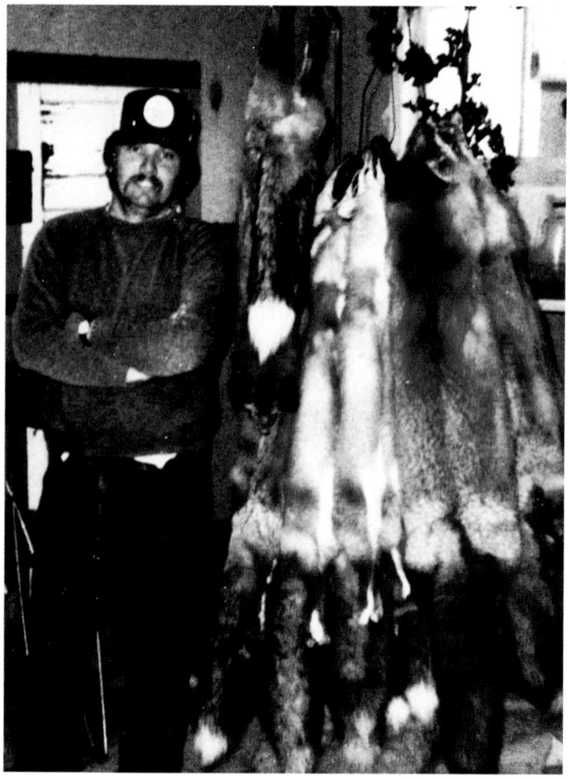
Stan Potts Photo

Whitetail pro Stan Potts poses in an early snap with some prime fox pelts.

Former Wild Turkey Federation president and Bass Pro Shops personality Rob Keck on the trapline teaching another generation of trappers.

FRONTLINE WARRIORS

Nice dawg taken by Greg Staggs.

Thank goodness there are trappers whose passion drives them into service of the trapping associations. Without state and national trappers associations, there would likely be no sport trapping at all today. I got involved back in the early 1980s in both the National Trappers Association (NTA) as well as Fur Takers of America (FTA) and I am glad I did. Both organizations have their expertise and missions to preserve and promote trapping. In my view, the NTA is the larger association and its mission tends more toward working with game departments and the legal issues that states battle to keep their trapping as well as humane trap initiatives. FTA is more a grassroots organization which concentrates on trapper training, benefit and jobs in the trapping arena like animal damage control.

Dave Hastings Photo

Nebraska teacher, trapper and FTA President Dave Hastings introducing students to the world of trapping.

Volunteering to work within state trapping associations is one way to give back to trapping and your heritage as a trapper. Talk to anyone who has volunteered, and most will tell you the experience has been rewarding. Of course, the purpose of any organization is to stand united and it's not easy when opinions vary and inevitably politics enters the arena. For some individuals this can be an issue, however for most, their service is dedicated to trapping and their duty is always focused on the best interest of trapping as a whole.

Just like trappers must fight to keep their privileges, so must hunters—it's seemingly a never-ending battle. Sportsmen tend to care about their individual interests and where trappers and hunters have like motivations in wildlife conservation, rarely do the hunters and trappers join forces. With activists nipping at the heels of all sportsmen, trappers are often considered the "low hanging fruit." Trappers represent one of the smallest groups of sportsmen and their traps which have been labeled "barbaric" add fuel to the fire and make trappers an easy target. One organization that attempts to bring all sportsmen together and fights for them all with a strong legal fund is Sportsman's Alliance.

Originally known as the Wildlife Legislative Fund of America, the organization formed in 1977 after Ohio Ballot Issue 2 threatened Ohio's trapping community. After leading the fight to successfully defeat the bill, U.S. Sportsmen's Alliance was officially incorporated in 1978 as the number one defender of sportsmen across the country. Although much of funding for the Alliance comes from hunter organizations, Sportsmen's Alliance still honors its roots and does much to defend trappers. I encourage joining and participating.

In the public eye for over 35 years, I have witnessed the savageness of animal activists using tactics of misinformation, character assassinations and pushes for natural resource preservation. Every hunter knows that our privileges are constantly under attack. But it's not just the activists and antis who attempt to divide and conquer. Many hunters and trappers inadvertently take up causes against each other over different opinions. Hunters are constantly fighting among themselves. Bowhunters argue over traditional archery and compounds. Hunters constantly challenge each other over the ethics of baiting, using hunting dogs, electronics and a host of other issues that foster resentment and divide our ranks. These discussions do nothing to protect our hunting privileges, in fact they give activists leverage against us.

Attending trappers conventions is one of the highlights of becoming a member of your state association. Often called a trappers meet, these association conventions are a who's who of top trappers as well as lure makers, trap suppliers and "tail-gaters" selling used traps, stretchers and everything trapping. Attending a convention is one of the best ways to meet other trappers and learn more about trapping. The national conventions are typically the all-star events of the year and always worth the effort to attend.

The NTA issues a quarterly magazine titled, *American Trapper* which contains timely articles and useful information compiled by trapper Rich Faler. FTA's *Fur Taker* magazine is issued monthly and a valuable resource on trapping compiled by trapper Eric Arnold.

Finishing my North America Super Slam was a huge milestone. It took 54 separate bow hunts over the course of 13 years to accomplish the goal. Subsequently it took eight months to compile all the footage and shoot the biographies and interviews that were needed to edit the DVD set. I had asked some of the bowhunters who had accomplished the Slam in years past if they would participate. All who I asked agreed, including Dr. John Jack Frost from Alaska, the first archer to take a Grand Slam of wild sheep. Also, Tom Hoffman from New York, the third bowhunter to take the Super Slam. And Frank Noska of Alaska. Frank is a United Parcel Service pilot and an amazing bowhunter. I also asked Grand Slam Club director Dennis Campbell to be in the documentary.

By November 2011 the video was complete. Five full DVDs. I sat down and watched it. After the screening, I realized that although the program was amazingly detailed—it was over eight hours in length. Too, too long. So, I decided to hold off the release and cut it down. The final program was 3 DVDs—320 minutes total running time.

Author's Photo

Tom Miranda's trophy room and his North American archery Super Slam display.

When the DVD finally released in late January 2012 it was a hit and flew off the shelves. Even today as I type this, it's the only fully documented archery Super Slam on video. Watching the program for the umpteenth time, I felt like the documentary was excellent, yet there were many details that hit the cutting room floor when I shortened it. I had kept such good records of my hunts, information that would help other bowhunters in their quests. Interesting facts and "how-to" were also cut to reduce length. I decided to compile the information and release a companion book.

My Adventure Bowhunter Super Slam is also available on Blu-Ray disc. One of the very few hunting programs ever presented in high quality HD Blu-Ray.

Adventure Bowhunter Tom Miranda's Quest for the Super Slam of North American Big Game, is a 384-page coffee table book I released in late 2012. Now there was a book and DVD companion set. There is still nothing like it on the market.

SAFARI CLUB

Soon after I finished the Super Slam, Ricardo Longoria, a Texas bowhunter and record book member with Safari Club International (SCI), contacted me. He congratulated me on the Super Slam and asked if I would consider going after the World Hunting Award (WHA) to help promote SCI. Ricardo had

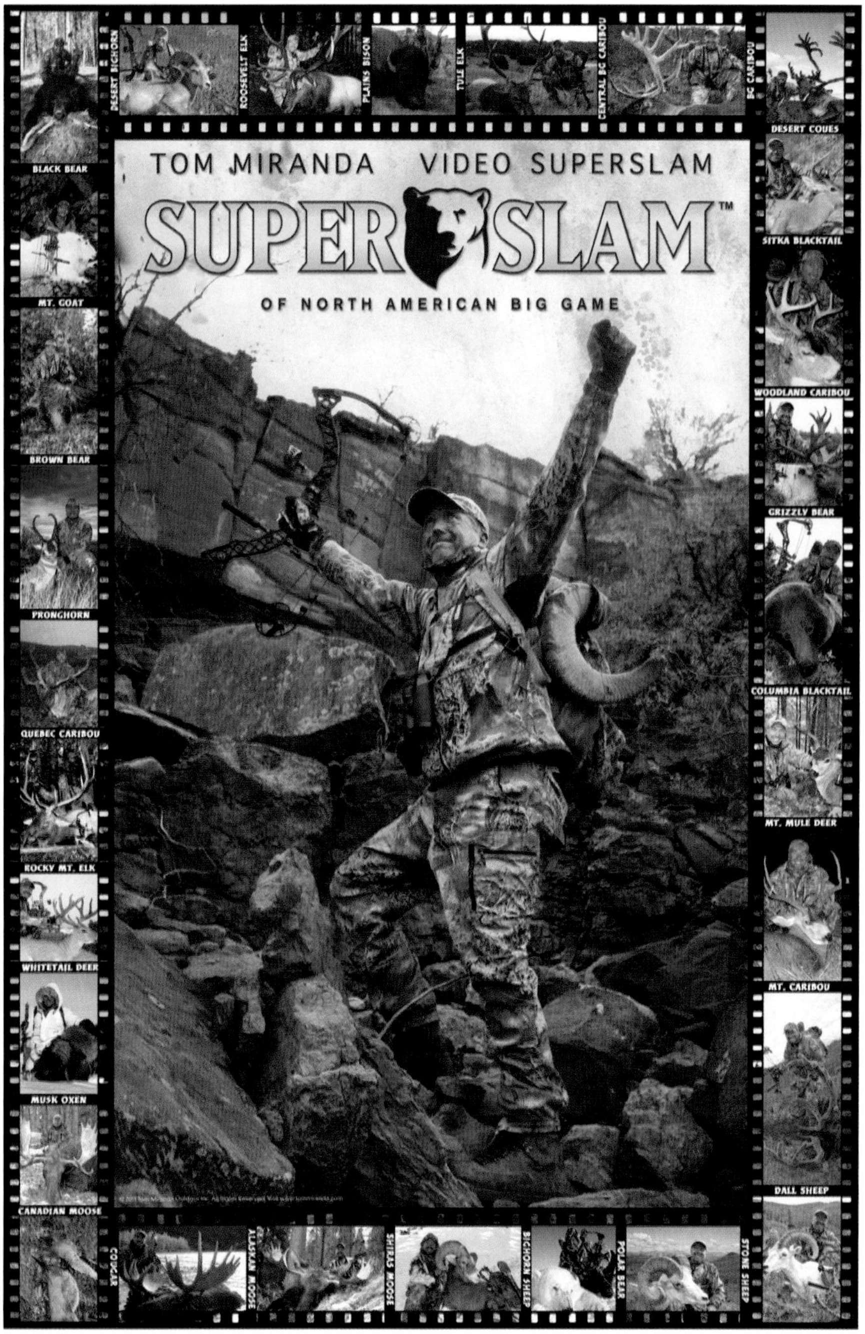

been watching my TV series and knew I was traveling extensively bowhunting in many areas of the world. At the time, I didn't know what the World Hunting Award was or how to go about pursuing it. Ricardo sent me some materials and a couple guys from the staff of SCI Record Book came to my home in an effort to document and score my animal, skulls, horns, antlers and tusks. For three days they measured and charted and came to the conclusion that I was 36 species away from achieving the WHA. Plus, all of the animals I had taken were documented on video as completed bowhunts. At that time, only four bowhunters had accomplished the feat including Ricardo Longoria, Byron Saddler, Gary Bogner and Archie Nesbitt.

The challenge had been made, so I decided to go for it. Most of the animals I needed were obscure species found on six continents. The most difficult would be African lion and leopard as well as mountain species like sheep, chamois, ibex, and a handful of tough small species like duiker and brocket deer. It had just taken me 13 years to nail down North America's 29, so another 36 species sounded like a huge proposition. But I had learned much about bowhunting and understood what I needed to do. Much of what I had learned during the Super Slam quest was that it was essential to find the target game as quickly as possible in the hunt and be aggressive. Accuracy at distance was also critical, as if I could make a 60-yard shot, I had a much better chance at success—every 10 yards closer magnified my success at least twofold. Sure, I would get lucky on some hunts and animals would walk into close quarters. Typically, the hunts were challenging and since I still had TV shows to produce, I was planning to record everything on video.

Proud night in the quest for Africa's big six most dangerous animals with this leopard taken near the Niassa Reserve in Mozambique 2012.

FINISHING AFRICA'S BIG SIX

I had been on four leopard hunts by this time and not taken one. The leopard was becoming a nemesis and I needed both a leopard and lion to complete the WHA. Activists around the globe were closing 'cat seasons and most outfitters refused to take bowhunters because of the difficulty. My South African PH Zak Grobler had secured a hunting concession in northern Mozambique and I would try for my leopard and lion there. Leopards are difficult hunts as most cats come to the bait at night when videotaping is difficult. Plus, the cats are quick and often spooky. Of the four hunts I'd done, I had missed two cats, two had jumped from the tree before the shot and on one full 14-day hunt—I never saw a leopard.

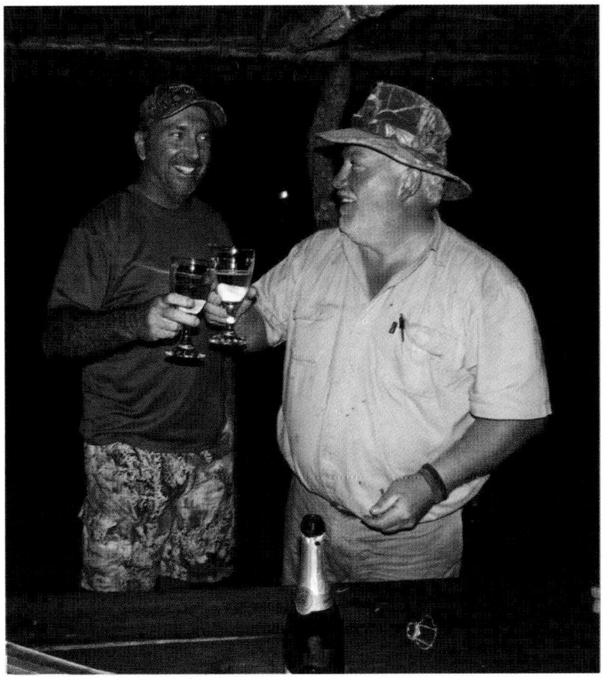

Author's Photo

PH Zak Grobler & Tom celebrate after the Mozambique leopard hunt.

In October 2012 I had three weeks to hunt the leopard and lion in Mozambique. We began with the leopard. Setting leopard baits is tedious work as you must not only collect bait but hang it in a tree and drag the area with a baited scent ball, then check the set daily for scouting camera photos. Female leopards aren't hunted so a male must hit the bait and many baits go unhit. We spent a week looking for leopard sign, talking with villagers and setting baits. Some of our baits were 150 miles from camp on rough roads so it took a full day to check baits after we had them set. If a leopard hits a bait, hunters only have a few days to score otherwise the full bait is eaten and the leopard gone. A bait was typically a quarter of a sable as these saber-horned animals are plentiful in northern Mozambique. We also used goats for bait which could be bought cheaply from villagers as many of the locals needed money for cigarettes or to pay their cell phone bills (of all things). Finally, in a little over a week we had a bait hit and it was a male. Zak and I immediately set up and camouflaged a pop-up blind about 30 yards from the bait. Then geared up and got into the blind. Zak would do the filming. Sure enough, that evening the leopard came back and I made the shot. It was very exciting and an intense hunt as there is only one chance and one shot. The target is about the size of a paper plate and in the dark it isn't easy.

We immediately began looking for lion sign and setting baits but by the end of my three-week safari we had nothing going. I told Zak I would return in 2013 to try for a lion.

October 2013 found me back in Mozambique. This time I had booked a full month to lion hunt and honestly hoped it wouldn't take that long. Zak had spent some time scouting and he had found lions in several areas where we would place baits. It's a long three days to get to northern Mozambique and about a five-hour drive into camp. We immediately started gathering meat and setting lion baits. On the third day I was in camp, I was not feeling well. I had gotten a cough and was carrying a fever.

Zak's wife Louise was also feeling ill and to add insult to injury, Zak had been bitten by a venomous spider. So, the hunt was not getting off on the right foot. We made a decision to make a three-day drive to Nelspruit, South Africa where there was a good hospital. On our drive south, we were stopped in a small town by the military. They said that a group of resistance fighters had been shooting drivers of cargo trucks and stealing the goods along the highway. The military's plan was to wait until a substantial group of vehicles had gathered and make the 100-kilometer drive through the dangerous area as a guarded convoy. We had no choice but to wait.

THE GAUNTLET

Eventually there were upward of 50 vehicles gathered and the military organized the convoy. We would be seventh in line with a military truck in front of us. Behind us was a bus and another 45 or so vehicles, buses and trucks farther behind. There would also be four armed Mozambique soldiers riding on the back of our truck, as well as in other vehicles.

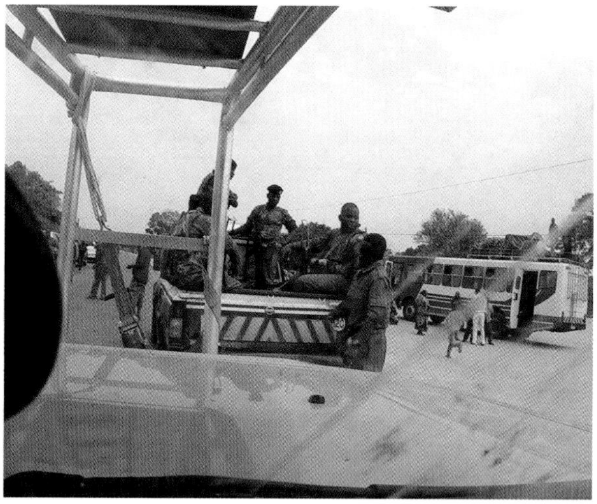
Author's Photo

Gearing up for the convoy.

As the convoy starts all is fine. Since Zak, Louise his wife and I all aren't feeling well, we are anxious to get to the doctor. Suddenly about 50 kilometers into the convoy, BAM! We are ambushed. A rocket-propelled grenade skips across the pavement in front of us and BOOM! Rapid machine gun fire came from the trees. The first bullet hits low just in front of my door, goes over my feet and into the transmission cowling.

Bullet holes in the Truck. The first bullet hit behind the left front tire in the quarter panel as seen. The second bullet struck low and back on the passenger door and is visible.

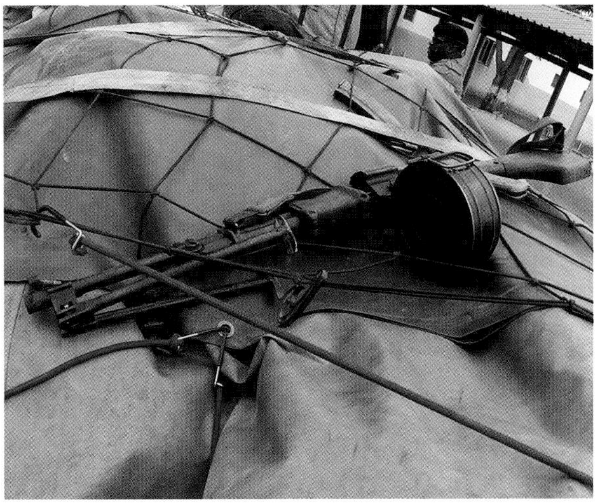

The machine gun of the soldier who was mortally wounded.

The soldier who was mortally wounded on the back of our Land Cruiser in the ambush- RIP.

Some of the damage of the bus which was following us during the ambush.

Another bullet goes through my door and into the lower seat—under and just behind me. Immediately I hear screaming as a soldier is hit by gunfire on the back of our truck. I'm yelling at Zak to go. Go! Go! The military truck in front of us has all but stopped where soldiers are returning machine gun fire. Zak swerved around the military truck and put the pedal down. It was another 50 clicks to the Save River bridge and the nearest town. When we arrived the soldier on the back was in grave condition and soon passed. We were all shell-shocked. Plus, my lower back had developed a deep and severe pain, a pain that I had experienced before. The stress and intensity of the event had released a kidney stone. My lion hunt was now becoming a nightmare.

The shorter version is that it took us another day and a half to reach Nelspruit, where I had the kidney stone removed by surgery. Plus, meds and a week of recoup. Of course, I can't tell this story without mentioning that in an attempt not to have my wife Sandy worry, I decided not to telephone her. Because of the remoteness of Niassa, she wouldn't expect a call. However, at the hospital, before the operation, I needed to pay $7 thousand (US) as my health insurance policy isn't valid in Africa. When the hospital ran my credit card for the surgery, American Express felt obligated to call and verify the charge, so Sandy found out from

Author's Photo

Tom Miranda poses with his hard won Mozambique bush lion taken with bow and arrow.

them. Soon Sandy called my cell, thinking I had been attacked by the lion, of course it wasn't the case. After some calming down everything was OK, however I didn't tell her about the ambush until I got home.

By this time, I still had nearly two weeks left to hunt, so Zak and I chartered a plane back to the lion camp. I honestly didn't want to risk the drive a second time, especially so soon after the ambush. Once in Niassa, we picked up where we left off and were lucky to get a tip from a local goat herder about a maned lion he had seen in the area. He showed us tracks and we set a bait—soon the bait was hit. Zak and I built a tree blind and the next night the brute came in. It was one very exciting hunt. We waited until the next day to look for the big cat and luckily no jackals or hyena found him. The village people were very happy, as was I because the beast had a pretty nice mane. Sometimes male lions who live in the bush areas have a short or spotty mane because of the thorns and briars constantly tugging at the long hairs. It was a grand finish to a long and complicated four weeks on the African continent. The moral of the story is never give up.

OTHER SPECIES

Finishing the African Big Six was a grand accomplishment, but there were many more animals on the list. Over the course of the next three years I would take all the species required to finish the World Hunting Award including trips to New Zealand for tahr, chamois and sambar deer. South America for buffalo, gray brocket deer, capybara, peccary, red deer and other species. In Europe I took the four different Spanish Ibex, roe deer, wild boar and alpine chamois. In Turkey the bezoar ibex. I returned to Africa to take dik-dik, klipspringer, duiker, steenbok—and more. In Zambia alone I needed puku, lechwe, defassa waterbuck and Lichtenstein's hartebeest. None of which are slam dunk bowhunts. It was a potpourri of species to be sure.

Tom Miranda with his first European species the Gredos Ibex taken in the Gredos Mountains of Spain.

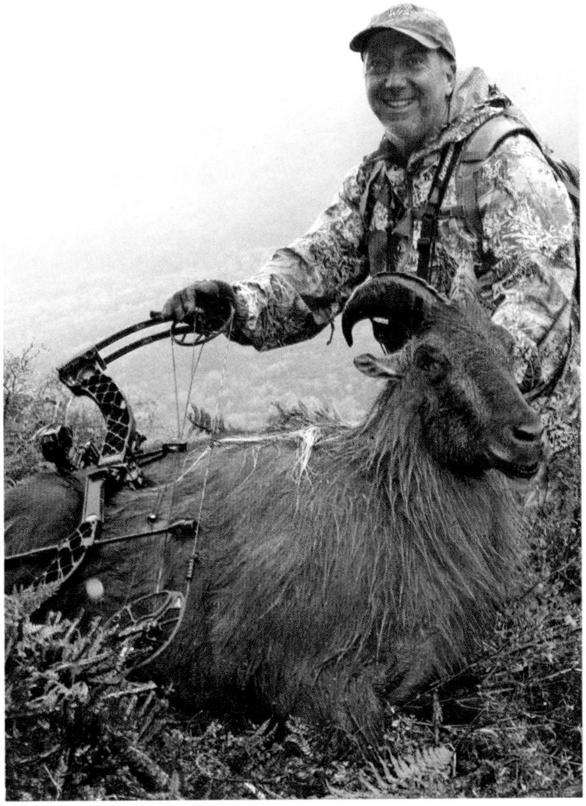

Author's Photo

Tom Miranda with a hard won New Zealand tahr taken near Fox Glacier.

Author's Photo

Awesome hunt for the elusive sambar deer near The Bay of Plenty on New Zealand's North Island.

Author's Photos

Tom Miranda and a dandy Puku arrowed in Zambia.

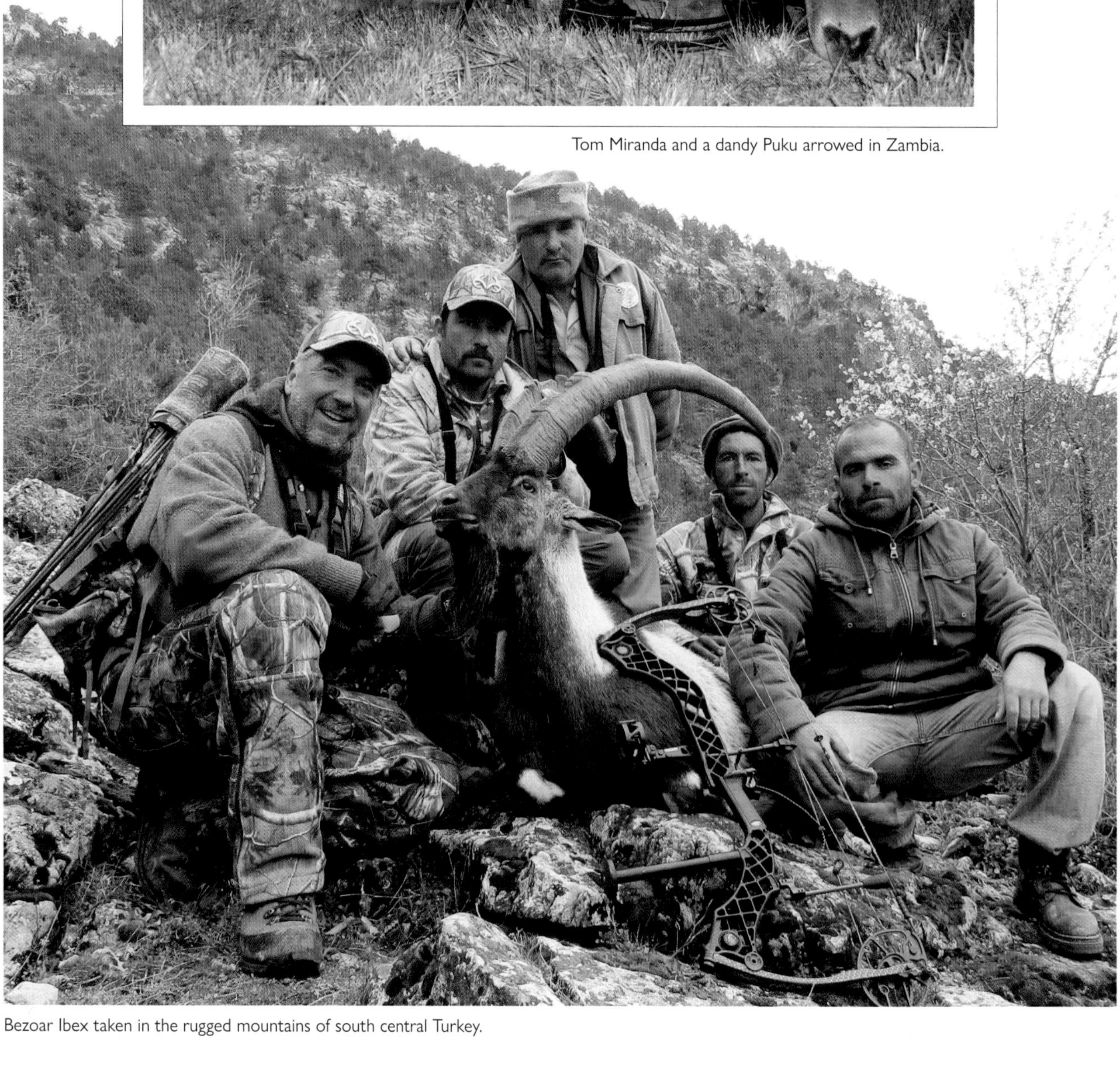

Bezoar Ibex taken in the rugged mountains of south central Turkey.

Oryx taken by Tom Miranda in the eastern Kalahari.

The largest rodent in the world, the capybara taken in northern Argentina.

Alpine chamois taken by Miranda in France.

Beceite Ibex taken by Miranda near the Castle of Molina de Aragón in Spain.

Author's Photos

Tom Miranda poses with his world record Kafue Flats lechwe taken in Zambia.

Whopper warthog taken by Miranda at his bowhunting camp on the Shelanti Game Reserve, Northern South Africa.

Tom Miranda poses with his brown-grey brocket deer taken in Argentina.

SCI's World Hunting Award with a bow requires 11 different Slams and 15 inner-circles at Diamond level. The toughest and most grueling are the animals of Africa inner-circle which includes 34 different African species. I was awarded my SCI World Hunting Award ring in January 2016, a little over five years from beginning the quest in late 2011. As a note, it took me 18 years to complete the Animals of Africa milestone, five years longer than the Super Slam. In 2017 I released my second SLAM DVD set, *Adventure Bowhunter Dark Continent,* which chronicles my 18-year-quest for the animals of Africa.

Author's Photo

Expert bowhunter Ricardo Longoria presents Tom Miranda the prestigious World Hunting Award ring achieved with bow and arrow January, 2016.

EVEN MORE BOWHUNTING

In 2016 I began to look back on my career and think about an exit strategy. I had accomplished much in the bowhunting world and had been doing bow hunts on TV for more than 25 years. There were two more possible accomplishments laying ahead and both where big commitments. One was Safari Club International's highest achievement, the World Conservation and Hunting Award, the other was the Grand Slam Club/ Ovis Triple Slam.

Adventure Bowhunter Dark Continent took 18 years to make and chronicles Tom Miranda's Archery Quest for the Animals of Africa.

SCI's World Conservation and Hunting Award includes 17 Slams and 25 Inner Circles at the Diamond level. I would need another 30-plus species. The Triple Slam requires 12 Capra goats taken in various areas from around the world and 12 Ovis "World Slam" sheep, including North America's Grand Slam of rams. Currently I am still in pursuit of these lofty goals, at this writing needing 7 additional "unique" animals to finish the SCI Conservation Award. For the coveted Triple Slam, I need 2 goats and 6 sheep.

In 2020 I released my third archery slam DVD set, *Adventure Bowhunter World Hunts,* which includes more than 40 additional bowhunts from around the world.

Author's Photos

This view of my game room shows the Africa Big Six as well as some of my other African trophies.

I became obsessed with books about old voyages and pirates while doing diving and spearfishing episodes for ESPN in the early 1990s. My Library has grown to over 4000 titles dating from the 16th century (1500s). Inset is a look at two of the most desirable pirate books.

EPILOGUE

Author's Photo

Here's a recent Miranda family portrait Jeremy, Tom, Sandy, Joshua, Tom Sr., Betty and Jennifer. Norwegian Cruise Lines December 29, 2018.

I know that some may look upon these type of hunting goals as a list of requirements and only a "tick of the box." However like trapping, bowhunting is a venture that consumes those who take it on as a lifestyle. Many bowhunters are happy to hunt only deer, or elk or feral hogs, and provide meat for their family. But these bowhunters are motivated by the same drive and emotions of the muskrats, mink, foxes, coyotes and 'catmen chronicled in this book. For me, the challenge of adventure bowhunting and the opportunity to record the journey for a television episode allows me to use my career to give a unique perspective of bowhunting in distant lands—and the cultures, animals and endeavors that exist for those craving more in their life.

Like trapping, bowhunting is conservation. International bowhunting gives wildlife living in distant lands value and brings tourism and income to rural communities where unique animals live. These animals are protected in these native lands for their value to sport hunting.

I carried this photo in my wallet for over 20 years. My children are very special to me.

I have been so blessed to enjoy a career outdoors. The privilege to grow up in America and to understand that freedom really does allow one to dream. The dreams I had as a youngster to become a wilderness trapper have evolved over time, yet I never lost sight of the real purpose. My life has been one in a million. Some might call me a lucky man, but the truth is we all make our own luck. During one's lifetime, there are many crossroads and many doors opened—the choices can become confusing. For some individuals, the risks of change are too great, for others the thirst for change is never quenched.

The average man today lives to be about 80 years old. That's about 29,000 days. The first 5,800 days are spent growing up. The middle productive years account for about 18,000 days, and the golden years an additional 5,200 days. What are you going to do with the days you have left? My parents taught me not to waste a single day. To follow my passions. To not be afraid to fail. To know that someone would always be smarter than me, have more success, have more money. Conversely someone would always be less smart and have less success. Our battles in life are not competitions with others, they are competitions with ourselves.

Those who strive to be the best they can be, know that failure is an integral part of success. If I had accomplished the Super Slam in 29 hunts, with 29 arrows it likely wouldn't have been a challenge or meant as much to me as the 13 years, 54 hunts and many missed opportunities. The character that comes from failure allows one to accept success more graciously. To appreciate the accomplishment for what it is.

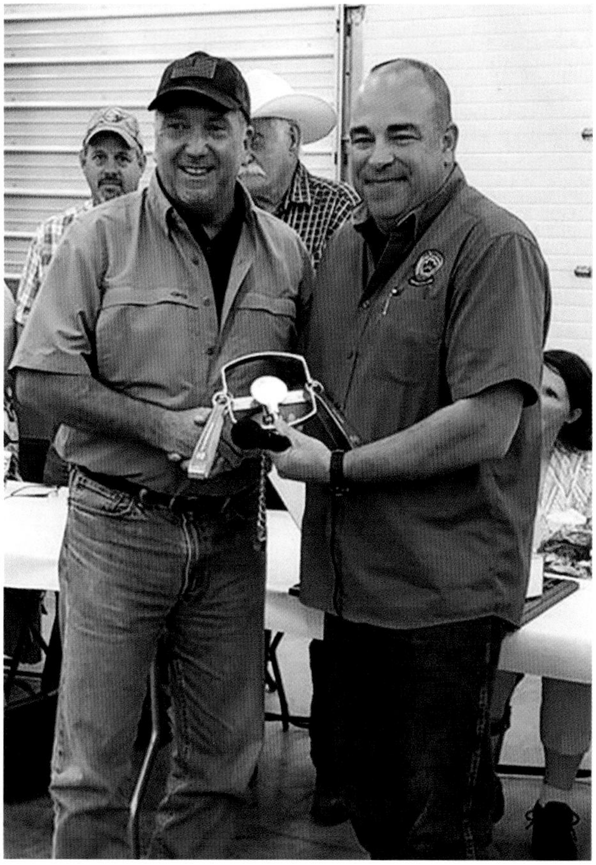

Author's Photo

Fur Takers of America's Todd Lang honors Tom Miranda as a 2019 inductee into the FTA Professional Trappers College Instructors Hall of Fame.

My goal with this book was to remind all trappers of their roots and the history of so many who followed the trapline. In a day of cancel culture and electronic books, history can be lost with the click of a mouse or the ravage of a book-burning society bent on their own ambitions. The industry of trapping in North America has a noble and romantic history and although some of our forefathers may have over trapped or exploited the animals and the wilderness, others realized the mistake and righted the wrong. The trappers who became teachers, lure makers, trap builders and biologists gave opportunity to all of us who followed them. This book wasn't written as the full history and record, but a slice of the history that affected me from a young age and a tribute to the trappers and outdoorsmen who inspired me to follow the trail less traveled.

To those mentioned in this treatise, I thank you for your inspiration and gifts to trapping. To those not mentioned, I wish this book not as an insult to what you have given to trappers and hunters, but a window into my life and those who molded my career—likely as some molded yours.

I look forward to the day when I retire my bow and return to the trapline. This time with thoughts of enjoying the challenges with a different perspective than I had during my trapping career and the years of molding my trapping skills and promoting my business. Life does come full circle and although I enjoy writing and sharing my adventures on both the printed page as well as television, I'll admit here that this trapper often reflects on the simpler days. I've traveled the world bowhunting but the joys and excitement I experienced while running my boyhood trapline are some of my most cherished memories afield. God bless the trapper in all of us.

Author's Photo

Tom Miranda proudly displays his National Trappers Association Trappers Hall of Fame Award. Miranda was inducted into the elite group of trappers in 2020.

Special Thanks

JOE GOODMAN

Some people discover their life's passion at an early age. Whether his passion came from an innate desire or a gift from the heavens, young Joe Goodman liked to draw. On a blank page, the corner of a homework assignment, even on a napkin. Joe would scratch out a figure or trace out an object. Some might call this doodling, but it's not "chicken scratches" when there's passion involved.

Running a small trapline with his father in northwest Ohio, 12-year-old Joe began learning about trapping and the outdoors. And immediately upon returning home, he began to sketch trees and ponds, traps and foxes. Discovering the pages of *Fur-Fish-Game* magazine ignited a fire within a young Joe Goodman. His imagination turned from muskrats to wolves and wolverine. Marten and beavers. Joe's passion was growing and so were his skills as an artist.

When Joe finished high school, he was still trapping—and yes—still drawing. His trapping had also graduated to red and gray foxes, mink and raccoons. Using the sets and methods gleaned from "Dakota Long-liner Garold Weiland, and Pennsylvania's Russ Carman's fox trapping books. Goodman enrolled in the prestigious Columbus College of Art & Design with a goal to hone his skills as an illustrator. Maybe he would follow in the footsteps of such greats as Frederic Remington or Norman Rockwell. Ambitious goals but the outdoor lifestyle was in Joe's blood and as the leaves changed and temperatures cooled, "College Joe" headed home to the woods for a two-week sabbatical for self-imposed trapping adventures.

Joe developed a personal interest in trapping history and the early fur trade. So, he began to sketch portraits of explorers, mountain men and trappers of these early eras. These works gained quick interest from others. Joe launched a website in 2004 to showcase his work. His limited-edition art prints became an instant sensation to trappers and readers of *F-F-G*. His merchandise line grew to include T-shirts and sportswear printed with his designs. It's likely if you visit the *National Trappers Association* Convention, you'll see Joe at his booth. He's easy to find, as his artwork in unmistakable.

> *"Running a trapline for muskrats with my dad during my early school years earned many fond memories that will stay with me forever."*
>
> *—Joe Goodman, 2020*

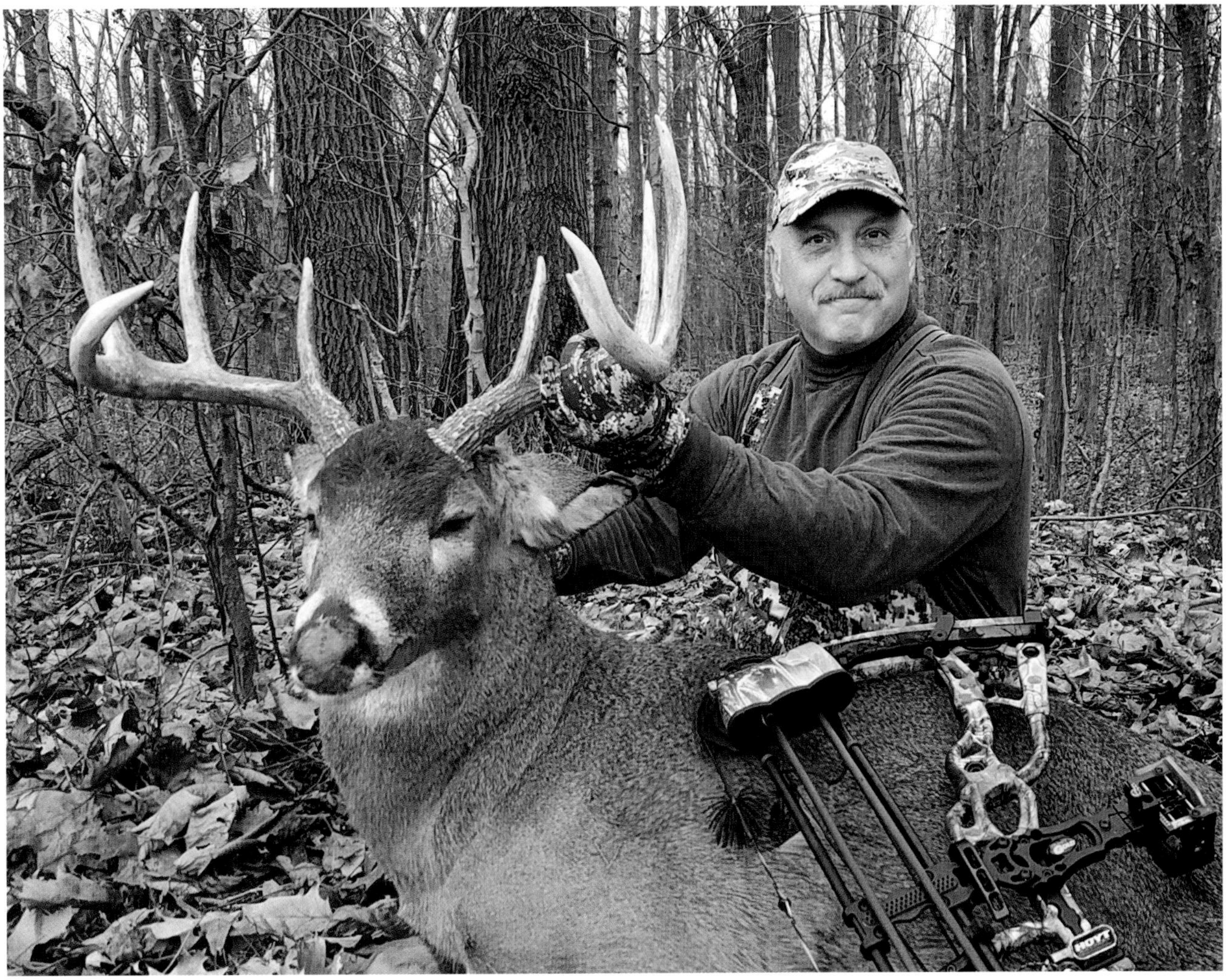

Master illustrator Joe Goodman poses with a great Ohio whitetail taken with archery tackle. Trappers make the best bowhunters!

After graduating from art college, Joe Goodman knocked on the doors of *Fur-Fish-Game* magazine, looking for work and eager to display his talents. Joe knew the difference between a coil-spring and a conibear, impressed the editor, and was given a tryout with two stories to illustrate. Goodman went to work. He knew this was what he was meant to do. Delivering his work on time, the editor was impressed, and Joe has never looked back. In fact, Goodman's work has appeared in each issue of *Fur-Fish-Game* since that pivotal first job.

Joe Goodman is also an avid bowhunter, which makes it pretty easy to see why his resume made him the perfect illustrator for this book. I'd like to thank Joe for supplying his talents and illustrations for *Master Trappers*. Find Joe Goodman online at JoeGoodmanPrints.com

—Tom Miranda